Communications Networks

Published by Online Conferences Limited, Uxbridge, England

Printed by Paca-Press & Co. Limited, West Drayton, England

Introduction

By D L A Barber, Director of the European Informatics Network and Chairman of The European Computing Conference on Communications Networks.

In the 25 years since they became commercially viable, the impact of computers on human affairs has been astonishing when compared with that of almost any other technical development. The promise to today's research has scarcely begun to be appreciated, yet it is abundantly clear that computers will change the shape of society more radically than has any tool hitherto conceived by mankind.

As society becomes more dependent on computers, two vital aspects emerge; the ability for the general public to interact with them assumes increasing importance, and the need for efficient communication between different computer systems becomes a necessity. This accounts for the spectacular growth of data communications.

The association of computing and communications began little more than ten years ago; since then, progress has been rapid and sustained and a remarkable development has taken place in the use of private data networks. The installation of public data networks offering features which will support advanced interactions on a national and, possibly, an international scale has begun. This surely opens a new prospect for us all.

The European Computing Conference on Communications Networks lights the way ahead with a series of authoritative papers covering the key issues under discussion today. Five sessions cover the main areas of general concern, and a further five parallel sessions look at some specialist topics in depth.

The session entitled Contemporary Systems covers features of today's private networks, the problems they are solving, and their likely evolution; while Future Facilities examines the plans of some authorised telecommunications agencies for new public switched data networks.

The necessity of designing networks to permit their future interconnection is, perhaps, the most urgent problem facing us now, if we are to avoid unnecessary future costs and restrictions. Also of vital importance, as we become more and more dependent on the complex systems now being created, are the subjects of Security and Reliability.

An indication of the impact of computers on society is given by the papers in Communications and People; the experiences and ideas discussed in this last main session give a fascinating foretaste of future possibilities.

The papers being presented in the five specialist sessions are of excellent quality. Their wide coverage indicates the range of topics that have now become relevant to the future of data communications, and those attending these sessions will obtain a good idea of the key issues currently under debate.

As Chairman of the Programme Committee for the Conference on Communications Networks it has been a pleasure to be so closely associated with Eurocomp 75, which will undoubtedly make a major contribution to a rapidly evolving area of computer science.

Derek Barber

Preface

This volume comprises papers presented at The European Computing Conference on Communications Networks — London, September 1975. To these have been added a number of other relevant papers for which there was not time for presentation at the Conference.

In order to ensure that the technical information is as up-to-date as possible, we have opted for direct reproduction of typed masters. For the same reason, these appear in random order throughout the book and are logically sequenced via the index.

Online wishes to thank Derek Barber, the General Conference Chairman, and all the under-mentioned Session Chairmen for their diligent assistance throughout.

J Arnould	Directeur General Adjoint, SESA, France
M Clayton Andrews	Director of Data Communications, IBM World Trade Corporation, Switzerland
G Dale	Head of Data Communications Division, Post Office Telecommunications, UK
D W Davies	Superintendent, Division of Computer Science, National Physical Laboratory, UK
S R Erdreich	Director, UNIVAC Development Centre, UK
P T Kirstein	Professor of Computer Systems, University College London, UK
D Kroneberg	SITA, France
L Pouzin	Directeur du Reseau CYCLADES, IRIA, France
P Schicker	Manager, Swiss Cost II (EIN) Project, ETH Computer Centre, Switzerland
T I Szentivani	Engineer-in-Chief, INFELOR, Hungary

This Conference was part of The European Computing Congress 1975 — EUROCOMP. Other conferences in this series investigate:

Business Data Processing
Interactive Systems
Systems Design and Implementation
Systems Evaluation

online

Online is Europe's leading specialist in the design and organisation of interantional congresses and conferences and advanced computing technology. Major regular events include: Eurocomp — The European Computing Congress, Medcomp — International Congress on Medical Computing, and Minicomputer Forum.

Online (Head Office)
Cleveland Road
Uxbridge, Middlesex
England
Telephone: Uxbridge 39262

Online Nederland
Regentesselaan 182
The Hague
The Netherlands
Telephone: The Hague 336004

Index

Communications and People

Designs in Detail

Modelling and Assessment

Operational Aspects

Services and Terminals

Protocols and Languages

Authors

Author	Organisation	Country	Page No.
Arndt G	Siemens AG	Fed. Rep. Germany	161
Baechi W	ETH Computer Centre	Switzerland	537
Bartlett K A	National Physical Laboratory	UK	95
Baum M	Eurocontrol	Netherlands	47
Belsnes D	Universitetet i Oslo	Norway	349
Beeforth T H	University of Sussex	UK	283
Borgonovo F	Politecnico di Milano	Italy	379
Bowie J A	Computer Analysts & Programmers Ltd	UK	129
Bright R D	Post Office	UK	567
Bürge H	IBM Research Laboratory	Switzerland	207
Cardy S	University of London	UK	177
Chandler A S	Computer Aided Design Centre	UK	583
Cotton I W	National Bureau of Standards	USA	433
Danet A	Centre Commun d'Etudes de Television et Telecommunications	France	331
Daniels M C	University of Sussex	UK	283
Davies G W P	Commission of the European Communities	Luxembourg	229
Dawes N W	National Physical Laboratory	UK	65
Despres R	Centre Commun d'Etudes de Television et Telecommunications	France	331
Dewis I G	National Physical Laboratory	UK	65
Duenki A	ETH Computer Centre	Switzerland	537
Fedida S	Post Office Research Centre	UK	261
Fitzhugh N S	Loughborough University of Technology	UK	519
Frampton J A K	International Computers Limited	UK	145
Franchi P	IBM Scientific Center	Italy	81
Fratta L	Politecnico di Milano	Italy	379

Gentry M	Computer Analysts & Programmers Ltd	UK	65
Gien M	l'Institut de Recherche en Informatique et d'Automatique	France	241
Goodlet J C	United Airlines	USA	35
Hebditch D L	Pliener Associates Limited	UK	567
Higginson P L	University College London	UK	25/453
Hinchley A J	University College London	UK	453
Jackson P N	Computer Technology Limited	UK	177
Jamet B	Centre Commun d'Etudes de Television et Telecommunications	France	331
Jenny C J	IBM Research Laboratory	Switzerland	207
Kashmeri S A	Regional Justice Information System	USA	467
Kirstein P T	University College London	UK	395/499
Kümmerle K	IBM Research Laboratory	Switzerland	207
Laws J	National Physical Laboratory	UK	241
Lloyd D	University College London	UK	499
McFadyen J H	IBM Corporation	USA	363
Maffioli F	Politecnico di Milano	Italy	379
Maier M	IBM Scientific Center	Italy	191
Mann D W	Logica Limited	UK	415
Meissner P	National Bureau of Standards	USA	433
Newman I A	Loughborough University of Technology	UK	519/549
Painter J A	Defense Communications Agency	USA	483
Pichon G	Centre Commun d'Etudes de Television et Telecommunications	France	331
Poncet F	SESA	France	301
Pouzin L	IRIA	France	603

Rettberg R D	Bolt Beranek and Newman Inc	USA	113
Roberts L G	Telenet Communications Corporation	USA	315
Scantlebury R	National Physical Laboratory	UK	241
Schicker P	ETH Computer Centre	Switzerland	537
Schwartz P Y	Centre Commun d'Etudes de Television et Telecommunications	France	331
Sommi G	IBM Scientific Center	Italy	81
Stemberger K	Siemens AG	Fed. Rep. Germany	161
Stokes A V	University College London	UK	25
Taylor D W	Loughborough University of Technology	UK	549
Teichholtz N A	Digital Equipment Corporation	USA	13
Thomas E M	IBM Corporation	USA	363
Trehan R K	The MITRE Corporation	USA	1
Tucker J B	Logica Limited	UK	301
Walden D C	Bolt Beranek and Newman Inc	USA	113
Wilbur S R	University College London	UK	395
Wilkinson P T	National Physical Laboratory	UK	95
Wood B M	Computer Analysts & Programmers Ltd	UK	129
Wood D C	The MITRE Corporation	USA	1

An assessment of the performance of packet switching networks

David C. Wood and Ranvir K. Trehan
The MITRE Corporation
USA

ABSTRACT

This paper assesses the performance obtainable by users of the Advanced Research Projects Agency computer network (ARPANET). Various factors which influence the performance, and indirectly the cost to the user, of such a network are identified and approaches for improving performance are discussed. Weaknesses of the present ARPANET architecture are described and an alternative network architecture with improved cost and performance characteristics is proposed.

INTRODUCTION

The Department of Defense Advanced Research Projects Agency computer network (ARPANET) has been in operation in the United States for about four years[1]. Its success, together with that of the network at the British National Physical Laboratory[2], has resulted in the planning and development of many packet switching networks around the world. Approximately twenty packet switching networks are in various stages of planning and development by research organizations, government agencies and common carriers.

Much of the published information, as well of the attention of network developers, appears to focus on technical aspects of the design of a packet switching communications system. On the other hand, the performance and economics of a packet switching network from the standpoint of the end user who accesses the network from a host computer or terminal has received limited attention. This paper is directed to a performance assessment of packet switching networks based on the authors' usage and experimentation on ARPANET during the last four years and on experience in the development of a similar network over the same period. The sensitivity of network overhead and performance to network protocols, software implementation and network use is identified. Network design approaches different from ARPANET and suitable for large scale networks for operational use are proposed with a view to improving performance and reducing cost.

Background

ARPANET is the only existing packet switching network of its size. The network comprises packet switches, known as Interface Message Processors or IMPs, and a great variety of computers or hosts. Each IMP is connected to two, or possibly three or four, other IMPs, to form a distributed network, and supports one or more hosts[3]. An augmented IMP, the Terminal Interface Processor or TIP, can additionally support terminals directly[4].

The network was begun in 1969 and entered an operational phase in 1971. Currently the network includes between 45 and 50 IMPs or TIPs, about equally divided, and over 50 hosts. In addition to nodes throughout the continental United States, there is a node in Hawaii and there are two nodes in Europe.

The IMP communications subnetwork provides for the delivery of messages of up to about 8,000 bits from one host to another host. The messages are partitioned into packets of about 1,000 bits for transmission through the network and reassembled in the correct order at the destination IMP.

Each host computer on the network has a Network Control Program (NCP) which manages communication with the IMP, constructs and interprets headers at the beginning of each message, distributes messages to or from other executing programs, and communicates with other NCPs according to the host-to-host protocol[5]. The host-to-host protocol uses separate messages between NCPs to establish logical connections and to manage buffer space for flow control. A receiving NCP allocates buffer space for each logical connection and periodically notifies the sending NCP, via an Allocate control message, of how much additional space is available.

Additional protocols have been defined and programs implemented using the NCP to provide network user capabilities[6]. One of these, Telnet, (for Telecommunications Network), enables a terminal at one host, or at a TIP, to establish a logical connection to a host elsewhere on the network, and appear as local terminal at that host. A file transfer capability enables the movement of files from one host to another host. A message service enables a terminal user to send a message to users at other hosts on the network; messages are stored in the recipient's mailbox file. The above three capabilities are implemented on practically all ARPANET hosts and are used extensively.

NETWORK OVERHEAD AND PERFORMANCE

The cost of using a packet switching network and its performance are highly sensitive to the amount of overhead traffic. Overhead traffic produces a processing load on host computers and consumes some of the bandwidth of the communications lines which is paid for by the user indirectly. Measurements on ARPANET of overhead traffic and network performance are described below. Revisions to protocols and to network software are identified which can substantially reduce the amount of network overhead and improve performance.

Line Overhead and Traffic Characteristics

Line overhead can be logically classified according to four categories[7]:

- Control of packet transmission between adjacent IMPs.

- Transmission control between source IMP and destination IMP.

- Message control between hosts.

- Background traffic overhead.

The overhead for the control of packet transmission between adjacent IMPs comprises the hardware generated framing characters, checksums and acknowledgments. Overhead between source IMP and destination IMP comprises the leader on each packet, and subnet control messages such as the Ready For Next Message (RFNM) which is returned from the destination IMP to the source host to indicate that a message has been received safely. Overhead for message control between hosts comprises additional header information on the front of each message as specified by the host-to-host protocol, and host-to-host protocol control messages such as Allocates. Finally, background traffic includes routing messages, messages which check line status, and status reports to the Network Control Center.

Data collected by the Network Measurement Center in May 1974 shows the percentage of line capacity attributable to the four categories of overhead (Table I). Because of the low line utilization, the projected

	ACTUAL OVERHEAD %	PROJECTED OVERHEAD %
CONTROL BETWEEN ADJACENT IMPS	0.89	35.22
CONTROL BETWEEN SOURCE & DESTINATION IMP	0.62	24.43
MESSAGE CONTROL BETWEEN HOSTS	0.32	12.59
BACKGROUND TRAFFIC	4.32	4.32
DATA	0.59	23.44
TOTAL	6.73	100.00

TABLE I

OVERHEAD AS A PERCENTAGE OF LINE CAPACITY
FOR CURRENT TRAFFIC CHARACTERISTICS

overhead characteristics of a saturated net, with the same traffic characteristics but no additional background traffic, are also shown.

The above analysis of overhead of average traffic data conceals wide variations in traffic characteristics, and therefore overhead, for various hosts and differing applications. Traffic characteristics which have a substantial influence on overhead are the actual message size and the number of host-to-host protocol control messages. These two traffic characteristics have been measured in detail for common applications, namely remote terminal access and file transfer, involving major hosts on ARPANET[8].

Remote terminal access uses the Telecommunications Network (Telnet) protocol, in addition to the host-to-host protocol, to provide a mechanism for a terminal on one host to gain access to another host on the network. Telnet traffic characteristics are influenced by the server host's transmission mode (i.e. whether it echoes input, and whether input is character-at-a-time or line-at-a-time), buffer sizes, and frequency of host-to-host protocol Allocate control messages.

Input from a terminal to a character-at-a-time system such as the PDP-10 TENEX, which sends an Allocate control message for every data message, produces traffic in which the actual data represents about one percent of the traffic associated with that logical connection, although the total volume is, of course, quite small. Input to a line-at-a-time system such as the Honeywell 6180 MULTICS, which sends infrequent Allocates, produces traffic in which the data represents about 20 percent. Table II shows the approximate percentage of each category of line overhead for Telnet input traffic to MULTICS with each user input assumed to average 12 characters. Characteristics of the output to a terminal from a timesharing system depend on various buffer sizes and the Allocate frequency, but typically the data represents about 30 percent of the traffic. The line overhead distribution for Telnet output in Table II assumes an average message size of 44 characters and an Allocate for each message.

	TELNET INPUT %	TELNET OUTPUT %	FILE TRANSFER
CONTROL BETWEEN ADJACENT IMPS	40	33	9
CONTROL BETWEEN SOURCE & DESTINATION IMP	28	22	7
MESSAGE CONTROL BETWEEN HOSTS	8	10	1
BACKGROUND TRAFFIC	4	4	4
DATA	20	31	79
TOTAL	100	100	100

TABLE II

OVERHEAD AS A PERCENTAGE OF LINE CAPACITY
FOR SPECIFIC TYPES OF TRAFFIC

The other common application, file transfer, is usually performed with full 8000 bit data messages. If the host has large buffers so that Allocates are infrequent, the line utilization for data is about 79 percent as shown in Table II. If Allocates are sent for every data message, the line utilization rate drops by about 4 percent.

The line overhead can be reduced both by more efficient use of the existing protocols and by improved protocols. Some ARPANET hosts send a host-to-host protocol Allocate control message for every data message received. In addition to the bandwidth required for the Allocate messages, this can also limit the effective bandwidth on a single logical connection because the source is waiting for notification to send. Although hosts with very limited buffer space, such as the TIP, cannot avoid frequent Allocates, larger hosts, particularly those with virtual memory, should be able to send Allocates less frequently.

An improved flow control scheme proposed by Cerf and Kahn[9] for the Inter-Network Working Group uses a moving window to describe the number of bits that can be sent. In addition, the commands from the destination which move the edge of the window are a standard part of the messages carrying data in the other direction.

Thus users and designers of networks should be aware that protocols, the way they are implemented, and the traffic characteristics, all have a substantial affect on the amount of overhead and hence the network's efficiency.

Host Overhead

An overhead in memory space and processing time on host computers is caused by the Network Control Program and other software such as Telnet which provides user-oriented network services. The amount of main memory utilized by the network software is usually easily available. Quantitative measures of processor overhead are difficult to obtain since at least part of the network software is generally integrated with the operating system. Few measures of processor overhead have been reported on ARPANET, but it is believed that the overhead is significant, particularly during file transfers. The overhead on a host is dependent on implementation characteristics of network software not only in that host, but in other hosts as well. For example, one host can be adversely impacted by another receiving host which sends frequent Allocates. The Telnet protocol causes excessive overhead because it requires each character in the data stream to be examined in order to find any control characters relevant to the protocol. Thus users should examine carefully the overhead of the network on their host computers.

Network Performance

Several performance criteria are of interest to network users. A low delay time for small messages is required by interactive terminal users. A high data rate is required for large volume file transfers. The original design requirement on ARPANET, of less than one half second round-trip delay for interactive traffic, was easily met for short messages[10]. Only as the network size in terms of nodes has grown have times started to approach one-half second.

No specific performance requirements for file transfers were established for ARPANET. In practice, the typical file transfer rate between two hosts ranges between about 7 kilobits per second (Kbps) and 20 Kbps. The transfer rate decreases the greater the number of hops through intermediate IMPS.

The main limit to file transfer performance is the host-to-host protocol, which currently permits only one 8,000 bit message to be in transit at a time on a logical connection. The average round-trip time, from a full message entering the IMP from the source host until the acknowledgement is returned, increases linearly as the number of inter-mediate IMPs to be transversed. Measurements show that the average round-trip time is about 200 milliseconds plus 60 milliseconds for each hop[8].

To achieve high throughput during file transfers, a modified protocol is required which enables several messages to be in transit at a time. In that case, either the destination IMP would have to be pre-pared to reorder the messages, or the host would have to assume that function. Thus network designers must develop more sophisticated pro-tocols for a packet switching network to provide large throughput rates for file transfers.

NETWORK ARCHITECTURE

The previous section has addressed areas for performance improvement within the existing ARPANET design. In this section, an alternative architecture is proposed for a large scale packet switching network suited to an operational organization. The proposed network architecture offers lower development costs and has the potential for improved per-formance.

Present Architecture

Although an IMP can connect up to four host computers and although the capability to connect non-collocated host computers has been devel-oped, the primary emphasis in ARPANET is to collocate an IMP (or TIP) with one or more host computers at a site. Since the traffic level does not justify more than the minimum number of lines for connectivity, the network is at present configured primarily as a ring of demand centers or processing units. This ring-like topology has been extensively used in electrical power transmission and distribution systems for decades. It pro-vides for two-connectivity of each node which is important for electrical power as well as data communications networks. However, this topology

and the resulting system architecture incurs economic and performance
penalties, particularly for a communications network with a large number
of nodes and having demand that is not uniformly dispersed over the entire
area but is rather clustered in regions.

Consider the present structure of ARPANET (Figure 1) to illustrate
the points.

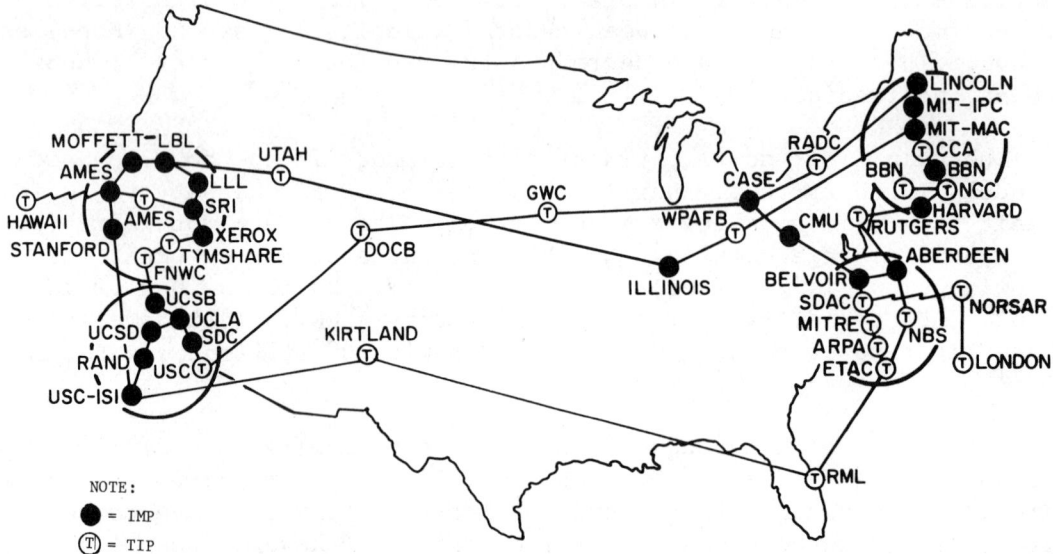

FIGURE 1

ARPA NETWORK, GEOGRAPHIC MAP, JUNE 1974

The network nodes, as well as incoming and outgoing traffic, are concentrated in four regional complexes, viz. Boston, Washington, Los Angeles
and San Francisco. In the Boston area, there are eight nodes all within
a radius of ten miles, and there is no limit on this number being larger
in the future. For the sake of illustrating our point in a simple manner,
let us assume (as all ARPANET topology studies do) that each of these
nodes does indeed have symmetric and uniform incoming and outgoing traffic,
both intra-complex and network-wide. Under these assumptions, a packet
whose source and destination nodes are both in the Boston complex will
traverse a mean of four hops which is acceptable from a response time
standpoint. For a typical inter-complex packet, the total number of hops
is likely to be much greater. For instance, the San Francisco complex
also has eight nodes. Thus a packet between Boston and San Francisco
complexes has a mean lower bound of eight hops, assuming direct connection between the complexes. Assuming three intermediate hops, inter-

complex traffic will experience a mean of 11 hops. With that many hops
the response time for interactive traffic becomes marginal, and the
throughput for file transfers is greatly reduced.

Thus it may be concluded that ring -like topologies of packet switched
networks do not take advantage of economics of aggregation possible because of the geographical clustering of demand centers/processing units.
Such economics are possible both by the reduction of the number of
IMPs/TIPs, and by the reduction in the number of communication circuits
which would be necessary to achieve higher connectivity to avoid large
hop traversals by a packet[11]. The present topology structure is also
highly sensitive to the distribution of traffic at various nodes within
a cluster. Thus a study of ARPANET, in retrospect, suggests the basic
philosophy, of treating every and any demand center/processing unit as
an entity on the communications network, may not be viable for large
scale computer network development.

Alternative Architecture

An attractive alternative network architecture would provide a
modular packet switch (rather than fixed capability IMPs/TIPs) as a node
on the communication network and connect to it by communications lines
all demand centers/processing units in a local region. The packet
switches may be multiprocessor configurations for higher reliability.
This approach would reduce the large number of packet switches and
excessive number of hops. As a result, round-trip times for messages
would be shorter, and fewer messages would need to be in transit simultaneously to maintain high throughput for file transfers.

The above discussion, coupled with our direct experience in the
development of a packet-switched network for an operational organization,
leads us to believe that the network architecture depicted in Figure 2

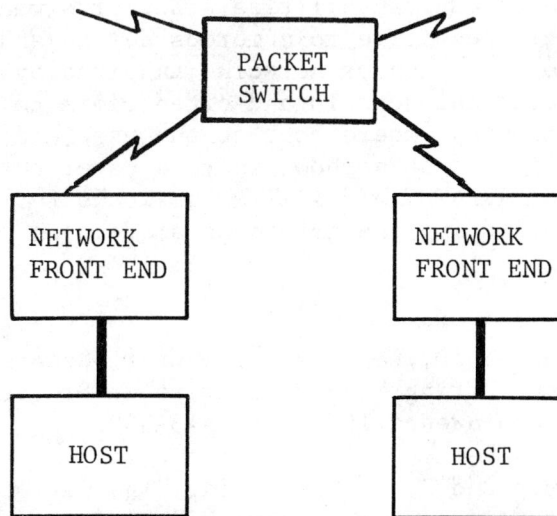

FIGURE 2

ALTERNATIVE NETWORK ARCHITECTURE

deserves strong consideration. In this approach almost all the network-related host software is resident in a Network Front End (NFE) processor rather than in the host computer itself. In this manner, the host network software development for an entire network can be consolidated in a standard NFE, uniformity of this software maintained throughout the network, and utmost flexibility for redesign of such software maintained without any impact on host computer operations. The only variation between NFE's on a network will be at the host computer connection end. The host computer connection may be achieved in a variety of ways such as "device simulation" or implementation of a special host to front end protocol.

An aspect in network design not explored in sufficient depth is the trade-off between 50 Kbps and 9.6 Kbps circuits[12]. It is generally believed that the per unit capacity costs of communications circuits decrease as a function of increasing capacity. There is however one exception. The 9.6 Kbps circuits in the U.S. are approximately ten times cheaper than 50 Kbps circuits, thus yielding a 2:1 diseconomy scale. For a given expenditure, the lower speed circuits could provide substantially higher connectivity and fewer hops. Such trade-offs offer another dimension to operators of commercial networks who may use the lower speed circuits for back-up purposes. The operator and customers of a commercial network may find it initially beneficial to operate in slower speed mode during infrequent higher speed circuit failures. It is recognized that 9.6 Kbps circuits can be dismissed as inadequate by imposing stringent response requirements; however, their use in large data transfer networks where throughput (achievable by multi-logical-link operation) is the major concern seems very appropriate.

CONCLUSIONS

The concluding thought of this paper is that although packet switching networks can provide unique capabilities, the performance and cost of those capabilities is highly sensitive to numerous design and usage parameters. Designers of the proliferation of networks inspired by ARPANET have been pre-occupied with technical details and often claim to be operating in an experimental environment where cost to the user and performance is not a priority. However, it has been shown in this paper that enough experience is now available from ARPANET and similar networks for an assessment of the impact of design and implementation parameters on cost and performance.

REFERENCES

1. L. G. Roberts and B. D. Wessler, "Computer Network Development to Achieve Resource Sharing," AFIPS Conference Proceedings, Spring Joint Computer Conference 1970, pp. 543-549.

2. R. A. Scantlebury and P. T. Wilkinson, "The National Physical Laboratory Data Communication Network," Proceedings of the Second International Conference on Computer Communication, August 1974, pp. 223-228.

3. J. M. McQuillan et al., "Improvements in the Design and Performance of the ARPA Network, "AFIPS Conference Proceedings, Fall Joint Computer Conference 1972, pp. 741-754.

4. S. M. Ornstein et al., "The Terminal IMP for the ARPA Computer Network," AFIPS Conference Proceedings, Spring Joint Computer Conference 1972, pp. 243-254.

5. C. S. Carr et al., "Host-Host Communication Protocol in the ARPA Network," AFIPS Conference Proceedings, Spring Joint Computer Conference 1970, pp. 589-597.

6. S. D. Crocker et al., "Function-oriented Protocols for the ARPA Computer Network," AFIPS Conference Proceedings, Spring Joint Computer Conference 1972, pp. 271-279.

7. L. Kleinrock et al., "A Study of Line Overhead in the ARPANET," Communications of the ACM, to appear.

8. D. C. Wood, "Measurement of User Traffic Characteristics on ARPANET," to be published.

9. V. G. Cerf and R. E. Kahn, "A Protocol for Packet Network Inter-communication," IEEE Transaction on Communications, Vol COM-22 No. 5, May 1974, pp. 637-648.

10. L. Kleinrock and W. E. Naylor, "On Measured Behavior of the ARPA Network," AFIPS Conference Proceedings, National Computer Conference 1974, pp. 767-780.

11. M. J. Gordon and R. K. Trehan, "ARPANET Economic Analysis," MTR-6890, The MITRE Corporation, McLean, Virginia, April 1975.

12. R. K. Trehan, "Considerations and Methods of Analysis for the Development of an Inter-Computer Network," presented at the Joint National Meeting of the Operations Research Society of America (ORSA) and The Institute of Management Sciences (TIMS), Atlantic City, New Jersey, November 1972.

Digital network architecture

NATHAN A. TEICHHOLTZ
Digital Equipment Corp.
U.S.A.

ABSTRACT

A principal advantage of computer networks is that they allow the coupling together of heterogeneous computers, each optimized around a different set of applications, in order to provide a complete solution for problems which cross the traditional domains (time sharing, real time and batch) of operating systems. This paper discusses the architecture used by Digital Equipment Corporation, to provide network capabilities within a wide range of computers (PDP-8, 11, 15, DEC-10), and operating systems. This architecture is general enough to accommodate all DEC systems, and consequently is adaptable to many non-DEC environments as well.

INTRODUCTION

In April, 1975, the Digital Equipment Corporation (DEC) introduced a new architecture for computer networks. Digital Network Architecture (DNA) is intended to accommodate a wide variety of network processors in networks configured to satisfy a variety of user environments. In this paper, we discuss the basic assumptions that lead to DNA, and present the major concepts of the architecture.

NETWORK APPLICATIONS

There are essentially three separate ways in which computer networks are used today. *COMMUNICATIONS NETWORKS* move data from one place to another, hopefully more rapidly than can be done by physical means. *RESOURCE SHARING NETWORKS* allow peripheral devices, data bases and programs to be shared amongst several machines; this is normally done to save money, but in some cases (e.g. data-base sharing) may be the only viable mechanism at any price. *DISTRIBUTED NETWORKS* allow many autonomous systems to coordinate their activities as they each work on various segments of a complex problem.

COMMUNICATIONS NETWORKS were the first type of network to be implemented, and are still the most numerous today. Such networks normally serve to interconnect a large number of terminals, usually geographically distributed, with a small number of large 'host' computers. Both interactive and batch (RJE) terminals must be accommodated. A major goal of such networks is to maximize the utilization of costly communications channels by data concentration and/or multi-drop (party-line) line techniques. A second goal of such networks is to unburden large mainframes of their communications processing load, by off-loading such functions onto a programmable front-end processor. A third goal is to provide improved reliability for the network as a whole, by dynamically compensating for the outages that are to be expected in the communications environment. An interesting characteristic of such networks is that normally very little preprocessing of data is done in the various communications processors; rather all the user's applications programs and data bases reside on the large network host systems. A typical communications network might have the following arrangement:

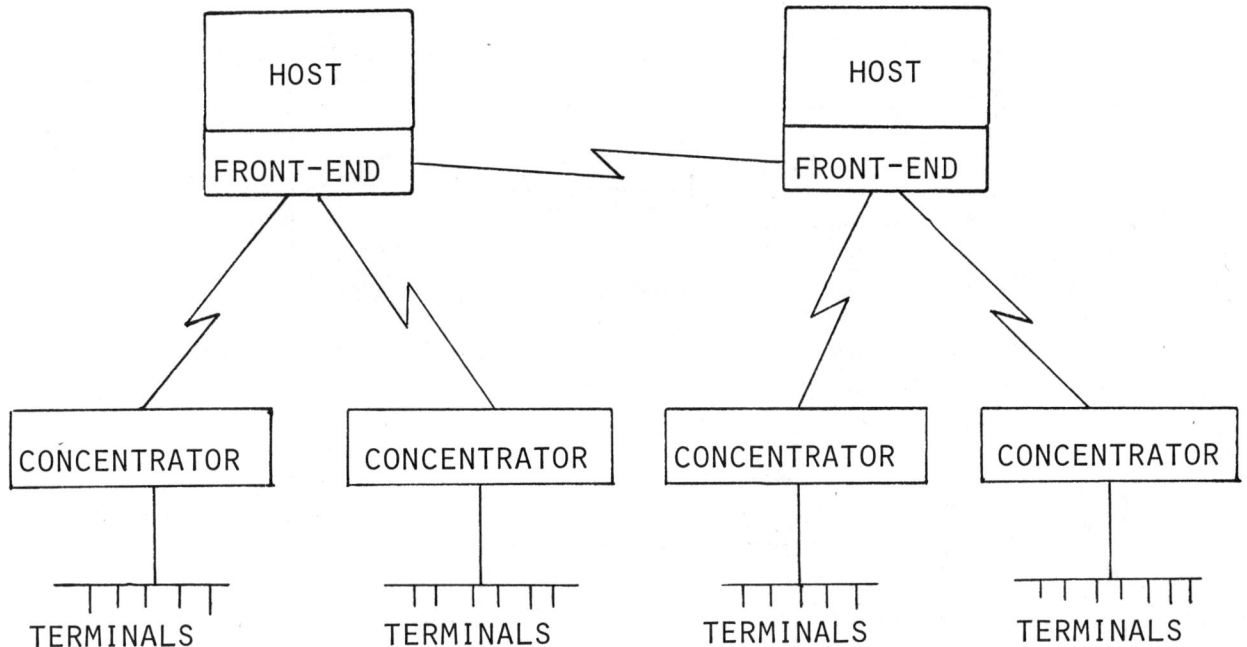

FIGURE 1

Communications Networks normally utilize both large host mainframes and small mini-computers, performing dedicated communications functions. Synchronous channels normally connect
the concentrators with the central sites, while high speed
parallel links or shared memory areas are used to connect
host computers with front-end processors.

RESOURCE SHARING NETWORKS allow the sharing of expensive resources among several (typically small) machines. In some
sense, the resource sharing network is the logical successor
to the conventional, single processor time-sharing system.
Originally the central processor (CPU) in such systems was a
scarce resource in need of multiplexing; today small CPU's
are sufficiently inexpensive so as to make such efforts unnecessary. Instead, each user can be provided with a dedicated CPU to execute his own applications programs. A central system controls the various mass storage devices and
other major peripherals, and provides resources to other
CPU's in the net on a demand basis. In effect, the central
system acts as a very smart peripheral multiplexor. A
typical resource sharing network might appear as:

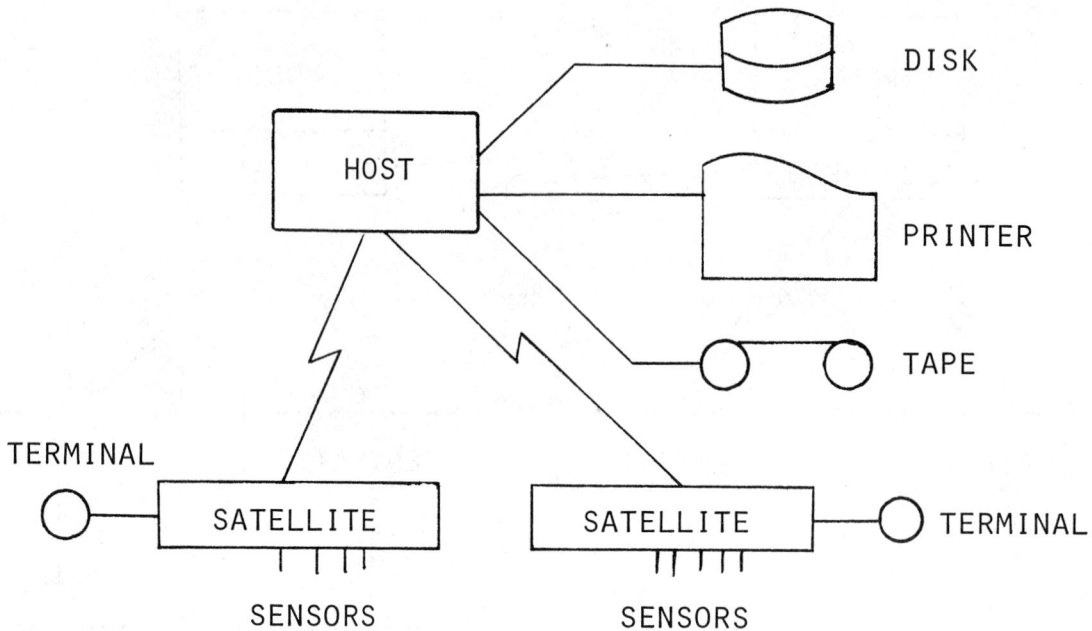

FIGURE 2

Resource Sharing Networks are often motivated by cost considerations, and thus the cost of the intersystem links is
often a major consideration. For this reason, asynchronous
links using private wires tend to be a common choice.

DISTRIBUTED COMPUTING SYSTEMS allow many autonomous computer
systems to cooperate in solving very complex problems, such
as the operation of a large manufacturing plant or a hospital.
There are many reasons why such an approach to computing is
increasingly attractive. First, it makes possible the dedi-
cation of machines in the network to specific functions.
This simplifies application program development, and makes
reliability analyses easier. Addition of new functions can
be handled by developing the new application off-line, and
plugging it into the network when it is fully debugged. A
major benefit of the use of distributed systems is to allow
the coupling of heterogeneous computers and/or operating
systems to solve different parts of an application most effectively. Every computer and/or operating system is optimized around a different orientation, and consequently does
some things more easily or inexpensively than others. A
distributed system allows each system to be used the way it
was intended to be used; there is no longer any need to try
to perform 'real-time' work on a timesharing computer (to
the probable detriment of both). A distributed network

allows real time tasks to be performed on a real-time system, and time sharing tasks to be run on a timesharing system, with tasks on both machines sharing a common data base.

Very often, distributed systems are implemented as hier-archies of computers, as shown below:

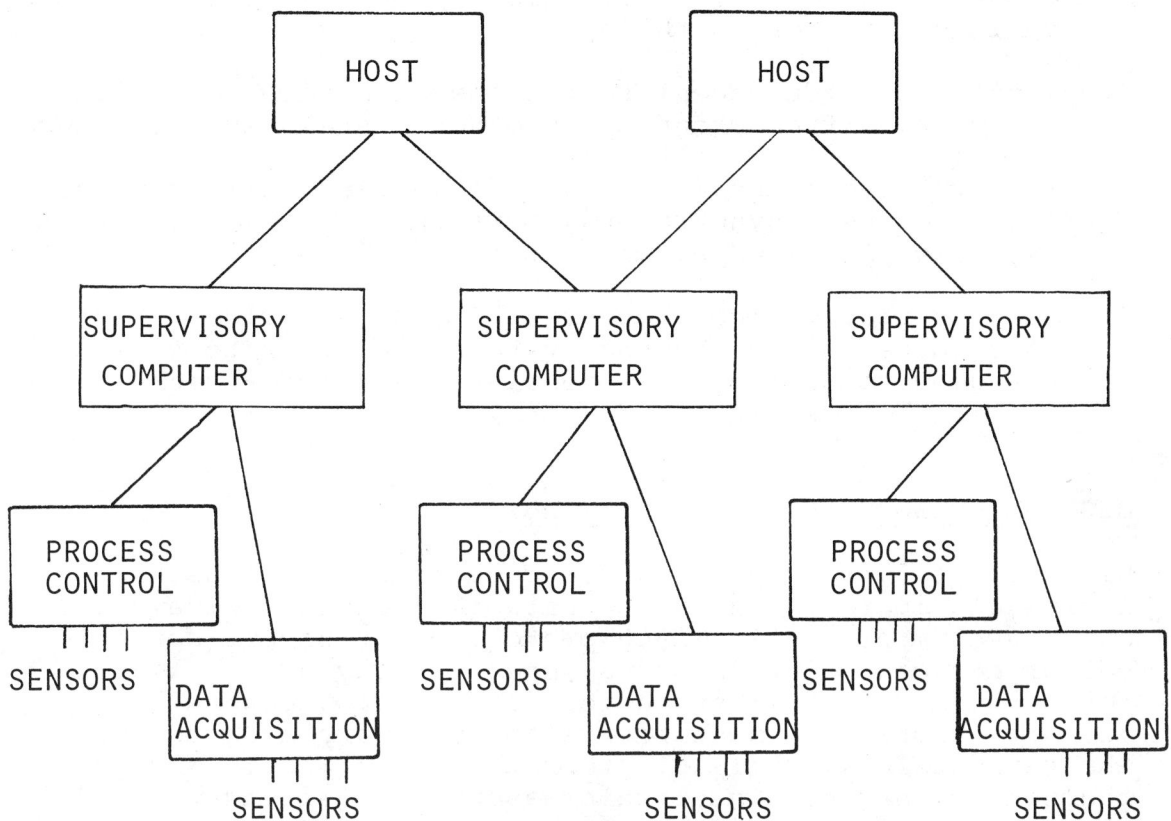

FIGURE 3

The hosts in such systems normally contain sophisticated pro-grams for dealing with both data and humans. The process control and data acquisition computers are sensor based machines, with only limited ability to manage local data bases. The intermediate machines are oriented towards supervisory functions, and perform such mundane functions as loading programs into the sensor based machines and switch-ing data from one low-level machine to the next. A variety of big and small machines, and fast and slow links, is necessary to implement such a network.

NETWORK ARCHITECTURE REQUIREMENTS

Given the applications described above, the following requirements were identified as being essential to the implementation of networks using Digital's (or any other manufacturer's) equipment:

1. Need to provide flexible communications paths between programs (including applications programs) operating on various machines in the network.

2. Need to provide access to peripheral devices and files on one machine from programs on other systems in the network.

3. Need to permit the use of a wide variety of link types (synchronous, asynchronous, parallel) in order to satisfy range of price/performance trade-offs.

4. Need to provide the above facilities in a wide variety of machines and operating systems, in order to permit the user to select an appropriate system for each application within the network.

DIGITAL NETWORK ARCHITECTURE (DNA)

Digital's solution to the above requirements has been to define and implement a set of network protocols within its major system products. Each protocol addresses a specific set of network related issues; specifically data reliability, network management (message routing and flow control) and resource sharing. The hardware and software architectures of the various individual DEC products differ widely amongst themselves (due to historical reasons), requiring that the elements of DNA be made quite general. Thus DNA is broad enough to operate with almost all known machine architectures, and is not limited to (or even oriented towards) any particular machine, word size, or other architectural parameter. The only fundamental requirement is the ability to handle eight bit data bytes.

DNA has three basic components, all of which must be implemented in orthodox network members. (Some unorthodox members have successfully omitted various layers with concommitant limits in functionality.) The basic components of DNA are:

1. *DDCMP* (Digital Data Communications Message Protocol). DDCMP is a link protocol, responsible for the integrity of transmitted data, and for link management functions in half-duplex and multidrop links.

2. *NSP* (Network Services Protocol). NSP provides network management services, including the routing of data messages between various end points in the network, and the management of message queues in each node.

3. *DAP* (Data Access Protocol). DAP provides resource sharing facilities in the network, by allowing user programs on one system to access files and devices on other members of the network. DAP compensates for the differences in input-output primitives and file structures which exist between many of DEC's operating systems.

These protocols work in concert to satisfy the needs enumerated earlier. Breaking out the various functions into separate protocols simplifies the implementation task, and often makes various elements of an implementation transportable to other systems. The following discussion provides more detail on the individual protocols:

DDCMP

DDCMP is a link protocol which operates efficiently over a wide variety of link types, including both half and full duplex links, and synchronous, asynchronous and parallel links. DDCMP utilizes conventional, character oriented communications devices, and does not require the new 'bit stuffing' devices necessary for the SDLC and HDLC protocols. DDCMP is effective on earth satellite links, which have long signal propagation delays and low error rates.

A typical DDCMP message consists of a header, user text, and a CRC-16 checksum:

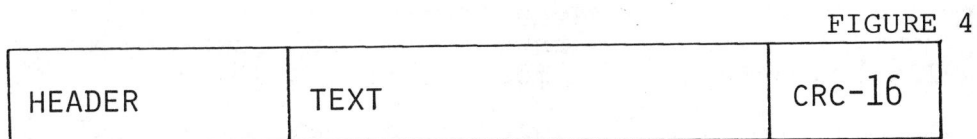

FIGURE 4

HEADER	TEXT	CRC-16

The header contains information relating to the acknowledgement of previous messages, the polling of stations (in a multipoint environment), and the length of the text field. The header has its own CRC-16 check, in order to maintain the integrity of the protocol. This information is arranged as follows:

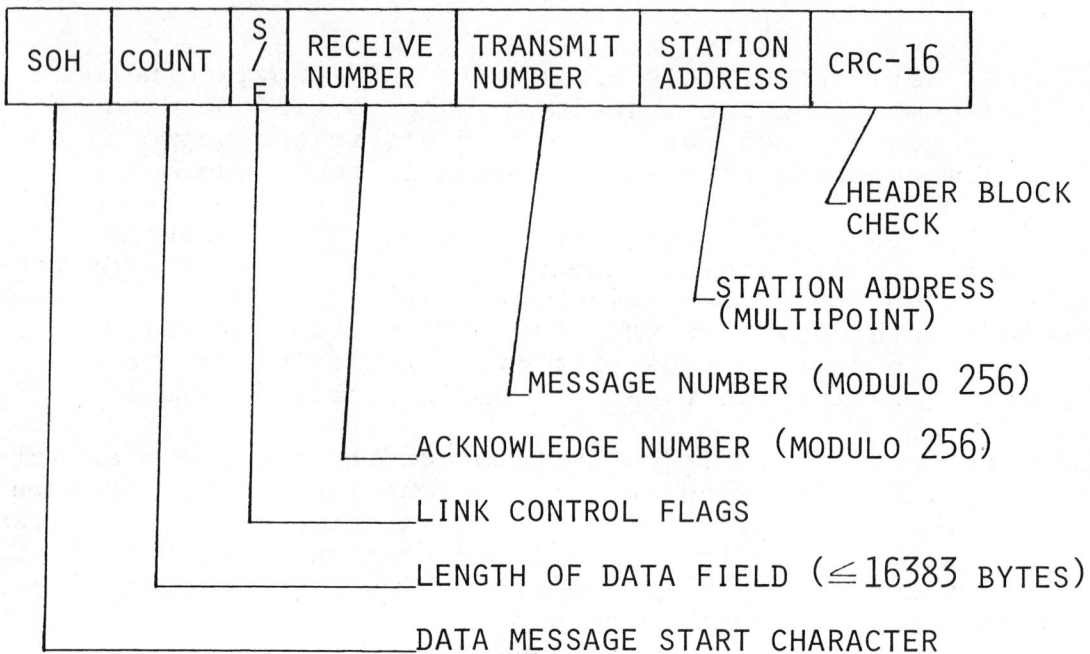

```
┌──────┬───────┬───┬─────────┬──────────┬─────────┬────────┐
│      │       │ S │ RECEIVE │ TRANSMIT │ STATION │        │
│ SOH  │ COUNT │ / │ NUMBER  │ NUMBER   │ ADDRESS │ CRC-16 │
│      │       │ E │         │          │         │        │
└──────┴───────┴───┴─────────┴──────────┴─────────┴────────┘
```

HEADER BLOCK
CHECK

STATION ADDRESS
(MULTIPOINT)

MESSAGE NUMBER (MODULO 256)

ACKNOWLEDGE NUMBER (MODULO 256)

LINK CONTROL FLAGS

LENGTH OF DATA FIELD (≤ 16383 BYTES)

DATA MESSAGE START CHARACTER

FIGURE 5

In normal protocol operation, messages are individually numbered and transmitted over the link without necessarily waiting for acknowledgements of previously transmitted messages.
If such acknowledgement is not received eventually, the
transmitting station can request a response from the receiver,
or it can assume the message was not received and merely retransmit the unacknowledged message and all its successors.

The acknowledgement scheme is such that acknowledging the
correct receipt of message N implies correct receipt of all
message up to N as well; thus it is not necessary to individually acknowledge each message received.

The count field in the header is used to provide transparency for the text field. The receiver will be aware how
long the intended message will be (useful for buffer allocation) and will know when the message has been received.
The header CRC check validates the count field. Since the
transparency feature doesn't require 'bit stuffing' techniques, it is appropriate for asynchronous and parallel
facilities as well as serial synchronous channels.

NSP

The Network Services Protocol is a 'logical link' protocol
within DNA. User programs on various nodes communicate via

NSP's logical link facilities. NSP handles both the multi-plexing of logical links onto physical links, and the flow control within the network.

NSP messages are wholly contained in the 'text' portion of DDCMP messages, and have the following format:

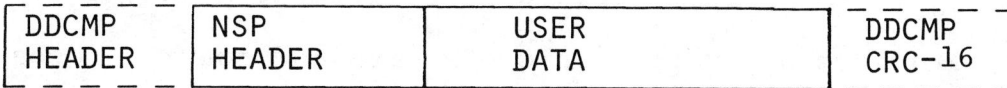

DDCMP HEADER	NSP HEADER	USER DATA	DDCMP CRC-16

FIGURE 6

The NSP header contains information necessary for routing messages within the network. This information is arranged as follows:

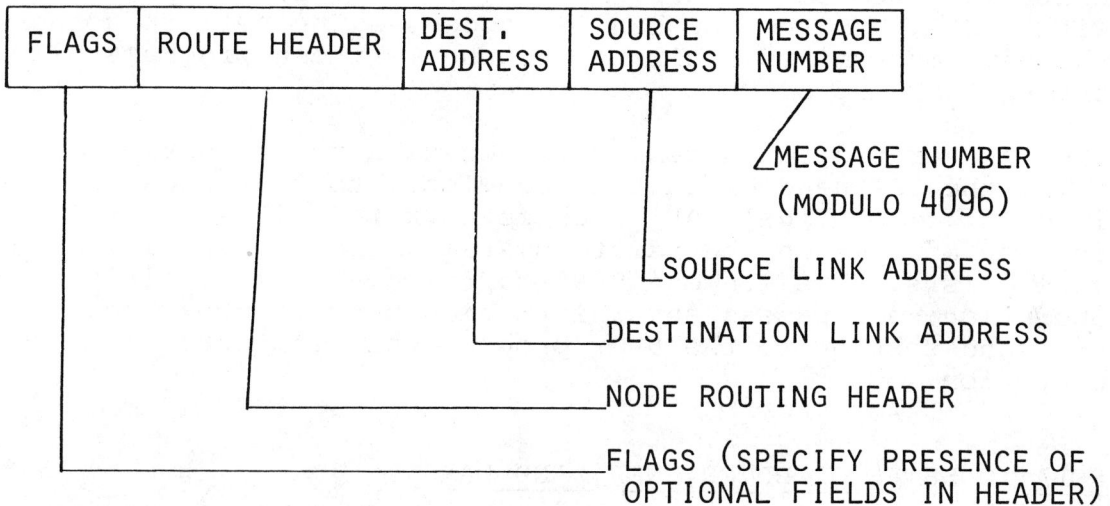

FLAGS	ROUTE HEADER	DEST. ADDRESS	SOURCE ADDRESS	MESSAGE NUMBER

MESSAGE NUMBER (MODULO 4096)

SOURCE LINK ADDRESS

DESTINATION LINK ADDRESS

NODE ROUTING HEADER

FLAGS (SPECIFY PRESENCE OF OPTIONAL FIELDS IN HEADER)

FIGURE 7

User programs wishing to communicate via the network do so via NSP. They have five basic primitives they use for network operations:

CONNECT -- This initiates the creation of a logical link to another program elsewhere in the network.

DISCONNECT -- This initiates the destruction of a logical link.

SEND DATA -- This is used to indicate the program wishes to transmit data over a logical link.

RECEIVE DATA -- The program uses this to indicate its
readiness to receive data. No data flows
over a logical link until one end has done a
'send' and the other a 'receive'.

TRANSMIT INTERRUPT -- This is used to send a small, non-
solicited message across the logical link.
No prior 'receive' need have been executed.

These primitives are mapped into NSP data and control messages,
and transmitted to the appropriate destinations.

DAP

The Data Access Protocol creates a machine independent format for data exchange with I/O devices and files within the
network. It is concerned with record and file formats, and
control of remote devices. DAP is a 'user level' protocol
within DNA, and the DAP handler accesses the network using
the same mechanisms available to user-written programs; i.e.
through NSP and DDCMP.

When a user program attempts to access a remote device or
file, the DAP handler on the node local to that program is
invoked. The 'local DAP' uses network facilities to talk to
the DAP modules on the remote system where the specified device exists. The 'remote DAP' carries out the specified
operation, and passes any information back to the 'local
DAP' and then on to the user program that initiated the
operation.

RELATIONSHIPS OF DDCMP, NSP, AND DAP

As previously noted, user programs have two basic mechanisms
with which to use the network. They can talk to other user
programs (using NSP as an intermediary) or they can utilize
remote resources by talking to DAP.

When user programs talk to each other, the flow of data
would be as follows:

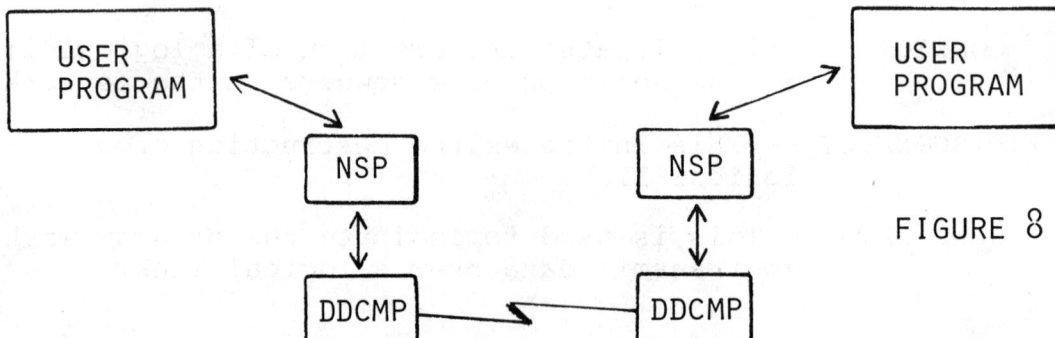

FIGURE 8

When a user program is utilizing the network to access remote resources, the picture would be slightly different:

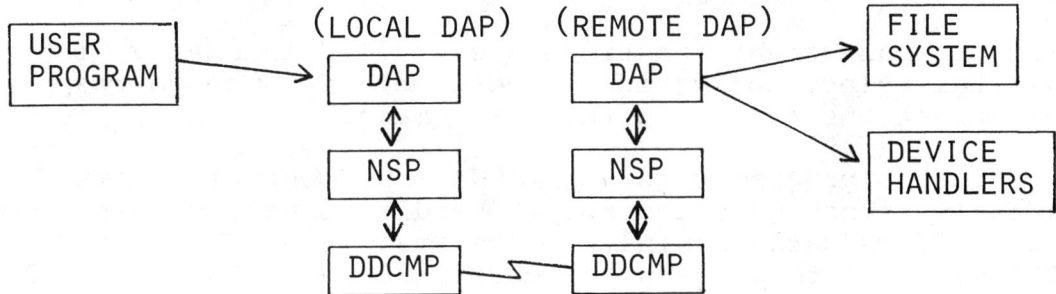

FIGURE 9

In actuality, user programs on each system can both be communicating with each other and accessing remote devices concurrently. Thus, the complete version of the above picture is the following:

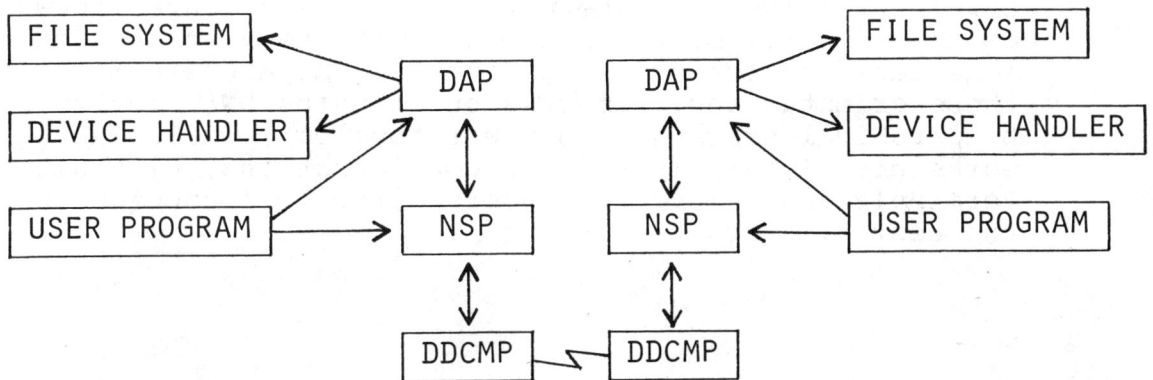

FIGURE 10

RELATIONSHIP OF DNA TO SNA

It is inevitable that the Digital Network Architecture will be compared and contrasted to IBM's announced Systems Network Architecture (SNA). There are many similarities and some significant differences.

Both architectures utilize a layered, functional approach to protocol definition. The link protocols (DDCMP and SDLC) have similar functional capabilities, but achieve these capabilities using different techniques. The DDCMP approach allows the use of synchronous, asynchronous, and parallel links, while SDLC is limited to synchronous links only. SDLC, conversely, has fewer protocol states, and requires slightly less hardware to implement.

Network management functions are handled in SNA by VTAM, the virtual telecommunications access method. The corresponding DNA functions fall into the NSP domain.

NCP is the program within the SNA implementation that actually runs the network. It handles lines, converts codes, and buffers data terminals. Its analog in DNA is the code DEC provides to process the DDCMP, NSP, and DAP protocols.

From a functional standpoint, there are two outstanding differences between DNA and SNA:

1. DNA is oriented towards *computer* networks. Its strongest point is providing the facilities for interprogram communication across system boundaries. SNA is oriented toward *terminal* networks. Its strongest point is providing facilities for user programs to talk to a variety of general purpose and specialized terminals.

2. DNA is oriented towards distributed control and distributed intelligence in networks. SNA is oriented towards central control of the network, with the distribution of some tasks to the outlying systems. As a consequence of these orientations, networks built using DNA tend to be hierarchical or random in their topology, while SNA networks are almost always star configurations, with all terminals and remote processors directly connected to the central system/370.

REFERENCES

Digital Equipment Corp., DDCMP Specification, December, 1974

Digital Equipment Corp., DAP Specification, April, 1975

Digital Equipment Corp., NSP Specification, April, 1975

IBM's Systems Network Architecture, J.P. Gray & C.R. Blair, "Datamation", April, 1975

IBM System Network Architecture, Auerbach Computer Technology Reports, May, 1975

The problems of connecting hosts into ARPANET

by

Adrian V.Stokes and Peter L.Higginson

Department of Statistics and Computer Science
University College London
UK

ABSTRACT

   The DEC PDP-9 at University College London is connected to a Terminal Interface Message Processor, the communication computer of the ARPA Network. It is also connected to the Rutherford Laboratory (RL) 360/195 and the Cambridge Computer Aided Design Centre ATLAS via leased lines. It is intended to connect the PDP-9 to other computers and networks in the near future. In this paper, we describe a novel approach to the problem of connecting Hosts to a computer network with particular reference to the RL 360 to ARPANET as a specific illustration. In our approach, all the network-dependent software is provided in the PDP-9, thus requiring only minimal changes to the software in the large computer. We describe the problems we have encountered and how they have been overcome. We mention that this approach is being used to connect other computers to ARPANET through the PDP-9.

1. INTRODUCTION

In order to connect a computer as a Host into the US Advanced Research Projects Agency network (ARPANET), it is necessary to write and test a considerable body of software (Ref. 1). This has a number of disadvantages, the major one of which is the probable interruption of services on the mainframe. In this paper, we describe an alternative approach whereby all the network-dependent software is written in a small computer and no software changes need be made in the main Host. In the case where only one large computer is connected to a network, such an approach has many obvious advantages, especially in a case such as ours where the large machine is not under our control. When more than one computer is connected, the approach is invaluable for a large number of reasons which we outline below.

In this paper, we describe how we have implemented a system whereby the IBM 360/195 at the Rutherford Laboratory (RL) was connected as a Host to ARPANET using a PDP-9 computer to perform the relevant protocol conversions. We describe the problems encountered in some detail and the solutions we have applied. We then describe briefly how this approach has been generalized to allow the connection of other machines.

2. HISTORICAL BACKGROUND

For a number of years, the DEC PDP-9 at University College London (UCL) has been connected via a 2400 bps leased line to the RL 360/195. In addition to the standard HASP batch facilities, it has a message switching system (MAST) which allows messages to be sent between on-line terminals and/or programs. In particular, this allows access to an interactive editor (ELECTRIC, Ref. 2) and to an output retrieval and graphics system (MUGWUMP).

The 360/195, under HASP/RJE, supports about 30 remote workstations (mainly GEC 2050 computers) which simulate, in most cases, IBM 1130 remote job entry workstations. A local modification to HASP allows terminal traffic to be multi-leaved with the standard peripherals i.e. card readers, punches, line printers and system console (Ref. 3).

The PDP-9 has 24K words (18 bit) of core, a 256K drum, two DEC-tape drives and various communication interfaces. It runs a locally written multi-programming operating system (Ref. 4) which allows program segments to be loaded dynamically from drum. It is connected to a standard ARPANET communications computer, the Terminal Interface Message Processor (TIP; see Ref. 5); this is a 28K word Honeywell DDP 516 which handles communication with the rest of ARPANET, attachment of keyboard terminals (directly or via the telephone network) and Host computers. The UCL configuration relevant to this discussion is shown in Fig. 1

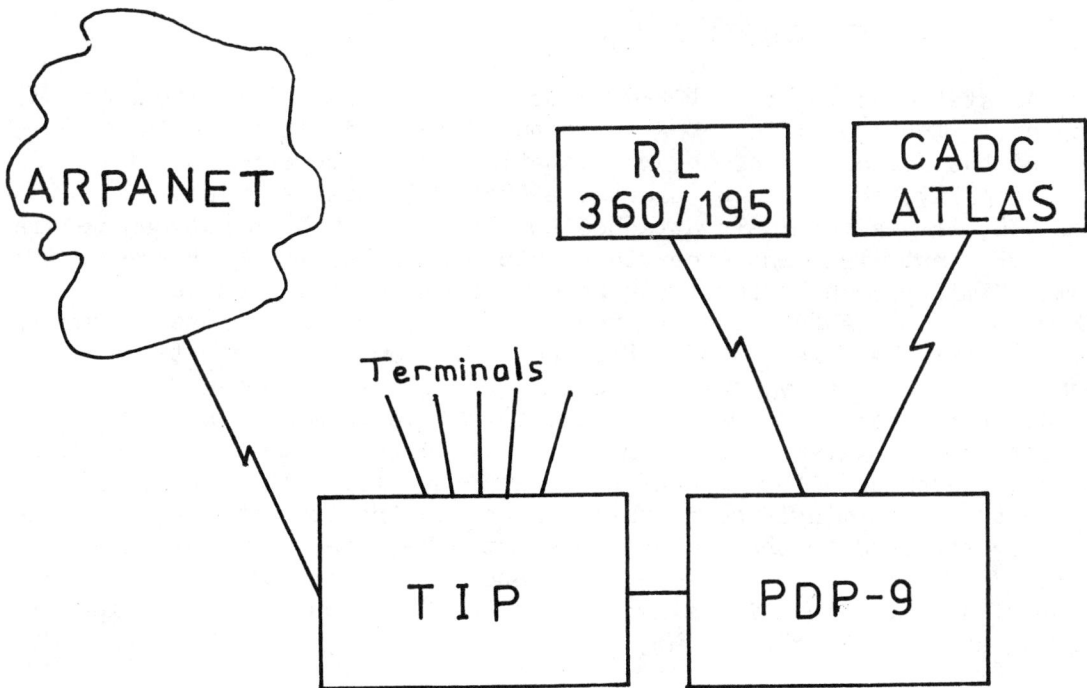

Figure 1:   UCL Computer Configuration

This PDP-9 may be viewed from a number of different aspects. From ARPANET (from henceforth, when referring to ARPANET, we will specifically mean the communications sub-network; similarly, when we refer to the protocols of the ARPA network, we will refer to them, for brevity, as the ARPA Protocols), it is a standard host, implementing all the low-level ARPA protocols. From the point of view of an ARPANET user, it provides an almost transparent front-end function to whichever large computer he wishes to access through it, implementing most of the server functions (see Sec. 3) of the higher-level ARPA protocols. From the RL 360 (and, of course, a similar point of view exists for any large computer connected in this way), the PDP-9 is simply a standard Remote Job Entry workstation. Finally, a user on the 360 sees the PDP-9 as, effectively, a local process providing the user functions of the ARPA protocols.

In reality, none of these viewpoints is complete. The PDP-9 consists of a number of co-existing and co-operating programs, each simulating the appropriate functions to the machine or network for which it is designed and between which it is possible to make virtual connections(Ref. 6). We now consider how such a function is performed in the specific case of the connection of the RL 360 and ARPANET.

3. THE PDP-9 SIMULATED WORKSTATION

As stated above, the PDP-9 simulates an IBM 1130 to the RL machine. The specific configuration simulated is shown in Fig. 2. Some of the capability of the work station is for members of the UCL group locally, the rest for users via ARPANET. Most terminal use, even from UCL, is via terminals attached to the TIP. Bulk output can be via the TIP, but is also done via printers attached to the PDP-9 or its drum. Similarly, bulk input can be done from the file stores on the PDP-9 or from ARPANET. Of the three pseudo line printers, one is reserved for the File Transfer Protocol (FTP) and the other two are for local use. Similarly, one of the card readers is reserved for the FTP and one for local use. Of the five interactive terminal streams, one is the HASP system console and is always directed to a local device; three are available for ARPANET users and the fifth is submultiplexed so that 360 terminal users (there is no distinction between terminals directly attached to the 360 and those attached via workstations) may access ARPANET. The 360 is, of course, totally unaware of such a mapping, any more than it is aware that the "card punch" used locally is, in reality, the PDP-9 drum.

In the other direction, we have the connection to ARPANET. In order to make such a connection, a number of protocols must be written and the levels of the various protocols and their inter-relationships are shown in Fig. 3. The lower-level protocols are mandatory (Host-Imp and Imp-Host). The next level, the Host-Host protocol is also mandatory (it is unnecessary if two Hosts have agreed on an alternative protocol; as almost all Hosts have implemented the standard protocol, this makes it effectively mandatory). At the highest level, the user level, it is completely optional which protocols are implemented. Furthermore, at this level, each protocol consists of two distinct parts, the Server function and the User function, and each may be implemented individually. Specifically, at the date of writing, we have implemented the User and Server TELNET protocols and the Server FTP. In practice, implementation of the Server TELNET gives access to the 360 terminal streams from ARPANET, the User TELNET gives access to ARPANET from 360 interactive terminals and the FTP allows files to be transferred to or from RL, at the initiation of another Host.

The above paragraph is an oversimplification of the true picture. Implementation of the Server TELNET specifically gives the ARPA user access to an interactive terminal stream on the PDP-9 and it is necessary to map this function onto the RL terminal streams. Also, it is necessary to define some protocols whereby the user may specify which machine he wishes to access and any optional parameters of the interaction, for example, to specify his terminal type. This problem exists even with only one large machine attached to the PDP-9, since the user may wish to have access to some of the (albeit highly restricted) PDP-9 functions.

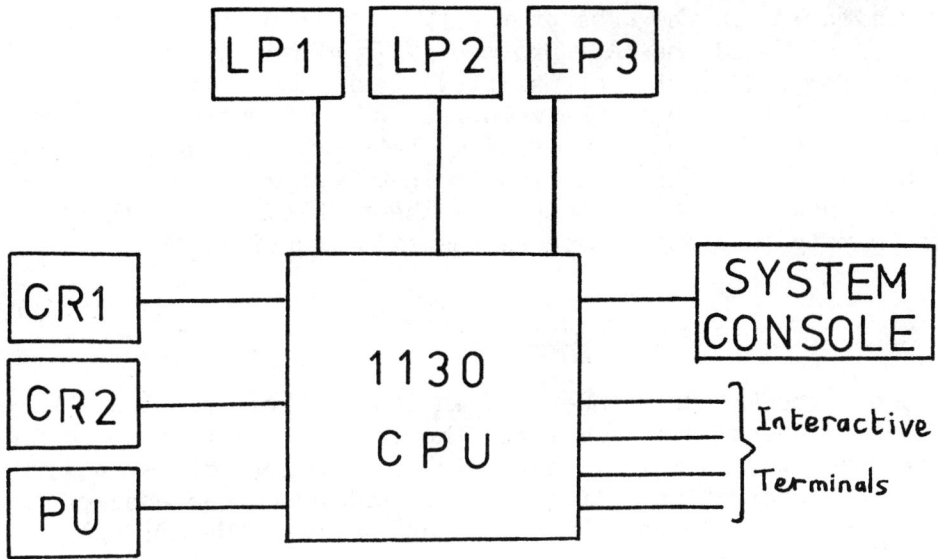

Figure 2:   The PDP-9 Simulated RJE Workstation

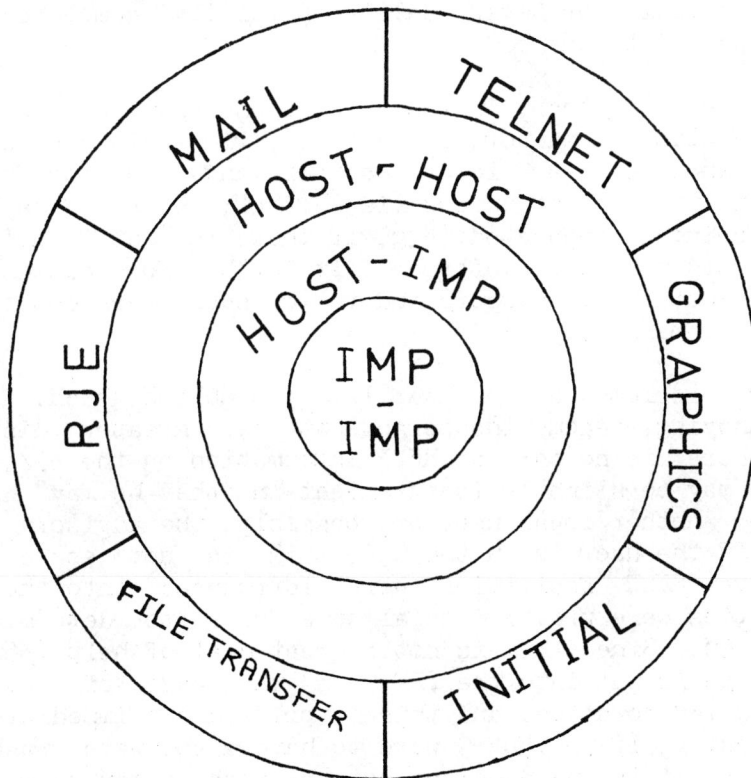

Figure 3:   Relationship of ARPA Protocols

Similarly, in the case of the FTP, it is necessary to map between the ARPA FTP and the HASP protocol. In general, it is a relatively straight-forward (but not simple) task to write the appropriate software to interface to the networks and computers mentioned above. However, the problem of mapping between the various higher-level protocols for the different systems is more complex and it is upon this that we now focus our attention. The problem may be divided into two parts, namely interactive access and file transfer.

4. INTERACTIVE TERMINAL ACCESS

Since the ARPANET concept of an interactive terminal stream and the 360 concept are similar, there is no basic problem in mapping between the two. However, there is one major difference. ARPANET views an interactive stream as a continuous sequence of characters (which may be interrupted at any point) whereas the RL operates on a line-at-a-time basis. Therefore, for data directed to RL, the PDP-9 reconstructs lines from ARPA users in addition to performing such functions as code conversion. Although this has some disadvantages, it does allow users to edit or even delete partially completed lines before they are passed to the 360.

A further problem is that, in the case of users who access the 360 in a more conventional manner, for example, via a dial-up port, the machine is aware when the user loses contact and can log him out accordingly. In the case of access via ARPANET, the PDP-9 may not be aware of a user being disconnected (e.g. if there is "Net Trouble") and hence the 360 could not be so informed. It is therefore necessary for the PDP-9 to time-out inactive users and to log such users out from the 360 in a controlled manner.

There are also problems at the user level; problems which, at short distances are annoying, become insuperable at far greater distances. For example, there is no on-line HELP information on the 360. For a local user, this may be slightly inconvenient in that he may have to telephone either another local user or, possibly, the advisory service at Rutherford. If the user is in the USA, this is not as easy and hence interactive HELP facilities were introduced into the PDP-9. Secondly, facilities were provided to allow a user to determine the status of the 360. Since this is not a great deal of help (360 IS UP or DOWN), a message is put into the PDP-9 in the case of any known problems or scheduled downtime, and this is printed out immediately any user logs in. Lastly, if the PDP-9 were to have a software crash while being used locally, it is inconvenient but the machine may be restarted easily. If the user is in America and the PDP-9 is unattended (it has no operator), such an event would be disastrous. Hence automatic restart facilities were provided in the PDP-9.

As far as 360 terminal access to ARPANET was concerned, more problems were encountered, mainly due to flow control. MAST has an extremely simple-minded flow control algorithm - namely that if the destination is unable to accept the message (or even if MAST has no spare buffers), it is returned to the source. Subsequent lines may or may not be accepted. In the case of an interactive user, this is a reasonable algorithm, although it may lead to problems. In the case where the origin is a program, a more sophisticated form of control is necessary. It may be noted that this facility is not specifically a requirement of ARPANET, but is necessary for any network connection.

The flow control algorithm implemented was a simple modification to that mentioned above, namely that, if a line could not be sent, all subsequent lines for the same destination in the current block were also rejected by the 360 and the source (PDP-9) was informed of the number of lines accepted in each block. This allows the PDP-9 to attempt to adapt to the flow control situation in the 360 by using the acceptance rate of the 360 to control the submission rate of lines.

The difference between the 360 and ARPANET interactive terminal concepts is more serious with use of ARPANET from the 360. Programs on ARPANET Hosts are frequently written to generate incomplete lines on output or require them on input. This means that the PDP-9 has to provide line reconstruction from ARPA in the case of lines to users on the 360. Similarly, it has to provide ways of generating lines that do not terminate in carriage return in the case of 360 users accessing other ARPANET Hosts.

5. THE PROBLEMS OF FILE TRANSFER

Unfortunately, the ARPA File Transfer Protocol does not map into a corresponding HASP protocol and this leads to many problems. In particular, the ARPA protocol assumes access to the file system, whereas the only access to files is via the batch stream on the 360, or, in the case of Electric files, via the interactive terminal ports. Therefore, two methods were considered for implementation. The first, that of reserving an interactive port, immediately ran into the problem of flow control mentioned above, especially since the solution only applied to terminal-to-terminal traffic. Also, only a limited number of terminal ports are available and there was no guarantee that one would be free when required (unless specifically reserved for the FTP, a solution which was considered to be too extravagant). Therefore, the second alternative was explored, namely to use standard utility programs via the batch stream. This suffered from the significant disadvantage that the job was likely to take a few minutes to run. In extreme cases (particularly on retrieving a file when two consecutive jobs must be run), the remote FTP User Process may time out, or, rather more likely, the remote user may become impatient and abort the transfer. This problem has been alleviated by having a high priority for such jobs, but nevertheless there is still a significant delay of up to a few minutes.

Another problem arose on retrieving a file, namely to indicate that the eventual destination of the file was ARPANET rather than the local line printer. This was solved by use of the HASP FORMS facility intended to enable an operator to load special stationery into a printer. By setting a (virtual) printer to special forms whenever the PDP-9 signs onto the 360, it can be ensured that all output for the FTP goes to that "printer" and hence may be distinguished by the PDP-9 and sent to its ultimate destination.

Finally, there is a problem of status information. Not only does the 360 not automatically provide this information, but the utility we are currently using gives a return code of zero (usually reserved for correct programs) irrespective of the faults encountered. This has been alleviated by allowing the user access to the output from the job via the interactive terminals, but this is not an elegant solution.

To overcome all the above problems, we are currently writing a utility program which will provide accurate status information (although this will still have to be requested explicitly by the PDP-9), will only require submission of one job and furthermore, will fully implement the protocol (there are a few cases at present where it is not possible to implement the protocol as specified; for example, the ARPA protocol specifies that the APPEND command should create a new file if one of that name does not already exist, whereas the 360 utility will not only not create the file, but will abort the job).

One advantage of using the batch stream for the FTP is that it has allowed us to implement a simple form of Remote Job Entry with no extra problems whatsoever. This is achieved by putting the "file" which is, in fact, a complete job, into the batch stream without modification. It is even possible to retrieve the output of such a job in a similar manner (the RETRIEVE command simply opens the data connection). Because of timeout problems, it is only practicable to retrieve output in this manner if the job is of high priority, otherwise its output should be directed to the filing system for retrieval at a later time (or to MUGWUMP for interactive access).

6.   THE CAMBRIDGE COMPUTER AIDED DESIGN CENTRE (CADC)

The CADC at Cambridge has an Atlas computer which is also connected to ARPANET via our PDP-9. In this case, te connection is not as sophisticated as that for the RL 360 but is nevertheless a considerable improvement over the other alternative, that of connecting it directly to the TIP. In the case of this connection, the PDP-9 simulates an interactive terminal to the CADC and conversely. However, because of the large buffer space provided in the PDP-9 (about 30 K characters for all buffering, allocated dynamically), it can communicate with CADC over a 1200 bps line. This connection is temporary and will be replaced by a connection via EPSS later this year.

7. SUMMARY AND CONCLUSIONS

In this paper, we have described the problems encountered in putting the RL 360/195 as a Host on ARPANET via a PDP-9. These problems have been minor and are far outweighed by the considerable advantages. Specifically, these are that only very minor changes have been made to the software of the larger machine (and these changes would have been necessary for connection to any other network) and that all software development has taken place on the smaller machine. Since all the ARPANET specific software is in the PDP-9, considerably less effort is now needed to put other Hosts onto ARPANET via the PDP-9. The University of London Computer Centre (ULCC) CDC 6400/6600/7600 complex has been attached in an experimental way and will soon be included in the standard system. In this case, the PDP-9 simulates a USER 200 terminal. Future plans include a connection to the Post Office Experimental Packet Switched Service (EPSS)

Acknowledgements

We acknowledge gratefully the support of the British Library, the British Post Office, the Department of Industry, the Science Research Council and the US Advanced Projects Agency which has made this research possible.

References

1.   -- , "Current Network Protocols", ARPA Network Information Center, NIC 7104, 1973.

2.   Burren J et.al., "Electric Users Manual", RHEL-72-03, Rutherford Laboratory, 1972.

3.   Girard, P., "HASP Remote Station Handling and On-line Console Support", RL-73-074, 1973.

4.   Gould, I.H., "PDP-9 Multiprogramming System Users' Guide", ICSP 130, Institute of Computer Science, 1974.

5.   -- , "User's Guide To The Terminal Imp", Report No. 2183, Bolt Beranek and Newman, Cambridge Mass., 1973.

6.   Higginson, P.L. and Hinchley, A.J., "The Problems of Linking Several Networks with a Gateway Computer", Proceedings of this Conference.

The UPARS Network: an extensive network servicing several diverse applications

THE UPARS NETWORK -
AN EXTENSIVE NETWORK SERVICING
SEVERAL DIVERSE APPLICATIONS

James C. Goodlett
Manager of Technical Services
United Airlines, USA

ABSTRACT

The United Airlines UPARS network is an extensive
data communications network. It services such applications as airline reservations functions, a training
package, a Food Services management information system,
and the Western International Hotels reservations system.
The network currently services 113 cities, 15 consolidated
reservations offices, 25 on-line hotels, and 21 food
service kitchens. It stretches approximately 57,000 miles
throughout much of the U.S.A., into Canada, and down to
Mexico City. This paper briefly describes the UPARS
network and some of its special features. Descriptions
are also given of two functions allowing a closer look at
specific solutions to unique application needs.

INTRODUCTION

The UPARS system is a large, real-time multi-application computer system. This system is United Airlines' version of the basic IBM PARS system. Using 360/195 computers, the Airline Control Program has been modified to handle several independent applications on a single processor. The applications functions are for airline reservations, hotel reservations, corporate training, and an MIS system for the Food Services Division.

The airline reservations application (APOLLO) actually is in itself a combination of numerous software packages performing such functions as booking reservations, fraud control, automated fare-quote and teleticketing, passenger check-in, and automatic teleticketing. The airline reservations system has handled a peak message traffic of 3,404,399 messages in a 24 hour period with a 10 second burst at 104 messages/second. The WIH hotel system (WESTRON) is a comprehensive reservations system for hotels. It contains a Guest Name Record and provides a full reservations capability along with internal administrative message switching. Future features of the system, currently under development, will provide accounting and billing capabilities.

The training function is a computer aided instruction (CAI) system accessible from all terminals on the UPARS system. It makes available an interactive training capability usable by all UPARS applications. CAI is primarily for the training of new agents and for training agents in the use of new or modified applications. The Food Services MIS system (FAMIS) is being developed as a comprehensive system to service the dynamic needs of the UAL Food Services Division. Phases I and II are operational at this time and encompass labor data collection, purchasing and receiving. Phases III and IV will be completed by 1977 and will fulfill food checksheets, profit/loss and liquor checksheet needs of the division.

Several thousand users of these applications are located in 113 city and airport ticket offices, 15

consolidated reservations offices, 25 hotels[1], and 21
Food Services kitchens. To connect these users with the
system, the network stretches 56,999 miles through much
of the U.S.A., into Canada and down to Mexico City.
    The UPARS system also has links to a Univac 1108
system (Unimatic) in Chicago which has its own nation-
wide network. While basically an airline operations and
maintenance system, the Unimatic system services some
airport and city ticket offices for APOLLO along with
handling corporate message switching and data communication to the 'outside' world. This network requires in
excess of 28,000 miles of dedicated leased lines and
services over 1,700 CRTs and printers.
    Three groups have been especially important to the
success of the UPARS network. The Technical Services
group has assisted in the design and implementation of
the network. They have also designed and, in some cases,
built special communications equipment. This equipment
has allowed some substantial cost savings while making
available special features for reliability and maintenance of the network. The Performance group, using
simulation models and deterministic methods, has successfully predicted the impact of suggested changes to the
UPARS system. Special on-line data collection of performance information has provided the ability to validate
models and forecasts along with suggesting ways to 'fine
tune' the system. The Operations group backed up by
Technical Services and Performance is the first line of
defense for debugging network troubles. Resolution time
of problems has been substantially reduced by careful
monitoring and investigation. By these three groups
working together, many new applications and equipment
with considerable network impact have successfully been
implemented.

THE NETWORK

    Structurally, the UPARS network can be viewed as a
star composed of 'backbone' 4800 Baud and 'prime' 2400
Baud lines. The current network is configured with
twelve 4800 Baud and forty 2400 Baud lines terminating

---

[1]The rest of the WIH chain, all outside the U.S.A., are
serviced by a reservations center in Seattle basically
through teletype communications.

at central site. The backbone is used in several ways.
High volume reservations offices such as Chicago, New
York, and San Francisco are serviced directly from the
backbone. Lower volume offices are serviced from one
side of a split backbone (multiplexed into two 2400 Baud
lines). The other side of a split line is frequently
used to service downline offices. Other backbone lines
are split into two connector lines both servicing multiple
downline offices. There are approximately sixty 2400
Baud multidrop lines currently in use off the backbone
lines.

Depending on the message volume of the drops serviced, Terminal Control Units (TCU) or terminals are
either connected directly to the connector line or to a
Line Control Unit (LCU). The LCU is a 4K mini-computer
servicing up to 16 low volume drops off of a 2400 Baud
line. It accepts a poll for all 16 units and only re-
directs the poll on to terminals with traffic; hence, an
increase in polling efficiency for low volume drops is
effected. A United developed unit called a Modem Sharing
Device (MSD) allows further hardware efficiencies on a
2400 Baud line by servicing up to four 2400 Baud lines
from one modem and an MSD. The MSD is used both to service numerous terminals in a given locality and to allow
consolidation of up to four 2400 Baud lines handling
diverse low volume traffic. A new version of the MSD
solves the problem of line equalization on a simply configured 4800 Baud multidrop circuit. Figure A is an
example of an MSD configuration.

An enhancement at the CPU end of the system comes
from use of a Port Sharing Device (PSD). This United
developed device allows a port on the central site communications controller (IBM 2969 or 2703) to be shared by
multiple prime lines. Thus, a single 2400 Baud port can
be shared by up to four 2400 Baud lines servicing connector circuits, LCUs or even dial-up facilities.
Additionally, this unit incorporates modem-eliminator
capability to hook up central site terminals on a digital
circuit without the use of modems. As is described later,
the PSD also enhances dial-up capabilities.

The network uses direct polling through IBM 2969 and
2703 controllers attached to an IBM 360/195 computer. An
additional controller (IBM 3705) is expected to be operational on the system in November 1975. This will allow
reconfiguration of the network to handle the peak 1975
traffic expected in December. To improve polling efficiency, a continuous poll was developed to overcome the

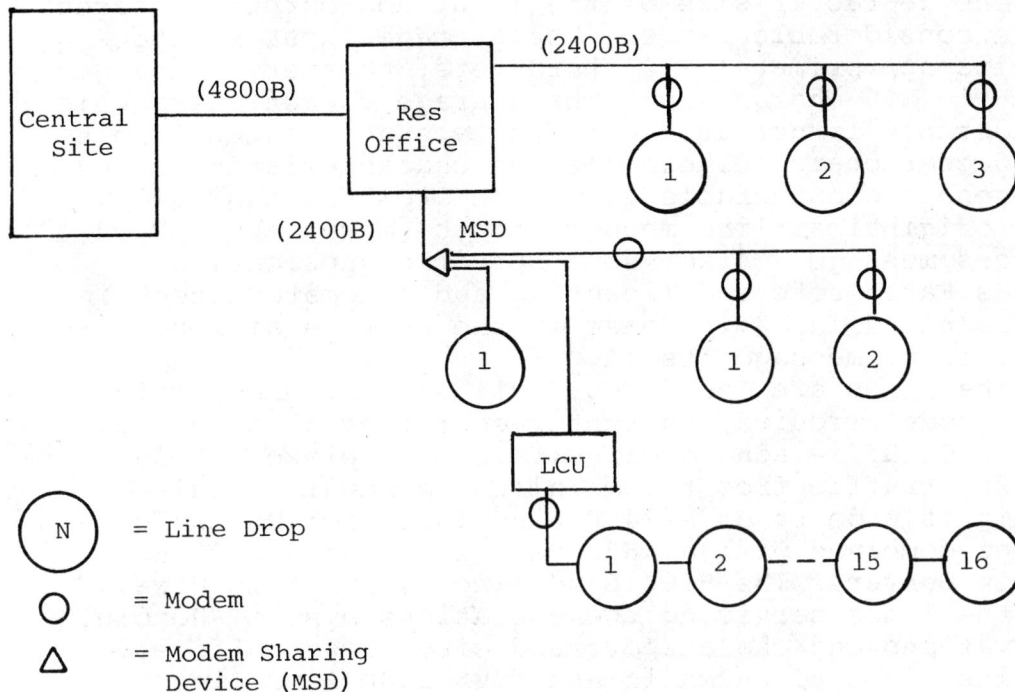

FIGURE A - SAMPLE MSD/LCU CONFIGURATIONS

delay caused by fixed time incremental polling. The
line discipline is the 6-bit PARS code sometimes referred to as SABRE Code (1). Messages are transmitted
in a continuous synchronous bit stream, serial by bit,
serial by character. Error checking is accomplished by
a Cyclic Check Character (CCC) which the IBM controllers,
RPQed for SABRE, are hardwired to handle (2). A clear
disadvantage of SABRE code is the restricted character
set (64 char.); however, for those systems not requiring
more, it is extremely efficient and reliable. This
efficiency is beneficial to a high performance system
both in terms of response times and line costs.

The UPARS system drives a variety of remote printer
and CRT terminals. There are over 2400 CRT's including
the IBM 2915, and Incoterm SPD 10/20 and 20/20 'intelligent' terminals. The approximately 1460 remote printers
include Vogue 810 ticket printers, Centronics 306
printers and teletype 28RO ticket printers. In addition,
many of the Univac CRTs and pagewriters are accessible
through the Unimatic link.

     The character size of the input and output messages
have a considerable range. The average input message
contains approximately 14 characters; however, it ranges
from 6 to 350 characters. The average output message is
considerably larger at 140 characters and ranges from 6
to 960 characters. These message characteristics have
undergone a considerable evolution from the basically
small original airline message to the much larger Food
Services message. Also, some specific applications
such as Fare/Quote and Ticketing and Automated Check-in
have resulted in an increase in the average airline
reservations message itself.

     The lines are dedicated, full duplex, unconditioned,
voice grade circuits, currently operating at speeds up
to 4800 Baud. A single circuit is multiplexed at 9600
Baud for traffic from the mainland to Hawaii. This
circuit is made up of a 2400 Baud line from Unimatic in
Chicago combined with a 4800 Baud line and a 2400 Baud
line in Denver. The 9600 Baud line is split in Hawaii
into the lines servicing the operations system, Honolulu
reservations and the airport and city ticket offices.
The link lines to Unimatic are four 2400 Baud lines
multiplexed into two physical lines operating at 4800
Baud. SABRE code is used on the link, even though the
dedicated Unimatic network uses the 8 bit ASCII code.
The link operates in a non-polled or 'free-wheeling'
environment. This multi-purpose link allows the UPARS
system to communicate with other airlines (through ARINC
and SITA), permits conversation between applications in
the two systems, and provides access to the reservations
system by Unimatic terminals.

REDUNDANCY AND BACKUP

     In order to reduce the chances of disservice due to
network failure, special redundancy and backup is provided to key elements of the network. Specifically,
each reservations office with its large concentration of
terminals is serviced by multiple lines. No one circuit
carries more than 60% of the offices' terminals. Alternate routing is employed to reduce the risk of losing
the whole network due to a cable failure from central
site. Two physical paths exit central site and connect
to the AT&T Denver office. Additionally, diversification
of the trunk lines helps minimize the risk of a total
office shutdown. Diversification is a telephone company

```
                    A
        ┌───────┐──────────┐──────────┐         ┌──────────┐         ┌───────┐
        │       │ Line X₁   │          │         │   X₁      │         │       │
        │       │     B     │          │         │           │         │       │
        │Central│           │  Telco   │         │           │         │  Res  │
        │ Site  │     B     │  Office  │         │           │         │ Office│
        │       │           │          │         │           │         │       │
        │       │ Line X₂   │          │         │   X₂      │         │       │
        │       │     A     │          │         │           │         │       │
        └───────┘──────────┘──────────┘         └──────────┘         └───────┘
              Alternate Routing                    Diversification
                    A/B                               X₁/X₂
```

Figure showing alternate routing between Central Site and Telco Office (Line X_1 B, Line X_2 A) and diversification between Telco Office and Res Office (X_1, X_2).

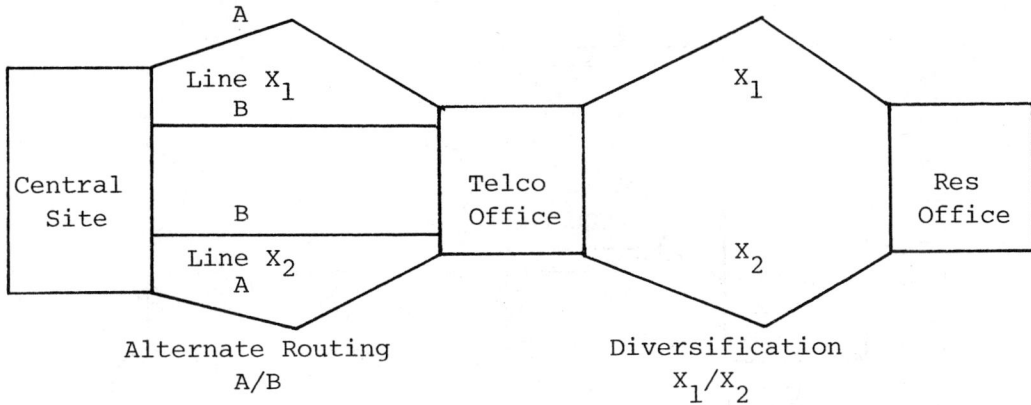

FIGURE B - DIVERSIFICATION & ALTERNATE ROUTING

term for a special guaranteed routing of two trunk lines
assuring that the two lines have only the terminator
points in common. Figure B shows a simplified example
of alternate routing and diversification.

Dial-up backup is supplied to key segments of the
network. To provide the 4 wire, full duplex capability
two phone connections are necessary. The PSD has special
application to this backup due to the elimination of
dedicated multiple ports for the dial-up lines. In
addition, the functioning drops on a multidrop line need
not be taken down to service only a portion of the circuit. Figure C shows a diagram of the multiple use of a
controller port with a dial-up link in use.

TWO SPECIAL APPLICATIONS

The Automated Check-in (ACI) application has a
requirement of very high reliability. First, two lines
service each ACI station. Second, to meet this requirement, hardware and software were developed at United to
automatically switch lines in case of line failure. The
software 'saves' the information in scratchpad storage
so that it is available after the switch to another line.
This software 'save' assures that the agent does not lose
information being developed on her terminal. Only the
information on the line can be lost in case of failure,
resulting in a minimal disruption to agent activity. The
switch is hardware programmed to recognize legitimate
line failure and to transfer the terminals from the
multiplexor on the failed line to the multiplexor

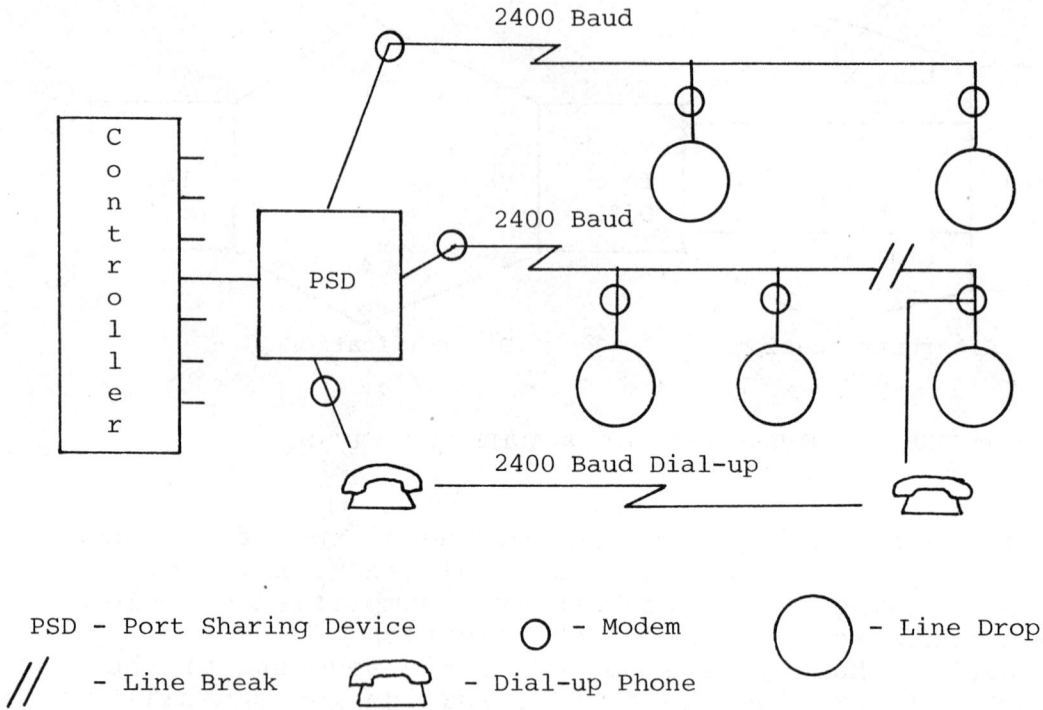

PSD - Port Sharing Device   ◯ - Modem   ◯ - Line Drop

// - Line Break   ☎ - Dial-up Phone

FIGURE C - PORT SHARING DEVICE CONFIGURATION

on the second line. From the standpoint of the controller, an unanswered poll results in three very rapid
retries followed by a 'SLO POLL'. The SLO POLL is
repeated thereafter every 15 seconds. The switch, using
multiple counters and timers, detects polls and times
the interval between them. Complexity is introduced due
to failure being possible on either or both the transmit
or receive side of the full duplex line. Once a SLO POLL
has been instituted by the controller a second one will
not appear until 30 seconds has elapsed since the suspected fault occurred unless normal operation has
resumed. The transfer to the good line takes place at
28 seconds, assuming normal polling has not resumed, in
which case the counters and timers are reset. In order
to avoid oscillation between two sporadically faulty
lines, the automatic transfers only take place once
until the switch is reset either manually or by operations at central site. Actually, unless a failure has
occurred only half the terminals are switched because
again, as in a reservations office, the two lines share
the complement of terminals.

United's Automated Teleticketing is an extension of an airline service to commercial accounts and travel agencies. The automation of this application removes the bulk of the manual handling previously required for teleticketing. This function is a service to customers with a need to have tickets printed at their place of business. A customer having the industry standard 28RO teletype printer calls reservations placing an order; at the request of the agent the system automatically prices the ticket from destination information given. The agent then routes the automatically formatted ticket to the customer's printer. These printers are on dial-up lines; thus, the system auto-dials the number, makes a connection, and prints the ticket at the requested delivery time. A combination of special microprocessors and modems are interfaced with automatic call units. This equipment is required to accept requests from the reservations system in SABRE code, buffer the message, extract the phone number, dial and make connection with the printer on low speed lines and finally perform the disconnect. The low speed lines are at 75 Baud using a 5-bit Baudot code to communicate with the 28RO printer. To minimize impact to central site facilities a PSD is used to handle multiple lines as well as other low speed traffic. Figure D shows a diagram of the basic teleticketing configuration. As in the ACI application above, both hardware and software developments were required to furnish this service.

OTHER SPECIAL HARDWARE

No discussion of the UPARS network would be complete without at least a mention of the central site patch panel developed by Technical Services. This panel provides computer operations many of the tools to debug and correct line problems. It also serves as the interface between the network and the controller, although it also plays a role between the controller and the CPU. A few of its features are the following:
1. By means of a switch changes alternate routing
2. Perform analog loop-back of any line
3. Allows switching communications controllers on and off-line
4. Patches any modem to any line
5. Has automatic audio-visual alarm system for line failures

```
          +-----------+              +-----------+
          |  Micro-   |==============|   ACU &   |-----\_____
          | processor |==============|  Modems   |          |
          +-----------+              +-----------+          |
+-------+                                                   |
| C     |                                                   | Bank
| o     |  +-----+                                          | of
| n     |  |     |                                          | WATS
| t     |--| PSD |                                          | and
| r     |  |     |                                          | DDD
| o     |  +-----+                                          | Phone
| l     |                                                   | Lines
| l     |                                                   |
| e     |          +-----------+              +-----------+ |
| r     |----------|  Micro-   |==============|   ACU &   |-\
+-------+          | processor |==============|  Modems   |  \___
                   +-----------+              +-----------+     |
```

PSD - Port Sharing Device   ACU - Automated Call Unit

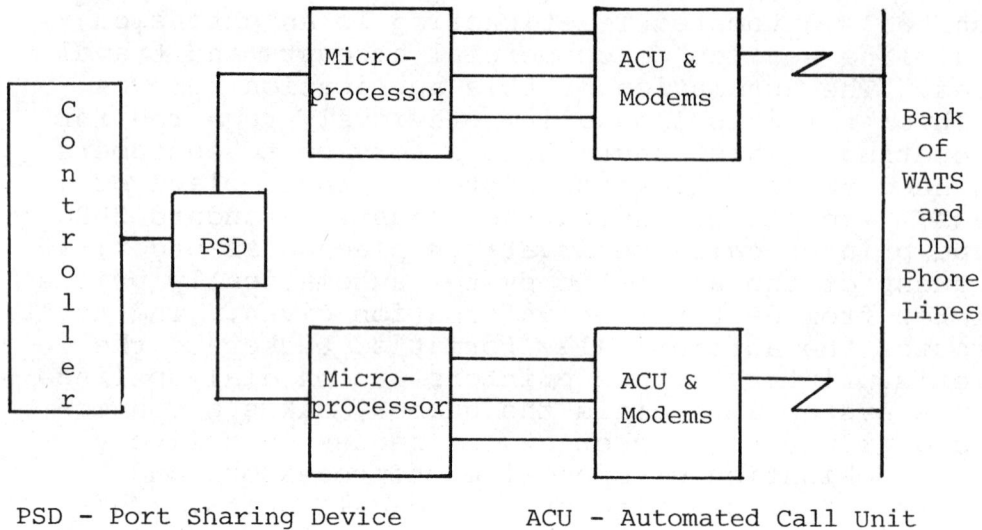

FIGURE D - AUTOMATED TELETICKETING

6. Displays various elements of line status
7. Allows digital and analog access to lines for
    testing and monitoring of lines
8. Patches dedicated lines to dial-up circuit.
In conjunction with this panel is a line utilization
counter to gather volume information.

   A new patch panel is currently under construction
to handle a 2 X 3 configuration of two 2703 and a 3705
controllers. Any two units will be on-line with the
third available for a test system and on-line backup as
needed. In addition to the features of the old panel
the new one will have provisions for
1. Switching to spare modems without recabling
2. Simplified Random Data Generator hookup to
    test out lines and modems
3. PSD interface and bypass
4. Selector for line monitoring without any cab-
    ling changes
5. Improved dial-up interface for connecting and
    monitoring.
Experience with the current panel has shown the need to
perform the various functions with a minimum of cabling
movement. Operations personnel monitoring and testing
equipment have little time to be switching cables around;
also, it adds an unnecessary element of risk.

Other hardware has been developed for use on the network such as a Supervisor's Console for testing hardware and switching out faulty components; a modem eliminator for digital circuits, a terminal tester; an LCU bypass switch; and a specialized dial-up unit. One final development is called a Pseudo Answer-back unit (PAB) for dial-up lines. This unit answers a PARS poll when no connection is available. When a dial-up line is connected, the PAB is automatically bypassed, resulting in an active circuit.

CONCLUSION

The UPARS network is a diverse, multifunctional network. Through a combination of unique hardware and software developments many innovative approaches to application problems have been employed successfully. As the applications continue to grow in number and complexity along with the inevitable changes in common carrier services, the demands on the implementers of networks will also grow. The challenges of the future are sure to be both severe and exciting.

ACKNOWLEDGEMENTS

The above material heavily references numerous internal United Airlines UPARS Operations' procedures, functional specifications and descriptions. Special thanks go to my secretary, Gloria Williams, and members of my Technical Services staff for their assistance.

REFERENCES

1) IBM Reservations Systems, Custom Feature Description, GL22-6960.
2) IBM 2969 PTI CPU Users Guide, GC28-6711.
3) United Airlines Mux Switching Unit, Technical Description and Procedures, March 13, 1975.
4) United Airlines Automated Teleticketing, Hardware description and Drawings, December 2, 1974.

DCTS: a data communication terminal system for the data exchange between air traffic control centres

by

M. Baum

EUROCONTROL Maastricht U.A.C.
The Netherlands

ABSTRACT

The Data Communication Terminal System (DCTS) is an autonomous front-end computer complex for the transmission of Air Traffic Service (ATS) and meteorological messages between MADAP and external centres. Data exchange between air traffic control centres plays an important role in the provision of up-to-date error-free information about flights which are to be controlled. Coordination between adjacent control centres in Europe means the adaptation of systems different in hardware, software and operation. Different transmission procedures used in national communication networks must be accepted, and this forces DCTS to process different transmission procedures in parallel and to translate from one to another. Compatibility requirements and data security have priority over response time aspects. DCTS is designed to run 24 hours per day, 7 days per week continuously without loss of data at any time. Thus, special attention is given to different steps of degraded functioning in case of malfunction of channels and of the system itself.

1. INTRODUCTION

Air traffic control systems need up-to-date data on the air traffic to
be controlled at any time : flight plans, meteorological and radar
data. These data are transmitted to control centres where they are
filtered, analyzed, correlated and processed into a visible form on
display consoles most suitable for the controllers who are responsible
for an effective flow of traffic and to prevent aircraft collisions.
Radar data are renewed and updated with each turn of the antennas, but
flight plan and meteorological data are transmitted once and are updated
only on changes of such data as departure times and estimates over reporting points. Therefore special care must be given to the safe and
error-free transmission of flight plan and meteorological data.

Maastricht U.A.C., a European air traffic control centre for the upper
area control of North-Germany, Belgium and Luxembourg with its highly
automated system MADAP (Maastricht Automatic Data Processing and Display
System), is surrounded by various national control centres with
different levels of automation. As air traffic passes from centre to
centre in very short times, data communication between the centres is
one of the most important origins of information. With increasing level
of automation of national air traffic control services specialized point
to point links and also networks as e.g. the DUEV-network have been
developed. As international standards for data communication in air
traffic control do not yet exist to a sufficient extent, developments of
communication procedures have been different for nearly every link.
Communication procedures or data link controls are hardware and software
protocols used to transfer data and control information between separated computing devices. They comprise conventions about the way of
establishing a link, the exchange technique, error recognition and
correction, block and message formats, code restrictions, etc.

Standardization and development of common communication procedures are
an aim for the future. As experience has shown, it takes too long to
wait for standardization in the development of communication procedures
which are needed now and in the very near future. Therefore the
decision was taken to develop a communication system which talks many
languages, i.e. can communicate in different procedures, transmission
speeds and codes and can translate from one into another.

The Data Communication Terminal System (DCTS) is designed as an autonomous front-end computer complex for the exchange of Air Traffic
Service (ATS) messages and meteorological data between MADAP and adjacent external centres. DCTS acts as a buffer for incoming messages and
in case of MADAP break-downs is able to continue accepting incoming
messages. In the event of longer break-downs, it is even able to print
incoming messages on printers reserved for such purposes.

2.   COMMUNICATION PARTNERS

MADAP

DCTS receives data from different external centres all destined for
MADAP. It concentrates these data streams after striping off procedure
- specific block and message envelopes. On the other hand DCTS also
distributes data from MADAP destined for external centres to the corresponding output channels after building a correct procedure envelope.
For the data exchange with MADAP a logical number of the external
station gives the reference to the sending or receiving unit. Because
of the concentration of different medium speed links to one flow of information directed to MADAP and the multiplexing of data coming from
MADAP, a powerful high speed link is required between MADAP and DCTS.
Via a Parallel Data Adapter, information is exchanged, in parallel, in
16 bit words which allows a transmission speed of 1.6 Mbps.

FRANKFURT

One of the most important external communication partners of DCTS is the
Frankfurt station of the data transmission and distribution system DUEV
(figure 1). DUEV Frankfurt is the centre of the star-type network of
the German administration for air traffic services (BFS : Bundesanstalt
für Flugsicherung). Via this network NOTAM bulletins (which inform
pilots about special conditions of navigation aids, control centres,
airports, etc.) and flight progress strips are exchanged between the
connected air traffic control and flight information services. In a
second phase the transmission of static flight plan information is also
foreseen which is done at present via the Aeronautical Fixed Telecommunications Network (AFTN). The link with the DUEV centre Frankfurt is
made via two full-duplex channels with a transmission speed of 4800 bps.

At present static flight plan information (AFTN) is exchanged between
DCTS and the AFTN network via the German switching centre A300 Frankfurt.
The AFTN network is a worldwide telex-type network based on 50 and 100
baud lines with a data concentration in national communication centres.
DCTS is connected with A300 switching centre via four 100 baud input
channels and two 50 baud output channels. Static flight plan information as transmitted in the AFTN network originates mainly at airports
where the pilots have to submit forms which describe the planned routes.

PARIS - KARLSRUHE

Links with the air traffic control centres for the upper area controlled
by CAUTRA Paris and Karlsruhe U.A.C., are planned for the exchange of
actual flight progress information just before the aircraft passes the
boundary between these areas and the Maastricht upper area. For the
link with Paris one 2400 bps line is foreseen whereas the link between
the EUROCONTROL centres Karlsruhe and Maastricht will be realized by
two 4800 bps lines in a code-transparent procedure. This is in order
to be able to exchange other information than real-time traffic data
such as documentation and statistics.

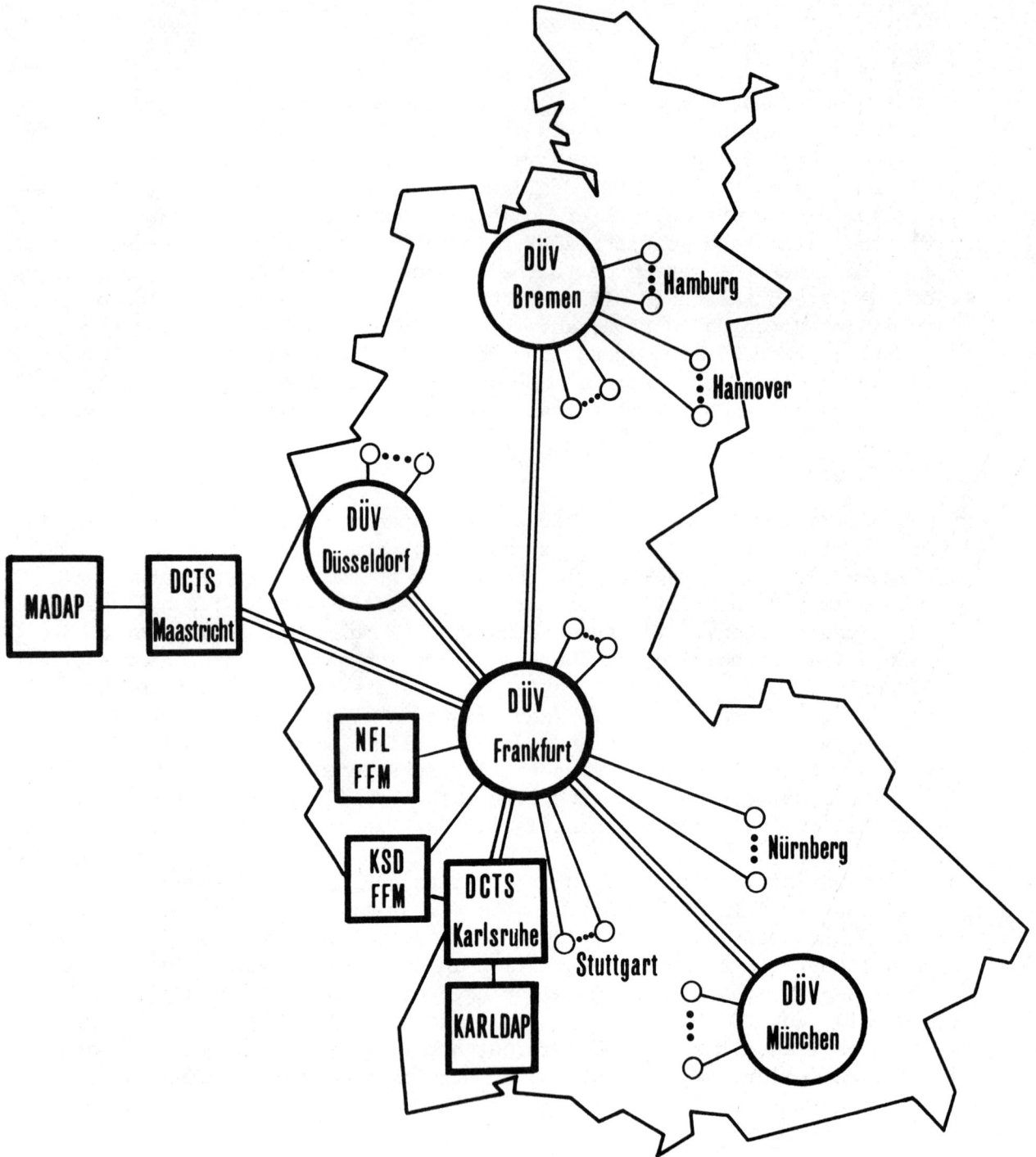

Figure 1: DÜV NETWORK

BRUSSELS

Finally a link is available with the Global Telecommunications System (GTS) which was planned by the World Meteorological Organization (WMO) according to an agreement of the General Assembly of the United Nations (figure 2). The three world meteorological centres Washington, Moscow and Melbourne which are connected by a main trunk are responsible for the international exchange of meteorological data. DCTS has an access to this network via the Brussels station which is connected to the regional centre Paris.

AMSTERDAM - LONDON

Further links are envisaged in order to be able to communicate with other air traffic control centres, as e.g. Amsterdam ACC and London ACC. Each of the mentioned communication partners uses his own technique of data transmission, however, standardization of transmission procedures will probably be achieved much later. Thus DCTS has to speak all their languages and must be prepared to convert between different procedures. This requirement enforces a very flexible hardware and software structure.

3. SYSTEM CONFIGURATION

In the following paragraphs a rough description of the DCTS configuration is given (figure 3). The system is based on a MITRA 15 minicomputer of 32 K, 16 bit words core memory with a fixed head SAGEM disc and two AMPEX magnetic tape units as backup. The system is duplicated because of reliability reasons, this means identical chains of MITRA 15 computers with their own discs and magnetic tape units.

For communication purposes three types of control units for the different transmission speed groups are available :

- A low speed control unit ESTG (Telegraphic Input/Output) for 24 input and 32 output channels of 50 or 100 baud multiplexes and demultiplexes incoming and outgoing characters.

- Two medium speed control units ESD (Medium Speed Input/Output) for 8 input/output channels of 2400 or 4800 bps process control characters such as STX, ETX, ETB, ACK, NAK, EOT and execute the vertical and horizontal parity check. In the case of code transparent procedures the ESD executes the flag handling instead of processing control characters.

- A high speed control unit EDP realizes the interfaces with the IBM Parallel Data Adapter. Each MITRA has two access paths to each main computer via these units. (EDP = Parallel Data Exchange).

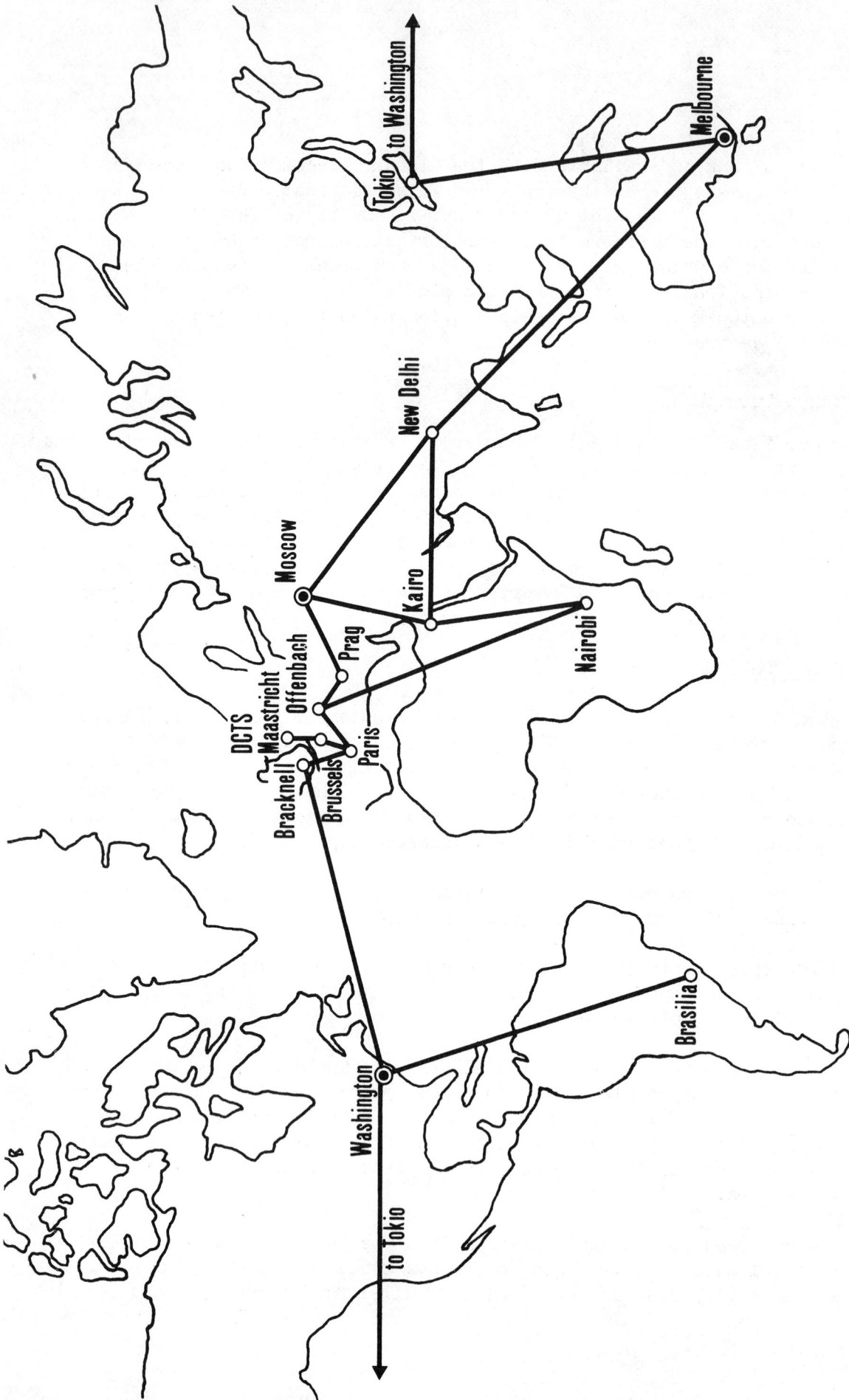

Figure 2 : GLOBAL TELECOMMUNICATIONS SYSTEM OF THE WORLD METEOROLOGICAL ORGANIZATION

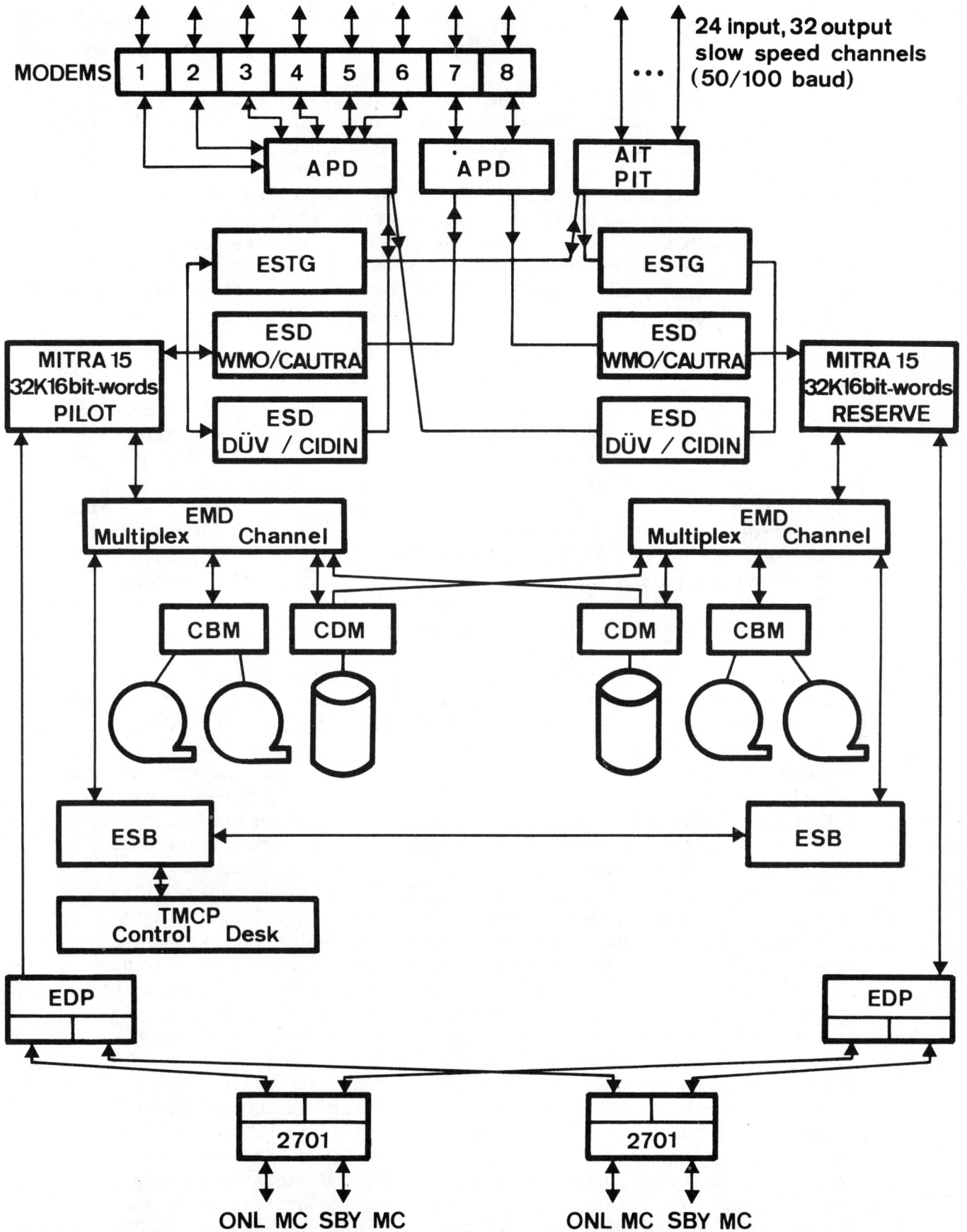

Figure 3 : DCTS SYSTEM CONFIGURATION

The control units APD (Medium Speed Data Duplication) and PIT (Telegraphic Input Duplication) take care that both chains are provided with
low and medium speed input in parallel. For the high speed link with
the IBM main computer the duplicated data transmission is controlled by
software. A central Technical Monitoring and Control Position consisting mainly of a control panel and an I/O printer is connected to both
chains. From this position all low, medium and high speed channels as
well as the essential system components of both chains as discs and
magnetic tape units can be supervised and switched. Â set of toggles is
designed for chain reconfiguration by operator decision.

4.   SOFTWARE ORGANIZATION

The basic software structure will be briefly sketched. DCTS is based on
a real-time supervisor consisting of a task scheduler, an overlay
processor for segments stored on disc, a dynamic core and a dynamic mass
memory allocator, a timer module and different failure routines. All
the I/O handlers for the slow, medium and high speed interfaces are also
core resident. On the other hand most of the application programs are
stored on disc and are swapped into the core by the overlay processor,
when the corresponding task is triggered. Messages passing through the
DCTS are stored both in dynamic core and disc zones. Articles are items
which describe a message in a certain processing state. They contain
all actual reference information of a message as result of the previously passed processing steps as internal number, input channel number,
reception time, storage address. Queues chain these articles which may
reside either totally in core, totally on disc or mixed in core and on
disc according to the time requirements of the corresponding message
processing. In all queues the 'first-in-first-out' rule is applied. The
incoming data are duplicated by hardware for the low and medium speed
interfaces and by software for the high speed interface and enter both
DCTS chains which process them in parallel. The reserve system does
not only check its hardware availability, but really processes the
messages up to the output queues. As only the pilot system may transmit
messages, the output queues of the reserve system are freed without
sending. Both computers have their own discs on which they write and
from which they read their messages and tables. Furthermore they can
read but not write from the opposite disc in order to synchronize the
queues at different levels of processing. On special disc zones each
computer, both pilot and reserve, writes messages destined for the
opposite computer which reads them triggered by an attention interrupt
from the writing chain. Via a telegraphic loop both chains send a
certain character to their own telegraphic interface and to the telegraphic interface of the opposite chain. By this means both chains can
detect, if the telegraphic interfaces of the both chains are working
correctly. Status information about starting and stopping a chain and
'who is pilot, who reserve' are exchanged via the control units ESB for
binary input and output.

5.   APPLICATION AND SYSTEM FUNCTIONS

In the following paragraphs a survey of the DCTS functions is given
(figure 4).

Message storage is required for different processing functions as mentioned hereafter. Furthermore messages are buffered on disc and after
a certain time also on magnetic tape in case of a link failure of an output channel. Within certain limits DCTS can resume the sending of the
buffered message, or it prints out these messages on own printers for
operator intervention. For messages exchanged in the unprotected AFTN
procedure a message retrieval for repetition purposes is required. Therefore all AFTN messages are stored at least one hour on disc.

Message switching means the distribution of incoming traffic according to
addresses given in the message header for different destinations. The
address fields are analyzed, and corresponding circuits and currently
available channels are determined. In the routing process different
priorities are obeyed by providing one queue per priority. Messages with
addresses which cannot be allocated because they are unknown or erroneous
are routed to a central correction position, where the message can be
reentered after address correction.

Message blocking and reassembly has to be done in the sense of packet
switching for certain transmission procedures, as the DUEV-, WMO- and
CIDIN procedure. Messages are subdivided into different blocks for
transmission and are reassembled after reception by DCTS before further
transmission.

Procedure conversion means that a message enters the DCTS in one transmission procedure and leaves it in another one. The envelope of the
input procedure is stripped off, the message is reassembled, subdivided
into blocks of the output procedure, and a corresponding block envelope is
generated. In some cases a code conversion is required.

Legal recording must be done in air traffic control for each message
passing through the system. All messages exchanged via the medium and
high speed links are recorded on magnetic tape for off-line evaluation on
an IBM batch computer. Slow speed traffic is recorded on-line on
printers because of the retrieval requirements, i.e. the operators must
have an immediate trace of transmission errors in order to verify that
messages have been received and emitted at certain times.

Statistics are presented for all medium speed channels comprising the
load (given in characters), the number of input and output messages per
hour, the number of transmission errors per hour and the present status
of the channels.

○   MESSAGE STORAGE

○   MESSAGE SWITCHING

○   MESSAGE BLOCKING AND REASSEMBLY

○   PROCEDURE CONVERSION

○   LEGAL RECORDING

○   STATISTICS

○   SERVICE MESSAGE INPUT

○   INTERFACE HANDLING FOR LOW, MEDIUM AND
        HIGH SPEED CHANNELS

○   CHANNEL SURVEILLANCE AND RECONFIGURATION

○   SYSTEM RECONFIGURATION

○   CENTRALIZED MONITORING AND CONTROL

Figure 4 : DCTS APPLICATION AND SYSTEM FUNCTIONS

The input of service messages is simplified by a DCTS program which produces a correct procedure envelope on an operator input comprising priority, destination address and message text only.

Interface handling for transmission procedures means the emission and reception of data in the form of blocks. The layout, the length, start and end characters are defined by each procedure. Some procedures foresee different block priorities, which allow the interruption of a block sequence by important information with a higher priority.

The security of data transmission is ensured by different checks at block reception : vertical and horizontal parity check and sequence of block numbering. The results of these checks are indicated in control blocks which are returned to the emitting station as response.

If a block is correct, a control block ACK is sent. If a parity error is found, or if a block is missed according to the received block numbers, a control block NAK is sent. At the reception of NAK a repetition trial is executed. After several repetitions without success the channel is taken out of service, and a channel reconfiguration is initiated if foreseen by the procedure.

Channel surveillance and reconfiguration. Certain procedures foresee a cyclic sending of test blocks, when no data blocks are transmitted, in order to check if channels are serviceable. Channel reconfiguration is possible, if a standby channel is available and serviceable.

System reconfiguration is triggered either automatically in the case of an irrecoverable error of the pilot chain or manually by an operator switch action. As both DCTS chains process all incoming data in parallel, a reconfiguration is done allmost immediately. In the case of chain reconfiguration only a flag is set which indicates the status of a pilot. A basic condition for such a reconfiguration is that pilot and reserve are synchronized, i.e. the reserve has updated its queues and tables according to information from the pilot.

Centralized monitoring and control of all DCTS functions is executed from a control desk consisting of a display panel, a set of function buttons and toggles and an input/output printer. At the display panel the status of all connected low, medium and high speed channels is indicated. The status of both chains is shown, warnings are given for hardware errors which are recoverable by repetition. Hardware faults which require immediate maintenance action as for instance irrecoverable disc and magnetic tape errors are indicated conspicuously. Function buttons are available for connecting, disconnecting, synchronizing and bypassing channels. Toggles are used for manual reconfigurations and the attachment of the input/output printer to the pilot or reserve chain.

6.   <u>COMMUNICATION PROCEDURES</u>

The various communication procedures which must be handled by DCTS are
described in the following paragraphs.

The <u>AFTN procedure</u> (<u>A</u>eronautical <u>F</u>ixed <u>T</u>elecommunication <u>N</u>etwork) is
an unprotected procedure used in the telex-type Aeronautical Fixed
Telecommunication Network. The transmission is asynchronous serial
full duplex, in which code CCITT2 is used, i.e. there are no parity
checks and no control characters. Message start and end are formed by
the character groups ZCZC and NNNN. The receiving station does not
positively acknowledge messages but informs the sending station only in
case of missing messages according to sequence number gaps by a service
message. As service messages asking for repetition of missing messages
can also be originated manually by other AFTN stations, all outgoing
messages must be stored at least one hour for retrieval purposes.
Transmission speeds are 50 and 100 baud only.

The <u>DÜV procedure</u> (<u>D</u>aten<u>ü</u>bertragungs- und <u>V</u>erteilersystem) is a synchronous serial line procedure for medium speed data exchange from 200
to 4800 bps with full duplex mode of transmission. DCTS uses the
highest possible transmission speed of 4800 bps. CCITT5 code is used
with odd parity and a longitudinal check character BCC. Blocks of 4
priorities can be mixed. The maximum block length is 402 bytes. A
standby line is foreseen which is controlled by sending BEL test blocks
each minute in both directions. A line reconfiguration is executed
automatically after three transmission trials answered by a NAK block
or not answered by an ACK block during a 4 second time limit.

The <u>INTERCAUTRA procedure</u> (<u>C</u>oordinateur <u>A</u>utomatique de <u>T</u>rafic <u>A</u>erien)
has the following characteristics : synchronous, serial, half-duplex
transmission in 2400 bps (figure 6). Either CCITT5 or EBCDIC can be
used as transmission codes. For the DCTS implementation CCITT5 is
chosen. Only one block priority exists. Error control is done both by
parity checks and a longitudinal redundancy check. There is no line
reconfiguration foreseen.

The <u>WMO procedure</u> (<u>W</u>orld <u>M</u>eteorological <u>O</u>rganization) has the same mode
of transmission as the INTERCAUTRA procedure except for being full-
duplex : synchronous, serial, 2400 bps, CCITT5. A speciality of WMO is
the utilization of 75 bps back-channels for the transmission of ACK/NAK
blocks.

The <u>CIDIN procedure</u> (<u>C</u>ommon <u>I</u>CAO <u>D</u>ata <u>I</u>nterchange <u>N</u>etwork) is the most
flexible of all line procedures implemented in the DCTS system (figure
7). It operates in transparent mode, i.e. any code or bit stream is
allowed. Before transmission of data, a zero bit is inserted after any
sequence of 5 one's and is removed on reception. The mode of

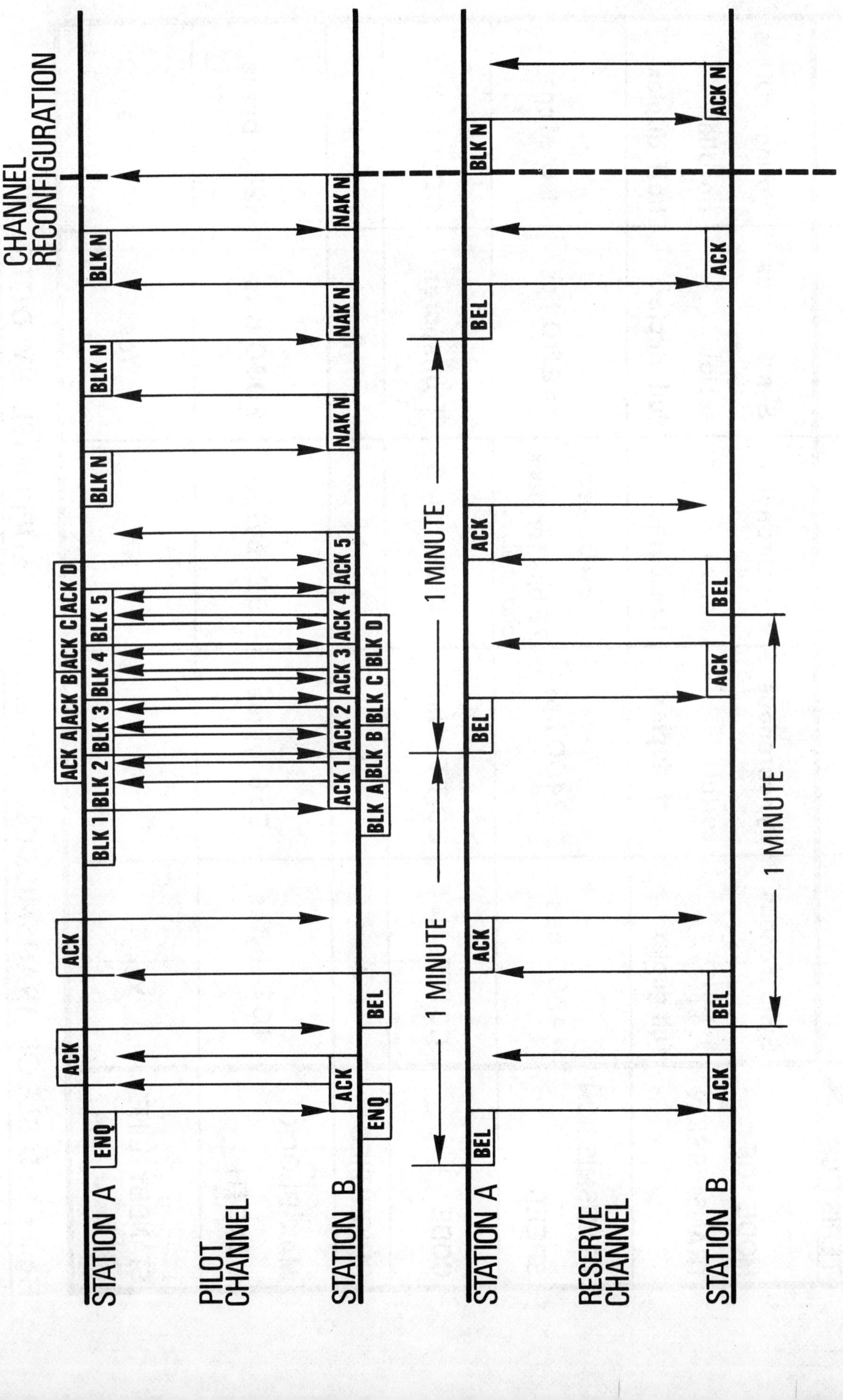

Figure 5 : DÜV PROCEDURE

PROCEDURE / CHARACTERISTICS	DÜV	INTERCAUTRA	WMO	CIDIN	MADAP – DCTS
MODE OF TRANSMISSION	Synchronous serial full duplex	Synchronous serial half duplex	Synchronous serial full duplex	Synchronous serial full duplex	Polling (200ms) parallel half duplex
TRANSMISSION SPEED	4800 bps	2400 bps	2400 bps 75 bps for back channel	4800 bps	1.6 Mbps
CODE	CCITT No.5	CCITT No.5	CCITT No.5	Transparent	CCITT No.5
PRIORITIES	4	1	1	2	1
MAX BLOCK LENGTH	402 bytes	756 bytes	192 bytes	2000 bits	1280 bytes
STANDBY LINE	Yes	No	No	Yes	Yes

Figure 6: TABLE OF TRANSMISSION PROCEDURES SUPPORTED BY DCTS

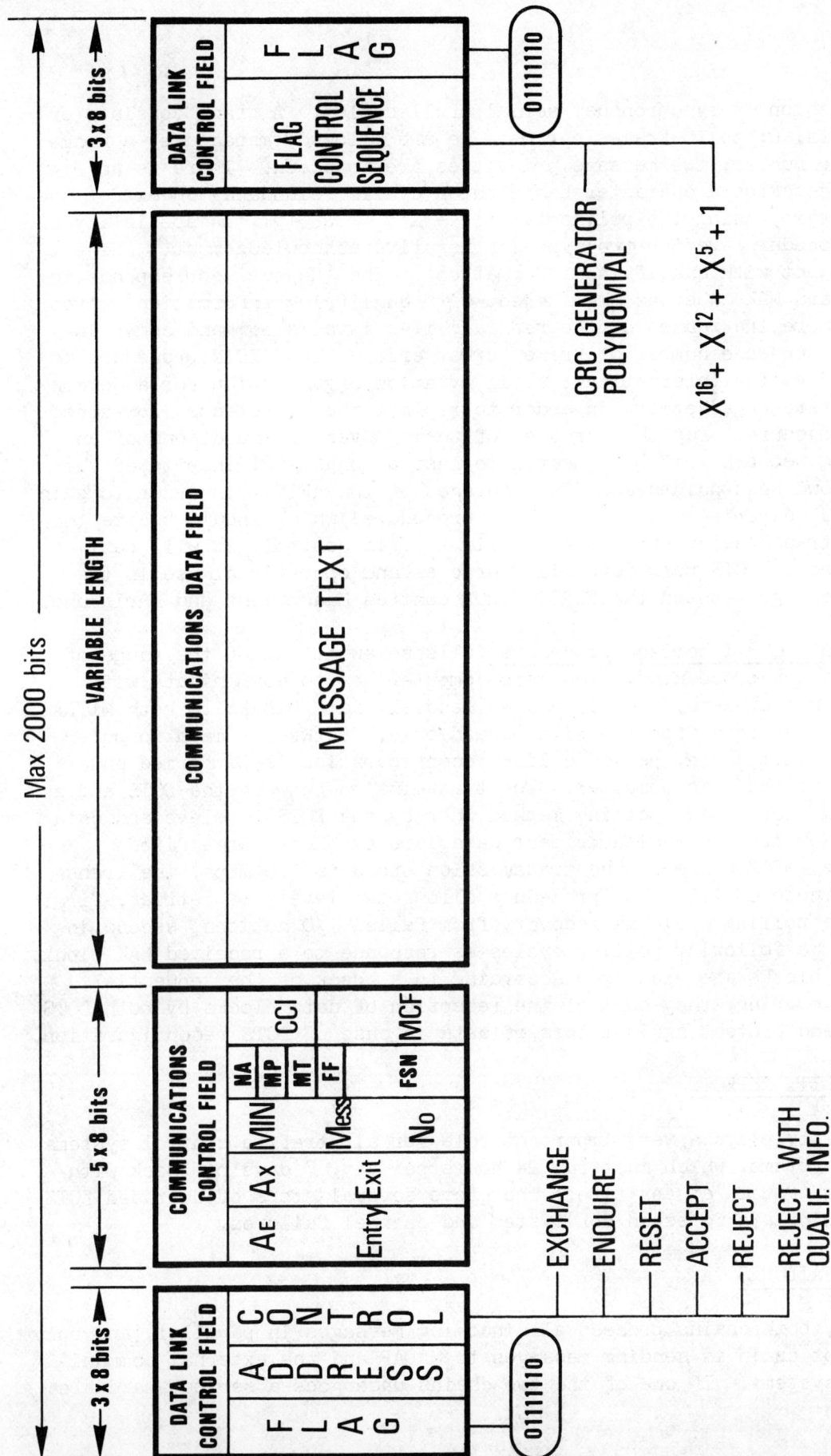

Figure 7 : FRAME FORMAT OF THE CIDIN PROCEDURE

transmission is synchronous, serial, full duplex. A frame consists of
2000 bits, up to 16 frames per message are allowed, managed by a frame
sequence number; two message priorities are foreseen. There is no
parity check on a character basis but a cyclic redundancy check for the
whole frame, using the polynomial $X^{16} + X^{12} + X^5 + 1$. A speciality of
this procedure are the two types of negative acknowledgement : 'Reject'
and 'Reject with qualifying information'. The 'Reject' corresponds to
a standard NAK, whereas the 'Reject with qualifying information' gives
furthermore the reason of the refusal, i.e. invalid command code, incorrect sequence number or frame format error. The CIDIN procedure is
designed by the International Civil Aviation Organization for a Common
ICAO Interchange Network in order to replace the unprotected low-speed
AFTN procedure. But this process of taking over the functions of an
existing network must be expected to last a long time, inspite of the
well known weak points and disadvantages of the AFTN. In order to gain
practical experience with the CIDIN procedure, which should become the
common transmission procedure for air traffic control, it will be implemented in DCTS both for trial purposes and operational use in the
data exchange between the EUROCONTROL centres Maastricht and Karlsruhe.

The MADAP-DCTS interface procedure falls somewhat out of the range of
transmission procedures. The main computer has to communicate with
both DCTS computers, i.e. it has to send all data blocks to both MITRAs
but receives data from the pilot chain only. Between a main computer
and the pilot chain, periodic link reconfiguration is performed under
control of the main computer. The transmission between the DCTS and a
main computer uses a polling method whereby the DCTS is slave and data
blocks, or if none available test data, are exchanged at a fixed
frequency of 200 msec. The transmission speed is 1.6 Mbps, the transmission code CCITT5. The procedure allows two levels of retries, first
within a polling cycle as recovery from failed I/O actions, second in
one of the following polling cycles as response to a received NAK block.
ACK/NAK blocks are exchanged according to a check of the sequential
block numbering, they control the reception of data blocks by both DCTS
chains and protect against loss of data in case of DCTS reconfiguration.

7.   RELIABILITY ASPECTS

Reliability plays a very important role for air traffic control systems
and subsystems, which must run 24 hours per day, 7 days per week without loss of data at any time. Therefore several steps of degraded DCTS
functioning are foreseen for system and channel failures.

SYSTEM FAILURES

Normally both chains process all incoming messages in parallel, and only
the pilot chain is sending messages to MADAP and the external communication systems. If one of the two chains undergoes a serious hardware

error, e.g. irrecoverable disc or magnetic tape failure, the other chain is restarted as reserve and will be ready for reconfiguration, when it is synchronized by the exchange·of various interchain messages.

For the low speed data a further step of degraded functioning is available, when both DCTS chains are down. Via a patch panel all 50 and 100 baud input and output channels can be connected with printers immediately, in order to prevent a loss of data exchanged via the unprotected low speed channels.

CHANNEL FAILURES

For the case of a channel failure different backup provisions are made. In some transmission procedures as the DUEV and CIDIN procedures a standby channel is available which is permanently controlled by exchanging test blocks periodically.

If the pilot channel fails, a channel reconfiguration is triggered automatically. After repair this channel will be reintroduced as standby channel.

If the link to MADAP or to one of the external stations breaks totally, DCTS is able to continue working for a time because of its buffering capacity. First a disc zone is filled which is swapped on magnetic tape when the available space is consumed. Dependant on time parameters, e.g. after 3 minutes for the link with CAUTRA, all messages waiting for output are printed on an overflow printer for transmission by telephone between the controllers involved. If the link is ready again before reaching the time limit, all messages are retransmitted automatically.

As a further step of link reliability DCTS network functions can be envisaged which e.g. allow to bypass the link to DUEV Frankfurt by the link to DCTS Karlsruhe or vice versa. This DCTS extension will involve a conversion between the DUEV and CIDIN procedures. The logic for bypassing a link by another one is realized in the DCTS software for the slow speed connections with the AFTN network and can be adapted for the medium speed links, too.

8. CONCLUSION

Standardization of communication procedures is an important aim for the interconnection of air traffic control systems. The development of a procedure for the Common ICAO Data Interchange Network is a first milestone in this development. The realization of the link between DCTS Maastricht and DCTS Karlsruhe with the CIDIN procedure should deliver practical experience as a second step of this development. Further implementation steps will require the replacement of some of the external communication systems by more powerful hardware and software.

In the meantime data communication between air traffic control centres must be realized with the existing systems and their communication procedures. Thus DCTS has to serve the AFTN, DUEV, INTERCAUTRA and WMO procedures but is prepared to become a switching node in the CIDIN network, to be implemented, hopefully, soon.

9.   <u>REFERENCES</u>

1. CIT-ALCATEL   Système de Commutation de Messages KLB5
                             Description Générale, CEM71/013, Ed. 4,
                             October 1971

2. CIT-ALCATEL   DCTS-Documentation Provisoire Programmation,
                             BK7717, March 1975

3. AEG-TELEFUNKEN   Datenübertragungs- und Verteilersystem
                             Systemkurzbeschreibung, January 1974

4. Gabel, J.   Datennetze für den Wetterdienst, NTZ-Kurier,
                             December 1972

5. International Civil   Automated Data Interchange Systems Panel,
    Aviation Organization   Report of the fourth Meeting, ICAO Document
                             9052 ADISP/4, May 1973

6. Watson, J.   MADAP - Software Aspects of Reconfiguration,
                             EUROCONTROL Maastricht U.A.C., May 1974

An EPSS interface service for the NPL data communication network

by

N W Dawes, National Physical Laboratory, UK

I G Dewis, National Physical Laboratory, UK

and

M Gentry, Computer Analysts & Programmers Ltd. UK

SUMMARY

This paper describes a system currently being
implemented within NPL to link the NPL and
EPSS packet switched networks.   The linkage
will enable users of either network to access
services attached to the other network.   The
main use will be, initially, for character
terminal access to interactive services.

1.   INTRODUCTION

A data communication network (DCN) has been operational
at the National Physical Laboratory for the past two
years.   Over this period, the number of terminals
connected, and hence the volume of traffic being
carried, has increased considerably.   However, a point
was soon reached when several users required access
to outside facilities such as computing bureaux.
Consequently, the Post Office's Experimental Packet
Switched Service (EPSS) was the natural choice as the
transport mechanism to enable such links to be made.

2.   THE NPL DATA COMMUNICATION NETWORK

Most readers will be familiar with the principles of
operation of the NPL DCN, which has been fully documented elsewhere [1], [2], [3].   Nevertheless, a
brief review may prove useful.

2.1   Logical structure

The logical structure of the network is a packet
switch at the hub of a radial series of links
to computers, called user machines   (UMs).
One of these UMs takes on a special role, that
of terminal processor (TP), allowing simple character
terminals to be connected.

Thus two types of terminal are distinguished.   An
intelligent terminal, particularly a computer, is one
which has the capability of correctly formatting data
into packets.   Simple terminals, such as paper tape
readers and teletypes, do not have this ability, and
thus depend on the TP to provide this function for them.

As a consequence of this differentiation, computers can
'multi-thread' packets to various destinations, whereas
simple terminals can only take part in one call at a
time.

2.2   Physical structure

Whilst the network is logically as described above,
physically the packet switch and terminal
processor reside in one machine, a Honeywell
DDP 516.   The advantage of this is that the transmission
hardware employed can be shared by both, which on a site
the size of that at NPL achieves considerable cost
reductions.

To allow compatibility between all connected devices, a universal interface is necessary, and the British Standard Interface BS4421 [4] has been employed. Each device plugs into a network termination unit, known as a peripheral control unit (PCU). There are two forms of PCU, corresponding to the two types of terminal: PCU-As (for simple terminals) and PCU-Bs (for UMs).

These PCU's are connected to the switching computer by a hierachy of multiplexors,or concentrators, which each have eight I/O ports. There are three levels of multiplexor, so that a maximum of 512 channels are available. A user's device may of course be connected to a multiplexer at a level other than the third, for example to achieve a higher throughput, but this would be at the expense of eliminating seven other channels.

3.   THE P.O. EXPERIMENTAL PACKET SWITCHED SERVICE

The British Post Office is providing its customers with an opportunity to evaluate the overall benefits of packet working via EPSS [5]. The authors prefer to call it a pilot network, not an experimental one, for its main purpose is not to conduct experiments into packet switching as such but to provide information about the commercial viability of a data communication system based on packet switching. The Post Office will gain experience in operational aspects, tariff structuring and trends in demand, all of which are necessary before a fully committed commercial service could be announced.

The EPSS network consists of three nodes or Packet Switching Exchanges (PSEs) to be situated in London, Manchester and Glasgow. Each PSE allows the connection of Packet Terminals and Character Terminals. Packet Terminals can handle data in packet format while Character Terminals only need the capability of operating in character mode. They therefore correspond to UMs and Terminals on the NPL network. Within each PSE character terminals are supported by a Virtual Packet Terminal (VPT) which corresponds to the NPL TP. A variety of line speeds are provided ranging from 50 bd for a character terminal to 48K bits/sec for a packet terminal.

The packet format is relatively complex, requiring each packet terminal to support, amongst other things, virtual calls, at least two levels of sequence numbering and a buffer allocation method of flow control.   Thus tight control is exercised over the use of the network which should enable high levels of reliability and integrity to be achieved.

This approach contrasts with that of the NPL DCN where the basic packet switched network has a minimal protocol requiring only the delivery address and size of data.   UMs are free to invent higher levels of protocol to give virtual calls, sequencing etc., but the control information for these protocols is part of the data as far as the DCN is concerned.

4.   OUTLINE OF THE INTER-NETWORK CONNECTION

4.1   Requirements of the interface service

A study was carried out in the autumn of 1974 to investigate the practicality of providing an interface service.   The implementation is based on the recommendations of the study.   The prime aim of the study was to propose methods of allowing character terminals on the DCN to access EPSS packet terminals. It was also desired, but of less importance, to allow EPSS character terminals access to NPL UMs; in particular, the NPL 'Scrapbook' information retrieval system.

It was not required to allow the more general connection between UMs and packet terminals or character terminal to character terminal conversations.   Additionally, the interface was not to get involved in enhancing either the services or the networks.

4.2   Configuration considerations

A basic linkage was already being developed to enable some pre - EPSS tests to be carried out.   This enabled a particular UM (a PDP8) to exchange information with EPSS provided that it handled the EPSS protocol itself. A CTL 'minimod' processor was being used to provide this linkage, appearing as a UM to the DCN and as a packet terminal to EPSS.   It had standard hardware interfaces to each network.   Thus if either interface were ignored the minimod appeared as a perfectly

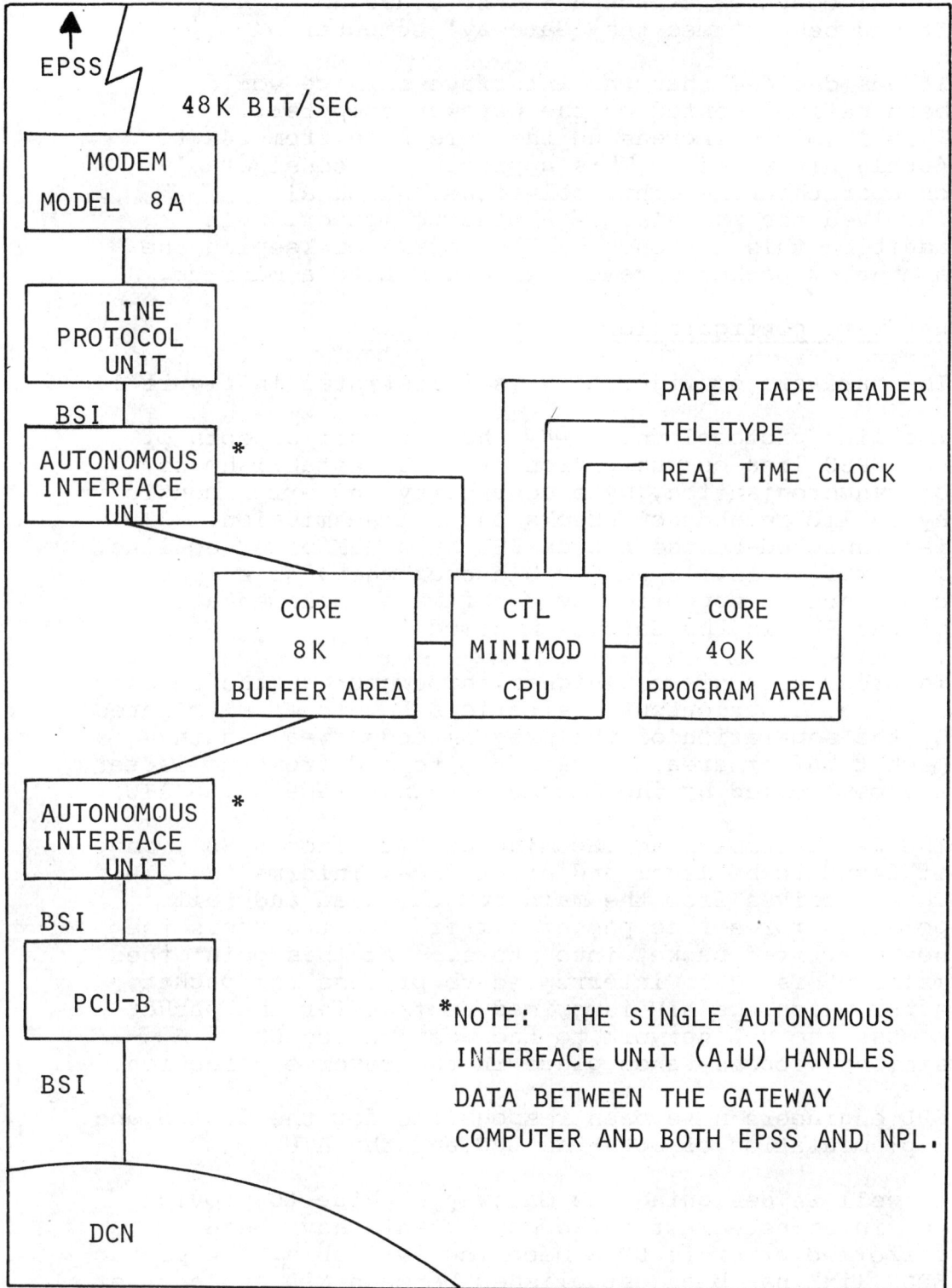

FIGURE 1:   THE HARDWARE CONFIGURATION OF THE GATEWAY

normal computer attached to the other network.
It has been termed the 'Gateway' computer.

It was decided that the interface service would
best be implemented on the Gateway computer.
This involved increasing the core size from 24K to
48K 16 bit words.   This approach was considerably
cheaper than the other solutions, which all
involved the purchase of another computer.   In
addition this approach had the merit of keeping the
amount of packet movement within NPL to a minimum.

4.3   Hardware configuration

The hardware configuration is illustrated in figure 1.

The line protocol unit (LPU) handles all aspects of
the EPSS line communication, such as establishment
of synchronisation, byte contiguity and error control
by cyclic redundancy checks and retransmission.   It
is connected to the London PSE by a 48K bits/sec line.
The traffic levels achievable over the 48Kb/s line
could not be supported by a software implementation
of the LPU in the Gateway minimod.

In order to achieve a higher throughput in the Gateway
machine, input-output hesitations have been eliminated
by the separation of the program code area and the
packet buffer area.   Transfers to and from the latter
are controlled by the Autonomous Interface Unit (AIU).

The LPU assembles an incoming packet (from EPSS), and,
if found to be legal and error free, informs the AIU.
This receives from the main cpu the head and tail
pointers for a free packet buffer, and transfers the
newly arrived packet into store.   At this point the
main cpu is again interrupted to process the packet,
after which the AIU is primed to transfer the packet
across the NPL network to the destination UM.   A
similar process takes place in the reverse direction.

NPL engineers have been responsible for the design and
implementation of both the LPU and the AIU.

As well as designing the Gateway machine to provide
the inter-network traffic path, tests have been
performed prior to EPSS becoming available.   A pseudo-
EPSS link has been established between NPL and another
EPSS customer - the Computer Aided Design Centre at
Cambridge.

EPSS is not a transparent network, and so these
earlier tests were only able to test a sub-set
of the EPSS protocols. To aid these pre-EPSS tests,
an additional hardware module has been built into
the line protocol unit to record details of the
various actions it takes under both normal and
error conditions, and these details are passed
to the processor for subsequent analysis.

4.4   Implementation constraints

It was necessary to implement the inter-connection
of the two networks within NPL in a manner which
involved no changes to EPSS, and preferably none
to the existing NPL network. The NPL DCN is a
single packet terminal as far as EPSS is concerned
even though it consists of a network connecting
several computers and many terminals. It was not,
however, practical for changes to be made either to
EPSS software or to EPSS user's software for the
purposes of communicating with the NPL DCN. For
example, the maximum packet lengths are different. NPL
could hardly request that the maximum EPSS data size
be reduced to match their own. Neither was it
desirable for EPSS participants to have to alter
their systems to fit the NPL maximum before calls
could be established between them and NPL. Therefore
it was up to the NPL interface with EPSS to cope
with large EPSS packets. It would have been possible
to make changes to the DCN and the DCN interface
software in the UMs if necessary but it was clearly
the best policy to maintain a stable interface with
the users. It was also more economical to concentrate
all work into one new machine instead of fragmenting
and duplicating it among already heavily used
computers.

5.   INTERFACE SERVICES OFFERED

5.1 Types of service considered

Several levels of service are possible, each offering
a different balance between degree of assistance and
flexibility.

The maximum flexibility is obtained with direct access
by UMs to the Gateway. In this case each UM acts as
an EPSS Packet Terminal but instead of exchanging
packets directly with the PSE, they transmit EPSS
packets across the NPL network to the Gateway in the

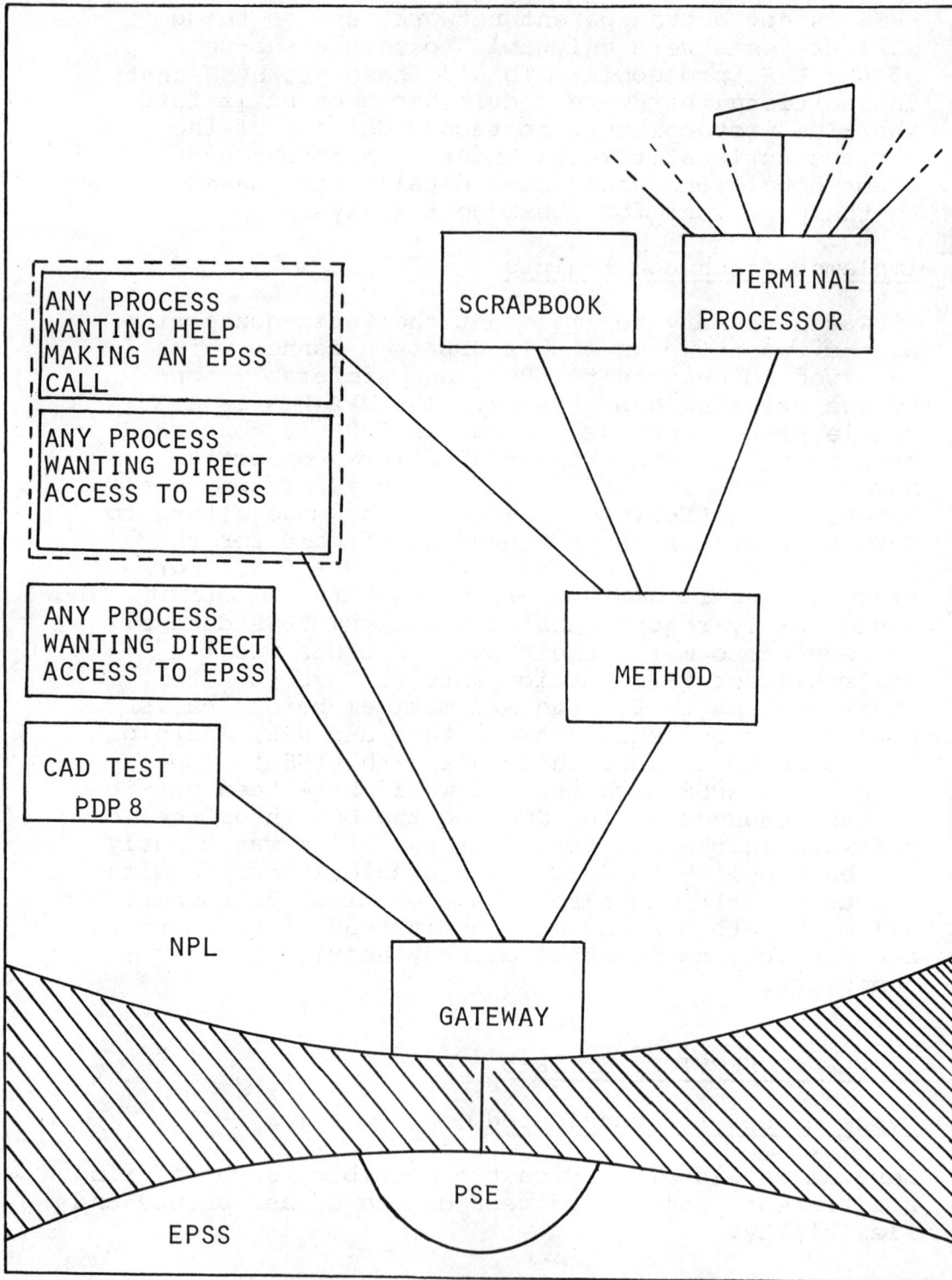

FIGURE 2:   NPL INTERFACE TO EPSS: LOGICAL CONNECTIONS

data field of NPL packets.   The latter concentrates
the flow over the single line joining the two networks.
Each UM, apart from having to operate with a given
subset of the address range, has as much control over
its EPSS calls as possible.   If a UM uses this
form of connection to EPSS it must itself handle
both the NPL protocols and the EPSS protocol.   This
would require considerable amounts of additional
software as the EPSS protocol is a good deal more
complex than the DCN protocols.

All other forms of service or connection offer some
degree of help or assistance to the NPL UM when making
an inter-network call.   For ease of reference it was
decided to call this service METHOD, an abbreviation for
Method for EPSS Terminal Handling On the DCN.   The
division between the simple Gateway connection and the
service offered by METHOD is logical.   Physically they
are very much integrated within the Gateway minimod
enabling the efficient use of many joint routines and
system functions.

In each case where assistance is given by METHOD, it
is METHOD that acts as an EPSS packet terminal.   Since
it is physically resident in the same machine as the
Gateway software, the overheads involved in transmitting
EPSS packets across the NPL network, between the Gateway
and METHOD, are avoided.   Figure 2 shows logical connections that can be made within NPL to gain access to
EPSS.   For simplicity the NPL DCN is not shown.   Note
that METHOD must communicate with EPSS via the Gateway.
Note also that, for generality, individual processes
within an NPL UM are shown using different access methods
to EPSS although this is unlikely to happen for some
time as NPL UMs tend to be mini computers dedicated
to single applications.

Minimum assistance occurs when the UM provides all the
parameters that are required to make an EPSS call.
METHOD makes and supervises the call as defined by
these parameters and acts as a remote extension to
the UMs own network control software.   Although the
UM is shielded from the mechanics of handling the call,
it must nevertheless be aware of EPSS characteristics.
For example, when setting up an EPSS call the two
parties must agree on the number of packet buffers to
be used during the call for flow control purposes.
EPSS allows any number between 1 and 8 to be used.

METHOD constructs the Call Originating Packet
(COP), used within EPSS to initiate the setting
up of a call but in the case of minimum assistance,
requires the NPL UM to define the number of EPSS
packet buffers.   This forms one of the parameters
within the COP.

Maximum assistance is given by METHOD when the UM
does not specify directly any of the EPSS call parameters.   METHOD utilises suitable default parameters
to handle the call.   In this case an EPSS Packet
Terminal would appear to the NPL user to be directly
connected to the DCN, thus the EPSS network would be
"transparent".   This option is the most attractive
because it avoids additional software in several
existing mini-computers.   Taking the same example
as used above when providing maximum assistance,
METHOD would choose a suitable number of packet buffers.
This would not necessarily be constant for all types
of call.   If the call was to an EPSS character terminal,
two buffers would be suitable whereas for a computer
to computer call, eight buffers may be most appropriate.

Between these two extreme forms of service METHOD
offers a whole range of flexibility by allowing UMs
to override individual control parameter default values
for each inter-network call.

5.2   Services implemented

The initial implementation allows METHOD to handle
calls involving either EPSS or NPL character terminals.
The direct Gateway connection is also included although
it was not specifically required.

Character terminal calls are handled with maximum
assistance, although NPL character terminal users are
given the opportunity to override relevant default
parameters.   Because METHOD controls the EPSS call
and the EPSS control parameters originate from either
METHOD or the NPL character terminal user, there are
no changes required to the NPL TP.   An NPL character
terminal user can make calls to any EPSS packet terminal.
This includes the VPTs and so character terminal to
character terminal conversations can be initiated by
NPL users.   An EPSS character terminal user can make
calls to NPL UMs supporting the standard UM to UM protocol.   The TP pseudo UM supports this protocol.   So
although not required, full character terminal to
character terminal conversations "fall out" of the
METHOD implementation.

The direct Gateway connection was also neither required nor expected to be used initially. It was implemented because METHOD needs nearly all the Gateway functions anyway, so for very little extra effort they could be offered to all NPL UMs. Thus any UM could, if it was wanted, control its own EPSS calls instead of having METHOD do it. This gives greater flexibility for long term developments.

The character terminal handling is designed around the EPSS Virtual Packet Terminal (VPT) system specification. NPL character terminals are handled by a subsystem of METHOD that mimics the VPT. Another subsystem forms a packet terminal suitable for handling calls to remote VPTs, so enabling NPL services, such as Scrapbook, to be used via EPSS character terminals. Some overheads in EPSS flow control were found in this area. Scrapbook allows the terminal user to input information at any time and the only practical way found to achieve this involved sending at best one empty control packet and at worst three empty control packets for a single data packet.

6.   IMPLEMENTATION

6.1 Incompatibilities between the two networks

Among the potential technical problems three areas were found to require serious consideration:

(a) Addressing

     Neither network explicitly allows in its address space for connection to other networks. However, in NPL's case the size of the network and the amount of internetworking expected were small enough to allow a simple address conversion table approach to be used. The critical factor here is not the amount of traffic but the number of different addresses accessed by NPL within the EPSS network and vice versa.

     The EPSS packet format allows 1000 different addresses (processes) within a packet terminal. No more than 256 character terminals can be connected to the DCN and as Scrapbook (and the other UMs) support no more than a handful of processes then it is possible to make a 1:1 address correspondence with plenty to

spare for future expansion.   EPSS users
wishing to access NPL will be given a
table showing, for example, that they must
address process 44 within the NPL packet
terminal to access Scrapbook.   METHOD
converts this by simple table lookup to
UM 4; Process O which is the real address
of the Scrapbook service within NPL.

A 1:1 address conversion table is also used
by METHOD to convert NPL processes into
EPSS addresses.   The NPL packet format
allows only 256 different addresses (processes)
within a UM.   As the EPSS network has
a much bigger population than NPL, it
is not possible for the table to hold
the addresses of all possible EPSS
processes that NPL users may wish to access.
However, in practice, it should hold all
the commonly used addresses and, as the
default override facility enables NPL
character terminal users to define EPSS
addresses directly, there is always a way
out.

(b)   Packet Length

NPL and EPSS packet lengths are incompatible.
This presents potentially large problems
within NPL but the nature of the services
to be connected in the first implementation
means that a general solution will not be
needed initially.

NPL protocol does not have facilities for
assembling packets into larger messages.
In theory an NPL service designed to process
single packets of data could behave incorrectly
when processing the two NPL packets arising
from a near maximum length EPSS packet.   It
would act on receipt of the first without
knowing whether a second was to follow.
Fortunately Scrapbook does not process packets
but regards its input as a continuous stream
of characters and searches for delimiters such
as "Carriage Return".   It was assumed that the
terminal users would also be able to sort out
any confusion on the rare occasions that
significant delay occurred between output of two
parts of an EPSS packet.   Therefore no extensions
are being made to handle messages bigger than
NPL packets.

(c)   <u>Flow Control</u>

There were two distinct problem areas associated with flow control. The first arose
because of differences in the control
techniques used by the two networks and the
second because of the lack of agreed standards
for the use the EPSS flow control techniques.

NPL flow control is not as precise as that used
by EPSS so METHOD cannot simply join the NPL
and EPSS calls directly together as if they
were, say, oil pipelines. Instead METHOD has
to act as a buffer area, storing, forwarding or,
very occasionally, dropping, packets. Whilst
this is, in theory, unsatisfactory, it is not
expected to be a problem in practice, especially
for character terminal users.

At the time that METHOD was being designed there
were no generally accepted standards for using
the EPSS flow control techniques. The problem
was being approached by some of the users in
Study Group Two but their recommendations had
not been finalised or accepted. This meant
that it was not possible for NPL to implement
the flow control aspects of a packet terminal
suitable for general packet terminal to packet
terminal working, because it was not known what
protocols would be adopted by the other EPSS
participants. Fortunately the flow control
protocol for the EPSS VPT had been defined by
the Post Office and so by using the same protocol,
and creating one to interface with it, METHOD
was able to support character terminal working
as initially required.

Among the other technical aspects that had to be
considered were character code, parity, terminal speed,
character echoing and the EPSS 'Reset' facility.
None of them presented any significant difficulty
because the networks were broadly compatible in these
respects.

6.2   <u>Implementation estimates</u>

The scale of effort involved was estimated at 6 man
years, spread over 1-1½ years, to produce 18K 16-bit
words of core resident code. Particular allowance
was made for the research nature of the project since

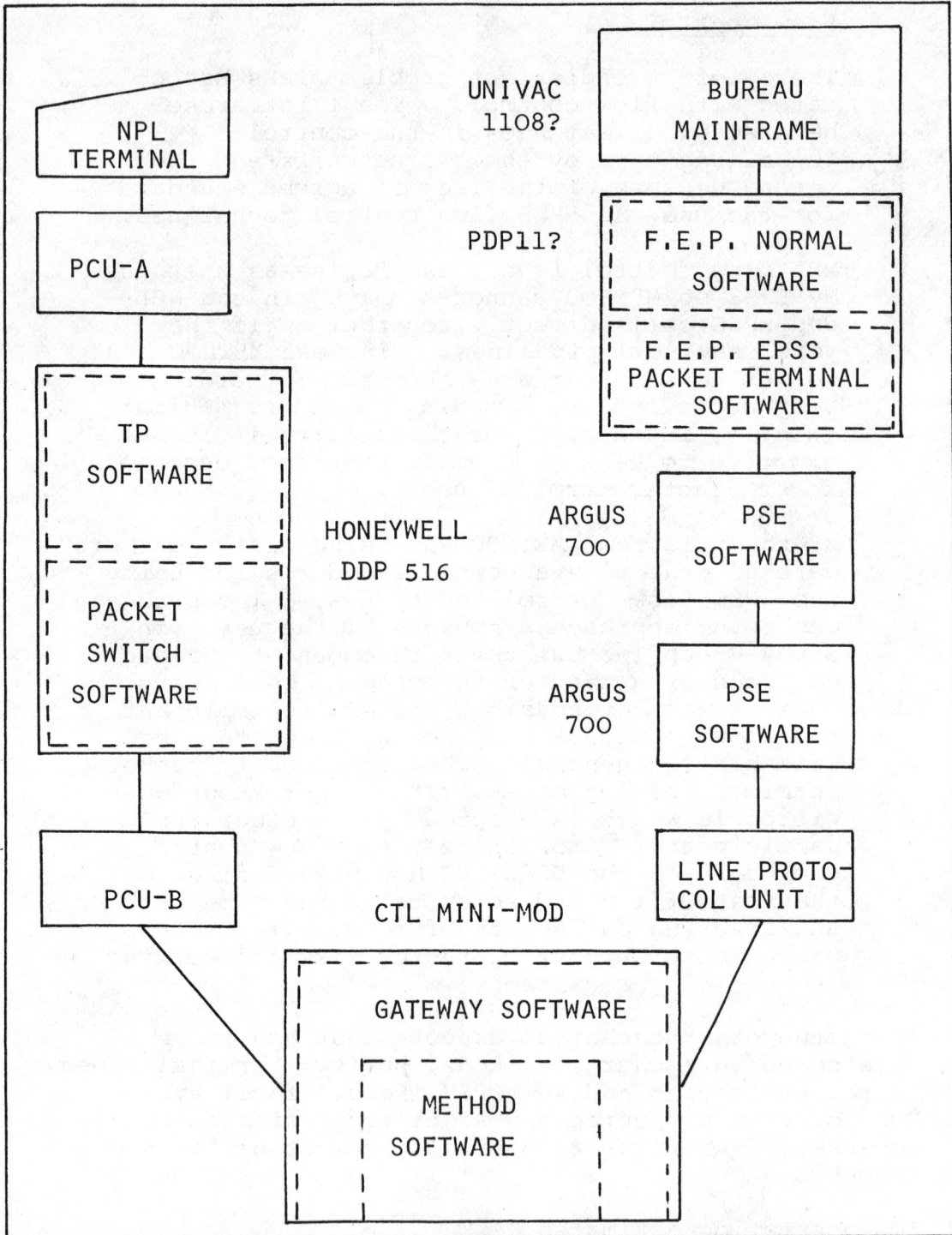

FIGURE 3:   SIMPLIFIED DIAGRAM OF THE HARDWARE/SOFTWARE
             INVOLVED IN AN INTER-NETWORK CALL

EPSS would not become available until the later
stages of implementation.   Also, because the
eventual uses of the inter-network connection
were difficult to predict, it was necessary to
make allowance in the software so that new services
or types of connection could be plugged in later.
Finally, the complexity of the hardware and the
software involved in an inter-network call necess-
itated generous allowance for system testing.
Figure 3 gives an indication of the hardware and
software units that must work together to enable
an inter-network call to be made.

It should be possible, at the time of the conference,
to indicate how closely the implementation will
follow these estimates.

6.   CONCLUSIONS

The study and initial design work have shown that
it is possible, on paper at least, to provide for
character terminal working between the NPL DCN and
EPSS.   Practical experience is necessary before
this can be proved.   More general inter-computer
working cannot be implemented until satisfactory
standards become widely accepted by EPSS participants.

REFERENCES

[1]   D.W. Davies et al.   A digital communication
       network for computers giving rapid response
       at remote terminals, Proc. ACM symposium on
       operating system principles, Gatlinburg USA 1967.

[2]   R. Scantlebury and P.T. Wilkinson.   The design
       of a switching system to allow remote access to
       computer services by other computers and terminal
       devices, Proc. ACM/IEEE second symposium on
       problems in the optimisation of data communications
       systems, Palo Alto USA 1971.

[3]   R. Scantlebury and P.T. Wilkinson.   The National
       Physical Laboratory Data Communication Network,
       Proc. ICCC Stockholm 1974.

[4]   BS4421: 1969.   A digital input/output interface
       for data collection systems.   British Standards
       Institution.   Sales Branch, 101 Pentonville Road,
       London, N.1.

[5]   D.J. Pearson and D. Wilkin.   Some design aspects
       of a public packet switched network, Proc. ICCC
       Stockholm 1974.

RPCNET features and components

by

P. Franchi and G. Sommi

IBM Scientific Center, Pisa, Italy.

Abstract

In this paper the general concepts of the REEL Project
Computer NETwork (RPCNET) are shown.
   A first functional distinction is made in three basic
layers: Communication Functions, Interface Functions and
Applications.
   Then, each layer is subdivided in different functional
boxes and these boxes are briefly described.
   Finally, the machines, hardware features and operating
systems on which the implementation is planned are listed.

1.- General Architecture.

Main purpose of RPCNET is to provide Computing Centers,
in the Research and Educational area, with a sensible way
of sharing their computational resources, such as
application programs, data sets, compilers, programming
subsystems and so on.
This objective should be attained without producing
unnecessary interference with the normal activity of the
Center and minimizing additional hardware and software
requirements. For these reasons, basic features of RPCNET
are:
                -distributed control topology,
                -dynamically variable configuration,
                -nonhomogeneous nodes.

Namely, this latter point means that in the Network both
Nodes with a "Front End Processor" (FEP) and Nodes without
an FEP, are considered. In this second case, the set of
functions which allow the internode communication is
performed by one of the HOSTs of the Computing Center. The
HOST subsystem which performs this set of function is called
LOGICAL FEP.
When a physical FEP is available, these functions are
developed by the FEP itself, which, in addition, may support
low speed, display and bulk I/O terminals. These terminals
are allowed to access both local HOSTs and remote Nodes.

The Attachment between an FEP and its HOST(s) is composed
of several independent communication subchannels, in order
to provide HOST's users with a variety of accesses to the
Network facilities.

The communication channel between adjacent Nodes is composed of non-switched, point-to-point telephone lines equipped with synchronous modems. The data rate which is first considered is within the range of 2400-4800 bps, but the upper bound is expected to increase in the time frame of the project.

The end-to-end data flow is accomplished with a Packet Switching technique [1]. The number and the geographical distribution of telephone lines allow more than one end-to-end data path between every pair of Nodes in the Network.

A User of the Network is every process (such as application program, terminal handler, user's task and so on) which wants to interact with a corresponding remote process (Server).

Each User is expected to know the location and features of its Server. User and Server are both Network Users, in a word, "Netusers".

The Network provides enquiry facilities, that help any User to find its Server, as well as connection facilities to establish communication between them.

For the whole duration of an activity between a User and its Server ("Session"), a "Logical Communication Channel" (LCC) is maintained by two classes of functions: "Interface Functions", in the boundary Nodes, and "Communication Functions", in the intermediate and boundary Nodes.

2.- Functional Components.

The main logical components that allow Network services to be provided are shown in Fig.1. For sake of convenience, in this figure the basic components of FEPs and HOSTs are not shown, such as: Monitor, Local I/O Handlers, Operator Command Processors and so on.

Already mentioned "Communication Functions" are further subdivided to better detail Network logical features.

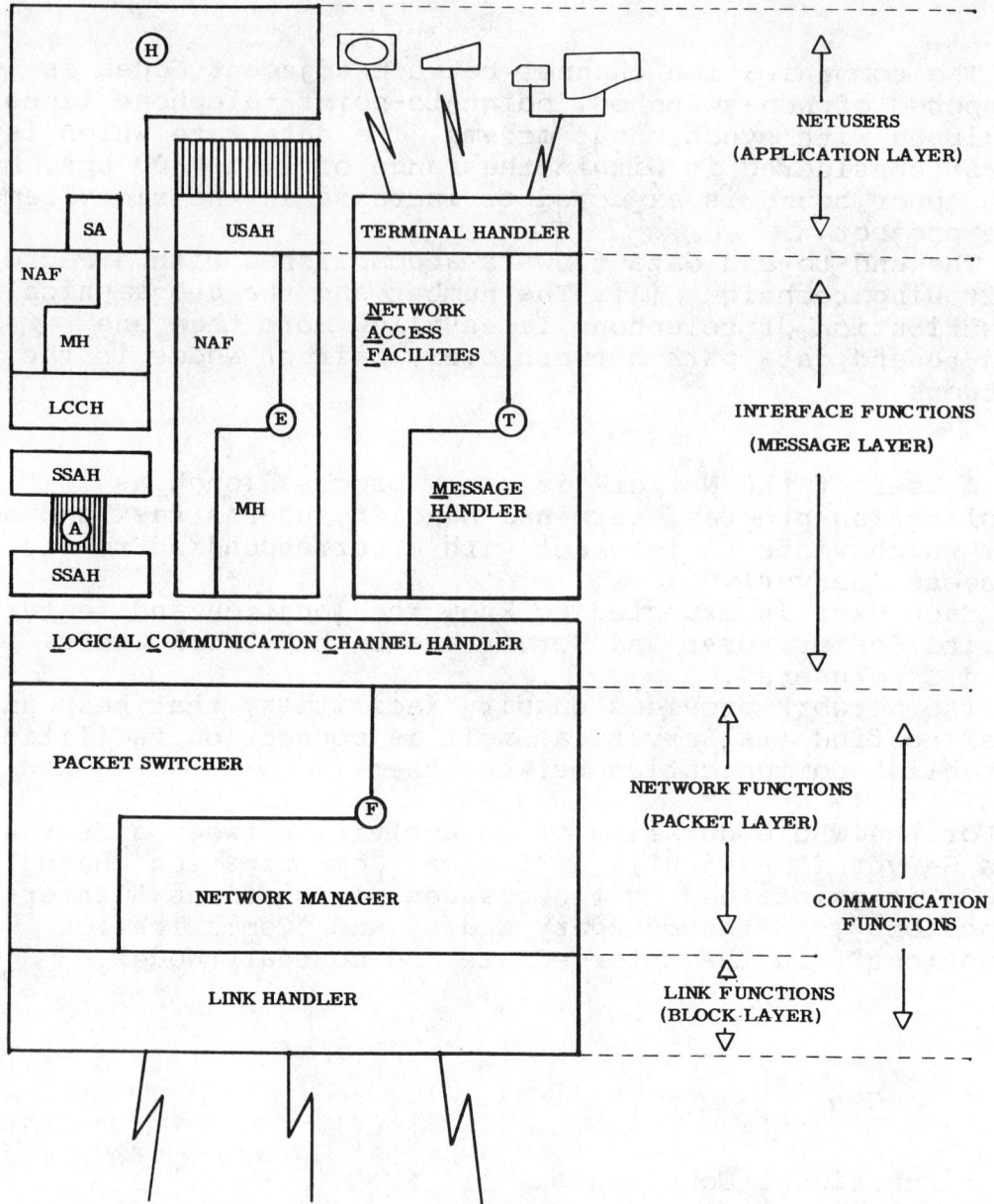

Fig.1. Node Components.

Namely, they can be splitted in: "Link Functions", which allow exchanging of Blocks (containing one or more Packets) from a Node to an adjacent one; "Network Functions" which comply with the task of routing Packets from origin Node to destination Node.

In Fig.1 the sets of components identified with H, A, E, F and T are related to the various Node configurations in RPCNET as shown in Fig.2.

The residence of the box H functions is the HOST processor, the residence of the box T functions is the physical FEP and the residence of the box A and E functions is the HOST-FEP Attachment. The box F functions can be implemented either by the HOST (LOGICAL FEP) or by the (physical) FEP.

3.- Communication Functions.

Regardless of their physical residence (FEP or HOST), the "Communication Functions" deal with the task of relaying every Packet to its destination.

3.1.- Link Handler.

The Link Handler (LH) component controls data links between adjacent Nodes. It performs framing of characters, according to the "Physical Protocol" of the communication channel and assures data integrity, by means of appropriate provisions ("First Level Logical Protocol").

Transmission of data is simultaneously made in both directions to take better advantage of the communication channel capacity (full-duplex technique) [2].

The out-of-sequence problem due to Block retransmission is solved by increasing the prority of the retransmitted Packets and checking the sequence of Packets at the destination Node.

The Link Handler maintains the active state of an idle link, by sending special Hello messages [3].

3.2.- Packet Switcher.

The Packet Switcher (PS) component relays Packets among various components of the Node, according to general rules and to the information carried by the Packets themselves ("Second Level Logical Protocol"). Packets which must be forwarded to other Nodes are submitted to the Link Handler in the appropriate input queue.

The choice of the appropriate link is based upon a "Routing Table" which relates each remote Node to a single adjacent Node.

In the first implementation a 'quasi-fixed' routing technique is adopted, in a sense that an alternative path is chosen only when a component deactivation or failure cuts the original optimal path [4].

An 'adaptive' routing technique is planned for future implementation. In that case, traffic information carried by incoming Packets will be used to update the Routing Table.

3.3.- Network Manager.

The Network Manager (NM) component maintains the Table in which the current topology of the Network is described ("Network Table") and updates the Routing Table as a consequence of any change in the Network topology [5].

The Network Manager is made aware of changes of state of the local links by the Link Handler, updates the Network Table and Routing Table and submits to the Link Handler reconfiguration messages to distribute the Network Table throughout the Network.

A special network process ("Tree Process") has been designed to perform this one-to-all distribution in an efficient and reliable way [4,6].

The reconfiguration message reaches every Node many times

from different paths, all starting from the sending Node.
The first time, every Node is reached from the shortest path
and in the fastest possible way. The set of the shortest
paths constitutes a "tree".

4.- Interface Functions.

The access of Netusers to "Communication Functions" is
allowed by a class of "Interface Functions", whose purpose
is to match a variety of Netusers with the standard set of
the "Communication Functions" [7].

4.1.- Logical Communication Channel Handler.

This component (LCCH) builds, maintains and releases the
Logical Communication Channels which begin and end at its
Node. Each LCC is described in a Table which contains all
the information to assembly in Packets the data arriving
from Netusers and to relay to the addressed Netusers the
Packets arriving from the Packet Switcher.

LCCH takes care of control Packets which are originated
by a Netuser in the course of its Session.
The Network Manager notifies LCCH of all component
deactivations and failures which could cause loss of Packets
or which make the LCC unrecoverable.
In the first case, LCCH retransmits control Packets not
yet acknowledged. In the second case, LCCH blocks
unrecoverable Sessions.

4.2.- Shared Subchannel Attachment Handler.

This component (SSAH) is present in a Node where HOST and
FEP are separate machines. It implements the HOST-FEP
communication by sharing a pair of Attachment subchannels

(two-way channel) among many Sessions at the same time.
    Data flow control, multiplexing and demultiplexing
functions are accomplished by SSAH by means of an
appropriate protocol [8].
    In this protocol, provisions are taken to protect the FEP
against an excessive input data rate.

4.3- Network Access Facilities.

    By this term (NAF) those conventions and facilities are
meant that provide a Netuser with a standard access to the
Network. This access method is called RNAM (REEL Network
Acces Method).
    On top of the RNAM level (Assembler Language) other
linking conventions may be developed, up to the level of
programming language library routines, operating systems
commands and job control language options.

    Among these facilities, the set of services is also
included that make it possible for a Netuser to enquiry
about the Network status.
    Primary objective of the project will be the
implementation of the RNAM macro language. Additional and
more user-oriented facilities will be developed when giving
access to the Network to particular applications (see
Section 5).

4.4.- Message Handler.

    This component (MH) serves the Netusers' request,
controlling the flow of information along the LCCs assigned
to the Netusers and sorting messages to and from the various
Netusers.
    The main task of the Message Handler is to implement the
functions of the RNAM macros SEND and RECEIVE, by which the
Netusers' "Basic Information Units" (BIUs) are sent to and
received from the Network.

The outgoing BIUs are segmented into Packets, according to the Communication Functions requirements. These segments are reassambled into BIUs by the receiving Message Handler, before being delivered to the receiving Netuser.

MH cooperates with LCCH to build at the sending side and to interpret at the receiving side the second level protocol part of the Packets.

5.- Applications.

Exchange of information between User and Server implies a previous agreement about data structure and control information ("Third Level Logical Protocol").

This control information is included in the BIU as a "User Protocol Unit" (UPU). The remaining part of the BIU is called "User Data Unit" (UDU).

When required, a BIU is splitted into its UPU and UDU part by the receiving Message Handler, before being delivered to the receiving Netuser.

An "Application" is constituted of one Netuser or more Netusers having the same physical residence and a single logical control.

The Applications build the UPU and UDU parts of BIUs and (via RNAM macros) send, receive and control the flow of BIUs.

In the Network there are as many "Third Level Protocols" as "Session" types. When implementing, two typical kind of activities are prioritized:

 -Interactive Session, or terminal-to-HOST activity;
 -Transfer of spool files, or spool-to-spool Session.

In order to allow taking place of the first type of Session, a specific third level protocol must be implemented between Terminal Handler at the terminal side and Attachment Handler at the HOST side.

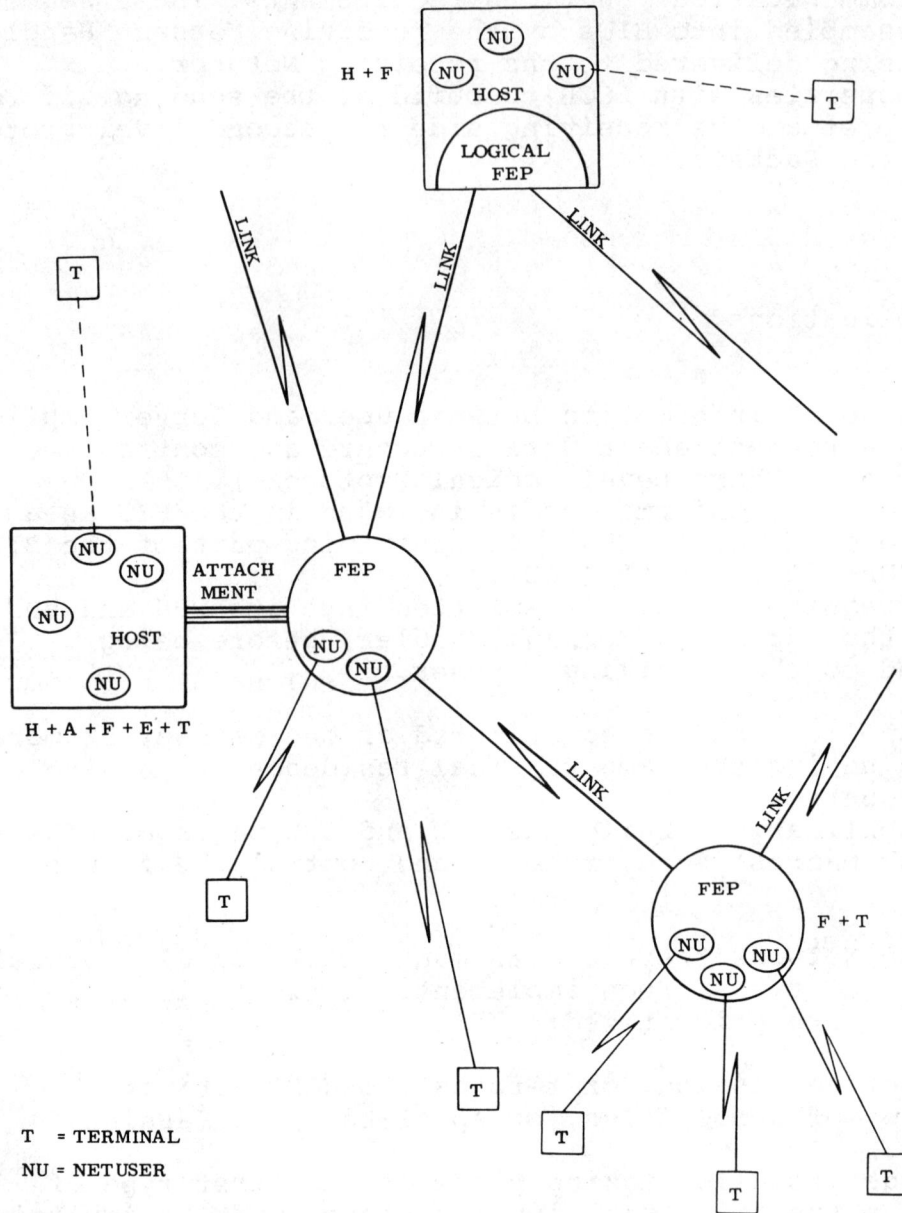

Fig.2. Node Configurations.

5.1.- Unshared Subchannel Attachment Handler.

This Application (USAH) manages a set of Attachment subchannels. These subchannels are unshared in a sense that they are in a one-to-one relationship with the corresponding remote terminals.

USAH resides in the (physical) FEP. At the HOST side, it implements the emulation of a subset of 2702 Telecommunication Control Unit I/O commands. At the Network side, USAH manages various LCCs via RNAM macros.

USAH allows the access to a HOST from terminals of another Node without any modification to the HOST operating system.

5.2.- Terminal Handler.

The privileged network partner of USAH is the Terminal Handler (TH) component. USAH and Terminal Handler cooperates to allow development of terminal-to HOST Sessions.

In the design of the terminal-to-HOST Session, two types of third level protocols are considered.

The first one is based on a request/response flow control. In this case the terminal is kept 'synchronous' with the sysyem, as it happens in the usual time-sharing star network.

In the second type, a limited number of I/O printing lines are allowed to be outstanding along the LCC. In this second case, the exchange of information between terminal and HOST is faster but the control of the Session is more critical.

5.3.- Host Applications.

The spool-to-spool activity is the second type of prioritized type of Session.

The Spool Application (SA) in a Node manages all the LCCs to the Spool Applications in the other Nodes. However, an

LCC is established only when a transfer of spool file is required.

In order to allow a faster spool transfer, the spool protocol has been designed in such a way that several spool blocks can be sent without requiring individual acknowledgments from the receiver [9].
Spool files are sent in their original format, if possible. When two communicating Spool Systems are nonhomogeneous, a common standard format is used.

6.- Hardware and Software.

While the overall architecture has been designed making reference to physical components and logical functions not related to a specific hardware or software, actual implementation is carried on making use of particular machines and operating systems.
These are: IBM System/7 as FEP; System/360s and System/370s running OS/VS and VM370 as HOSTs.
The System/360/370 Channel Attachment (RPQ D08112) provides the capability of attaching the System/7 to the HOST processor.
The System/7 Teleprocessing Multiplexer (RPQ D08011) provides the communication interface of the Front End Processor.
The LOGICAL FEP manages Network data links via Telecommunication Control Units of the 270x series or 370x series in 270x emulation mode.

Acknowledgments

The design of RPCNET shown in this paper is the result of a cooperative effort on behalf of several individuals.
Namely, many thanks are due to C. Johnson and his team (IBM CSC), to L. Lenzini and his team (CNUCE) and to all the people of the IBM PSC involved in the project.

References

[1] - Donald W. Davies and Derek L. A. Barber, "Communication Networks for Computers". John Wiley and Sons, 1973.

[2] - L. Lenzini, "Full-duplex Data Link Protocol: a Proposed Design". RPCNET Internal Document IS004-01, August 1974.

[3] - L. Lazzeri, "Link Handler Specifications" RPCNET Internal Document UG011-00, October 1974.

[4] - P. Franchi, "Internode Communication Functions: Initial Design". IBM Scientific Center Technical Report 513-3527, April 1974.

[5] - P. Franchi, "Modeling and Analysis for Reconfiguration Procedures in a Distributed Computer Network". Proceedings of the European Computer Workshop on "Distributed Computer Systems", Darmstadt, October 1974.

[6] - William D. Tajibnapis, "The Design of A Topology Information Maintenance Scheme for a Distributed Computer Network". Proceedings of the ACM Annual Conference, November 1974.

[7] - M. Maier, "Network Interface Functions: Problems and Proposed Solutions". RPCNET Internal Document UG008-01. November 1974.

[8] - A. Fusi, L. Lenzini and R. Matteucci, "System/360/370 to System/7 Local Attachment Protocol: Proposed Design" RPCNET Internal Document IS006-00, September 1974.

[9] - P. Bertaina, M. Magini, C. Paoli and F. Tarini, "Spool to Spool Protocol: Initial Design". RPCNET Internal Document IS007-01, October 1974.

The effect of a data communications network on a large laboratory site

by K.A.Bartlett and P.T.Wilkinson
National Physical Laboratory
UK

The NPL Data Communications Network has been operational for over two years, during which time it has become an essential site service. Because it acts as a common-carrier and offers a range of very general communication facilities, it has allowed the development of several interdependent remote access services including an alphanumeric database and a central file store. The network's influence has been apparent in such diverse areas as the increased utilisation of small computers and a reduction in the demand for typing services.

Experience gained in using the network has pointed the way to further developments in distributed computing utilities and remote uses of computers.

1. Introduction

The development of a packet switched data communications network
serving the National Physical Laboratory site has had a profound effect
upon the type and organisation of the computer services available to
terminal users. The network, which is described in more detail in
Section 2, supports a large number and variety of terminal devices
through which the users expect to be able to access these services
directly. The use of paper tape and cards as intermediates has largely,
if not yet entirely, died out.

Rather than perpetuating the usual situation in which one central
computer complex attempts to offer all types of service to all users,
the network has promoted the development of a distributed system in
which several more specialised services are provided by smaller
computers, any of which may be accessed from each user terminal. The
main features of these services are outlined in Section 3. They include
an information storage and retrieval system (Scrapbook, Section 3.1); a
central file store (Section 3.2) and a general purpose editing system
EDIT, Section 3.3).

The final three sections of the paper discuss some of the network
implications for these service computers and for their subscribers, the
network terminal users. The way in which these services have evolved
since joining the network, and are continuing to evolve, is considered,
as is the consequent need for the network itself to expand, both in
capacity and geographical extent in order to keep pace with the
changing needs of its users.

2. The main features of the NPL network

The NPL Data Communications Network is a general purpose system serving
a multi-disciplinary laboratory site. The site, which is about a half
mile long, accomodates some 200 administrative personnel and 700
engineers and scientists working in such fields as as Numerical
Analysis; Chemical Standards; Acoustics; Radiation Science; Metrology
and Computer Science.

The network acts as a common carrier, operating on the store-and-
forward basis that has become widely known as "packet switching". The
NPL network was constructed as an isolated 'local area' of a
hypothetical multi-node system (Ref.1). Thus, although it serves a
relatively small site and contains only one central control computer,
the network organisation takes no advantage of these facts, having all
the significant features of a full-scale system as far as its users are
concerned.

Subscribers are connected to the network by a purpose-built hardware
system of eight-way concentrators and serial line transmission units
(Ref.2). The subscribers are divided into two classes. The first
consists of computers which are able to create and interpret packets as

required by the network. These are known as 'User Machines'. User machines communicate with each other by transferring packets through the 'Local Packet Switch', to which each one has a single link. Since each packet is an independent entity (this is the nature of packet switching), a User Machine may be involved in many simultaneous interactions through the network by using its single connection to carry interleaved streams of packets.

The second class of subscriber to the network is the simpler character organised terminal which actually requires a User Machine to handle the packet assembly and disassembly. Thus a special User Machine (known as the Terminal Processor) offers a "virtual call" service to these simpler kinds of subscriber peripheral devices (generically referred to as "terminals"). One terminal may establish a call to another through the Terminal Processor but each terminal is permitted to be involved in only one call at a time.

In addition, terminals may communicate with User Machines; this involves the Terminal Processor in generating and interpreting packets on behalf of the terminal users, these packets being exchanged with other User Machines via the Local Packet Switch. During a virtual call, a terminal may exchange arbitrary amounts of data with the other party. The use of a standard interface (the British Standard Interface, BS4421) to connect peripheral equipment to the Terminal Processor communications hardware permits the attachment of a great variety of terminal devices to the network.

Connection of User Machines to the Local Packet Switch is made by means of the same hardware standard interface and a set of very simple procedural and packet format standards (that is, a communications protocol). Because this protocol is a standard imposed by the network, once a User Machine has connection to the Local Packet Switch it may interact with any other User Machine. Thus the network behaves as a common carrier at this level. Because the protocol and hardware interface are very simple, it is relatively easy to connect computers to the network. In particular, the amounts of code and data storage required by the "network control programs" within each User Machine are very small (typically a few hundred words).

Communication between the Terminal Processor and a User Machine requires an additional level of protocol in order to effect the virtual call mechanism. This "virtual call protocol" is also very simple so that a relatively small extension to the "network control program" of a User Machine (again, of the order of a few hundred words of program code plus tables) enables it to engage in virtual calls with terminal devices. Since this protocol standard is imposed by the Terminal Processor, it does not constrain other types of inter User Machine communication. However, the protocol has sufficient generality to make it useful in this situation also. It has been adopted by most of the User Machines on the present network as the basis for general computer-computer communications and resource-sharing activities.

Incidentally, it is quite possible for computers to be connected to the
Terminal Processor as "simple terminals". This method of attachment has
the advantage of avoiding any alteration to the basic software of the
computers (since interaction is then made in terms of a simple input
and output character stream, as though from a directly connected
device) but at the cost of permitting only a relatively small number of
simultaneous interactions and of using up this number of terminal
ports. The more network-oriented services such as Scrapbook, EDIT and
the Central File Store are connected as User Machines to the Local
Packet Switch, with the much greater flexibility that this implies.

The Local Packet Switch and Terminal Processor "functions" are in fact
implemented in the same central computer and share the communications
distribution network. This central computer is a Honeywell H516 with
32,768 words of store. The Local Packet Switch function looks after all
the User Machines while the Terminal Processor function caters for the
terminals. The Local Packet Switch software occupies under 2,000 words
of store and can handle a mean throughput for traffic passing between
User Machines of from 250 to 500 packets per second, depending on the
average amount of user data carried in each packet (the maximum being
255 8-bit bytes).

The Terminal Processor software takes somewhat less than 5,000 store
locations and can support an average terminal to terminal traffic of
from 250 to 330 data blocks per second. Since the H516 is time-sharing
the Local Packet Switch and Terminal Processor functions, it is not of
course possible to get both these maximum transfer rates
simultaneously. Traffic between terminals and User Machines also
imposes a greater load upon the control computer and the average
maximum rates fall in the range 150 to 250 packets per second.

The network has been operating in its present form since June 1973 and
at the time of writing has 140 devices connected of which 19 are
mini-computers and 75 are Visual Display Units. The remainder is
composed of tape readers, punches, line printers and special- purpose
devices. It is currently available for 12 hours each day during which
time it handles about 300,000 packets.

3. The services available over the network

3.1 Scrapbook

This is a computer-based information retrieval system for alphanumeric
data (Ref.3,4). The system is most frequently accessed via VDU's which
are connected to the Scrapbook computer through the network for the
duration of the interaction. Original text is entered into a file or
"record" by the author or a typist from a keyboard or it may be read
from paper tape. This record may then be retained as part of a personal
information system or selectively broadcast to interested parties -
again through VDU's - for information, comment or annotation. The final
text may be retained in the system for future reference; archived or,

if absolutely necessary, printed out as hard copy.

The system is designed to be used with rapid access visual display units which can quickly display a suitable quantity of information when used in a rapid 'page-turning' mode. Records are therefore structured as strings of "frames", each of which can hold enough information to fill the average display screen.

Scrapbook offers considerable assistance to the creator and editor of records, one of its principal design objectives being to provide a highly user-oriented interface at the keyboard/display terminal. Operations may be carried out on lines, frames or complete records. Examples of line based operations are GAP, DELETE and PACK whereby words on a line may be moved to allow extra words to be inserted; lines or parts may be deleted and words - as delimited by spaces - may be packed into the smallest possible number of lines.

This last operation can apply over a complete frame. Other frame operations include TRANSFER, ERASE and SPLIT which enable the order of frames within a record to be changed; complete frames to be removed and two frames created by dividing one at a specified point. Complete records may be copied or transferred within Scrapbook or printed out. A referencing and linking system allows short-form instructions to be planted within frames which then allow rapid access to other frames or records. These latter facilities are very important since they turn Scrapbook into a system for general information manipulation and retrieval. This indeed was another of the primary objectives of its designers.

Scrapbook, along with all similar terminal-oriented services, is accessed by first establishing a virtual call via the Terminal Processor; this is achieved by using the terminal to send the network address of the service User Machine to the Terminal Processor. Once the call is set up, the computer and terminal operator can exchange data until one or other of them terminates the call by sending a special signal to the Terminal Processor. When the call is first established, Scrapbook proceeds to determine the identity of the user by requesting a password. In this way access to restricted information can be controlled.

A MESSAGE facility allows records to be assembled into a message file which is displayed to the recipient whenever he logs on to the system. This is being developed into a full conferencing system which will allow a 'chairman' to receive submissions on a subject and control the insertion of these into a conference record.

This is displayed to all current conference delegates. Private conversations are possible between the chairman and delegates which may not become part of the conference record. As conferences often continue for days or weeks, the chairman may suspend his special role and allow all contributions to be entered on to the conference record. References are easily constructed so that relevant frames of the conference record may be quickly accessed. Each delegate to the conference has a record maintained for him by the system of his contributions to the conference and all private messages sent by him during the conference. In addition, records are maintained of all messages received during the conference. The main conference record is backed up by two administrative records listing the terms of reference and the identities of logged on participants.

Scrapbook was originally created on a single Modular One computer with 48,000 words of direct access memory and 28 megabytes of disc but the demand for the service has been such that a second system of the same size has now been installed. The service has 140 subscribers who maintain 2000 records between them. The average record length is 20 frames (10,000 characters). The Scrapbook computers between them handle about 40,000 packets per day.

Scrapbook is used to retain information, pass messages and write reports. This last application is very important. The ease with which sections of text may be erased, inserted or transferred between records has meant that report writing has become an interactive on-line process. Very often, the computer based print-outs are sufficient for the hard copy requirements but if hand typed, well formatted copies are required then the typist is only involved at the final stage – never during editing.

The message passing facility within the system has resulted in a greater interchange of information between groups and individuals. The existence of recorded information in an easily accessible and transferable form has meant that experimental results, statistics, budgetary data and staff levels, once recorded, can be quickly passed to a number of people and assimilated into local reports and working documents without manual transcription.

The natural tendency to browse through the Scrapbook system has also meant that there is a wider dissemination of secondary information – that which would not be directly sent for your attention but is available for your inspection. The abilty to restrict access to records to specified groups means that secure or sensitive information cannot be gleaned in this way.

For historical reasons, Scrapbook is used rather more in some sections of the laboratory than others and in these sections, the demand for typing services has decreased dramatically as has the time taken to produce reports. One factor which may limit the eventual coverage of the system is its inability to cope with anything other than straightforward alphanumeric data. It is difficult to represent subscripts and other notation used in mathematical formulae. The production of simple character-symbol diagrams is possible although not particularly convenient; Scrapbook was never intended as a graphics system.

3.2 The Central File Store

The Central File Store (Ref.5) was designed to act as a common backing store for the multiplicity of small computers around the site. It consists of a Honeywell H516 control computer to which are attached three head-per-track disc units with a total capacity of 60 megabytes. Two magnetic tape drives are used to provide security dumping and file archiving.

The file store was intended specifically for use by other User Machines via the network. It is accessed by means of a relatively simple coded command language which is carried by packets transmitted according to the Local Packet Switch and Terminal Processor protocols. Thus an extension to the network control program of a User Machine will permit the programs executing therein to make use of the file store.

The file store has a number of 'users', characterised by user identifier and password. A 'user' may be another User Machine or an individual on whose behalf such a User Machine is accessing the file store. Each of these users is allowed to own a collection of uniquely named files. A system of access controls is provided to make reading from (and possibly writing to) the files of other users possible by privileged users.

Since the file store is intended as a backing store to hold information without regard for the structure or meaning of that information, it follows that the files must be very simple objects at the level of the file store operations and that the latter must be of a very general nature. A file in fact is treated as an addressable byte space which has an associated name and access controls. File store operations include commands for reading or writing a string of bytes (8-bit characters) of a given length starting from a given byte address. Sufficient disc space is allocated to hold a file whose last byte has the largest address specified in a write operation.

The file store command interface is not suitable for use as a standard for the direct transmission of files between other pairs of User Machines (it was not intended to be used in this way). However, most intercommunication of files between User Machines takes place using the central file store as an intermediary. Conventions as to the naming of files, their formats and the use of additional special control information stored within the files themselves (such as checksums) have been established by the users for this purpose.

The central file store is a passive system, performing its operations only in response to commands received from other network User Machines. The command interface is completely unsuitable for use from normal keyboard terminals, which therefore need the intervention of another service computer to perform the function of accessing the file store. This limitation was deliberately adopted in order to expedite the development of the file store software; such a division is only possible when the system components are linked by a general-purpose communications medium which has adequate transmission bandwidth.

At present, there are over 200 users registered with the system but the majority of these access it only indirectly as a result of using another service – EDIT. The file store is used as a backing store by seven computer systems on the site. In one case, an operating system (PS-8) for the DEC PDP-8 computer with a small local disc has been modified by the addition of a new pseudo-disc driver so that, in effect, the amount of storage space available to its user was considerably increased.

There are 20 megabytes of data stored on the central file store discs, representing about 2000 files, and a further 20 megabytes on magnetic tape. The file store handles around 80,000 packets per day, which accounts for almost one third of the traffic transmitted through the network.

3.3 EDIT

EDIT (Ref.6) was intended from the outset as a service that would take advantage of the flexibility of the NPL network. It offers a comprehensive and powerful set of text manipulation commands that is basically line-oriented but which includes facilities such as context editing and systematic string replacements throughout a file. It was also intended to make use of, and to act as a "front-end" to the Central File Store. EDIT consists of a DEC PDP11/20 with small local discs for main store swapping and for holding the files that have been opened by logged-on users. However, the Central File Store is used for all long-term file storage. A complete file is read down from the file store on first being referenced by the user. On receipt of a command from the keyboard operator to preserve a copy of the edited local file, the complete file is written back to the file store via the network.

Because of its basic role as a file and text handling system, EDIT has some characteristics similar to those of Scrapbook. For example, it may be used for information transmission among its subscribers and it is to a considerable extent self-documenting. However, the overlap between EDIT and Scrapbook is not very great and the "information utility" aspects of the former have not been particularly emphasised because the primary objectives of these two systems are significantly different.

EDIT provides a text output mechanism which formats text prior to output to one of a number of different hardcopy printers. This includes code-changing where necessary. Another of its functions is to act as a "logical lineprinter", accepting a stream of characters from a calling terminal such as a paper tape reader and spooling the input onto its local disc in preparation for later output to an actual printing device.

It is worth noting that the network makes possible the sharing of a

great variety of computer peripheral devices, like lineprinters, paper
tape readers or graph plotters, amongst all the subscriber computers.
It also allows such equipment to be conveniently located for the users.
These attributes are particularly valuable when the shared devices are
expensive and/or require continuous manning. However, it is still
preferable to have centralised control, in a manner typified by EDIT's
logical lineprinter service, since this then permits the user computers
to proceed with their operations without having to wait for an
arbitrary length of time while an attempt is being made to "seize" the
physical device by making a network call.

EDIT also permits character stream input or output to take place
between a nominated user file and a network peripheral, such as a paper
tape reader or punch, under the control of the user at another network
terminal. By making use of the virtual call protocol, this mechanism
will permit file transfers to take place between EDIT and a program
running in another User Machine. The input/output programs in EDIT do
not need to know anything about the characteristics of the other party
to the call in this situation.

The service also provides a set of graphical formatting and output
utilities which will process suitable data files for output either to
graph plotters or graphical storage displays connected to the network.
This set of facilities has been extended by the addition of a very
powerful microfilm plotting device (the Laserscan HRD1) connected to a
PDP11/50 computer. This second PDP11 is not attached directly to the
network, but is joined to the original computer in a store-sharing
arrangement – effectively an enhancement to the EDIT system.

At the time of writing, EDIT has more than 100 different users in any
week, up to 16 being able to use the system simultaneously. It handles
daily almost 200,000 packets, which is approximately two thirds of the
total network traffic. Of this traffic, over 100,000 packets pass to or
from the Terminal Processor and over 70,000 to and from the file store.

3.4 The KDF9 computer services.

The main computing service within NPL is provided by a pair of English
Electric KDF9s running under the 'ELDON' operating system, one of which
provides simple interactive editing for terminal users, with program
execution being performed non-interactively through foreground and
background queues. The second KDF9 is used mainly for batch job
execution. The online machine has a PDP-8 front-end to which 30
Teletypes are connected by means of dedicated low speed (10 characters
per second) lines; this computer service antedates the NPL network.

Both KDF9s are connected to the network as single "terminals" (ie using
the virtual call mechanism). The ELDON service is also linked via the
PDP-8, again as a single "terminal" connection, so that it can be used
from other suitable network terminals. The KDF9 computers are not
integrated into the network as User Machines; this would have been a

relatively major task, unjustifiable because of their limited remaining
life.

However, the addition of a few KDF9 utility programs accessible by
terminal users or by running programs has allowed the transfer of input
data or program output between the KDF9s and other network devices,
which may either be peripherals or other computers. Such transfers may
either take place directly across the network or the central file store
may be used as a Poste-Restante for input or output files. It is
possible to involve EDIT or other network services in input
preprocessing or output postprocessing, so minimising the terminal load
on the KDF9s and making use of a wider set of resources. In fact a
major part of EDIT's network traffic comes from KDF9.

A natural extension of this scheme is the use of EDIT as a front end to
KDF9; a KDF9 utility program periodically accesses EDIT and reads job
descriptions and files, which are then inserted into the local job
queue. Results can be returned to the Central File Store. It can be
seen from the foregoing account that EDIT has in fact become the
central service on the network, tying together several other systems.

3.5 The PDP-8 BASIC service.

With so many keyboard terminals around the site, it was clear that some
central form of simple programming and calulation service should be
made available. BASIC was a fairly obvious solution to this demand and
a PDP8 computer using standard DEC multiaccess (5 user) software was
connected to the network to provide a limited service.

There was not sufficient effort available at the time to modify the
front-end software to work in packet-switched mode and so five separate
virtual-call connections were made to the network Terminal Processor.
The network then appeared to the software as five separate
teletypewriters. One (of the many) disadvantages of this connection
method was that in the absence of a network control program in the
PDP8, capable of inspecting the data stream for control characters,
every character transmitted by the service had to be a complete
(one-character) packet.

The system is used quite extensively for short calculations and is
especially popular with the Design and Drawing offices. To some extent
it is competing with the desk or hand-held calculator and has held down
the number of these devices which have been purchased.

The BASIC service runs on a machine without a local disc, so that
programs cannot be saved or loaded rapidly, although they can be input
and output in a non-interactive mode from a peripheral such as a tape
reader. Since EDIT also offers character stream input/output
facilities, it is straightforward to make use of these from a terminal
in conjunction with the BASIC system, so that manually driven program
dumping and restoring can be achieved in this way.

3.6 Other facilities offered over the network

Among the many other terminals and services connected to the network, the most useful are probably TIME; ECHO and the Documents scheme.

TIME is a clock terminal which, upon being called, transmits a sixteen character message giving the day of the year and the time of day in hours minutes and seconds. The inaccuracy is limited to the one-way transit of the network from TIME to the requesting terminal and since this is normally (but not guaranteed to be) much less than one second, it may be used to initialise sytems down to one second accuracy. The overhead involved in making the network call and the wait — of up to one second — before the time is returned means that TIME is not used to replace conventional minicomputer clock systems.

ECHO is a terminal with a small store which will accept a packet from the network and return it. This is very useful when testing out new network terminals or driver software where a computer is being used as a terminal but has the limitation that it cannot be used to test anything other than the existence of a virtual call through the Terminal Processor.

The Documents scheme is a computer based interactive keyword system which allows paragraphs from documents to be retrieved and inspected. The database scanned by this system is held on the central file store, and is at present limited to internal computing documentation. The Documents computer is another H516.

4. The effects of the network

It is almost certainly true to say that Scrapbook, EDIT and the other network services have had a much larger effect upon the community of computer users within NPL than has the data communication network itself. These services are the aspects of the total system that are in direct evidence to the user. The communications system on the other hand is simply an access mechanism whose presence should be essentially invisible to the terminal user. This point is vitally important and it is worth reiterating that the communications system must intrude as little as possible upon the normal activities of a terminal user. The adoption of the store-and-forward mode of operation raises some problems in this area which have had to be faced in the design of the network.

The influence of the data network, as far as the majority of users are concerned, is therefore of a more indirect nature, in that it affects the functions and organisation of the services available to these users and greatly increases the possibilities for the enhancement and evolution of these services.

The requirement for the communications subsystem to be unobtrusive cannot apply to User Machine subscribers, since all the significant

properties of the network must be taken into account by the designer
when specifying the functions of the network control program. This
program must, in particular, implement the two levels of protocol
imposed by the network. It is clearly a matter of great importance that
the interfaces and protocols of any network should be fully and
precisely defined in order that these programs may be implemented
quickly and effectively. This requirement to be concerned with the
details of network protocols does not necessarily extend to the user
programs executed by the subscriber computer, however, since these
should be able to avail themselves of the network control programs in
order to make use of the network.

Thus the network control program may make communications facilities
available to user programs through the medium of standard operating
system mechanisms. For example, attachment and operation of peripheral
devices through the network may take place in precisely the same way as
for local devices. Again, a file referenced by a user program may be
available from local storage or it may have to be transferred through
the network. This transfer could take place with or without the user
being aware of it.

The effects of the network — or, more directly, the effects of the
services offered over the network — are seen in such diverse areas as

> a reduction in the demand for typing services;
> — due to the 'Telex' facilities of the network and the
> facilities offered by Scrapbook
>
> an increased number of reports and their quicker
> production
> — due to the ease with which they may be created in
> SCRAPBOOK and EDIT.
>
> easier access to data for both humans and machines
>
> greater utilisation of small computers;
> — due to the access provided by the network and the
> storage provided by the Central File store.

This last point is illustrated by a number of programming systems for
small computers which are based on remote centralised facilities rather
than dedicated ones. For instance, a gateway between the NPL and
external networks has recently been created. The program source text
for this system was produced, edited and stored in Scrapbook. It was
compiled in a machine linked to Scrapbook and only transferred across
the network to the target machine as binary code. As with all offline
programming systems, this left the target machine free to be used for
testing programs without interfering with program development but the
ability to teleload large programs without handling paper tape proved
to be of considerable assistance.

In addition to the programs being developed away from the target machine, the application system also made use of the network. As with many systems, a time-stamp is required at initialisation and reset. This is obtained by a network call to the TIME terminal and thus enables the machine to be run unattended even through crashes.

The effects which are not yet in evidence are the standardisation of file structures and commands. The commands for equivalent operations in Scrapbook and EDIT are not the same. This is because the two systems were created independently for specific types of work. The use of the two systems by one operator at a common terminal has emphasised the need to invoke common actions by common commands. These comments apply also to the file structures of the two systems, although there do exist some agreements as to the format of files held on the central file store.

One significant effect that the network has had upon the computer services connected thereto arises from the great variety of peripheral devices used to access these services. It is more usual for such services to deal with only one type of terminal device. However, Scrapbook and EDIT accept connections both from a number of typewriter-like peripherals and from visual display terminals. Of the latter, there are a number of different types in common use, with various screen sizes, incompatible control operations and so on.

The network does not inform the service computers as to the type of the connected terminal (indeed, it is completely transparent to the device type because of the use of a standard interface to effect the attachment of the device). These computers therefore either have to ask the user for a terminal type code at log-in time (which Scrapbook does) or maintain a local table from which the type code can be looked up using the network address of the calling terminal (which EDIT does). In both cases, however, the bulk of the terminal handling software has to be written in terms of a standard "virtual terminal" with a "front-end" which performs the appropriate virtual to actual terminal mapping.

There are two alternative solutions to this problem. The simplest is to enforce standardisation of terminal devices. Such a policy might be acceptable in the long term, and to some extent the existence of general purpose data networks will tend to encourage this standardisation. The other possibility is to move part of the virtual terminal to actual terminal mapping function out to the Terminal Processor. The service computers are thus relieved of at least a part of this task, although at the expense of having a more complex "virtual terminal protocol" in the place of the present very simple protocol.

5. Evolution of the NPL network

The network can in theory support 256 terminals and 128 User Machines. However, the limitations of main store and processing capacity of the control computer make it unlikely that more than about 200 subscribers

of both types can be supported, assuming a reasonably high level of
activity on the part of these subscribers. The network is much in
demand - there are presently 40 unfulfilled requests for connection -
and this demand will soon reach the practical capacity of the present
system in terms of the number of subscribers that can be connected.
However, the traffic handling limits of the present system are actually
greater than the computing and terminal handling power of the attached
services.

Ideally, it should be possible to extend the network in an incremental
fashion and to introduce new technology into parts of the system whilst
maintaining the existing facilities in other parts. In fact, such an
evolutionary approach is possible with the NPL network because the
design of the logical network structure, protocols and software
expressly took into account the need for extension.

The flexibility inherent in the present structure is that it permits
the physical splitting up of Local Packet Switch and Terminal Processor
functions into separate processors. The virtual call protocol and
Terminal Processor software is additionally designed in such a way that
two or more Terminal Processors may be connected to the Local Packet
Switch. Thus it would be possible to add a second Terminal Processor as
a physically distinct User Machine connected to the Local Packet
Switch. Functionally, this extended network would appear identical to
all subscribers, with terminal to terminal calls being made in the same
way whether or not the two devices were connected to the same Terminal
Processor.

This development could be taken a stage further using "cluster
controller" Terminal Processors for smaller groups of terminals or for
devices which are all of the same type, so permitting various economies
to be made or providing extra facilities for users. The limit to this
logical progression is to have one Terminal Processor per terminal.
With the advent of microprocessors, this idea is not as ridiculous as
it might at first appear.

This evolutionary approach will even make it feasible, ultimately, to
change the technology of the central Local Packet Switch. Thus the
computer, and also the distribution network hardware if necessary, may
be replaced without affecting the existing terminal system. It is most
important to realise that the network is an essential part of
laboratory life and that its removal, even for replacement, is
unthinkable and continuous evolution is necessary.

One way in which the network can and must evolve is outwards, that is,
to allow users to access services outside the NPL site and conversely
to allow outside users to access NPL services where appropriate. This
is taking place in an indirect manner through the linkage of the NPL
network to external large scale networks that are just becoming
operational. The networks to which initial connections are being made
are the UK Post Office Experimental Packet Switched Service (EPSS,

Ref.9) and the French CYCLADES network (Ref.8); the latter connection
will eventually be replaced by one to the European Informatics Network
(EIN, Ref.10).

The mechanism by which this network interconnection is to be achieved
is the use of a so-called "gateway" computer. Thus, two gateways are at
present under construction at NPL, one for EPSS and one for
CYCLADES/EIN (Ref.7). In both cases the gateway is a User Machine
attached to the NPL network Local Packet Switch, and performing a
translation from the protocols of the NPL network to those of the
connected system.

6. Evolution of the computer services

There have been several examples of the requirement to create temporary
facilities involving more than one party, at the request of the user.
One example of this has already been quoted where the program loading
facility was added to the BASIC service using EDIT and the Central File
Store. The three essential elements in this transaction are the store -
represented by the Central File Store; the network executive -
represented by EDIT and the user job machine, which in this case is the
PDP8 running the BASIC service.

One concept which is being examined is that of combining these last two
functions in a general way. This gives rise to the 'network bare
machine concept' in which a minimal executive and loader are resident
in a computer attached to the network. The executive may be used by a
remote operator to load and run a program in the machine - the program
being called down from a store elsewhere on the network such as the
Central File Store. If that program is a compiler and errors are found
during compilation, an editor may be called down to correct the source
code either in that machine or another. Transfers of information are
handled by the machine or machines subservient to the operator at the
time.

The obvious evolution is that to off-site specialised services rather
than remaining dependant upon in-house expertise for every requirement,
and the development of gateways to other networks, mentioned above,
will make this evolution possible. The growth of public, switched data
communication networks and the standardisation that these will bring in
access methods and command languages will make it possible for networks
like that at NPL to be used merely as local terminal access networks to
these larger systems (like Private Branch Exchanges in Telephony).

It is of interest, finally, to chart the evolution of Scrapbook, which
was initially conceived as a stand-alone system offering a specialised
multiaccess service to keyboard/display terminal users. This is the
normal state of affairs for computer services today. Thus, Scrapbook
used the network merely as a mechanism for terminal access although the
network control programs were implemented in a general way. Because of
this, it became possible to make use of the network to gain access to

computer peripheral devices such as printers and paper tape readers. Thus facilities were added to allow users to send or receive continuous streams of data from Scrapbook in addition to the normal interactive access mode.

The great variety of interactive terminal equipment was another outcome of joining the network which had to be faced by the service implementation team; this problem has already been mentioned in Section 4. The next stage in development occurred when it was decided to make use of the central file store for archiving purposes. The Scrapbook system maintains disc backup copies of user data but has no archiving facilities of its own. Commands were therfore added which allow a user to transfer files to and from the file store and thereby to implement a non-automatic archiving facility.

The next stage in the evolutionary process, which has recently begun, has been forced by the need to expand both the processing power and storage capacity of the system. Unlike EDIT, which made no use of the network to achieve its expansion, Scrapbook has been enhanced by the addition of a second system directly onto the network. Initially the two systems will be entirely independent and the user population divided into two.

The service will therefore fall short of one of its primary objectives, namely that of acting as a general information utility, while it remains in this form since it will be more difficult (although by no means impossible) for the two groups of users to intercommunicate. Thus it is planned to gradually make changes to the software of the two systems in order to effectively merge them together as far as their users are concerned. The ideal will be to end up with a service which is indistinguishable from the single system described above.

Acknowledgements

The NPL data communications network and the many equipments attached to it represent the work of a large number of people. In particular we thank David Schofield and David Yates for their help in preparing this paper. We also thank Mark Dowson for allowing us to include a brief description of his Scrapbook conferencing system.

References

1) Scantlebury, R A and Wilkinson, P T
   The National Physical Laboratory Data Communication
   Network.   Proceedings ICCC, Stockholm 1974

2) Bartlett, K A
   Transmission Control in a Local Data Communications
   Network.   Proceedings IFIP, Edinburgh 1968,
   North Holland Publishing Company.

3) Robinson, M G and Yates, D M
   The Scrapbook information system.
   J Inst Information Science, Vol 4 (1973)   pp135-143.

4) Cashin, P M, Robinson, M G and Yates D M
   Experience with Scrapbook, a non-formatted data base
   system
   Proc IFIP 1974 Congress, Stockholm, August 1974.

5) Bailey, P A and Wood, B M
   A central file store for the data communication network
   at the National Phsical Laboratory
   Proc 2nd International Conf. on Computer Communications
   Stockholm, August 1974   pp229-238.

6) Schofield, D and Hillman A L
   EDIT user manual.
   Internal document, Division of Numerical Analysis and
   Computing, National Physical Laboratory.

7) Gien, M, Laws, J and Scantlebury, R A.
   The interconnection of packet switching networks, theory
   and practice.   (This conference.)

8) Pouzin, L
   Presentation and major design aspects of the CYCLADES
   computer network.
   Proc 3rd ACM/IEEE Data Communications Symposium,
   Florida November 1973, p80.

9) Belton, R C and Smith, M A
   Introduction to the British Post Office Experimental
   Packet-Switching Service (E.P.S.S.) Post Office
   Electrical Engineer's Journal Vol. 66 p.216 Jan 1974.

10) Barber, D L A
    Progress with the European Informatics Network
    Proc ICCC Stockholm 1974 p215.

Gateway design for computer network interconnection

David C. Walden and Randall D. Rettberg

Bolt Beranek and Newman Inc.
Cambridge, Massachusetts USA

Abstract

Issues associated with the interconnection of packet-switching networks via entities called gateways are discussed. A gateway virtual network is proposed, and a prototypical implementation is described.

1.   Introduction

The work done to date on the interconnection of computer networks has usually assumed a configuration such as

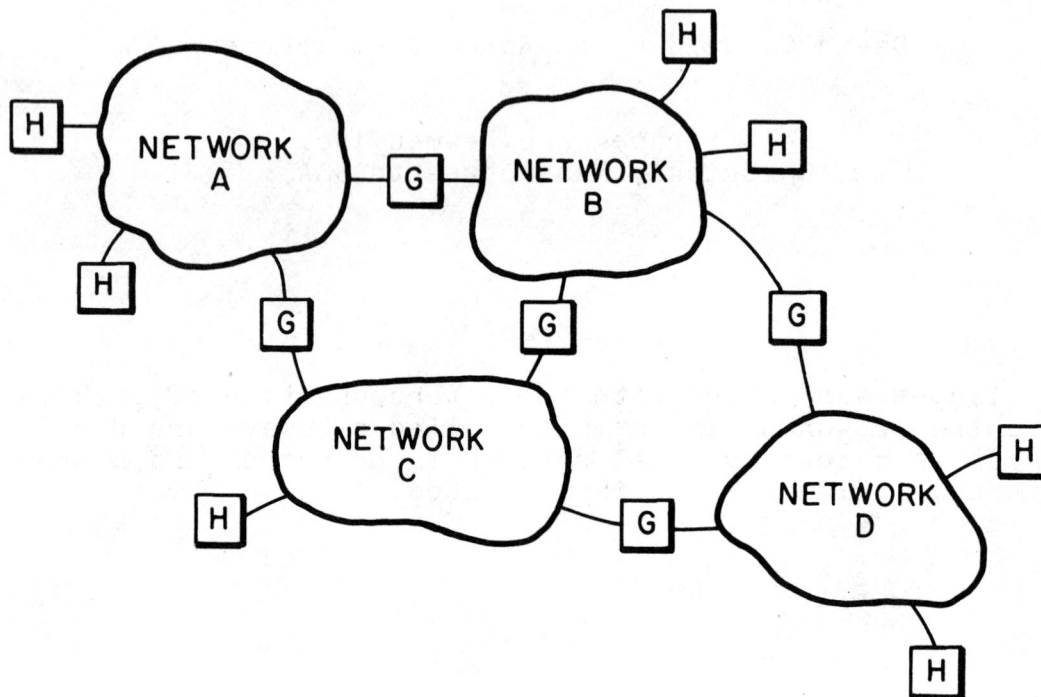

Figure 1 -- Networks Connected by Gateways

that shown in figure 1. (In this paper, our discussion refers only to networks of the the packet-switching variety, and assumes the reader to be familiar with packet-switching terminology.) On each network there are hosts (denoted by H in the figure) which desire to communicate with hosts on other networks. The networks are connected together by units (denoted by G) called "gateways."* The gateways must in some way convert traffic in the format of one network into traffic in the format of another network.

- - - - - - - - - -

*Note that this is a different use of the term "gateway" than in conventional international telephone system interconnection, where the term is used to refer to an artificial site from which it is convenient to establish tariffs).

Because host-to-host protocols differ from one network
to the next, and because these protocols are generally complicated and incompatible, many researchers (including ourselves) believe that hosts on different networks wishing to
communicate must do so in a common protocol. Much of the
work to date in network interconnection has been to specify
such a standard protocol: see for example [Cerf 74a],
[Zimmerman 74], [McKenzie 74b]. While there has not yet
been agreement on the standard protocol, for the purposes
of this paper we assume the terminology and protocol
described by Cerf and Kahn [Cerf 74a], [Cerf 74b]. In this
protocol the logical entity in the host which performs the
protocol functions is called the Transmission Control Program or TCP.

While there has been considerable work on the standard
host protocol, there has been less work on the function and
structure of the gateway. For the most part it has been
assumed that the gateway will forward traffic between networks (and across networks) without specifying how this
would be done. In this paper we consider the functions the
gateway should perform and how it should perform them.**

2.   Gateways as Hosts vs. Gateways as Nodes

One of the outstanding questions of network interconnection is whether the gateways should connect networks at
the packet or host level. By packet level, we mean that a
portion of the gateway would actually become a node on each
of the networks being connected. By host level, we mean
that a portion of the gateway would actually be a host on
each of the networks being connected. We feel that the
gateways should connect at the host level primarily to
maintain the sovereignty of the networks involved [Crowther
72]. Furthermore, it is unlikely that a standard packet
format can be found, at the present state of ongoing development of all of the packet-switching networks that might
be connected, which would permit packet level connection.

By network sovereignty, we mean that connection to the
networks must be done at a point where the interface is
both well defined and well controlled by the constituent
networks. If the point of connection is the host level
just mentioned, each network can protect itself against
activities of the gateway to the same extent as it may protect itself against the activities of any other host.

- - - - - - - - - -
**[Burchfiel 74], [Lloyd 75], and [Belloni 74] have also
addressed this issue. The latter two of these references
came to our attention late in the writing of this paper.

As already mentioned, we believe that it will be
impossible, in general, for the gateway to convert between
the host-to-host protocols of two communicating networks.
Thus, rather than communicating in the host-to-host protocol of the network, the gateways should communicate with
nodes of the network in the lowest form of host/network
protocol supported by the network. Transmissions in the
network interconnection protocol of the TCPs should be the
text of these host/network protocol messages.

Notice that a host on a given network might find
itself having to implement, in addition to the host-to-host
protocol of its own network, the standard internetworking
host-to-host protocol for communication with hosts in other
networks. Of course, one can hope the internetwork standard will eventually prevail throughout the world and the
host-to-host protocols of the individual networks will
eventually wither away.

To summarize, hosts involved in internetwork communications must adopt a common protocol, and gateways should
connect to networks as hosts using the lowest level of
host/network protocol. Further, protocols have already
been specified [e.g., Cerf 74a] for the former task and the
protocol for the latter task is specified by the network
for any network to which a gateway is to be attached [e.g.,
BBN 74].

If the gateways connect to the networks as hosts, then
the format of the messages passed to the network is specified by the host/network protocol. This protocol is then
used to permit transparent transmission of segments of an
internetwork transmission. This can be done by embedding
the internetwork segment in the text of a message in the
host/network protocol as shown in figure 2. Such a composite message has two leaders and potentially two trailers.
The outermost leader and trailer provide information for
the network. The leader will specify the address of the
gateway host to which the message should be delivered, any
allocation or sequencing information which is used by the
host/network protocol, and any further information demanded
by that protocol. An example of a trailer that might be
required by the host/network protocol would be padding and
a checksum. Within this outermost leader and trailer is
the internetwork data segment with its leader and trailer.
The internetwork leader specifies such information as the
ultimate destination, sequencing, and reassembly information. The actual data which is being transferred is the
text of this message.

HOST/NETWORK HEADER *	INTERNETWORK HEADER	TEXT	INTERNETWORK TRAILER	HOST/NETWORK TRAILER *

DATA

INTERNETWORK SEGMENT
(HOST/NETWORK TEXT)

HOST/NETWORK MESSAGE

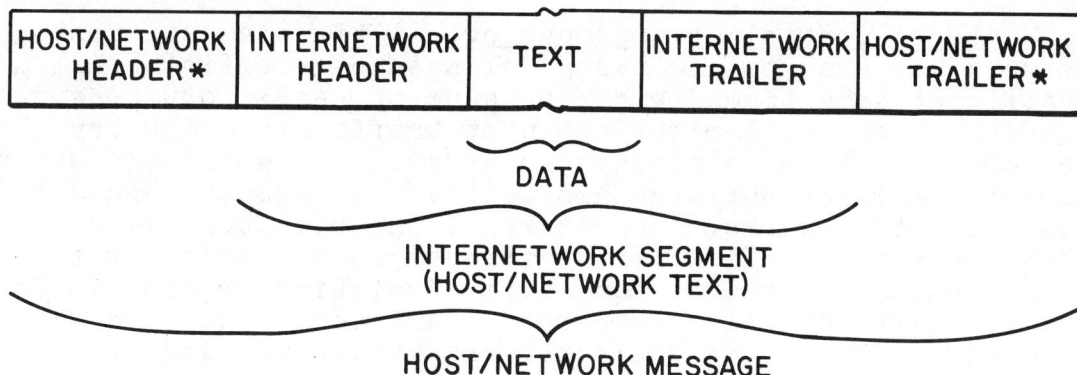

*THIS VARIES FROM NETWORK TO NETWORK

Figure 2 -- An Internetwork Segment Embedded
in a Network Message

3.   Gateway Characteristics

We will now examine some of the characteristics a
gateway must have in addition to being able to pass messages between two networks. The gateway must have:

-a capability for inter-gateway routing

-access control and accounting mechanisms

-a capability for fragmentation

-control of congestion at the gateways

-in some cases, a capability for inter-gateway
retransmission

In the following paragraphs we elaborate on each of these
points.

Routing. Inter-gateway routing is desirable for all
of the standard reasons one desires routing. For example,
for reliability one must have alternate paths over which
traffic may be routed; for achieving higher bandwidth than
is available over any single path, one wants to be able to
route traffic over parallel paths; different classes of
traffic should be able to follow different routes (e.g.,
traffic requiring low delay should be routed around networks which insert large delays).

Access Control and Accounting.   A given constituent
network may wish to limit some classes of traffic or all
traffic at some times (e.g., because of regulatory considerations, country A might not want traffic from country B
to country C to pass through country A's network).   Also, a
given user might not wish his traffic to pass through some
constituent networks.   For example, the U.S. Defense
Department might allow its traffic to go to England via
Canada but not via Cuba for obvious political reasons.   In
any case, the constituent networks are very likely to want
to monitor the use of their network by internetwork traffic.

For efficiency of routing and access control, in large
networks with hundreds of hosts and gateways, the routing
algorithm will probably need to have a hierarchical structure knowing about logical and/or physical areas.

Fragmentation.   Because of the differences in message
size of the constituent networks connected by a gateway,
the gateway must have the ability to fragment a larger message arriving from one network into smaller messages which
are acceptable by the next network.   When such fragmentation occurs, the message stream must eventually be reassembled into its original structure.   The protocol proposed in
[Cerf 74a] provides the reassembly function at the destination host.

Congestion Control.   Congestion will inevitably occur
at the gateway unless specific measures are taken to prevent it.   This congestion can occur as a result of speed
mismatches between the networks connected by a gateway,
because several gateways on a network may simultaneously
transmit traffic to the same other gateway, because traffic
may have to be held during a period of recovery from a
failure, and so on.   One specific kind of congestion
results from deadlocks, such as when gateway A is full of
traffic for gateway B which is full of traffic for gateway
A.

Retransmission.   When a message is lost in the network
between two gateways, one can either retransmit the message
between the two gateways or assume that the message will be
retransmitted from the source host to the destination host.
It has been shown [NAC 73] that hop-to-hop retransmission
is more efficient than source-to-destination retransmission
if the possibility of message loss is appreciable; and even
when there is little possibility of message loss, the variance of retransmission delays is less with hop-to-hop
retransmission than with source-to-destination retransmission.   While some networks deliver messages very reliably,

other networks rely on source-to-destination retransmission
and in some cases are quite cavalier about throwing away
messages. Thus, the gateways should have the ability to
retransmit messages across lossy networks. It seems that
at least when the hosts on a network are normally responsible for retransmission across that network, the gateways
ought to provide retransmission across that network.
([Mader 74] supports the notion that end-to-end timeout and
retransmission can be unduly inefficient.)

4.   The Gateway Virtual Network

     Notice that the characteristics of a gateway described
above are very similar to the characteristics of a node on
a packet-switching network [Crowther 75]. This leads one
to the notion of a gateway virtual network wherein the
gateways act as nodes and the network spanned by the gateways acts as virtual lines fully connecting all the gateways on that network. This concept is illustrated in fig-

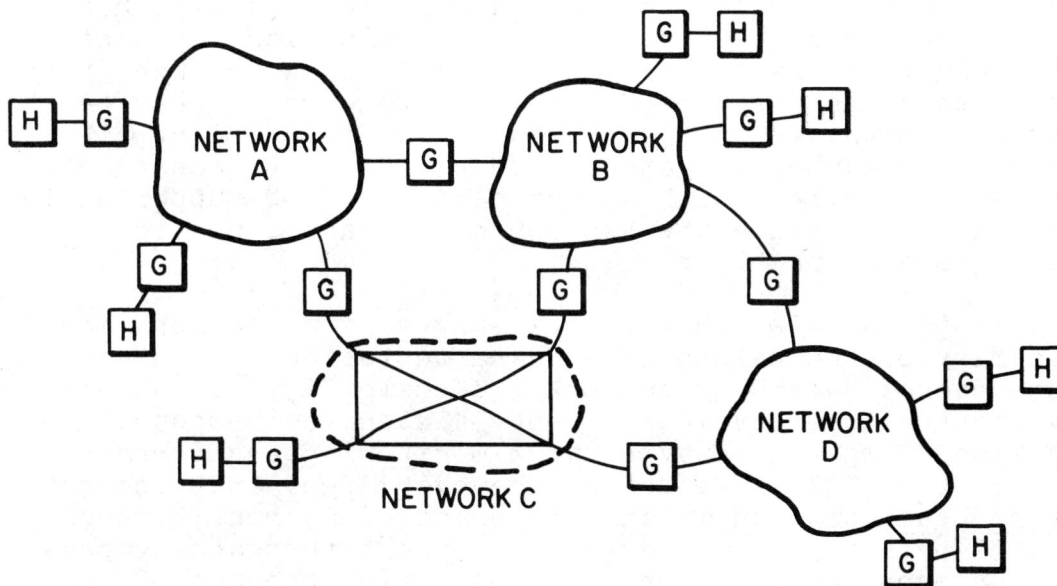

Figure 3 -- Gateway Virtual Network

ure 3, where network C has been replaced by the virtual
lines it provides. Further, notice in the figure that
logically there is a gateway associated with each host
attempting internetwork communication.

Although the figure shows a separate gateway for each
host, we do not mean to imply that the gateways must be
physically separate machines or that there need necessarily
be a one-to-one correspondence between hosts and gateways.
For instance, the logical entity that is the gateway may
take the form of a program running in a host computer.
Alternately, the gateway could be in a stand-alone machine
connecting two networks or serving one or more hosts. On
the other hand the gateway connecting two networks could
even take the form of a program running in a host which is
connected to both networks. In general, a gateway should
be able to connect any combination of hosts and networks.
(The political and economic issues relating to whether the
gateway should reside in a host or a separate gateway
machine are discussed in [Kuo 75].) Furthermore, it is
entirely possible for a host not to have its own gateway at
all, preferring to use a gateway elsewhere in its network
to perform the gateway functions for the host. In this
case, the host would simply know the address of a couple of
gateways in its network and would send its internetwork
traffic arbitrarily to one of these gateways for routing
and forwarding. Note that the gateway arbitrarily chosen
may not be on the best path to the destination, and this
gateway may, in fact, forward the traffic to another (better) gateway in the same network for forwarding outside the
network. Although this approach may be inefficient, it
reduces the number of gateways that have to be constructed.
Further, we believe both approaches should be supported in
the long term; since the two approaches are compatible,
this causes no problems.

It is our view that the gateway virtual network should
have many of the maintenance characteristics of a stand-
alone packet-switching network [McKenzie 72]. It should
have centralized development and maintenance responsibility, including a gateway network monitoring and coordination center (GCC). We do not, however, feel that the gateway program must run in any one brand of machine; indeed,
it will probably be necessary to support the gateway program on machines of several nationalities because of the
international extent of these networks.

The gateway virtual network is a general solution to
the problem of interconnecting networks which is not highly
dependent on the nature of the networks being connected.
Because of this we expect that networks which are connected
in the future will not require modification to facilitate
connection. While one can conceive that a simpler but less
general form of interconnection may be possible through
modification of the current networks, future networks may
be much less amenable to such an attachment and therefore

require major modifications to themselves or even to the
previously interconnected networks. Furthermore, the gateway virtual network, with its adaptive routing, congestion
control, and gateway-to-gateway retransmission capability
provides for high performance host-to-host communication
across multiple networks (note that this approach is in
contrast to [Opderbeck 74], which advocates sacrificing
such efficiency for simplicity).

5.   Division of Functions Between the Gateway and TCP

     Just as in a stand-alone network there is a question
of the division of responsibility between the hosts and the
nodes (i.e., should reassembly be done by the hosts or
should the nodes deliver traffic in order), in the gateway
virtual network there is a question of the division of
responsibility between the TCP and the gateway. It is best
to implement these functions in either the gateway or the
TCP, rather than blurring the implementation across the
boundary between them. Some points are quite clear. For
instance, reassembly must be done by the destination TCP,
as traffic traversing the virtual network may be fragmented
and pieces routed on alternate paths to the destination.
Thus, the ultimate destination TCP must be prepared to
rearrange the communication stream into the correct order
and reassemble it into the internetwork data segment. (The
reassembly problem is further aggravated when intervening
networks do not maintain ordering.)

     Second, the differences in message or packet size
between constituent networks mean that it may be necessary
for messages to be successively fragmented into smaller and
smaller units as they pass from one network to the next.
It seems natural that this task should be done in the gateway since it knows the message and packet size characteristics of the networks to which it is connected. Even at the
source host, the TCP can leave any necessary fragmentation
of the message stream to the gateway.

     Just as clearly, the gateways must be responsible for
the routing calculation, since only the gateways have the
global knowledge necessary to make a sensible routing decision.

     The access control and accounting functions should
also be in the gateway since these functions are desired
between the networks.

     It is less clear whether the gateways or TCPs should
perform the congestion control and retransmission func-

tions. One alternative would be for the gateways not to worry about retransmission and to solve any congestion problems simply by discarding traffic, in each case relying on the source and destination TCPs to provide the necessary recovery mechanisms ([Belsnes] advocates this). In fact, the TCP of [Cerf 74a] does provide such recovery mechanisms. On the other hand, if much traffic is discarded by the gateways to control congestion, or if there is even one network which loses traffic frequently, then we believe relying on source-to-destination TCP retransmission will be prohibitively inefficient and will also be expensive, both in direct (network-imposed accounting) and indirect (TCP overhead) costs. For this reason we think it is incumbent on the gateways to shoulder the burden of controlling their own congestion and for the gateways to provide the option of retransmission across a lossy network. Of course, even though the gateways provide these functions, the TCPs should retain the end-to-end retransmission capability at their level for reliability, since retransmissions performed by the gateway level are for efficiency rather than for complete reliability.

The remainder of the functions performed by the [Cerf 74a] TCP are properly the functions of the TCP and not the gateways, as these functions are concerned with end-to-end issues, user process level issues, etc., while the gateways are properly concerned only with traffic switching issues.

There does have to be some communication between the TCP level and the gateway level. Most obviously, the TCP must specify the address of the destination TCP to which the gateways are to route the traffic. This particular communication can be effected simply by having the gateways understand the TCP traffic formats which include such addressing information. Another area of communication required between the TCPs and gateways is to specify certain transmission characteristics for the traffic (e.g., networks through which the traffic must not be routed, maximum acceptable delays, and average throughput required over a period of time). This area has not been explicitly addressed previously and requires further study.

At present we have no opinion on whether the security function should go in the gateway or the TCP. Current U.S. military communications security standards appear to require pairwise encryption between source host and destination host. If such standards are maintained, then the security function must obviously reside with the TCPs. Alternatively, there has been much discussion of so-called "link encryption." Use of link encryption would lead one to place the security function in the gateways. A third alternative would be to place the security function between the source and destination TCPs and their gateways. In this case the TCP "header" must be in the clear, permitting the gateways to access the information. There are elaborations of all the above schemes and other schemes are possible.

6.   A Prototypical Implementation

A prototypical implementation of the gateway is illustrated below. It consists of modular structures which carry on communications at a message level with various networks, modules which transform a particular network message format into a TCP type packet and vice versa, and modules which perform message routing and other centralized message processing functions such as flow and access control.

The purpose of each of these elements of the gateway will be clear if we follow a message as it is processed by

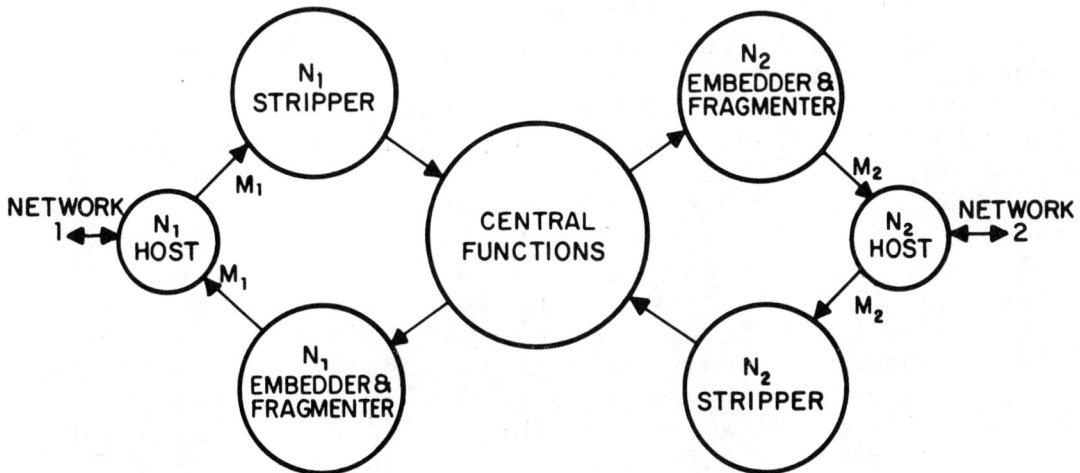

Figure 4 -- Components of a Gateway

the gateway from Network 1 to Network 2 in figure 4. The line to Network 1 is operated by the code labelled "N1 Host". This code acts as a host on that network, passing the required control information and transferring messages to and from other hosts on that network according to the lowest level message protocols of that network. In the case of a connection to the ARPA Network, this code would implement the standard Host/IMP protocol [BBN 74]. Incoming messages received from Network 1 are passed to the "Network 1 Stripper," where the Network 1 message leader is removed. The result is an internetwork protocol segment. This segment is passed to the central portion of the gateway, which examines the address specified in the segment and queues it for output to that network. The "Network 2 Embedder and Fragmenter" takes these internetwork segments and converts them into messages in the Network 2 format. In this case, once again, the format will be ARPA Network messages. If the internetwork segment does not fit within the text of a network message, it will be fragmented and re-formatted until all parts fit into network messages. Finally, the message is presented to the Network 2 message interface for delivery to the appropriate gateway host.

The control function will be responsible both for determining where to route an individual internetwork segment and for performing the distributed routing functions in cooperation with the other gateway nodes. In operation, this distributed routing can be accomplished in the following way. Each gateway exchanges routing packets, containing information about all gateways in all networks, with every other gateway on each network to which it is attached. The gateway is given the host addresses of all other gateways on each of the networks to which it is attached in an internal table which will be used eventually for the access control logic. This is similar to the way an ARPA Network IMP exchanges routing packets with its immediate neighbors, where the packets contain information about every possible destination [McQuillan 74]; the other gateways on the same network are logically the immediate neighbors in the gateway network. In this case, however, it is necessary for each gateway to contain internally the network address of the other gateways in the same network, because while an ARPA Network IMP has at most five neighbors, a network has potentially many hundreds of hosts, a large fraction of which may be gateways.

The information passed in the routing messages can contain at least three types of measurement about the network: delay, bandwidth, and delay variability. For instance, gateways can accumulate delay and estimate bandwidth for the network connection between each pair of gateways in the same network. The gateways can then maintain a structure similar to that used by the ARPA IMP for routing. For each potential destination gateway, the intermediate gateway to which messages should be addressed for minimum delay and maximum bandwidth can be determined along with the expected delay and bandwidth. Periodically, the gateway reports to each of the other gateways on the same network the expected delay and bandwidth via this gateway. The other gateway then adds the delay to that gateway and determines the minimum of the bandwidth through that gateway and the bandwidth on the path to that gateway, to determine the delay and bandwidth which may be expected along this path to the destination. Through this mechanism, each gateway can have the necessary information to route packets. Priority letters could be routed for delay, while others could be routed for bandwidth.

We recognize that this sample routing scheme suffers from an inability to accurately determine the expected delay and bandwidth along a path, particularly as the actual path across a network may change unbeknownst to the gateways. This is intrinsic to the implementation of gateways as hosts rather than as nodes, since only the nodes of a network normally have the necessary state information (e.g., line speeds between node pairs or the number of packets queued for a line), and so far, no network passes this information to its hosts. We believe that the reasons mentioned previously in this note for connecting gateways at the host level are very important, and that the way to improve the routing efficiently between gateways is for the networks to pass expected delay and bandwidth information, for example, to their hosts. Even without the issue of gateway routing, it might be useful for hosts on a network to receive such delay and bandwidth information to improve their use of the network (e.g., deciding whether to send a large file now or later).

We have suggested that in general a gateway will be required in association with each TCP. Since these gateways form a network of their own, routing and formatting packets, and since there may eventually be many of them, it is advisable to keep them as identical as possible. We therefore suggest that the gateway routines be specified in some reasonably universally available higher level language. If possible, the gateway code should be machine compiled from that specification. Otherwise, the routines can be hand compiled from the higher level language specification. We hope that in this way, the implementation effort and variability will be minimized in implementations at the various hosts.

7. Backwards Compatibility

Although gateways permit the interconnection of networks and communication across network boundaries, the ability of a host on a foreign network to use the facilities of a local network is limited by the form of network interconnection used. Since all communication across network boundaries, as described in previous sections of this paper, must be in the form of TCP segments, it is impossible for a foreign host to participate in the same levels of communication in which a local host might participate. There are some instances where it is desirable to permit a foreign host to communicate at (or near) the host/network protocol level. For example, a local host may communicate with other, less powerful hosts in the lowest level of host/network protocol, but a foreign host cannot communicate with those hosts no matter how hard it tries or no matter how willing it is to accept inefficiencies in the communications. In this case, the less powerful host may be provided by the network itself (such as the statistics hosts in an ARPA Network IMP [BBN 74]), and it may be impossible to have it understand the internetwork protocol.

Remote use of the host/network protocol can be made possible by including a TCP in the gateway between networks. To send a message in the format of the destination network, the foreign host would embed the destination network message in an internetwork segment addressed to the TCP in a gateway on the destination network. At that gateway, the internetwork leader and trailer would be removed, leaving a message in the proper format for the destination network. The gateway would then insert any leader information necessary to identify the foreign source of the message so that replies to the message may be embedded in internetwork framing and returned to the foreign host.

To communicate with some host on the local network, the foreign host should set up a "mailbox" in a gateway to the local network through communication with the TCP in that gateway. The foreign host would then notify the local host of the address of the mailbox to be used. Messages originating in the local host would then be sent to the mailbox; the gateway would forward them to the foreign host.

This type of connection is much less efficient than the methods described in the previous sections; however, it provides a capability which is not available in any other way.

Acknowledgments

This work has been supported by the Information Processing Techniques Office of the Advanced Research Projects Agency (ARPA) of the U.S. Department of Defense under Contract No. FO8606-73-C-0027 and Contract No. FO8606-75-C-

0032.   The ideas we have presented in this paper have evolved through interactions with a number of other workers in the field, particularly V. Cerf of Stanford, R. Kahn of ARPA, and R. Binder, J. Burchfiel, W. Crowther, N. Liaaen, A. McKenzie, and J. McQuillan, all of Bolt Beranek and Newman (BBN); and to them we are grateful. We are also grateful to R. Brooks of BBN for his help with the preparation of the manuscript for this paper.

References

BBN 74.
Bolt Beranek and Newman Inc., "Specifications for the Interconnection of a Host and an IMP," BBN Report 1822, revised December 1974.

Belloni 74.
A. Belloni, M. Bozzetti, and G. Le Moli, "Routing and Internetworking," International Working Group Protocol Note 10, August 1974 and February 1975.

Belsnes 74.
D. Belsnes, "Flow Control in Packet Switching Networks," INWG Note No. 63, October 1974.

Burchfiel 74.
J. Burchfiel and R. Tomlinson, "An Experimental Simulation of a Satellite Gateway," INWG Experiment Note 2, August 1974.

Cerf 74a.
V.G. Cerf and R.E. Kahn, "A Protocol for Packet Network Intercommunication," IEEE Transactions on Communications, Vol. COM-22 5, May 1974, pp. 637-648.

Cerf 74b.
V. Cerf, Y. Dalal, and C. Sunshine, "Specification of Internet Transmission Control Program," INWG Note 72, revised December 1974.

Crowther 72.
W.R. Crowther and D.C. Walden, "Response to INWG Note 6," INWG Note 10, December 1972.

Crowther 75.
W.R. Crowther, F.E. Heart, A.A. McKenzie, J.M. McQuillan, and D.C. Walden, "Issues in Packet-Switching Network Design," to be presented at the AFIPS 1975 National Computer Conference.

Kuo 75.
F.F. Kuo, "Political and Economic Issues for Internetwork
Connections," Computer Communication Review, Vol. 5, No. 1,
January 1975, pp. 32-34.

Lloyd 75.
D. Lloyd, M. Galland, and P. Kirstein, "Aim and Objectives
of Internetwork Experiments," INWG Experiment Note 3,
January 1975.

McKenzie 72.
A.A. McKenzie, B.P. Cosell, J.M. McQuillan, and M.J.
Thrope, "The Network Control Center for the ARPA Network,"
Proceedings of the First International Conference on Com-
puter Communications, pp. 185-191, October 1972.

McKenzie 74a.
A.A. McKenzie, "Some Computer Network Interconnection
Issues," Proceedings of the AFIPS 1974 National Computer
Conference, pp. 857-859, May 1974.

McKenzie 74b.
A.A. McKenzie, "Internetwork Host-to-Host Protocol," INWG
Note 74, December 1974.

McQuillan 74.
J.M. McQuillan, "Adaptive Routing Algorithms for Distributed Computer Networks," BBN Report 2831, May 1974.

Mader 74.
E. Mader, W. Plummer, and R. Tomlinson, "A Protocol Experiment," INWG Experiment Note 1, August 1974.

NAC 73.
Network Analysis Corporation, "Comparison of Hop-by-Hop and
End-to-End Acknowledgement Schemes," Packet Radio Temporary
Note 7, January 1973.

Opderbeck 74.
H. Opderbeck and L. Kleinrock, "The Influence of Control
Procedures on the Performance of Packet-Switching Net-
works," National Telecommunications Conference Proceedings,
San Diego, December 1974.

Zimmerman 74.
H. Zimmerman and M. Elie, "Transport Protocol. Standard
Host-Host Protocol for Heterogeneous Computer Networks,"
INWG Note 61, April 1974.

The design of host and terminal interface systems for data communication networks

B M Wood and J A Bowie
Data Communications and Teleprocessing Group
Computer Analysts & Programmers Limited
UK

Summary

As data communication networks become more widely
available, the efficiency and cost of interfacing
to them will become increasingly significant factors
in their use. The paper looks at some aspects of the
design of interface subsystems in order to define an
approach which reconciles the need for high performance
at reasonable cost with a system structure which
separates in a clear and simple way the levels of
control involved in the operation of a network.

1. INTRODUCTION

In most computer networks it is possible to trace a common
logical subsystem structure, though the boundaries between
the subsystems may at times become blurred. This structure
comprises (Fig. 1):

- a Communications Subsystem;

- Host Interface Subsystems;

- Terminal Interface Subsystems;

- Host computers;

- a terminal population.

A Host Interface Subsystem provides access to processes in
a Host from terminals on the network or processes in other
Hosts. A Terminal Interface Subsystem provides control of
a terminal network, local terminal facilities and access
through the Communications Subsystem to other terminals and
to processes within Hosts. Both kinds of interface have
been provided in a variety of ways: in some cases incorporated
in another component of the network (e.g. an interface implemented entirely within a Host) and in some cases as stand-
alone systems (e.g. the ANTS terminal on the ARPAnet, Ref.1).

This paper looks at some aspects of the design of stand-
alone interface subsystems. It attempts to define a design
approach which reconciles the need for high performance
(whether defined as throughput or terminal handling capacity)
at minimum cost and the need for a system structure which
reflects directly and simply the levels of control necessary
in the network.

2. BASIC SYSTEM STRUCTURE

It is a golden rule in the design of any system that the
structure should be fitted to the functions in the simplest
and most direct way possible. The basic functions of the
systems discussed in this paper are:

- the efficient reception of data over transmission links;

- the execution of control functions which depend on the
  data received;

- the efficient transmission of data.

The control functions involve limited amounts of processing
to reformat data, update control tables and allocate
resources. There is also a need for system control and
monitoring activities, but these can be provided by sequences
of functions each of which requires only a limited amount of
processing.

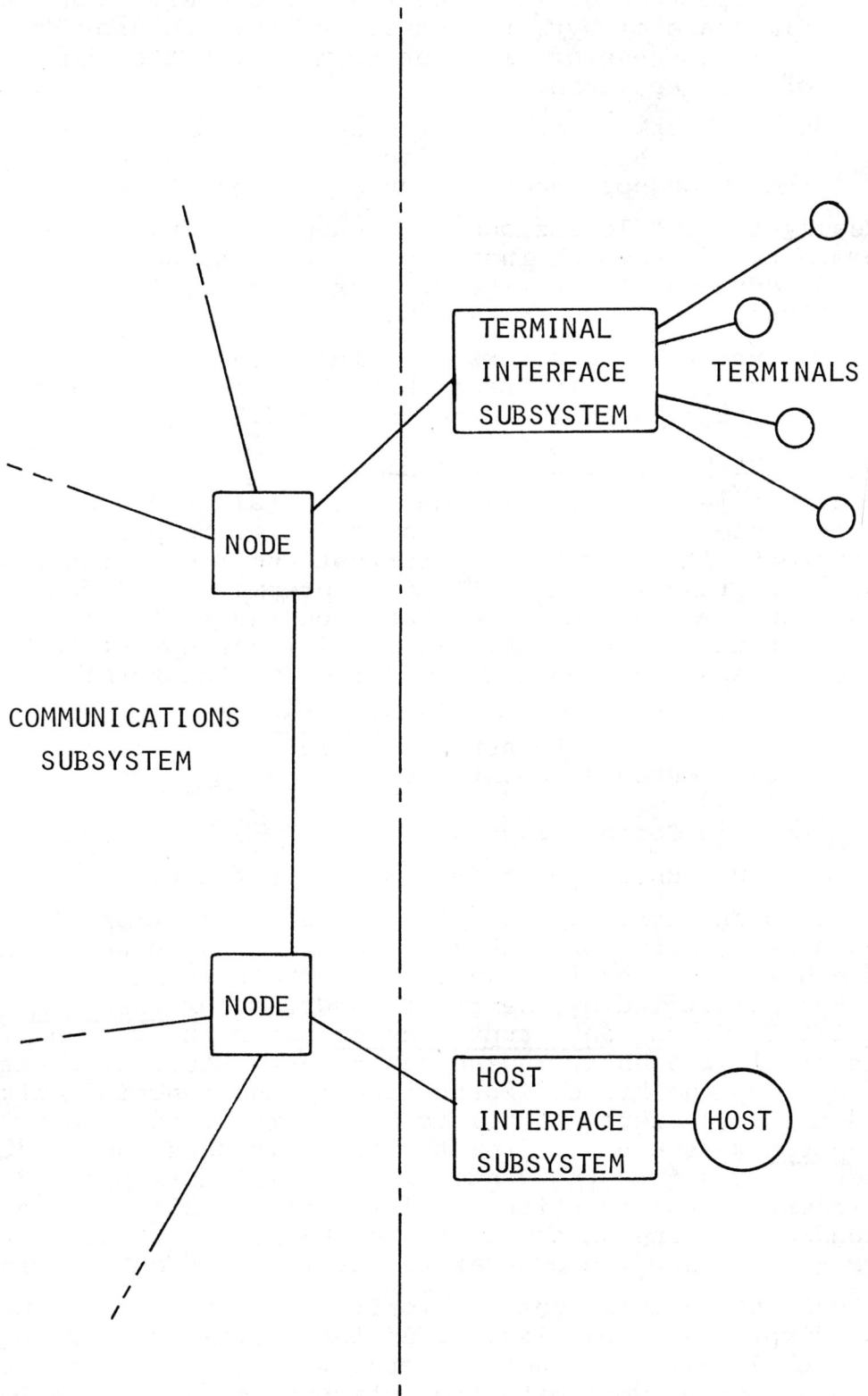

FIG 1 : THE LOGICAL STRUCTURE OF A COMPUTER NETWORK

Thus two basic levels of operation must be considered:

-   interrupt level at which functions operate in the
    timescale of byte transmission times to provide
    efficient use of lines or to meet the time constraints
    of line servicing;

-   normal task level at which functions must operate in
    the timescale of data block interarrival times to meet
    the throughput demand, but are single threaded.

Ideally the two levels operate independently, except for
communication through input and output chains of data blocks
and scheduling of activity at task level by interrupt level
functions.

A structure will be described which gains simplicity through
the use of executable dispatch tables similar to those described by Hergenhan and Rochkind   (Ref.2).

2.1   Interrupt Level Scheduling

Interrupt level processing has a crucial effect on system
performance.   Therefore, it is essential to provide an
efficient link between an interrupt and the corresponding
interrupt function, and efficient preemption of functions.
A suitable mechanism can be based on the system described
in Reference 2.   For a single level interrupt system this
uses a dispatcher table with entries of the form:

```
Word 1  NOP or Branch to dispatch routine
     2  Branch to next table entry
     3  Program counter save area
     4 ⎫
     ⋮ ⎬ Context save area
     n ⎭
   n+1 Entry point for Interrupt function
```

There is an entry in the table for each interrupt function
and a last entry for task level processing in which the
branch instruction is always set.   The current entry is
always identified by the return address for dispatch.   On
an interrupt the interrupt handler saves the current function
context in its entry and schedules any interrupt functions
by setting the branch instruction in the function entries
and then transfers control to the start of the table.   When
dispatch gets control from the table it uses the return
address to set up the context, enables interrupts and enters
or reenters the function.   All functions exit through a
standard routine which resets the branch instruction to an
NOP and the program counter to the function entry point.

With hardware implemented priorities between interrupts,
the dispatcher table is divided into sections corresponding
to each level.   Each section starts with instructions to
load a control word with the interrupt mask for the level,
and the handler for the level enters the table at the start
of the section.   Dispatch uses the control word to enable
interrupts.   If the interrupt for a given level is enabled

within the corresponding table section, function preemption can take place within the level. Otherwise functions for a given level will always be scheduled together when processing falls to a lower priority.

2.2 Network and Host Link Control

Control of network links takes place at interrupt level; it is considered in some detail because it can be affected significantly by the standards imposed for the network. Control of Host links will have similar characteristics: operating in terms of data frames with checking procedures on the frames. Simplicity and efficiency depend upon the interrupt interface, the line control procedures and the interface to the task level.

Interrupt Interface

Typically, there are a number of links with the same servicing requirements. Operation can be simplified if each interface, after transferring data by direct memory access communicates with the control function via a control word buffer and a common interrupt. The interface puts the line identifier and a condition code in the buffer and raises an interrupt. Once the control function has been entered, it runs until the buffer is empty.

Line Control

An ARPA-type line control procedure (Ref.3) allows a very simple organisation of control actions. In this procedure a line is divided for acknowledgement purposes into a number of logical channels. Each packet in one direction carries a channel number and phase bit and packets in the reverse direction carry a set of acknowledgement bits. On input the line number will indicate a control block holding a set of control values, and the actions are:

- set up a mask using the received channel number and phase bit, and test the receive phase register for a duplicate (OR under mask);

- if the packet is not a duplicate, set the receive phase register using a single bit channel number mask (EXOR operation);

- test for acknowledgements using the acknowledgement bits with the transmit phase register and set the register;

- if the packet is not a duplicate, schedule the task level function with the packet buffer address as parameter;

- if there are acknowledged packets, schedule the task level function with the line number and detected acknowledgements as parameters;

-    initialise the interface for input to the next buffer.

Thus the input function runs autonomously, driven by the line interrupt. It provides control information for output (detecting of acknowledgements of frames and recording correct reception of frames) and schedules actions at the task level.

The output control function is also interrupt driven by the output line interface. It communicates with the input control function via the line control block and accepts input from the task level in an output buffer chain. Empty frames are transmitted in the absence of data - a minimum byte interval is imposed by the line interface. The basic output control actions are:

-    access next output buffer;

-    get the logical channel number from the control block and set the phase bit (EXOR operation);

-    put the logical channel number and phase bit in the frame header;

-    put the receive phase register in the header as the acknowledgement bits;

-    initialise the interface to output the buffer.

Data could be protected on transfers to and from a Host by similar procedures operated through a communications interface, thus providing a standard which applies whether the link is local or remote.

Task Level Interface

The interface between interrupt level and task level is formed by the task dispatcher table and input and output buffer chains. The operation of the dispatcher table is described later under the organisation of the task level.

The input and output chains are manipulated by task level functions; interrupt level functions operate on buffers without removing them from the chains. Buffers are removed from an output chain by the task level function scheduled by input control when the packet which they hold has been acknowledged. A retransmission is either scheduled explicitly as a result of detecting an unacknowledged packet in processing acknowledgements or occurs automatically when there are no new packets to transmit and there are unacknowledged packets in the output chain.

2.3 Task Level

Task level functions operate within the timescale of frame interarrival times and processing can be single thread with consequent gains in simplicity and efficiency. The system is based on the use of executable tables (function schedules) to specify processing sequences either within a task or between tasks.

Function Schedules

The form of a function schedule is shown in Fig. 2. It consists of a header, a body and a tail. The header holds three items:

- next function pointer;

- exit pointer;

- exit instruction.

The body comprises a sequence of two word function slots. All function slots except those pointed to by exit pointer hold a subroutine branch to a function procedure and a parameter (e.g. data pointer); the slot identified by exit pointer holds the exit instruction. The tail location holds a branch instruction to the beginning of the body. The length of a table is a power of two and the start is located on the appropriate boundary.

The next function pointer indicates the next function slot to be executed; the exit pointer indicates the location following the last function currently scheduled; and the exit instruction is an instruction to be executed when the table is entered and no (new) functions are scheduled.

A function is put into the schedule by an enter procedure. This stores the function entry branch and parameter in a function slot, increments the exit pointer to point to the next slot and stores the exit instruction in the new slot.

The schedule is entered at the address given in next function pointer and function execution starts as a result of the subroutine branch. The return address is used to access the parameter location. Then it is incremented and stored in a system location associated with a function exit sequence which is the return path for a function procedure. The sequence uses the return address to generate the base address of the function schedule, stores the return address in next function pointer and executes an appropriate return instruction.

The Task Dispatcher

Task level processing requires priority ordering between tasks and the task dispatcher is formed by a set of function schedules in priority order. The schedules are linked by the return instruction and the exit instruction:

- return instruction: this is a branch indirect on the next function pointer in the top priority table;

- exit instruction: for schedule $i, i < i_{max}$, this is a branch indirect on the next function pointer in schedule $(i+1)$; for schedule i_{max} this is a branch indirect on the next function pointer in schedule 1.

WORD 0

1

2

WORD 2N-1

| NEXT FUNCTION POINTER |
| EXIT FUNCTION POINTER |
| EXIT ACTION |
| |
| ENTRY BRANCH: TO FUNCTION |
| PARAMETER OR POINTER |
| |
| EXIT ACTION |
| |
| BRANCH: TO WORD 3 |

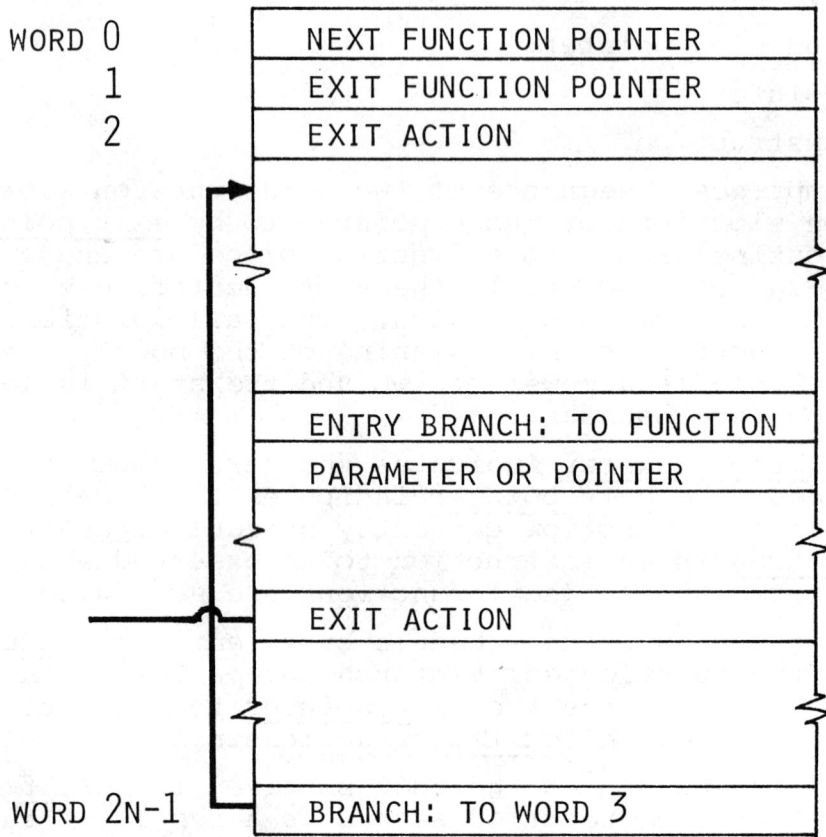

FIG 2 : LAYOUT OF A FUNCTION SCHEDULE

Thus on return from a given function the set of schedules are executed from the beginning, until a function entry branch is met.

Task Function Schedule

A separate function schedule is used to specify dynamically a control path for a specific task. In this case the <u>exit instruction</u> is a branch indirect on the <u>next function pointer</u> in schedule 1, and the return instruction in the <u>function exit sequence</u> is a branch indirect on the <u>next function pointer</u> of the task function schedule. Thus on exit from the first function called from the task dispatcher, the return address is stored in the <u>next function pointer</u> of the appropriate schedule and the <u>return instruction</u> then enters the task function schedule. It executes there until the <u>exit instruction</u> is met and control is returned to the dispatcher. Thus a function itself executes independently of the schedule from which it is called. This is illustrated in Fig. 4, Section 3.1.

3.   FUNCTIONAL ORGANISATION

This section discusses the organisation of the functions provided by the interface subsystems and their relationship to the system structure outlined in Section 2. The Host Interface Subsystem is considered first.

3.1   The Host Interface Subsystem

The Host Interface provides, in fact, a link between network systems: the communication network and the logical networks of processes in Host computer systems. As a result the functional structure is symmetric with interface functions for Host and communication network linked and administered by central control functions (Figure 3).

Control Levels

Assuming protocols similar to those proposed by Zimmermann and Elie (Ref.4), control of the network interface can be divided into three major levels:

-     Communication Control;

-     Port Control;

-     Connection Control.

Communication Control administers the reception and transmission of packets and carries out basic routing - between communication network links, and transport stations for Hosts or internal services. (The term transport station is used as in Ref.4 for the logical entity identified by a network address. A Host interface may link several Hosts through a common address, or each Host may be identified by a separate address). It provides the functions of a simple packet switch requiring only information on the existence and status of local links and on internal and external network addresses.

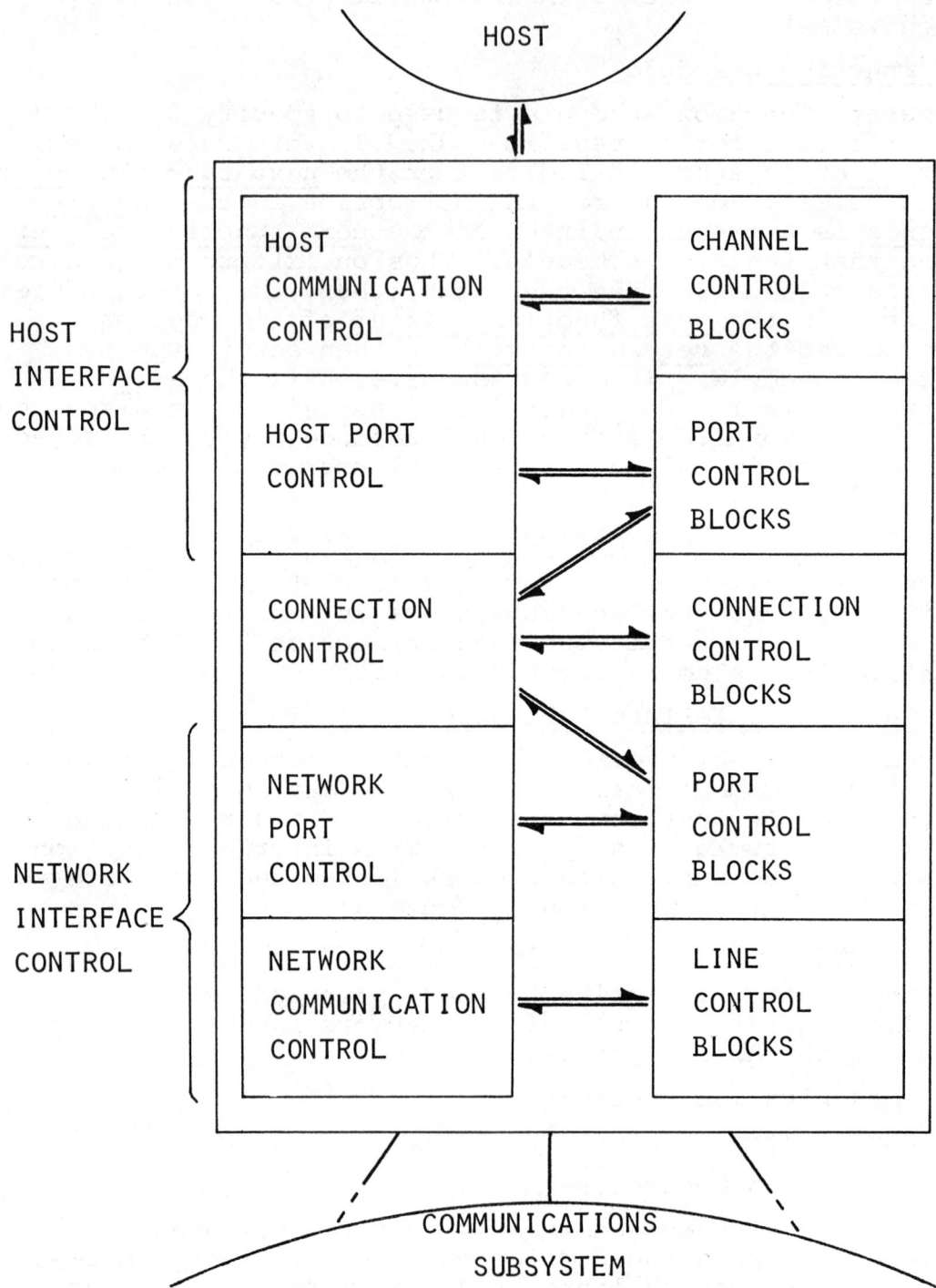

FIG 3 : HOST INTERFACE SUBSYSTEM - FUNCTIONAL ORGANISATION

Port control administers logical data flows multiplexed on to the physical data streams directed to and from the network. Logical data flows take place to and from ports which are identified by addresses within an address space assigned to a transport station. There are two kinds of data, administered differently by Port control:

- event data, which are carried in single packets and can be transmitted or received on an existing port at any time;

- message data which are carried in message units comprising a number of packets and can only be exchanged between ports for which a call has been set up.

Event data is used mainly for control purposes, e.g. setting up and closing down calls, error conditions etc. The normal data flow is carried in messages. There are a number of levels of service for message data: flow control, sequencing, and error control.

Port Control operates on the basis of control information passed to it by Connection Control. Thus the activation of ports, call set up and breakdown and setting of flow control parameters are carried by Connection Control. Flow control is a crucial problem and is discussed in more detail later.

Communication over a Host link is basically similar to that over a link to the network. A number of logical channels will be multiplexed on to the single physical link; relatively short block sizes must be used if short messages are not to be delayed by long messages. Thus the major levels of Host interface control will be the same as for Network interface control with a Port control level to administer channel flows. The complexity of the functions required depends upon the degree of control exercised by a Host over the logical channel space. A simple system can operate using a fixed set of logical channels with fixed assignments; a general system will require a connection dialogue between Connection Control and the Host to assign a channel for a call.

Control Functions

In the system structure discussed in Section 2 the normal processing of a data frame passes from an input function at interrupt level to a sequence of processing functions at task level which may end again in an output function at interrupt level.

When the functional organisation is mapped on to this path, each control level is implemented as one or more processing functions defined by a set of procedures and associated control information (Figure 3).

Passing control from one control level to another operates
through the task function schedule. The control block or
section of a control block for a given level (e.g. line/link
control block, routing table, station (port) control block
etc.), holds the entry instruction for the function in its
base location so that the function is scheduled by passing
the block address to the enter procedure to set the function
in the schedule (Fig. 4).

Alternatively it may be necessary for a given function to
schedule a number of lower level tasks, for example, where
a number of packets for a message are to be transmitted.
In this case a number of executions of the appropriate
function are scheduled through the task dispatcher, so that
packets of higher priority may be interleaved with packets
of the message.

Flow Control

The interface should operate without buffering complete
messages since this avoids placing restrictions on message
lengths while limiting the buffer requirements and message
delays. This implies a two level system in which Connection
Control is aware of the buffer limit specified by the message
destination (either local Host or remote destination) but
controls the buffer authorisations for input to the interface (within the message limit) according to the availability
of interface buffers.

Flow control over a connection can follow the approach put
forward in Ref. 4 in that each port transmits authorisations
to send depending upon the buffer space available, but it
is necessary to operate at the level of the data frame
(packet). Buffer space allocation is logical and not
physical - since a specific frame cannot be identified
until it has been received.

3.2   The Terminal Interface Subsystem

This subsystem exhibits a similar structure to the Host
Interface Subsystem, but the Host Interface Control
functions are replaced by the terminal control functions -
Virtual Terminal Control, Device Control and Line Control.

Virtual Terminal Control (VTC) provides the link between
the logical full duplex connection for each call, and the
physical connection for each terminal. This may mean
handling the terminal as a half duplex connection, as
would most likely be the case for a remote batch terminal.
VTC must therefore link port addresses to physical terminal
addresses, and vice versa. It is also responsible for
requesting calls to be set up or broken down by Port Control,
and for controlling the flow of data between the terminal and
the remote connection point. It can therefore be seen that

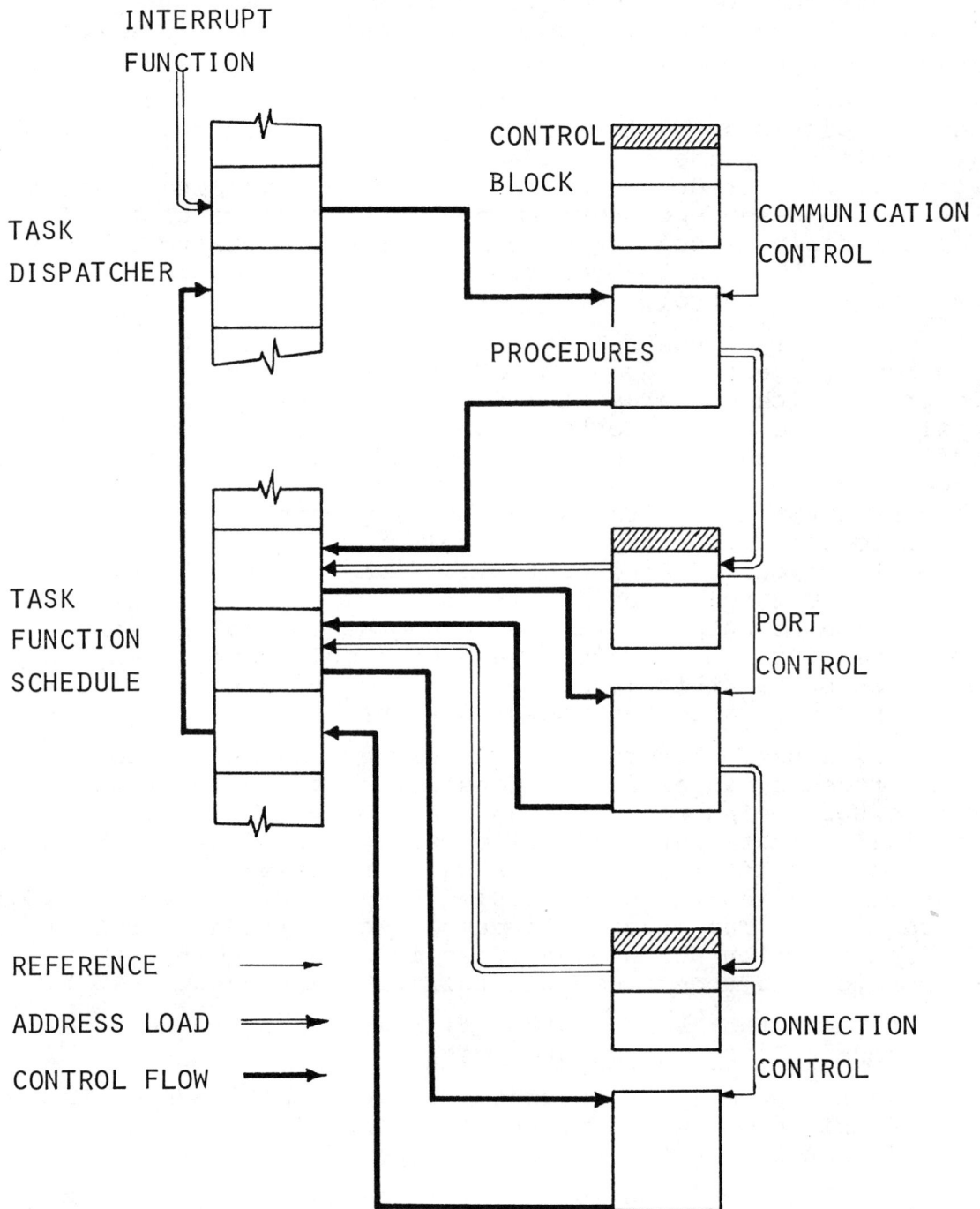

FIG 4 : A CONTROL PATH FOR PACKET PROCESSING

VTC exercises control over a Terminal Interface Subsystem in much the same way as Connection Control does in a Host Interface Subsystem.

VTC operates in terms of a "virtual terminal". Device Control provides the interface between the virtual terminal as specified by the network and the physical devices actually connected. The purpose of this level is to cater for device-dependent requirements such as code conversion, special dialogue control or character block control. If it is present, Device Control will always be scheduled between VTC and Line Control.

Higher levels of control are isolated from the physical problems of getting data to and from terminals by Line Control, which operates at two levels. The interrupt level will schedule Device Control functions when a complete bufferful of characters, or a control character, has been received. For lines that deliver one character at a time, the interrupt level itself may be responsible for buffering characters and identifying control characters. The task level functions of Line Control, which may be scheduled by Device Control or by the interrupt level, deal with initiation of output on a line, and the control of line protocol; thus polling terminals on a multipoint line would be organised at this level, as would responding to requests to transmit in a contention situation.

The relationship between the functional levels can be illustrated by an example. Consider a connection to a remote Host being requested and used by a terminal. Initially, characters are collected by Line Control. When the last character of the message is received, a Device Control function may be scheduled to perform data conversion as required. The message is passed to a Virtual Terminal Control function which identifies it as a request for connection and undertakes the following actions:

-      request that Port Control allocates a port and sets up a call to the remote Host;

-      when the reply is returned, a "go-ahead" message is compiled and passed to Device Control for processing and output to the terminal;

-      if the connection to the terminal is half duplex, no buffer space is allocated at this point for packets incoming from the Host. This means that the logical full duplex connection through the network is being used as a virtual half duplex connection, since the only packets for this port that will be received are those containing event data.

Virtual Terminal Control is now able to accept character strings from Device Control, packetise them, and request their transmission to the remote Host. When the last packet has been acknowledged by the remote Host, VTC has a choice of two actions:

- It may set up buffers for receiving data and pass them to Port Control. This implies that the call is to be kept open for the reply from the remote Host, and would be the normal case if an immediate reply was expected.

- It may request that Port Control breaks down the call, but keeps the port address allocated for a reply. This could be the case when data from a remote batch terminal is added to a long jobstream in a remote Host, and the reply may be delayed for a considerable time. This action is vital if the port address is the only identification available to the remote Host interface; physical terminal address is meaningless in an environment that permits dial-in connections for terminals. When the packet containing event data heralding the reply is received, it may be necessary for Line Control to re-establish the physical connection to the terminal before Port Control can be authorised to accept the call.

4.   CONCLUSION

As the use of computer networks grows, the need will grow for interface subsystems which provide high capacity and reliability at reasonable cost. To meet this need it will be necessary to develop hardware and software which are specialised rather than adapted from general purpose systems. This paper has proposed some directions for such specialisation. There are three points which are worth underlining.

First, it is clear that there are a number of functions which are common across the subsystems in a network: communication control functions in interface subsystems and switching nodes, port control functions in the interface subsystems etc. Implemented on a suitable machine range, these could be the building blocks for a variety of network configurations.

Secondly, there is the parallel between the functions of the Host Interface and those of a Gateway Exchange. This may help to clarify to functions of such an exchange. It also reflects the fact that the interface subsystem cannot completely replace the network functions in a Host. For example, the dynamic allocation of logical channels requires a connection dialogue between Host and interface subsystem. Thus, strictly speaking, the complete interface must include functions which remain within the Host.

Finally, there is the problem of routing data to and from applications in the Host. Even with a message interface (which is undesirable) it is usually necessary to identify the destination and move the data after it has been received. One way of improving these data transfers would be through an I/O controller which could use logical channel numbers to scatter/gather data frames; an alternative would be to provide direct access to the Host memory from the interface, although this would present greater protection problems. Unfortunately, since it involves mainframe hardware, this is likely to be an area where progress is slow.

5. REFERENCES

[1]   W J Bouknight, G R Grossman and D M Grothe

The ARPA Network Terminal System - A New
Approach to Network Access

Proc. 3rd Data Communications Symposium 73 (1975)

[2]   C B Hergenhan and M M Rochkind

The Multipurpose Batch Station (MBS) System -
Software Design

Proc. National Computer Conference 1974

[3]   J M McQuillan et al.

Improvements in the Design and Performance
of the ARPA Network

AFIPS Fall Joint Computer Conference, 1972

[4]   H Zimmermann and M Elie

Transport Protocol. Standard Host-Host
Protocol for Heterogeneous Computer Networks

Reseau Cyclades SCH 519.1, April 1974

The impact of prospective public data network facilities on terminal design

J.A.K. Frampton
International Computers Ltd.
UK

Abstract

The advent of digital techniques in telecommunication has led to
proposals for purpose-built public data networks. The paper assesses
the impact such developments will have on terminal design (both
processor-end and remote terminals). The assessment takes into
account the time factors between pilot development and availability
on a global scale in the telecommunication sphere so that, as a
starting point, there is no special preference implied for any of the
possible new facilities - leased, circuit-switched and packet-switched.
To make the assessment as meaningful as possible, the proposed new
facilities are, where practical, compared with their existing counter-
parts on public telephone, telegraph and Telex networks, the comparison
being based on an already published concept of system structure.

Introduction

To date, facilities for data transmission through public data networks
have been limited in that existing telephone and telegraph facilities
have had to be adapted to satisfy the new requirements. Although such
adaptation has been successful - data transmission services are now
accepted throughout the world - there are inevitably significant
limitations. The constraints applicable to the original service,
necessarily designed without any consideration for future adaptation
to the requirements for data transmission, cannot be wholly removed.

In recent years, technology has advanced to the point where it can be
more economical to use digital techniques for transmission rather than
analogue. This is to be seen, for example, in pulse code modulation
(PCM) of speech. It has also been recognized that such techniques
could form the basis of a purpose-built public data network service
which would, ideally, be wholly digital. To date, substantial
agreement has been reached internationally on the form that such a
service would take and plans for pilot development are at an advanced
stage in some countries.

This paper assesses the impact that new public data network services
will have on terminal design but since the anticipated services are
probably not widely known (and are, in fact, still being considered in
many points of detail at this time) and since a description of the
services as such will no doubt be available elsewhere, the assessment
will be in the form of a comparison with existing telephone, telegraph
and Telex facilities, as adapted for data transmission. The intention
is not to detail all the possible changes but rather to isolate some of
the more significant effects on the overall system as viewed at the
terminal. Note particularly that the term "terminal" in this paper
encompasses processor ends.

Assumptions Concerning the Availability of Public Data Network Services

The capital investment in the telecommunications industry is vast and
it is not possible to introduce a new facility such as a new data
network overnight. Inevitably, all new developments must be
evolutionary rather than revolutionary. The time interval between the
introduction of some new service on a geographically limited scale and
the availability of that service at all places in that country (or
throughout the world) must be many years.

From the point of view of the terminal designer, this is an unfortunate
limitation. The transition from one design for one type of network to
another for a new network may, in fact, last for longer than the life
of the product. And it is the user of the terminal who determines
where it is to be located and consequently (although indirectly)
determines the available facility. There is no choice than to offer
an appropriate degree of flexibility.

But even more significant, when new networks are being considered for
which the implicit changes in design are somewhat greater than those
applicable merely because some new, more sophisticated modem has been
introduced, is the fact that the new services will themselves evolve,
not necessarily in technical detail but rather in terms of relative
cost, convenience and availability. Who can predict whether packet-
switched, circuit-switched or leased digital data services will
predominate ten years or more from now? It may be that all three will
be available with equal merit, tariff-wise but who could then predict
the most convenient when assessing the users' needs in twenty years'
time? Will closed user networks be the norm or will such networks
require occasional, or perhaps frequent, access to other user networks
via say a public switched data network service?

These questions cannot be answered now. Even market surveys have
limited value because it is a changing world and the availability of
a particular facility may cause further change. But one thing is
certain; the capital investment in telecommunications is such that
rapid change is not possible. There is an order of time difference
between development in telecommunications and development of terminal
applications. Decisions taken today on future data network services
will be relevant at the end of this century.

The premise, then, for assessing the impact of public data networks on
terminal design must be without consideration of the importance of any
one facility relative to another. All facilities must be judged
initially as of equal merit. From this, we can explore the
difficulties, if any, in modifying our present-day concepts of terminal
structure to suit any one, or all of the new facilities. Hopefully,
we will be able to see the advantages, from the terminal point of view,
of any one facility as against another so that, when the users'
applications are considered we do at least have an understanding of the
possible benefits new services may provide. Indeed, it is only by
understanding the problems as well as the benefits in all the design
areas - network, terminal and user application - that we can hope to
obtain the best return from any investment in something new.

Terminal Structure

An obvious difficulty when assessing the effects of new network
facilities on terminal design is that there is no agreed yardstick upon
which such assessments can be based. The fundamental characteristics
of data communication are not necessarily fully appreciated. For
example, a common error is to assume, by apparent analogy with the way
the telephone is used, that the process for establishing a call and
for talking through the network to the called party is indivisible,
simply because we, as humans, do not consciously have to separate the
two activities. A further point of confusion arises with packet-
switched networks - the distinction between an end-to-end function to
which the network is transparent (for example, the text field of the

packet) and one that is network dependent (for example, the sequence number, conveyed end-to-end, in the packet header) is often not made clear and yet such distinctions are fundamental.

Misunderstandings of the nature of the data communication system can be resolved by adopting functional models as a means of separating the fundamentally distinct components that form the communicating system. This approach is an essential first step if a proper understanding of the changes implicit in data network services is to be made.

A recent paper[1] has demonstrated that the concept of structure, in the form of a functional model, can be applied to the representation of a network. The base model chosen in that paper was one for a circuit-switched network but an outline of the modifications needed for leased facilities and for packet switching was also included. The basic model for a circuit-switched network is reproduced below in its simplified form (that is, it assumes an ideal network with a notional exchange and only one direction of call connection set-up).

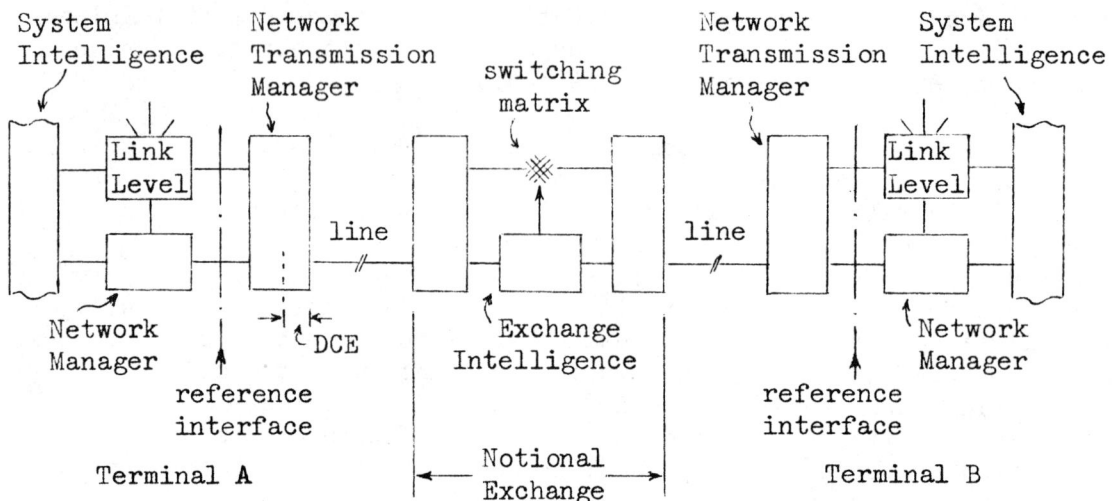

FIG. 1

In this diagram, the "reference interface" represents the dividing line between that part of the system responsible for information interchange and that part responsible for the transport, or rather the alignment, of units of information (as data). It is a distinction between the information conveyed and the means for conveying the information. The alignment functions are necessary because the transmission process is bit serial.

The concept is simple. The important interface is that called the reference interface, not that which divides the Data Terminal Equipment (DTE, or terminal) from the Data Circuit-Terminating Equipment (DCE, commonly a modem) - the latter divides the module called Network Transmission Manager. To clarify this concept, the **framing** procedure in HDLC* (mentioned later in this paper) contains Flag (frame delimiter), zero-bit stuffing and idle definitions all of which are concerned with frame alignment and therefore reside below the reference interface; the "information" conveyed end to end, the genuine frame consisting of the A (address), C (control), Information and FCS (frame check sequence) fields, is generated and acted upon at Link Level (Figure 1). (The FCS can, if preferred, be conceived of as an encoding level between Link Level proper and the Network Transmission Manager module. The model does not, of course, define the implementation method; in particular, it does not define the hardware-software interface.)

It is to be noted that the Network Transmission Manager module has to multiplex the two communicating paths, end-to-end and terminal-to-exchange. Hence, the reference interface itself operates at two distinct "levels".

Public Data Network Facilities

The analysis is presented by considering first the end-to-end user facility as applicable to both leased and circuit-switched services. The requirements for establishing and controlling calls on circuit-switched networks are then examined and finally, the requirements for packet switching.

End-to-End User Facility, Point-to-Point (Leased and Circuit-Switched)

The majority of existing data processing systems operate either with start-stop encoding or with a synchronous procedure such as Basic Mode (as standardised by ISO+), or a variant of Basic Mode. For these systems, two-way alternate operation is usual (although start-stop differs in that a simultaneous return path may be needed for a "break-in", or interrupt, facility). Proposals for a different procedure (known as HDLC*) have been put forward and at this time a draft international standard for the frame structure has been prepared (but not yet ratified by ISO). This new procedure permits two-way simultaneous operation.

In principle, no modifications to any of the above procedures will be necessary on leased and circuit-switched public data network facilities. However, existing facilities at rates of 600 bit/s and above are constrained to half-duplex (or asymmetric duplex) operation on the public switched telephone network and this constraint will wholly disappear on public data networks. (Equivalent leased facilities on the telephone network are usually 4-wire presented in which case the constraint does not apply. It is to be noted that the fact that two-way alternate operation may apply for information

---

* High-level Data Link Control (procedures)
+ International Organisation for Standardisation

interchange does not prevent use of the full-duplex characteristic such
that carrier, on analogue facilities, can be maintained so as to reduce
the turn-round overheads.)

Obviously, relatively minor changes to accommodate the new DTE/DCE
interface (CCITT* Recommendation X20 for start-stop, X21 for
synchronous[2]) will be required. For example, the synchronous classes
will have network-defined bit timing on a single interface interchange
circuit. It follows that, to ease the problems of transition from one
network to the other, the equivalent modem interfaces can be readily
created except that, if an existing terminal is designed solely for
switched telephone network operation, the half-duplex constraint will
(for true equivalence) have to be simulated by the network (and this
implies additional control communication outside the user's data, for
example, network control signalling via the status bit in an 8+2
network envelope structure). However, many terminals may be designed
also to operate on 4-wire presented leased lines, a configuration that
would permit better exploitation of the inherent data network
characteristics. Note that compatibility for call establishment on
circuit-switched facilities is discussed separately below.

For the synchronous classes, not only will the symmetric duplex
characteristic be an inherent feature of the new networks but also bit
sequence independence. This last point is not normally significant
with Basic Mode procedures because it is common to transmit odd parity
with each (7-bit) character so that continuous streams of like data
bits do not occur in data. However, for HDLC, the information field in
the frame is not constrained and, notwithstanding the zero-bit stuffing
component in the framing procedure, the data transmitted to line may
contain long sequences of consecutive zero bits; for a few types of
modem a technique such as that known as zero-complemented differential
encoding then has to be used but this will not be required on the new
networks.

All the above can be represented pictorially as follows:

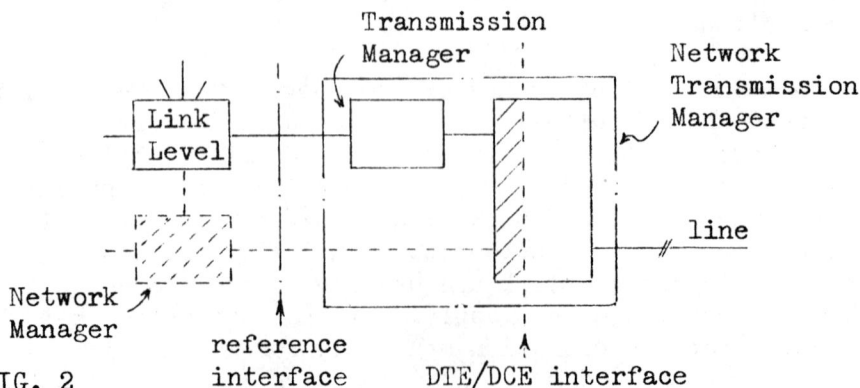

FIG. 2

* International Telegraph and Telephone Consultative Committee

In relation to Figure 2, the Link Level component is essentially unchanged as also is the frame alignment function represented by the module called Transmission Manager (a sub-module of Network Transmission Manager). The major area in which modifications for interfacing to the new network will be required is represented by that shown shaded in the diagram.

A simplification, not shown in Figure 2, is that, since there is no analogue to digital converter (modem), the second level of connection (called Transmission Connection in the aforementioned paper[1]) has disappeared. Not only is there no imposed half-duplex limitation but also it is no longer possible to monitor the absence of carrier and thus convey intelligence at this level (for example on a leased line, that the terminal is not powered) so that, if an equivalent function is to be defined and not provided by the network, it must be defined in the data, for instance, by distinguishing between continuous Flag and continuous one-bit (Idle) transmission in HDLC.

For the future, there is one aspect that should not be overlooked. If public data networks provide an independent end-to-end control facility for use during the data phase, the framing procedure represented by Transmission Manager in Figure 2 could be integrated with the functions contained in the remainder of the Network Transmission Manager module. (An end-to-end control facility has been suggested for networks based on an 8+2 network envelope structure in which the two extra bits are assigned one for network envelope alignment and one for use as a status bit, and for which the network envelope alignment is made visible at the DTE/DCE interface in the form of a "byte timing" interchange circuit - a facility that may be offered as an option in some countries.) For example, the HDLC framing procedure can be specified in the form:

... F [A, C, Information, FCS] F ...

where F (Flag) is a unique 8-bit pattern, herein referred to as the frame delimiter; and the part in square brackets (herein referred to as the "frame") contains the Address (A), Control (C), Information (if applicable) and Frame Check Sequence (FCS) fields, all of which are subject to a zero-bit stuffing rule so as to prevent the frame delimiter (Flag) from appearing in the data transmitted to line other than as an intended delimiter. Given an end-to-end control function, equivalent to a ninth bit for 8-bit data, the Flag could be encoded via the ninth (status) bit and eliminate the need for the zero-bit stuffing rule. The apparent restriction to 8-bit structured data is not necessarily significant because the final Flag could be encoded, via the ninth bit qualifying the other eight, to indicate the number of padding bits (necessarily less than eight) in the final octet of the genuine frame.

- Multipoint (Leased)

With a very few exceptions, the Link Level carries a multiplex of
several logically different streams (communicating entities) through
a single link. This is indicated in Figure 1 by the multiple paths
emerging from the Link Level module. A multiplex below Link Level (in
concept below although not necessarily seen in the implementation as
such) is applicable for multipoint configurations - a leased line
connecting more than two terminals together. Considering the usual
case where one terminal controls all the others, the network has to
provide branching amplifiers which broadcast data from the control
terminal outward to all the others and in the inward direction
effectively logically OR's the data from the other terminals.
Necessarily, only one remote (relative to control) terminal must be
transmitting at any one time.

In analogue networks, there is no knowledge of data structure at the
branching points but the transmitting terminal can be identified by
the presence of carrier so that there is no difficulty in providing
the necessary logical functions. In digital networks there is no
carrier and either the transmitting terminal must be identified by
independent control signalling (compare last paragraph of previous
section) or the non-transmitting state must be defined in the user's
data. The latter is possible because the data structure will be
visible at the branching point; for example, the HDLC framing procedure
defines the transmission of contiguous one-bits (if sustained) as an
Idle state so that a simple logical AND at the branching point will
provide the OR function (the inverse logical operation being effective
because the "one" state is defined as Idle).

If the second method described above is used, the equivalent modem
interfaces (which could be provided on the new network to assist
transition from old to new) will present, at the receiver of the
controlling terminal, the equivalent of the mark-hold clamp option
(CCITT Recommendation V24[2]) on the received data interface circuit
(that is, a sustained one-bit state) when no remote terminal is
transmitting. It is possible (although unlikely) that incompatibility
problems might ensue.

- Start-Stop

The aspects so far detailed are in principle applicable to start-stop
systems. Two further points should also be mentioned. First,
telegraph and Telex facilities have characteristics similar to those
of the equivalent start-stop services proposed for public data
networks. The implications on design are therefore relatively minor;
for instance, the number of data rates and start-stop character
envelope structures available for use in the data phase (end-to-end)
will be limited whereas there are no such restrictions (up to the
maximum permitted rate) on telegraph facilities (as also applies on

modem facilities).

Secondly, dependent on tariffs, it may be more convenient to transmit asynchronously generated data via the synchronous class of service. This can be done, for example, by defining a synchronous idle character (to be transmitted when no data is available, and discarded at the receiver). Some extra buffer would be required and obviously the synchronous bearer rate would have to be faster than the required asynchronous rate. A possible disadvantage is that the idle character so defined could not be used as a data character. Alternatively, for networks providing end-to-end control signalling this could be avoided if the ninth (status) bit were used to define the idle state. Moreover, such a technique would make it possible for the network to provide conversion from start-stop to synchronous bearer as a service, a facet which could substantially simplify the physical connection at a multi-line installation (for example, a processor connected to many different start-stop terminals). Rather than have a multiplicity of individual interfaces for each line, it would be possible to exploit the byte-interleaved multiplex proposed to be used on the bearer from the exchange which, if capable of 48 kbit/s, can be subdivided to provide a maximum of eighty 600 bit/s channels. At the processor, one interface to the network would then suffice. The mean rate of insertion of the synchronous idle condition at the processor would, of course, have to be equal to the difference between the bearer rate and the maximum permitted received information rate at the remote terminal. These physical considerations would also apply if the user himself converts asynchronously generated data for transmission via the synchronous class of service.

- Multi-Line Connection

To conclude thia part of the analysis in this paper, the benefit of multiple line connection via a single interface is to be noted not only for the instance quoted but also as one of general application which could lead to even greater simplification of the means of connecting to the network than just the elimination of modems. That is, a mix of remote terminals operating at any of the rates 600, 2400 and 9600 bit/s, independent of whether the individual facilities are leased, circuit-switched or packet-switched, could be connected, at a common processor or network node, via one 48 kbit/s bearer, the number so connected being limited only by the capacity and permitted sub-multiplexes of the bearer.

Circuit-Switched

Referring to Figure 1, the component that has not so far been considered on circuit-switched networks is the module called Network Manager. The fact that it is shown as a unit in the model does not necessarily mean it has to be implemented as part of the logic of the terminal as will be evident in the following analysis.

- Manual Control of Connection

Some existing systems rely on external operators to control the
establishment of calls on switched networks (telephone or Telex). An
equivalent facility could be provided on public data networks. Note
that it is immaterial here as to whether the manual facility should be
provided as part of the DCE or as part of the DTE, as indicated in the
following diagram (compare Figure 2):

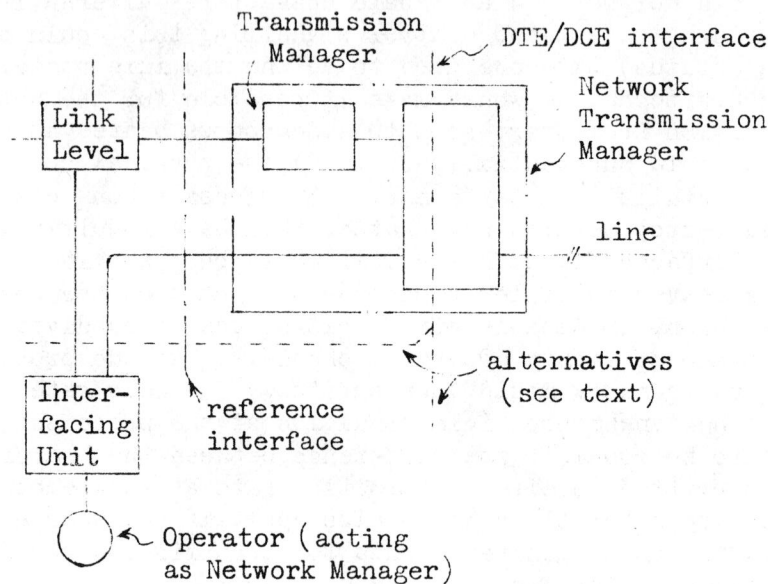

FIG. 3

It seems hardly necessary to dwell on this form of control because it
is unlikely to be a requirement once the transition period is over
except perhaps for the lowest cost manually operated terminals.
However, since there is no speech facility, there is no exact equivalence with similar existing systems although the only significant
problem is that of identification (particularly, calling to called, but
also vice versa as confirmation that the required connection has been
set up). This can be resolved by incorporating the optional "remote
line identification" facility in the interfacing unit. Nevertheless,
this merely adds to cost and should be compared with the alternatives
given in the next sections.

Unlike the switched telephone network, call clear-down at one end will
be signalled by the network to the other end so that some simplification in terminal design will apply.

For leased lines, there is no circuit switching but where there is an
alternative use for the line (for example, speech) the logic function
represented by Network Manager in Figure 1, although reduced to a
primitive form, is not eliminated. Obviously, this is another area of
simplification with data networks (but the convenience of speech

communication for, for example, maintenance should not be forgotten even if it becomes more economic to rely on independent public switched telephone network facilities).

- Manual Establishment of Calls with Automatic Answer

This category is considered separately because it is common to provide automatic answer facilities in existing systems but rare to provide automatic calling.

In principle, automatic answering requires:

1) recognition of the incoming call signal from the exchange

2) appropriate response to the calling signal (call confirmation)

3) recognition of "connect through" signal.

Space precludes an examination of these requirements in detail but, in principle, the new system is analogous with existing systems (implying some obvious changes in the interfacing mechanism but no significant change at the higher levels in the terminal system) with one noticeable exception. Other than for Telex (for which an answer-back facility is provided) there is no mechanism available for identifying the subscribers to each other (on the telephone network there is the added complication that a human operator will, in general, have set up the call and he requires a specific tone response to indicate "connect through"). The new data network will, however, provide (as an option) a remote line identification facility. Study of the model in Figure 1 indicates that such a facility is in no way equivalent to any existing facility provided as part of the Link Level protocol for similar purposes. This is because remote line identification is part of the call establishment process and therefore operates at a different system level. Moreover, the fact that it operates at a different level indicates that it provides a much greater degree of security than anything that can be provided at Link Level. For example, an unwanted subscriber can (at least theoretically) break into an existing system from his own terminal by calling in from any telephone location if he can obtain, inter alia, the relevant passwords. The expedient of "calling back" to protect against this is cumbersome compared with the virtual elimination of the possibility on the new network - the unwanted subscriber has to call from the same data terminal location. In addition, remote line identification provides a ready-made universal basic description.

Since a terminal may represent many different logical entities at a higher system level, the need for identification procedures at Link Level does not, of course, wholly disappear.

- Automatic Calling and Answering

At the present time, there is no requirement to be able to reconfigure a system rapidly because of data communication requirements through public network facilities. Even if reconfiguration is required because a particular communications facility is being used from time to time for different logical entities (that is, calls to different terminals) and the call establishment function is automated, the time taken to establish the call is such that there is nothing to be gained by operating with a call hold time short relative to call set-up time. But for public data networks, the call set-up time will be relatively short in comparison with the present-day switched telephone network. (It is not easy to quantify because it is dependent on many factors such as data rate and distance but it is reasonable to assume it will be less than one second for most calls except those at very slow data rates. For shorter distances, especially at the higher data rates, it may be of the order of 200 ms or even less.) Dependent on tariffs and the costs of modifying the terminal system, it may become economic to reduce the call hold time even to the point where it is of the same order as the call set-up time. For instance, a transaction could be divided into message input on one call with the reply on another, later and separate call. Whether or not such radical changes in operating strategy are going to happen is not material to this paper (it will in part depend on the optimum scheduling rate in the terminal) - the significant factor is that the possibility of such changes should not be overlooked.

The potential impact on terminal design can be summarised by saying that, at present, the connection functions that could be performed automatically by Network Manager (Figure 1) have a time factor in existing systems that is large in comparison with the scheduling rates performed by most present-day operating systems but that the differential between the two will, in the future, be reduced so that, to benefit from circuit-switched public data network services, it may be necessary to modify, to a greater or lesser extent, the operating system characteristics to take into account the operating characteristics dictated by the network. Note that this would substantially affect the modus operandi at Link Level (Figure 1).

Apart from such overall system considerations, it is to be noted that, although there are similarities between establishing calls automatically on existing networks (telephone and Telex) and likewise on public data networks, the similarities can only be seen at the higher system levels. Moreover, existing networks have some inherent limitations (for example, the absence of remote line identification, and indication of remote call clearance on the switched telephone network is not provided) and these limitations will not apply to public data networks so that, call set-up time considerations apart, it is largely unrealistic to think of modifying existing designs for compatibility with the new services. This is emphasised by the fact that the DTE/DCE interface will be very different (compare, for example, CCITT Recommendation X21 for synchronous services with its telephone counterpart, Recommendation V25[2]).

As a final point, the new networks must define an alignment procedure
to enable the interchange of "information" between the terminal and the
data switching exchange (for example, call selection digits). The
alignment procedure is a component of the Network Transmission Manager
module shown in Figure 1. For simplicity, it would be ideal to have
essentially the same alignment procedure for both end-to-end as well as
terminal-to-exchange interchange. This is easy for start-stop services
in which the character envelope structure for both uses is rigidly
defined. For synchronous services, the ideal is unlikely to be
attained because more than one procedure currently exists - whichever
is chosen cannot be suitable for all terminals. In this context, the
remarks already made on possible future end-to-end procedure developments are relevant.

- Closed User Groups

Mention should be made of closed user groups which is likely to be
offered as a facility. The implication is a simplification in the
calling and answering procedures. Note that the limiting case when
only one connection is permitted (Direct Call) is not identical to a
leased facility because the network may return a supervisory response
to a call request.

Packet-Switched Network

It has already been indicated that if, for tariff reasons, it is
desirable on circuit-switched networks to ensure that the call hold
time is not unduly long in comparison with the call set-up time, it
may be necessary to modify substantially the modus operandi at Link
Level. In the limit, when only one frame is transmitted per call, it
would evidently be more logical to include the end-to-end data with
the initial request to the exchange to set up the call. If, then, no
acknowledgement from the remote terminal is required we have a packet-
switched service which has been called "datagram". On the other hand,
if an acknowledgement from the remote terminal is required, to be
delivered by the network at some later time, we have a packet-switched
service which has been called "virtual call". Since, in general, an
acknowledgement from the remote terminal will be required (and may
include a reply message which may lead to further packet interchange)
the difference will usually be one of deciding whether the end-to-end
control will be network supported (virtual call) or network independent
(datagram). There are other differences, of course, the most important
of which is concerned with packet flow control but which it is not
necessary to consider in any detail here.

A method of examining the implications is to consider the structure of
the conventional Link Level when several logical entities are multiplexed through the resources of a single link. It has already been
stated that the structure of the Link Level frame in HDLC can be
specified in the form:

$$\ldots \mathrm{F} \left[\; A_1 \; C_1 \; \text{Information} \; \text{FCS} \; \right] \; \mathrm{F} \ldots$$

The reason for adding the subscripts will become evident.

The A_1 field represents an addressing field below the C_1 field which controls the link, one control entity for each individual A field. Considering the simple case where the link is point-to-point and there is no multiplexing below the level of link control, the A_1 field becomes null. But since, for the example, multiplexing exists above the level of link control, there must be a further addressing field (A_2). If the information field is structured for the higher levels in the same way that the link is structured, the complete format becomes:

$$\ldots \mathrm{F} \left[\; A_1 \; C_1 \; \left(\; A_2 \; C_2 \; \text{Information} \; \right) \text{FCS} \; \right] \; \mathrm{F} \ldots$$

The relationship between this and that required for packet switching can be seen by considering the following diagram which is a representation of the structure required for packet switching, drawn for virtual call control:

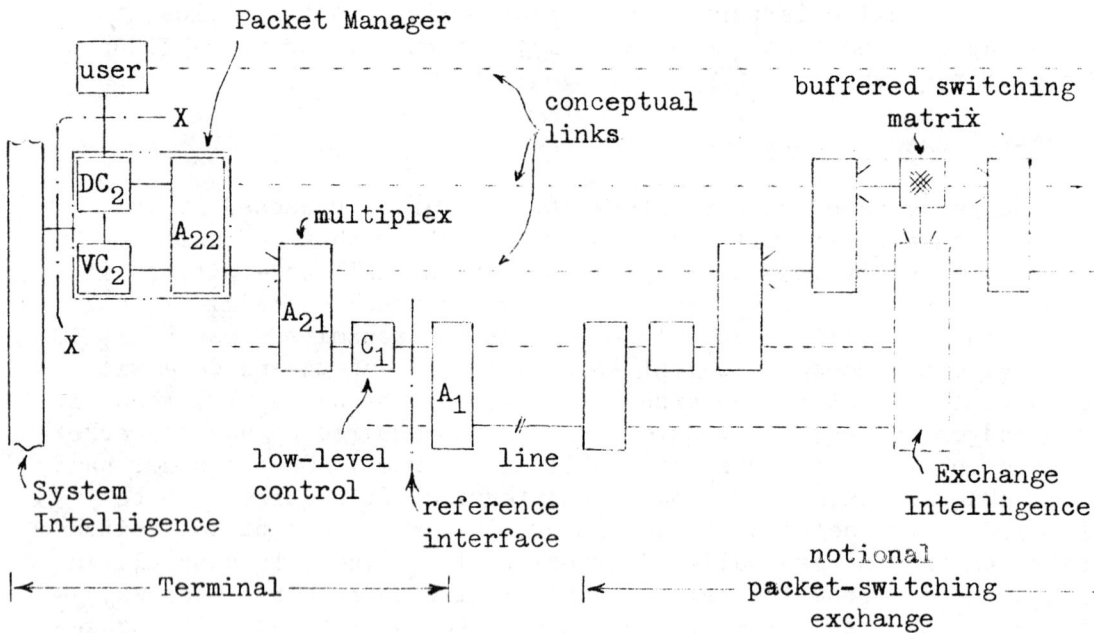

FIG. 4

VC_2 represents virtual call control. For datagrams, DC_2 (end-to-end control, network dependent) does not exist (the equivalent facility, if required, being provided by the user).

It can be clearly seen that C_1 corresponds with the Link Level of Figure 1 but is now defined as the means of exchanging packets with the packet switching exchange (PSE). The A_2 level is represented by two components, A_{21} for identifying a number of separate paths between the terminal and the exchange (when applicable), and A_{22} separating virtual call control from end-to-end control. The combination of DC_2 VC_2 and A_{22} (called Packet Manager, per logical entity) should be compared with Figure 1. The analogy should be obvious but whereas, for circuit switched, the system can be complicated when a few exchange lines are shared between many more users, for packet switching the complication reduces to a simple scheduling algorithm (represented by A_{21}) provided a single base link can handle the total traffic.

The implication of all the above is not to suggest that packet switching necessarily introduces a new dimension into terminal design so much as to indicate the need to re-appraise, and substantially modify, existing techniques. If this is not done, then the operating constraints in an existing implementation will most likely prevent full exploitation of the new facilities; indeed, response times at the user level may even be markedly inferior. In practice, it is likely that the majority of the required changes will be to software, hardware being usually limited to the A_1 (and possibly the C_1) level.

It does need to be stressed that the analysis is much simplified - for example, there is no attempt in Figure 4 to separate the two directions of transmission. Thus, the A_1 field is, strictly, not null because it is necessary to distinguish (in each direction) between packets in transit to (or from) the exchange and acknowledgements to packets sent in the opposite direction - the low level control (C_1) incorporates the function of re-transmission when transmission errors occur.

In Figure 4, the overall control functions that could exist at each multiplexing level (A_1, A_{21}) are not shown. For example, packet switching could be superimposed on a circuit-switched facility in which case the call establishment and control module would be attached at A_1 as in Figure 1. This does not, of course, then constitute the functional model for character mode operation as provided in EPSS*[3] (as an alternative to packet mode) - Packet Manager is then contained in the exchange so that the line interface is, conceptually, that between the user and Packet Manager, marked X-X in Figure 4 (supported, of course, by appropriate link procedures). Note that this interface includes the link from "System Intelligence" (effectively, the terminal's resource scheduler), that is, it includes the control functions for defining the existence of a virtual call. In packet mode on EPSS, study of the content of the packet header indicates consistency with the model here presented (Figure 4) but note that the fields are not ordered according to level (for example, the sequence number applicable to the low-level control, C_1, is defined in a sub-field of two bits in the third octet of the packet header).

---

* U.K. Post Office Experimental Packet Switched Service

Conclusion

Although it has not been possible to include more than a few of the more important effects that public data networks will have on terminal design, nevertheless it should be evident that the impact will depend very much on the degree to which new facilities are exploited. The impact will be least on end-to-end user procedures applicable to leased lines and to the data phase on circuit-switched facilities. The impact will be greatest with packet switching for which there is no equivalent on existing public facilities and for which a revision of the terminal's operating strategy is implicit.

The implications are not limited to the operating procedures used in the terminal but extend also to physical aspects, particularly to the potential simplification for multi-line connection to the network.

It is hoped that this paper has shown that it is possible to relate the proposed facilities with the concepts applicable to terminal design so that features common either to existing facilities or across the various facilities on new networks or both can be recognized so as to minimise the effects on design. This is especially important when the uncertainties concerning the availability of new services within the next few years are considered.

Acknowledgement

The author expresses his appreciation to International Computers Ltd. for permission to publish this paper.

References

1. Frampton, J.A.K.: Circuit-Switched Networks - a Structured Model of the Network applicable to the Design of Terminal Equipments. Proc.IEE 1974 Computer Systems and Technology Conference, p.123.

2. The International Telegraph and Telephone Consultative Committee (CCITT) Green Book, Vol.VIII, V-Series and X-Series Recommendations. The International Telecommunication Union, 1973.

3. Experimental Packet Switched Service (EPSS): U.K. Post Office publication.

Practical experience with the telephone used as a data terminal

G. Arndt
Project Manager
Research Laboratories, Siemens AG,
Federal Republic of Germany

K. Stemberger
Systems Analyst
Research Laboratories, Siemens AG,
Federal Republic of Germany

Abstract

Because of its wide distribution the telephone has great
potential as a data terminal. It would give practically
everyone access to data services with no significant increase in terminal-equipment costs. The people using the
telephone "data terminal" will have had no experience with
computers, so a special system was developed and put into
operation in a large PABX (21 000 extensions) as part of a
trial project. The application in question is a computer-
controlled call number information system, which permits
the extension users to conduct a dialog with the computer
from their own telephones to obtain information about the
call numbers of other users connected to the same PABX.
Special recording programs were run to produce data on the
operation of the system, and an evaluation of these data
showed that the telephone would be entirely suitable as a
medium for conducting computer dialogs of this type.

Introduction

When it comes to making the telephone network serve as a
data communications network, the idea of using the simple
telephone as a data terminal presents a challenge from both
the economic and technical standpoint. On the one hand,
practically everyone - in the highly developed industrial
nations at least - has access to the telephone, and on the
other hand the telephone used as a data terminal is totally
different from the data terminals currently employed in remote data processing. The data are fed in via the dialing
equipment, which in the vast majority of cases is a rotary
dial. The minority type, the pushbutton telephone equipped
with 10 digit buttons and 2 special buttons, which is better
suited for conducting a data dialog, is becoming more widespread. The data are fed out in the form of audible tones
or via a computer-controlled voice output. In view of the
simplicity of this interface to the data-processing system,
the telephone functions best as a data terminal in cases
where the data dialog involves a small number of input data
and short answers. This is frequently the case with various
types of information systems, simple ordering systems and
data-collection systems with highly decentralized collection points.

In order to test the suitability of the telephone used as
a data terminal we deleloped a special information system
which can be operated via the telephone and used it as the
basis of a practical trial. The following report gives an
account of this system, the results of the trial and our
experience with the telephone "data terminal".

The System

This particular system is an automatic call number information system for the large PABX with approximately 21.000
extensions serving our Munich complex. Each of the extension users is able to conduct a dialog with the computer
from his own desk telephone in order to find out the call
number of any other user. This type of information service
is of special interest, because the information provided can
be easily kept up-to-date, in contrast to the information
contained in internal telephone directories which is soon
out-of-date. Moreover, it offers the prospect of rationali-
zation in view of the fact that the users have direct access
to the EDP system when conducting the information dialog;
this drastically reduces the manual activity at the information office.

Fig. 1 shows the hardware configuration of the information
system. All the connected telephones have rotary dials. The
vocoder system /¯1,2,3_7 is used for the voice output. The
data of the 21.000 users are located in a disk storage file
and occupy 300 Kbytes. The digital vocabulary is also lodged
in a disk storage file, and occupies 39 Kbytes corresponding
to a voice output lasting 130 s.

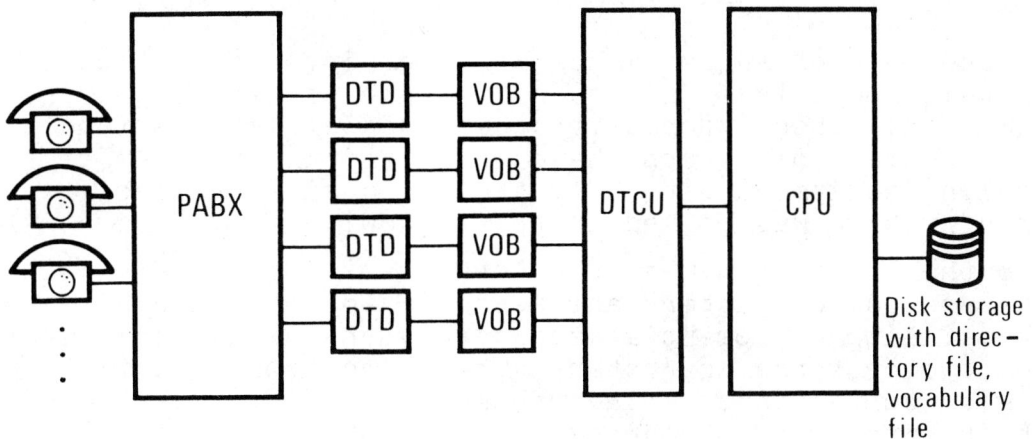

DTD	Data Transmission Device
VOB	Voice Output Buffer
DTCU	Data Transmission Control Unit
CPU	Central Processing Unit

Fig. 1   Hardware configuration of the call number infor-
         mation system

The information dialog proceeds as follows: The user dials
the number of the automatic call number information service
and is connected to one of the four inputs at the EDP system
which are served by the information program. The dialog
with the computer can now begin. Via the computer-controlled voice output the information system requests the data
which are required for identifying the subscriber in question. The user replies by feeding in the relevant data via
the dialing equipment on his telephone. The first information which the system requests is always the desired party's
last name. If this is sufficient to establish the correct
call number, the caller is informed of the number via the
voice output. If it is not, the dialog is continued. The

system asks the caller to supply additional data relating to the person in question and information which
serves to localize him within the organization served by
the PABX (e.g. group, department, office). After each
reply has been fed in, a check is made to see whether
sufficient data are present to identify the subscriber
or whether the dialog must be continued. Many of the
questions asked by the information system require only
a 'yes/no' answer. The user may also reply with 'not
known'.

In the case of automatic call number information accessed
by telephone, it is a special feature of data input that
names and other information comprised of letters (and a
few special characters) have to be fed in by means of the
dialing equipment with only the ten digits available.
This problem was solved in the following way:

For the input of names, the letters of the alphabet plus
two special characters are assigned to the ten digits on
the dialing equipment in such a way that each digit stands
for two or three characters. The allocation of letters to
digits corresponds to the scheme on the digit/letter disks
which have been introduced in some countries, with the
addition of the missing letters and special characters.
Fig. 2 shows the chosen allocation. A suitable digit/let-
ter disk was made and given to the users to place over
the standard digit disk on their telephones. (Fig. 3)

1	2	3	4	5	6	7	8	9	0
−	A	D	G	J	M	P	T	W	Z
␣	B	E	H	K	N	R	U	X	O
	C	F	I	L		S	V	Y	Q

- hyphen   ␣ space

Fig. 2   Allocation of letters and special characters to
the digits on the digit disk

Fig. 3　Telephone equipped with digit./letter disk for
the automatic call number information service

The names are indicated according to the "ambiguous letter input" method, whereby the user feeds in the digits
to which the particular letters (special characters) have
been assigned. This gives rise to a certain degree of inaccuracy in the input data since each digit stands for
several letters, of course, and it may happen that different names will generate the same digit sequence. The
system can only treat such cases as identical names, a
fact which in principle further restricts the already

limited selectivity as regards last names. However, this has little effect on the average number of dialog steps required to identify a particular terminal, as is demonstrated in the following.

Fig. 4, section A, shows the distribution of last names among the parties connected to the PABX. This indicates that less than half of all the users can be unambiguously identified on a last-name basis. If an unambiguous letter input method were chosen, the dialog would have to be continued about every other time a request for information was made in order to identify the desired party. Turning now to section B in Fig. 4, which shows the distribution of the digit sequences corresponding to the last names in the case of ambiguous letter input, we can see that with this method there is only a very slight deterioration as regards the requisite number of dialog steps. On the other hand, this method permits a rapid data input since the dial only has to be actuated once for every letter.

A   Last names
B   Digit sequences
     The digits indicate the frequency
     of the last names
     or the digit sequences

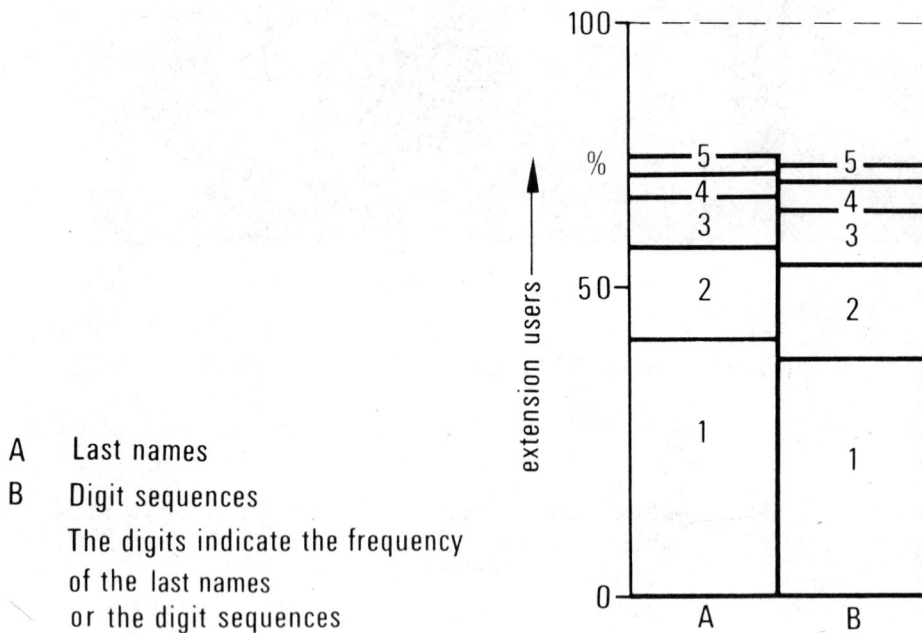

Fig. 4 Distribution of last names and digit sequences among extension users

A few comments on the dialog formalities:

Each data input must be concluded by keying in an end-of-block character. The digit combination '11' was chosen for this,because the digit 1 does not represent any letters and because the input time must be short on account of the frequent use of this signal.

Fig. 5 shows the possible responses which the user can make to the system's requests for data. To clarify the dialog formalities we have given an example of the procedures involved in a dialog for call number information in Fig. 6.

NAME11	Last name or first name of required party
J11	Yes
N11	No
11	Not known
1711	Request for repetition of last announcement
	(11 designates the end of an input block)

Fig. 5 Input data which can be fed in by users of the automatic call number information service

User: Connection setup to the
         information service

         Computer: "This is directory information,
                    Siemens Munich. Please give the
                    last name."

User: "LEMANN11"

         Computer: "Is the party you require a
                    gentleman?"

User: "J11" (≙ yes)

         Computer: "Please give the first name."

User: "11"   (≙ not known)

         Computer: "Does the party you require work
                    for the telecommunication group?"

User: "N11" (≙ no)

         Computer: "The number is 44175."

User: "1711" (≙ repeat announcement)

         Computer: "The number is 44175."

User: Replace telephone handset

Fig. 6   Sequence of steps in a computer dialog

The Results

The PABX extension users have been able to avail themselves of the automatic call number information service all day since the beginning of September 1974. So far an average of 500 dialogs have been conducted everyday. From September to March, special recording programs were in the EDP system simultaneously with the information program so as to produce a record of all the details of each dialog. An evaluation of the recorded data yielded an objective assessment of the rotary-dial telephone's performance when used as a data terminal and of the inexperienced user's ability to conduct a data dialog.

Correctly evaluating the data provided by the recording programs was no easy matter. It was necessary to allow for the numerous instances of experimentation with this freely available and easily accessible service, which meant that the dialog data recorded when people were "playing around" gave a distorted picture of the user's behavior and of the telephone for use as a data terminal.
Because of this, all dialogs which had obviously not been conducted with the aim of obtaining call number information were excluded from the evaluation. During the first few months these accounted for approx. 50 % of all calls.

An evaluation of the sifted dialog records produced the following results:

The successful and unsuccessful dialogs were contrasted schematically (Fig. 7), showing a very positive result. Only about 8 % of the dialogs failed to produce the desired information due to errors on the part of the users and were discontinued. A total of 6,7 % of all the inputs were formally incorrect.

discontinued by user —

6%

2%

discontinued by the
system due to serious
formal errors,
exceeding of time limit

22%

successful with corr. error(s) —

70%

— successful without errors

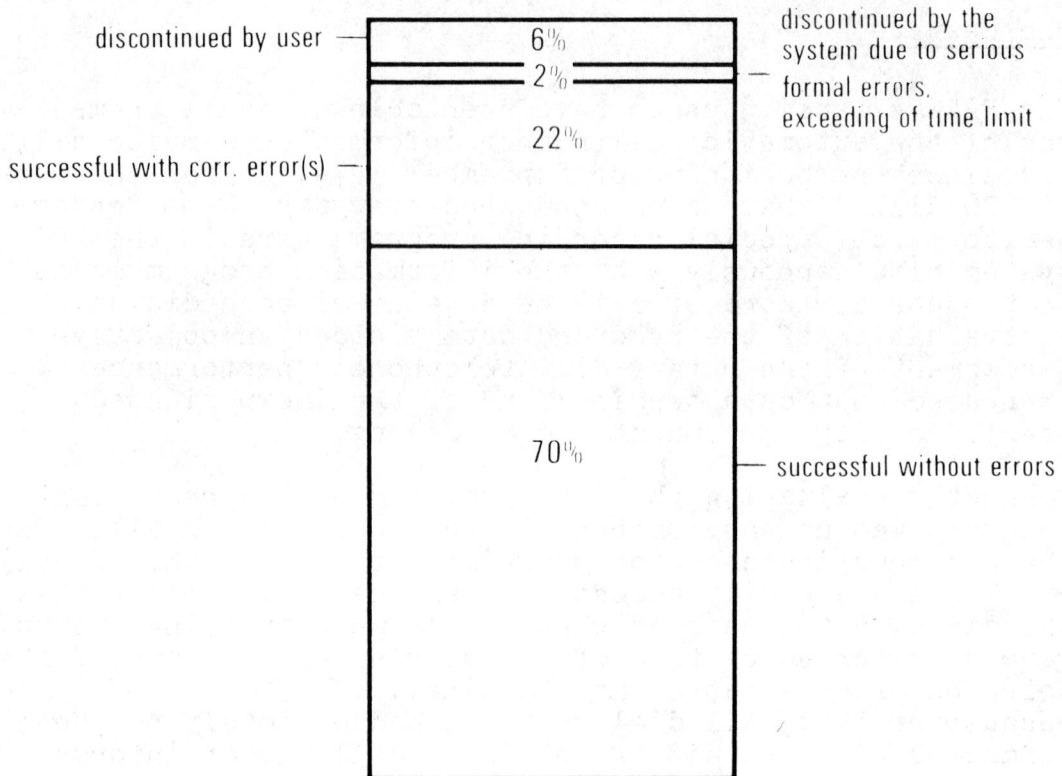

Fig. 7   Dialog success rate

Figs. 8 and 9 contain information about the length of
the dialogs. Fig. 8 shows how many dialog steps were
needed to obtain the required information. The diagram
proves that the users were quite capable of conducting
a long question-and-answer dialog with the computer without making mistakes.

Although the diagram shows a decrease in the number of dialogs as the number of dialog steps increases, it must not
be concluded that relatively more mistakes were made in the
case of longer dialogs. Understandably fewer long dialogs
have to be conducted than short ones. This is clear by
Fig. 4.

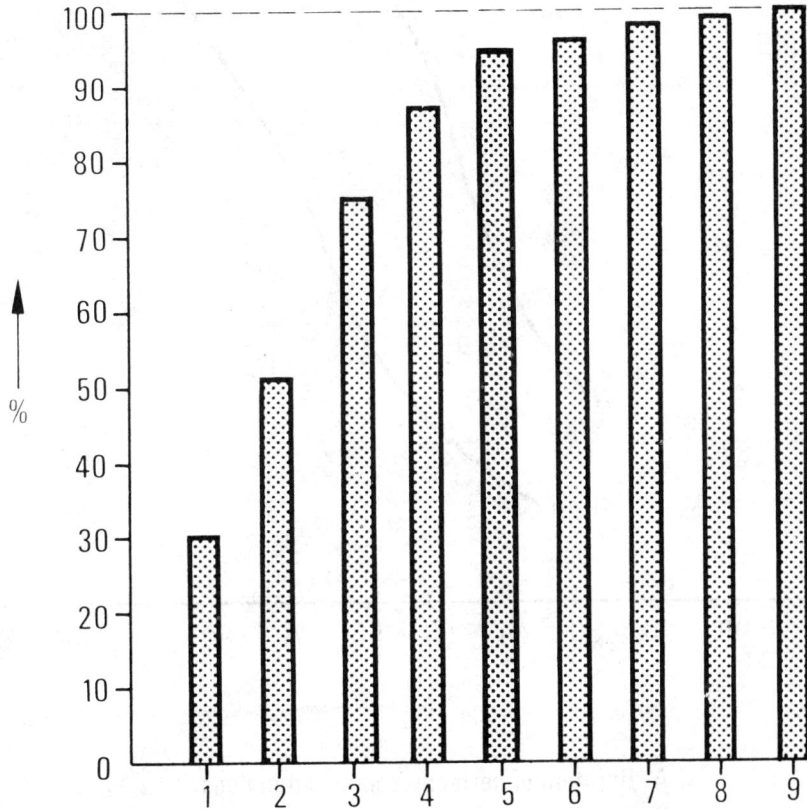

Fig. 8 Distribution of the dialog steps among the
perfectly conducted dialogs

The average duration of the dialogs was 50 s. Fig. 9
shows the relationship between perfectly conducted dialogs and dialog duration. It also shows how mistakes increased the duration.

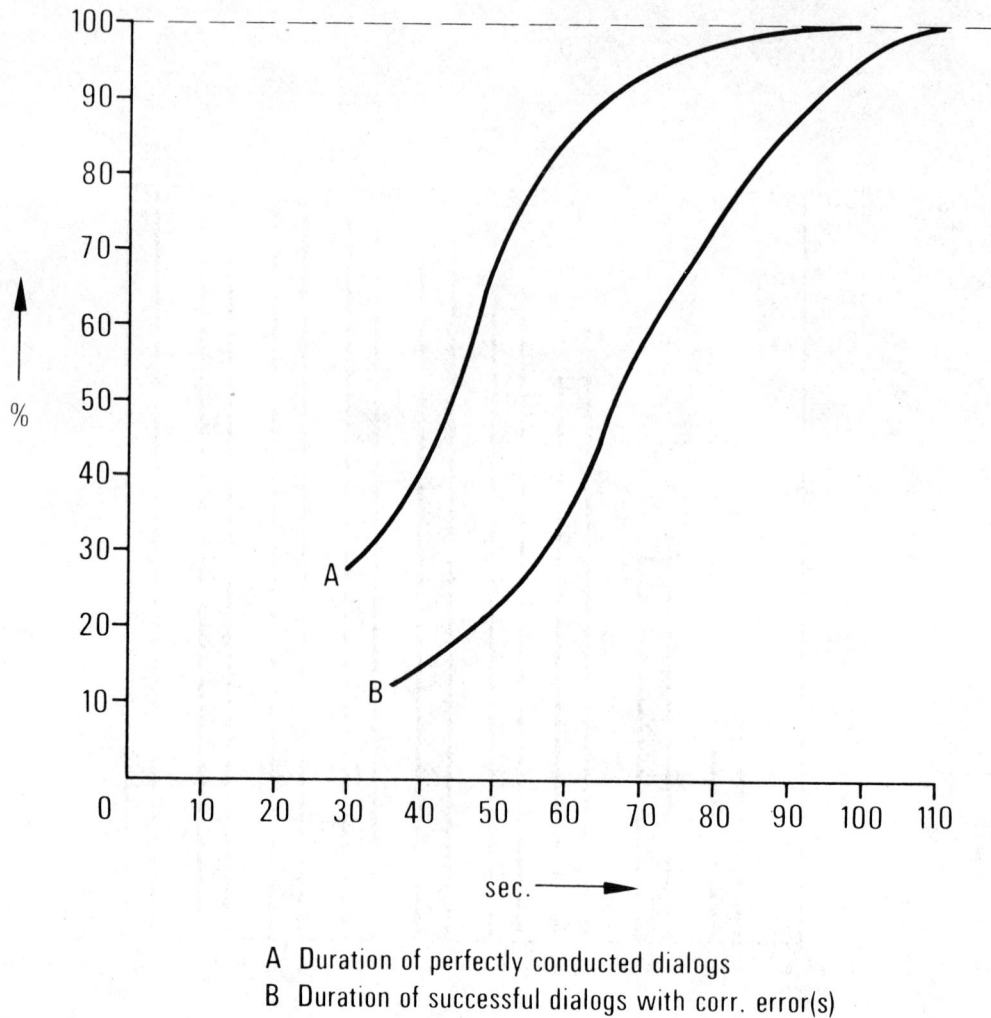

A Duration of perfectly conducted dialogs
B Duration of successful dialogs with corr. error(s)

Fig. 9 Duration of the dialogs

Another investigation was carried out to find out how
well the users coped with the ambiguous letter input;
after all, they were not used to dialing long sequences of letters. The time taken to feed in names was
measured and compared with the time normally required
to dial call numbers consisting of digits. (The time
data relating to call-number dialing via a dialswitch
were taken from /‾4_7 and /‾5_7.) Fig. 10 shows the

result. It can be seen that there is little difference
between ambiguous letter input and call-number dialing,
and that the differences which exist are largely due to
the longer prepause associated with the letter input.

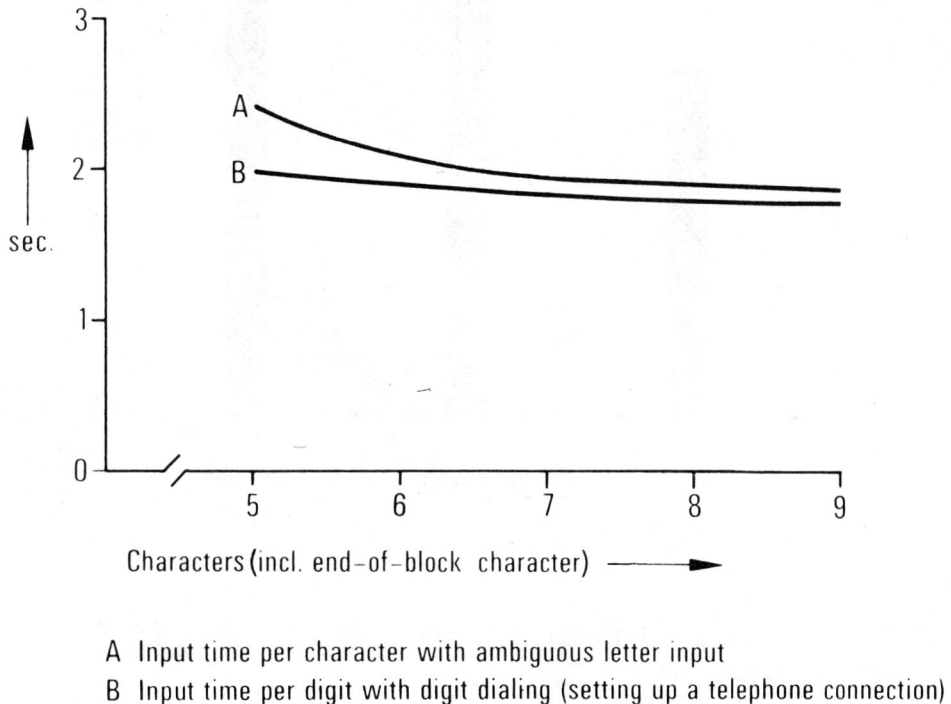

A Input time per character with ambiguous letter input
B Input time per digit with digit dialing (setting up a telephone connection)

Fig. 10 Time data of letter input

Fig. 11 supplements Fig. 10 by showing the average time
required for the input of special dialog control characters.

A final comment concerning the digital voice output:

The system can output a total of 33 questions and standard
announcements. Very seldom did the users request a repetition of these announcements. The repetition rate lay between 0,2 % and 1,1 % depending on the particular announcement. This demonstrates the good intelligibility of the
voice output.

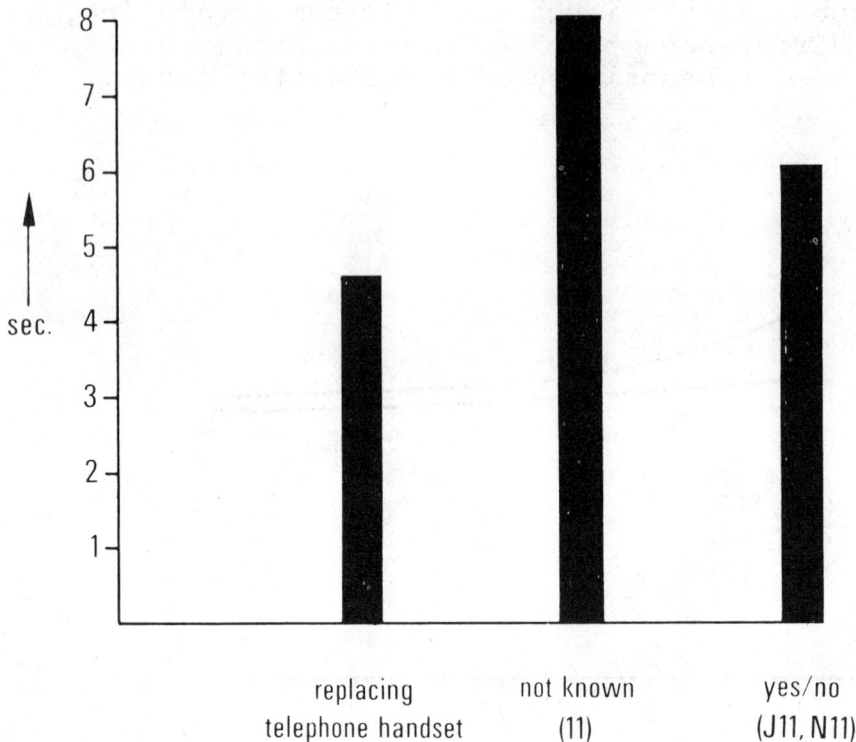

Fig. 11   Average duration of special dialog control
          characters

Understandably, requestes for a repetition of the call
numbers showed a much higher rate (repetition rate approx.
18 %).

It can be concluded from the results of the trial operation of the automatic call number information service
that the telephone would be very efficient as a terminal for operating a similar, if somewhat more sophisticated information system. Even people who have had no
experience with computers are managing to cope with the
data dialog very well.

When asked to comment, the users expressed surprise at dis-
covering how easy it was to operate the information system
using such a primitive terminal, and were of the opinion
that it could be used for still more applications.

References

/¯1_7   Christiansen, H.M.; Schweizer, L.;
         Sethy, A.; Hoffenreich, F.
         New Correlation Vocoder
         J. Acoust. Soc. Amer. 40 (1966), pp.
         614 to 620

/¯2_7   Schreiber, A.: Der Computer lernt sprechen
         Siemens Data Report 6 (1973) No. 5, pp.
         5 to 9

/¯3_7   Arndt, G.; Hülters, H.: Hardware and Soft-
         ware for Realizing Telephonic "Speech Dia-
         log" with EDP Systems
         Siemens Reports on Telephone Engeneering
         VIII (1972) No. 1, pp. 46 to 49

/¯4_7   Rothert, G.: Influence of dialing and
         Push-button calling on error rate and
         call number transmission time
         TELETEKNIK, Vol. 7 (1963) No. 2, pp.
         59 to 66

/¯5_7   Masakazu Suzuki: Customer Dialing Beha-
         viour During Push-Button Dialing, Field
         Trial Test in NTT. 4. International
         Symposium on Human Factors in Telephony
         Bad Wiessee, 23. 9. 1968, pp. 191 to 199.

Inter-mainframe communication via spooling RJE machines

Mr. S. Cardy, programmer, Computer Unit, Westfield College,
    University of London, UK

Mr. P.N.Jackson, programmer, Computer Technology Limited, UK

Abstract

   We discuss the problems associated with transferring files
between mainframes and conclude that there is a need for a mechanism
which makes use of already existing facilities. Such a mechanism is
possible if we postulate the existence of an interface between batch
terminals connected to different mainframes, and we show how the
existence of spooling RJE terminals makes possible the provision of
this interface. We then describe a piece of software which performs
the interfacing, and discuss the implications.

1.   Introduction

For some time now the trend has been toward the establishment of large computer centres which offer facilities both on-site and via remote links to various kinds of terminals. These can range from low speed interactive terminals (teletypes and VDUs) to high speed batch terminals which provide a convenient method of handling large volumes of data. Examples of batch terminals are the CDC U200 station, which is effectively an interactive terminal with associated card reader and line printer; IBM 2780, which is a remote card reader and line printer; IBM HASP workstation which has multi-leaving capability; ICL 7020 which is similar and the CDC high speed batch terminal, which is effectively a means of distributing mainframe intelligence.

The fact that a remote site often has access to several mainframes means that a user has a choice of mainframe to use, according to his various applications. In this situation it is often helpful to be able to transfer information between mainframes. This has been achieved in two ways:

1)   Originally the only means available was to transfer physical copies of files on, for example, cards, paper tape, magnetic tape or discs, and this method is still widely used. Simple though this is, it is not without its problems: it is often the case that mainframe coding conventions differ, and one is also restricted to using a medium acceptable to both mainframes which may not be ideal for transportation. There are long delays involved in transferring files this way (of the order of days) and this is clearly unacceptable for many applications.

2)   More recently much work has been done in setting up elaborate communications networks which have large computer centres as nodes. [1,4,5,12]. These nodal mainframes use a standardised protocol for communicating with other nodes, often while retaining the usual protocol for their own terminals. [2,8,11] . Each node must possess software for interfacing with the standard protocol, which may be resident in the mainframe itself or in a dedicated mini-computer; this effectively makes the mainframe aware of the network. (Fig. 1). Clearly the addition of N different new nodes entails the provision of N different such pieces of software. We feel there would be a saving of effort if it were possible to utilise the existing communications software which drives the mainframes' own terminals. We will now discuss how this may be achieved.

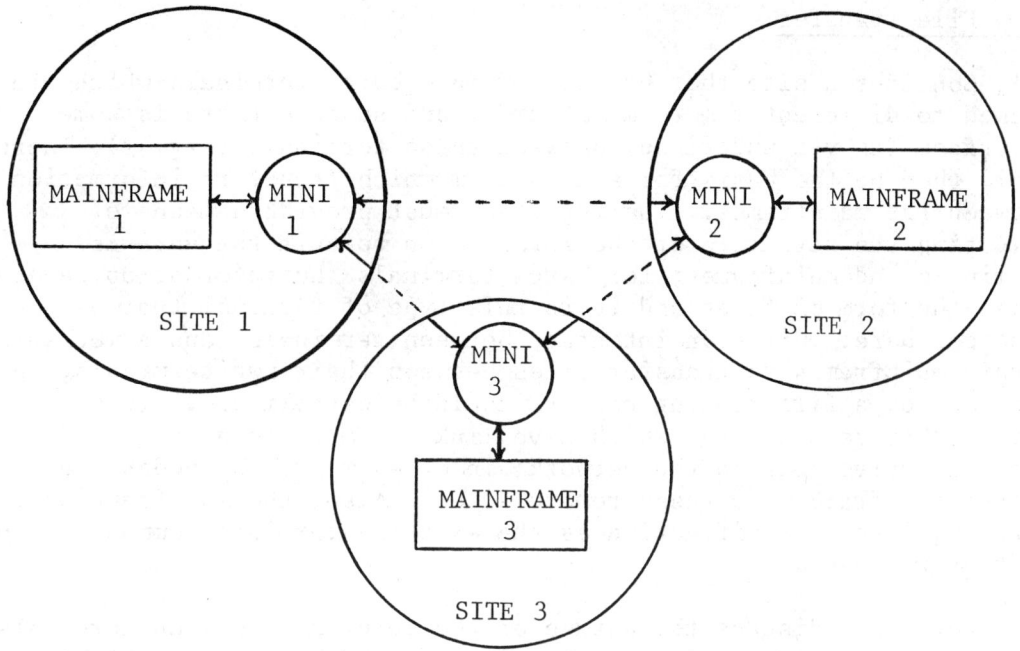

Fig. 1

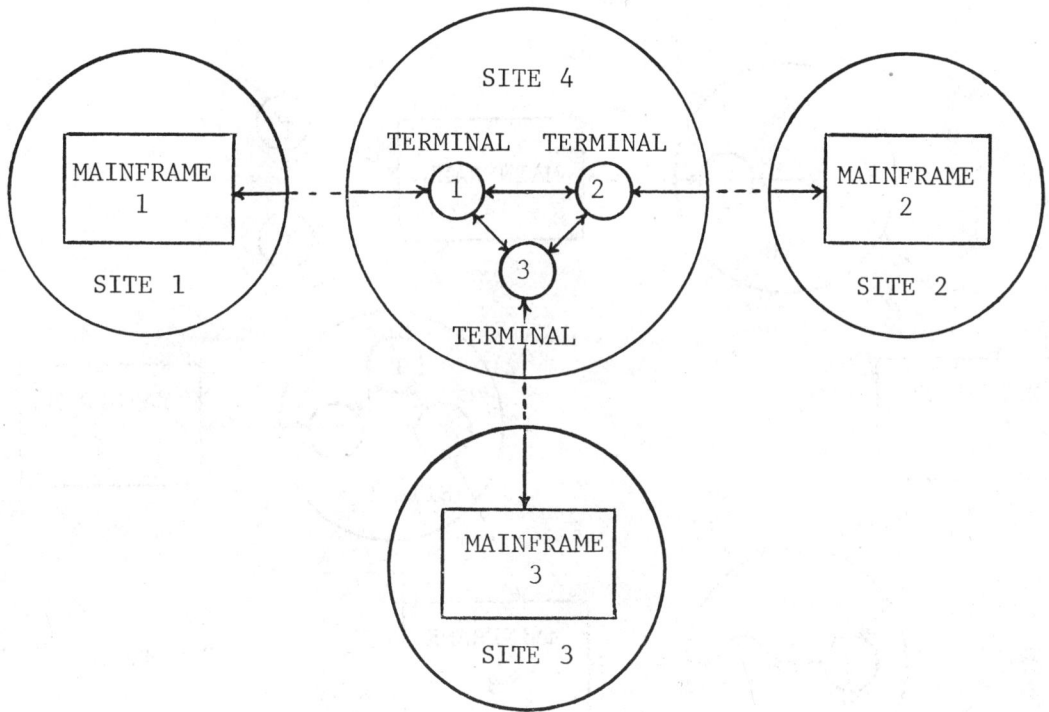

Fig. 2

2.   File transfer

Consider a site that has two or more batch terminals which are
linked to different remote mainframes, and suppose there is some
interface (as yet undefined) between these terminals (Fig. 2). There
would then be the basis for a mechanism which transfers information
between the mainframes. The interface must provide a means of
adjusting the structure of the information to suit the various
terminals and mainframes; for batch terminals the information generally
takes the form of files and it is this type of terminal that we
consider here. Given an interface between terminals, and a mechanism
within mainframes to transfer files between their own terminals, we
can see how a file routing network could be established. (Fig. 3).
Notice that remote sites which have links to more than one mainframe
play an active role in the network; in other words the nodes consist
of the mainframes and these remote sites. Also, the mainframe software requires no modification as the existing terminal communications
software is used.

Before we discuss the nature of the interface between terminals,
it is necessary to examine the types of batch terminals available
today.

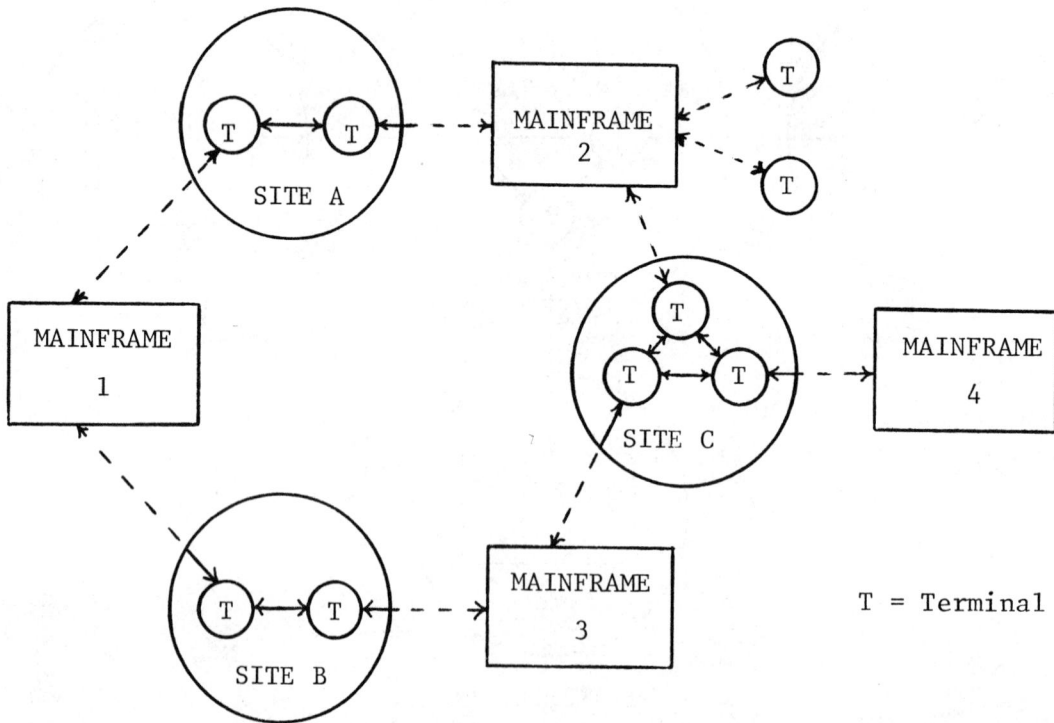

Fig. 3

3.   Batch terminals

Many batch terminals were originally hard-wired devices which were inherently inflexible, providing a fixed set of facilities. In recent years manufacturers have been providing emulators for certain of the larger mainframe RJE (Remote Job Entry) terminals. These emulators while replacing the hardwired terminals, may also provide an enhanced set of facilities such as an extended range of peripherals on the terminal. (Fig. 4). Originally these emulators were stand-alone programs on small configuration machines, but more recently a manu-facturer has produced RJE facilities as part of a larger system providing local processing capability and spooling of I/O files (the CTL MODUS 4 system [3]). (Fig. 5). It is an important development because this system is capable of supporting more than one emulator and, since I/O is spooled, the files used and produced by the emulators have a common structure; to the best of our knowledge this is currently the only manufacturers system providing such a range of facilities. Thus the terminals at a site which are connected to remote mainframes can effectively reside within the one machine, and the filing system can provide the basis for an interface between them. (Fig. 6). Naturally an output file from one mainframe cannot be transmitted to another mainframe without modification: a software system is needed to make it acceptable to the second mainframe. This system must be general enough to allow the transfer of files between any two emulators.

4.   FRAME

FRAME is a program which is being developed to run on a CTL MODUS 4 system. It performs the following three functions, either singly or in any combination:

(1)   Assemble a file from pieces taken from various sources
      which can be named files or real peripherals.

(2)   Split a file and route the pieces to various destinations
      which can be named files, queues of files, or real
      peripherals.

(3) Reformat parts of a file.

These functions are of use when constructing files for batch execution, or when obtaining the output from a batch run for further processing. For example, suppose a user has a local file on the RJE machine which he wants to supply as data to a program which runs on a remote mainframe. By the facility offered by (1) he can input part of his batch job on the main input medium (e.g. cards) and insert the data from the local file into the correct place. By the facility offered by (2) he could then (without splitting the file at all) submit this complete file to a queue of files for transmission to the

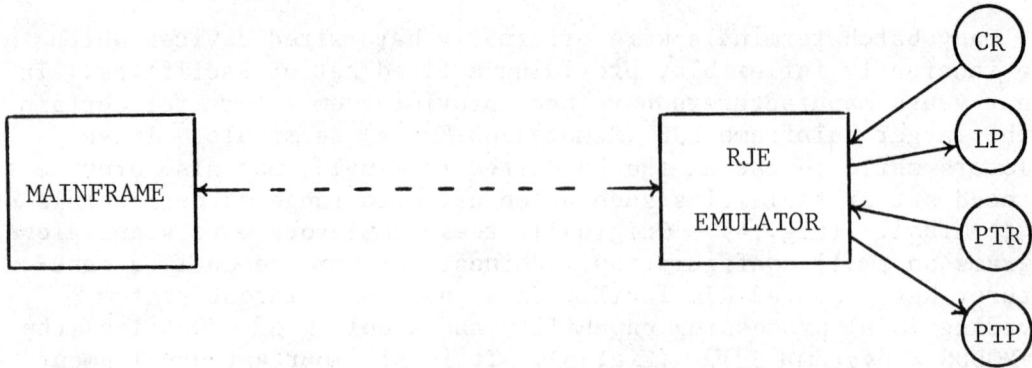

Fig.4

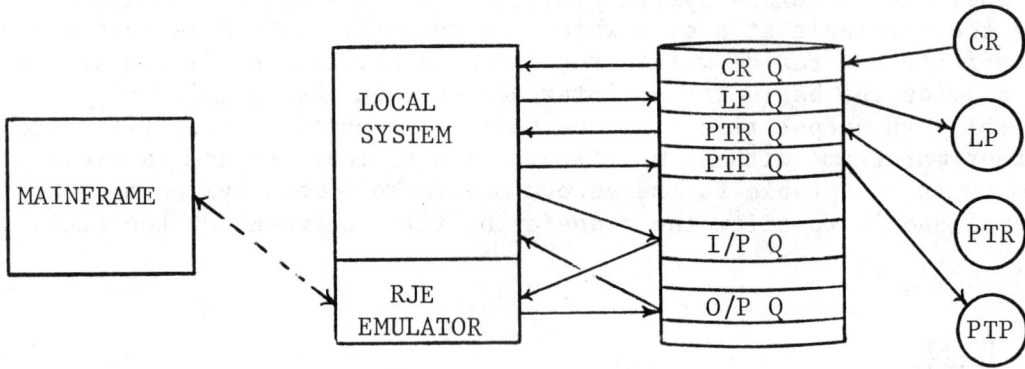

Fig.5

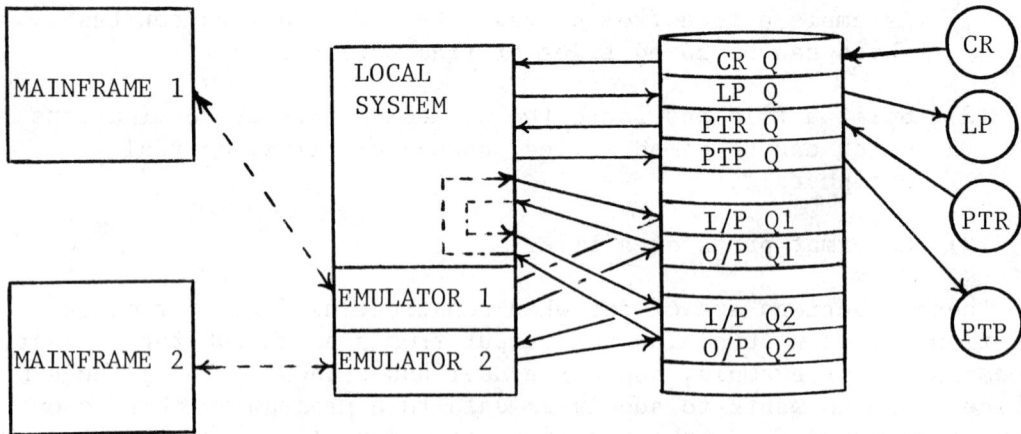

Fig.6

Q = queue of disc files

mainframe. The facility offered by (3) is for code conversion, etc. and will not concern us further here. The same user may wish to place part of the output from the mainframe job into another local file for further processing. This could be achieved by using the facilities offered by FRAME on the output file returned from the mainframe. (Fig. 7).

FRAME was originally designed to provide local file manipulation [9], but it is sufficient to provide the interface between the RJE facilities of the local machine, thus providing the mechanism for inter-mainframe communication.

5.   How FRAME works

FRAME begins by taking input from a file and copying it to a default output file, while scanning the data for embedded directives. Directives, which are not copied to the output file, are of three forms, corresponding to the three functions described in section 4:

1)   Switch to a new input file. Processing of the old input file may later be resumed from its current position. FRAME will accept further directives from the new input file as well as copying it. When an input file is exhausted, processing will continue from the previously defined input file, if there was one.

2)   Switch to a new output file. As with input files, output files are 'remembered' by FRAME and one can later resume out-putting to a previously used output file at its current position.

3)   Reformat the contents of input files in some standard way before copying. (E.g. code conversion, or coding binary information.)

FRAME continues processing until the original input file is exhausted. For example, consider a file called FILE A containing the following information:

```
ABCD
EFGH
<FRAME command to switch output to FILE B>
IJKL
MNOP
QRST
<FRAME command to switch to input from FILE C>
4
<FRAME command to switch output back to default output file>
567
89
```

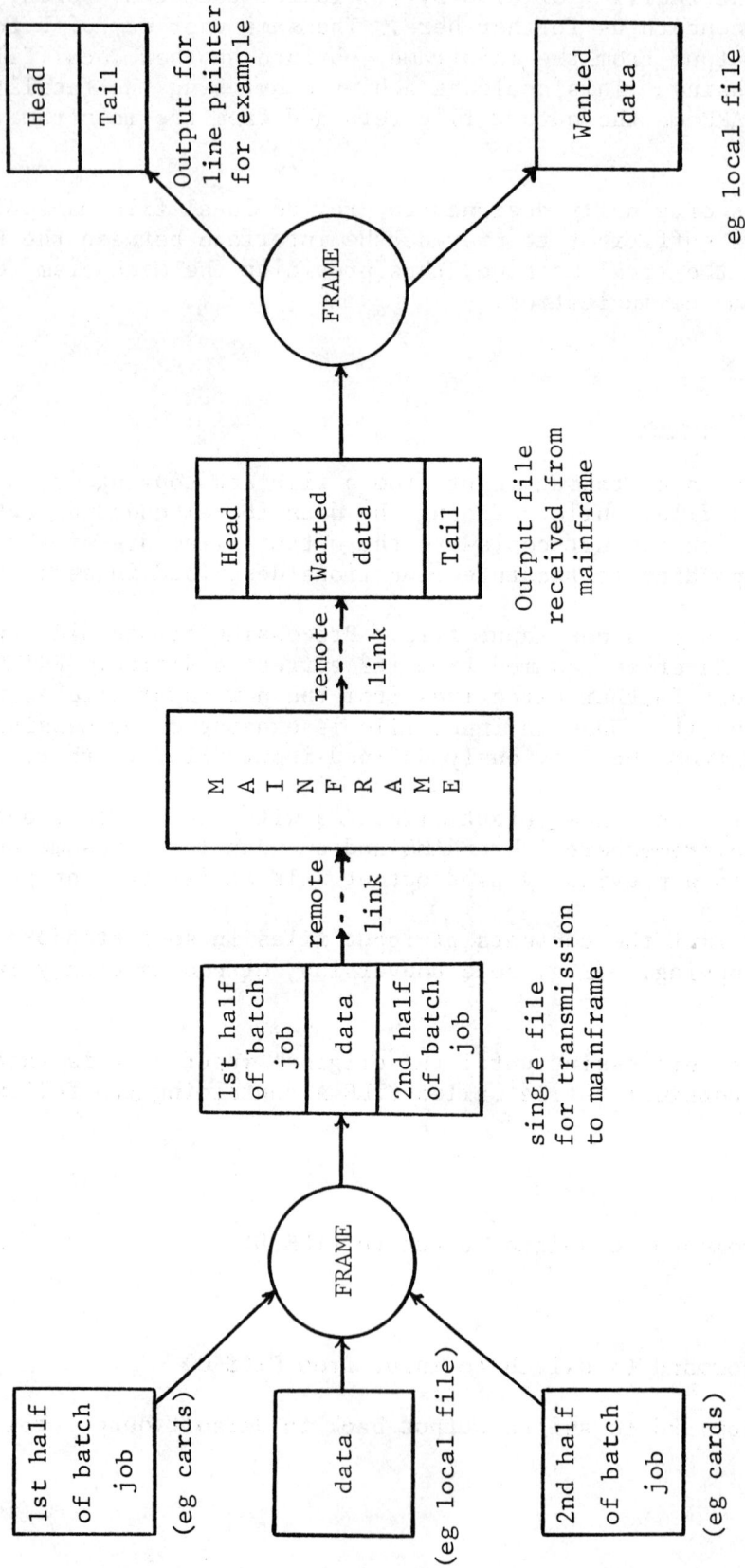

Fig. 7

and suppose FILE C contains:

```
UVWX
⟨FRAME command to switch output back to default output file⟩
YZ
⟨FRAME command to switch output to FILE B⟩
0123
```

After FILE A has been processed by FRAME, using FILE D as the default output file, FILE D will contain:

```
ABCD
EFGH
YZ
567
89
```

and FILE B will contain:

```
IJKL
MNOP
QRST
UVWX
0123
4
```

6.   Inter-mainframe communication using FRAME.

FRAME can be used to modify the output from one mainframe to produce a file suitable for input to another mainframe. In general terms this is achieved by using FRAME directives to strip off the unwanted parts of the output file and to add the extra sections which may be required to make a file acceptable for transmission to another mainframe. This means that a user must arrange that the appropriate FRAME directives appear in his output file. As an example, consider the problem of transferring the output from a program run on mainframe A to be processed by another program run on mainframe B. The user may arrange that the file transmitted from mainframe A to the spooling RJE machine has the following format:

(1)   ⟨file header provided by mainframe A⟩

(2)   ⟨program listing etc.⟩

(3)   ⟨FRAME directive to change the current output file to one for submission to the input queue of the emulator servicing mainframe B⟩

(4) ❬FRAME directive to change the current input file to a
     local file containing JCL for mainframe B❭

(5) ❬output from program run on mainframe A❭

(6) ❬FRAME directive to change the current input file to a
     local file containing the terminating sequence for the job
     for mainframe B❭

(7) ❬FRAME directive to change the current output file back to
     the original (default) output file❭

(8) ❬file tail provided by mainframe A❭

After processing locally by FRAME, the output returned to the
user from mainframe A consists of items (1), (2) and (8), and mainframe
B is sent a job consisting of the results of items (4), (5) and (6),
items (4) and (6) serving to insert the contents of complete local
files.

In the above example the job was initiated at, and returned to,
an RJE machine directly connected to both mainframes A and B (as
terminal Y in Fig. 8). However it would be possible to arrange more
extensive networking of files by using FRAME at each spooling RJE
machine (if there is only one type of machine used this involves
only supplying a copy of FRAME to each of them). For example, a job
could be run on mainframe B having been transmitted from terminal X
and the output could be routed to another terminal Z connected to

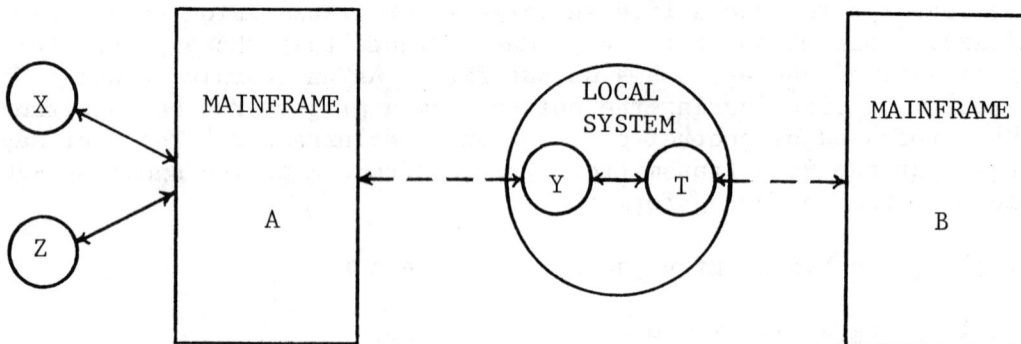

Fig. 8 : Y and T are batch terminal emulators on the local
          machine.

mainframe A. (Fig. 8). Note that no mainframe software modification is needed to achieve this; indeed the mainframes are completely unaware of FRAME and the network since all the file manipulation is done on the RJE machines. FRAME is in effect providing a high level protocol for the transmission of files. This system on its own, however, has the disadvantage that a large number of FRAME directives would be required for work of any complexity; this is inconvenient and leaves wide margin for user error. So far we have not discussed anything which needs mainframe software modification, but the above situation improves if we provide mainframe JCL to insert FRAME directives into a user's output. JCL for inserting FRAME directives could also be provided on the RJE machines, and this would greatly simplify the task of routing files around the network. Perhaps, if such JCL could be standardised, it could provide the basis for a network language. [10]. This will be discussed in a further paper.

There have been other attempts at providing an interface between batch terminal emulators running on an RJE machine, but in our opinion these would have one or other of the following drawbacks:

(1) The system does not support spooling [6] so that bottlenecks can occur if two nodes connected to the RJE machine both want to access a third node at the same time: one of these two nodes must be made to wait until the other is finished. With a spooling system both can send their files to the RJE machine, where they are stored until they can be transmitted. Similarly this aids throughput if the 'destination' machine is down.

or (2) The system is dedicated to particular mainframes [7] and the interface between terminal emulators is not flexible enough to easily allow connection of additional mainframes to the network.

A preliminary version of FRAME has been used to successfully transfer files between an IBM 360/65 and a complex of CDC 6000/7000 machines at different sites in London University. We have thus demonstrated the feasibility of using FRAME for inter-mainframe communication, and our experience in doing this has revealed several areas in which further work needs to be done, in particular the provision of further FRAME directives and the study of flexible error recovery procedures.

7. Summary

We have described how we can take advantage of the facilities offered by spooling RJE machines to provide a mechanism for transferring files between mainframes, by the provision of only one new piece of software, FRAME. Although such a network can be inherently slow and deals only with batch files (and we are not suggesting that a network using FRAME would perform better than any other network) it does have several advantages:

(i)   It is a single piece of software which can be distributed to the RJE machines involved.

(ii) It makes use of already existing lines of communication, both hardware and software.

(iii) No modification of mainframe software is necessary.

This means that a batch network using FRAME could be implemented at less cost than a traditional network and could be used in situations where one would not be able to consider implementing a full-scale network.

We have also mentioned how it may be possible to use FRAME as the basis for the implementation of a network language.

References

1.   Abramson,N. Packet switching with satellites. Proc. AFIPS National Comp. Conf. 42 (1973) 695.

2.   Carr,C., Crocker,S., and Cerf,V. Host/Host communication protocol in the ARPA network. Proc. AFIPS SJCC 36 (1970) 589.

3.   Computer Technology Ltd. MODUS 4 System operating handbook (TP 381/9N/2A1).

4.   Dennis, J.B. A position paper on computing and communications. Communications of the ACM 11 (1968) 370.

5.   Frank,H., Kahn,R.E., and Keinrock,L. Computer communication network design - experience with theory and practice. Proc. AFIPS SJCC 40 (1972) 255.

6.   Ghezzi,C., Moli,G., and Mezzalira,L. Introduction to Poli computer network design. International Computer Symposium (1973) 271.

7.   Griffiths,M. A disc-based twin emulator providing host-to-host link capability. 1974 Modular One software workshop, Liverpool.

8.   Heart,F., Kahn,R., Ornstein,S., Crowther,W., and Walden,D. The interface message processor for the ARPA computer network. Proc. AFIPS SJCC 36 (1970) 551.

9.   Jackson,P.N. The transmission and reception of non-standard files via a U200 emulator. M.Sc. project report, Westfield College, London.

10. Kriloff,H.Z. A high-level language for use with multi-computer networks. Proc. AFIPS National Computer Conference 42 (1973) 149.

11. Ornstein,S., Heart,F., Crowther,W., Rising,H., Russel,S., and Michel,A. The terminal IMP for the ARPA computer network. Proc. AFIPS SJCC 40 (1972) 243.

12. Roberts,L., and Wessler,B. Computer network development to achieve resource sharing. Proc. AFIPS SJCC 36 (1970) 543.

Out-of-sequence problem in a packet switching network: a simulation approach

Mauro Maier

IBM Scientific Center, Pisa, Italy

Abstract

In this paper we present a simulation approach to the out-of-sequence problem in a packet switching network.

First of all, some generalities on components and functions of a network interface are given. In this context, the characteristics of Logical Communication Channels, Basic Information Units and Message Handler are analyzed.

Then the problem of diagnosing loss of packets is taken into consideration and stochastic methods are discussed, based on timeout and out-of-sequence concepts.

Finally, the simulation model used to gather statistics is described and some results, concerning the out-os-sequence phenomenon, are reported.

§1 - INTRODUCTION

When a user logs in a computer network, the main
service he wants is the utilization of an end-to-end
communication channel in order to exchange information with
a partner.

To allow a user to access a communication channel in an
implementation independent way, the network must provide an
interface (access method) to the communication subsystem
(subnetwork). The main task of this interface is to offer
communication channels and to control information flow
through them.

Most of the problems for the network interface arise
when the end-to-end data flow is accomplished with a packet
switching technique [3]. In fact, packet switching networks
may deliver packets in more than one copy or not deliver
them at all. They may expand or contract the interval time
at which packets were submitted by the sending interface, so
causing timeout problems. They may destroy the order in
which packets were submitted, so causing out-of-sequence
problems. Both timeout and out-of-sequence conditions
require recovery procedures based on stochastic parameters.

In order to define suitable recovery procedures in the
frame of RPCNET [8], a simulation study has been decided on.
The main objective of this study is to gather statistics
about the most important variables representing the
behaviour of a packet switching network.

§2 - GENERALITIES

Before describing the simulation model used in that study, let us briefly analyze the characteristics of some components and functions of a packet switching network which are involved in timeout and out-of-sequence problems [7].

§2.1 - Logical Communication Channels

In a packet switching network the flow of information from the sending to the receiving user goes through a communication channel that is, in general, not in a one-to-one relationship with a communication hardware.

A Logical Communication Channel, as designed in RPCNET, has the following main characteristics:

LCC.1: it has only two ends, each of them being associated with only one user; it is able to transfer bit strings from one end to the other in both directions, but in only one direction at a time;

LCC.2: it is able to transfer bit strings not longer than a maximum value, this value being due to the maximum length of the bit string ("Packet") transportable along a physical communication link;

LCC.3: there exists a certain probability for packets to be delivered in an order different from that one in which they entered the Logical Communication Channel;

LCC.4: while it is practically impossible for a packet to be altered during the transfer, there exists a non zero probability for a packet to get lost or to be delivered in more than one copy.

Characteristics LCC.1 and LCC.2 come out from design choices; the other two characteristics need a more detailed discussion.

Characteristic LCC.3 is a direct consequence of the chosen link protocol and of routing and reconfiguration mechanisms.

Let us suppose we are using full-duplex links controlled by a protocol which allows the forwarding of packets without any respect to possible relationships between them [4] [5]. In this case, it may happen that a sending node takes notice of the need to resend a packet after having already forwarded other packets. If some of the forwarded packets pertain to the same Logical Channel of the packet in error, an out-of-sequence condition has been originated.

Under certain circumstances routing and reconfiguration mechanisms may cause changes in the path followed by packets of a Logical Channel [2] [6]. The new path may allow a faster transferring, so that packets can reach their destination out of sequence.

Characteristic LCC.4 is related to the probability for a node to go down.

If in the failed node there is the only copy of a packet, this failure results in an unrecoverable loss of the packet in concern. While, if the packet has been already forwarded to the following node, but not yet acknowledged to the previous one, two copies will be delivered to the destination. In fact, in this case, the node waiting for the acknowledgment from the failed node must forward its copy of the packet along another path, while the copy that passed successfully the failed node continues to flow to the destination.

Duplicates can be generated also if a data communication link fails. Also in this case, the sending node could not receive the acknowledgment of a packet, but this packet could have successfully passed the failed link.

§2.2 - Basic Information Units

With "Basic Information Unit" (or simply "Information") we refer to the whole bit string passed by a user to the network with a single send request. The network must deliver this string to the destination user in its integrity.

A basic information unit compatible with the RPCNET

design has the following characteristics:

BIU.1: it may consist of one or two substrings: "Protocol" and "Data" respectively; if only one of these components is present, it can be either protocol or data;

BIU.2: both protocol and data cannot be longer than a maximum; this maximum is completely unrelated with the maximum length of a packet (§2.1 - LCC.2).

While characteristic BIU.2 is due to technical design factors, characteristic BIU.1 comes out as a user requirement.

As a matter of fact, while the protocol substring often can reside in the same storage area during the entire communication session, data are generally stored in different buffers (e.g. file transfer session). In this case, it is very suitable for the user to be able to notify to the network interface both protocol and data substrings with only one send/receive request. With this facility the user is not required to pack both the substrings in a logically contiguous storage area in order to send/receive them as a single information unit.

§2.3 - Network Services

Services offered to the user by the network can be arranged into three main classes: General Network Activities, Logical Channel Control and Logical Channel Utilization.

Services of the first class are exploited outside any Logical Channel; they can be services like enquiries, warning messages etc..

Services of the second class are: setting up and cancelling of Logical Channels, i.e. connect and disconnect services, or testing Logical Channel status, i.e. test Logical Channel and test activity services. All the services for Logical Channel control are offered by the Logical Communication Channel Handler (LCCH) component.

Services of the third class are: sending and receiving

basic information units through a Logical Channel, i.e. send
and receive services. These services for Logical Channel
utilization are carried out by the Message Handler (MH)
component.

§2.4 - Segmenting and Reassembling

As previously seen (§2.2 - BIU.1), with a single send
(receive) request a user can pass to the Message Handler one
or two storage addresses and lengths identifying one or two
buffers containing (set up to contain) either protocol or
data or both.

The main task of the sending Message Handler is to
verify if the information to be sent can be transferred as a
single packet or needs to be segmented into more packets
(§2.1 - LCC.2 and §2.2 - BIU.2).

The main task of the receiving Message Handler is to
reassemble incoming packets pertaining to the same
information in order to be able to pass to the receiving
user the correct originary bit string(s). In order to do
that, the receiving Message Handler needs to be able to
recognize packets pertaining to the information under
reassembling. That is possible only if the sending Message
Handler has marked every packet with a label (information
name), identifying the information to which the packet
pertains, and values (packet number and length or
equivalents), identifying the packet position into the basic
information unit. Moreover, to recognize when a bit string
is completed, the receiving Message Handler needs to be able
to recognize the last packet of both protocol and data; so,
the sending Message Handler is charged with the task of
marking these particular packets with a special
identification.

§3 - LOSS OF PACKETS

It has already been pointed out that packets may get lost during their journey through the communication subnetwork (§2.1 - LCC.4).

If a packet gets lost, the receiving interface becomes unable to reassemble the corresponding basic information unit, and, therefore, it must give a reception error to the destination user.

The problem for the receiving interface is then to become aware that a packet has got lost. But, due to the reasons exposed in §2.1, it is impossible for an interface to make an exact diagnosis of loss. It can only make assumptions based on some stochastic methods.

§3.1 - Timeout

From a logical point of view, the simplest algorithm, on which an evaluation of the probability of packet loss can be based, is to compare the time elapsed from the last reception occurred with a maximum time interval (timeout). Then, when timeout value is elapsed, the network interface can reasonably suppose that the missing packet has got lost, otherwise it has to keep waiting for the packet in concern.

This method is based on the following statistical considerations. Let "τ" be the random variable representing the time interval between receptions of two contiguous packets pertaining to the same basic information unit. The variable τ is such that:

(1) $$\lim_{t \to \infty} \text{Prob} \{ \tau > t \} = 0$$

then it is possible to find a time interval T so that:

(2) $$\text{Prob} \{ \tau > T \} < \text{Prob} \{ \text{packet loss} \}$$

from which it comes out that it is completely useless for
the receiving interface to be waiting longer than a time
interval T for a missing packet.

An estimate of T can and has to be made only by the
receiving interface, packet delays being due to the
communication subnetwork only.

This method becomes a little more complex when a basic
information unit has been completely reassembled and no
packet of the next information has arrived. In this case the
delay is due to two factors: the first is the one seen above
and due to the communication subnetwork, the second is due
to the interval time elapsed between two send requests made
by the sending user.

An estimate of timeout value T', taking into
consideration this second factor, can and has to be made
only by the receiving user. The resulting timeout value used
between arrivals of packets pertaining to different basic
information units can be exactly the sum of T and T'.

§3.2 - Out-of-Sequence Condition

Characteristic LCC.3 of Logical Channels, i.e. the
possibility of packets being delivered out of sequence, is,
perhaps, the main problem in reassembling basic information
units.

Let "p" be the last packet received in sequence through
a Logical Channel. If the next packet is packet "q"
(q > p+1) and not packet "p+1", successive of packet "p",
what kind of actions has the network interface to make in
order to face this situation?

Of course, it is not suitable for the user that the
network interface disregards packet "q" arrived out of
sequence. Then, let us suppose we have a certain number of
buffers associated to the Logical Channel in concern. In
this case, after having stored packet "q" in a buffer, the
receiving interface can keep waiting for the missing packet.
But how long?

Obviously not longer than a time interval T, as shown
in §3.1.

Let "ν" be the random variable representing the number of packets arrived after packet "p" and before its successive "p+1" along the same Logical Channel. Then, the variable ν can be used as measure of the delay associated with the packet "p+1". The distribution function of the random variable ν satisfies the relation:

$$(3) \qquad \lim_{n \to \infty} \text{Prob} \{ \nu > n \} = 0$$

from which it results possible to find a number N so that:

$$(4) \qquad \text{Prob} \{ \nu > N \} < \text{Prob} \{ \text{packet loss} \}$$

The similarity between (2) and (4) is evident, and also in this case it seems useless for the receiving interface to keep waiting for a missing packet after having received more than N packets out of sequence. Then the out-of-sequence method can be combined with the timeout one in order to solve satisfactorily the problem of missing packets.

An estimate of N can and has to be made only by the receiving interface, out-of-sequence conditions being due to the communication subnetwork only.

§3.3 - T and N Estimates

An estimate of T and N is a very hard problem, since it is very difficult to know the distribution functions of τ and ν, and practically impossible to quantify the probability of packet loss.

A remark has to be made on the above mentioned methods for loss diagnosis: due to their statistical basis these methods may cause an interface to consider a missing packet as lost, even if it has been simply delayed more than a time T or an out-of-sequence N, but it is not actually lost.

Now, let E(T) be the event representing the arrival of a packet with a delay greater than T, E(N) the event representing the <u>arrival</u> of a packet with an out-of-sequence greater than N, and <u>E(L)</u> the event representing a packet <u>loss</u>.

The probability P of a reception error due to the network is then:

(5) $P = Prob \{ E(T) + E(N) + E(L) \}$

If we take into consideration that events E(T) and E(N) represent delayed <u>arrivals</u>, it is clear that they are mutually exclusive to E(L). Then, equation 5 can be written as follows:

(6) $P = Prob \{ E(L) \} + Prob \{ E(T) + E(N) \}$

and finally

(7) $P < Prob \{ E(L) \} + Prob \{ E(T) \} + Prob \{ E(N) \}$

An estimate of T and N must tend to minimize the corrective term in (6) and practically to minimize the probability of the events E(T) and E(N), as shown in (7).

On the other side, due to performace goals, T and N must be as little as possible, since it is obviously pointless to keep waiting after an excessively long blackout period or after too many out of sequence receptions. So it seems suitable to act on the forwarding mechanism in the communication subnetwork in order to minimize the variance of the random variables τ and ν.

§4 - SIMULATION APPROACH

A simulation approach is a suitable way to reach a good knowledge of the stochastic behaviour of a computer network. Such approach gives a flexible tool to the designer in order to investigate how the system reacts upon certain choices, and, then, to evaluate their suitability [1].

§4.1 - The Simulation Model

A simulation model has been built following the characteristics of RPCNET [8].

This model is described by means of the General Purpose Simulation System (GPSS) language [9] and may run on IBM S/360 and S/370 machines under OS/360, OS/VS, DOS and DOS/VS operating systems.

The main objective of this model is to furnish statistics on the behaviour of the communication subnetwork.

In order to simulate a distributed control over the network, equi-hierarchical "Nodes" have been defined as addressable units at the communication level. Each Node is responsible for a set of application clusters ("Hosts"), each of them being responsible for a set of "Logical Communication Channels".

The model allows only full-duplex links between Nodes and full-duplex attachments between each Node and its Hosts.

A Node may have any number of links and attachments, limits being those of the GPSS language as far as the required core storage is concerned. A Host may have only one attachment with only one Node. The number of active Logical Communication Channels controlled by a Host is limited only by the required core storage.

Nodes are able to carry on parallel activities on any number of attachments and links.

Each link is considered to be composed of two lines, one for each direction. All the lines have the same speed. The model allows specifying the number of bits per second the lines are able to transfer.

As far as attachment speed is concerned, it has been considered not comparable with line speed. Then, the time required to transfer a packet over the attachment has been assumed to be one millisecond, no matter how long the transferred packet is.

Due to the high speed of the attachment, a gate has been defined in any Node in order to slow down packet flow from the Hosts. When the number of busy buffers in a Node passes over a certain value, the gate blocks the input from the attachments. Hosts will be again allowed to send packets as soon as the number of busy buffers in the receiving Node goes under a certain other value.

Packets are forwarded by each Node via a routing vector obtained and maintained by means of a suitable updating algorithm [2] [6]. The model allows testing of any type of updating algorithm in order to compare their effects on the system.

Packets are enqueued for transmission on a priority basis. The priority of a packet depends on the type of the session to which the packet pertains. This priority may be increased by the forwarding mechanism when a packet transmission fails and a requeueing takes place. In any case, the priority of a packet is always reset in each Node to its original value before the first enqueueing for transmission.

Failures may happen during packet transmissions over links but not over attachments, this second case being of no interest due to the attachment characteristics.

Acknowledgments are exchanged between adjacent Nodes adding a certain number of bits to each transmitted packet. When an output queue is empty and some packets have been received, a local packet is generated in order to send back appropriate acknowledgments [4] [5].

Sessions may be divided into priority classes with the possibility to define, parameters for each of them. These parameters are: distribution type and average of the session length (number of basic transmission units transferred during the session); distribution type and average of BIU length; priority and percentage of sessions in each class.

A mechanism has been included in the model in order to

simulate coming up or going down of the network components (links and Nodes).

§4.2 - Preliminary Results

This study being started at the beginning of this year, only preliminary results have been obtained. The topology used for the first runs is reported in figure 1, where circles represent Nodes and square symbols represent Hosts.

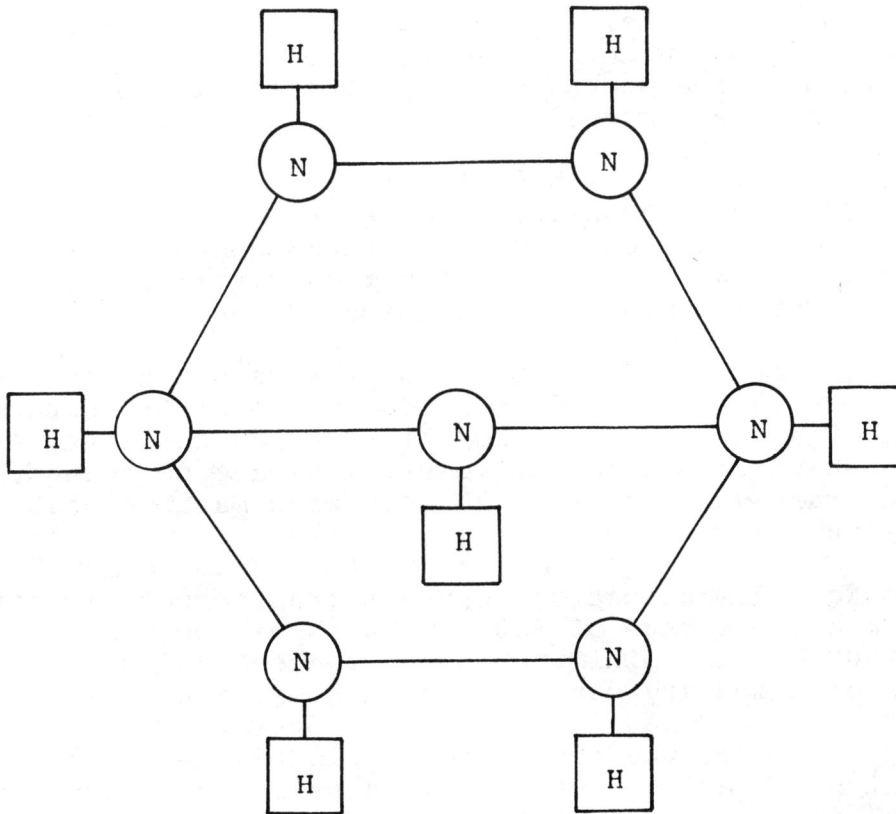

FIGURE 1

The following values were assigned to some network
parameters: line speed = 4800 bps, error rate = 10^{-6} errors
per bit, maximum packet length = 2048 bits, transmission
overhead = 128 bits.

Three classes of sessions were defined: heavy batch
(with low priority), light batch (with medium priority),
interactive (with high priority). These classes were defined
in order to simulate file transfer, process-to-process and
conversational sessions respectively.

Sessions were generated at the rate of one every five
minutes in each Host. Percentages of sessions into the three
classes were: 20% for heavy batch, 40% for light batch and
40% for interactive.

One hour of network operation was simulated. In this
time, about 28,000 packets were transferred for a total of
about 70 million bits. The mean load on the communication
lines was 550 bps with peaks over 4750 bps (99% of line
utilization). Such peaks were experimented for periods not
shorter than one minute.

For the first runs only fixed routing was implemented
in the model, and reconfiguration problems were not taken
into consideration. Under these circumstances, only 30
packets (over 28,000) reached their destination out of
sequence. The maximum out-of-sequence value was "2".

The interarrival time between packets of the same basic
information unit resulted in a mean value of 600 msec and a
maximum of about 3000 msec for heavy batch sessions. As far
as light batch and interactive sessions are concerned, the
mean interarrival time was 400 msec with maximum values of
about 2000 msec.

Logical Communication Channels transferred bit strings
at the mean data rate of 3000 bps with maximum values of
about 4400 bps and minimum values of about 500 bps (as
results of temporary congestions on communication lines).

At the end of the simulation period 17 heavy batch,
30 light batch and 14 interactive sessions were completed,
while 11 interactive sessions were still open.

§5 - CONCLUSIONS

As we already mentioned, only few experiments have been carried out with very reduced topologies. Nevertheless, some conclusions can be reached.

First runs were intended to emphasize the influence of transmission errors on the out-of-sequence problem. From the obtained results it comes out that the effects of a packet retransmission can be consistently reduced by increasing the priority of the packet in error. As a matter of fact, with this simple mechanism, the maximum out-of-sequence values resulted of the same order as the number of Nodes crossed by a packet during its trip.

The effective data rate of Logical Communication Channels and the actual load of the communication lines resulted to be spread over a large interval. In fact, the first resulted ranging from 500 bps to 4400 bps, and the second resulted ranging from 550 bps (11.5% of line utilization) to over 4750 bps (99% of line utilization). Such a wide dispersion of values is substantially due to the fact that, using a fixed routing, no optimization of the traffic load is attempted.

It will be of great interest to investigate how dynamic routing techniques will affect the distributions of both the traffic load and the data rate along Logical Communication Channels. As a matter of fact, a better utilization of the communications facilities is expected to reduce the variance and, may be, the average of the mentioned distributions.

Dynamic routing is also expected to introduce a new cause of out-of-sequence, but not to alter the possibility of keeping the maximum out-of-sequence values to suitable levels.

Experiments related to the dynamic routing techniques are in progress and results will be object of a future paper.

REFERENCES

[1] - L. Kleinrock "Analytic and Simulation Methods in
      Computer Network Design" AFIPS SJCC, May 1970

[2] - G.L. Fulz and L. Kleinrock "Adaptive Routing Technique
      for Store-and-forward Computer Communication Network"
      INFOTECH, Report 6, 1971

[3] - D.W. Davies and D.L.A. Barber "Communication Networks
      for Computers" John Wiley and Sons, 1973

[4] - L. Lenzini "Full-Duplex Data Link Protocol:
      Proposed Design" RPCNET Internal Document IS004,
      July 1974

[5] - L. Lazzeri "Link Handler Specifications"
      RPCNET Internal Document UG011, August 1974

[6] - P. Franchi "Modeling and Analysis for reconfiguration
      Procedures in a Distributed Computer Network"
      Proceedings of the European Computer Workshop on
      "Distributed Computer Systems";
      Darmstadt, October 1974

[7] - M. Maier "Network Interface Functions: Problems and
      Proposed Solutions" RPCNET Internal Document UG008,
      November 1974

[8] - P. Franchi and G. Sommi "RPCNET Features and
      Components" Proceedings of the European Computer
      Conference on Communications and Networks,
      September 1975

[9] - "General Purpose Simulation System V - Introductory
      User's Manual" IBM Corporation, White Plains,
      New York, Form Number SH20-0866

Network node with integrated circuit/packet switching capabilities

Christian J. Jenny, Karl Kümmerle, Helmut Bürge
IBM Research Laboratory
Data Communications Center
Switzerland

ABSTRACT

Present and future public data networks use or plan on using one of two switching methods, circuit switching (C/S) or packet switching (P/S). The low predictability of future requirements clouds the issue which of the two methods is better suited in the long term. As a consequence flexibility should be a primary objective for the near term design.

The approach proposed to meet this objective is integration of circuit switching and packet switching into a single public network. P/S is to be achieved based on a C/S network. The portion of packet switching facilities not shared with the C/S facilities must be a minimum Δ :

$$P/S = C/S + \Delta.$$

This report addresses the switching node in such a public network. A novel node concept is presented which – analogous to the integrated network concept – imposes packet switching on a circuit switching node structure.

Very small and simple processors built into storage modules perform the packet handling. Their number, may exceed forty (40) modules for the environment considered. The well-known saturation effect of multiprocessor systems, i.e., decreasing incremental throughput per additional processor module with an increasing number of processor modules, is overcome by a new concept of intermodule communications, taking advantage of the particular data communications environment. The system throughput is analysed and shown to be nearly a linear function of the number of modules.

1. INTRODUCTION

Todays and future data networks use or plan on using either one of two switching methods, circuit switching (C/S) or packet switching (P/S).   Both methods – when compared against each other – offer a wide range of advantages and disadvantages depending on factors like subscriber traffic, user applications, interface complexity, transparency.   The low predictability of future requirements clouds the issue which of the two methods is better suited in the long term.

Potential developments may take any of the following paths:

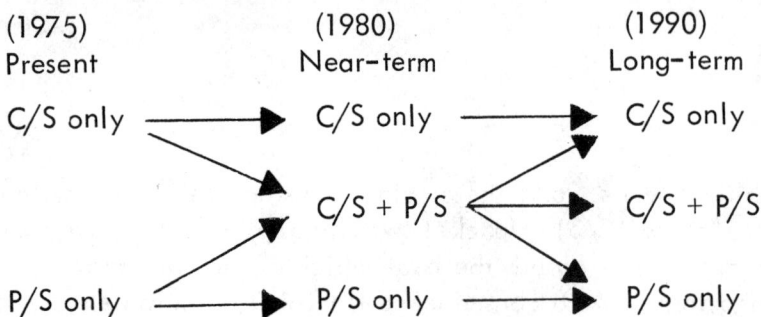

(1975) Present	(1980) Near-term	(1990) Long-term
C/S only	C/S only	C/S only
	C/S + P/S	C/S + P/S
P/S only	P/S only	P/S only

A network employing only circuit switching today may require both techniques in the long-term future (e.g. 1990) as new users with new requirements want to attach to the network.   Conversely, a presently planned packet switched network may no longer require any packet switching by 1990 as all users may have changed their needs for circuit switching facilities only.   Or, of course, all users attaching to a circuit-switched network at present may never require any other switching facility.

As a consequence, flexibility should be a primary objective for the near term design.   A solution must be found which allows migration into the best, still undetermined future solution, be it circuit switching, packet switching, or both. The approach proposed to meet this objective is integration of circuit switching and packet switching into a single public network.   Any required mix of circuit switched and packet switched traffic shall be provided for.   Each subscriber will have his own choice whether to use the circuit switched or the packet switched facilities according to costs and performance.

We base the <u>strategy for a solution</u> on the perception that circuit switching is a traditionally existing service, offering a large number of facilities which are prerequisites for implementing packet switching. We thus achieve integration by establishing P/S as an expansion of the C/S network. Economy and efficiency dictate that a maximum of functions and resources required by both methods shall be shared. The remaining portion of packet switching facilities must be a minimum $\triangle$. The integrated public network concept we strive for can thus be formulated as:

$$P/S = C/S + \triangle \, , \ P/S \cap C/S = large, \ \triangle = small.$$

Integration in a public data network encompasses a number of problem areas, such as:
- Network Architecture
- Network User Interface
- Network Management
- Trunk Multiplexing
- Switching Node

The network concept $P/S = C/S + \triangle$ can be applied to each of these problem areas.

This report addresses the problems concerning the <u>switching node</u>. A novel node concept is presented which – analogous to the integrated network concept – achieves packet switching as an expansion of its basic circuit switching node structure. Any integrated traffic mix up to about 1200 packets/sec or 2 Mbits/sec can be handled.

The next chapter discusses the first major concept of this structure, the separation of functions like connection set-up and node control, communications-link access, and packet processing, into groups of separated modules; chapter 3 deals with the second significant concept of the presented new node structure: the avoidance of throughput saturation arising from both the requirements of high throughput and modularity.

2. PRINCIPLE OF INTEGRATION

2.1 Integrated Network Concept

In this section a network solution according to the strategy outlined in the preceeding chapter will be introduced in several steps.

The most straightforward solution is to provide completely separate networks for circuit switching (C/S) and packet switching (P/S) as indicated in Figure 1a, where the transmission lines, the switching nodes, the functions available and the access to the networks are clearly separated. Obviously, such a solution does not comply with the strategy suggested, since P/S is not achieved as an expansion of C/S.

Shared access to the networks for C/S - and P/S - users (Figure 1b) is a first step to overcome the shortcomings of the previous solution. The transmission and switching resources, however, are still separated. The access to the P/S network is achieved via C/S-channels. Similar approaches, to expand C/S-networks by adding to the network a separate P/S-facility which can be accessed through C/S-channels, have been suggested by several countries (1, 2).

A further step towards maximizing function/resource sharing between C/S and P/S and minimizing Δ is shown in Figure 1c. There, in addition to the shared network access, the transmission resources are fully integrated and only the control and switching facilities are separated (3, 4).

Finally, a fully integrated solution (Figure 1d), featuring:
(i)   Shared access to the network
(ii) Shared transmission resources, and
(iii) Shared control and switching functions,
promises to yield the smallest increment Δ for those P/S facilities which cannot be shared with C/S. At the same time, any traffic mix (C/S and P/S) can be accommodated, since the full integration allows a flexible assignment of the network resources (trunks, nodal storage capacity, nodal processor power) according to the momentary demand.

2.2 Integrated Node Concept

The concept of an integrated network meets the objective stated in the first chapter: to provide a near-term network solution which can migrate into the best, presently still unknown, future network solution. The strategy which has been applied to arrive at the network concept will now be adapted to a switching node in such a network:
-   Achieve P/S based on C/S
-   P/S = C/S + Δ
-   Maximize function/resource sharing between C/S and P/S
-   Minimize in the non-shared P/S facilities Δ.

Before developing the node concept proper, the design decisions will briefly be discussed which came from the other problem areas listed in chapter 1 but have an impact on the node structure. (i) A connection is defined as the agreement between two users, i.e., terminal-host or terminal-terminal, to communicate via a communications link provided by the network. (ii) A call consists of three distinct phases: call set-up phase, data phase and disconnect phase. (iii) In the C/S case a user signals to the network during the call set-up phase and provides the network with information, which (after processing) results in the establishment of a real channel between both ends. (iv) P/S and C/S have common call set-up/disconnect procedures. (v) In the P/S case a user signals to the network during the call set-up phase in the same way as a C/S-user, and provides the network with information which relieves him from sending path information in the data phase. As opposed to a real channel in the C/S case, in P/S a virtual channel is set up.

Assumption of a virtual channel implies that the network has obtained information for resource allocations prior to the data phase.   Message delimiters, identifiers and information for the control of the packet flow are received during the data phase by means of the packet headers.   The possibility exists of also implementing P/S with a service mode not requiring the establishment of a virtual channel prior to the data phase.   Each packet then contains all necessary information for performing resource management and the routing and switching functions. Whereas the node concept presented here easily accomplishes the handling of such a service mode we concentrate our attention on the more general case of P/S services which require establishment of a virtual channel.

The first possibility of an integrated switching node is depicted in Figure 2a.   The assumptions of a common call management for both switching techniques and of the traffic integration on trunk lines allow the sharing of functions and resources in the communications processor and in the communications link access module (represented by the cross hatched areas).   As has been indicated, the assumption of a common call management and the notion of a virtual channel come from other problem areas, i.e., the user-network interface.   It is interesting to realize that the condition of maximising function/resource sharing between C/S and P/S in the switching node would lead to the same assumptions, independently from other areas.

The increment $\triangle$ has a software and a hardware component.   The software component consists of the storage management for packets and of the programs necessary for packet processing.   The hardware component consists of both additional storage space and processing power.

Due to the virtual channel concept for P/S, the packet handling functions to be performed in the data phase are very simple, but the load imposed on the communications processor by these functions can constitute a substantial part of the total workload.   Based on these facts, it can be shown (section 2.3) that the $\triangle$ required for P/S can best be achieved by a configuration as shown in Figure 2b.

The main characteristic of the configuration depicted in Figure 2b is the separation of the packet processing/storage module from the node controller.   Three modules can be distinguished in the structure:
- Communications Link Access Module (CAM)
- Node Control Module (NCM)
- Intermediate Storage Module (ISM).

The Communications Link Access Module (CAM) interfaces a variety of communications links, such as multiplexed trunk lines of various speeds, non-multiplexed lines and local loops to the node.   It contains the necessary logic and registers for exchanging data and control information with the other modules.

The Node Control Module (NCM) contains the software necessary to perform connection management and to monitor a connection. At the same time, it contains all node control functions, the routing algorithms, as well as auxiliary functions for accounting, logging, etc. Also, the NCM's error control procedures will be called upon to handle failures or other abnormal conditions in the ISM or CAM which cannot be managed by these modules alone.

The Intermediate Storage Module (ISM) provides buffer storage and processing capability for packet switching in the data phase.

All modules interconnect via the Information Transfer Bus (ITB). External data and control information as well as node internal control information and data are transferred over the same bus.

In the remaining part of this section the nodal operation in the C/S and P/S-mode will briefly be described.

C/S-mode.   During the call set-up/disconnect phase the dialogue between user and node, besides the CAM's, primarily involves the NCM. At the end of the call set-up phase a real channel has been established through the network. This means for each node involved that the registers of the CAM's concerned have been loaded with addresses in order to route the C/S data flow through the node. It is an important feature of the solution that once the channel has been set-up the data flow is completely managed by the CAM's without intervention by the NCM (see dashed line in Figure 2c).

P/S-mode.   During the call set-up phase the dialogue between user and node, subsequently referred to as source node, is the same as for C/S. At the end of the call set-up phase a virtual channel has been established between both ends, i.e., between the caller attached to the source node and the callee attached to the destination node.   The NCM in the source node provided its ISM with all information necessary to build packet headers, allocated buffer space for one packet and loaded the address of the buffer into an address register in the CAM which handles the incoming line.   In the destination node a buffer area for that particular virtual connection has been allocated as well.   Transit nodes (i.e., the nodes between source and destination nodes in a packet's path) are left unaware of the virtual channel established.

Data are assumed to be transmitted in blocks between the user and the source node, where the block size may be less, equal or greater than the maximum packet size.   The ISM in the source node detects the beginning of a message, assembles a packet, builds the header and dispatches the packet on the appropriate outgoing line.   In the case of message blocks being greater than a packet, it also allocates additional buffer space.   The ISM in a transit node detects the beginning of a packet, allocates buffer space, stores the packet, checks for transmission errors, analyzes the header and dispatches the packet.   The ISM in a destination node detects the beginning of a packet, stores the packet, checks for transmission errors, analyses the header and delivers the packets of the same message in correct sequence to the destination. It has to be pointed out that also for P/S, the NCM is not involved during the data phase provided no failures occur (solid line in Figure 2c).

2.3 Separation of Packet Handling Functions from Node Control Functions

For the 1980's, high data rates are expected. A packet rate, averaged over all industry sectors, of about .07 packets/s (in and out) can be derived from data projected in the Eurodata Study (5) for 1985. A larger European country may have around 220×10^3 terminals and between 10 and 30 switching nodes at this time. This results in throughput requirements for a node which may well be above 2 Mbit/s or 1200 packets/s (packet length 1600 bits).

Figure 3 represents a map of the communications processor shown in Figure 2a: the processor modules (several will be necessary), the major software modules, tables, and data storage space. Software modules are executive systems (multi-processor scheduler, storage management, I/O-handler, language processors), utility programs (diagnostics, statistics, error recovery procedures), switching and routing functions and the packet handling functions in the data phase (packet assembly/disassembly, packet dispatching, header analysis, header editing).

A detailed investigation of the major functions to be performed for packet handling in the data phase shows that: (i) the functions are very simple from a computational point of view (primarily table look ups, read in/out of buffers, comparisons), (ii) there is a great number of identical tasks to be executed at the same time, (iii) the tasks have short execution times, ranging from about .5 to 5 ms, (iv) the tasks are independent and disjoint, i.e. they operate only on private data and are not synchronized.

An expected packet throughput in the order of 1200 packets/s imposes on a communications processor a workload in the order of 6 to 7 MIPS not counting overhead. This is a very high figure, usually only encountered in large scientific data processing systems. A way must be found to accommodate this workload requirement at a fraction of the costs of a large scale computer. The properties of the major functions listed above in addition to the very high workload suggest a solution: splitting off the packet handling functions(Figure 2b).

Separating the packet handling functions from the other node functions (control functions, connection management, error recovery functions, auxiliary functions) and executing them in a separate module has several advantages:
- Avoids wasting of expensive processor cycles on simple operations.
- Reduces the size and/or the number of node control modules.
- Requires only a simple processor for packet handling due to the fact that the packet processing tasks are short, simple and independent from each other. A simple processor also is a point of great importance to LSI technology.
- A few executive routines suffice; no complicated operating system is needed. Short routines save programming expenses since it is well-known that

programming costs per instruction increase with the size of a program (6).
- Increased reliability: simple programs and simple procedures are less doom-
  ed to failure.   Furthermore, a structure with separated functions is capable
  of continuing the operation on connections already established, even with
  all node control processors disabled.

3.   MODULAR PACKET HANDLING TECHNIQUE FOR HIGH DATA THROUGHPUT

3.1 Modular Packet Handling

The "single" ISM approach shown in Figures 2b and 2c, and discussed in the preceeding chapter has several disadvantages:

- The processor must be very powerful in terms of processing speed, since it
  has to be capable of handling the whole range of throughput requirements.
- There is no modularity and, consequently,
- System expansion is not easy, and
- Reliability is still weak, since an ISM failure can stop the whole P/S opera-
  tion.

In order to overcome these disadvantages, the packet handling capability has to
be provided in modular form.   At the same time, the $\triangle$ necessary for packet
switching will be further reduced.   The resulting node structure is represented
in Figure 4a.

The functions performed in the node control module (NCM) and in the communications link access modules (CAM) are the same as outlined in section 2.2.   The
information transfer bus (ITB) interconnects all modules.   It employs a decentralized bus control with a daisy chain scheme, a flexible priority structure, asynchronous bus communication and fixed length blocks for the information transfer.
The bandwidth of the bus is designed to be sufficient for all potential needs.

The intermediate storage modules (ISM) now consist of very small and simple processors built into a storage module.   Such a step is suggested by the particular
workload characteristics: the many identical and independent tasks lend themselves quite readily for parallel execution by identical programs in identical
parallel operating modules.   The modularity allows an easy adaptation of the
number of ISM's to the workload to be processed and also satisfies the requirement for reliability.

We will now briefly discuss the packet switching operation for a transit connection via the trunk lines A, B (see Figure 4b).   When the first character of a
packet arrives at CAM 2 via trunk A, CAM 2 sends a request① to ISM 2 to
allocate the required buffer for that particular trunk.   If the request can be
satisfied, an acknowledgement ② containing the buffer address will be sent back
to the originating CAM.   Any further characters are immediately forwarded to
ISM 2 to be read into the buffer ③.   Once the entire packet has been assem-

bled, ISM 2 performs error and sequence checks, analyses the packet header in order to obtain the number of the outgoing trunk and, finally, signals a "ready to readout" ④ to ISM 3.   Once trunk B is ready, CAM 3 sends a request ⑤ to ISM 3 which indicates that a next packet can be placed on the trunk.   Subsequently a request for packet ⑥ will be forwarded to ISM 2.   The packet is sent from ISM 2 to CAM 3 character by character ⑦ and ISM 3 is informed of the first character transfer by a message ⑧ .   ISM 3 receives an acknowledgement ⑨ as soon as the packet is properly transferred to the next node.   It then releases the buffer ⑩ in ISM 2.

3.2 Solution to Throughput Saturation

3.2.1   Definition of Throughput Saturation

The high throughput demand for the packet-switched traffic together with the requirement of modularity may lead to node configurations with up to thirty or forty ISM's.   This raises the problem of operating a great number of modules such that the well-known saturation effect of multiprocessor systems does not occur, at least not in the range of throughput values to be considered here.   Subsequently, we will focus on this problem and develop a distributed control concept to over-come the saturation effect of the ISM's.   Questions concerning either the node control module (NCM) or the communications link access modules (CAM) will no longer be discussed.

The saturation effect is defined as: decreasing incremental throughput per addi-tional processor with an increasing number of processors.   When a new processor is added to the system, the throughput increases by the processing power of the new processor but, at the same time, is also reduced by the additional overhead of exchanging information (communicating) with it.   The saturation point is reached when the additional overhead outweighs the gained throughput.

3.2.2   Existing Approaches

Existing approaches to multisystems are all known to show throughput saturation. The first type of multisystems, multiprocessor systems, is usually encountered in general purpose computers like (7, 8, 9).   Multiprocessor systems are composed of processor and centralized memory modules which can be freely interconnected depending on the processing requirements.   A common executive system with centralized scheduler, storage management, tables, etc., "covers" all modules and makes them appear as an entity.   Using the abbreviations and conventions introduced in Figure 3, Figure 5a schematically shows this approach.

The overhead leading to throughput saturation is caused first of all by processor delays due to access conflicts to the various memory units shared by all processors. The relatively small number of different program modules and tables required for packet handling were to be used by all processors.   This either requires reentrant usage of programs, thereby increasing access conflicts considerably, or the use of many copies of the same programs.   The latter possibility, however, is not in accordance with the idea of shared memories and rather points towards multicomputer structures which will be discussed below. If cache memories were to be used in order to reduce the amount of memory accesses, the well-known multiple copy problem would tremendously increase the overhead. Secondly, overhead is caused by the executive system which (i) has to schedule all processors, (ii) has to manage all resources and (iii) is responsible for synchronizing the usage of programs and tables.

This has the consequence that if the high throughput in the order of 1200 packets/s has to be achieved, the processors have to be very powerful in order to keep the number of modules small. Obviously, this is contradictory to the desired modularity and to the simplicity of the packet handling functions. Therefore, such an approach has to be ruled out.

A second type of multisystems, multicomputer systems, is usually encountered in special purpose applications such as avionics (10). An idealized multicomputer strucutre where all modules are completely autonomous is represented in Figure 5b. Each module contains all information which is necessary to perform any task, or to be more specific, to handle any pair of incoming/outgoing lines. The executive system residing in each module is much simpler as compared to the one which is necessary in the multiprocessor configuration because (1) it has to control a single processor configuration and (2) the functions to be performed are very simple. The notion of completely autonomous modules implies that each module needs up-to-date information on all lines. Therefore, such a configuration is characterized by an extremely high amount of overhead due to an extensive exchange of information among all modules in order to keep them up-to-date and to have them prepared for taking any action on any packet or on any line. Again, the overhead causes saturation.

3.3.3   New Approach

a)   Outline of Basic Concept

The key to the solution consists of finding ways to reduce the overhead, i.e., to find an appropriate structure between the two extremes outlined in the previous section: avoiding both a common executive system and a pure multicomputer configuration with completely autonomous modules.

The essential idea of the new approach is depicted in Figure 5c. In contrast to the multicomputer structure Figure 5b, autonomy of each module is deliberately kept incomplete. This means each module has the capability of performing all packet handling functions in the data phase provided the operational data were available. The complexity of the executive system, the code required for the packet handling functions and the space for the major tables are the same for the multicomputer configuration and the new solution. Each module, however, only contains operational data pertaining to lines it is handling at this moment. Figure 5c represents this by the smaller data areas and by the thinner arrows for intermodule communications.

The idea of keeping the autonomy of each Intermediate Storage Module (ISM) incomplete provides the basis for drastically reducing overhead: only two modules are involved in handling the switching of a particular packet. Intermodule communications are reduced to the cooperation of two processor modules. They are referred to as <u>pairwise cooperating</u> modules. The first module referred to as "packet processing ISM" provides <u>buffer space</u> for the packet to be handled and performs the <u>processing</u> required for accepting data from the incoming channel, assembling the packet, analysing and editing the packet header, and for releasing the data. The second module referred to as "associated ISM" is responsible for <u>controlling</u> the dispatching of the packet on an outgoing channel after the first module has signalled a "ready for readout". The packet data itself is routed directly from the packet processing ISM to the communications line attachment without ever being moved through the associated ISM. A significant source of overhead, the moving of packet data within the processor is thus ruled out.

As each ISM handles a multitude of connections at a time it is evident that each ISM must be capable of performing both functions, packet processing and controlling the dispatching, simultaneously. Subsequently, we refer to these two functional capabilities as packet processing and associated (controlling) mode. Mode assignment for a particular pair of ISM's is always with respect to a particular connection (i.e. it only makes sense to talk about a pair of cooperating modules with respect to a particular connection).

Intermodule communications has been reduced to the cooperation of two modules, making them an autonomous pair for a particular connection. Hence, the number of information exchanges and the amount of information transferred during each information exchange has become nearly independent of the total number of ISM-modules attached to the system. The overall system overhead has been significantly reduced. As a consequence, the system throughput for fixed processor utilization is nearly a linear function of the number of modules, the deviation being less than 10% over the range of interest as will be shown in section 3.3.3. The significant result of this is that we can achieve the modularity desired, that we can use many modules of modest processing power instead of a few powerful processors and – at the same time – that we are not restricted by the saturation effect.

b. Allocation of Modules

The node control module (NCM) originally assigns to every ISM the mode of associated ISM with respect to a group of one or more communications link access modules (CAM's). In the example represented in Figure 6a to 6c, the following associations are assumed: ISM 1 associated to CAM 1 and CAM 2, ISM 2 associated to CAM 3, ISM 3 associated to CAM 4 and ISM 4 associated to CAM 5 and CAM 6. The mode of associated ISM remains permanently assigned with respect to a group of CAM's and is only changed or cancelled in case of ISM failure or

significant changes of the workload.   Assignments are made on the basis of obtaining as equal a load distribution as possible.

An associated ISM is responsible for managing the outbound traffic for a particular connection leaving the node via CAM and communication line assigned to it.
It is important to note that the associated mode implies only supervisory but no
packet processing functions.

Packet processing ISM's in cooperating pairs are responsible for managing the incoming traffic.   They are appointed for local lines (source and destination) when
a virtual connection is set-up, for low speed trunk lines when the first character
of a packet arrives and for high speed trunk lines when the trunk becomes active.
Subsequently, we will consider three examples for appointing an ISM as packet
processing ISM for a particular connection.

The CAM handling the incoming line, CAM 2 in Figure 6a, first sends a resource
request block (= request for buffer) to the ISM associated to it.   Provided the
request can be satisfied, the address of the buffer area (page address) is sent back
to the originating CAM.   By virtue of this action ISM 1 is considered as packet
processing ISM for that particular connection.

Since it has been assumed that the outgoing line is attached to CAM 4, ISM 3 is
assigned as the associated partner in the pair.

In Figure 6b, the incoming line is attached to CAM 5.   In order to assign a packet processing ISM, CAM 5 sends a resource request block to ISM 4 which has
been associated to it.   Suppose the request cannot be met.   Then ISM 4 forwards
the resource request block to ISM 3 or in other words the request overflows from
ISM 4 to ISM 3.   If the request can be satisfied there, as assumed in Figure 6b,
ISM 3 is the packet processing ISM for that particular incoming line.   The appropriate buffer address is loaded into CAM 5 so that data can be sent to ISM 3 without involving ISM 4 further.   In the case that ISM 3 has no buffer available, the
request overflows to ISM 2, etc.   The policy of sending the resource request
block to the respective associated ISM first, prevents overloading of certain
ISM's and distributes the load equally.   The operation of forwarding requests
which overflow to the next ISM is identical to a loop operation.   We therefore
denote it as overflow loop.   Note, that overflow activities beyond a certain
threshold – they occur when congestion builds up in the node – will be prevented
by a flow control mechanism residing in the NCM.   Finally, it has to be pointed
out that the same ISM, ISM 3 in Figures 6a and 6b, simultaneously can act as
associated and packet processing ISM in different pairs.

It also may occur that a connection involves a single CAM only as shown in
Figure 6c.   Provided the first request for buffer space can be met, ISM 3 hosts
associated and packet processing ISM for a connection.   The interaction between
the pair takes place in a single module.

3.3 Calculation of Throughput

3.3.1 General Outline

The objective of section 3.3 is to calculate the throughput of the multiple ISM configuration suggested in the previous section as a function of the number of ISM-modules.   If no overhead existed the relationship would strictly be a linear function.   Therefore, the method to find the actual relationship between through-put and number of modules is to determine the overhead occurring when the con-figuration is operated under a certain workload.

In the context of the following discussion overhead is understood as the number of instructions executed per unit time due to the fact that more than one ISM-mod-ule is involved in handling a particular packet.   We can distinguish between three different sources of overhead:

(1)   Overhead due to ISM-ISM communication (communication between cooper-ating pairs).   This overhead comprises all those actions which were not necessary if a single module would be sufficient to handle a particular packet or in other words if no communication between corresponding data areas (see Figure 5c, 6) were necessary: prepare message for other ISM, send message, receive message, interpret message, etc.   By means of flowcharts the average overhead is found to be in the order of 600 ISM instructions for each packet handled(*).

(2)   Overhead due to ISM-NCM communication (communication between associ-ated ISM and NCM).   Because of the separation of the packet handling functions in the data phase from the node control functions residing in the NCM some com-munication is required between these modules which otherwise was not necessary: for each packet handled a message is sent from an associated ISM to the NCM. Accordingly, the NCM sends an acknowledgement back which has to be received and interpreted.   The overhead per packet is in the order of 90 ISM instructions. Additionally, the NCM updates the routing tables in all ISM's every 500 ms. However, the overhead caused by this activity can be disregarded for our present purpose.

(3)   Overhead due to ISM-storage overflow.   If a request for packet buffer space cannot be satisfied by a particular ISM, say ISM No. i, then this ISM will issue a new request and send it to its neighbour ISM, ISM No. i+1.   If the request can-not be satisfied by ISM No. i+1, it will be passed on to ISM No. i+2, etc.   In this case the overhead consists of actions like unsuccessful buffer search, issue new request for buffer, interpret request in next ISM, buffer search in next ISM, etc.

3.3.2 Overflow Model

In order to obtain the overhead due to ISM-storage overflow quantitatively, an analytical model will be used which is known in traffic theory for the dimension-ing of alternate routes in telephone networks (12).   The model will only yield

---

*   This relatively high number is due to handling intermodule message blocks with a very primitive instruction set.

approximate results. Its limitations will be explicitly discussed.

The model is represented in Figure 7.   Request for buffer space arriving originally at ISM No. i, that is, not overflowing from another ISM, constitute a statistical process.   These requests come from two different sources: requests for the establishment of virtual channels and requests from trunk lines.   For the present investigation each of these request streams is assumed to be of the Poisson type. Consequently, the traffic A_p originally offered to ISM No. i is (11).

$$A_p = \lambda_{vc} \cdot b_{vc} + \lambda_T \cdot b_T \tag{1}$$

where λ_{vc}:   mean request rate for establishment of virtual channels

λ_T: mean request rate from trunks

b_{vc}:   mean buffer holding time due to virtual channel request

b_T: mean buffer holding time due to trunk request.

Furthermore, we assume that the composite buffer holding time distribution is negative exponential.

An overflow from ISM No. i to ISM No. i+1 occurs if a new buffer request cannot be satisfied since all n packet buffer-pages are already allocated. The overflow traffic is bursty and will be characterized by its mean value R_i and by its variance coefficient D_i, i.e., variance minus mean value (12):

$$R_i = A_p \cdot \frac{A_p^n / n!}{\sum_{i=0}^{n} A_p^i / i!} \tag{2}$$

$$D_i = R_i \cdot \left(\frac{A_p}{n+1 - A_p + R_i} - R_i \right) \tag{3}$$

Now, the traffic offered to ISM No. i+1 consists of the traffic A_p originally offered and of the traffic R_i overflowing from ISM No. i.   The variance coefficient of the traffic A_p is zero, since it is assumed to be of the Poisson type.   Therefore, the total traffic offered to ISM No. i+1 can be characterized by:

$$R = A_p + R_i \tag{4}$$

$$D = D_i \tag{5}$$

The probability that ISM No. i+1 will overflow is given by:

$$B_{i+1} = \frac{R_{i+1}}{R} \tag{6}$$

where R_{i+1} is the traffic overflowing from ISM No. i+1.

The goal of the overflow calculation was to obtain the overflow probability B_{i+1} since it can be used as a weight for calculating the number of instructions executed per unit time due to ISM-storage overflow. At this point several comments seem appropriate in order to clarify the accuracy and the shortcomings of the model:

- The overflow probability B_{i+1} will be used for each ISM.
- In reality ISM No. i does not only receive the traffic A_p but overflow traffic from ISM No. i-1 as well. Therefore, the overflow probability B_{i+1} is somewhat optimistic. The accuracy, however, can be considered adequate as long as $B_{i+1} < 0.05$. For greater values the model has to be refined.
- The fact that multiple overflow can occur is not taken into account in this model. This again can be justified for $B_{i+1} < 0.05$. As will be discussed later, an appreciable amount of multiple overflow will significantly reduce the throughput.

3.3.3 Numerical Examples

In this section some numerical examples are presented. The assumptions are listed below and in Table 1. The results are compiled in Figure 8.

Assumptions

- ISM processor speed: 500,000 instructions/s.
- ISM memory sizes: 48 K Byte, 64 K Byte, 96 K Byte.
- ISM processor utilization: approximately 60% in order to meet response time requirements.
- Packet rate per terminal (in and out): 0.07 packets/s.
- Packet length: 1600 bit.
- Traffic balance: the locally generated traffic stays to 30% local, 70% are long distance traffic going out. Both the long distance traffic arriving and being destined for the node considered and the transit traffic equal the long distance traffic generated locally.
- The traffic A_p (see equ. (1)) originally offered per ISM is $A_p = 54.6$ Erl.
- The following table contains the number n of buffer pages available in each ISM for storing packets when the memory sizes stated above are assumed and when various assumptions about the total number of terminals attached, or what is a consequence of that, about the total throughput required are made.

3.3.4 Discussion of Results

The ideal throughput characteristic is a strictly linear function without any limitation with respect to the number of modules. Unfortunately, such a characteristic cannot be realized because of intermodule communications overhead.

The throughput characteristic of the multiple ISM solution suggested in section 3.2.3 holds under the assumption that all tasks to be performed in each ISM have

Total no. of Terminals	1000	2000	5000	10000	20000
Total Throughput Packets/s	80	160	400	800	1600
Total no. of ISM's	2	4	10	20	40
Storage required for programs per ISM in K byte	32	32	32	32	32
Buffer pool in K Byte	4	4	4	4	4
48 K Byte memory; Storage required for tables K Byte	2	3.5	6.5	11.5	23.5
Number n of pages per ISM	40	34	22	2	-
64 K Byte memory; Storage required for tables K Byte	2.5	4	7	12	24
Number n of pages per ISM	102	96	84	64	16
96 K Byte memory; Storage required for tables K Byte	3.5	5	8	13	25
Number n of pages per ISM	226	220	208	188	140

TABLE 1:　Assumptions

the properties discussed in section 2.3. The solid line holds for an ISM memory size of 96 K Byte, the upper dashed line for an ISM memory size of 64 K Byte and the lower dotted line for an ISM memory size of 48 K Bytes. Note that the solid and the upper dashed lines coincide for the range of up to 20 ISM modules.

The significant result is that the throughput characteristic is almost a linear function of the number of modules, the deviation being not greater than 10% for up to 20 modules in the case of a 64 K Byte memory or for at least 40 modules in the case of a 96 Byte memory. However, in contrast to the ideal throughput curve, the number of intermediate storage modules cannot be increased unlimitedly.

The purpose of increasing the number of ISM's to provide additional throughput capability if more terminals and trunk lines are to be attached or, in other words, more traffic has to be handled. As can be seen from the Table 1, the number of pages per ISM which is available for storing packets decreases with a growing number of terminals and lines. The reason therefore lies in the fact that with a growing number of terminals and lines the tables contained in each ISM grow as well and, as a consequence, reduce the amount of buffer space for a given memory size. Fewer pages for storing packets, on the other hand imply a higher probability of ISM buffer overflow. Since the load has been assumed to be equally distributed among all ISM's, the same situation holds for all modules. Moreover, the fact that the overflow model described in section 3.3.2 cannot be applied for overflow probabilities being greater than 5%, high overflow probabilities have a significant impact on the throughput characteristic.

Suppose we have a high probability for buffer storage overflow in each ISM (high meaning greater than 5 to 10%). This has two consequences: first, the traffic overflowing from a particular ISM increases and second, overflows over two or more ISM's become very likely. This, however, has two disadvantages:

(i) Significantly increased overhead due to additional communication between modules and execution of a lot of unsuccessful and time consuming search procedures. It can be expected that this additional overhead grows much more than proportionally with the number of modules.

(ii) The allocation of a buffer area has to take place within certain time constraints. In the case of multiple overflow, say if more than three ISM's were involved, it will be difficult to service the request for buffer in time.

For an ISM memory size of 48 K Bytes the probability for buffer storage overflow is greater than 50% over the whole range considered and, consequently, multiple overflow is very likely to occur frequently. Hence, the real overhead will be significantly greater than the overhead calculated according to the model in section 3.3.2. Therefore, the lower dashed curve in Figure 8 is by far too optimistic (a forthcoming report will contain more accurate results). A satisfactory operation seems to be impossible with such a memory size. For an ISM memory size of 64 K Bytes the linearity of the throughput characteristic holds until 20 to 22 modules. With an increasing number of modules the overhead due to ISM storage overflow increases more than proportionally. Again, the dashed line is too optimistic. For an ISM memory size of 96 K Bytes the saturation point definitely lies beyond 40 modules. This clearly indicates that by means of additional memory the maximum number of possible ISM modules is increased.

4. CONCLUSION

Three key ideas have been put forward in this report:

(i) It is an open question whether C/S or P/S is better suited for a future public network. The objective is to remain flexible. Proposed is the integration of C/S and P/S into a single network. Integration is achieved by packet switching based on circuit switching:

$$P/S = C/S + \triangle \quad \text{with } \triangle \text{ being a minimum.}$$

(ii) Connection set-up and node control functions, communications-link access functions, and packet processing/storing are performed by groups of functionally separated modules, similar to the integrated network concept. Functional separation:

- Avoids wasting expensive processor cycles on simple operations.
- Keeps node adjustable to changes in traffic load and traffic mix.
- Requires many simple processors but only few complex processors.
- Permits to share a maximum of functions common to C/S and P/S.
- Reduces design and programming costs.
- Increases reliability.

(iii) The saturation effect of multiprocessor systems is overcome by a distributed control concept. Packet handling modules (ISM's) are cooperating in pairs as autonomous units with respect to a particular connection. Each ISM is responsible for allocating and scheduling its own resources and is oblivious to resources allocated in other modules. Resource request blocks are dispatched directly to a required module except in the case of an overflow when resource request blocks are passed on in a loop. Intermodule communication – and therefore overhead – has been significantly reduced and is shown to be independent of the total number of modules attached to the system. Systems throughput for fixed processor module utilization is nearly a linear function of the number of modules, the deviation being less than 10% over the range considered.

5. ACKNOWLEDGEMENTS

We wish to thank Dr. E. Port and our colleagues of the Data Network Research Group, Zurich Research Laboratory, for many stimulating discussions and for reviewing the manuscript.

6. REFERENCES

1. Nippon Telegraph and Telephone Corporation, Study and Development Planning of Digital Data Switching Systems, CCITT Special Study Group D, Contribution No. 75-E, February 1974.
2. Itoh K. et al.: An Analysis of Traffic Handling Capacity of Packet Switched and Circuit-Switched Network. Proceedings of the Third Data Communications Symposium, Florida, November 1973, pp. 29-37.
3. Kümmerle, K.: Multiplexor Performance for Integrated Line- and Packet-Switched Traffic. ICCC 74, Stockholm, pp. 507-515.
4. Zafiropulo, P.: Flexible Multiplexing for Networks Supporting Line-Switched and Packet-Switched Data Traffic. ICCC 74, Stockholm, pp. 517-523.
5. European Computer and Communications Markets 1973-1985, published jointly by PA International Management Consultants and Quanterm Science Corp., London and New York, 1973.
6. Dunn, D.A. et al.: Patterns of Technology in Data Processing and Data Communications. SRI-Report No. 7379B, Menlo Park California, 1969.
7. UNIVAC 1108 Multi-Processor System. System Description. Sperry Rand UP-4046 Rev. 2, 1968.
8. Barnes, G.H., et al.: The ILLIAC IV Computer. IEEE Transactions on Computers, Vol. C-17, No. 8, August 1968, pp. 746-757.
9. Wulf, W.A. and Bell, C.G.: C. mmp – A multi-mini-processor. FJCC 1972, pp. 765-777.
10. Anderson, G.A.: Interconnecting a Distributed Processor System for Avionics. 1st Annual Symposium on Computer Architecture, University of Florida, December 9-11, 1973, pp. 11-16.
11. Cooper, R.B.: Introduction to Queueing Theory. The Macmillan Company, New York, 1972.
12. Wilkinson, R.I. and Riordon, J.: Theories for toll traffic engineering in the U.S.A. ITC 1955 and Bell Syst. Tech. J. 35 (1956), pp. 421-514.

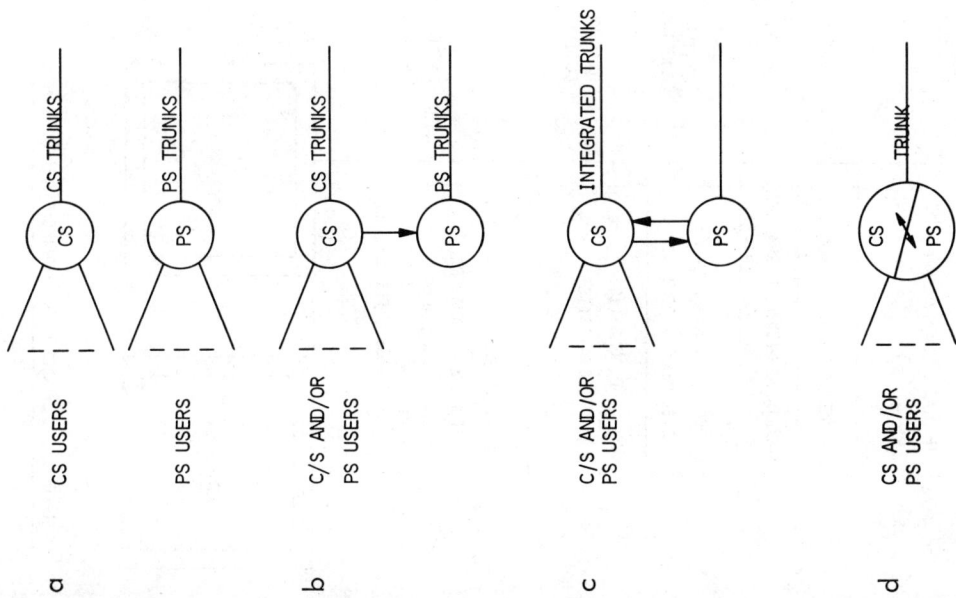

Figure 2: Integrated Switching Node

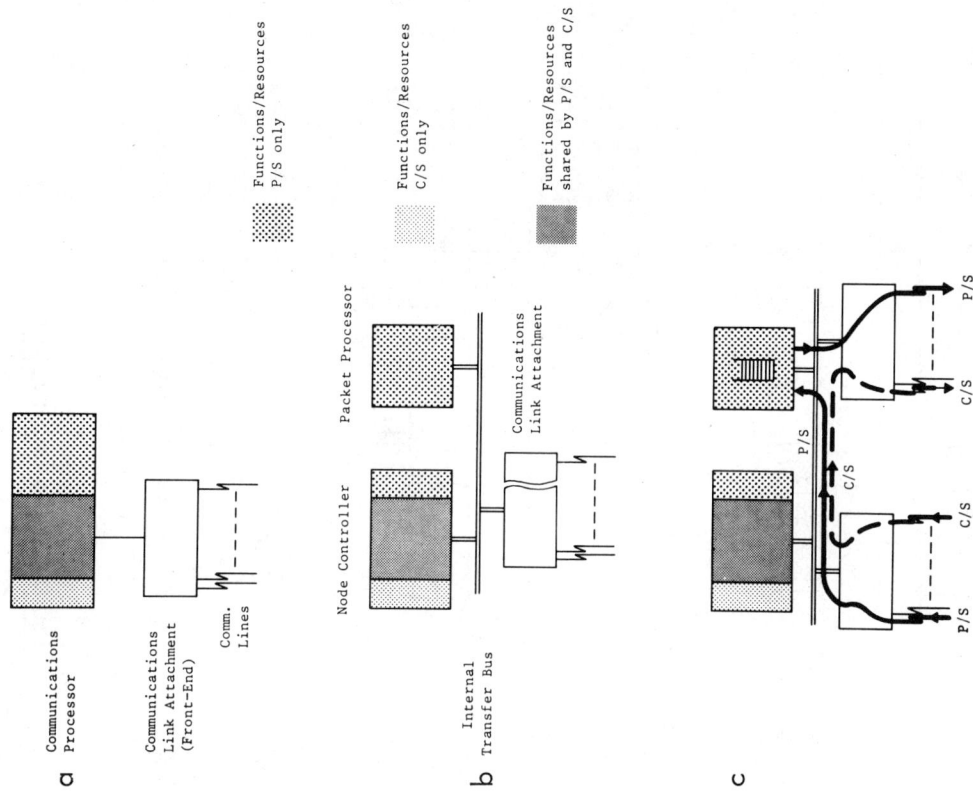

Figure 1: Integrated Network Concept

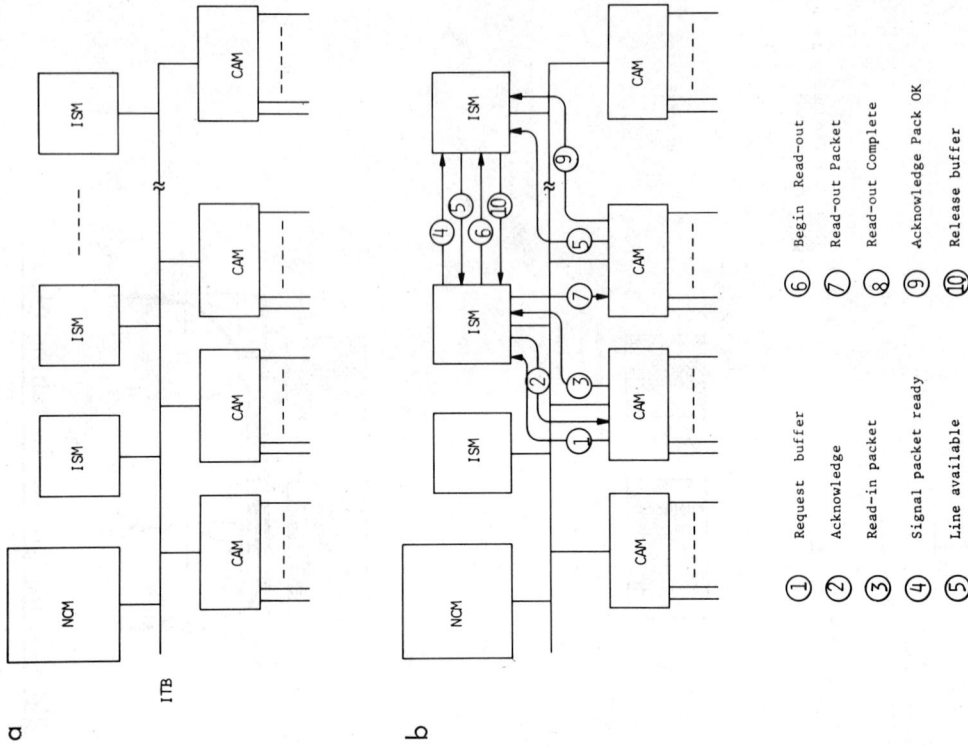

Figure 4: Node Structure

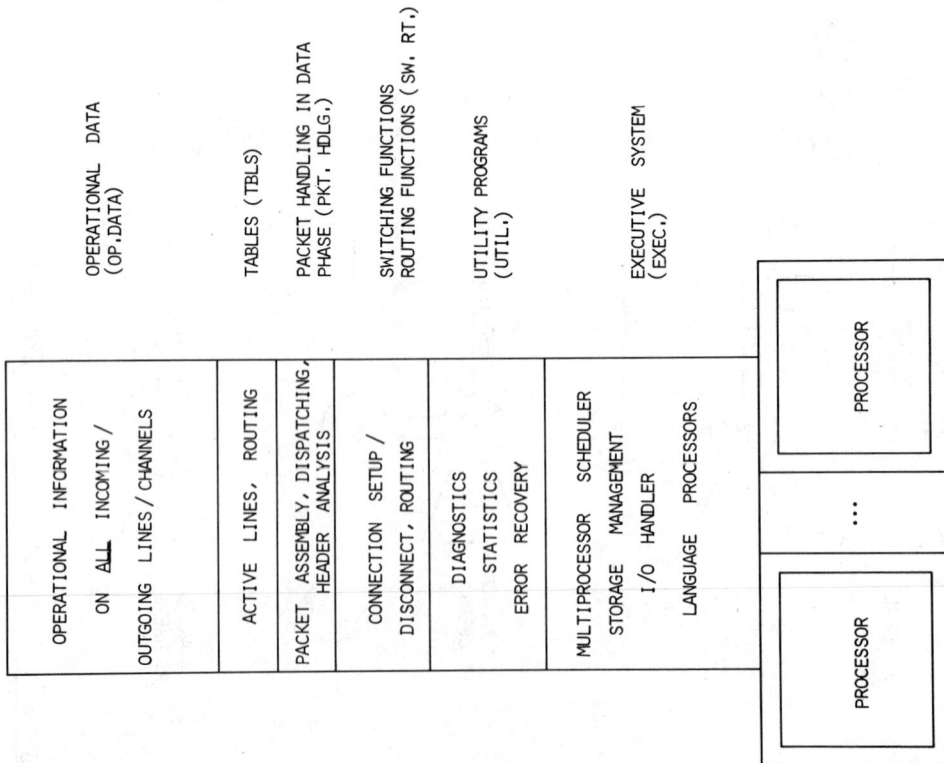

Figure 3: Organization of Functions

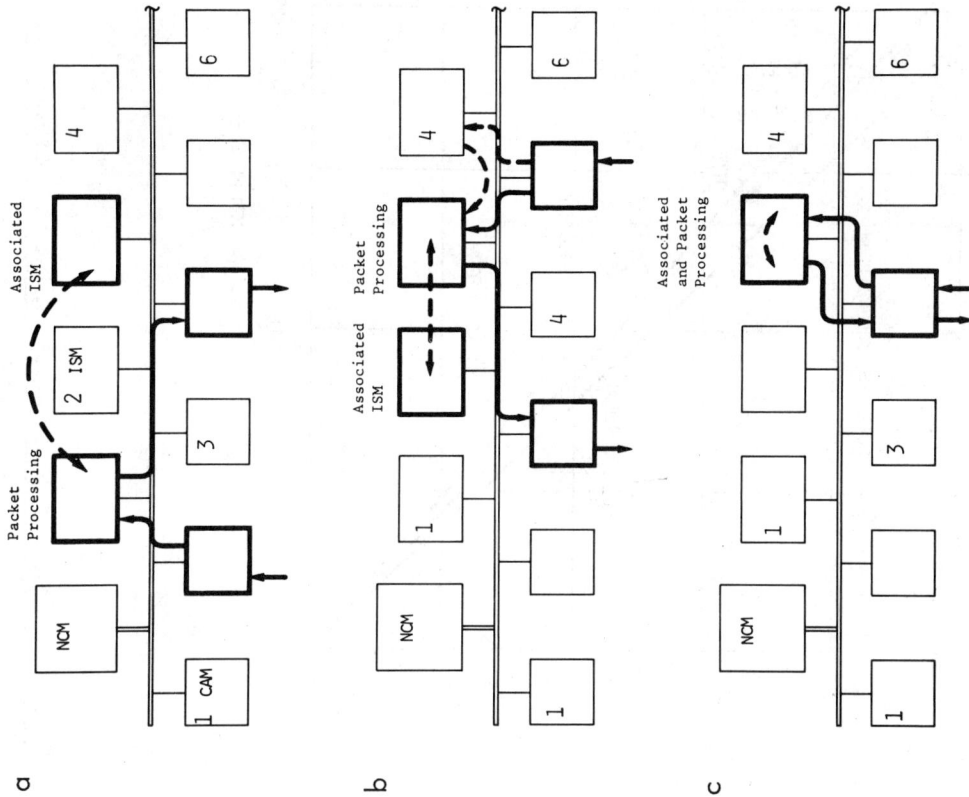

Figure 6: Examples for Pairwise Cooperation

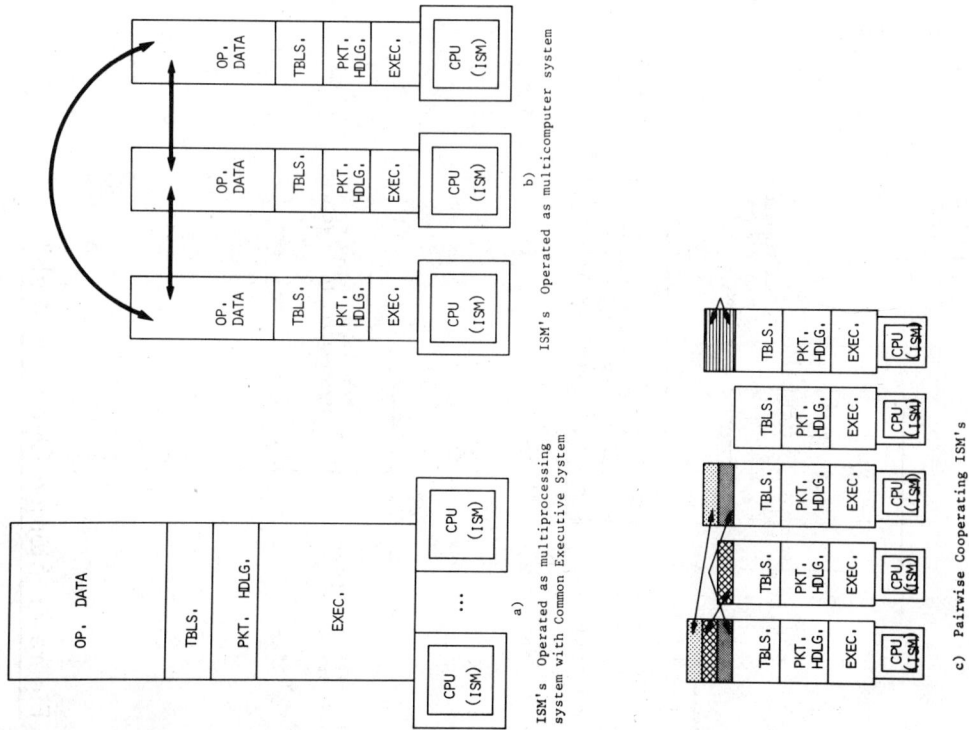

Figure 5: Multiprocessing/Multicomputer–Approach vs. Pairwise Cooperating Modules

THROUGHPUT
M BIT/s

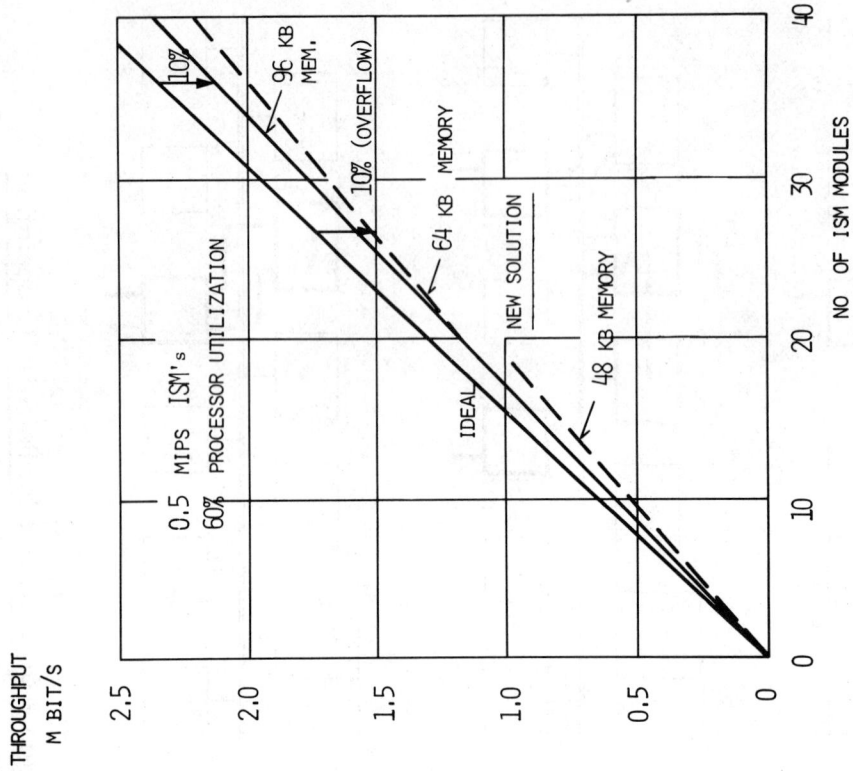

Figure 8: Relation Throughput vs. Number of Modules

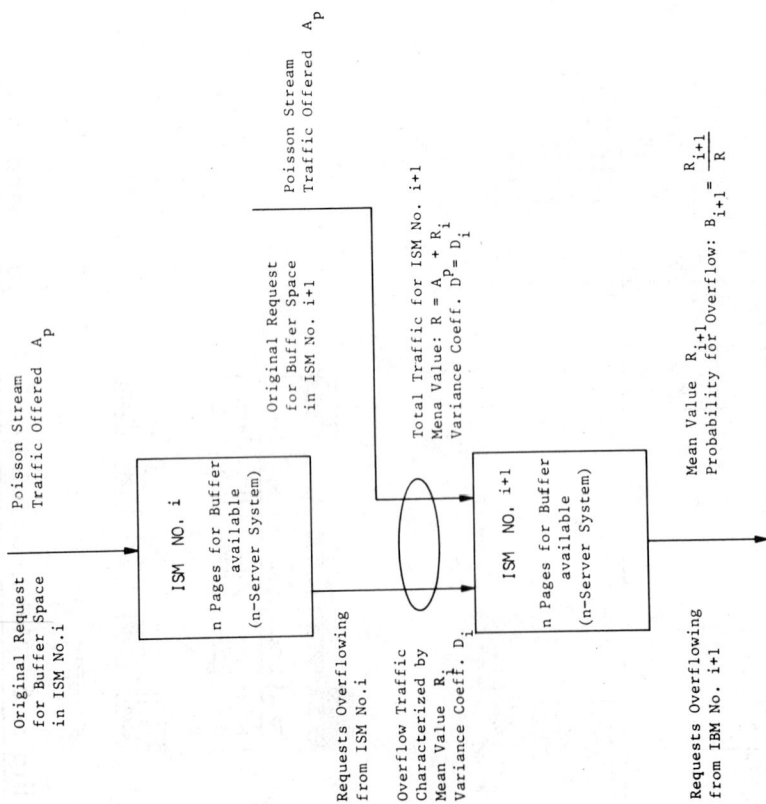

Poisson Stream
Traffic Offered A_p

Original Request
for Buffer Space
in ISM No.i

ISM NO. i

n Pages for Buffer
available
(n-Server System)

Requests Overflowing
from ISM No.i

Overflow Traffic
Characterized by
Mean Value R_i
Variance Coeff. D_i

Poisson Stream
Traffic Offered A_p

Original Request
for Buffer Space
in ISM No. i+1

Total Traffic for ISM No. i+1
Mena Value: $R = A_p + R_i$
Variance Coeff. $D^P = D_i$

ISM NO. i+1

n Pages for Buffer
available
(n-Server System)

Requests Overflowing
from IBM No. i+1

Mean Value R_{i+1}
Probability for Overflow: $B_{i+1} = \dfrac{R_{i+1}}{R}$

Figure 7: Storage Overflow Model

Euronet project

G.W.P. Davies

Commission of the European Communities
Luxembourg

Abstract:

A network (EURONET) for scientific and technical information is being
developed for the European Community. A 3-year Plan of Action
to establish EURONET is now being implemented, the goals of which
include the development of data base systems in specific subject fields,
the creation of a shared network for information handling and the
promotion of information retrieval technology. This paper describes
the main activities underway in the EURONET programme, placing particular
emphasis on the various ways in which the design is being influenced
by the wide range of requirements of the potential user population.

1.   Background

In June,1971, the Council of Ministers of the European Community
passed a Resolution with a view to "coordinating the action of the
Member States regarding scientific and technical information and
documentation". In particular, they asked the Member States to co-
operate with regard to the following areas:

(a)   the creation and rational development of systems for scientific
       and technical information and documentation, so that a European
       network could be established

(b)   the establishment or rules and procedures to ensure the
       cohesiveness of such a network

(c)   the training of specialists and the education of users

(d)   technological progress in the science and processing of
       documentation.

The Resolution further specified that the creation of the network
is to be achieved by the "most modern methods" and to provide services
"to all persons needing to use such information, under the most
favourable conditions as regards speed and expense", thereby indicating
a European-wide network making full use of modern telecommunications
and computer technology.

2.   The Action Plan

Since the original decision of the Council of Ministers, a complex
process of consultation has been undertaken between the Member States
and the Commission, the latter having been charged with the responsibility of implementing the Resolution. A special committee was established, known as the CIDST (Committee for Information and Documentation
in Science and Technology), which is composed of persons responsible for
drawing up policy on scientific and technical information in each of the
Member States together with representatives of the Commission. This
Committeehas been, and still is, central to the formulation of the
policies for implementing the Resolution and supervises the work of
various task groups set up under its auspices. However, the scope of
the Resolution was so wide that the CIDST by necessity also interacts
with many other organisational units, particularly those illustrated in
Exhibit 1 .

As a result of this consultation process, a 3-year Action Plan has been
prepared, covering the period 1975-77. The overall strategy of this
Action Plan is based on three main areas:

-    development and creation of systems in the various subject fields
     (e.g. agriculture, physics, etc.)

-    creation of a physical network for information handling

-    development of skills and tools in information technology

EXHIBIT 1
EURONET ORGANISATIONAL
RELATIONSHIPS

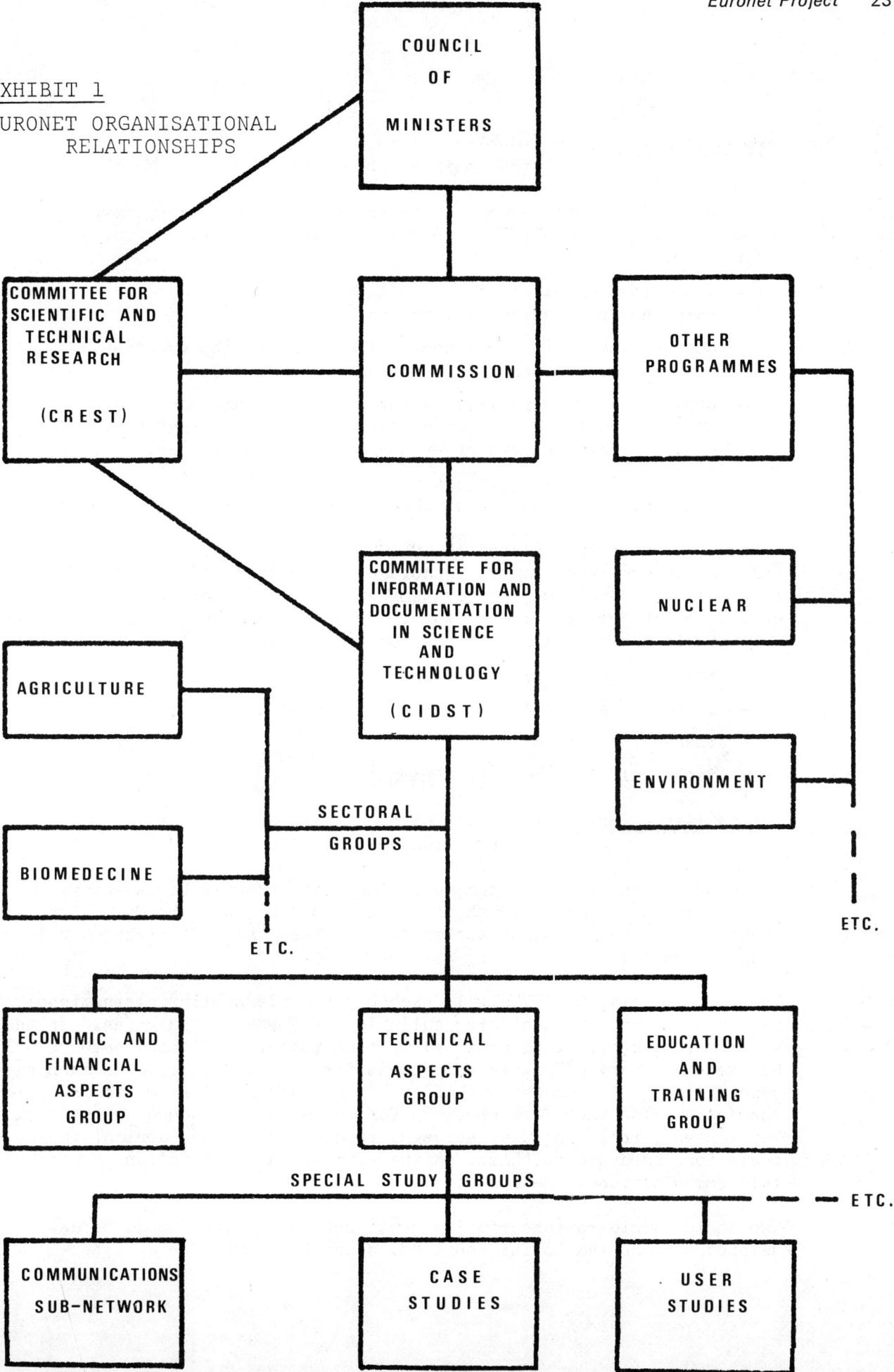

COUNCIL OF MINISTERS

COMMITTEE FOR SCIENTIFIC AND TECHNICAL RESEARCH (CREST)

COMMISSION

OTHER PROGRAMMES

COMMITTEE FOR INFORMATION AND DOCUMENTATION IN SCIENCE AND TECHNOLOGY (CIDST)

NUCLEAR

ENVIRONMENT

AGRICULTURE

BIOMEDECINE

SECTORAL GROUPS

ETC.

ETC.

ECONOMIC AND FINANCIAL ASPECTS GROUP

TECHNICAL ASPECTS GROUP

EDUCATION AND TRAINING GROUP

SPECIAL STUDY GROUPS

ETC.

COMMUNICATIONS SUB-NETWORK

CASE STUDIES

USER STUDIES

2.1   Action Plan – Part 1   (Development and creation of systems in the various subject fields)

For many subject fields, working groups exist, e.g. agriculture, environment, and the CIDST gives guidance to these groups, particularly with regard to:

- improving, adapting to common standards and rationalising existing information systems and services;

- cooperating (with other sectoral groups) in the creation of new systems and services, as and when required;

- providing better facilities for processing and accessing information and data, especially by "Europeanising" national centres and/or services, by way of European referral facilities, etc. ;

- cooperating in the use of non-Community information resources.

However, part of the role of the CIDST is to identify gaps in information provision and to encourage, where appropriate and when possible, the development of systems outside its direct influence, e.g. those of commercial operators. In addition, the Action Plan calls for work in those areas which are common to all subject fields, notably:

- indexing and retrieval tools

- inventories of data available, R&D projects, etc.

- thesauri development

- technical standards (e.g. formats).

2.2   Action Plan – Part 2   (Creation of a physical network for information handling)

Some form of physical telecommunications network will be necessary to provide the means by which users distributed among the Community countries can gain on-line access to data bases also distributed widely geographically.

In 5 to 10 years, the PTTs will probably provide public international services for data transmission suitable for EURONET's purposes. In the meantime, however, it is expected that an interim dedicated network will be needed. Every effort is being made for the PTTs to take as much responsibility in the management of such a network right from its inception. The Action Plan therefore provides for the normal processes of network development, including user surveys, feasibility study, design, implementation, hardware purchase, software creation and adaption, rental of telecommunications lines, etc.

Two basic considerations require that such facilities should be developed on a shared basis: cost and service to users.

The EURONET programme is based heavily on the practical concept
that existing systems must be the keystone to a developing network.
However, such systems themselves are tending to cause the introduction of a multiplicity of small networks to provide users with
access to them. Rough estimates indicate that if three or four
networks cover the same geographical area, the telecommunications
costs alone are more than twice that of a shared network. Savings
of a similar proportion could presumably also be made by sharing
management, staff and other costs. In the light of trends for
individual data base services to initiate their own networks, the
creation of a cooperative network is a logical step to substantially
reduce the overall level of public expenditure required.

2.3   Action Plan – Part 3 (Development of skills and tools in
                            information technology)

It was recognised at an early stage in the creation of the Action Plan
that success will depend not only on the data bases and the network
itself but also on a variety of other important factors. Notably
these include:

- education of users and training of specialists

- provision of multilingual tools

- data base technology

The Action Plan therefore provides for research, coordination and
promotion of activities in these and other similar fields, in order
to develop the necessary infrastructure for the successful implementation of the network.

3.   Key Concepts in the Implementation of the Information Network

The following describes certain basic concepts which are crucial to
the design of the planned information network:

3.1   Meaning of "scientific and technical information"

This was explicitly defined by the Council of Ministers as consisting
of "scientific, technical,economic and social documentation and data".
This encompasses a broad area of information and further definition
work has identified the inclusion of such fields as patents, dentistry,
education, etc.

3.2   Machine-readable and non-machine readable data.

Apart from this provision of access to on-line data, clearly the provision
of documents is a key factor for success. Nothing is guaranteed more
to frustrate a user than to give him a reference to a document he
cannot obtain. A satisfactory on-line service can only be obtained
through a blend of computerised and non-computerised systems and services.
Extensive cooperation with libraries is therefore a prerequisite for a
successful network.

3.3   Approach to non-Community involvement

The range of computerised information services to be included
should be as wide and as diversified as necessary, with some
produced within the Member countries, some by the Community and
some in countries outside the Community or by international
organisations wider than the Community.

3.4   Types of information

Most on-line systems now operational in the field of scientific and
technical information are based on bibliographic references, sometimes providing abstracts, sometimes not. EURONET will, however,
not be restricted to this kind of information but will aim to include direct fact retrieval, numerical data banks, graphical data,
etc. It is envisaged that, particularly with regard to graphical
data, facsimile transmission will eventually become technically
and economically feasible enough to be incorporated into the network
services.

3.5   Types of service

Services currently available through data base operators will
naturally determine the range of services offered through the network.
Initially, these will inevitably be primarily of the retrospective
search type. In the long term, however, it is feasible to consider
a much broader range of services, possibly including the following:

a) Retrospective search (up to 2 years back)
b) Retrospective search (more than 2 years back)
c) Retrospective search – distribution of results
d) SDI profile construction and updating
e) SDI-distribution of results
f) Numerical data retrieval from stored tables
g) Fact retrieval, ie: file interrogation with minimal processing
h) Question-answering, ie: logical processing based on files
i) Computational retrieval, ie: the incorporation of retrieved
    data directly into the user's processing environment
j) Library selection and acquisition support
k) Library reference service support
l) Library cataloguing and holding file support
m) Referral of users to data bases and services within EURONET
n) Referral to people, places and conferences
o) Mail-box, ie: system-user message facility
p) Data base transfer to systems outside EURONET, eg: specialised
    information centres
q) User file services, eg: personal use bibliographies
r) Document ordering for users (search related) from libraries
    or other centres
s) Facsimile transmission of text and other images to users

4. Major factors influencing the design of the network

4.1 Potential User Population

One of the first activities undertaken as part of the detailed planning work for designing the network was to commission a study to forecast the likely demand for on-line services in scientific and technical information. This took place over the period July-November, 1974, and the results (§) are providing important input for a variety of design decisions. Among the highlights of the results are:

The demand for on-line services for scientific and technical information in Europe is expected to increase dramatically, as indicated by the forecast number of users:

1976	60.000
1980	960.000
1985	2.350.000

These figures relate to users who initiate searches to meet their information needs. They may not necessarily carry out the searches themselves. In many cases this will be done by a mediator – usually a librarian or information officer.

Furthermore, the average annual frequency of uses per user in terms of retrospective searches per annum is expected to increase through the forecast period, from about 1.7 in 1976 through 2.8 in 1980 to 3.7 in 1985. The distribution of use is highly uneven and a small number of users has a very high frequency of use, while a large number makes only very occasional use of information retrieval facilities.

User demand in 1976 will be dominated by medicine and chemistry, which together are expected to account for around 56% of all users at that time. By 1985 this percentage is forecast to have fallen to about 20% but medicine will still be the largest user sector(12.5% of all users) generating at that time nearly one million searches per annum in the Community countries as a whole.

(§) "Forecast of users of on-line retrieval services for scientific and technical information in Europe 1976 – 1985", prepared by P.A. International Management Consultants Ltd., November, 1974.

4.2   Pricing policy

This area is the subject of a special group working within CIDST. This group has identified the following principles with regard to a pricing policy for scientific and technical information:

1. Any pricing policy for scientific and technical information should be designed to lead gradually to a reasonable balance between costs and revenue so that its degree of financing from public funds should diminish in the course of time.

2. The price asked must be related to an accurate view of the true costs of the services provided.

3. In order to implement a pricing policy based on the foregoing principles it is essential to harmonise national policies within the Community, to avoid problems of competition that might arise if different national pricing policies were applied.

    Among the aspects which the pricing policy of EURONET will have to take into account are:

    Location of users. Community users should not be penalised for being located at places remote from data bases they wish to access, even though the telecommunications costs for those users may be higher than average.

    Ownership of the data base. Not all the data bases in EURONET will be owned by public authorities. Users will also want to access commercial data bases and appropriate charging schemes must therefore be developed.

    Category of user. It is possible that different charging policies will be applied to different categories of user, for example, users within and outside the Community, government and commercial users, etc.

4.3   Compatibility factors

A characteristic of the EURONET environment is the wide variety of potential users, data base suppliers, hardware, types of service, etc. This inevitably means that a considerable amount of effort will have to be devoted to overcoming problems of incompatibility.

These will include:

-   Information formats. Among the many factors to be harmonised here are data record formats, terminology and indexing routines. The optimisation of data base use for EURONET users will call for the ability to extract parts of data bases, to form subsets and to allow merging of data bases and subsets; this can only be achieved if compatibility of information formats exists.

-   Telecommunications protocol. The communications sub-network will naturally operate under a precisely defined set of procedures for the movement of data. These procedures will have to **inter-lock** with those of the many different machines, which will be connected to the network.

- Command language interface. Although it is planned to provide
a standard command language, this will have to interface with
existing command languages and indeed with non-standard command
languages associated with data bases to be incorporated into the
network.

4.4 Telecommunications network

A special study group investigated this aspect over the period
April – December,1974. The results indicate that until suitable
public international PTT data transmission facilities become
available a multiconnection ring structure of nodes will be needed,
with high speed transmission lines between the nodes. Terminals
will then be able to use the network by connecting either to a
local host computer or directly through a concentrator. Hence
the specification of the communications sub-network involves
definition of:

- traffic through-put capacity
- response time
- error rate
- reliability
- recovery procedures
- geographical distribution of lines and nodes
- hardware characteristics of nodes and communications equipment
- user protocol
- network protocol
- standards (transmission, interface, etc.)

If at all possible, existing proven hardware, software and network
technology will be chosen.

4.5 Multilingual aspects

A unique feature of the EURONET environment is the need to provide
services on a multilingual basis. Exactly what is needed is in the
process of being investigated by a special study group. Areas for
investigation include: machine-aided translation, limited syntax
languages and multilingual thesauri.

5 Outlook

It is planned to commence the first pilot operations of EURONET by mid-1976
with a limited number of services and to expand the network and the
services it offers from there. The future expansion of EURONET will
include links to other networks, both national and international.

Current trends in scientific and technical information, as illustrated
in Exhibit 2, indicate that the users of the 1980s will require a much
wider range of data bases and types of service than those of today. It
is hoped, indeed expected, that EURONET will play an important role
in meeting the needs of these future users of scientific and technical
information in Europe.

1966 – 70	1971 – 75	1976 – 80	1980 – 85
Increasing Awareness of the Information Explosion	Council of Ministers' Resolution, 1971	Harmonisation of National Policies in STI	Integration of International STI Networks
Increasing Expenditure on R & D	Greatly Improved Technology	Greatly Reduced Unit Costs for STI Services	Greatly Widened User Base, Especially in Soft Sciences
Introduction of Many Batch STI Services	Introduction of On-line STI Services	Wide Expansion of On-line STI Services in Traditional Fields	Proliferation of Data Bases and Creation of Specialised Services
STI Activity Mainly at National Level but Beginnings of International Effort	Initiation of 3-Year Action Plan of the Community, 1975	Build-up of Services available Through EURONET	Rapid Trend to Use of Numerical and Factual Data Banks
			Introduction of Cheap Facsimile Transmission

EXHIBIT 2

Some major trends and events in scientific and technical information in Europe, 1966 – 1985

Interconnection of packet switching networks: theory and practice

Gien, M.   Software Research Engineer, l'Institute de
                Recherche en Informatique, France

Laws, J.   Senior Scientific Officer, Computer Science
                Division, National Physical Laboratory, UK

Scantlebury, R. Principal Scientific Officer, Computer
                Science Division, National Physical Laboratory, UK

Abstract:

There is now a fair number of " computer networks " employing
the packet-switching technique and inevitably, at some point,
the question arises of connecting some of these together, so
that users can get at the resources of other systems via their
own. Ultimately this must be done by providing a common
communication function, possibly put together from the
communication systems of the existing networks, but eventually
provided on properly designed communication networks. The
perennial question is how to move from the present position to
the desirable end, without sacrificing the present investment.
An experiment is being conducted by IRIA and NPL in the
interconnection of the CYCLADES and NPL networks, not only at
the communication network level, but also at the level of
standard procedures used between the computers attached to the
networks.

1.　Introduction

The past few years have seen the emergence of a fair number of computer networks or "tele-processing" systems. Many of these computer networks require a switching capability as well as data transmission facilities and the timescales have been too short for the Telecommunication Authorities themselves to provide such data switching systems. This has resulted in the designers of these networks providing their own switching systems, and one of the advantages of the packet-switching technique is the relative ease with which it can provide an economic and timely solution.

Perhaps the best known example of such a system is the ARPA network in USA (1) which has been in operation for over six years.

This is not to say that the various national Telecommunication Authorities have not taken the requirement for data switching networks seriously. Indeed the Experimental Packet Switched Service of the British Post Office opens this year, the French PTT have announced their Transpac system and Bell Canada propose to open their Datapac system in 1976.

Inevitably the communication facilities of various networks differ both in the services offered to the subscribers (ie their external appearance) and in the details of their internal operation. This fact leads to problems when it is required to interconnect such networks so that users of one network can communicate with users of another.

At this point it should be noted that the word "network" occurs in the literature to mean either a series of computers and/or terminals connected together for some purpose, or a communication system employing transmission bearers and switching devices. Sometimes the use of the word in the first case subsumes the second. In what follows we will endeavour to be explicit.

2.　The Packet-Switching Schism

Most of the packet-switched communication networks that have been designed fall into one of two broad categories. This is because the particular designs relate to the kinds of device for which the system is to cater. For example, in the case of the ARPA, CYCLADES (2) and NPL (3) computer networks, the original aim was to achieve resource sharing between computer installations. This led to the adoption of packet-switched communication networks which do not embody the notion of a "call" but simply pass the packets as unrelated events. The association between processes in one machine and processes in another is undertaken by a special program called the Network Control Program (NCP) or Transport Station (TS) resident in each of the subscribing computers. This led to an hierarchical design philosophy in which the communication mechanism between computers as provided by the

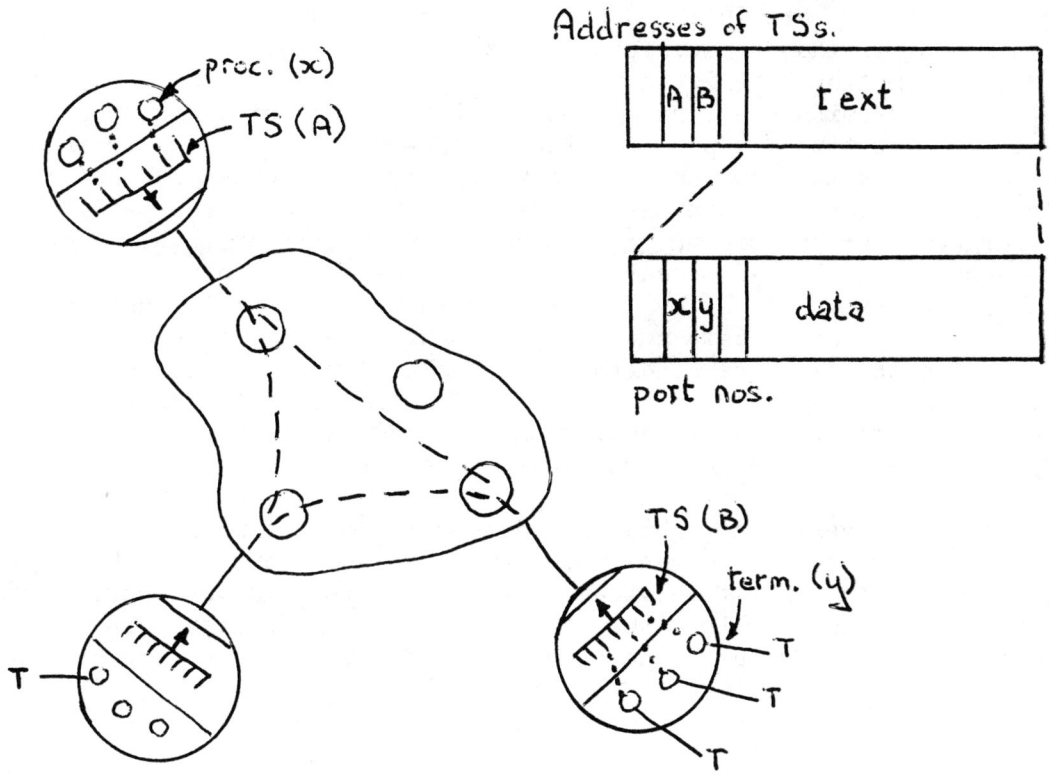

FIGURE 1

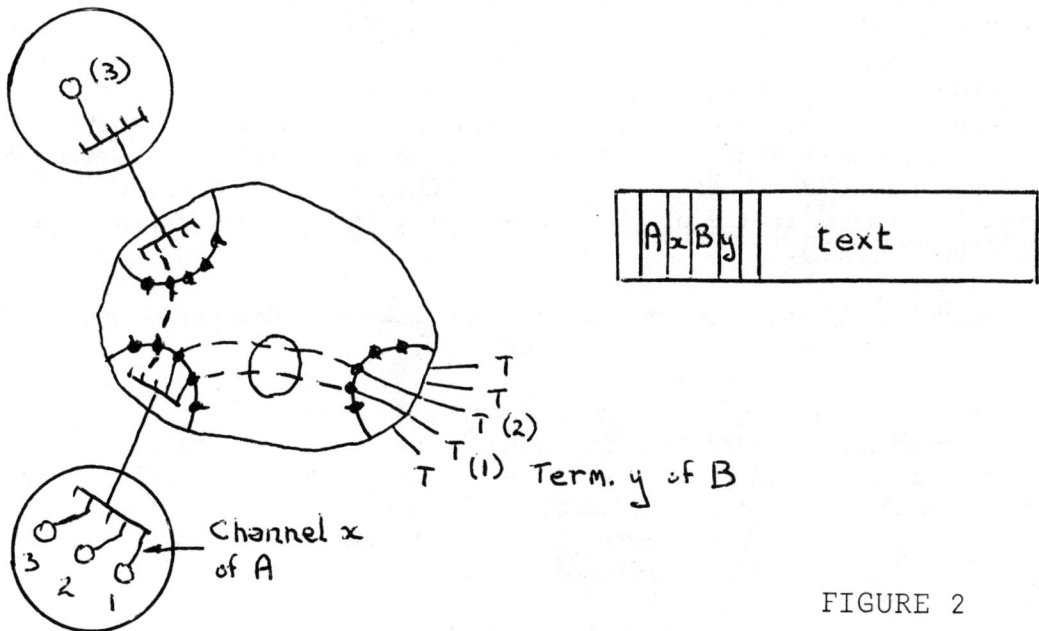

FIGURE 2

communication network is independent of the mechanisms employed for
establishing liaison between remote processes (4)(5) Fig 1. A
further assumption here is that human access to the system is via
programs or terminals attached to subscribing computers, and is not
directly evident to the packet-switched sub-system. However in the
case of some communication networks where terminal access for human
users is a primary concern, as for example in EPSS and Transpac it has
been argued that the communications should be "call" oriented. Now in
some sense a "call" can be said to exist above the NCP or TS level as
in the ARPA case, but in the EPSS the intention is that the call is
known not only to the data switching exchange handling simple terminals
but also to the exchange handling the "packet interface" customer, Fig 2.
This has lead to a monolithic structure for the "packet-subscriber" in
which the customer address and sub-channel address he uses is known
and/or administered by the communication network.

Space does not permit an exhaustive discussion of the merits and de-
merits of these two approaches here, but merely to point out that they
are different and that they give different services to the subscriber.
However the authors believe the first scheme is inherently more
flexible and that further experience is needed before the services that
ought to be offered by public networks can be agreed.

3.   The Interconnection of Networks

The purpose of interconnecting two computer networks is presumably to
allow users on one network to access the services of the other.
Between two private networks one could conceive of a solution whereby
one "service" is a subscriber to both networks. This subscriber would
act as a 'Gateway' between the networks and could contain a number of
functions. One such function would be to handle any differences
between the two parochial communication systems, including the
addressing mechanisms. Another could be to carry out a conversion of
the subscriber-to-subscriber procedures used in one network so as to
match those used in the other (for example, the HOST-HOST protocol of
the ARPA network).

The objective of this scheme would be to make any foreign computer
network appear just like the home network.

At first sight this notion might appear attractive particularly to well
established subscribers, but is actually untenable in the long term.
The conversion would have to be done for every pair of connected networks and the service to the users would become increasingly turgid as
the communications with remote sites was 'strained' through various,
and perhaps ill matching protocol transliterations.

Catenet

It seems a laudable aim to be able to inter-connect communication
networks so that a subscriber to one can communicate with a subscriber

to another, possibly via a third, in such a way that the concatenated communication networks appear like a single communication entity.

Setting aside for the time being the reductio-ad-adsurdum case of all communication networks becoming identical both in their internal and external operations, there is the possibility of the constituent communication networks adopting a common standard for a packet format (and a common mode of subscriber access) at least for inter-net traffic. Theoretically such packets could be used in addition to the usual format within each network, and their use might lead to an eventual international standard.

This notion is the basis of Pouzin's idea for Catenet (6) but has the disadvantage that some of the existing networks would have difficulty in implementing the changes internally. As it happens, it is not actually essential that the internal formats of a constituent network conform to some standard, since the important feature of Catenet is the commonality of external service provided to subscribers and to other communication networks.

The Common User-Services Network

If amongst their customer services two communication networks offer a common service, and if the means for interworking between the two networks exists such that this service can be mutually exchanged, then there exists the basis for the interworking of their subscribers using that service.

At the August 1974 meeting of the IFIP Inter-Network Working Group it was made known that a group of European Telecommunication Administrations had prepared a paper for submission to CCITT proposing a set of services that might be offered by public packet-switched networks. If such services were to be provided by all communication networks, then a real basis will exist for general interworking.

So far two basic services have been identified namely the 'Datagram' and the 'Virtual Call'. They arise because of the different approaches taken to the systems design by the public nets like EPSS and Transpac, and the private nets like ARPA, CYCLADES and NPL. Despite this potential schism mentioned above, a measure of agreement was reached in INWG which applauds and supports this proposal.

To illustrate how the above services could be used to effect Catenet, let us consider the following example.

In the CYCLADES network, the various participating centres exchange messages with each other, which are broken up into packets by the 'Transport Station' within the subscriber for transmission via the communication network (Cigale). Message fragmentation and reassembly is therefore a subscriber function as is the identification of subchannels. The interface with the communication network is therefore one in which individual and unrelated packets are exchanged. The addresses on packets refer only to Transport Stations since Cigale plays no part in the identification of sub-channels.

A similar state of affairs exists in the NPL and ARPA nets, but in the case of the latter, the external unit (hereinafter called the EXDAT) exchanged between the HOST and the IMP is called a message and this is further fragmented (into INDATS) by the IMP for handling as packets within the communication network.

Although message fragmentation and reassembly occurs within the ARPA communication network, there is still an EXDAT which we can equate with the notion of the Datagram.

Thus two networks whose EXDATS can be made compatible can potentially facilitate communication between their respective subscribers. The Datagram is therefore the definition of a common service whereby all conforming networks can freely pass the message contents of their respective EXDATS. The mode of operation would be that at the gateway between two networks the arriving EXDAT would have the proprietry envelope of the one network removed, yielding the message contents, which would be rewrapped in the proprietry envelope of the second for onward transmission.

One of the essential features therefore of the Datagram service is the agreement of a maximum size of message that can be so carried. If the EXDAT size of a constituent network is less than that of its partners, it would be obliged to fragment the message and to reassemble it before passing it on to another net (or even to a subscriber if appropriate). However, the present proposal is to adopt a maximum of 255 octets for the message portion of a Datagram, which fits in with the operation of virtually all the existing or proposed networks.

The definition of the Virtual Call service has not yet been finalised, but in an analogous manner calls between two networks offering this service could be exchanged at their boundaries. The gateways between networks would relay the call set-up, call control and breakdown, features from one network to the next.

4.   Subscriber-to-Subscriber Protocols

The Cerf-Kahn Proposal

Messrs Cerf and Kahn of the ARPA community, have proposed a scheme (7) which not only provides an experimental inter-net HOST-HOST protocol but also suggests a strategy to be adopted at gateways between networks.

It is based on the Datagram principle and assumes that each HOST has a Transmission Control Program (TCP) which provides the certain services to user processes within the HOST.

The TCP provides for the transmission of messages, of finite but un-bounded strings of characters (octets), which are fragmented into units suitable for handling by the local communication network.

Cerf and Kahn argue that since a fragmentation scheme is required in the HOSTs it is possible to use it to take account of the different sizes of EXDATs in different communication networks by allowing the Gateways to participate in the same scheme. A Gateway receiving from one network an EXDAT which was larger than the EXDAT of the next net-work could further fragment the message and, by creating new values for the octet pointers accompanying the message, would render to the eventual recipient of the several EXDATs the ability to reassemble the octet steam as if the fragmentation had occurred in the original HOST.

The advantage of this ploy is to allow those communication networks with large EXDATs to utilise them fully while not precluding the inter-connection with networks having small EXDATs.

The disadvantages are threefold.

* Once fragmented into tiny pieces by one network it is impractical for subsequent networks to reassemble to larger fragments which they might otherwise carry with less overhead.

* The Gateway must be party to the HOST-HOST protocol which in any case might change.

* Extra complication is involved at the Gateway if more than one HOST-HOST protocol is in existence.

It is very unlikely that the providers of public networks would agree to the above requirements. It was pointed out in the INWG forum that a desirable aim is to decouple the HOST-HOST protocol from the Gateway issue and by adopting the proposed Datagram service this end can be achieved.

This does not invalidate the Cerf-Kahn protocol, which indeed is being experimented with in the ARPA community. It merely means that Catenet subscribers on different networks must avoid sending EXDATs to each other longer than the specified maximum length.

The Elie-Zimmerman Protocol

An alternative 'HOST-HOST' protocol has been proposed by Elie and Zimmerman of the CYCLADES project (8). Currently a version of this is being implemented experimentally between the NPL and CYCLADES networks, and is proposed for use in the European Informatics Network (9).

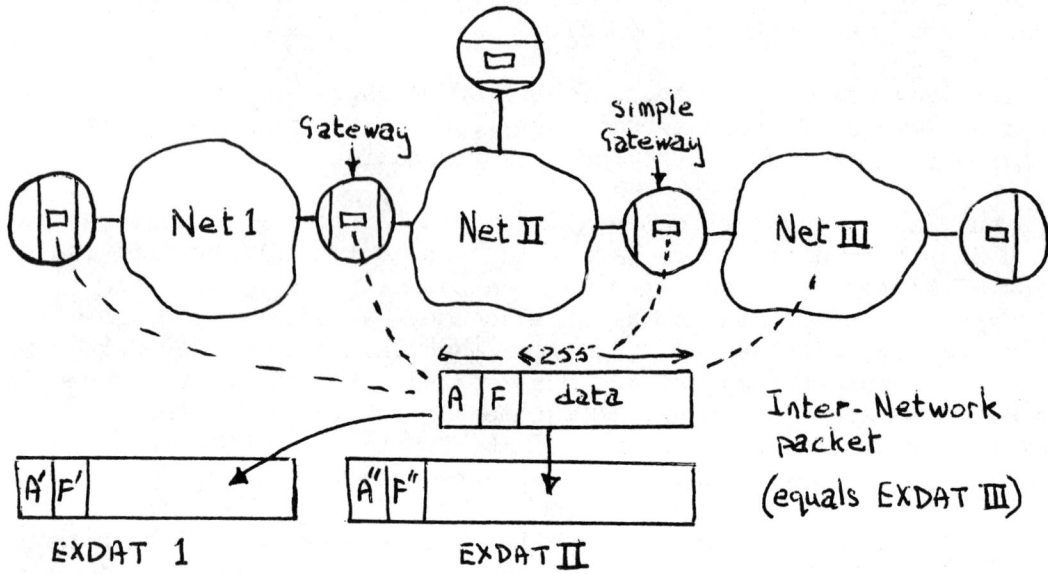

FIGURE 3

Octet 0	1	2	3	4	5	6	7	8	...
FL-LT	CRD-NB	DEST	PT-NO	SRCE	PT-NO	YR-REF	MY-REF	EOL/FR-NO	FR-TEXT
FL-AK	CRD-NO	"		"		YR-REF			
FL-TG		"		"		TG-TEXT			
FL-INIT		"		"		SERVICES AND PARAMETERS			
FL-TERM		"		"		REASON			

FIGURE 4

This too calls for a control program, called a Transport Station which is resident in the subscriber computer and which provides a set of services to user processes. There are certain similarities with the Cerf–Kahn protocol but the fragmentation of the users' data stream is handled in a different manner.

The basic unit of currency to the user is the 'letter' which has some bounded but negotiable length up to say several thousand octets. This is fragmented (as necessary) for transmission as EXDATs. Here it is assumed that the fragment size will be that of the Datagram service. Before describing an actual TS implementation we will expand a little further on the Datagram and Gateway theme.

An Inter-Network Packet Format Proposal

It was observed that in any inter-net HOST–HOST protocol there would be the necessity to be able to name or address HOSTs or TSs in foreign networks comprising Catenet. It was therefore suggested that whatever the particular message format that will be associated with a particular experimental protocol, it would be an advantage if the addressing portion of the formats could be standardised. (A in Fig 3).

This idea was extended by Pouzin to the point where he proposed a universal header format that could also be used as a packet header within a communication network. Such networks which could adopt the format would then be in the position that the INDAT and EXDAT would be the same thing. This would greatly simplify the Gateway function.

Networks which could not or would not accept such a standard would have to wrap this format as a message within their own EXDAT. In order to accommodate this suggestion it was pointed out in INWG that the total length of the message, which includes the universal or inter-network header as well as the data, must fit into the data portion of the EXDAT. i.e. to be able to be sent as a Datagram through Catenet. The present suggestion is that the data portion of a Datagram shall not exceed 255 octets.

This means that in the above case some of the addressing information could appear twice, i.e. both in the parochial Datagram header and in the universal header, as part of the message.

This may be inevitable in the cause of reaching agreement on principles between all parties.

IRIA-NPL Experiment

An experiment is in progress linking the CYCLADES and NPL networks, based on the foregoing principles. A 'Gateway' situated at NPL, links the two communication networks at the Datagram level and experimental Transport Stations exist in computers on each network.

5.   The NPL/Cyclades Network Gateway

The NPL Data Communications Network (DCN) and the French Cyclades network are connected via a 'Gateway'. This Gateway is a structure comprising software and hardware elements.

The functions of the Gateway are:-

a)   to accept data packets of either network and transform them into the appropriate data packets for transmission into the other network;

(b)   to handle the packet communication protocol of each network.

Gateway hardware elements

The central element is a Computer Technology Ltd. (CTL) Mini-Mod composed of a processor, 24K (16-bit) words of semi-conductor store, control teletype, paper tape reader and a BS4421 (10) interface (BSI) module supporting four source/acceptor pairs. The BSI operates an asychronous 8-bit parallel data transfer between source and acceptor, and is driven by software a single byte at a time.

The connection of this computer to the NPL DCN is established via a BSI source/acceptor pair into a Network Termination Unit (NTU). The NTU permits a full duplex flow of packets between the Gateway and the DCN.

The Gateway/Cyclades connection is via a BSI source/acceptor pair into a line serialiser unit and then onward to a CODEX 9600 b/s modem attached to a 4-wire audio circuit (M102). The line takes the connection over to a Cyclades network node situated at IRIA near Paris. The line and Modem have the capability for full duplex working, but are used logically as half duplex by the present line transmission protocol software.

The use of the BSI confers a distinct advantage. If the packet stream flowing in any of the connections or the operation of the line protocol are thought to be suspect, the BSI cable connections can quickly be broken and a variety of hardware diagnostic aids inserted to monitor the traffic.

Gateway Software Elements

The major components of the software are the CTL E2 executive and the application programs for performing the detailed Gateway functions.

The E2 executive provides facilities for inter-program/task communication and multi-programming scheduling.

The Gateway application programs are written in CORAL 66 (11) with assembler code inserts (permitted by CORAL) as necessary to use the E2 executive facilities. An application program is formed from a set of CORAL source code modules; the main program of the first module being the entry point. Code and data declared within one module may be used within other modules provided that explicit Library declarations are made. The CORAL compiler produces a program with a single entry point.

Gateway Application Programs

The Gateway application decomposes naturally into a number of asychronous tasks. At first sight it might appear that each task would have to be written as an independent program, due to the constraint of only one entry point for a CORAL program. Inter-task communication would then be via the facilities of the E2 executive. However, considering the necessity of servicing the Modem line at a peak rate of about 1200 bytes per second, we decided that this form of inter-task working would present an unacceptable overhead.

Some software has been developed so that at run time, a CORAL program may assign itself additional entry points to each task. This has the advantage of allowing tasks to share global data structures. Access protection to the common data must be performed by the tasks, but is a small penalty to pay. Semaphores can be implemented on the Mini-Mod using the accumulator/store exchange instruction.

Code could still not be shared between tasks because of the way the CORAL compiler lays out the link word, parameters etc. into the data segment. Thus, each task had to declare its own copy of a common procedure within its own code module. This was found to be expensive in space. Procedures declared to be "Recursive" use a software stack, but the compiler only assigns one stack for the whole program. We have developed some software, so that at run time the single stack may be segmented into a number of stacks, each of which is uniquely assigned to a single entry point (task). Common procedures are then declared to be Recursive and use the stack segment assigned to the calling task.

The Gateway software is implemented as two application programs — one for DCN i/o and the other for Cyclades i/o and packet conversion. The two programs communicate with each other through the E2 executive.

DCN i/o Program

This program operates the NPL DCN packet protocol. The DCN packet protocol is full duplex and has a simple flow control mechanism.

The program is structured as three tasks. The service task handles requests to send/receive DCN packets made by the other program. A request for service, and the packet buffer, are placed on the appropriate send/receive queue. The sending task examines the send queue and transmits packets into the DCN via the BSI and NTU. When output has been completed the other program is informed that the packet buffer is free, by setting a flag in its data segment. The receive task accepts packets from the DCN and signals the other program that input has been completed. If a received packet is marked as being in error, then it is discarded. If a packet is received, but no request for it has yet been made by the other program, the packet is held for a time awaiting such request. At timeout the packet is discarded.

Cyclades i/o and Packet Conversion Program

This program is in three levels. The line protocol level, the Cyclades packet protocol level and the packet conversion level.

The line protocol level is composed of four tasks. This level handles the 9.6 Kilo-bit line connecting the Gateway to the Cyclades network node. A very much modified IBM BSC-HASP line protocol is used. This protocol is half duplex and has facilities for retransmission of packets that have been received in error. In this protocol packets are framed by "SYN" characters and a Cyclic Redundancy Check (CRC). In addition, flow control is provided in that either end may request the other to stop transmitting. The detection of the leading SYN character of a packet received from the line is performed by the line serialiser. All other functions, including SYN generation on outward packets and CRC verification and generation, are performed by the line protocol software. It is accepted that this approach places a heavy burden on the processor, but we wished to be in a position to adapt quickly to new versions of the line protocol. This adaptability would be less if the protocol had been frozen into hardware. (Currently a full duplex HDLC line protocol, is being implemented).

This level has a very simple interface with the Cyclades packet protocol level. The interface is a single buffer queue for the next packet to be transmitted to Cyclades, and a double buffer queue into which packets are to be received from Cyclades. Semaphores are used to indicate when a buffer has been completed in sending or receiving. The need for double buffering on the receive side was found to be necessary for efficient working of the line protocol.

The Cyclades packet protocol level is a single task. Its interface with the packet conversion level is again very simple and is via two queues (send and receive) whose length is bounded only by the availability of free buffers. On the transmit half of the cycle, a packet is taken from the queue of packets awaiting transmission (passed down by the packet conversion level) and is placed in the send queue of the line protocol level. In the event that no data packet has been passed down for transmission, a dummy packet (called a "bubble") is generated and sent. The receive half of the cycle attempts to maintain two buffers in the receive queue of the line protocol level. It also determines if the received packet is a "bubble" or a data packet. The latter is placed on the receive queue of the packet conversion level.

The packet conversion level is structured as two tasks, one for each direction of flow. The receive task removes packets from the Cyclades receive queue. The Cyclades packet header is examined and a DCN packet header generated in front of the Cyclades header. The DCN i/o program is then requested to send the packet into the DCN. The send task requests a DCN packet from the DCN i/o program. When received, the DCN header is removed exposing the Cyclades packet header. The packet is then placed on the Cyclades send queue.

The Cyclades packet protocol and packet conversion levels obtain receive buffers from the free buffer pool. If a buffer is not available then the receive task in the level must wait until one is returned to the pool by a send task completing its packet output. An overall control is placed on these two levels, so that a burst of data packets in one direction does not take all the free packet buffers and so degrade the performance in the reverse direction.

It is observed from the above, that the packets sent into and received from the DCN by the Gateway, carry the Cyclades packet header within them as part of the data field of a DCN packet. Due to the restricted addressing capability of the DCN packet header, we had to carry additional address information within the data field of the packet. Rather than create another header, we elected to adopt the proposed inter-network packet header, which has also been adopted by Cyclades as its own packet header. Packets exchanged with Cigale must therefore be restricted to 255 octets maximum overall length including the inter-network header.

The store occupied by the software elements is as follows:—

E2 executive		12 K bytes
DCN i/o program:	code	5 K bytes
	data	3 K bytes
Cyclades i/o, conversion program:	code	10 K bytes
	data tables	3 K bytes
	20 packet buffers	5.5 K bytes

6.   The Transport Station

The End-to-End Protocol used in the CYCLADES-NPL network interconnection is the "Transport Protocol" defined by H Zimmerman/M Elie in (8).

This protocol consists of a multiplexing-demultiplexing function, which provides packet communication between Ports on top of which a Port-to-Port protocol performs fragmentation and reassembly of letters into packets as well as Error and Flow Control on letters.

Transport Station (TS): The Transport Station is in charge of multiplexing this interface between the "processes" and adds some more services and control to the basic packet switching function. There can be more than one Transport Station on a physical machine. Transport Stations co-operate according to the Transport Protocol. The Format of the exchanged commands is given in Fig. 4.

Multiplexing and Demultiplexing Functions: A Transport Station has an address, known by the communication network. This address is located in the packet header. Each TS owns a set of Ports (PT) identified within the TS by a 16 bit Port Number (PT-NB). These Port Numbers will be allocated to processes, for inter-process communication purposes, as statically as possible. Dynamic allocation of Port Numbers is not considered in the implementation described below.

The assocation of a pair of Ports is called a flow (FL) or liaison (LI) and is controlled by the Port-to-Port protocol.

The first function of a Transport Station will be, then, to multiplex-demultiplex the sub-network interface (e.g. a line) between the different flows.

Letters and Telegrams: A Letter (LT) is a variable length block of information with a maximum size presently fixed to 4000 octets, intended for transfer of data. The letter is given as a whole by the sending process; it is divided as necessary into a number of fixed length Fragments (FR) (except for the last one) each fragment being sent in one packet with appropriate control information. It is reassembled upon arrival by the receiving TS and then delivered as a whole to the receiving process. Since packets may get lost, reassembly is protected by a Time-Out (TO1) associated with each letter under reassembly. A Telegram (TG) is a fixed length piece of information (16 bits) intended for interrupt like use.

Error Control: This is performed on a letter basis (not on Fragments) on top of fragmentation-reassembly. The sending TS sends letters with (cyclicly re-used) sequential references 'MY-REF' and expects acknowledgement within a maximum delay (TO3) after the last Fragment has been sent. The receiving TS acknowledges letters after the last Fragment has been received, sending back 'YR-REF' meaning that letter with that reference and all preceding ones have been received

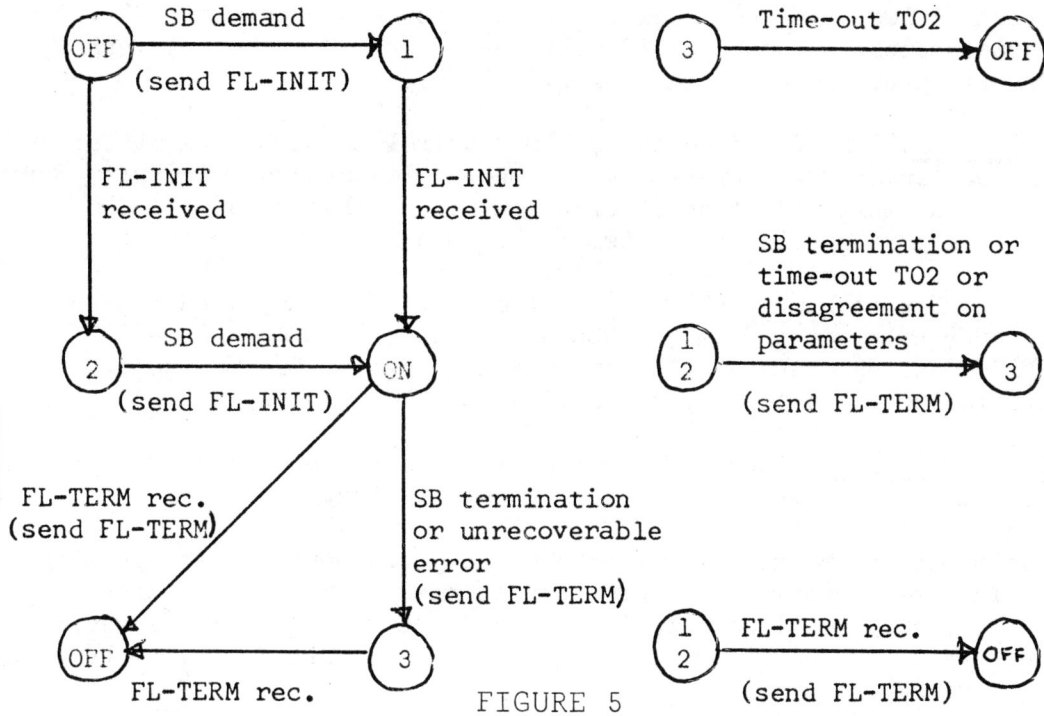

FIGURE 5

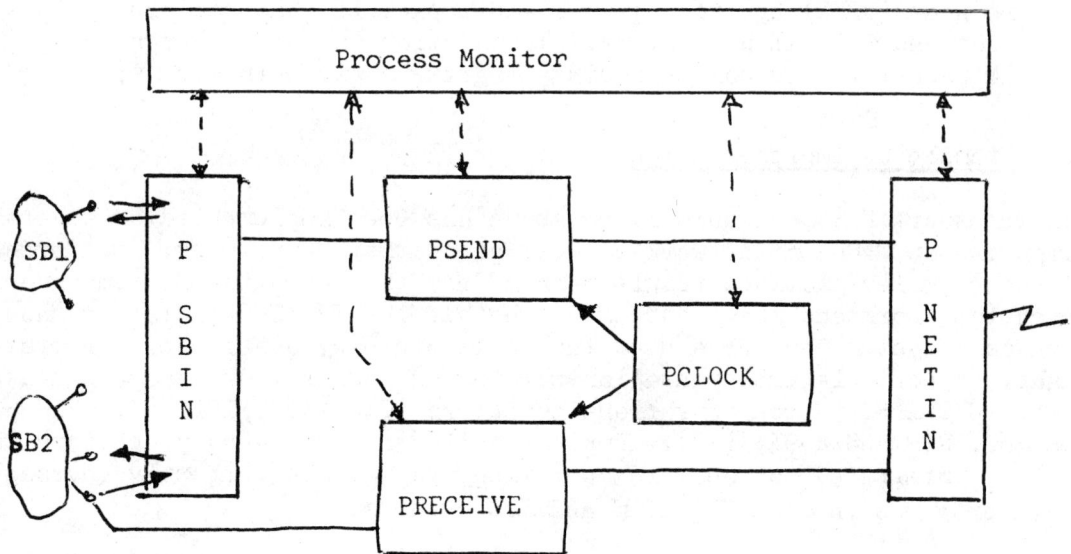

FIGURE 6

correctly and passed to the receiving user. If acknowledgement is not received by the sending TS within TO3, all unacknowledged letters will be presumed lost and sent again. If a letter has been sent 'N' times without success, the sending TS will declare an unrecoverable error, inform its user and close that flow.

<u>Flow Control</u>: As Error Control, Flow Control is performed at letter level, on top of Fragmentation-Reassembly. It is associated with Error Control. At initialization of flow control, both ends of the flow agree on a maximum size of letter to be sent in each direction.

The 4 bit Credit Number (CRD-NB) sent means: "You may send letters with references going from (YR-REF) +1 up to (YR-REF) + (CRD-NB)" unless CRD-NB = 0 which means "don't send any more letters". The sending TS restricts itself to this upper limit.

<u>Optional Set of Services</u>: Error and flow control on flows are optional services; users have the following possibilities.

- Basic Service where the TS performs only fragmentation-reassembly. No initial exchange of information is needed prior to sending a letter, only local declarations (OPEN) are required. This Basic Service can be considered as a kind of "Lettergram" service between processes ports.
- Error control on letters.
- Error and Flow Control on letters.

For the two optional services, the required initialization is done on user request (OPEN) by exchanging FL-INIT packets that contain options asked for and initial parameters. Termination is done by exchanging FL-TERM packets. The corresponding diagram is given in Fig. 5.

7.   <u>Example of Implementation</u>

The Transport Protocol summarized above has been implemented on several computers on CYCLADES network as well as on the NPL network. Differences in these implementations result mainly from the Operating System under which they work and the choice made whether the Transport Station should work as a System task or a User task accessible by other users or system tasks. A portable implementation working as a User task has been made within CYCLADES to run on various computers (CII 10070/IRIS 80, IRIS 50, IBM 360, SIEMENS 4004) (12). Implementation in front-end processors as well as integrated to the main operating systems are currently envisaged or in progress in some CYCLADES and EIN centres.

<u>Transport Station Structure</u>: (Fig. 6) A Transport Station consists of five processes.

- Receive demands from the users (PSBIN): This process is in charge of receiving Demand Blocks from the users, to control them, and take proper actions. These actions can consist of handling completely the

Demand and give a response to the user (local actions) or handle partially the demand and signal to another process that there will be "something to do" for that user (e.g. a letter to be sent).

- Prepare and send packets (PSEND): This process is in charge of two functions. As flows are competing for the use of the network communication resource, it must choose from among the flows having something to be sent, the one that will get this right. This selection is done according to one of several criteria – (multiplexing function). When a flow has been selected, it prepares the packet to be sent and passes it to the sub-network interface process (see below).

- Handle received packets (PRECEIVE): This process analyses the received packet to determine to which flow it is addressed, (Demultiplexing function) and then takes the action corresponding to the contents of that packet, and the state of the flow (e.g. continue the reassembling of a letter, signal acknowledgement to be sent on that flow, open a flow with services from a distant request, give a response to a completed user demand such as whole letter received, etc.)

- Handle a clock and perform Time-Out actions (PCLOCK). This process is awakened at each clock interrupt; it updates all posted time-outs and takes proper actions corresponding to those that have expired (e.g. signal that a letter has to be retransmitted on that flow, tell the user that an error has occurred due to time-out expiration, etc.)

- Sub-network Interface (PNETIN): This process handles the communication line(s) with the sub-network and the corresponding procedures. It takes and gives packets from and to the PSEND-PRECEIVE processes. It should be noted that this process could reside in a task or machine other than the TS, and that it could multiplex the line(s) and demultiplex received packets for different TS using the same network interface. Actually, this process (or Task) has in fact the function of a partial gateway exchange, between the packets handled by the TS and the sub-network. Where a standard packet format has been agreed, every TS would handle only this kind of packet, the wrapping-unwrapping of those packets into local sub-network format being done by this network interface process. In the NPL-CYCLADES interconnection experiment, this process on the CYCLADES machine does not do anything more than handling the line, the packet format handled by CIGALE being the same as the one known by the TS processes. On NPL machines, this process has the added function of wrapping and unwrapping packets to and from the TS, into NPL network packet format. (See above on the gateway exchange).

In addition, there are some re-entrant service subroutines used by the preceding processes. A flow context table (TBFLCTX) is associated with each active flow. These Tables can be accessed from an Active Flows Table (TBFLACT).

User Interface

The User Interface can be implemented in different ways depending mainly on the facilities offered by the Operating System under which the TS is working.

The set of primitives given to the user in our implementation, for communication with the TS is listed below:

OPEN-PT: This allows the user to start receiving on a local PT, given as a parameter without specifying any distant port. Actions taken from this command are only local and consist mainly in the initialization within the TS of a Port context.

RECV-PT: Where the user gives a buffer to receive a letter on that port from any distant port. The TS will give to the user a received letter for which no explicit flow has been opened (see below). This command and the one following must have been preceded by an OPEN-PT command. (The first RECV-PT emitted could play the role of an OPEN-PT but for simplicity of implementation and conformity with flow commands we prefer to have separate commands for different functions).

RINT-PT: Where the user signals that he is prepared to receive interrupts (TG or distant initialization = INIT) from any distant port.

CLOSE-PT: To terminate receiving on a Port and release associated resources within the TS.

OPEN-FL: This allows the user to start sending and receiving on the mentioned flow. This command will also initialize optional services on that flow if required.

SEND-FL: Where the user asks for a letter to be sent on the flow.

RECV-FL: Where the user gives a buffer to receive a letter on the flow.

RINT-FL: The user signals that he is prepared to receive TG on the flow.

SNTG-FL: To send a TG on the flow.

CLSE-FL: To terminate communications on the flow and stop optional services if any.

Responses from the TS to the users are given as events associated with each command and posted with a completion code or as messages put into user queues associated with each type of command, depending on the implementation.

Implementation Figures

On the CII-IRIS 80 (IRIA) the TS has about 8K instructions. (One instruction takes 32 bits). It is written in a macro-language used for portability (13). Tables on buffer space are not included. Space needed for this purpose depends very much on the choices and constraints of implementation (e.g. How many active flows are going to be handled simultaneously? Buffer space used belongs to user tasks or to the TS etc.) It is also clear that more rigid and static choices in the implementation of a TS for limited purposes (e.g. within a Terminal concentrator) would lead to the need for much less code.

The NPL experimental version, implemented on a CTL Modular One computer also occupies about 8K instructions (but of 16 bits). It is written in CORAL 66. This figure also does not include Tables and Buffer space as in the above case. As an indication however, maintaining a Flow uses about 20 words. The context of a user demand (SEND or RECEIVED) needs about 8 words (without Buffers).

8. Conclusion

The definition of the datagram service for packet-switched networks could be quite easily agreed. The interconnection of existing networks by means of such a universal service is then a simple matter. Present subscribers could interwork in terms of this service and would then require to agree a suitable "HOST-HOST" protocol.

The feasibility of this approach has been demonstrated by the NPL-CYCLADES experiment reported above.

Acknowledgement

The authors gratefully acknowledge the work of H Zimmerman, K Danq-Quoc and M Riou (IRIA), and of J Sexton and D Baker (NPL), on which this paper is based.

References

(1)   Roberts, L.G. and Wessler, B.D.   "Computer network development
      to achieve resource sharing",   Proc. AFIPS 1970 SJCC pp 543-549.

(2)   Pouzin, L.   "Presentation and major design aspects of the Cyclades
      computer network", Proc 3rd ACM/IEEE data communications
      symposium, Florida   Nov. 1973 p.80.

(3)   Scantlebury, R.A. and Wilkinson, P.T.   "The National Physical
      Laboratory data communication network",   Proc. ICCC Stockholm
      1974 pp 223-228.

(4)   Scantlebury, R.A. and Wilkinson, P.T.   "The design of a switching
      system to allow remote access to computer services by other
      computers and terminal devices".   Proc. ACM/IEEE Second Symposium
      on problems in the optimisation of data communication systems,
      Palo Alto, USA 1971 pp 160-167 .

(5)   Le Moli, G.   "A Theory of colloquies",   1st European Workshop on
      Computer Networks.   Arles April 1973 pp 153-174.

(6)   Pouzin, L.   "A Proposal for interconnecting packet-switching net-
      works",   Proc Eurocomp May 1974   pp 1023-1036.

(7)   Cerf, V.G. and Kahn, R.E.   "A protocol for packet-network inter-
      communication".   IEEE Transac. comm.   Vol. Comm. 22 No. 5.   May
      1974 pp 637-648.

(8)   Zimmermann, H. and Elie, M.   "Transport protocol: Standard Host-
      Host protocol for heterogeneous computer networks".   IFIP WG 6.1
      doc 61   April 1974.

(9)   Barber, D.L.A.   "The European computer network project".   Computer
      communications: impacts and implications.   S. Winkler ed.
      Washington, Oct 1972 pp 192-200.

(10) BS4421:1969.   A digital input/output interface for data collection
      systems.   British Standards Institution, Sales Branch,
      101 Pentonville Road, London N1.

(11) Official definition of CORAL 66.   HMSO London 1970.

(12) Zimmerman, H. et al.   "Spécifications de réalisation de la Station
      de Transport ST2 portable".   IRIA Technical Report SCH 536
      Oct 1974.

(13) Gien, M. and Seguin, J.   "Langage de macro FANNY et portabilité"
      Rapport project CRIC, CII Grenoble, Jan 1973.

Viewdata: an interactive information service for the general public

S FEDIDA   C.Eng, B.Sc(Eng), MSc, FIEE, MBCS, ACGI

Manager, Computer Applications

Post Office Research Centre, UK

ABSTRACT

The concept of VIEWDATA, a computer-based information medium and
service, suitable for non-computer users, is explained by reference
to the "total cost-effectiveness" of computer-based information
systems. The means of implementing such a system includes the design
of a low-cost, yet of pleasing appearance, rugged and reliable terminal connected to the telephone system, together with its associated
keypads, a distributed but interconnected computer system giving
access to internal and external data bases, a "natural" protocol for
information retrieval requiring no training whatsoever for its effective
use and a software structure designed to maximise throughput and hence
minimise costs.

System studies and experimentation to-date indicate that the majority
of the system design objectives have been met and also provide good
grounds for believing that the remainder can also be met.

1   INTRODUCTION

A large number of attempts have been made in recent years in the design
and establishment of computer based information systems. The main emphasis has been on the whole to provide information for managers -
information that they may find useful in the conduct of their businesses.

The design of these systems has been motivated principally from the
need to ensure maximum cost effectiveness. This requirement has been
usually expressed in terms of reducing storage needs to the minimum,
and ensuring commonality between the various users of a data base.
Thus while each user has an interest in perhaps one or two areas of
a data base, the totality of users are interested in all the aspects
of the same data base. Thus the data base organisation is so chosen
as to be capable of being configured in many different ways, according to usage.

The emphasis on cost-effectiveness as expressed in the above terms has
resulted in extremely sophisticated developments of integrated databases, which in the event can only be used by the specialist programmer
or else persons specifically trained in the (usually) very complex
protocol of the data base.

VIEWDATA has also been designed as a computer based information system
with a very great emphasis being placed on "total" cost effectiveness
as will be seen later. By "total" cost effectiveness we mean cost
effectiveness judged against the whole system background, ie users and
computer and not just computers. Thus we find that "total" cost
effectiveness is reflected in a different set of criteria.

One of the major requirements has been to make the data base accessible
by all manner of users who might be interested in the information contained therein, but without requiring that they should be specially
trained to use the system. Hence the emphasis has been on making the
information system easy to use, rather than on providing a wealth of
extremely sophisticated logical search facilities, which in the opinion
of the writer are frequently greatly overrated and indeed seldom used.
Nevertheless the structure of the system is such that many sophisticated search facilities may be easily accommodated as the system expands,
as we shall see later.

The underlying concept of VIEWDATA which has led to the "ease of use"
requirement being placed at the top of the list of priorities in its
implementation, apart from the overriding importance of "total" cost
effectiveness, is the belief that by and large the potentially
immense beneficial impact of the computer on modern society has not
yet materialised to any great extent. If anything, the impact has
been in many ways rather unfavourable.

We may regard this development as a third stage in the industrial-
isation of modern society. This began as we know with the exploitation of energy resources and the development of machines to replace
the muscular effort of man, and to enhance it by many orders of
magnitude. The second stage, begun some 50 years ago, has been concerned with the automation of the manufacturing and distributive
processes. We are now reaching the third stage, which, matching the
growth of the service industries in modern society, in relation to
the production of goods, is the automation of services, which, to a
very great extent, are essentially concerned with the creation and
distribution of information.

In order that this new kind of automation should succeed and become
part of the fabric of society, it is essential that it should be
accessible to all members of society, that it should use "natural"
modes of communication with its members and that it should not require
extensive or specialised training.

So how do we see VIEWDATA fulfilling these ambitious requirements -
or at least being a first step in the open ended development which is
now required?

We first see VIEWDATA as a centralised information source. This does
not imply that VIEWDATA will need to incorporate immense data banks on
each and every topic, but rather that it would provide the first point
of entry to a wide diversity of information requirements. Much of
this information is already in existence in a variety of newspapers,
magazines, books of reference, timetables etc.

The problem however is that it is not always readily available when
one needs it. It is not generally classified or structured in such
a way that retrieval of specific items is easy. It is fragmented in
many source texts. It is frequently out of date and sometimes of
dubious quality.

We are all of us innundated with published information of all kinds.
Some of it we read and digest at the time and then discard. A small
part of it we keep for later reference. We have neither the time,
the energy, the inclination, nor indeed the patience and special
skills needed to catalogue and file it for future reference. Thus
we find ourselves unable to get at the information when we really need
it. Thus VIEWDATA would become the first reference point for this

information. By being available all the time, we can get the information when we want it. By being catalogued, filed and indexed we
can retrieve just what we want with the minimum of effort. By being
versatile we would obtain information, the existence of which we frequently may not even be aware of. Also the quality of the information
is likely to be very high and it would be up-to-date.

Secondly, we see VIEWDATA as an intelligent interface with specialised
data banks, which by their nature need to have fairly complex protocols
for access and use. Thus VIEWDATA would translate the requirements of
the user according to the protocol and language specific to the data
bank. This may well only occur infrequently initially, but as these
data banks increase in size, complexity and versatility, the intelligent interface requirement will become increasingly important.

Third, we see VIEWDATA as a communication machine for passing messages
between individuals via an intelligent machine and between individuals and machines. After all, messages are a subject of information
services and as such they may be handled in the same way.

Fourthly, we see VIEWDATA as a temporary or semi-permanent store of
information for an individual's own use, which he may need to access
frequently wherever he might be - perhaps aunty's telephone number.
It is not suggested at this stage that sensitive information should
be kept in a computer file, although this may come later, if and when
adequate safeguards to protect privacy are evolved.

Fifthly, we see VIEWDATA as a new information medium which, like any
other medium, is made available to those private and public agencies
that make it their business to distribute information for profit or
as a public service. For example, it could be a new medium for
classified advertisements and a new medium for distributing information relating to parts of the apparatus of government.

Sixthly, we see VIEWDATA as providing a powerful channel for education
in the home, for which its interactive nature makes it ideally suited.

Seventhly, we see VIEWDATA as providing an advanced calculator service
somewhere between the capability of a pocket calculator and that of
a powerful computer. We regard this as also being information in a
wider sense.

I shall not continue to ennumerate the range of possibilities but
we can see clearly that they are very wide.

VIEWDATA as an information machine.   Perhaps one thing should be
made quite clear at this stage. VIEWDATA is seen to be more an information medium than an information service. The establishment of a
VIEWDATA network would put at the disposal of all, individuals and
organisations alike, the means of disseminating information and of

communicating by electronic means. The information banks are not, and need not be, part of the medium, and frequently will not be. As with all media, the presentation of the information must be compatible with the way the medium operates and the way it is used. This is in a sense the major contribution of VIEWDATA to the dissemination of information, ie in the provision of a well defined, nation-wide, perhaps in due course world-wide, information medium, with compatible interfaces with information sources and a simple and well proven interface with the user.

2   THE VIEWDATA SYSTEM

The VIEWDATA system comprises the following components.

A low cost terminal connected to the telephone system and associated keypads

A distributed network of interconnected computers

A set of data bases, some internal, some external, and a range of information services

A 'natural' protocol for information retrieval

A software organisation for maximising throughput and a set of processes to support the various services.

2.1   THE VIEWDATA TERMINAL

The primary requirement here is for a low-cost device, of pleasing appearance, rugged and reliable and suitable for domestic or professional use in offices. These requirements are met by video terminals, based on the use of standard and unmodified television receivers. Printing terminals are more expensive and not suitable for both domestic and professional environments.

The adaptation of a television receiver for use as a VIEWDATA terminal is carried out by the VIEWDATA adaptor, which, assuming large scale manufacture and the adoption of LSI techniques, meet the low cost and reliability requirements.

The prime function of the adaptor is to store the signals received from the telephone line and after suitable conversion from ASCII code, using a matrix type of character generator, to a form suitable for a line-scan display, drive the television set, and thus refreshes the display 50 times per second. A UHF modulator is used where the input to the television set is via the aerial socket. Where TV sets have been designed to provide an input socket for video input, modulation to VHF

is not required, video injection being used. The VIEWDATA adaptor
also provides the necessary line and frame synchronising signals, which
are added to the video signal before being offered to the UHF modulator, or to the video input of the TV set.

An additional component of the adaptor is the line modem. In the
experimental model shown this accepts an input from the telephone line
at 1200 bits/second and transmits to the telephone line at 75 bits/second,
both channels being capable of operating simultaneoulsy.

A number of additional refinements are also envisaged.

Character rounding is one of them. This can provide a substantial improvement to the appearance of the display, by rounding the staircase-
like appearance of characters when these are generated by a 5:7 dot
matrix, as in the current experimental model. Other facilities such as
flashing characters or other features, and special graphical symbols
are also clearly possible. They add little to the cost of the terminal,
if one postulates large scale integration (LSI), which will clearly
be the case if the service is successful.

A colour display is also another refinement which enhances greatly the
pleasing effect of the display and provides added dimensions of editorial
freedom. In many cases colour increases the intelligibility of the
text, by providing natural breaks. Colour may be added quite simply
and here again the extra cost is small. It is, however, very difficult
to design a UHF adaptor with this facility. Instead it is necessary
to resort to video injection either from an external adaptor, if TV
receivers are provided with the necessary input facilities at video
for the three colour channels, or alternatively the adaptor must be
integral with the TV receiver. It is anticipated that in due course
TV receivers with integral VIEWDATA adaptors will be commercially
available, at reasonable cost, but this will take time. In the meantime the most economical terminal consists of a standard unmodified
TV receiver and an external adaptor using video injection (if the TV
set provides video input facilities) or UHF injection.

The second component of the terminal is the keypad. In the simplest
or basic terminal the keypad is fitted with only 12 keys, the 10
numerals 0 to 9 and the two international keyphone symbols * and # ,
the purpose of which will be explained later. Also in the basic
VIEWDATA terminal, the connection is first established by dialling
the local VIEWDATA computer, using the telephone. In the majority of
cases this will be fitted with a rotary dial, but in certain cases it
may be fitted with a push button keyset.

Where the telephone is already fitted with a push button set, this
may be used instead of the basic keypad, if the telephone is situated
in a convenient position with respect to the television set, so as to

enable signalling the VIEWDATA computer while observing the TV display.

Other versions of the basic keypad are envisaged. In a slightly upgraded version, an additional key, marked VIEWDATA, enables the user
to dial the VIEWDATA computer automatically just by pressing this
button.

For users requiring the full range of VIEWDATA facilities a keypad
of approximately the same size as the basic keypad is provided, but
this, the ALPHAPAD, has a full complement of keys to provide the
full alphabet and punctuation symbols together with arithmetic symbols
and a small number of function keys. Views of both keypads and alpha-
pads are shown in photos 1 and 2.

The normal connection of keypads to the VIEWDATA adaptor or integral
display is provided by means of a coaxial cable, the encoding of the
command signals being carried out in the keypad. It is envisaged
that some versions of the keypad will dispense with the cable
connection and use instead an ultrasonic or infra-red link to the
VIEWDATA adaptor thus allowing freer operation untrammelled with
trailing cables.

When VIEWDATA is used in an office environment, an integral instrument, incorporating VIEWDATA and telephone facilities, the VIEWDATA-
PHONE will be found more convenient (photo 3). This is based on the
use of a small screen television set to which have been added the
VIEWDATA adaptor, the telephone and the keypad, thus providing the
whole range of communications facilities in one set. The VIEWDATA-
PHONE may also be used to receive television broadcasts.

A number of important add-ons are envisaged for the future, for
both standard VIEWDATA and VIEWDATAPHONE. They include a matrix
printer, when hard copy is an essential requirement. This is most
likely to be of importance in the business environment. Another
add-on of great importance is a cassette recorder. This would enable
a large volume of data to be transferred from the computer to the
cassette tape, at high speed, and to be replayed at leisure when
required. This would also offer the facility of transmitting the contents of private files from cassette to computer if required.

The amount of storage provided at present in the experimental VIEWDATA
system is limited to one page of display. This is a total of about
600 characters and an upgraded version is available with a storage
capability of about 1000 characters. This, however, is only the beginning. With the cost of semiconductor storage going down steadily,
further improvements are planned in this area. Increased local storage
to, say, 10 000 or 20 000 characters would provide the capability of
displaying considerably more information, in particular detailed

graphical information, such as complex maps, diagrams, etc, would become possible. This enhanced capability is of particular value in the professional environment compared with the small extra cost of the additional storage.

A block diagram of the VIEWDATA adaptor, and keypads is shown in figs 1 and 2.

2.2   THE VIEWDATA COMPUTER SYSTEM

The design philosophy of VIEWDATA is that access to all information should be available using the public switched network (PSTN) as it exists at present, and that appropriate modifications are introduced to keep pace and take advantage of enhancements as and when they are introduced. Thus no modifications are required to the telephone system before the system can be put in operation.

VIEWDATA is best implemented as a distributed computer system rather than a single centralised one. There are many reasons for this. One of them is to keep telephone call charges to the minimum, preferably to the level of a local call charge. Another is to provide for the expansion of information services with a local flavour, and to develop local interest in the service. This is best done if the computer is not centralised.

Another very important reason is to keep individual data banks to a small (not too small) size in order to simplify control and updating procedures.

In addition, a distributed system provides a higher degree of reliability than a centralised system. Alternative routings and some limited duplication of data banks on a local basis is easily arranged. Other problems such as traffic congestion at a few points are also minimised.

The major criterion however remains that of overall cost to the user. Studies carried out in the past few months have indicated that given an appropriate computer architecture, operating system and applications software, computer connect charges may be kept down to a level about equal to the local telephone call charge (about 1p per minute). Under these circumstances a further reduction in computer connect charges, brought about by the centralisation of computer resources is counter productive, as it can only lead to a greatly increased total cost to the customer due to the increased telephone call charge. The only important exception to note here is the case where the value of the information to the user is so high that call charges and connect charges become insignificant. This may apply for example to financial information in times of high volatility. The regional centre concept explained below, provides the half way house designed to cope with this situation. In such cases the user would connect up to the regional centre for this limited range of services.

A typical VIEWDATA computer with duplicate appears to be capable of supporting about 300 to 400 simultaneous users, which might imply an effective user population of some 10 000 to 20 000.

The VIEWDATA system viewed at the local connection level would be as shown in fig.3. This illustrates the VIEWDATA terminal connected to the local VIEWDATA computer by way of one or more local exchanges. Further connections would be established from the local VIEWDATA computer to other computers and where the demand exists to one or more specialised data banks.

At the network level, it is possible to envisage a number of regional centres, as in fig.4, in each of which four or five VIEWDATA computers would support local users, with a regional centre distributing information and updating the data stores resident in each computer. Regional centres would accept information of local interest for distribution to the individual local VIEWDATA computer. Such a regional information network might support a user population of perhaps 100 000 to 200 000.

Several regional centres would be necessary to provide the nationwide service, the size of each regional centre being approximately as indicated.

At the wider level a national information centre, which would be fully manned, would provide the inflow of national information to the individual VIEWDATA computer via the regional centres. The national centre would accept input from the information supplier, hopefully in a ready formatted form, to be distributed to the local centre. It could also provide the necessary connection to the individual data banks established for the specialist.

A national network of this type would probably be designed to cater for the needs of, say, a 1 million to 2 million user population. Clearly it is also possible to design this network for a considerably larger user population.

It is envisaged that communication between the regional centres and the local VIEWDATA computers would be by means of medium speed data lines, say 2400 to 9600 bits per second, mainly for the updating of fairly static information, such as yellow pages, classified ads etc. Communication between the national centre and each regional centre would be at a higher data rate, say 48 k bits per second, mainly to ensure the transmission of high value of information which is likely to change very frequently. Since this information is not intended to be relayed down to the local VIEWDATA computers, the latter do not need the higher speed communications links to the regional centres.

2.3   THE DATA BANKS

We have already mentioned the point that VIEWDATA is more an
information medium than an information service. The major implication of the statement is that it is available to information
suppliers to enable them to disseminate their product to the users.
Thus information suppliers would collect, collate, edit and input
the information to the medium. The users would retrieve this information according to their needs.

The physical storage of some of this information may be in the hands
of the information suppliers or within the VIEWDATA system. Clearly
it is more economic to store this information in the local VIEWDATA
computer thus minimising the cost of its retrieval to the user. Thus
high-usage, low-cost information is likely to be stored in a storage
medium local to the VIEWDATA computer. This includes yellow page
information, directory information, news, sports results, entertainment,
classified advertisements, travel etc.

More specialised information, usually high intrinsic value, but lower
total usage, may be stored at a regional centre, or at the national
centre, or may even reside at the information suppliers own data bank.
We have already mentioned that financial information may reside at the
regional centre. Even more specialised information, such as library
information, may reside in the information suppliers own storage.

Apart from information provided by professional information suppliers,
VIEWDATA will also accommodate stored information which is intended to
be passed on from one user to one or more other users, eg messages to
be transmitted from one person to another or to many others. Other
information may be input by a user for his own benefit. Clearly these
banks of information will be stored in VIEWDATA's own computers. It
is not difficult to visualise the development at some later date of
warehouses of information, similar to warehouses for physical goods.
These warehouses will provide a storage service and possibly an access
service. VIEWDATA, by virtue of its networking ability, would also
provide a channel of access to these information stores, according to
the desired protocol.

A range of information services for which VIEWDATA has been designed
to provide the means of distribution and retrieval is very wide. It
will be seen from fig.5 that it covers the almost entire range of
information needs of society. At one end of the scale we have general
information services of a topical nature, such as news, sports results,
financial news and entertainment information, and also information of
a reference nature such as timetables, directions and yellow pages.
Information on leisure activities such as DIY, recipes, hobbies, would
also come under the same heading.

At the other end of the scale the information services are extended to services capable of taking advantage of the user interaction facilities provided by VIEWDATA, such as education services, calculator services and reservation transactions. Classified advertisement services may also be extended by interaction to the request of sales literature, prices etc and even to ordering.

In between the two ends of the range there are a host of services to the business and domestic users. Messages services in particular provide a fast and economic modern electronic equivalent to the telegram service. Other potentially important services are those of interest to the business user, or in the public services where the information is required for use in-house, or to be distributed to large numbers of outside customers on a regular basis.

The extent of the locally stored data bases, and hence the range of services provided will depend primarily on demand. The physical storage of this information does not appear to present serious problems, at least for the foreseeable future. Given a modest 20 Mbyte disc for the information store, a total of at least 20 000 pages (1000 character pages) of information may be provided. This figure may be doubled using fairly simple storage savings techniques. Thus local information centres may be expected in due course to have available something of the order of 200 000 pages of information for immediate access. This is a great deal of data. For example the complete listing of stocks and shares prices in the back pages of the Financial Times would occupy under 150 pages.

2.4 THE "NATURAL" PROTOCOL

The major obstacle which stands in the way of users of computer-based information and communications systems is the protocol, ie the set of rules and procedures which govern access to and use of the computer. For the professional frequently using a specific computer for a narrow range of activities, the protocol presents no long term problem; only short term problems remain which, given sufficient enthusiasm, tenacity, sagacity and deductive intelligence, the dedicated computer user is able to overcome satisfactorily.

Part of the protocol is made up of code words and observations which are designed to reduce the work load of the computer and hence increase its cost effectiveness. The trained computer user has no difficulty in using these abbreviated codes; indeed he frequently creates new abbreviations, so as to speed his own work. Nevertheless before he is able to use the computer-based information service effectively he must be thoroughly trained in its protocol. Different computers have different protocols and additional training must be done when a subsantial change to the data base protocol or to the supporting computer is carried out. For these reasons it is clear

that the normal computer protocol is not suitable for the majority of
potential users of the information and communications services provided
by VIEWDATA. These potential users, whether they be in the domestic
or the business environment, cannot be expected to submit to extensive
training to learn and memorize the necessary protocols, nor to remember every minute detail of it whenever they need information.

The use of manuals has also been excluded on principle. Manuals have
a habit of starting small and then growing in size out of all recognition and usually out of keeping with the needs of the users. Thus
manuals would tend to erode the basic simplicity of VIEWDATA and would
in time subvert it to look like any other computer-based information
system - very useful, but difficult to use.

Therefore in VIEWDATA there are no manuals and no protocol. There is
however a small set of basic instructions - exactly five in number,
which are printed on a small card, the VIEWDATA card, and also engraved
on the keypad in use.

These instructions tell the user how:

(a)   to access the system, ie which telephone number to use and the
      user number. With automatic dialling keypads this instruction
      is not necessary.

(b)   to recover from errors, eg what to do to correct a miskey, how
      to return to the top of the selection tree, how to go back to
      an earlier page.

(c)   to bypass much of the selection tree procedures, for users who
      have already used the system several times and already know
      the page number of the information they are seeking.

Essentially the "natural" protocol consists of nothing more than
giving numerical responses, by pressing appropriate keys on the keypad, to the computer to indicate a choice of the alternative routes
offered to the user, the one selected usually ending at a point where
the information the user is seeking is presented to him.

We may look at this selection process in one of two ways.

In certain cases it represents a model of the data structure itself,
which is arranged on the basis of a selection tree, each branch
giving access to a different classification of the information. For
example, if the data base is classified according to fig.5, then
the first page of the selection tree would offer the choices indicated by the headings. Each choice is identified by a numeral
between 0 and 9 and the user would enter the next lower level of
selection by keying the appropriate number.

The selection tree may also be looked at from a different point of view. It may be considered to be a questionnaire to elicit from the user precisely what information he desires. Once this has been ascertained a code is built up by the VIEWDATA computer according to the specific protocol of the particular data base the user wishes to access. The questionnaire is not a model of the data structure, but it elicits the necessary keywords which are necessary to access the data base. For example, one may have a sequential data structure, each record consisting of, say, a person's name, address, occupation, etc. The purpose of the VIEWDATA protocol is to elicit from the user the appropriate key words and offer these to the data base in the correct format.

This approach is of course not new, but in VIEWDATA it has been developed into a general purpose selection system, applicable to the majority of retrieval cases.

You will have seen a demonstration of this system on a large variety of information topics and there is no doubt that it works. Users learn very quickly how to use the information base, indeed within seconds of taking hold of a keypad. Also by providing a jump facility to a frequently used page, the more experienced user does not need to go through the whole selection procedure. In the cases so far demonstrated, the selection procedure is indeed a model of the data structure, but the alternative methods of structuring the data base is currently under investigation, specifically using a telephone directory enquiry system - as an example.

2.5 SOFTWARE DESIGN

In the more usual and simpler case of where the selection tree is a model of the data base organisation, information retrieval can be extremely efficient, in terms of minimising the amount of processing required to locate and output the information.

The process of locating and outputting information consists of three parts. Given that a page of information containing a list of choices and the corresponding numeral responses offered to the user has been displayed on the screen, the following tasks follow in succession:

1   The acceptance of a numeric response from the user

2   The matching of the response with the address of the next page in disc storage

3   The transfer of this next page to primary storage

4   The output of this next page to the user

Using a standard RTE operating system in a mini-computer the timings
of the operation are approximately as follows:

1   Deciding the next page to be output, from user's response:
     approx 1 msec.

2   Fetching page of information from disc: approx 63 msec.

3   Outputting page using standard interrupt driven driver:
     120 msec (for 960 character page).

The transmitting time at 1200 bits per second of a 960 character page,
using start stop asynchronous signalling, is approximately 9 seconds.
Allowing, say, 3 seconds for a response to be given by the user, we
might take it that on the average a new page is to be output to each
user about every 12 seconds.

From the timings shown above one bottleneck is likely to be the disk
transfers, which would limit the number of simultaneous users to an
absolute maximum of about 200, more likely 100, to ensure an adequate
computer response time. Another bottleneck is clearly the output to
line, which places an even lower limit to the total number of simultaneous users, an absolute maximum of 100, more likely 50.

The output bottleneck may be overcome quite simply by moving away from
an interrupt driven output mechanism, which handles characters one at
a time, to a continuous polling mechanism which clears the page buffers
onto the line buffers, at a rate just below the output transmission
rate, thus ensuring the line buffers never overflow. The polling
mechanism may be improved in efficiency, if, for example, more than
one character at a time is transferred to line buffer. The polling
mechanism shown by the flow diagram of fig.6 is based on the use of
a conventional minicomputer, now much established in the UK.   It
handles two characters at a time at an average CPU time of 12.5 μsec
per character, thus requiring 12.5 msec to output a 1000 character
page. Given this order of performance the major bottleneck is now
in the disk transfer arrangements, rather than in the output arrangements. The use of larger line-buffers, which would make it possible
to transfer several characters at a time from page buffers to line
buffers, would reduce the significance of output timing even further.

The disk transfer time indicated above is almost twice as long as it
needs to be, because the standard software available on the experimental machine only handles $\frac{1}{2}$ page at a time (one disc sector). To
maximise disk throughput it is clearly more advantageous to transfer
a full page at a time, from disk to core. This would reduce the disk
transfer time to 32.5 msec on the average. At the same time, by
using appropriate software to optimise disk throughput, a substantially
lower time per disk transfer may be achieved. One such system consists

of sweeping the seek area of the disk mechanism unidirectionally, first from the periphery to the centre, then back to the periphery, and transferring records on the way. Such an optimisation system would reduce average disk timing to less than about 20 msec, thus giving an absolute maximum number of simultaneous users of about 600. A computer simulation of the whole timing system is now in progress and it is anticipated that a single medium size mini-computer should be able to support comfortably well over 200 simultaneous users.

3   CONCLUSION

An experimental study of a computer-based information distribution and retrieval interactive medium, called VIEWDATA, has been carried out with a view to investigating the potential of such a medium to providing a nation-wide information and message service to the general public and to the professional user.

The medium, which is based on the use of low cost television type displays and a very simple and "natural" protocol, can support a very large number of information and message services and can lend itself to a great variety of interactive information services. It has been demonstrated to be very easy to use and to require no training whatsoever on the part of the users, to extract the maximum benefit from it. Special hardware and software enhancements to the experimental system are planned for the purpose of optimising its operation and improving its cost effectiveness. It is confidently expected that they will result in an economical and reliable system which may form the basis of a completely new and beneficial service.

ACKNOWLEDGEMENTS

The writer wishes to thank the Director of Research, Post Office Research Centre, for permission to publish this paper. Also to acknowledge gratefully the constant support and encouragement of the VIEWDATA Project Director, and the unstinting help he has received from all the members of the VIEWDATA team and many others who have contributed to subsequent implementation of the experimental system.

May 1975

FIG 1   BASIC KEYPAD

FIG 2   ALPHAPAD

FIG 3   VIEWDATAPHONE

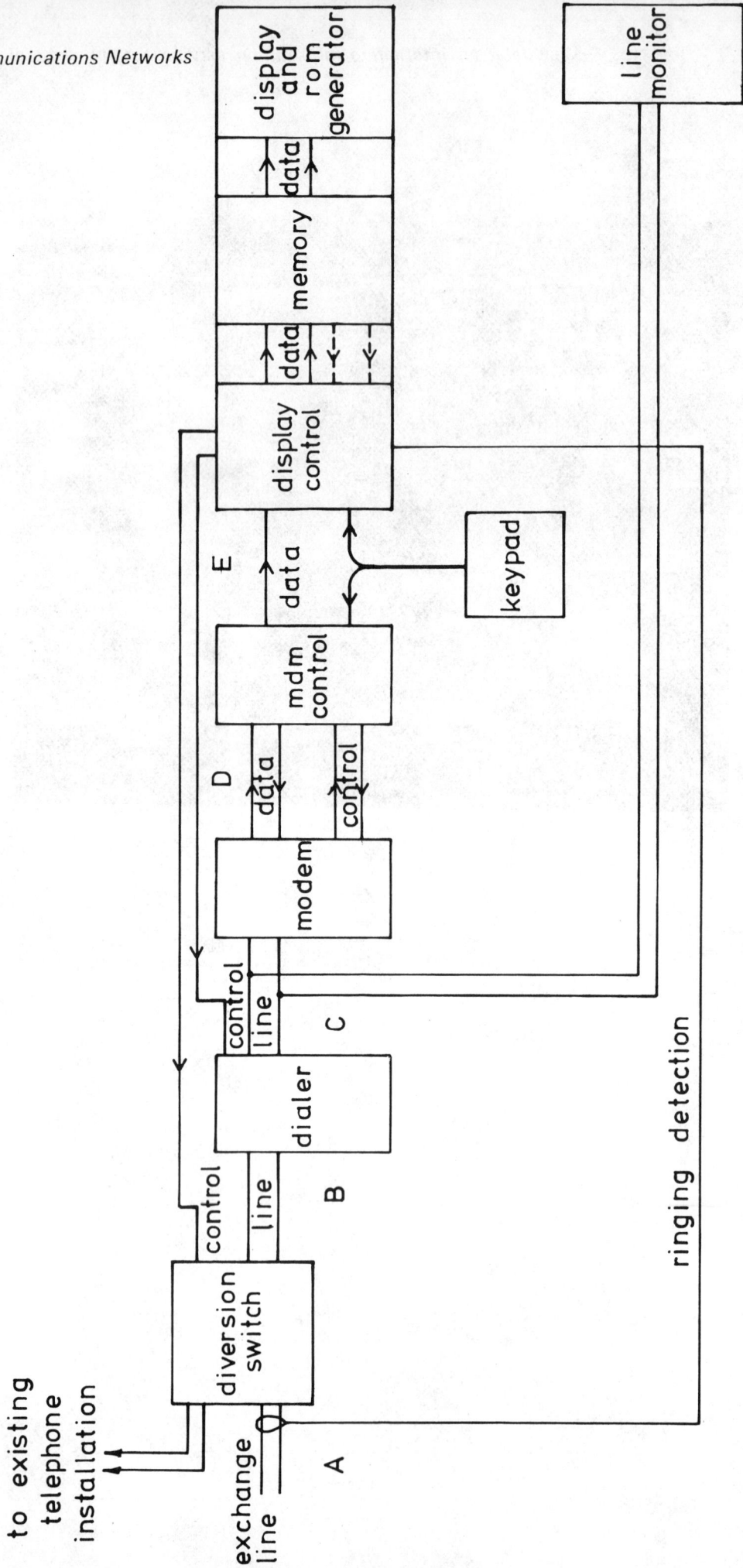

FIG. 1.

FIG. 3   VIEWDATA CONNECTIONS

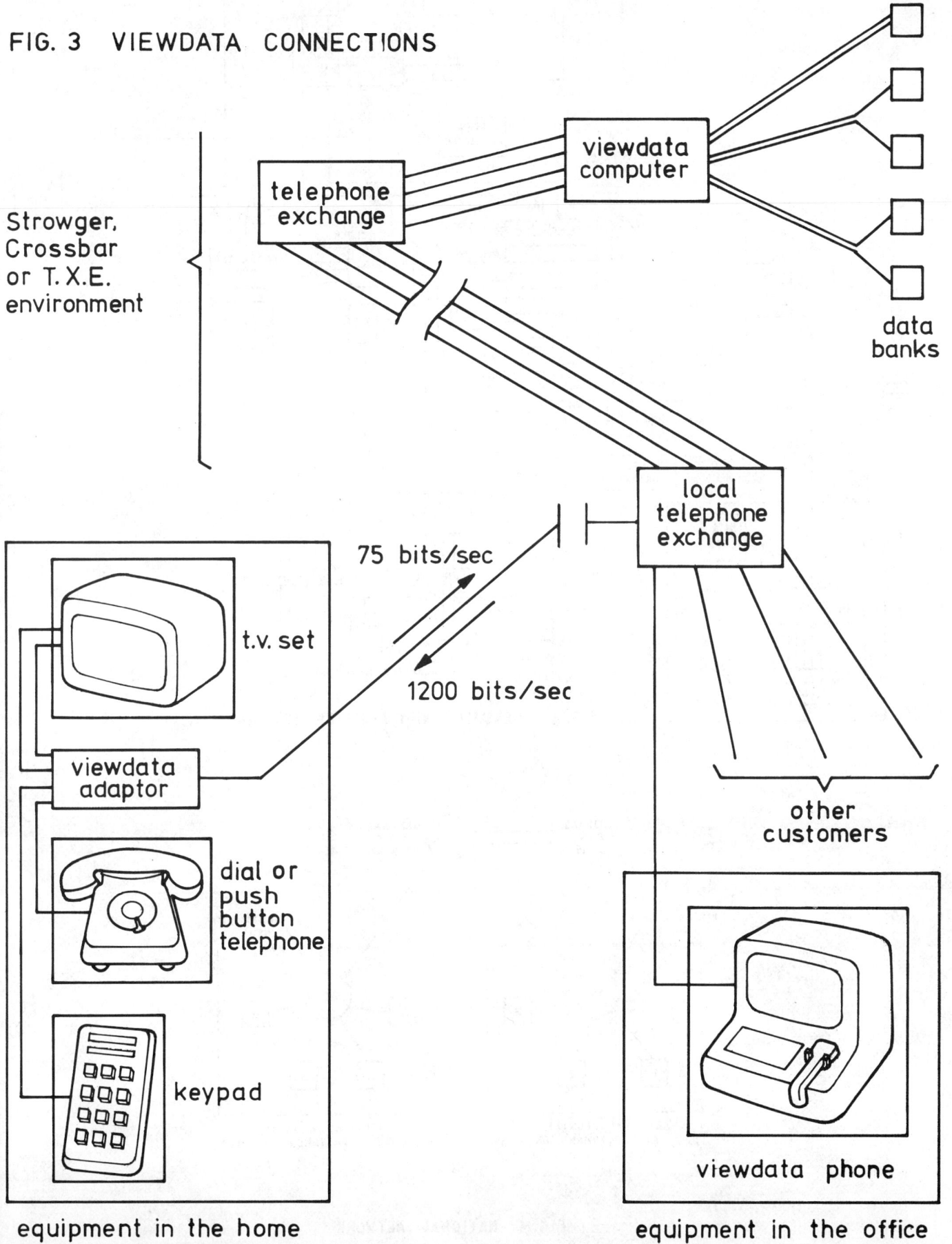

Strowger,
Crossbar
or T.X.E.
environment

telephone exchange

viewdata computer

data banks

75 bits/sec

1200 bits/sec

local telephone exchange

other customers

t.v. set

viewdata adaptor

dial or push button telephone

keypad

viewdata phone

equipment in the home

equipment in the office

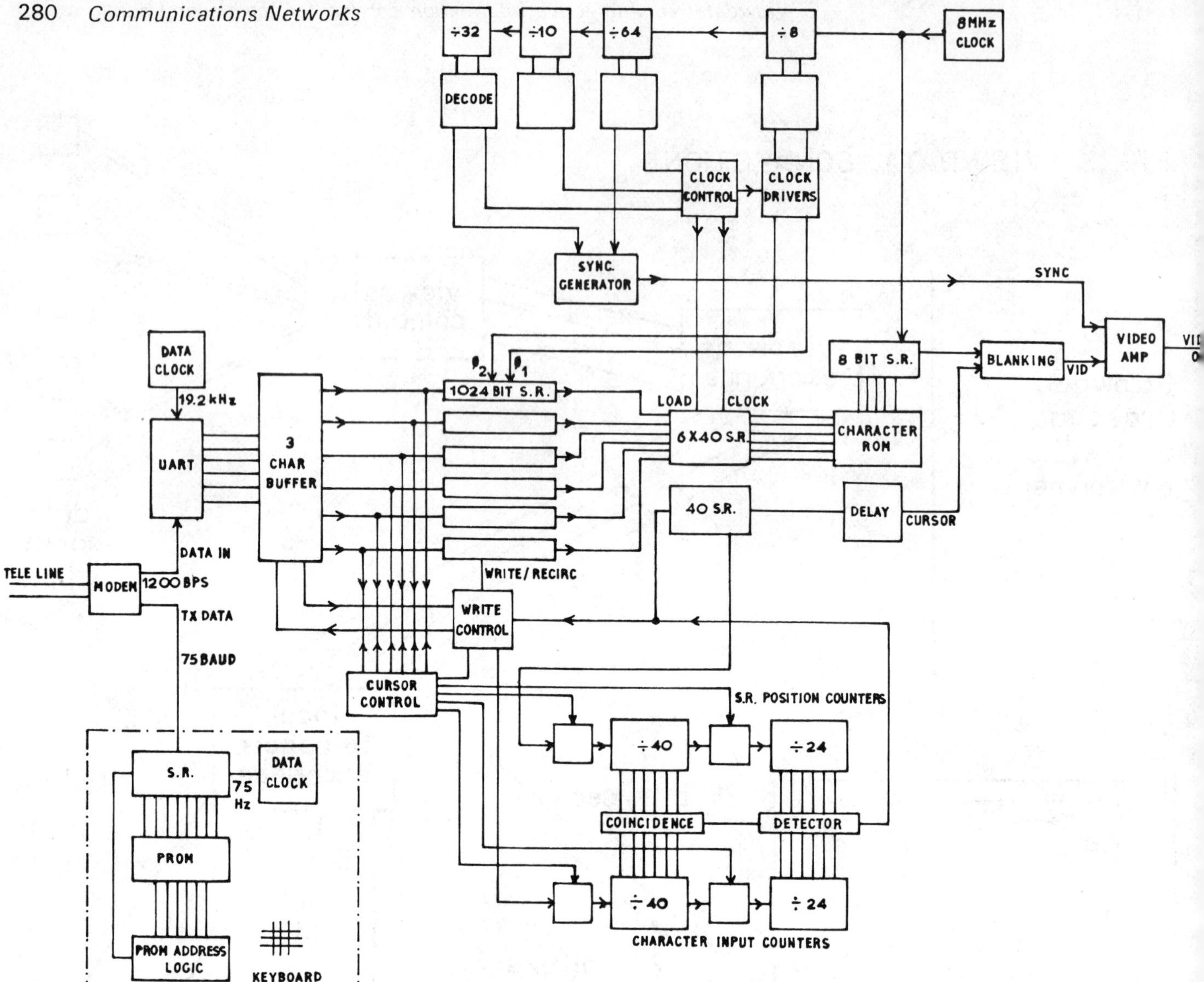

FIG. 2   VIEWDATA SHIFT REGISTER TERMINAL

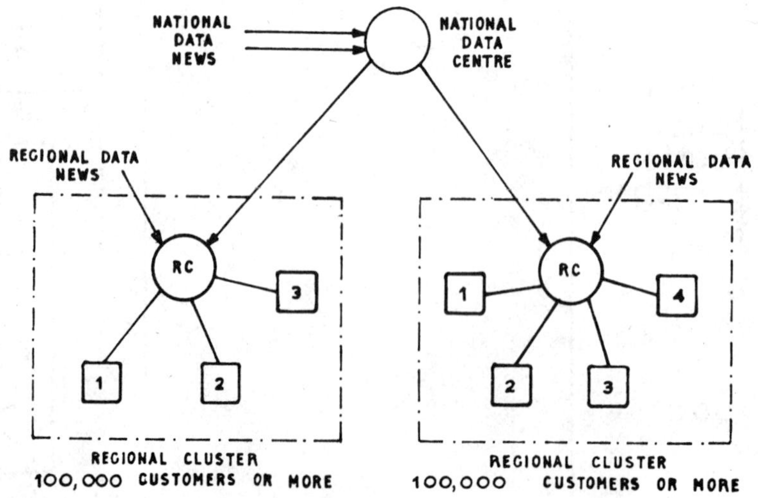

FIG. 4   NATIONAL NETWORK

1. General Info Services	2. Classified Ads	3. Professional Info Services	4. Business Applications	5. Message Communications Aids	6. Shopping Aids	7. Education	8. Calculator Service	9. Reservations
News	Properties	Components data	In house info services	Electronic telegram	Market prices	Courses at home	Slide rule service	Hotels
Sports	Employment	Literature retrieval	In house phone directories	Telex connection	Special offers	School homework service	Business calc.	Cars
Financial	Services	Technical info	Business info	Newspaper reporting	Mail order	Special coaching	Technical calc.	Travel
Entertainment	Articles for sale		Secretarial service	Phone for deaf		Adult education		Holidays
			Circulars					
Time tables			Accounts info					
Phone directories			Personnel					
Yellow pages								
Leisure								
D.I.Y.								
Recipes								

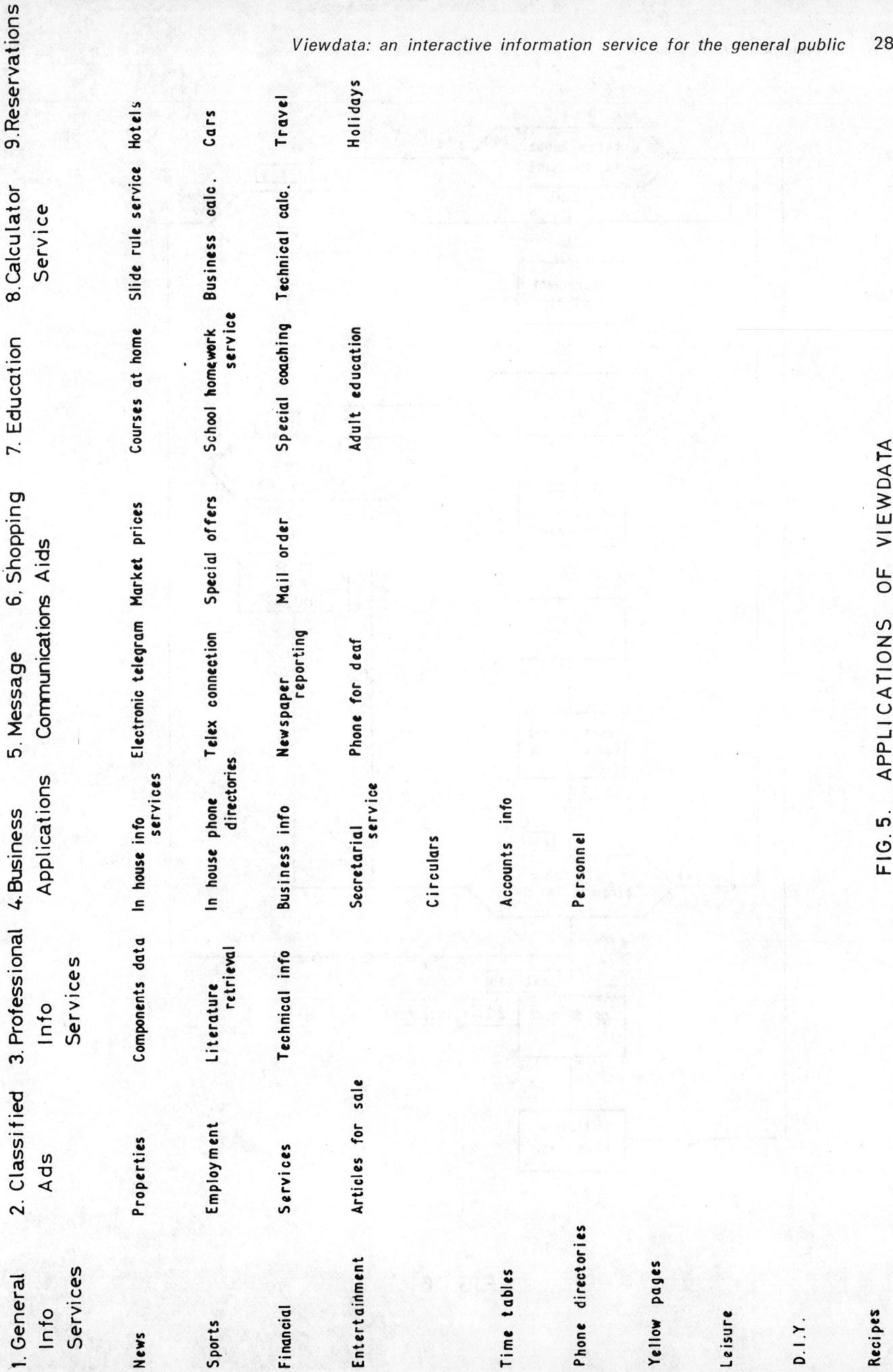

FIG. 5.   APPLICATIONS OF VIEWDATA

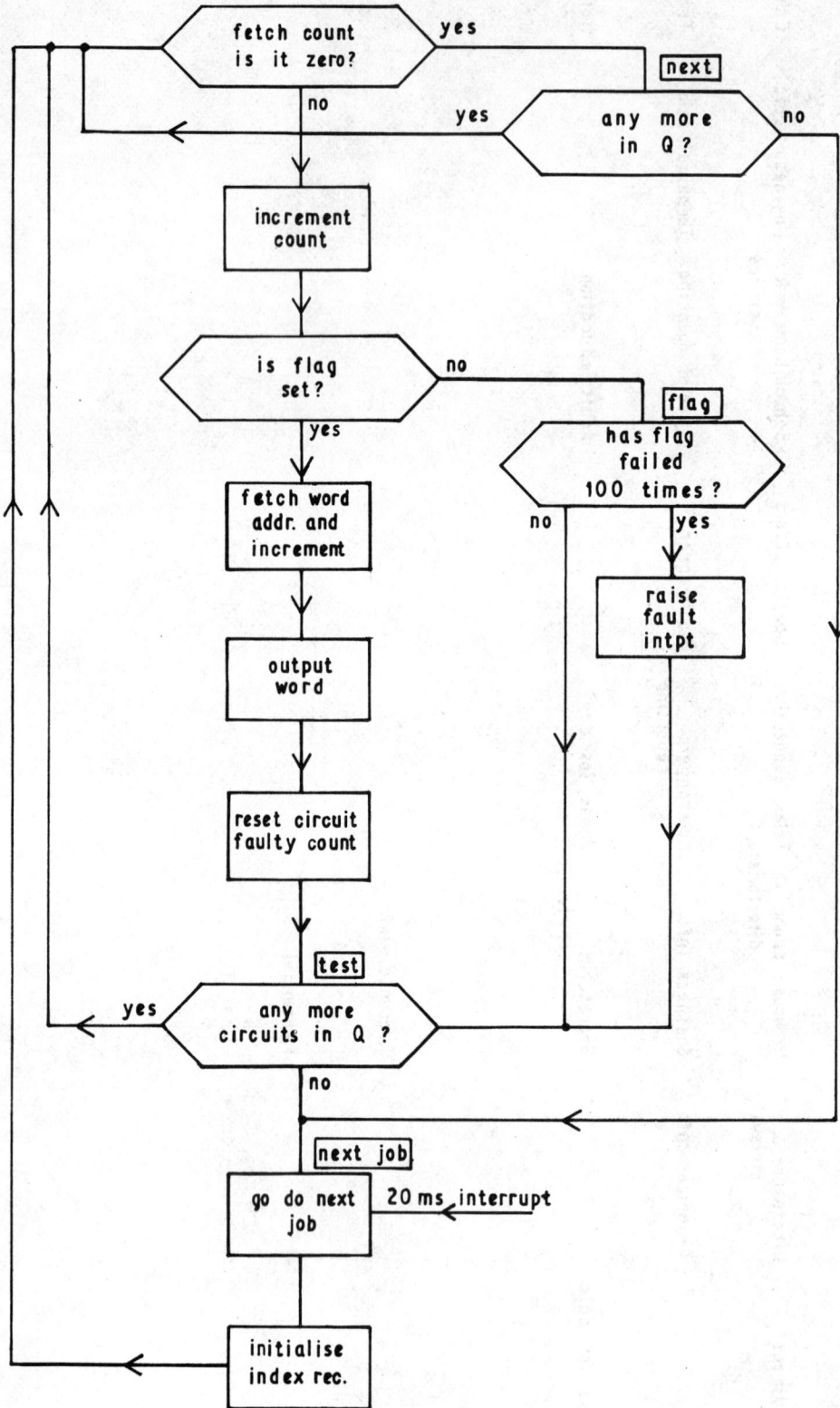

FIG. 6

Simulation of a data communication network

T. H. Beeforth and M. C. Daniels

University of Sussex, U.K.

This paper describes simulations of a data communication network with special reference to different routing methods.   The simulation is applied to a 25-node network and the effectiveness of the routing methods is assessed by considering the resultant system response to traffic demands under varying load conditions.

Predetermined routing was simulated first, in which there is only one specified route between any pair of exchanges.   If any part of that route is not available no alternatives are considered.   System performance is of course very dependent on the original route specifications.

Two types of adaptive routing methods were simulated.   In the centralised version, one exchange in the network maintains up-to-date network statistics which are then used every time there is a request for a route.   System congestion can be very greatly reduced in this way and high values of system utilisation obtained.   In progressive methods, routes are determined by selecting the most appropriate forwarding link from each exchange encountered, according to the prevailing local conditions.   Link selection may be simply by availability and directness, or by a weighted consideration of all available forwarding links.

Results obtained for adaptive routing methods were in general found to be better than those of predetermined routing but not as good as with centralised routing.   Routing effectiveness is however only one factor to be taken into account when choosing a routing method, and other relevant factors are discussed.

Introduction

In many data communications systems, both proposed and already implemented, data messages are split into standard-format packets for transmission through a network of exchanges (refs. 1, 2). The data packets of a given message then travel to their destination comparatively independently of each other: in some systems every individual packet is responsible for finding its own way to the destination, whereas in others, all the packets of a given message are constrained to follow the same route (ref. 3).

A more significant distinction here between different systems is in their response to increasing traffic demands. In some systems virtually all data for transmission will be accepted whatever the current loading, so that the user becomes aware of a heavily loaded system through rapidly increasing system delays (ref. 4). Alternatively further traffic may be accepted only if the network has sufficient resources still available to ensure an acceptable response, so that as the system loading approaches its maximum so an increasing proportion of intending-users simply finds the system engaged.

In all of these systems however, a fundamental problem is that of determining the most appropriate routing philosophy, and there is considerable debate on the relative merits of different approaches in different circumstances. Where all traffic is accepted, the effectiveness of a routing method may be conveniently assessed in terms of the delays experienced by packets travelling through the system (refs. 5, 6), but another viewpoint, particularly useful where traffic demands may be rejected, is provided by considering the variation of traffic acceptance with system loading. A typical relationship for a packet type system is shown in fig. 1. At light system loading all requests for routes can be accepted and the acceptance rate is 100%. At 100% loading no further routes can be allocated and the acceptance rate of new calls has fallen to zero. The striking and quite typical feature of fig. 1, however, is the break point above which the acceptance of further traffic demands falls abruptly below 100%. Clearly, with a given network it is important that an operating philosophy shall be chosen that will maintain 100% traffic acceptance to as high a system loading as possible, and this paper is concerned with the development and comparison of different routing methods with that objective in mind.

Although this paper refers specifically to the routing of standard format packets through a data communication system, it will be apprec-

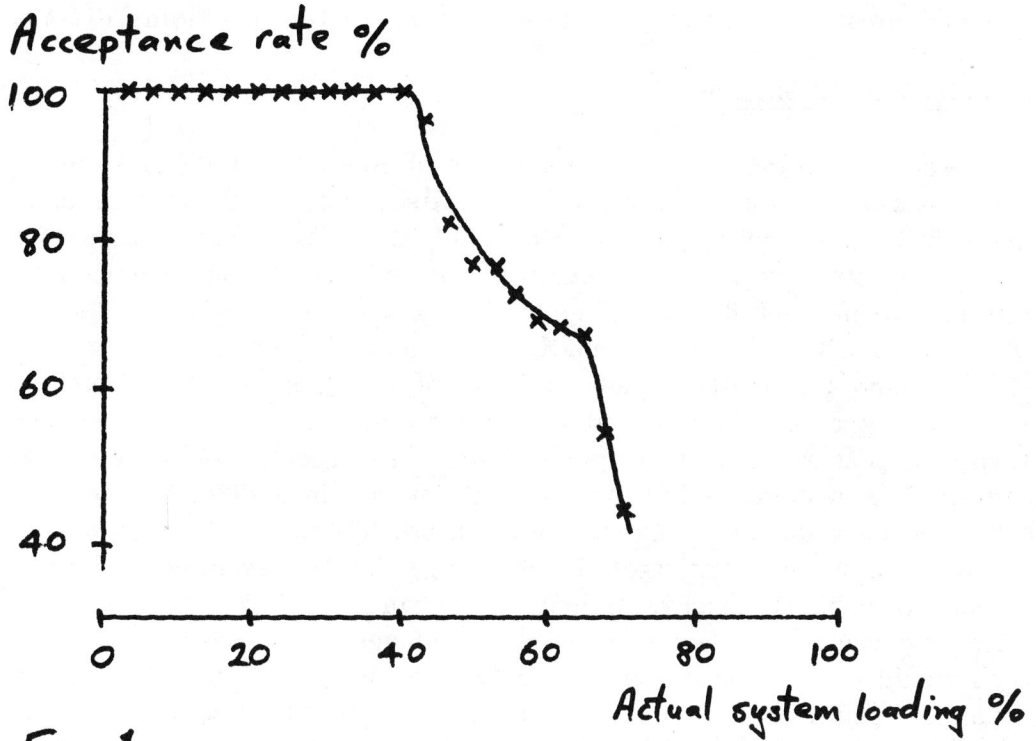

Fig 1

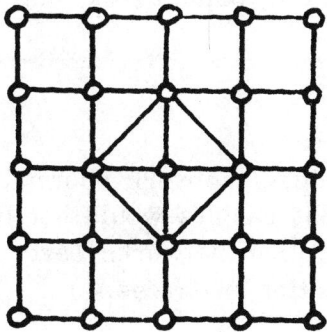

Fig 2

Network number three

iated that the techniques and results described may be of relevance to
any communication or transport system where routing problems exist.

The Principles of Routing

Acceptance-rate break-points occur at less than 100% system
loading because of the development of localised congestion and the subsequent failure of routing methods to avoid it.   The basic objects of a
good routing strategy must therefore be to circumvent congestion, but
preferably to prevent it developing in the first place.   Ideally, the
routing philosophy will be continually optimising the match between
traffic demand and available network capacity.   If both demand and
network are precisely known and do not vary at all, then a simple predetermined routing method is appropriate.   All routes could be decided
in advance of system implementation and entered in a directory to be
read out when required.   On the other hand, if the traffic demand is
uncertain and the network itself is changing, due for example to break
down or other short term variations in exchange or link capacities, then
an adaptive routing method may offer advantages.   In adaptive routing,
routes would be decided on demand only after reference in some way or
another to conditions existing in at least the relevant parts of the network
at that particular time.   The advantage of pre-determined routing is its
operational simplicity, but its disadvantage is that there is no facility for
coping with significant changes in either the traffic demand or in the
system itself.

The main value of simulation is to allow comparisons of the
technical effectiveness of different routing philosophies before actual
implementation.   There is never a simple answer to the question 'which
is the best method?' since this will depend on the particular network
topology, the 'cost' of including more complex routing methods, and on
many other individual factors, but a valuable starting point to the discussion is provided by advance simulation results.

The Simulations

The simulations refer to the 25-node high level network shown in
fig. 2.   A symmetrical network was chosen so that results would not be
influenced unduly by topological peculiarities, but other networks have
been studied by substituting the appropriate connection matrices.

Each simulation starts by assuming the network empty, and then steadily increasing the loading until the acceptance rate breakpoint is reached. In this way, various characteristics of the system will be found as functions of the system loading, such that it may then be possible to develop improvements to the routing method being tested.

System loading is built up from zero by generating route demands and attempting to establish a route from each source to destination according to the method being used. Route demands are generated by selecting a random source-destination pair of exchanges, according to a rectangular distribution, but such that consecutive sequences of 600 demands include every one of the 25 x 24 different source-destination pairs possible in the network. Individual calls connected are assumed to occupy one unit of system capacity, so that when a route search is successful the loadings of the corresponding links and exchanges are incremented by one. No calls are disconnected, so that with further route connections the system loading steadily increases towards 100%. Eventually, some route searches must fail, and the traffice acceptance rate falls from 100%, as indicated, for example, in fig. 1.

In each simulation the capacity of the system is set so that over 10,000 route-demands can be accepted. This is a sufficiently large multiple of the basic set of 600 different routes to smooth out any statistical fluctuations within the random generation of each set.

Limiting Factors to System Capacity

System capacity will be influenced primarily by exchange processing power and inter-exchange link capacity. Ideally, these two factors would contribute equally, so that exchange and link loadings would be evenly balanced, but in practice, it may well be that the overall system loading will be limited predominantly by either one of them.

One attraction of simulation is that such parameters may be varied quite easily, and hence the effectiveness of different routing methods under the different conditions readily compared.

Predetermined Routing

In predetermined routing only one specified route between each pair of source destination exchanges is permitted. If any part of such a route is found to be blocked that route search is unsuccessful.

Clearly, the effectiveness of such a method depends greatly on the original selection of routes.   Fig.1 shows a graph of acceptance rate as a function of system loading for one selection where it can be seen that route searches begin to fail at the comparatively modest overall system loading of 43%.

If the various individual link and exchange loadings are examined at the break point loading, it will be found that some parts of the system have reached 100% loading, causing a subsequent fall in acceptance rate, but that other parts of the system are still very lightly loaded.

An improved performance results if the original allocation of routes is designed to spread the load more evenly over all parts of the network.   For a network of 25 nodes this allocation proves quite difficult, even when the methods of linear programming are employed, but the consequent improvement in the network performance is considerable, fig.3(a). More subtle approaches to predetermined routing are available and with a constant pattern of traffic demand some further improvement in acceptance rate can result.   Such improvement must however be treated with some caution: the routing methods are, in effect, being tailored to fit a particular traffic pattern to a particular network, and as there is none of the inherent flexibility associated with adaptive routing, the methods are not immediately able to cope effectively with fluctuations in demand distribution, or with changes in the network.

Adaptive Routing

The distinctive feature of adaptive routing methods is that the current state of the network is taken into account at the time of each demand for a route.   Adaptive methods may conveniently be categorised into centralised or progressive.

In centralised routing methods one exchange acts as central control to which all route demands are referred.   This exchange maintains an up-to-date record of the loading of every link and exchange for reference by the route search method being employed.

On the other hand, in progressive routing methods, packets are forwarded from exchange to exchange in a progressive attempt to estab-

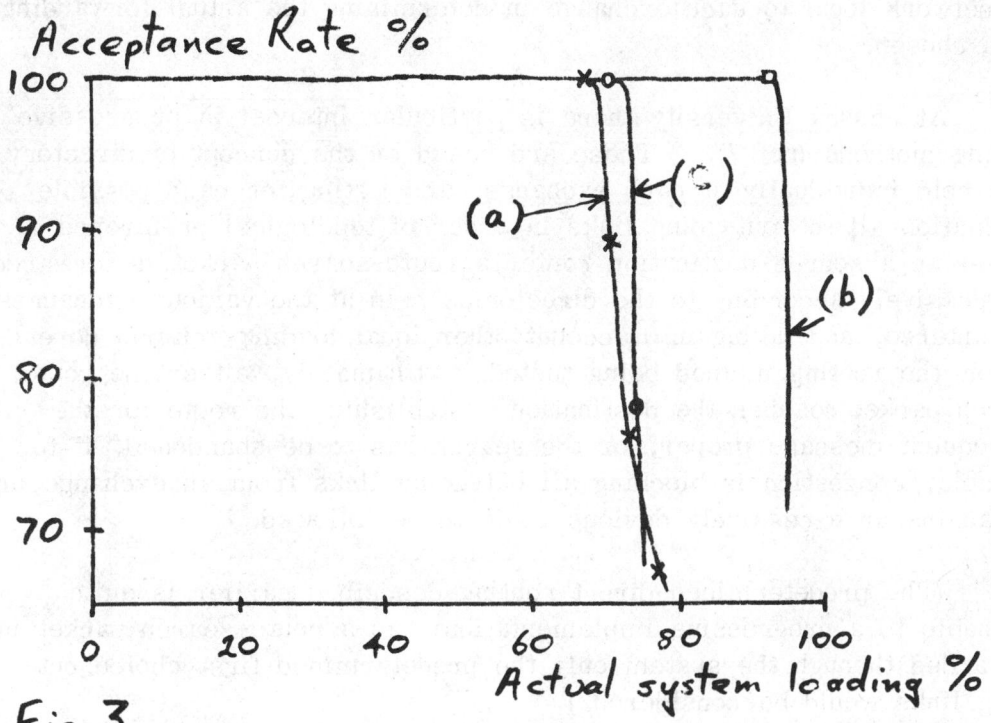

Fig 3

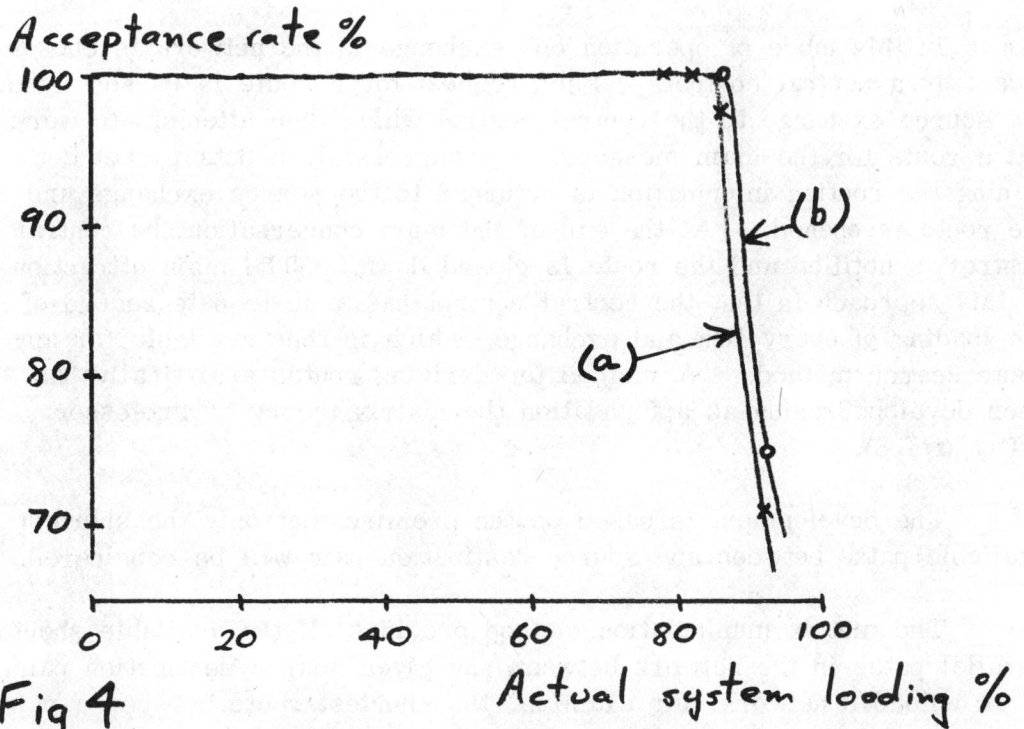

Fig 4

lish a route from source to destination, taking into account the state of the network local to each exchange in determining the actual forwarding links chosen.

At Sussex University there is particular interest in progressive routing methods (ref. 7).   These are based on the concept of directory lists held individually at each exchange, and listing for each possible destination all the out-going links in order of topological preference. To set up a source-destination route, a route-search packet is forwarded progressively according to the directories held at the various exchanges encountered, and taking into account other local loading criteria dependant on the routing method being tested.   Ultimately, either the route search packet reaches the destination, establishing the route for the subsequent message proper, or the search has to be abandoned, if for example, congestion is blocking all out-going links from an exchange or is causing an excessively devious route to be followed.

(The predetermined direct routing described earlier is quite amenable to a progressive implementation: as a route-search packet is forwarded through the system only the predetermined first choice out-going links would be considered.)

Centralised Routing

In this mode of operation one exchange in the network is chosen to act as a central control.   Each request for a route is passed from the source exchange to the central control which then attempts to work out a route for the main message.   If successful, a data packet containing the routing information is returned to the source exchange and the route is opened.   At the end of the main conversation the central control is notified and the route is closed down.   The main attraction of this approach is that the central control has an up-to-date record of the loading of every link and exchange, which is then available for any route search method.   A method for deriving routes analytically has been developed using as a foundation the matrix theory of Professor I. Paz (ref. 8).

The development is based on the premise that only the shortest available paths between any source destination pair will be considered.

The matrix manipulation method provides all the available shortest parallel paths in the network between any given source-destination pair. In an unloaded network, for example, the shortest route between a pair

of nodes may be three links.   However, if these links prove to be
blocked when the network becomes loaded then routes of four links length
will be found.   The process can be repeated until either a route is
found or it is decided not worthwhile to proceed.   For example, in
network three, fig. 2, the longest of the direct routes contains seven
links and there are 18 possible choices of route.   It is not considered
profitable to allow more devious paths as most of the relevant links will
already have been taken into account with the previous 18 choices.

The choice between the parallel paths found can be made on
several different criteria.   These may be a simple arithmetic total of
the loading of each link or a combination of the mean loading of each
route and the standard deviation.   The most satisfactory has been the
first method, that is choosing the route with the greatest total amount
of capacity still available regardless of the distribution of the loading on
the individual links.

A graph of the route search results for network number 3 is
shown in fig. 3(b), and the breakpoint of over 90% is typical of centralised routing methods.

Although as expected, centralised routing results in a very effective use of network resources there are nevertheless serious disadvantages.   As with any centralised control, the system is very vulnerable
to failure in the control area, and also, its effective capacity is significantly reduced by the overheads involved in transmitting routing information and network statistics to and from the control area.

For these reasons little further work was carried out on centralised routing methods, but the results achieved did at least set a useful
target for non-centralised methods.

Progressive Routing

In progressive adaptive methods the choice of forwarding links
from each exchange is made only after specified local conditions have
been considered.   For example, the selection criteria may be that only
forwarding links heading most directly to the destination shall be considered and that where there is more than one such link the choice will be
simply the least loaded.   In this way all routes will follow the shortest
path between source and destination but flexibility is introduced where
alternative routes exist.

Fig. 3(c) shows the performance of the network using the above method and it can be seen that the introduction of a comparatively small amount of flexibility has again raised the break point to somewhat over 70%, virtually the same as with the improved predetermined method, fig. 3(a).   However, the performance of adaptive routing may be further improved by introducing more sophisticated selection criteria whereas it is difficult to visualise much scope for further improvements to the predetermined methods.

Sequential Routing

This is a simple and obvious development of adaptive routing, but one which introduces some of the complications present in more elaborate methods.   The directory in each exchange lists all the links from that exchange in order of topological preference for every destination, so that if the first preference link is already fully loaded or out of action then second or third choices and so on may be considered.

Fig. 4(a)   shows the acceptance rate characteristic compared to that of adaptive direct routing.   Clearly a useful improvement appears to have been achieved.

Since routes may now deviate from the most direct, the first complication that arises is a possibility of routes going round in circles. The simple example of this, where messages are shuttled back and forth between the same two exchanges (ping pong), is readily detected in practice since exchange processors need only compare the intended forwarding link to the arrival link.   If they are the same then the next forwarding link suggested by the directory list must be considered or the route search abandoned.

To   detect circling around several exchanges is more difficult. Route-search messages could carry their route history with them, or alternatively, each exchange could record the identity of every route search passing through.   The solution adopted in the Sussex system is for the total deviation from the most direct route to be arbitrarily limited.   This is effected by including in each route search packet a route control number, R.   R is initially set at the source exchange and is reduced every time the route search is forwarded by links other than the most direct.   If R falls below zero before the destination is reached, the route search is abandoned.

Simulations using various values of   R   showed that the highest acceptance rates were obtained if R has a value about the range 7 to 10, and fig 4(a) is a typical result with R = 10.   If R is too small, the ability to circumvent congested areas is unduly restricted: in the limit, with R = 0, the method reverts to one of the direct routing methods.   On the other hand, too large a value for R results in unduly devious routes being allowed.

The second complication in analysing results of adaptive routing methods is that direct comparisons between for example figures 3 and 4(a)   are in general misleading.   Since adaptive routes will usually deviate from the most direct, a given traffic demand involves the use of more system capacity.   It is essential therefore to distinguish useful, or equivalent loading from actual system loading.   The equivalent loading may be defined as the actual loading that would be observed if the same traffic were constrained to equivalent direct routes.   Hence, in general, equivalent loadings will be less than actual loadings.

This effect is not too serious in the above example, and at the breakpoint, the 85% actual system loading corresponds to an equivalent system loading only one or two percent lower - with other adaptive methods much larger discrepancies may be observed.   The effect is slight here because routes take no evasive action to avoid congested areas until the first choice links are fully loaded.   By that stage the network is approaching its breakpoint anyway so that the subsequent, comparatively few, deviating routes do not unduly influence the loading distortion.

Fig. 5 confirms this point by showing the deviation ratio, of actual route lengths to equivalent direct ones, as a function of system loading, and it can be seen that significant deviations occur only as the break point is approached.

Collective Routing

Traffic acceptance breakpoints occur when links become loaded to their maximum capacity.   Premature falls in acceptance rate will therefore occur whenever the loading in critical areas of a network is allowed to build up faster than elsewhere.   If the system loading were made to build up with a completely uniform distribution, no link would overload while there was any significant capacity elsewhere, and the acceptance rate breakpoint would rise to 100% actual system loading.

In collective routing, forwarding links are chosen only after all

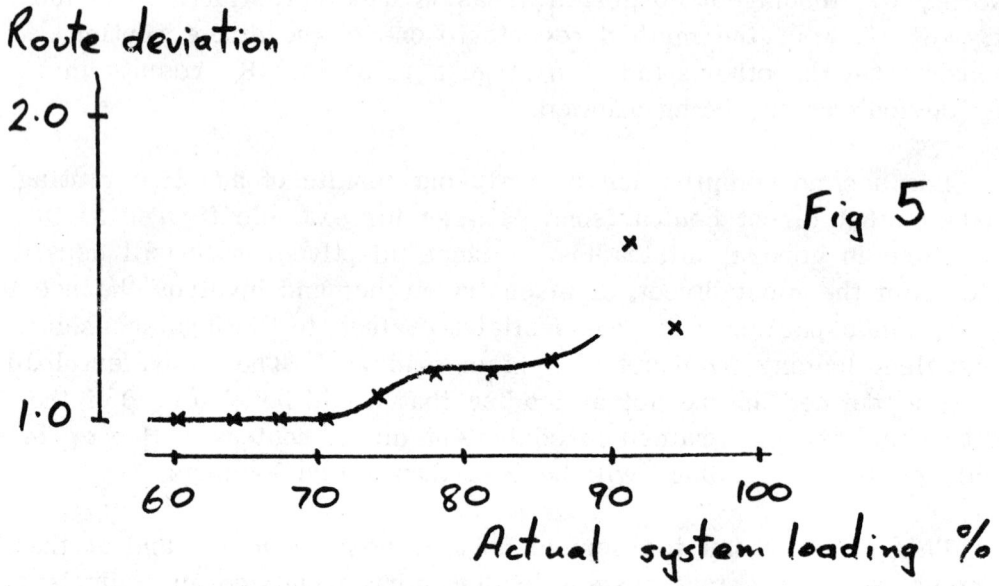

Fig 5

Route deviation

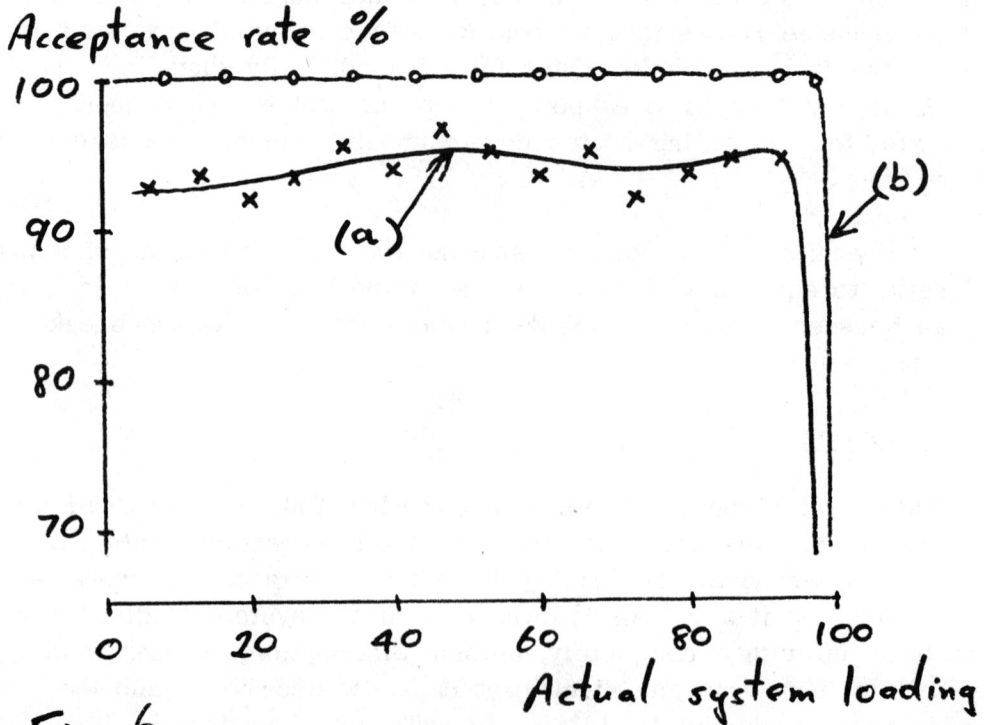

Fig 6

outgoing links have been considered collectively in a suitably weighted manner, dependent on both their topological directness and their current loading.

The first simulation of collective routing used a weighting ratio of 2 to 1, giving the forwarding links, in order of topological preference, weighting-factors of 1, 2, 4, 8 etc. The links chosen at forwarding exchanges are the ones found to have the minimum value of weighting-factor current-loading product.

The optimum value of R was again found to be around 10, and figure 4(b) shows the result of the simulation with that value. The immediate observation is that there is not a great deal of difference between this result and that obtained earlier using sequential routing, fig. 4 (a) Again, the actual and equivalent system loadings differ by only about 2%, and routes were found to deviate from the most direct only when the system loading was above 75% or so.

A weighting ratio of 2 to 1 is in fact very limited in the extent to which the load may be uniformly spread. Once adjacent link loadings are within a ratio of 2 to 1, no further spreading takes place, so that at the break point some links .will be 100% loaded, but adjacent links could be little more than 50% loaded, and more remote links even more lightly loaded, corresponding to an actual system loading well below 100%. It was in fact found that the least loaded links were carrying about 60% of their capacity at the acceptance rate breakpoint.

A measure of. the effectiveness of routing methods in spreading the system loading uniformly is provided by the mean deviation of individual link loadings from the system average. In the above simulation the deviation remained reasonably constant at around 16% as the system loading increased from zero to the breakpoint.

In contrast, figure 6 (a) shows the result of a 1 to 1 weighting ratio, (again with R=10). The forwarding links chosen are then simply the least loaded, with no consideration of topological preference. The breakpoint has been raised to 95% actual system loading, but the maximum acceptance rate has fallen below 100% even under lightly loaded conditions. This unacceptable fall in acceptance rate is due to the complete lack of directivity in the routing combined with too low a value for R . With the same weighting ratio, but a higher value for R, such that routes may wander virtually indefinitely until the destination is found, or congestion causes their abandonment, the acceptance rate is found to vary as shown in figure 6(b).

With a 1 to 1 weighting ratio, an acceptance rate of 100% can be maintained up to 99.5% actual system loading, the individual link loadings deviating from the mean by only 0.2% !   Unfortunately, the complete lack of directivity leads to route lengths being in general considerably longer than the most direct (route lengths of over one hundred links were observed) so that the useful, or equivalent system loading at the break-point was only 39%.

Further simulations were carried out with weighting between 2 to 1 and 1 to 1.   Sample results are summarised below: (B.P. = Acceptance rate breakpoint.)

Weighting ratio	Route length		System loading at B.P.		
	Max.	Mean	Actual	Equiv.	Deviation
2 to 1	8	3.0	86	84	$\pm$ 15%
1.5 to 1	8	3.0	86	84	$\pm$ 13%
1.1 to 1	12	3.2	91.5	84	$\pm$ 5%
1.01 to 1	21	3.8	99	77	$\pm$ 0.7%
1.00 to 1	116	7.5	99	39	$\pm$ 0.2%

Unexpectedly, there was no improvement in the equivalent system load being carried at the breakpoint.   Although a more even load distribution was being achieved with the lower weighting ratios, the intended advantages were being more than balanced by the increasing deviation of routes away from the most direct.

Control Route Deviation

Further simulations were carried out in which a steadier control of individual route deviation was applied.   The control route deviation described above is very crude in that routes are allowed to deviate quite freely until either the destination is reached, or R 'runs out' whereupon the route search is abruptly abandoned even though a route may ultimately have been found.   The first simple modification was that after R 'runs out' route searches could continue, but only along the most direct links still available, irrespective of the local loading pattern. This control is still uneven in that a route may deviate quite freely and then become suddenly constrained to the most direct available.   In the final simulations control was applied by re-evaluating R at each exchange encountered, dependent on the length of the most direct route still apparently available, and then using R such that as the destination was approached so an increasing bias would be applied against selecting forwarding links other than the most direct available.   This approach automatically embraces a common 'ad hoc' feature in other routing proposals, namely that on arrival at an exchange adjacent to the final destination, packets must then go along the most direct link (ref. 9).

Although the above approaches were expected to improve the performance of the network, preliminary results show that any improvement is hardly significant, the break points still occurring around 84% equivalent system load.   Indeed the arguments behind these later routing methods may themselves be somewhat specious.

Conclusions

A number of different routing philosophies have been simulated and a comparison made of the effective system loadings above which acceptable system performance can no longer be maintained.   It has been shown that unacceptable service will occur at quite low system loading if an inappropriate routing method is chosen, resulting in a serious underutilisation of network resources.   More effective use of the network results if routes are carefully determined in advance, although 100% utilisation could only result if the traffic demand, network facilities and routing determination were exactly matched to each other. Such methods are basically inflexible, and therefore sensitive to changes in any of the above factors.   In the simulations, there was no particular attempt to match demand to network, and the highest network utilisation at which the service degraded seriously was found to be about 70%.

Under the same conditions, comparable and superior results were obtained by progressive adaptive routing methods, dependent on their complexity.   In the final adaptive routing simulations, acceptable network performance was maintained to over 99% system loading, although because of deviating routes the highest equivalent effective loading achieved was only 84%.

As anticipated, the most effective use of network resources resulted from adaptive centralised routing.   Acceptable service could be maintained to considerably over 90% actual system loading corresponding to an equivalent loading only three or four percent lower.

Although simulations such as the above provide useful comparative data, routing effectiveness is however only one factor to be taken into account when choosing between routing philosophies.   Cost of implementation must also be considered, and almost inevitably the more effective routing methods are the more sophisticated, and the more expensive to implement.

A further relevant factor influencing the choice of routing method is the ability to cope with localised failures.   Adaptive routing methods seem inherently better suited to recovery than predetermined methods, since facilities are already available for pursuing alternative routes. If predetermined methods have been chosen then additional facilities would have to be specially provided for routing under failure conditions, and it might then seem preferable to use these facilities even under normal working conditions so that the further advantages of adaptive routing could be enjoyed.

References

1.   L. G. ROBERTS, B. D. WESSLER.
       Computer network development to achieve resource sharing.
       AFIPS Spring Joint Computer Conference, 1970, pp. 543-9.

2.   R. D. BRIGHT.
       Experimental packet switching project of the UK Post Office.
       Proc. Advanced Studies Institute on Computer Communication
       Networks, 1973, pp. 435-444.   Noordhoff International Publishing.

3.   FLT. LT. D. J. SILK.
       Routing doctrines and their implementation in message-switching
       networks.
       Proc. IEE. Vol. 116, No. 10, Oct. 1969, pp. 1631-38.

4.   W. L. PRICE.
       Design of data communication networks using simulation techniques.
       Computer Aided Design, Vol. 6, No. 3, July 1974, pp. 171-5.

5.   W. L. PRICE.
       Simulation studies of an isarithmically controlled store and
       forward data communication network.
       Information Processing 74 - North Holland Pub. Co. (1974) pp. 151-4.

6.   L. KLEINROCK.
Analytic and simulation methods in computer network design.
AFIPS SJCC. 1970, pp. 569-579.

7.   T. H. BEEFORTH, R. L. GRIMSDALE, F. HALSALL, D. WOOLLONS.
Proposed organisation for packet-switched data communication
networks.
IEE. Proc., Vol. 119, No. 12, Dec. 1972, pp. 1677-82.

8.   I. M. PAZ.
Pathfinding through a communication network.
Proc., Vol. 114, No. 1, Jan. 1967, pp. 76-78.

9.   D. W. DAVIES and D. L. A. BARBER.
Communication networks for computers.
Pub. John Wiley, pp. 442-443.

The design of the packet switched network for the EIN Project

F. PONCET

Ingénieur Principal

SESA

France

J.B. TUCKER

Principal Consultant

Logica Ltd

UK

Abstract

The role of the packet-switching network in supporting the
research of the EIN project is examined. The requirements for the network are stated, and how the design
meets the problems is explained. Particular reference
is made to the problems of communications standards.

THE DESIGN OF THE PACKET SWITCHING NETWORK FOR THE EIN PROJECT

1. INTRODUCTION

The European Informatics Network (EIN) project began
in November 1971 with the COST 11 agreement between
several European countries and Euratom to set up
a network of computer centres engaged in a collabo-
rative program of research. The project has two
principal aims : research into resource-sharing
in a network of dissimilar computers, and research
into the interconnection of networks.

At the time of writing, five centres have firm
plans to participate in this research :

National Physical Laboratory (NPL) : Teddington
England.

Institut de Recherche d'Informatique et d'Automatique (IRIA) : Rocquencourt France.

The Federal Institute of Technology (ETH) : Zurich
Switzerland.

Politecnico di Milano : Milan Italy.

The Joint Research Centre, EURATOM : Ispra Italy.

A packet-switching network of Network Switching Centres (NSCs) has been commissioned from SESA/Logica
in order to provide the EIN centres with a communications service ; the computers connected to the
NSCs are known as Subscriber Computers (SCs). Some
of the SCs will provide network services for users
some may act as gateways into other networks (NPL,
CYCLADES).

For simplicity, we shall use "the network" in the
remainder of this paper to mean the packet-
switching communications network of NSCs.

2. THE NETWORK SERVICE

SESA/Logica are currently developing the software for the NSC system and the installation of the first five NSCs is sheduled for completion by April 1976.

The NSC computer is a CII Mitra 15 containing specially developed line interface hardware.

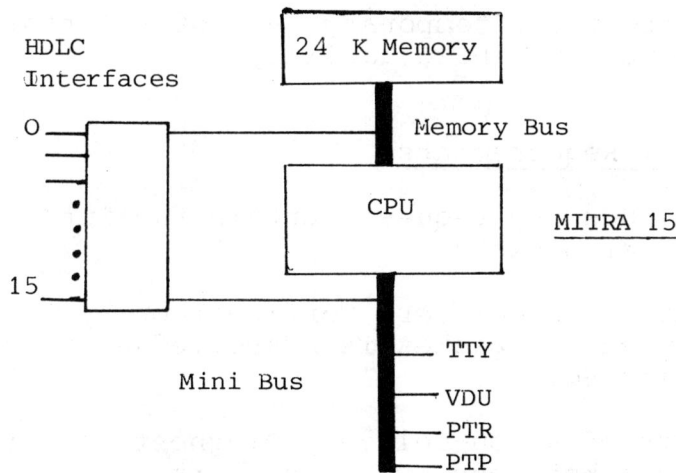

Figure 1 : The NSC Configuration

The packet-switching network is intended to provide a fast, efficient and flexible communications service to the EIN centres. It is not itself a research project : in fact, an important design objective has been to lean heavily on the work performed in other network projects and to adopt as far as possible procedures and mechanisms already proven in network operation. But no two networks have the same objectives and the body of networking knowledge is growing all the time ; so the EIN packet switching network has its own distinctive features.

The requirements which most significantly influenced the design are set out below.

2.2 Communications Requirements

- The network should support line speeds of
  up to 48 kbps.

- SCs may have links to more than one NSC.

2.3 Communications Flow Requirements

- Normally, packets are unordered - i.e. they are
  treated as independent data items. However, SCs
  may request the network to deliver certain
  streams of packets in order.

- SCs may request a temporary halt of all traffic
  from the network (hold facility).

2.4 Packet-Level Requirements

Optionally, SCs may request certain facilities
for individual packets :

- the return of a Delivery Confirmation by the
  network when the packet is acknowledged by the
  destination SC.

- the return of a Non-Delivery Diagnostic in the
  event of packet loss by the network.

- the return of a Trace packet from every NSC
  though which the requesting packet passes.

2.5 Service Facilities

NSCs should contain certain service facilities
directly addressable by SCs. These are :

- ECHO, which returns packets sent to it.

- DROP, which discards packets sent to it.

- TIME, which returns to the requesting SC
        the current network time.

Such facilities are not related to the communi-
cations-handling part of the NSC system, but are
in fact analogous to service facilities provided
in SCs. Thus each NSC contains a 'virtual SC'
(VSC) which itself contains several processes
(VSCPs).

3. PACKET FORMAT

In a purely private network with no intention of
talking to anyone else, the packet format may be
dictated by purely local requirements. But the
prospect of interconnecting networks raises
questions of incompatibility of packet format.
Unfortunately no 'standard packet format' exists.
However, the International Network Working
Group (INWG, IFIP/TC6/WG6.1) has produced an informal
standard for internetworking experiments, the D-
format ; and this format complies with the proposals
for a Datagram service currently under consideration
by CCITT. It has therefore been adopted.

Its structure is shown below.

Numbers of bits

```
        2    2    4        8
      ┌────┬────┬──────┬──────────────────┐
      │    │ 10 │ 0100 │                  │
      └────┴────┴──────┴──────────────────┘
```

Local PSN format type

Inter network format type

Header length (-8 octets)

Message length

```
      ┌────────────────────────────────┐
      │        Message identifier       │
      └────────────────────────────────┘
```

```
        3   1 1        11
      ┌────┬─┬─┬───────────────────────┐
      │    │ │ │                       │
      └────┴─┴─┴───────────────────────┘
```

Local PSN facilities

Gateway echo
Node trace

Reserved

```
        4        4        4        4
      ┌──────┬────────┬────────┬────────┐
      │ 0001 │        │  0001  │        │
      └──────┴────────┴────────┴────────┘
```

Destination PSN ads. length
Destination PSN address
Source PSN ads. length

Source PSN address

```
      ┌────────────────────────────────┐
      │   Local destination address     │
      └────────────────────────────────┘
```

```
      ┌────────────────────────────────┐
      │   Local source address          │
      └────────────────────────────────┘
```

```
      ┌────────────────────────────────┐
      │             TEXT                │
      │        (0-255 octets)           │
      └────────────────────────────────┘
```

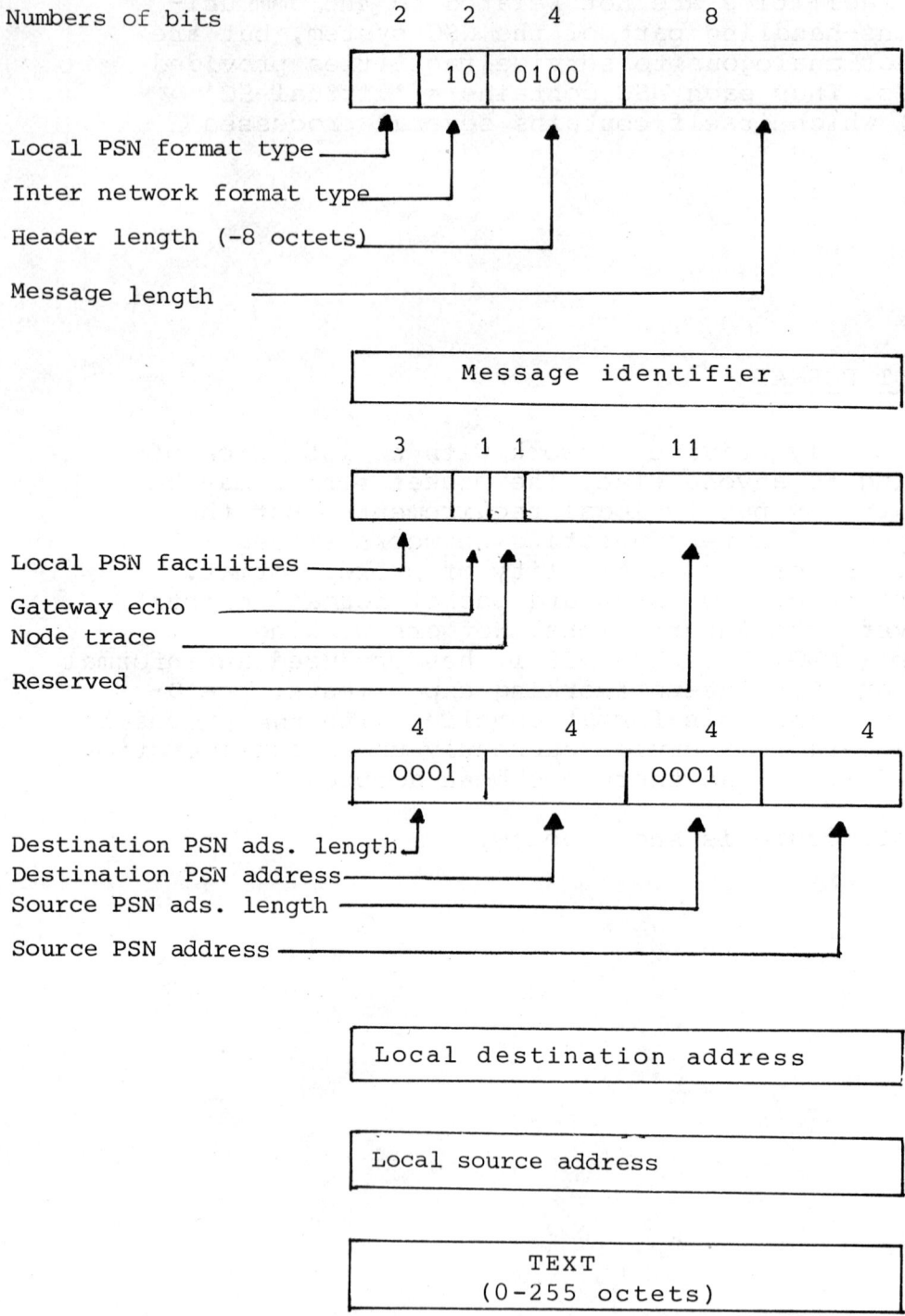

Figure 2 : The D-Format

6. LINE-LEVEL PROCEDURES

Another problem of standards appears at the level of
line-handling, and it is all the more important in
that interface hardware is involved. No international standard exists for full-duplex transparent
data transmission, but the High Level Data Link
Control (HDLC) procedures are on their way to
becoming standards. However, at the time when the
design choices had to be made; the HDLC proposals
were still in an uncertain state.

The transport level of HDLC, for achieving transparent transmission of frames with error detection,
was fairly widely accepted, but the higher-level procedures required for error correction, general
transmission control and recovery from failure
were still far from definition. Nevertheless, it
seemed that a set of HDLC standards would emerge.

The choice made was to adopt the HDLC transport
level specification as it then stood, and to
implement it in special-purpose interface hardware ;
but to ignore any suggested higher-level HDLC proposals
and to implement instead, by software, the logical
channel scheme used in the ARPA network - a scheme
which is simple and very efficient and which recovers
extremely quickly from error conditions.

So packets are transmitted in HDLC frames (illustrated below), the definition of which is now
a Draft ISO Standard (DIS 3309). By suitable software
modifications it will be possible to adopt
high-level HDLC procedures when they emerge.

Flag 01111110	Address 8 bits	Control 8 bits	Information	FCS 16 bits	Flag 01111110

Figure 3 : The HDLC Frame

The complete format of data on a SC-NSC communications circuit is thus made up to three components ;
an HDLC frame ; an ARPA-like error correction portion
and a D-format packet.

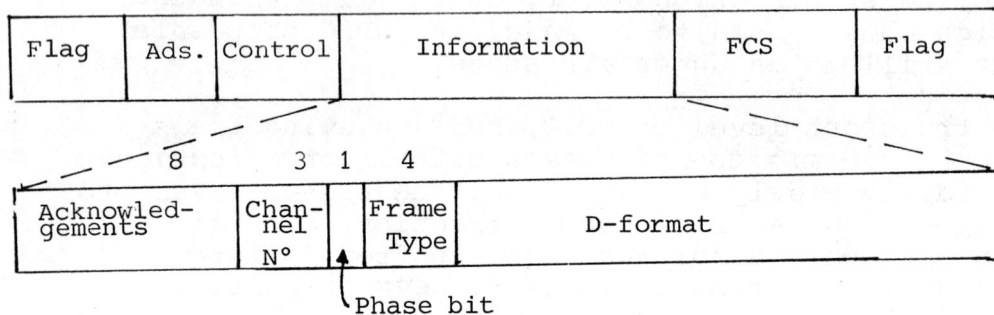

Flag	Ads.	Control	Information	FCS	Flag

8	3	1	4	
Acknowled-gements	Chan-nel N°		Frame Type	D-format

Phase bit

Figure 4 : SC-NSC Packet Format

Between NSCs, there is yet another component, as
will be described in sections 5.

Packets are not the only blocks of information
transmitted on lines, however. Certain exchanges are
necessary (in a network context) to test the
lines in the absence of any data packets, to carry
routing information etc. Transmissions of this
kind use the HDLC frame but do not use the D-format
They are service frames, not packets.

5. OPERATION OF THE NETWORK

If a packet-switching network is to be robust, i.e.
if it is to cope with internal failures and unbalan-
ced and widely varying traffic loads without unnecessary disruption to the communications service, the
nodes must   collaborate in some procedures.

The simplest is perhaps end-to-end-end error detection.
If some NSC has a memory or interface fault whose
only visible effect is to corrupt packets in
transit, this fact - and the NSC concerned - must
be quickly identified. For this reason, the NSC
where a packet enters the network (the NSC-O)
calculates a software checksum on the packet and
includes it in an internal header addition. This
checksum is verified in all NSCs though which
the packet passes.

If a line fails, or an NSC fails or becomes very
heavily congested, traffic should be diverted to
bypass the affected area. This is the province of
the routing algorithm. Following the principle
stated in section 2 viz. that tried and tested
procedures be adopted where possible; we have substantially implemented the current ARPA routing algorithm
- a distributed adaptive algorithm whose objective
is to minimize packet transit times though the
network. While implementation details will obviously
differ, the principles of the EIN algorithm are
those of ARPA. It should be noted that best routes
are chosen to NSCs, not to SCs ; this is simply
to keep the management overhead of the algorithm down
to reasonable proportions. It is therefore necessary
for the NSC-O to choose an NSC-D for each packet
which enters and to write its address into the
header addition. If the destination SC is connected
to more than one destination NSC (NSC-D), the choice
is made on the basis of the delay estimates produced
by the routing algorithm.

A more contentious area is that of congestion
control. It is undesirable for a network to get
into a state where an increase in input traffic
decreases the throughput ; and a network should
ideally be in some sense 'fair' to its users -
user A should not experience serious performance
degradation simply because user B suddenly

generates a high traffic load. To attack
such problems, an end-to-end protocol (between
NSC-O and NSC-D) has been developed. For each
NSC-D separately, the NSC-O gives a
sequence number to all packets destined to the
NSC-D, and restricts the numbers of packets in each
NSC-O/NSC-D 'pipe' to a certain maximum. The
NSC-D acknowledges packets by returning a spe-
cial end-to-end acknowlegement to the NSC-O. No
packet ordering is implied by this mechanism.

However, some such mechanism is needed if the
network is required to deliver some packets in
the order in which they were input ; and in fact the
EIN packet-ordering facility is implemented through
the use of an analogous order sequence number, which
however is applied to just those packets which
request the ordering facility.

An end-to-end protocol also offers the detection
of lost or duplicate packets, which can easily
arise when lines or NSCs fail.

However, the use of the protocol requires end-to-
end acknowledgement packets, which take up line
space, CPU time and core. The Elie/Zimmermann
host-host protocol, which will be used by SCs,
itself duplicates some of the features of the
end-to-end protocol ; and therefore the network
packet-ordering facility is not expected to be
used initially. So a second version of the
NSC system will be provided - a version
without the end-to-end protocol. The reaction
to congestion of the second version will be to discard
packets and to allow the host-host protocol
to take the necessary remedial action.

The exsitence of these two versions of the NSC system
will present an opportunity for controlled experimentation in the use of end-to-end protocols. Here,
therefore, is an area where the packet-switching
network itself may be used as a research tool.

We now illustrate the format of a packet on an NSC-
NSC line.

Flag	Ads.	Control	Information		FCS	Flag

	8	3	1	4		
A		C	P	F	Internal Addition	D-format

cf. Fig 5

16	8	8	8	8
Software checksum	NSC-O	NSC-D	Sequence N°	Order N°

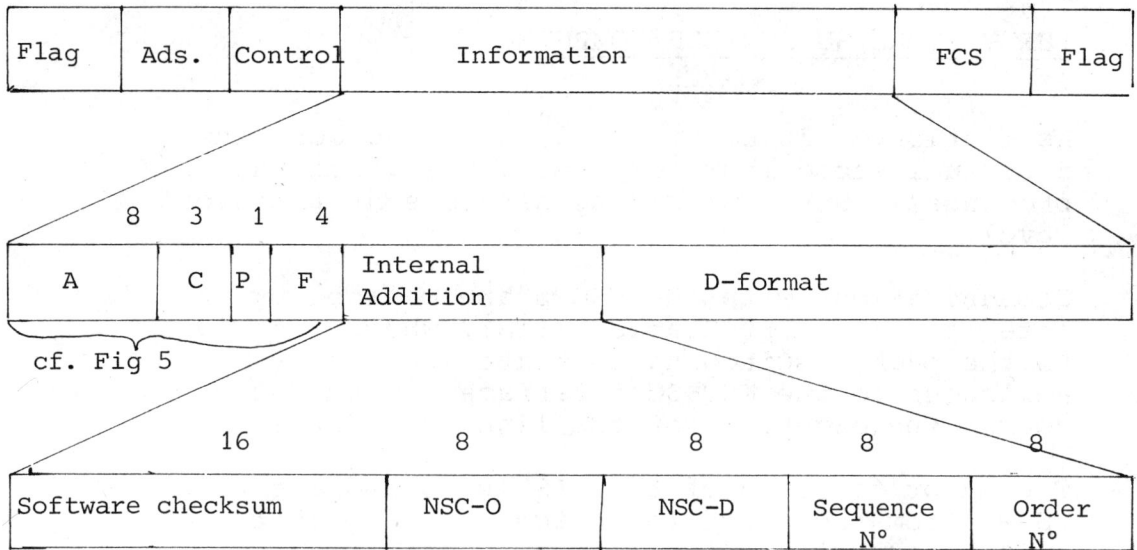

Figure 5 : NSC-NSC Packet Format

6. THE VIRTUAL SUBSCRIBER COMPUTER

As mentioned in section 2.5, each NSC contains
a virtual subscriber computer (VSC) which has
processes (VSCPs) providing services at the user
level.

Communications with the VSCPs are managed by an
Internal Transport Station (ITS), whose interface
to the packet-switching software is exactly
analogous to the NSC-SC interface - with, of
course, the exception of the line procedures.

The major function of the ITS is to isolate the
VSCPs from the characteristics of the packet-
switching system. It will, on request from
VSCPs, ensure that packets are retransmitted
in the case of loss -using the end-to-end
protocol if it exists, or its own mechanisms if
not.

In addition to the VSCPs ECHO, DROP and TIME,
which are accessible from SCs, the NSC contains
several 'private' VSCPs :

- MONITOR   Statistics collection and
                          reporting, snapshots, gene-
                          ration of NSC status log.

- STATUS CONTROL   Line and peripheral status
                          control, shutdown, system
                          dump.

- COMMAND LANGUAGE   Command and reporting inter-
  INTERPRETER   face with local consoles,
                          enabling operators to use
                          VSCPs.

- OUTPUT   Bulk output handler to local
                          peripherals.

At the time of writing there is no commitment
to the development of a Network Control Centre
which could be responsible for various centralized
functions such as :

- initiation of maintenance

- collection of statistics

- release of new software/modifications to old

- remote control of network configuration.

However, the VSCPs MONITOR,STATUS CONTROL and
DEBUG have been developed in such a way as to
operate under the control of a centralized
or even distributed Network Control Centre should
one be implemented.

REFERENCES

1. Barber D L A – Progress with the European Informatics Network
    ICCC Conference August 1974, Stockholm. Pgs 215–220

2. SESA/LOGICA – Specification of the Interface between Subscriber
    Computer and Network Switching Centre
    7104/5 2240–2000 1/03 and
    7104/5 2240–2001 1/01 (March 75)

3. Elie M and Zimmermann H – Transport Protocol Standard Host
    –Host Protocol for heterogeneous computer networks INWG note 61,
    CYCLADES SCH 519 1 June 1974

4. Pouzin L – CIGALE, the packet switching machine of the CYCLADES
    computer network. IFIP congress 74 Stockholm

5. Heart F E et al – The Interface Message Processor for the ARPA
    Computer Network – SJCC 1970 Atlantic City N.J.

6. McQuillan J M et al – Improvements in the design and performance
    of the ARPA network. FJCC 1972, Anaheim California.

7. Pouzin L – Efficiency of Full–duplex synchronous data link
    procedures. INWG Note 35. CYCLADES TRA 510 June 73.

8. Protocol Committee of IFIP. TC–6 WG6.1 (INWG) Doc 1.
    Experiment in Inter–Networking. Basic Message Format.

9. ISO/DIS 3309. High level Data Link Control Procedures
    Frame Structure Dec 1973

10. ISO/TC 97/SC 6 Doc 1010. Proposed Amendment to DIS 3309
    Oct 1974.

11. ISO/TC 97 SC 6 Doc 1005. High level Data Link Control
    Procedures. Proposed draft International Standard on Elements
    of Procedures. Oct 1974

12. ISO/TC 97/SC 6 Doc 1014. Proposed Amendment to ISO/TC 97/SC
    6 Doc 1005.

13. McQuillan: J M – Adaptive Routing Algorithms for Distributed
    Computer Networks. BBN Report 2831. Harvard Doctoral
    Thesis May 1974.

Telenet: principles and practice

Lawrence G. Roberts

President

Telenet Communications Corporation

USA

Abstract

The advances over the last decade in electronics and computer technology have substantially changed both the market requirements for data communications and the technology for implementing communications systems. The rapid decrease in the cost of computation is swelling the demand for interactive and transaction-oriented data communications at an ever increasing rate due to the economy of automating a great many previously manual operations. This same trend in the cost of computation has permitted the rapid development of totally automated communications systems utilizing the principle of packet switching which far more efficiently handles transaction-oriented data traffic. Packet switching has now emerged from the private network development phase and is being introduced in many countries as a publicly offered carrier service. The market response to the introduction of Telenet's packet switching service in the United States has been exceedingly positive with many users finding for the first time a data communications service offering which can serve their entire corporate requirements.

TELENET: PRINCIPLES AND PRACTICE

Most major countries in the world are in the process of
developing or inaugurating a public switched data network to
satisfy the rapidly growing demands for a complete data
service. Recently the predominant choice of technology for
providing this service has been packet-switching, based on a
number of successful private network experiments. However,
until these networks have been in operation for several
years, the question remains "What is the market impact of
packet switching and where is it most effective?" Telenet's
experience with the first packet-switched data communications
service in the United States may be of use in gaining preliminary insight into this question.

First one must understand the very unique situation in the
United States with respect to common carriers. Unlike most
other countries there is not just one supplier of communications, there are several competing carriers, all regulated
by the Federal Communications Commission. By far the largest, AT&T provides the dial telephone service and supplies
the majority of the long-haul transmission facilities. In
addition, there are a number of competing transmission
suppliers providing service by both satellite and microwave.

In 1973, in order to encourage the technological development
of new data services, the FCC established a new class of
common carriers called "value-added carriers." These new
carriers, of which Telenet is one, lease communications
facilities from the other carriers and add switching to
provide an overall communications service to the end user.
Since it makes no difference technically whether one makes
or buys the transmission facilities in the modern data communications network, Telenet's business is very similar to
that of any other carrier, except that its goals are more
sharply oriented toward improving the overall service to
the customer and reducing the overall cost of communications
by eliminating inefficient usage of transmission capacity.
In Telenet's view, packet switching is the ideal technology
with which to reduce the transmission capacity wasted to a
minimum and provide the most complete and responsive data
communications service to today's computer user.

Telenet's initial service offering provides a wide range
of data communications services to the entire continental
United States by leased line and dial access to a central
packet net operating in seven cities as shown in Figure 1.

TELENET 7-CITY NETWORK CONFIGURATION

FIGURE 1

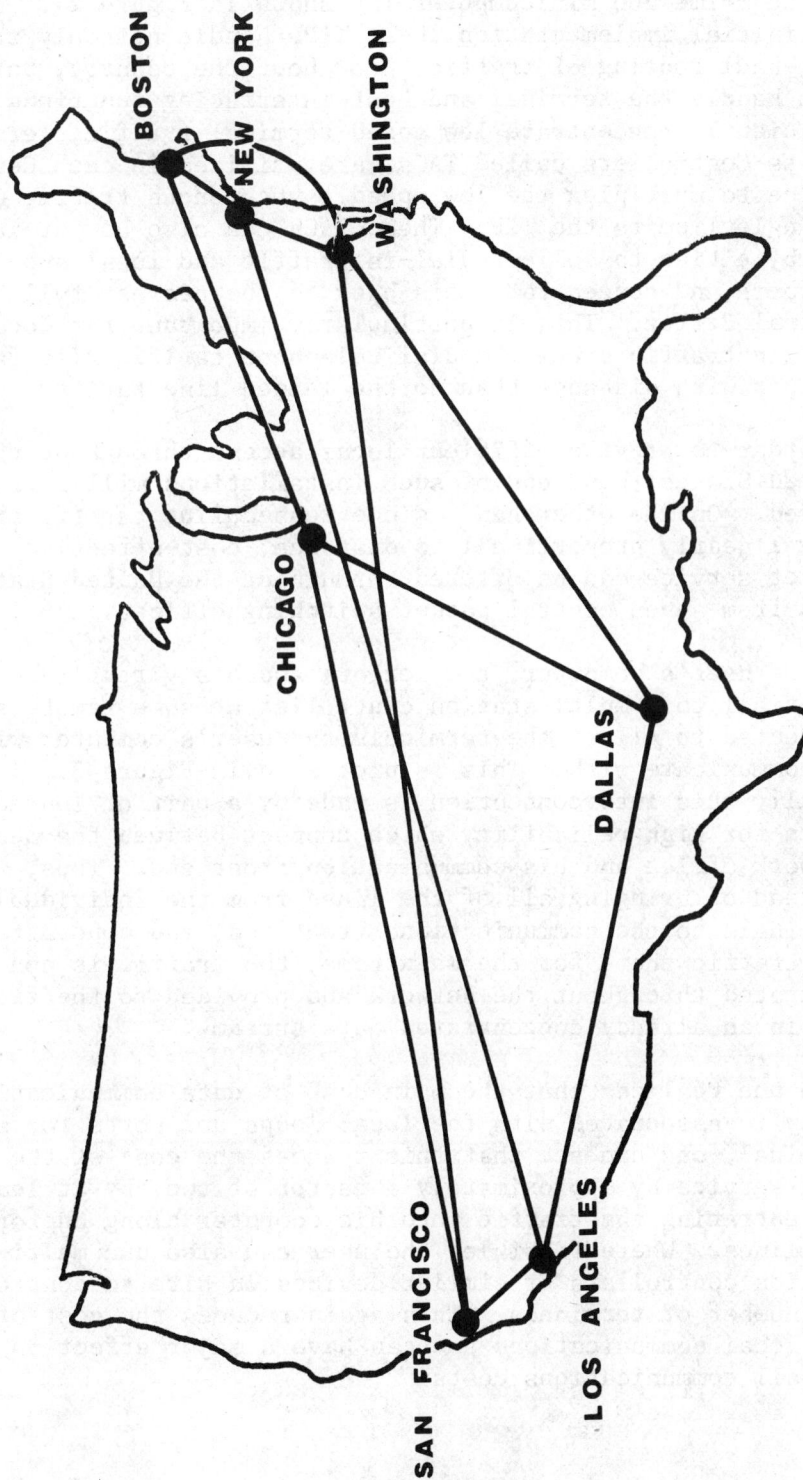

In each of these cities Telenet operates multiple packet switches called Terminal Interface Processors (TIPs), based on the Prime 200 minicomputer (as shown in Figure 2). In the initial implementation these TIPs handle not only the long-haul routing of traffic throughout the country, but also handle the terminal and host interfacing functions. To efficiently concentrate low speed terminal traffic, Terminal Access Controllers called TACs, are utilized in each Central Office to multiplex the low speed asynchronous traffic onto a single line to the TIP. These TACs can also be put in nearby cities to collect dial-in traffic and local subscribers and concentrate this back to the nearest full Central Office. This is particularly important for local dial-in traffic since the dial telephone tariffs rise far steeper with distance than do the leased line tariffs.

In order to provide efficient local access throughout the United States, hundreds of such installations will be required. On the other hand, since leased line tariffs are only linearly proportional to distance, cost-effective packet service can be offered throughout the United States even from seven central packet switching offices.

To the user's computer, the network appears virtually identical to a multi-station controller at some remote spot connected to all of the terminals the user's computer wishes to communicate with. This is protrayed in Figure 3. Usually this interconnection is made by a pair of leased lines for high reliability which connect between the nearest network office and his communication front end. Thus, instead of bringing all of the lines from the individual terminals to the communications front end, and concentrating the traffic there for the mainframe, the traffic is concentrated throughout the network and provided to the front end in an already concentrated data stream.

When one realizes that the main cost of data communications today is associated with the local loops and ports for each terminal, one can see that this reduces the cost of the network service by approximately a factor of two, by at least concentrating the traffic into his computer along one or two lines. Where feasible, the user can also use multi-station controllers or similar devices on site to control the number of terminals. This again reduces the cost of the local communications and can have a major effect on overall communications costs.

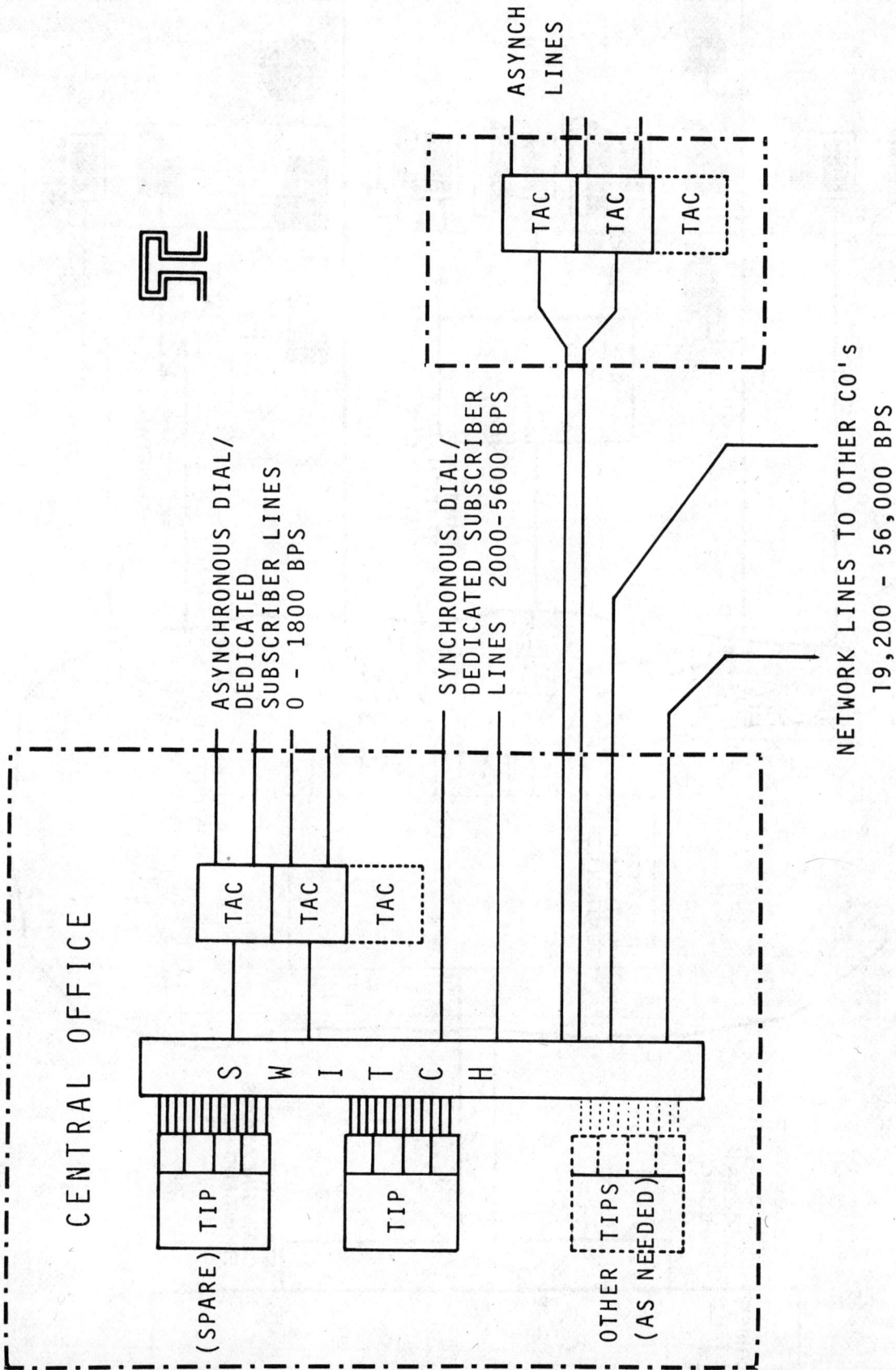

ASYNCH
LINES

TAC
TAC
TAC

ASYNCHRONOUS DIAL/
DEDICATED
SUBSCRIBER LINES
0 - 1800 BPS

SYNCHRONOUS DIAL/
DEDICATED SUBSCRIBER
LINES 2000-5600 BPS

NETWORK LINES TO OTHER CO's
19,200 - 56,000 BPS

CENTRAL OFFICE

TAC
TAC
TAC

S W I T C H

(SPARE) TIP

TIP

OTHER TIPS
(AS NEEDED)

Figure 2

INITIAL CENTRAL OFFICE CONFIGURATION

Figure 3

TELENET HOST INTERFACE

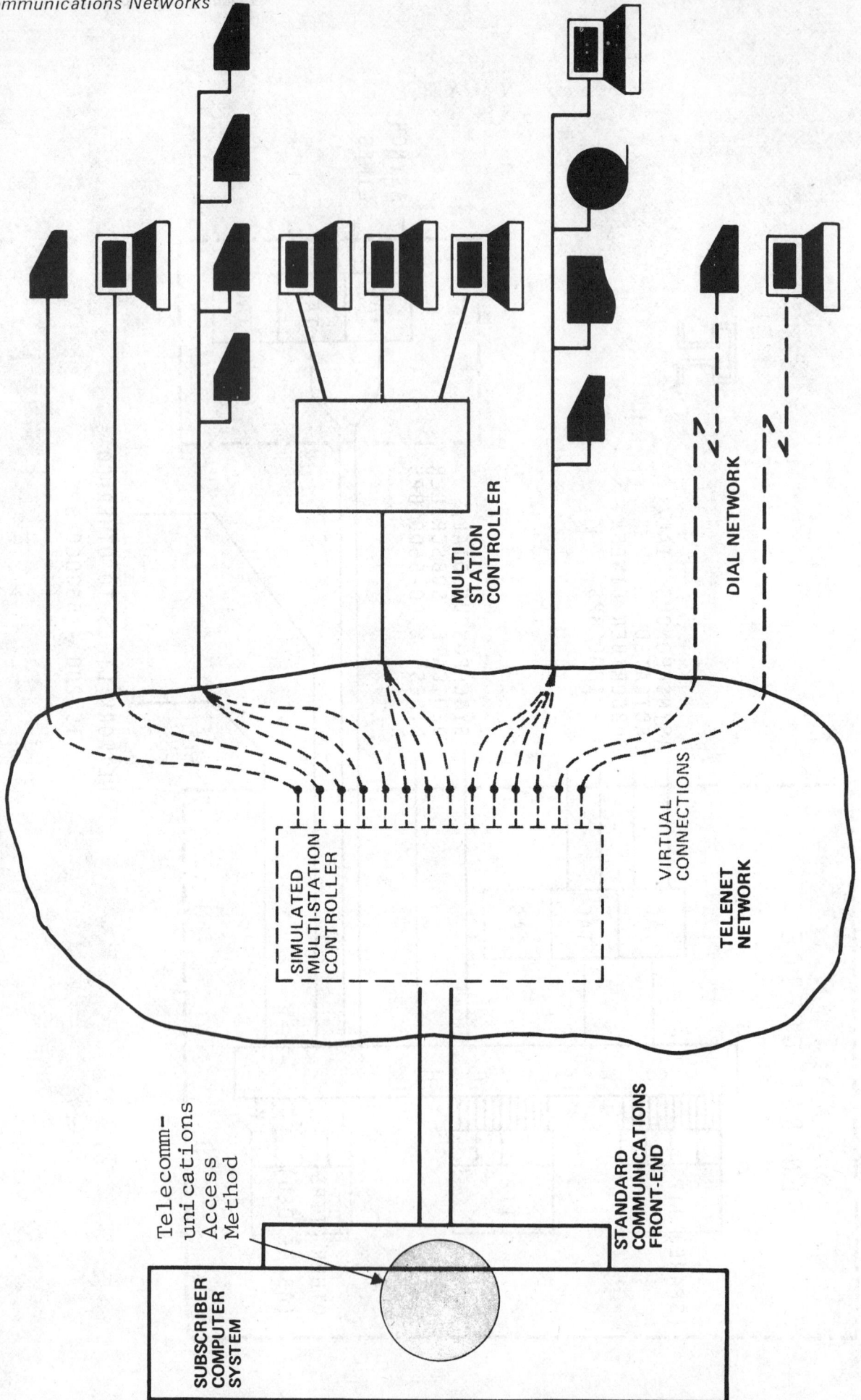

Over the communications line between the network and the front end processor, a host interface protocol is utilized as shown in Figure 4. The first element of this protocol is the Basic Link Unit, or BLU, permitting error-free transfer of information between the host and the network. This is purely a line control discipline and may operate in conjunction with a standard BSC or SDLC hardware. Embedded within the BLU is the Telenet Information Unit, or TIU. This provides the multiplexing of the information from the various terminals and contains the control information for flow control and error control. It also permits the computer to request the switching capability made available to it by the network, connecting or disconnecting from remote computers and terminals.

Since most computers and front ends today were designed without consideration of packet switching, Telenet TIPs provide a virtual call mechanism which completely frees the computer from worrying about packets in any way. The flow between the network and the front end is purely a multiplexed data stream of blocks to and from various terminals and computers within the network. There is no requirement for duplicate detection or sequencing at the computer, thereby permitting the interface process to be totally self-contained within the front end processor. For example, the IBM package which has been developed for the 3705 front end processor, loads with the 3705 emulator program and makes the entire network appear transparent to the 360 or 370 computer, the operating system, and the application programs.

The situation is changing rapidly, however, and computer manufacturers are integrating packet switching network functions into their front ends and computers at an ever increasing rate. IBM's SNA architecture and the Digital Equipment Corporation's DECNET architecture are two major examples of this. As these systems and those of other manufacturers progress, it will become progressively easier to make full use of packet switched network capabilities in their fullest with software provided directly by the manufacturer.

By far the most important facet of packet switching is the ability to have a pricing structure which does not depend on time or bandwidth. With a packet switched system the supplier is not dedicating bandwidth across the country to a user who has requested a connection. Instead, only a small block of connection information is required at either end of

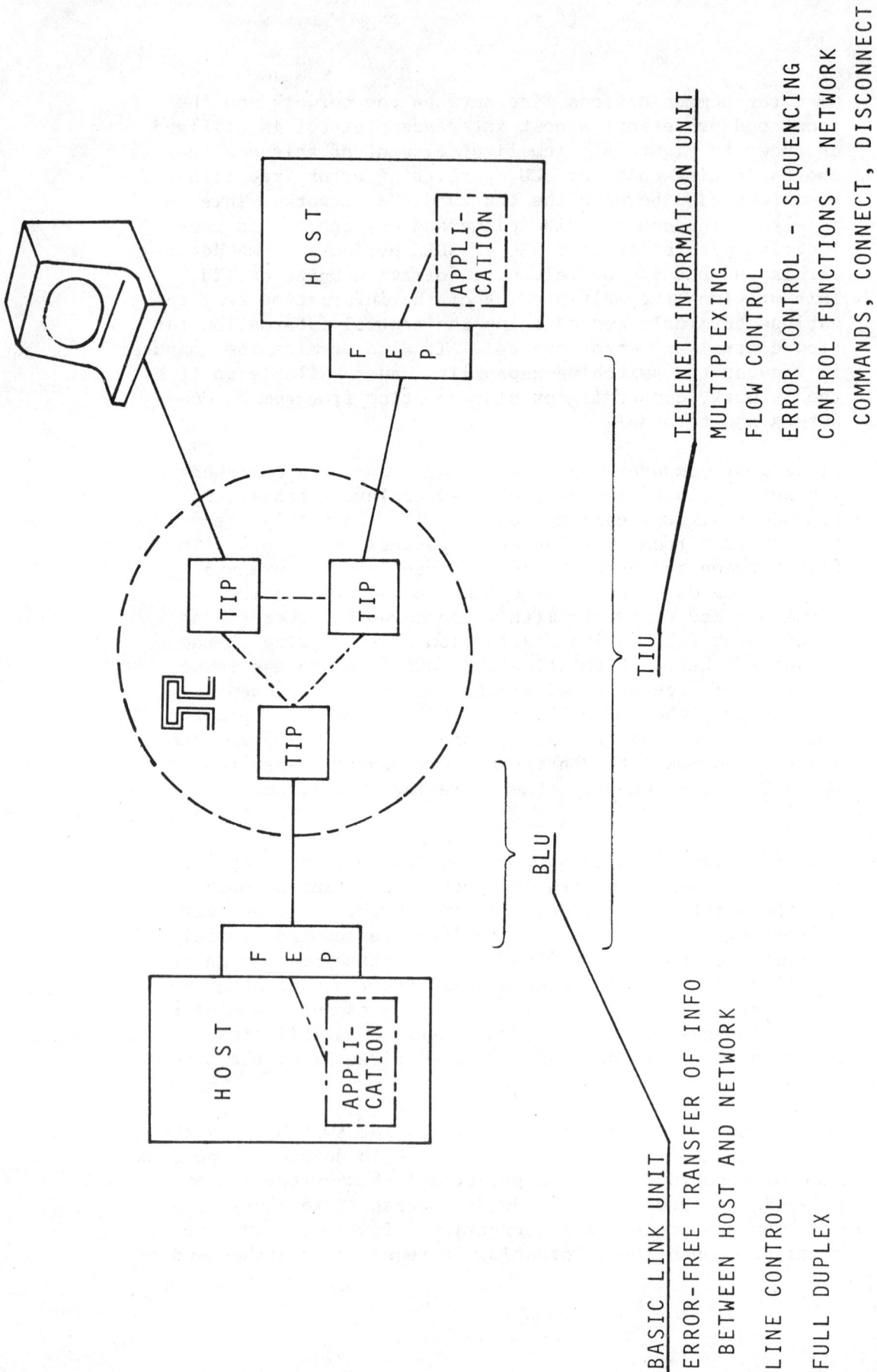

TELENET INFORMATION UNIT

MULTIPLEXING

FLOW CONTROL

ERROR CONTROL - SEQUENCING

CONTROL FUNCTIONS - NETWORK

COMMANDS, CONNECT, DISCONNECT

TIU

BLU

BASIC LINK UNIT

ERROR-FREE TRANSFER OF INFO
BETWEEN HOST AND NETWORK

LINE CONTROL

FULL DUPLEX

Figure 4

TELENET HOST INTERFACE

the network and transmission bandwidth is only utilized
when actual data is sent. Therefore the tariff structure
can be volume dependent rather than time dependent.

Additionally, since the dependence on long-haul communication is drastically reduced, there is no requirement for a
distance dependent component in the tariff either. In fact,
the distance dependent component of Telenet's cost is less
than one percent (1%) of the total cost. Based on this fact
and the fact that private user networks are also largely
distance independent, Telenet has chosen to make its tariff
structure completely distance independent.

There are two basic cost components: Network access charges
and volume charges. These charges are shown in Figure 5.
The volume charge is sixty cents (60¢) per 1,000 packets,
where each packet is up to 128 characters in length, or
1,024 bits. This corresponds to about one cent (1¢) per page
of text.

For leased line access, the leased line charges are passed
through to the customer and an additional port charge of $75
to $200 a month is added. Alternatively, for dial-in access
the user may lease a dial port in any city for $100 to $400
a month. The lease of a dedicated dial port permits the
user to have a permanent connection established from this
port to his computer so that the response in answering the
port is from his computer, rather than Telenet. Or if he
does not have the demand for a set of ports of his own in
each city, he may use the demand dial 300-baud ports which
Telenet supports, for $1.40 per hour. When a user dials in
to one of these ports, he must respond with the address of
the host computer he wishes to connect to. The normal
method of connecting a computer to the network is with a
multi-connection port and a leased line to the computer.
The multi-connection port charge is $400 a month, and a
leased line may be any speed from 2.4 kilobits to 56 kilobits.

The dramatic price advantage permitted with a common user
packet network service is demonstrated by the cost of low-
speed dial service for a 300-baud dial-in terminal accessing
a central computer anywhere in the United States as shown in
Figure 6. The cost of dial telephone service has long since
become uneconomic for most large system users. Several
years ago it became quite advantageous economically to build
private concentrator star networks rather than pay the very
high cost of the voice dial telephone network. Typically
these networks are constructed with multiplexers or small
minicomputer concentrators operating in a star-like arrangement permitting local dial access in each city being served.

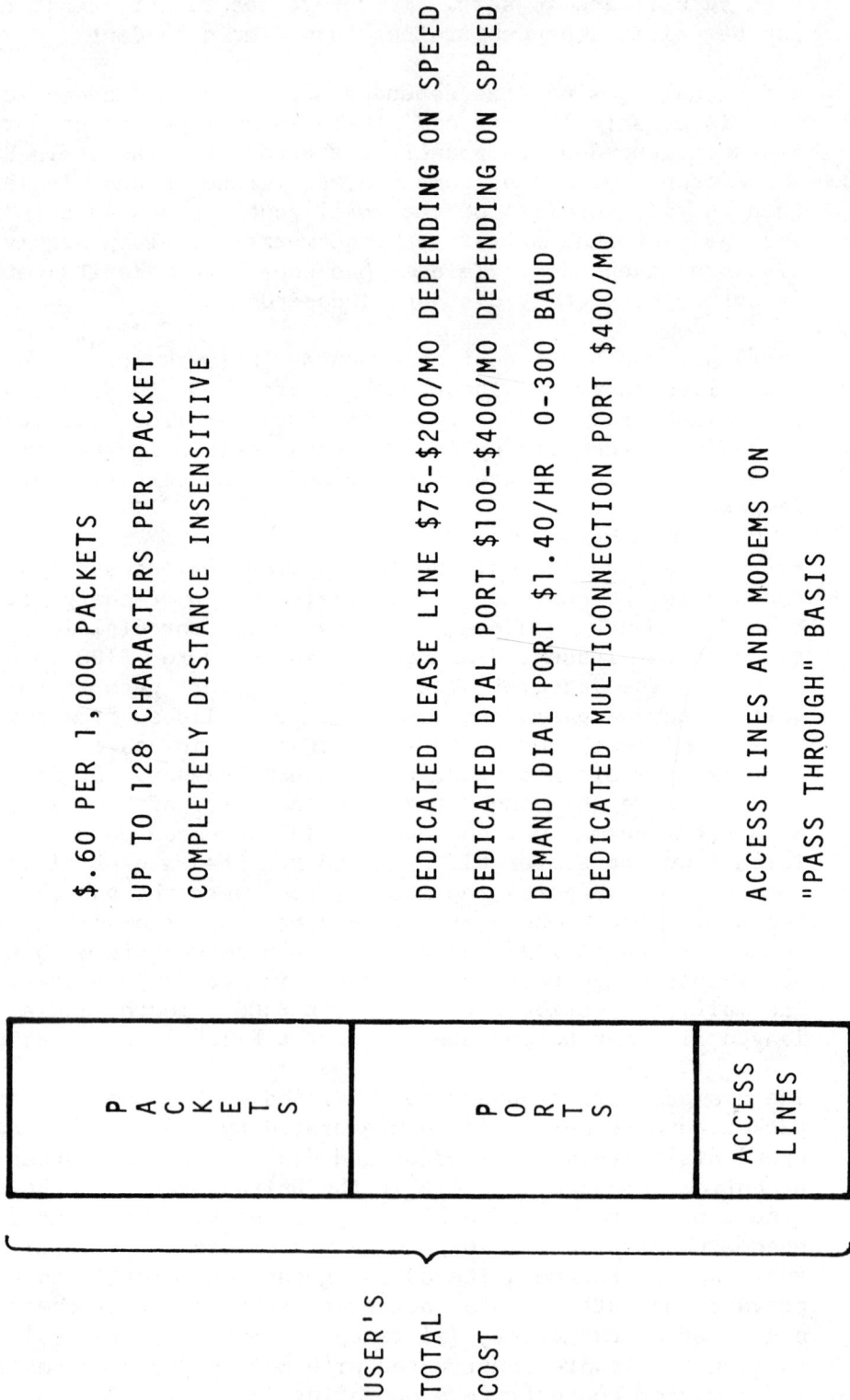

TELENET PRICE STRUCTURE

Figure 5

$.60 PER 1,000 PACKETS

UP TO 128 CHARACTERS PER PACKET

COMPLETELY DISTANCE INSENSITIVE

DEDICATED LEASE LINE $75-$200/MO DEPENDING ON SPEED

DEDICATED DIAL PORT $100-$400/MO DEPENDING ON SPEED

DEMAND DIAL PORT $1.40/HR 0-300 BAUD

DEDICATED MULTICONNECTION PORT $400/MO

ACCESS LINES AND MODEMS ON

"PASS THROUGH" BASIS

PACKETS	PORTS	ACCESS LINES

USER'S TOTAL COST

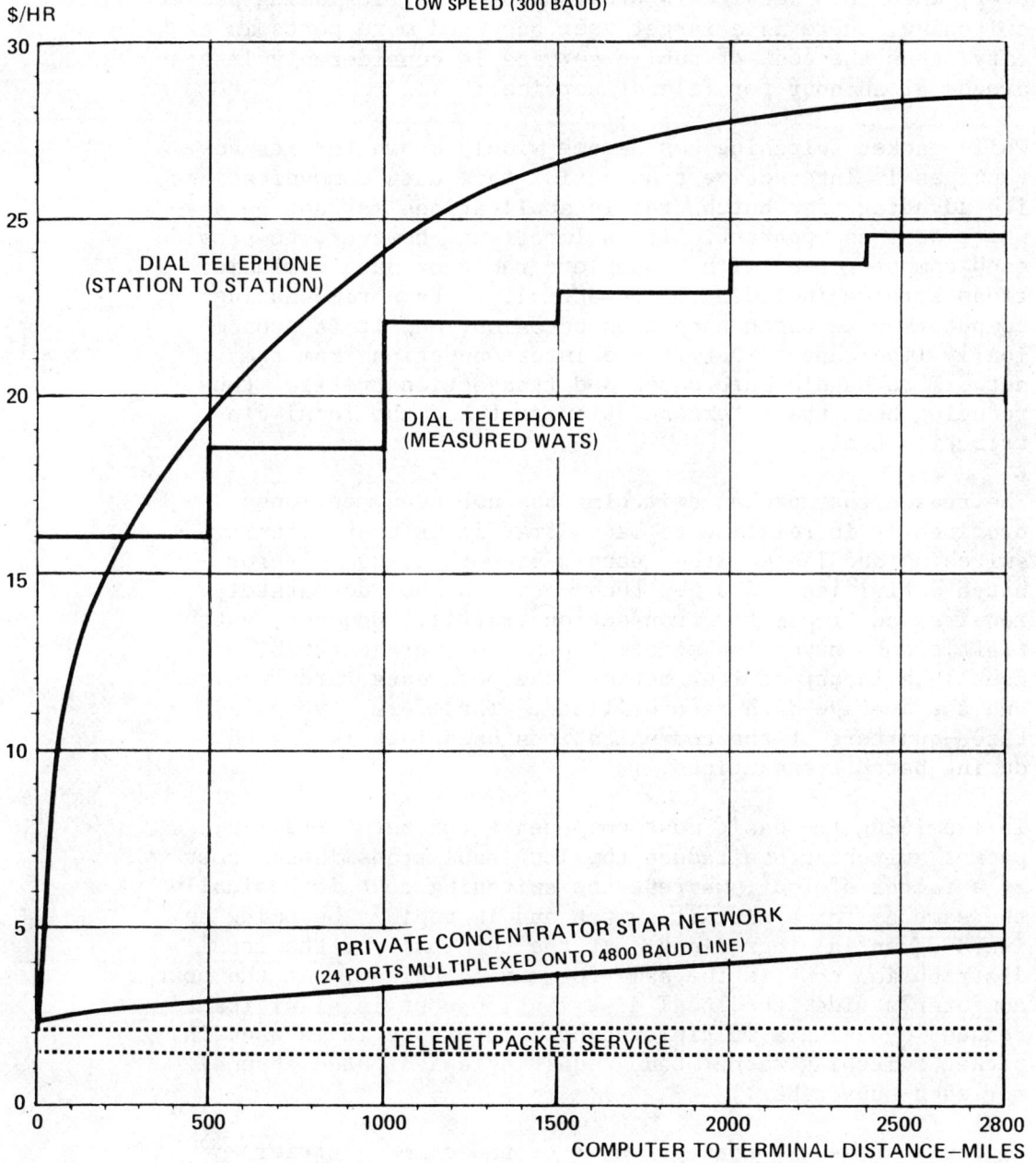

HOURLY COST OF DIAL-IN TERMINALS
ACCESSING A CENTRAL COMPUTER
LOW SPEED (300 BAUD)

Figure 6

The cost of service for this arrangement is not heavily
distance dependent and varies between about $3 and $5 an
hour if 24 ports can be multiplexed in one location. However, when this service is provided by a carrier using packet
switching, there is a larger user base and more ports in each
city, thus the cost of public service is considerably less --
around $2 an hour for Telenet service.

While packet switching has become widely known for its advantages in interactive transaction type data communications,
its advantage for batch traffic applications may not be anywhere near as apparent. It is important, however, to provide
each computer user with a complete range of data communications service including batch activity. Even timesharing
computers have batch output on occasion, and it is economically important to permit one interconnection from the
network to handle both batch and transaction traffic, thus
reducing both the interconnection cost and the local distribution cost.

The reason that packet switching has not been mentioned
prominently in relation to batch traffic is that circuit
switching and leased line techniques work adequately for
batch activities and a new technology was not desparately
required as it was for transaction traffic. However, batch
traffic does have a substantial peak to average ratio,
usually a factor of four between the peak data rate required
and the average data rate utilized. Therefore, typically
three-quarters of the communications bandwidth is wasted
during batch transactions.

In examining the basic cost components for batch traffic,
packet switching can reduce the long haul transmission cost
by a factor of four, whereas the switching cost is basically
the same as for a circuit switch and is rapidly becoming an
inconsequential ingredient. At the terminal end the local
distribution cost is the same for any technique. At the host
computer's side, the local distribution cost is significantly
reduced by using a multiplexed host interface as is used in
packet switching rather than requiring a dedicated channel
for each subscriber.

Figure 7 shows the cost per hour of the common carrier
service options available within the United States. The
example is for a 2400 bit per second remote batch terminal
operating into a large computer handling 20 such devices.
In order to compare leased lines within the same graph, it
was necessary to assume a use pattern of three hours per day
for the terminal, however, this primarily affects the slope
of the leased line service. Clearly the cost per hour of the

REMOTE BATCH COMPARISON

2400 bps - 3 HRS/DAY

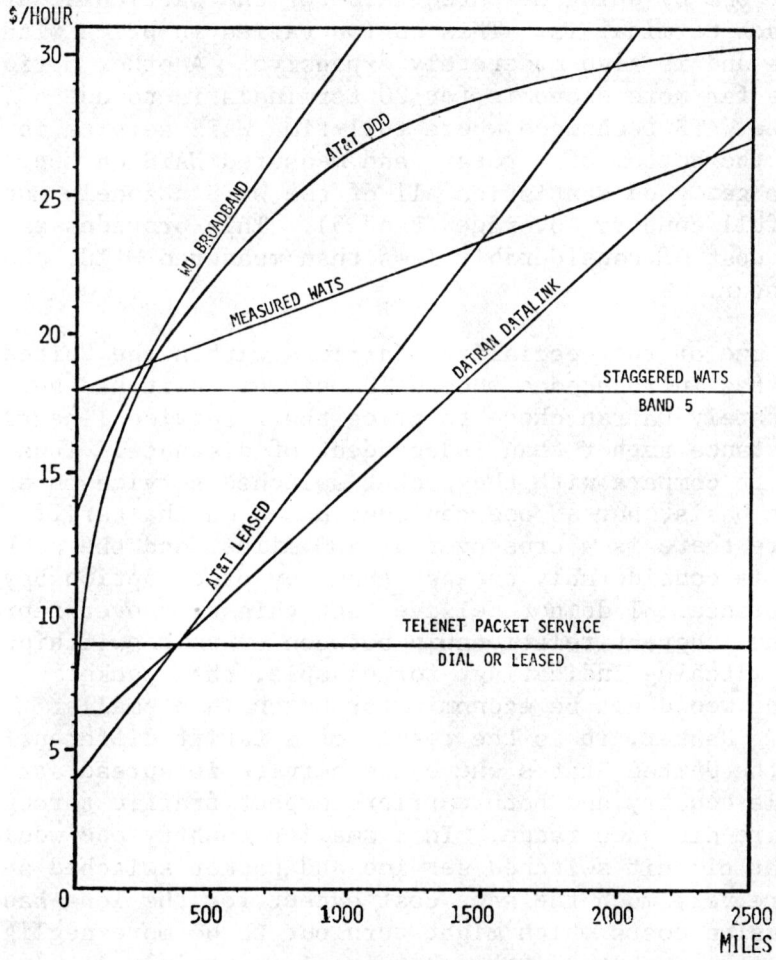

Figure 7

leased line option decreases as the terminal is used more
each day. As with the dial telephone service for 300 baud
use, the voice dial network (AT&T DDD) is one of the most
expensive options, costing between $25 and $30 an hour for
most distances. There are two ways of organizing WATS
service, one by using measured WATS for the particular area
where each terminal is. This option varies in price with
distance and is also moderately expensive. Another option
which is far more economic for 20 terminals is to use a
staggered WATS technique where full-time WATS service is
used on the bottom of a rotary and measured WATS on top. In
order to get good statistics all of the WATS channels must
be the full country coverage (Band 5). This provides an
average cost of considerably less than measured WATS, about
$18 an hour.

DATRAN, one of the specialized carriers within the United
States, has introduced a modern TDM circuit switched service.
Unfortunately Datran chose to price their service linearly
with distance rather than independent of distance. Thus it
is hard to compare with the packet switched service on a pure
economic basis, but as one can see, based on the tariff
structure there is a crossover at 400 miles, and the packet
service is considerably cheaper than any other option beyond
this distance. I do not believe that this crossover represents any inherent relationship between circuit switching and
packet switching indicating, for example, that packet
switching would not be economic for batch in a smaller
country. Rahter, it is the result of a tariff differential
within the United States where the service is spread across
the whole country and both carriers expect traffic throughout
the entire distance range. In a smaller country one would
find that circuit switched service and packet switched service were very much the same cost except for the long-haul
transmission costs which might turn out to be more negligible.
However, the packet switched service is certainly no more
expensive than the circuit switched service even under such
circumstances and can quite adequately compete as the most
effective overall data service for all purposes. Clearly in
the interactive area for low speed terminals and in the
transaction area for credit transactions, reservations and
stock exchange quotations, packet switching is the obvious
and preferable technology.

Even though Telenet is a small and new carrier within the
United States, the market response to its packet switched
service offering has been nothing short of fantastic. Even
before tariffing the service and starting official operation,
many thousands of U.S. corporations wrote Telenet requesting
sales literature and information. This includes virtually

all of the major corporations within the country. Telenet's marketing staff has met with a large number of these organizations and priced the service for their requirements. For the vast majority of applications the service has proven to be cost competitive with not only the current system being utilized, but their hypothesized private networks as well.

However, even more importantly, the packet network service helps the company organize its total data communications requirement within one service, connecting terminals wherever and whenever they are needed, and not building vast overlaying networks of leased lines and specialized communications processors. It is this total network service incorporating all of the requirements for message switching, order entry, reservations service, inter-company document and credit transfer, as well as virtually all data processing terminal requirements, that is necessary within any data communications service if it is really to meet the needs of tomorrow's business world.

Packet switching in a public data transmission service: the TRANSPAC network

A. DANET, R. DESPRES, B. JAMET, G. PICHON, P.Y. SCHWARTZ

C.C.E.T. - Centre Commun d'Etudes de Télévision et Télécommunications - FRANCE.

(Common Research Center of the french PTT and of "Télédiffusion de France", the french Broadcasting Agency).

ABSTRACT

A public packet switched service has a few specific requirements :
- simplicity and steadiness of customer protocols
- good security and grade of service even in case of faulty or malicious use
- interconnectability with other networks without requiring a control
- suitable tariff structures for various traffic patterns.

This paper provides a description of the main choices decided for TRANSPAC, taking in account the current work of CCITT on packet mode of operation, the economics of the service and the considerations above.

The basic service available to customers is the handling of Virtual Circuits (Switched or Permanent) for packet transmission. In the case of multiple access terminals the network exercises selective flow control. Thus data never have to be destroyed by the network and no virtual call can block another due to buffer obstruction.

TRANSPAC's architecture is based on 6 to 20 switching nodes, with local and remote multiplexors or concentrators.

Regarding the possible addition of a Datagram service, further studies are made in the fields of congestion control, quality of service and charging principles.

1. INTRODUCTION

The study of a new Public Data Transmission Service has been decided
in November 1973 (1) by the French PTT Administration, under the technical responsibility of its research center in Rennes (C.C.E.T.T.).
The choice of the packet mode of operation for the network and an
objective of several tens of thousands customers constituted a major
step in the french plans for data transmission ; but today, the present
state of development of such networks and the discussions on a international level indicate that this choice is also made by other Administrations or Common Carriers.
Following this decision, the C.C.E.T.T entered a first technical and
economic study of TRANSPAC and wrote the specifications of the network
(2) after discussions with customers and hardware manufacturers. A
public call for tenders was issued in February 1975, for the design
and implementation of a network with six national switching centers.
This paper gives the provisional planning of TRANSPAC's realization,
the main charasteristics of the services which will be proposed on
the network and general information on its internal mode of operation
and management.

2. OBJECTIVES AND PLANNING OF TRANSPAC

The November 1973 decision resulted from the following circumstances
  - customers motivation for a new Data Service (evolution of custo-
    mers quantitative requirements, study by large companies of na-
    tion wide networks ...)
  - economic interest of the packet mode of transmission (use of
    non-specialized hardware, sharing of the transmission lines ...)
  - technical experience (knowhow obtained more specially on RCP
    the experimental network of the French PTT Administration (3)(4),
    and of existing or studied networks : ARPA, CIGALE, GERCIP ...).
However an economic evaluation of TRANSPAC was in order to fix the
objectives of the project. This was done during the first six months
of 1974 as described on figure 1. First a global estimation of the
cost of a packet switched network was done for the data traffic foreseen
in the EURODATA study in 1976. This study resulted in a set of tariff
hypotheses which were used in a second step to perform a detailed
analysis for all the applications listed in the EURODATA data base
and this for 1976, 1980 and 1985 objectives. The size of the network
and its throughput were then determined from the list of the applications for which TRANSPAC would be of interest, for economic and technical reasons.

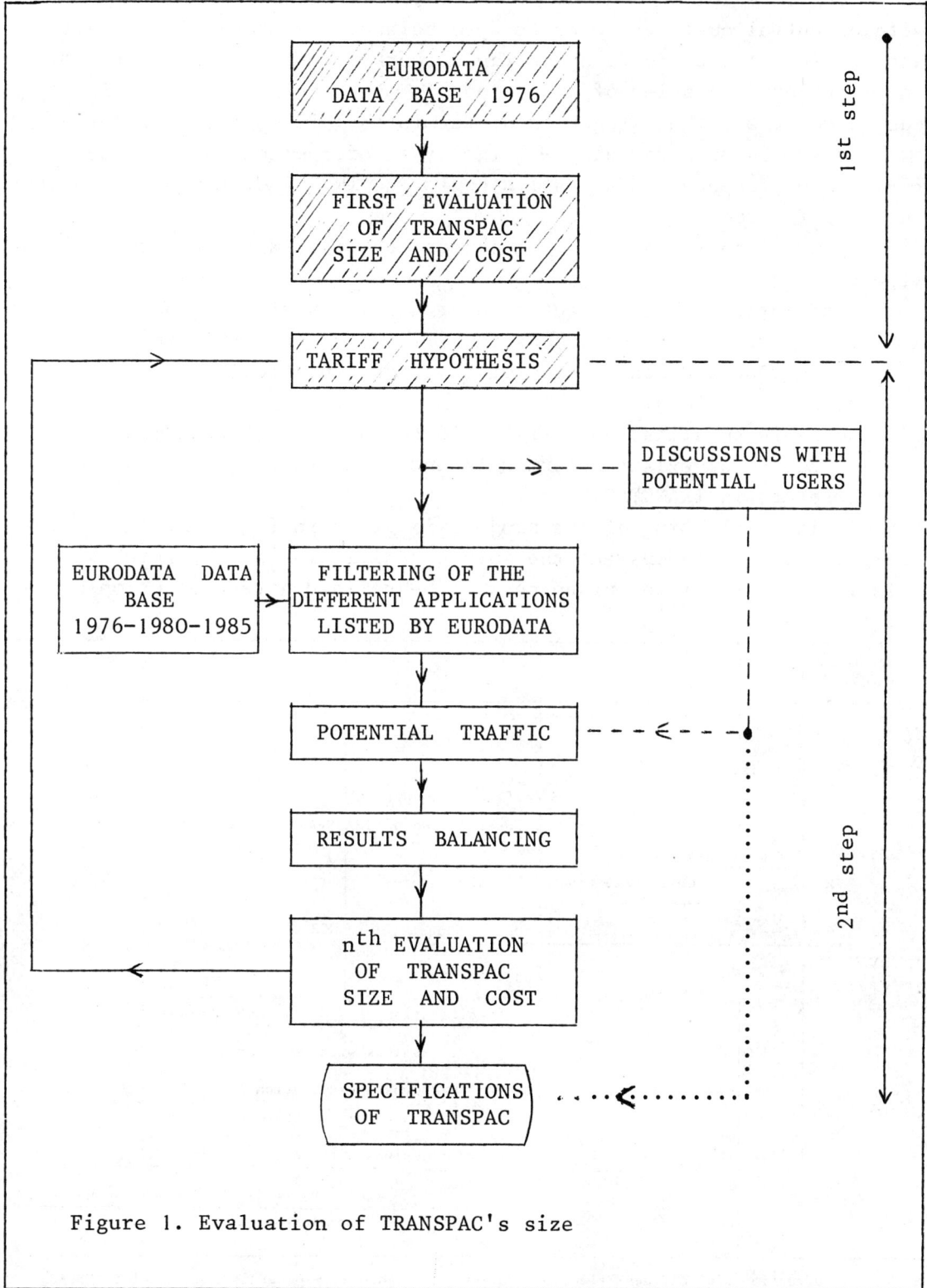

Figure 1. Evaluation of TRANSPAC's size

In order to refine this global approach, a few direct discussions
with potential customers permitted to balance the preceeding results
and provided the basic data for the network size as presented in §5.
An important conclusion of this study is that the proposed service
has to cover all the categories of terminals (DTE of the CCITT) from
50 bauds to 64 kb/s and also all the types of applications. Up to
75 % of the foreseen data traffic could use TRANSPAC, depending on
the tariff structure.

Under theses conditions the main objectives of TRANSPAC are the following :

- realization and implementation of a network with a global throughput of several hundred kb/s in 1977 and several Mb/s in 1980.
- definition and realization of a standard protocol to access the
  network services.
- possible substitution of TRANSPAC to the present transmission
  circuits for existing terminals and software by using protocol
  adapters in TRANSPAC.

A provisional planning of the project is given in figure 2. It covers
the preliminary studies and the future realization of the network ;
this latter part of the planning will be refined after reception of
the tenders.

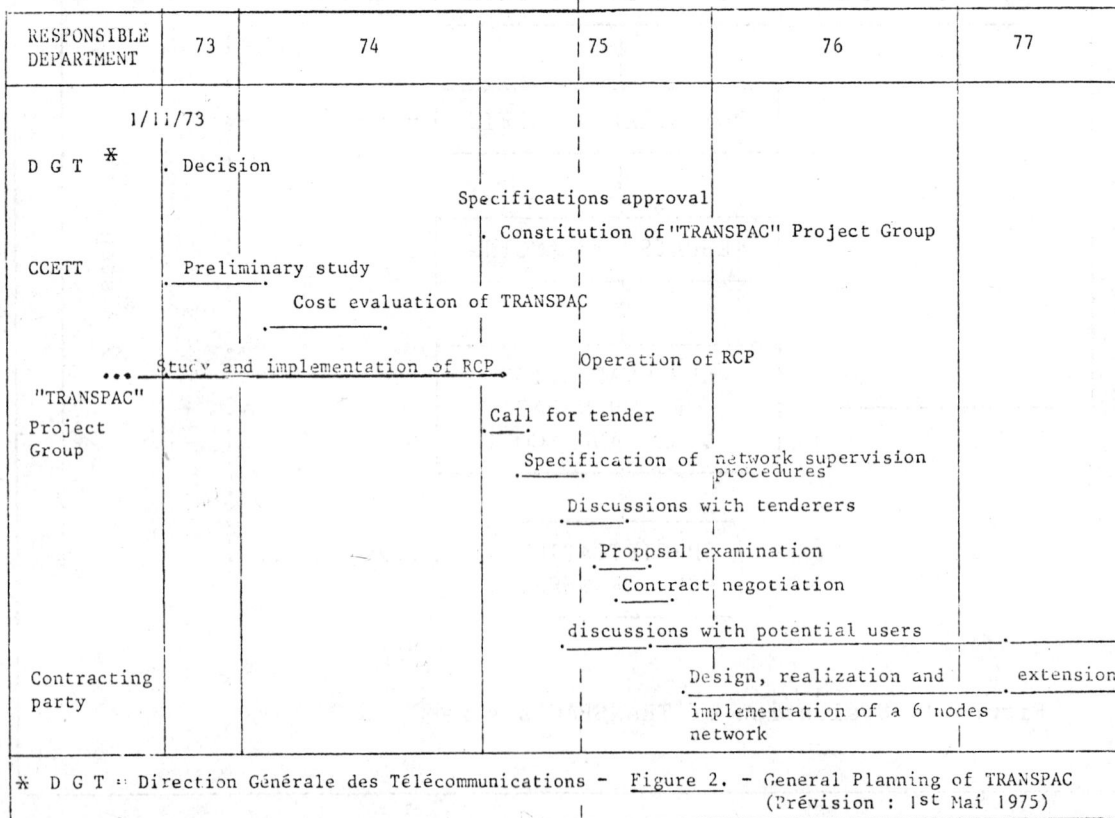

RESPONSIBLE DEPARTMENT	73	74	75	76	77
D G T ✳	1/11/73 . Decision		Specifications approval . Constitution of "TRANSPAC" Project Group		
CCETT		Preliminary study Cost evaluation of TRANSPAC			
...		Study and implementation of RCP	Operation of RCP		
"TRANSPAC" Project Group			Call for tender Specification of network supervision procedures Discussions with tenderers Proposal examination Contract negotiation discussions with potential users		
Contracting party				Design, realization and implementation of a 6 nodes network	extension

✳ D G T = Direction Générale des Télécommunications -   Figure 2. - General Planning of TRANSPAC
(Prévision : 1st Mai 1975)

3. BASIC SERVICES

The basic mechanism offered by TRANSPAC is the handling of virtual circuits.

A virtual circuit is a communication established through the network between two logical channels, each one of which provides a connection from one DTE to the network.

A virtual circuit may be <u>permanent</u>, allowing data transmission between two particular DTE's at any time whithout having to request the network to establish it, or <u>switched</u> (virtual call (8) established or released using DTE to network signalling).

TRANSPAC offers standard access protocols for both permanent and switched virtual circuits.

A virtual circuit, as seen by the DTE, has the following basic characteristics :

- it enables two DTE's to initiate and carry out a two-way exchange of strings of messages, each ones of which is composed of any number of octets.
- messages are sent and received by the DTE's in the form of a series of packets, with network end to end preservation of sequence order.
- The rate at which DTE's transmit data is controlled by the network in a manner acceptable for both network and receiving DTE. This flow control applies for each individual virtual circuit (selective flow control).
- A signalling system enables one DTE to set-up,confirm or clear down a virtual call.

TRANSPAC allows the connection of both single and multiaccess DTE's (multiaccess DTE's are allowed to have several virtual circuits in operation at the same time).

Access to the network is possible either directly on packet switching nodes, for synchronous DTE's using standard access protocols, or through connecting units (concentrators) for the others.

The connecting units contain some protocol adapters allowing the connexion to the network of DTE's using asynchronous or synchronous protocols which are not the standard ones.

Asynchronous DTE's for which access protocol is provided are Teletype and compatible, telex, and IBM 2740 model 2. Access is possible through :

- synchronous leased lines operating in full duplex from 2400 to 64 000 bit/s.
- asynchronous leased lines normally operating in full duplex at 1200 bauds.
- the switched telephone network (at same speed and format combinations as for asynchronous leased lines up to 300 bauds).
- the telex network (only at 50 bauds).

All asynchronous access are made via time division multiplexors capable of automatic speed and character format recognition.

At the subscription time or with each "call request command" the customers can choose :

- the charged party
- the maximum throughputs in the two directions
- the adherence to a closed user group.

The relationship between maximum throughputs, maximum packet lengths and number of packets allowed for immediate transmission are determined from a customer table which is entered in the connecting switching node at subscription time (see § 4 below).

Main performances expected of the network are the following :

- average transit time of a packet from starting node to ending node is less than 0,2 s.
- on a given link, different virtual circuits may be used with quite different traffic patterns. Maximum throughputs are specified at calling time.
- the rate of undetected transmission errors is very low, ranging from one bit in 10^{10} on subscribers lines to one bit in 10^{12} on trunk lines.

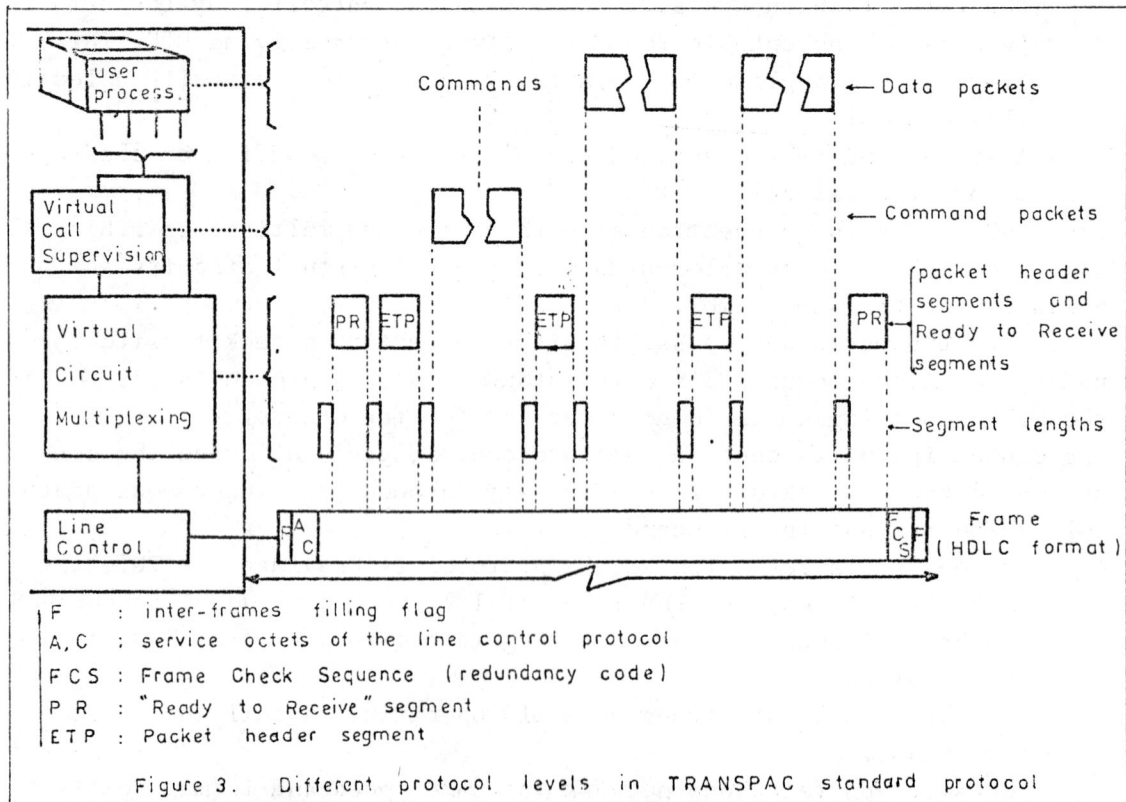

F   : inter-frames filling flag
A,C   : service octets of the line control protocol
FCS   : Frame Check Sequence (redundancy code)
PR   : "Ready to Receive" segment
ETP   : Packet header segment

Figure 3.   Different protocol levels in TRANSPAC standard protocol

4. THE TRANSPAC STANDARD PROTOCOL FOR MULTI-CHANNEL DTE

This protocol (5) is employed by TRANSPAC for DTE's which want to communicate simultaneously with several correspondents (these DTE's being connected to the network by a synchronous line).
It has three levels : the frame level, the packet level and the command level (refer figure 3).

4.1. Link Control Procedure : the frame level

This permits simultaneous bi-directional transmission of data blocks on a line, with error control, local flow control and sequential order maintenance, each block containing one or several "packets" handled by the second level of the protocol. The standard frame format is described on figure 4. A particular frame ("RAZ") initialise the line. It is characterised by a bit $Z = 1$. Initialisation is not complete until both the DTE and the connecting node have received this frame without error. For each direction the receiver controls the transmission from the sender by the Sr, Nr and Mr fields of the frame wich are returned to the sender. The sender for its part, gives indications about the frames it transmits in their Se and Ne fields.

4.2. The packet level protocol

The packet level of the TRANSPAC protocol transforms the frame procedure tool in another capable of handling one or several virtual circuits. Each circuit is associated with a so-called "logical channel" identified by a channel number.

Different types of segments are defined for implementing the functions of Virtual Circuits : transmission of data bytes, flow control, initialization.
We can distinguish four types of segments :
- RAZ : Reset segment for initialising the channel
- PR : "ready to receive" segment. One more data-packet can be sent one this channel in the other direction.
- ETP : packet header segment. The next segment in the frame is implicitely an Information Packet IP.
- IP : information segment of packet (Data or Command).

A packet includes a packet header segment and an information segment. The formats of these different segments are described on figure 5.
As for the frame level, the initialization of a channel is complete only when the two ends have received an RAZ segment. For this purpose, each responds with such a segment if it receives but has not yet sent one.
After the initialization of a channel each end receiving PR segments keeps a count of the number of data-packets which it is authorised

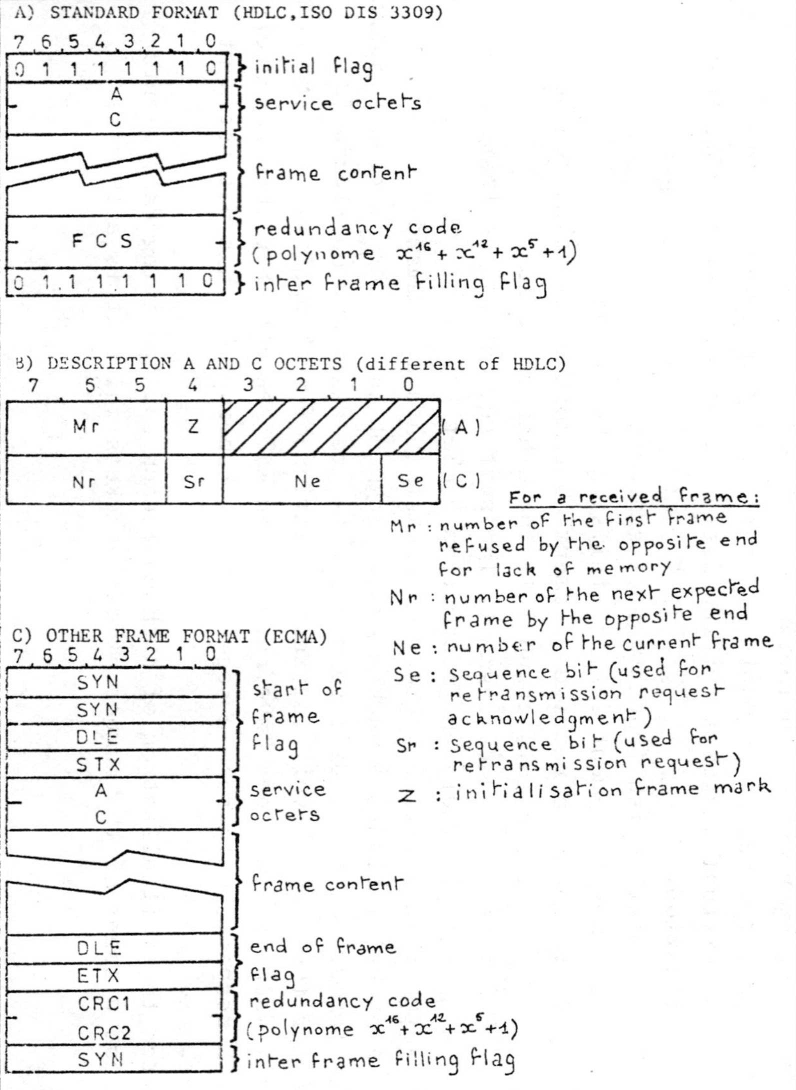

Segment type	Format	Comment
Reset R AZ	type = 0 / logical channel number / Reset cause	Reset cause = o if it is a reset confirmation
Ready to Receive PR	type = 1 / logical channel number	One data packet more can be sent in the other direction on this channel
Packet header ETP	D S / type = 2 / logical channel number	The next segment in the frame is an information segment. S=1 if it is a command information segment. D=1 if it is the last data-packet of a message
Information I P	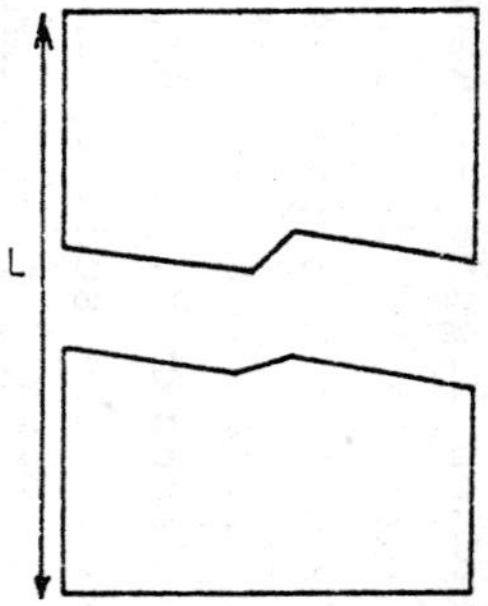 L	if LP stands for the packet length, L= LP for data-packets which are not the last packets of messages. L≤LP for data-packets which are marked "last of a message"

Figure 5. Segment formats

A) STANDARD FORMAT (HDLC, ISO DIS 3309)

7 6 5 4 3 2 1 0

0 1 1 1 1 1 1 0   initial Flag

A / C   service octets

frame content

F C S   redundancy code (Polynome $x^{16}+x^{12}+x^5+1$)

0 1 1 1 1 1 1 0   inter frame Filling Flag

B) DESCRIPTION A AND C OCTETS (different of HDLC)

7 6 5 4 3 2 1 0

| Mr | Z | Se | (A) |
| Nr | Sr | Ne | (C) |

For a received frame:

Mr : number of the First frame refused by the opposite end for lack of memory

Nr : number of the next expected frame by the opposite end

Ne : number of the current frame

Se : Sequence bit (used for retransmission request acknowledgment)

Sr : Sequence bit (used for retransmission request)

Z : initialisation frame mark

C) OTHER FRAME FORMAT (ECMA)

7 6 5 4 3 2 1 0

SYN
SYN
DLE
STX   start of frame Flag

A
C   service octets

frame content

DLE
ETX   end of frame Flag

CRC1
CRC2   redundancy code (Polynome $x^{16}+x^{12}+x^5+1$)

SYN   inter frame Filling Flag

Figure 4. Frame format

to transmit on this channel. Thus the correct reception of all data
packets transmitted is guaranteed. The flow control on each channel
is assumed by means of these PR segments. The maximum number of PR
segments which can be accumulated on a channel without transmission
of data is a parameter called "anticipation degree". In order that
the two ends of the link agree about anticipation degree and packet
length, a table is fixed at subscription time for each terminal, to
determine which maximum packet lengths and anticipation degrees apply
to its virtual circuits as a function of maximum throughputs.
There is only one entry in the table for terminals which handle only
one packet size and use always the same anticipation degree. There
are more entries for terminals with varying traffics and optimized
resources allocation.

The maximum packet lengths used are : 8, 16, 32, 64 and 128 bytes.

Two customers exchange messages on a virtual circuit. These messages
are split into packets, the length of which is equal to the maximum
packet length. Only the last packet of a message can be shorter This
last packet is marked "last of its message" (bit D = 1 in ETP segment).

NOTE   The maximum packet lengths can be different at the two ends
       of a virtual circuit ; the network can easily regroup or
       split packets because the maximum lengths always have the
       form 2   (See example on figure 6).

4.3. The command level

This level exists only with the switched virtual circuits. The
part of the command level is the setting-up and clearing-down of
virtual calls. Each command is associated with a logical channel and
is transmitted in a command packet. A command packet is characterised
by a bit S = 1 in the packet header segment.

There are four types of commands which are :

A : command for call request
C : command for connection confirmation
L : command for clear down
L' : command for clear down confirmation.

A call request includes the following items of information :

- address of the called customer (the "callee")
- address of the calling customer (the "caller")
- a collect call flag
- an indication about closed user group
- maximum send and receive throughputs used by the caller.

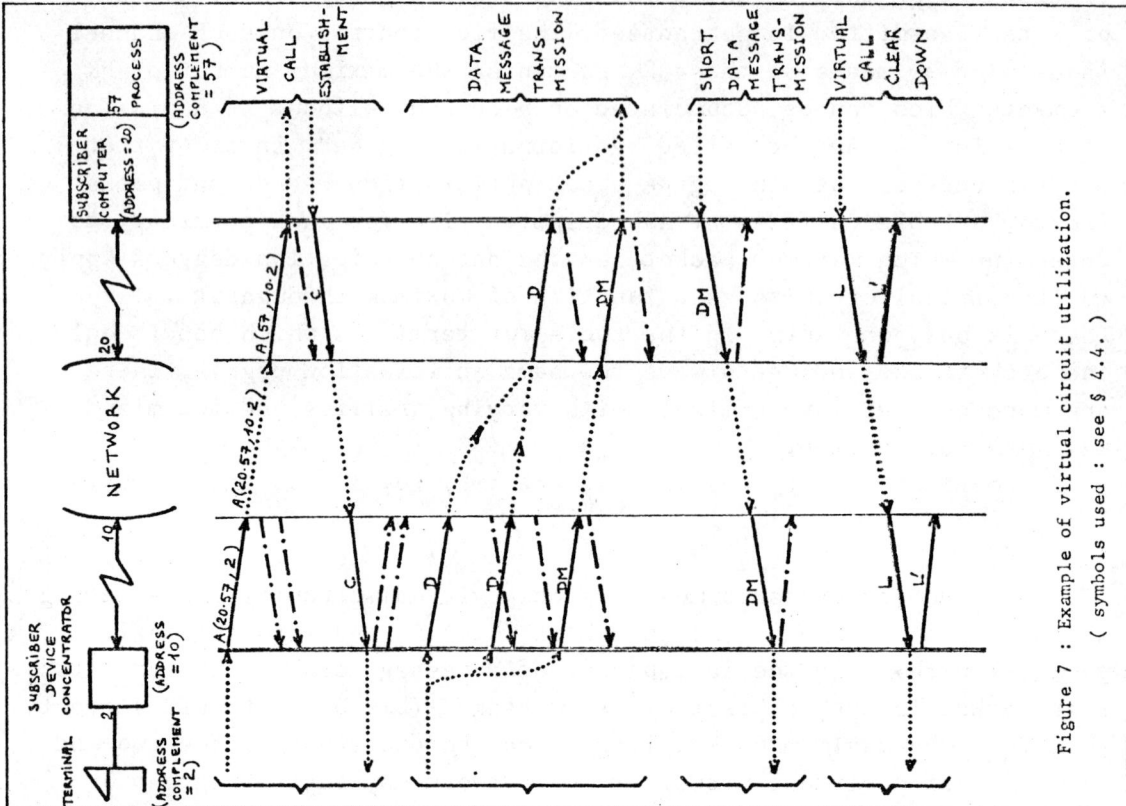

Figure 7 : Example of virtual circuit utilization.
(symbols used : see § 4.4.)

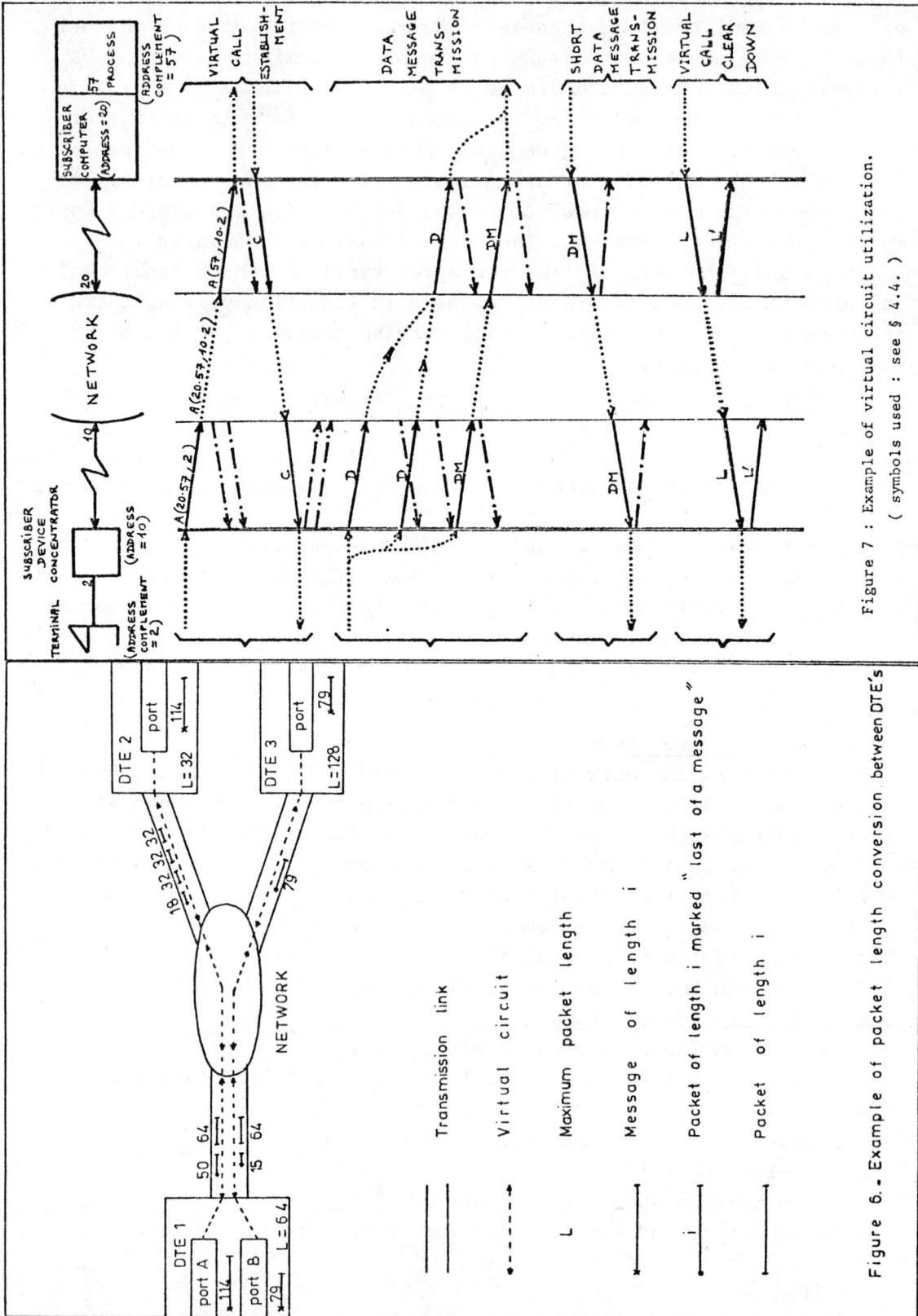

Figure 6.- Example of packet length conversion between DTE's

Adress of the callee : This address has two parts. The first gives
                       the identification of the callee within TRANSPAC
                       and the second gives an address complement
                       used by the callee itself if it needs further
                       identification.
Address of the caller :Its content has the same structure as for
                       the address of the callee.
Collect call flag   : If this flag is set, the callee must be charged
                       for the call.
Closed user group   : This field allows the caller to specify one closed
                       user group to which it belongs and is applicable
                       to the call. If the callee does not belong to that
                       group, the call is cleared down by the network.
Maximum send and receive throughputs : The maximum throughput appearing
                       in the call request have the form 2^k bytes/s
                       with k ranging from 0 to 15. Using these
                       informations and the table fixed at subscription
                       time, the network find the maximum packet length
                       and anticipation degree which allow for these
                       throughputs for each direction.

A connection confirmation is returned by the callee when it accepts
                       the call request.
A clear-down command can be sent at any time by any customer involved
                       in a virtual circuit or also by the network
                       itself in case of failure.
                       It has the effect of re-initialising the logical
                       channel. Any data which were left in the virtual
                       circuit are destroyed. A customer is always
                       informed of clear down and it can have an expla-
                       nation by looking at the clear-down cause which
                       is transmitted with the clear-down signal.
A clear-down confirmation is sent when a clear down command is received.

4.4. Example of a virtual circuit utilization (see figure 7).
   For this example the caller is a device connected to a device concentrator and the callee is a task in a computer. The network knows
only the device concentrator (subscriber address = 10) and the computer
(subscriber address = 20). Address complements 2 (for the device)
and 57 (for the task) are used for further identifications.
   Maximum packet length is supposed to be 16 octets between the concentrator and the network and 32 octets between the network and the

subscriber computer.

Symbols used

$\xrightarrow{X}$	Symbolizes the transmission of a packet X
$-\cdot-\cdot\rightarrow$	PR segment transmission (ready to receive)
$\cdots\cdots\cdots\rightarrow$	Internal exchange of informations.

A (nA, nB) : Call Request (Called address, calling address)

C   : Connection confirmation

L   : Clear down command

L'   : Clear down confirmation command

D   : Data Packet

DM   : Data Packet "last of its message".

5. NETWORK ARCHITECTURE

The network will be built using modular units for switching, transmission and control. Its general organization has been designed in
order that the failure of a particular component, (hardware or software), will not spread in the entire network and affect communication
not related to the component in failure.

5.1. Functional structure of the network

The functional structure of the network is given in figure 8.

The nodes are of two kinds. National nodes handle local, incoming,
outgoing and transit traffic and have some personnel which can control
and monitor the node and all its remote dependancies through a local
control point. Regional nodes have no personnel and do not perform
transit routing. They are under the control of remote national nodes.

Each node includes a switching unit which performs routing and
transmission of packets. Subscribers may be connected directly to
the switching center if they are synchronous and use the standard
protocol (see § 4.), or otherwise via a local or remote connecting
unit, which performs lines concentration and protocol conversions
when needed. Asynchronous terminals may access TRANSPAC through direct
leased lines, public telephone or telex networks, via a local or remote
time-division multiplexor for up to 50 asynchronous lines, connected
to a connecting unit by the mean of a parallel interface.

Connexion units use for their links to the switching center the
same protocol that is proposed to subscribers and used between switching nodes (described in § 4). The frame level however is different and applies to several lines in parallel : thus a single line
failure has no other effect than a reduced throughput.

The management centers collect all statistical and charging infor-

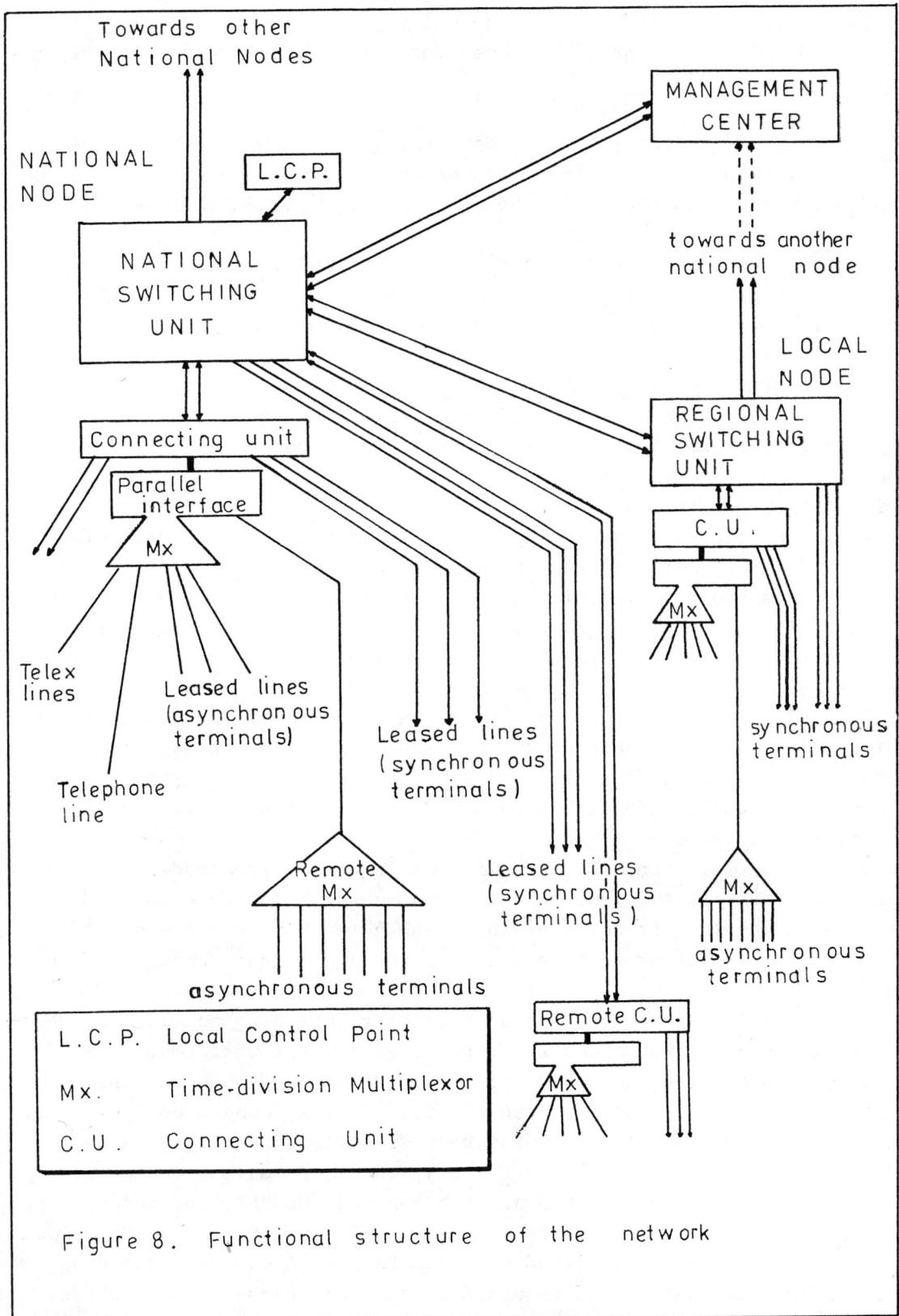

Figure 8. Functional structure of the network

mations, in view of processing and editing.

All network nodes are interconnected by at least two primary groups
at about 64 Kbi/s.

5.2. Size of the network

Two steps are already planned concerning the network development.

In the opening stage (1977) the network will have 6 national nodes
and one management center located in Rennes. Switched throughputs
of nodes will range from 100 to 500 kbts/s.

In the next stage (after 1978) the network will have 7 national
nodes, 6 regional nodes, and two management centers. Switched throughputs of nodes will range from 50 to 2 000 kbits/s.

6. SOME ASPECTS OF INTERNAL OPERATIONS

Some of the original features of the TRANSPAC design are now discussed.
However, finalized design details will not be know before the con-
tractor has fully specified the technical options that are left to
him in the specifications.

One specificity of the design is that virtual circuits are materialised throughout the network, in a succession of logical channels
on the subscriber's and inter-node links, connected by "transit points",
located in the switching nodes. Attached to the transit point is the
buffer storage affected to the virtual circuit. At least in a first
stage memory is not shared between different virtual circuits. Transit
points are created at call set up time and destroyed when call is
cleared down. Thus a good control of the traffic can be exercised.
A saving on transmission also results from the possibility of using
abbreviated packet identifications throughout the network.

6.1. Call set-up

As far as switching and transmission functions are concerned, operations are exactly the same in the nodes subscribers are connected
to and in the transit nodes of the trunk network, since protocols
for call supervision and data transmission are unique throughout the
network.

When a call request command arrives in a switching node, with the
logical number i from the link A, routing is first performed (see
§ 6.3.), which gives the outgoing link B to be used to reach the
callee. Then a free logical channel number, j, is chosen on this link.
A transit point is created, which records at least the links A and
B, the logical channel numbers i and j, the four maximum packet lengths
to be used for each direction of each logical channel, and incorporates
the buffers for each way of transmission. Sizes of buffers and maximum
packets lengths are determined by consultation of tables, according
to the maximum throughputs required in the call request command for

both directions. Those tables are constructed, either by the network
designer for trunk links, or by agreements between the network authority and the customer for subscriber's links (as explained in §
4.2.), in order to obtain a good compromise between various parameters,
such as queuing delays, processing time, buffer space, overhead in
store and on links, store management simplicity.

When the call is cleared, the transit point is killed, the channel
numbers i and j are freed ant the buffers are restituted to a common
pool.

6.2. Data transfer

Let us consider the direction from link A to link B in the transit
point established in § 6.1.

Attached to this direction is a "permits counter" which is incremented each time a ready to receive segment arrives from link B on
logical channel j, and decremented each time a data packet is sent
on logical channel j of link B.

As soon as there are enough data in the corresponding buffer to
make a packet of maximum length, or an packet marked "last of its
message", and the permits counter is non-zero, packet is sent on link
B with logical channel number j. Each time buffer space is freed in
such a manner, a ready to receive segment is sent on logical channel
i of link A.

By this way, one never needs to destroy data by lack of buffer
space, since buffers are reserved prior to the arrival of data packets.
Packet length conversion is easily done when needed.

When RAZ segments (refer § 4.2.) are exchanged all data in the
buffers for both directions are killed and permits counts are reset.
Then the adequate number of ready to receive segments are sent in
both directions.

6.3. Routing of call request messages
6.3.1. Numbering scheme

Details of numbering scheme are not yet wholly fixed. Provisions have been made to ensure :

. international interconnexions (without any need for knowing
TRANSPAC number before it is internationaly agreed).

. independance of subscribers' addresses and network topology.

6.3.2. Selection of appropriate destination node

By consulting a table, a node determines, among the network
nodes or subnetworks it knows, which one a call has to be routed to.
For this purpose, it looks through the callee's address, going more
or less far down the successive hierarchical fields, according to
the remoteness of the destination. (For example, a node may know each

switching node in a neighbouring area, but only a main node in a remote
area.

6.3.3. Selection of appropriate route

When the destination node has been chosen, the last problem
to solve is to select an outgoing link towards this destination.

A set of fixed routes is predetermined (off-line), classified
by levels of priorities, for each destination. The level of resources
(memory, loads of the lines, etc...) still available for each route
are known as a result of internodes exchanges of informations. These
resources, expressed in terms of available throughput, are quantified
into a few different levels. Among the routes which are at the highest
level of resources, the one of highest priority is chosen.

This routing method, as detailed in (6), permits altogether that
external operators can know and regulate routing mechanisms (by acting
upon the routing tables), and that calls may be rerouted when links
or nodes are overloaded (or reach a predetermined degree of load)
or fail.

6.4. Multiline link protocol

To improve reliability of the links between the different elements
of the network (switches, connecting units, management centers),
the use of multiline links will be generalised. A multiline-protocol
has been defined for this purpose.

The aims of this protocol are :

- to make of a set of lines a unique full duplex data link, with
  a maximum available throughput equivalent to the sum of the individual throughputs of the different lines.
- to allow that some of the lines may fail without any loss, inter-
  version or duplication of data.
- To work in an efficient way with any type of links (number of
  lines, speeds, propagation delay, ranging from direct metallic
  wires to satellite connections) and frame lengths distributions.

A simplified line protocol allows the two ends to close or open
line simultaneously, when it detects abnormal or normal transmission
properties on the line.

The link protocol controls the transmission of frames. When it
decides that a frame has to be sent, it chooses any of the open lines.

Three numbers (modulo 64) are carried by each frame :

- number of the frame
- number of the expected frame in the reverse direction, which
  acknowledges all the frame up to that number. (lower bound of
  reception window)
- number of the first frame which cannot be accepted from the reverse
  direction, which performs the flow-control function (upper bound
  of the reception window).

For detailed description of multiline protocol, see (7).

7. EXTENSIONS AND CONCLUSION

Some extensions concerning the fields of available services and the
capacity to satisfy the foreseen data traffic expected in the near
future are planned and studied.

Conversions of protocols will allow early customers to convert their
present or planned private networks, by the use of virtual circuits
instead of leased or switched lines (even if multipoints) without
any major change in their commmunication software and hardware systems.
The list of protocols that will be accepted by TRANSPAC is to be defined
according to commercial, technical and economic considerations.
Customers who want to improve throughput and reliability of their
connections to the network will be allowed to use a multiline link
with the protocol described in § 6.4.

A datagram service - i.e. transmission and switching of independant
packet of 255 octets at most -, as defined by C.C.I.T.T. (8), is under
study. It is intended to accept the present users of the CIGALE network.
Flow-control and independance of users are crucial problems. Transit
time of datagrams, number of datagrams simultaneously in the network
per subscriber and number of datagrams queuing for delivery to a customer
are limited by the network, by dropping datagrams if necessary.

By the mean of its wide spread geographical extension, its
broad range of available services and connections possibilities, its
good reliability and performances in terms of call set-up time and
transit delays, TRANSPAC is hoped to meet the requirements of most
teleprocessing users.

REFERENCES

1. "Les Télécommunications et l'Informatique" - L. J. LIBOIS, Congrès
   AFCET 1973 - Séance solennelle.
2. "Spécifications du réseau TRANSPAC" - January 1975. CCETT - DIR/T/8/74.
3. "RCP : 1e Réseau Expérimental à Commutation par Paquets des PTT".
   R. DESPRES - A. BACHE - A. PUISSOCHET - A. HENRIOT - Congrès AFCET 1973
7-9. Novembre 1973. Tome 2. p. 223 - 236. English Translation can be
found in - National Physical Laboratory - Com. Sci. TM 84. March 1974.
4. "RCP, the experimental Packet-switched data transmission service of
   the french PTT". R. DESPRES - ICC Stockholm - August 1974. T. 1266
p. 171.186.
5. "Protocoles standards d'accès au Réseau TRANSPAC"- February 1975 -
   CCETT* - TPC/R/DT/6/75.
6. "Informations sur le routage" - April 1975. CCETT* - TPC/R/DT/29/75.
7. "Protocole Multilignes" - March 1975. CCETT* - TPC/R/T/75/BJ.
8. C.C.I.T.T. - COM VII - Point C. n° 129 - August 1974.

* CCETT - BP 1266 35013 RENNES CEDEX.

Flow control in the packet switching networks

Dag Belsnes
Ass. Professor
EDB-sentret
Universitetet i Oslo
Norway

Abstract

In data networks that are used to transfer large files,
flow control is required to prevent congestion in the net.
The window scheme, which allows for end-to-end flow control
of each connection, can also be used to avoid global
congestion. It is shown how the sending side can set the
window size so that good throughput is achieved and
overloading of the net is avoided. A discussion of how the
buffer space in the host computer should be used, is also
included.

1. INTRODUCTION

In a communication network, where the traffic mainly consists of short messages (typically in conversational computing), there is little need for an end-to-end control of the transmission rate. However, control is needed to ensure reliable transfer of the data. The sender can send messages as soon as possible, with little probability of causing serious congestion in the net. Of course, many connections could simultaneously be in operation, so that the net has difficulties in handling all the traffic. Such overload situations should be resolved by either updating the network to a greater capacity, or by having some means for intermediately rejecting some of the customers, thus providing some kind of a congestion control mechanism. However, if the network is also used to transfer large files, some kind of end-to-end flow control is required. Otherwise, even high capacity networks may easily be congested by a couple of fast data sources.

In the ARPANET, the so-called RFNM-message is used to prevent one connection from flooding the net. Originally only one message could be transmitted on a connection (link) before a RFNM was returned from the receiver. In many cases this reduces the throughput over the connection drastically. At present the ARPANET permits more messages (currently 4) to be outstanding at a time between any pair of source-destination nodes (IMPs). Operbeck [OP 74] has, however, shown that serious throughput degradations can still occur. In the French CYCLADES [PO 73] network, and in a protocol proposed by Cerf and Kahn [CEKA 74], there is another end-to-end flow control scheme. Briefly this mechanism works as follows.

Assume that the characters (or packets) on a data stream are numbered sequentially. A window, described by a left and right edge, restricts the sequence numbers of characters the sender may transmit at any given instant. The receiver responds to data with a positive acknowledgement which causes the sender´s window to move ahead. The window scheme is also used for error control, duplicate detection, and sequencing of packets into correct order by the receiver.

While short delays are the important issue for interactive traffic, high throughput is the objective for file transfers. The main problem in flow control is, on the one hand, to prevent sources eagerly trying to get high throughput from delivering so much data into the net that the net gets jammed, or that the receiving processes can not cope with the high data rate. On the other hand the restrictions caused by the flow control should not have the effect of unnecessarily reducing the throughput.

Investigations in the form of simulations described in D. W. Davies [DA 71] indicate that the total throughput in a store-and-forward packet switching network increases with the load until about half of the storage capacity of the net is in use. If the load is increased beyond this threshold, then the total number of packets delivered decreases rapidly caused by congestion in the net. Of course, the throughput also depends heavily on the topology of the net and the actual traffic pattern.

Davies [DA 71] has proposed an interesting overall network congestion control scheme. The total number of packets in the net is kept constant through the use of empty packets. Such a network is called an isarithmic network. The empty packets flow in the net in a random fashion, and when needed the sender picks an empty packet from the net and replaces it with a data-carrying packet, and the receiver gives empty packets back to the net. Thus, global congestion is prevented at the cost of empty packet management. This solution, however, has some deficiencies:

Traffic might be slowed down just because empty packets are not available when they are needed.

The overhead due to the traffic of empty packets takes bandwidth from ordinary connections.

If the traffic pattern is such that bottlenecks arise, packets will pile up so that the number of packets for other connections may get very small.

It is hard to keep the total number of packets in the net unchanged in connection with node failures.

In the following sections we will discuss how the window mechanism can be used as a flexible and robust tool for tuning the data flow over a connection.

II. CONTROL OF FILE TRANSFERS

Consider a connection over which we want to transfer a file. We want to be able to control this flow of data so that a high throughput rate is achived without overloading the network or blocking other data connections. For the moment we will make some assumptions in order to simplify the situation, and later we will discuss the consequences when these assumtions are not satisfied.

Many of the problems disappear if we can assume unlimited buffer resources in the source and destination host computers. We also assume that both producer and consumer user processes are fast compared to the network, so that the throughput is mainly determined by the performance of the net. Furthermore, the assumption is made that the flow in the net has stabilized. Let c be the average capacity offered by the net for our connection, measured in packets/packet time. Here packet time is the time it takes the net to accept one packet from a sender, and we will, for convenience, use this as a rough unit for time. Of course, this unit depends on the size of the packets and the speed of the transmission line, but for a file transfer we can assume that the packet size is about constant, and it is just as well to keep the line speeds out of our discussion.

If there is much traffic in the net, the capacity c will typically be less than 1. On the other hand, if we have a lightly loaded net with multiple paths from sender to receiver, then c might be greater than 1.

If the sender transmits packets with a rate greater than c for some period, the only result is that additional load is put on the net without any gain in throughput (or a gain will be achieved with significant reduction for other connections). Thus, in order to get good throughput, the sender should send packets with a rate close to c, but should not be allowed to transmit much faster. This is a major problem in end-to-end flow control.

Let RT be the average round-trip time (the time taken to receive an acknowledgement from the instant the packet was sent) measured in packet time. It is also assumed that the traffic in the net has stabilized. During a long file transfer both c and RT will in general vary, but we hope that our flow control scheme will dynamically compensate for such variations.

The round-trip time mainly depends on the number of nodes between the sender and receiver, on the current load, and the need for retransmissions between nodes.

If the variance of the capacity and the round-trip time is very small, an ideal window size would be:

$$w = c \cdot RT$$

This will result in the "pipe" between the sender and receiver containing enough packets to maintain a bandwidth of c. With a smaller window the throughput is reduced because the sender often is delayed waiting for acknowledgements. See Figure 1.

Fig. 1, iii) illustrates how a sender may flood the network with packets without obtaining any better throughput. Observe that the throughput is closely related to the rate at which acknowledgements are received by the sender, and not with the rate at which packets are injected into the net.

III.   VARIATIONS IN CAPACITY AND ROUND-TRIP TIME

Normally both the capacity and the round-trip time will show variations during a file transfer. This may be caused by changing load conditions in the net, variations in the packet distribution across the net, packets that have to be retransmitted because of transmission errors, alternate routing of packets, etc. In order to take advantage of (or not lose bandwidth because of) such variations, the window size should be somewhat larger than $c \cdot RT$. How much larger is difficult to determine as it will depend on the characteristics of the variations.

Fortunately the sender is in a good position to estimate both the capacity and the round-trip time. The round-trip time for each packet can be directly measured, and a good estimate of the capacity is the incoming rate of acknowledgements (assuming that enough data packets are given to the net).

This makes it possible for the sender to determine a well-suited window size. A simple rule would be to start off by sending packets into the net at a high rate. When an acknowledgement arrives, the sender sets the window size. This will have the effect of reducing the output rate to the rate at which acknowledgements are received. The window size will also tend to be greater than $c \cdot RT$. Figure 2 is an illustration of this rule of determining the window size. Figure 3 gives an example of the effect of variations in the round-trip time. Note that this scheme does not require any calculation by the sender of the capacity or the roundtrip time.

Because of the possibility of a bad estimate of the window size, or because of a change in the mean capacity or round-trip time, the sender should regularly update the window size.

time

(unit packet time)

1 2 3 4 5   6   7   8   9   10   11   12
Sender

A1 A2 A3 A4 A5 A6 A7 A8   Receiver

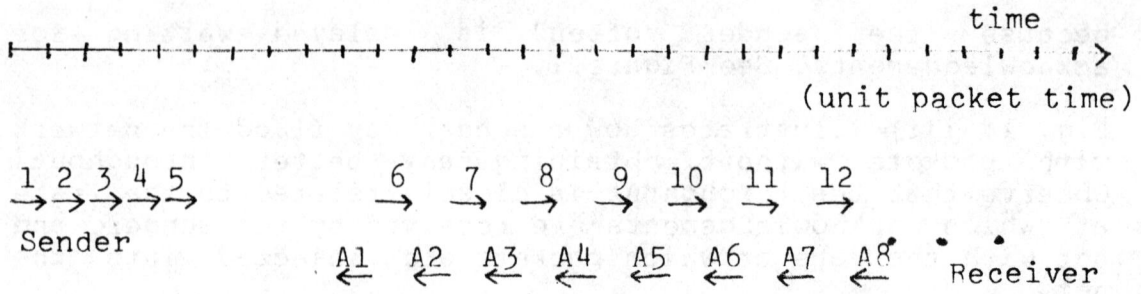

i) $c = \frac{1}{2}$ RT=10   w=5

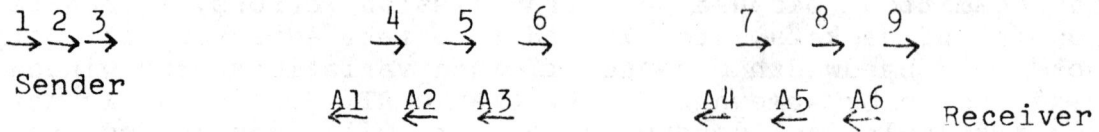

1 2 3   4   5   6   7   8   9
Sender

A1 A2 A3   A4 A5 A6   Receiver

ii) $c = \frac{1}{2}$ RT=10   w=3

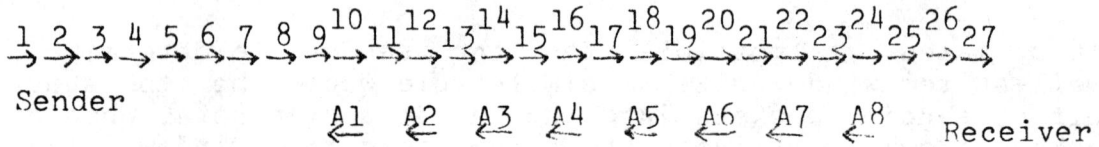

1 2 3 4 5 6 7 8 9 10 11 12 13 14 15 16 17 18 19 20 21 22 23 24 25 26 27
Sender

A1 A2 A3 A4 A5 A6 A7 A8   Receiver

iii) $c = \frac{1}{2}$ RT=10   w= ∞

FLOW OF PACKETS ON A CONNECTION WITH DIFFERENT WINDOW
SIZES WHEN THE CAPACITY AND ROUND-TRIP TIME ARE
CONSTANT.

FIG. 1

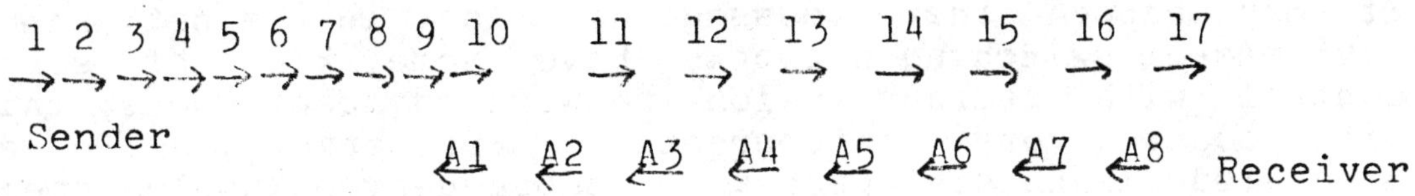

1 2 3 4 5 6 7 8 9 10   11   12   13   14   15   16   17
→ → → → → → → → → →   →   →   →   →   →   →   →

Sender   A1   A2   A3   A4   A5   A6   A7   A8   Receiver

$c = \frac{1}{2}$ RT = 10   W becomes 9

WINDOW SIZE SET WHEN ACKNOWLEDGEMENT IS RECEIVED
CONSTANT CAPACITY AND ROUND-TRIP TIME.

FIG. 2

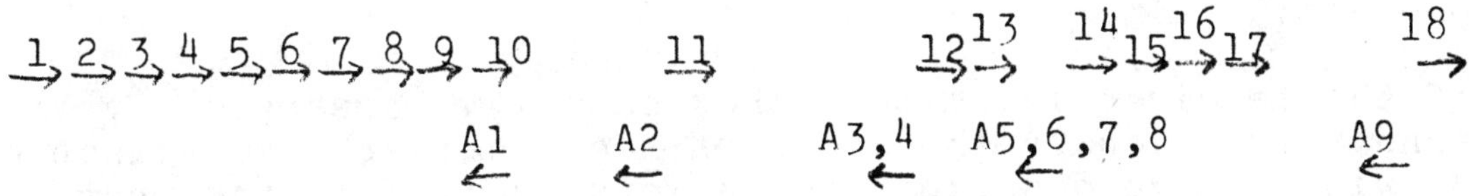

1 2 3 4 5 6 7 8 9 10   11   12 13 14 15 16 17   18
→ → → → → → → → → →   →   → → → → → →   →

A1   A2   A3,4   A5,6,7,8   A9
←   ←   ←   ←   ←

$c = \frac{1}{2}$ RT = 10   w becomes 9

PACKET FLOW WITH VARIATION IN THE ROUND-TRIP TIME
(SAME AVERAGE).

FIG. 3

It may happen that a message gets lost in the net. Since most packet switching networks have some kind of error control with retransmission between adjacent nodes, this will occur very infrequently. Furthermore, if an acknowledgement disappears, a subsequent acknowledgement from the receiver will resolve the situation for the sender. Thus, it will be sufficient to have a very long time-out for retransmission by the sender, and the loss of bandwidth will still be small because this happens so seldom. A long time-out has the advantage of avoiding unnecessary retransmissions. A clear distinction should be made here between retransmissions between adjacent nodes inside the network (increases the reliability of the subnet), and retransmissions by the sender (caused by packets lost or delayed in the subnet, or because the receiver has dropped a packet).

IV. SLOW USERS

In most cases where a file is moved from one computer to another the sender and receiver will be faster than the net. However, if I/O equipment, for instance, is directly connected to the net, the user may be the bottleneck. If it is the sender, there is no problem with the flow control in the net as the window normally is ahead of the sender process.

If the receiver is slow, the capacity observed by the sender is given by the speed of the receiver. The selection of window size described above works well for the net in the sense of avoiding congestion in the net. However, the network module in the receiving host will use a lot of buffer space for such a connection. Data is received in order, but the user is not ready to consume the data. Therefore, the receiver may want to shorten the window size in order to reduce the load on the local buffer resources. Also a normally fast user may want for some reason to reduce the transmission rate for a period of time. Hence, the transmission control must include a way for the receiver to reduce the window size (perhaps to zero).

In the next paragraph we will look closer at problems connected with limited buffer resources in the host computers.

V. BUFFER ALLOCATION

During the transportation of data from a producer process in one host computer to a consumer process in another computer, there is need for buffer space in both hosts. When a sender delivers data to the network, the data must be available in the host until an acknowledgement is returned from the receiver. This is necessary because of a possible need for a retransmission.

Since packets may arrive at the receiving host out of sequence, this computer must be prepared to store packets until data can be consumed by the user in correct order.

We assume that a host computer contains a Transmission Control Program (TCP) that acts as an interface between the user and the packet switching network. In [CEDASU 74] such an interface module is described in detail. The data flow between the user and the TCP goes in finite length letters. When a user has data to send, it delivers a letter to the TCP in a user buffer (a buffer included in the user's data space), and the user is informed when the letter is successfully transmitted by the TCP. A receiving user requests a letter by giving a user buffer to the TCP. When a complete letter has been received, the buffer with the letter is returned to the user.

If the TCP receives a packet out of order, the data can not be stored in the letter buffer because the packet may be a part of another letter. Hence, the packet has to be saved in a TCP buffer. Thus, we have two types of data buffers in the host, the user buffers and the TCP buffers which are buffers to be shared among all the network users in the host.

For most host computers buffer space is a valuable resource. The TCP in many implementations may have an additional restriction on the amount of buffer space since the TCP can be regarded as a part of the operating system. It is important to share this limited buffer resource among the users in a way that does not reduce the total throughput too much.

Earlier in this paper it is established that the sender often wants to use a large window size in order to obtain a good bandwidth through the net. This has some implications on the treatment of the TCP buffers.

Consider first a transmitting user. He gives the letters to the TCP in user buffers. Before the data is sent into the net the character stream is broken up into packets with necessary header information added. Since a packet may have to be retransmitted, it is convenient to store the packets in TCP buffers until acknowledgements are received. However, with large window sizes this will require many TCP buffers. Furthermore, retransmissions from the sender occur infrequently with good flow control (the receiver seldom has to discard packets), and the data for reconstruction of the packet is available in the user buffer containing the letter. Hence, unless TCP buffers are cheap, it is not reasonable to use TCP buffers on the sending side.

On the receiving side a packet that arrives at the TCP in sequence can immediately be put in the user's receive buffer (if it exists). On the other hand, packets that are received out of order has to be kept in TCP buffers (or discarded). The need for TCP buffer space is difficult to estimate. It depends on the size of the window and the probability of long packet delays in the net. (We assume that special action is taken if many TCB buffers are used because of a slow user.) In the worst case about one window's worth of data can be out of sequence on a connection.

A safe way of allocating the buffer space is to equally distribute the TCP buffer resource among all connections, and set the window size on a connection equal to the reserved amount of buffer space. Then the TCP will always be able to store all out-of-order packets. However, this will often result in too small window sizes, which in turn will reduce the bandwidth. It is natural to believe that packets will in general arrive with only a small degree of disorder. Hence, the average need for buffers will be significantly less than the window sizes.

Sometimes a packet may get a very long transit time because of many retransmissins or an unfortunately chosen path. This causes an acute need for buffers on the particular connection.

Altogether this indicates that the available TCP buffer space should be organized in a pool of small buffer blocks, and that blocks be assigned to the connections according to need. Then the sum of the window sizes for the active connections can be substantially larger than the TCP buffer resource, without increasing too much the probability of rejection of a packet by the TCP.

VI. RETRANSMISSION

When a packet is discarded by the receiver, this may be done without notifying the sender. The way to recover is to let the sender have a time-out for retransmission. As mentioned earlier such a time-out is also required when packets are lost in the network. It is a delicate problem to determine the length of the time-out interval. If it is too short, bandwidth is lost because of unwanted retransmissions. If it too long, the reduction comes from the delays caused by the sender. The time-out should not be a fixed number of seconds, but rather be based on the sender´s current estimates of the round-trip delay on the particular connection.

The retransmission will often include more packets than the original rejected packet. We will illustrate this with an example.

Let the sender´s window size be 20, and assume that packet 1 gets a long delay in the net. Many packets arrive out of order, and let us say that the receiver must throw away packet 10. Then 1 arrives, and the receiver sends an acknowledgement for packets 1 to 9. This will cause the sender to transmit up to packet 29. But since packet 10 is gone, all the packets 11 to 29 arrive out of sequence. Most likely some of these also will be discarded. Thus, when the sender times out on packet 10, the sender can as well retransmit the whole window (packets 10-29) in order to avoid a new time-out. Note that after a retransmission the communication will proceed normally. The phenomenon described in [OP 74], where ARPANET can be trapped in a retransmission situation (reducing the throughput to one-fourth of expected), will not occur.

An alternative retransmission scheme is to let the receiver send a notification to the sender when a packet is discarded. This negative acknowlededement will make it possible for the sender to retransmit only that packet without any time-out. The recovery will in this case be very inexpensive in terms of throughput. Hence, this alternative seems to be more attractive.

Frequent retransmission on a connection is also an indication to the sender that there is some problem on the connection, and the sender can in such cases try to reduce the window size.

VII. SUMMARY

In data networks that are used to transfer large files, flow control is required to prevent congestion in the net. The window scheme, described in [CEKA 74] allows for an end-to-end flow of each connection and can also be used to avoid global congestion of the communication network. The network will at every instant offer to a connection a certain capacity and round-trip delay. The amount of data that the sender should allow to be outstanding is closely related to the product of the capacity and the round-trip time.

Since these quantities can best be estimated by the sender, it should be the sender's responsibility to determine the window size.

A simple and promising way to determine the window size is to let the sender start sending packets into the net at a high rate. When the first acknowledgement arrives, the sender sets the window. Then the window size normally is good in order to achieve the best bandwidth for the connection under the current load on the subnet. Furthermore, this window size prevents the sender from giving too much data to the net, which has the effect of reducing global congestion in the net and will give good total throughput for active connections.

Since this window setting is easy to do and since the load on the net may change, the sender updates the window size regularilly.

An exception to having the sender set the window size is the case where the receiving user is slow compared to the net and the sender. In order to reduce the need for buffer space in the receiving host, the receiver may request the sender to use a smaller window. Hence, the transmission protocol should allow for this.

The available TCP buffer space in the host should mainly be used to store packets which arrived out of order. This means that most often it is too expensive to use TCP buffers to store packets transmitted but not acknowledged, or packets received in order but waiting for a slow user.

By sharing the TCP buffers among all active connections, the sum of window sizes can be much larger than available buffer space, and still the probability that the receiving TCP must discard a packet can be kept low.

If retransmission from the sender is controlled by time-outs, this can have a significiant effect on the throughput. It will be a time-out delay (which cannot be too small because of unwanted retransmissions), and in many cases a whole window of data may have to be retransmitted. This retransmission overhead can be reduced if the transmission protocol allows the receiver to inform the sender when the receiver discards a packet.

VIII. FURTHER WORK

Most of the ideas expressed in this paper are based on intuition. The next step would be to work out the details of the window setting protocol, and then to simulate the system under different load conditions. Comparisions should be made with other alternative solutions and modifications to the flow control scheme.

Acknowledgements

The author wishes to thank Vinton G. Cerf, Yogen Dalal, Torstein Haugland, and Carl Sunshine for many fruitful discussions about problems in data communication and for many suggestions and corrections of the work in this paper.

REFERENCES

DA 71
  D.W. Davies, "The Control of Congestion in Packet Switching Networks," Second ACM Symposium on Problems in the Optimization of Data Communications Systems, 1971.

CEKA 74
  V. Cerf and R. Kahn, "A Protocol for Packet Network Intercommunication," IEEE Trans on Communication, Vol. C-20, No. 5, May 1974, pp. 637-648.

CEDASU 74
  V. Cerf, Y. Dalal, and C. Sunshine, "Specification of Internet Transmission Control Program," Stanford University, Dec. 1974, INGW Note #72.

OP 74
  H. Opderbeck, "Throughput Degradations for Single Packet Messages," unpublished memo, available from the Network Information Center, NIC No. 30239, 1974.

Concepts of System Networks Architecture

J. H. McFadyen, E. M. Thomas

International Business Machines Corporation
Systems Development Division
Kingston Laboratory
USA

ABSTRACT

Data processing systems have rapidly evolved from a central processing unit with a few peripheral devices to elaborate information processing networks. As network configurations and application programming became more complex, an increasing lack of adaptability hindered further system evolution. More significant, however, was the absence of a unified network structure on which more versatile network designs could be based.

This paper begins with a synopsis of network evolution, outlining the changing relationships between the user and the data processing system. The paper then introduces the concept that a network of programmable products should be viewed as a system that provides services in response to a user request. Systems Network Architecture is a unified network structure developed to support user requests for services. A discussion of various types of services is followed by examples of recently-announced IBM products based on these concepts. The paper concludes with a summary of the fundamental concepts of Systems Network Architecture.

INTRODUCTION

In the course of a few decades, computer systems composed of a central processing unit and a few input/output devices have evolved into complex information processing networks. Further network evolution has been impeded by various factors such as design incompatibilities among network products. The development of new or improved network applications has also been handicapped because the detailed characteristics of the physical network have been integrated into many application programs. By divorcing network management from the data processing of interest to the user, a unified network system structure can conserve and enhance valuable application development resources. Systems Network Architecture (SNA) allows the application programmer to concentrate his efforts on specific user applications while the SNA communication subsystem assumes responsibility for the details of network management and data transmission. The communication subsystem adapts to configuration changes without requiring modification of the application program.

Network restructuring is also simplified for the owner of the SNA network because the network is designed to be both flexible and extendible, reducing the resources required for reconfiguration, network expansion and the introduction of new products. Such restructuring is particularly burdensome in networks where both computers and control units are programmable, and network modifications affect the application programs. On the other hand, a network of programmable products offers the greatest potential for providing the user with convenient access to a wide variety of information processing services. The user of a properly implemented network system need not be aware of any physical products beyond the device with which he interacts in requesting services.

Systems Network Architecture details the format and protocols of information interchanges among the various computers and programmable control units that comprise an SNA network. To ensure that networks are capable of accommodating an increasing variety of configurations, services, and growth requirements, the structure of the architecture is based on a few fundamental concepts. This paper describes the concepts of services and requests that form the foundation for the functional capability and structure of SNA products.

EVOLUTION OF INFORMATION PROCESSING NETWORKS

Before discussing the concepts underlying the structure of SNA products and networks we will describe the development of the current teleprocessing environment. Five simplified stages of system evolution can be used to illustrate the essential features required of a comprehensive network management structure. This brief discussion of network evolution is included to show that application-to-device relationships as well as system configurations have become more complex during the evolution of network capability. The concepts of SNA address both aspects of network design.

Figure 1 shows the first three evolutionary stages of information processing systems. In the first stage the system consists of a computer containing a single application program and a few locally-attached Input/Output (I/O) devices. The application program manages the operation of the I/O devices through unique attachment mechanisms and supplies a data processing service to the user of the system. The user typically interacts with the system by submitting a deck of data cards and receiving printed pages of information at the conclusion of the "job." Job orientation was typical of early computer systems and remains characteristic of many contemporary computer operations.

In the second stage multiple applications coexist in a single computer and the locally-attached devices are distributed among the applications. An Input/Output Supervisor (IOS) program manages the sharing of the local attachment channel so that devices attached to the same channel can be dedicated to different applications. The application retains control of the assigned device for the duration of a job step. Device control is some-what simplified for the application because differences between similar devices are masked by the methods used to access the devices. Multiple devices and services are concurrently available to different users but the user interface has remained essentially unchanged.

Teleprocessing (TP) devices ("terminals") and lines appear in the third stage. The terminal and the telephone line connecting it to the computer are managed as a combined resource. This resource is allocated to an application in the same manner as a

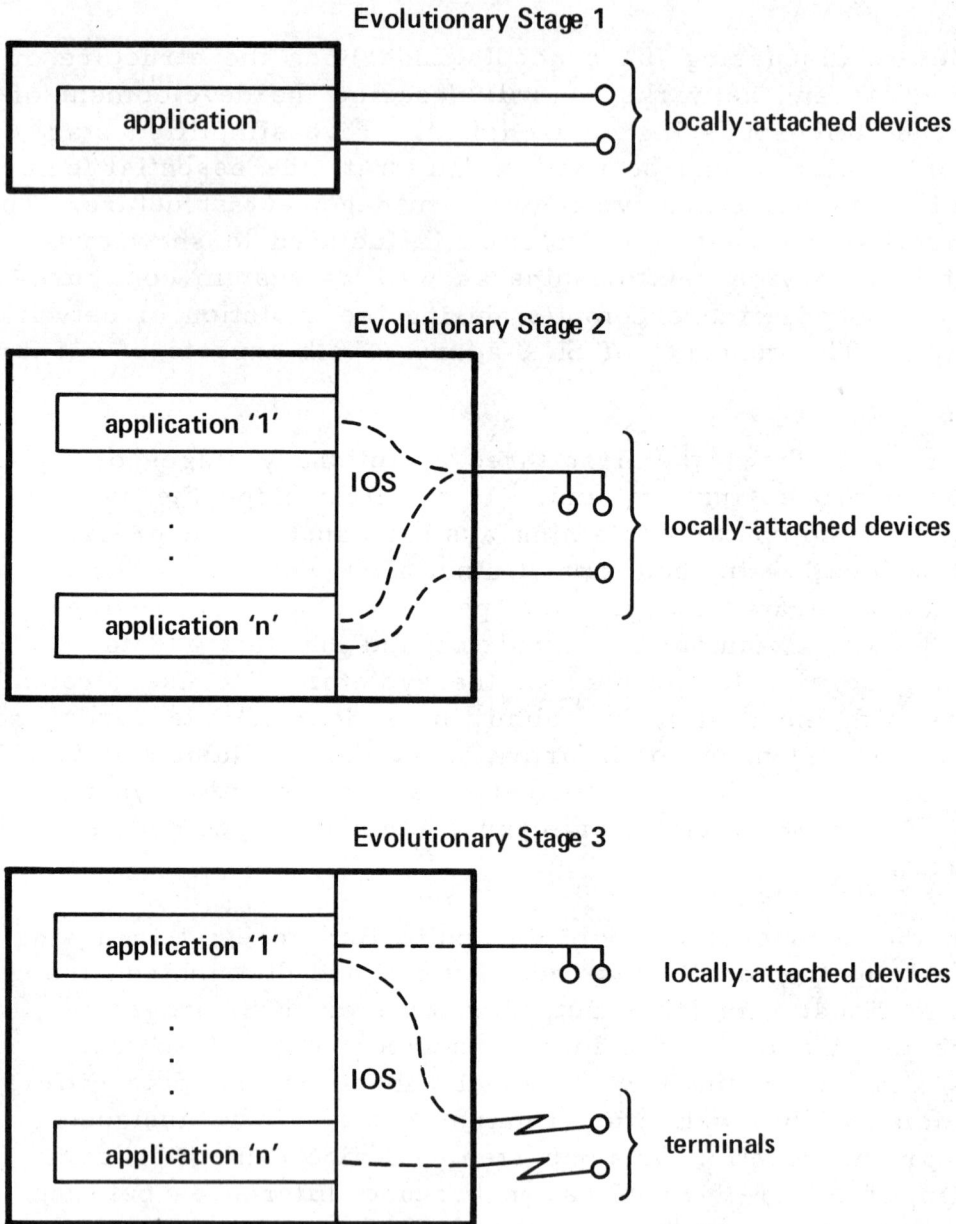

Figure 1. The first three stages of system evolution

local device but is managed differently because the TP line protocol combines line control and device control functions.   If a terminal becomes inoperative, the user cannot access the application services from a terminal on another line unless support for that type of terminal and line has also been designed into the application program.   The duplication of functionally equivalent facilities increases the cost of information processing services in terms of maintenance, storage, and performance.

In this stage, however, the user can interact with the application while it is in progress rather than receiving results only at the conclusion of the job.   The user can also obtain data processing services from a remote location.   Both of these capabilities require the user to understand a new interface to the system.   The operation of a typewriter-like terminal and the protocols for communicating with the application differ from those of locally-attached devices such as card readers.   In some instances the operational differences of two functionally-equivalent terminals result in additional operator training requirements.

Figure 2 shows two further stages of system evolution and complexity.   In the fourth stage multiple terminals coexist on a single TP line, but TP line protocols prevent devices with incompatible protocols from sharing the same line.   A line manager program, Teleprocessing Input/Output Supervisor (TPIOS), assumes the responsibility of managing the TP lines, permitting terminals on shared lines to be distributed among applications.   The somewhat simplified applications manage the terminals using device control functions that TPIOS combines with line control functions.   Since the applications continue to support specific device types, a user may be required to move from one terminal to another to obtain a service from a different application.   Device-dependent programming and incompatible terminals result in the duplication of expensive TP facilities that may not be fully utilized.

In the tree-structured network of the fifth stage, the terminals can be separated from the computer by multiple control units.   TPIOS manages the paths between computer and terminal so that the application is unaware of intervening communication control units, device control units, and multiple TP lines.   Specialized device control functions in the application continue to manage the operation of the terminals.

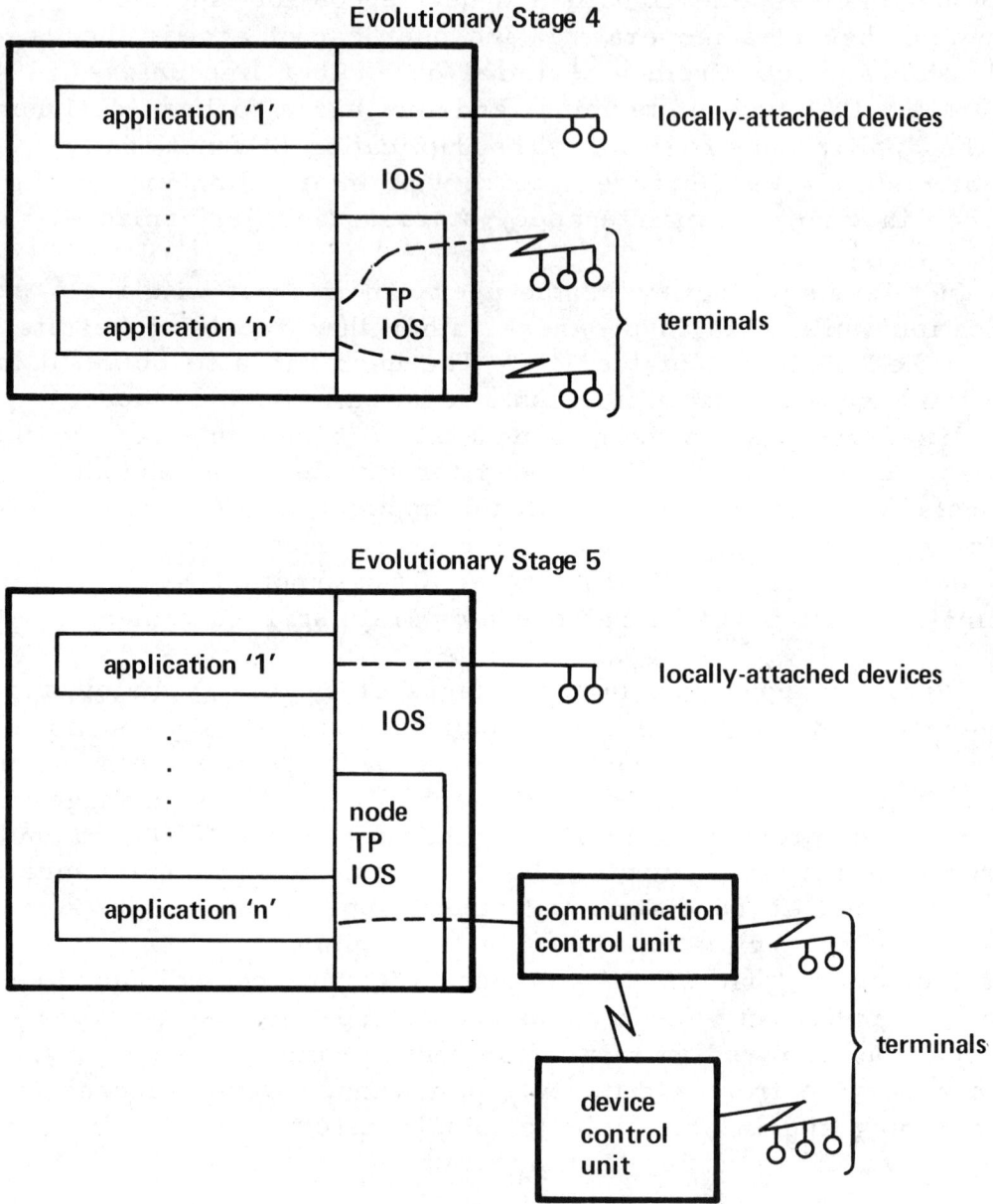

Figure 2. Stages 4 and 5 of system evolution

The availability of programmable control units encourages the movement of device control functions out of the computer into other network products. Although programmable control units offer potential advantages such as improved system performance and dependability, the management and utilization of a network of these products becomes more complex. Functions can be arbitrarily distributed in a network, but unless the network structure assures a functional consistency among applications, multiple applications cannot share a programmable control unit. It is at this stage of evolution that a comprehensive network architecture becomes essential to the design of an effective communication subsystem.

SERVICES AND REQUESTS IN THE SNA NETWORK

A user should have the ability to view a network of programmable products, regardless of configuration complexity, as an integrated system from which he can readily request information processing services. With the appropriate network system design, the communication subsystem can accomplish the transmission of requests for services without direct involvement of the user or application program. The communication subsystem of an SNA network conveys requests of various types from one programmable product to another programmable product: user requests for information processing services, application requests for device control services.

A user can access a wider variety of services when the system is composed of a diverse set of products; however, the details of the network operation and configuration should not intrude on his ability to readily obtain the desired services. As implied by Figure 3, terminals should be adapted to the user's specific requirements. The user's interaction with a terminal should be relatively uncomplicated and defined by the services he requires rather than by network characteristics. These objectives are achievable throughout the network system only when a formal structure exists for all network system products. SNA achieves this formal structure by defining the system capability of a network in terms of a hierarchy of functional layers; the user and the application belong to the outermost layer as shown in Figure 4. The communication subsystem conceals the actual location of the application from the user.

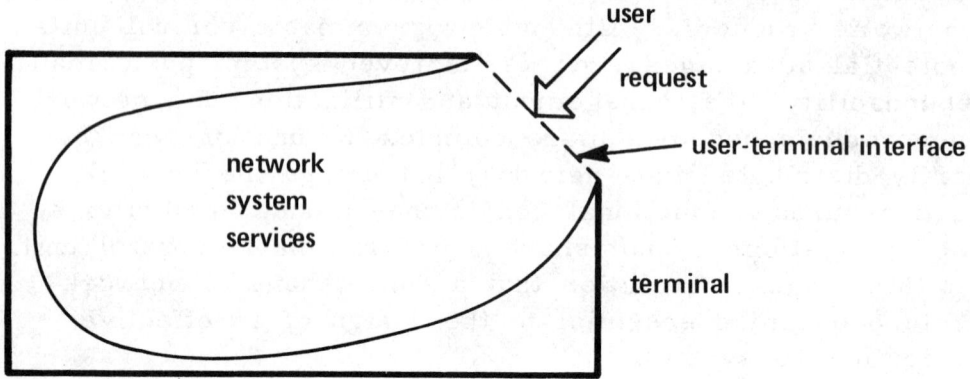

Figure 3. User perception of the SNA network system

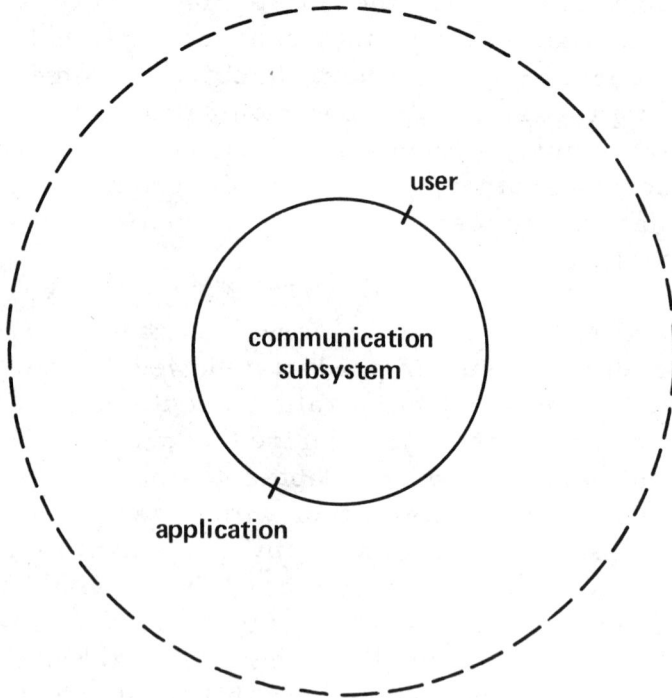

Figure 4. Conceptual view of an SNA network system

The user distinguishes different services in an SNA network by their unique network names. By addressing a request to a specific network name the user can access a service knowing neither the actual physical location nor the implementation details of the network product supplying the service. Similarly the application directs its communication to the user by specifying the user's network name as the destination. SNA refers to the collection of all network names as the "logical network," which extends into all SNA products. As shown in Figure 5, the SNA network connects a user to an application by establishing a logical point-to-point path between them. The path through the logical network is provided in such a way that the specific products and transmission facilities are not visible to either the user or the application.

A set of basic transmission services includes a basic information flow protocol and control functions to manage, recover, and maintain the request flow on the logical path. These services are independent of the actual physical locations of users and applications and provide a level of support common to all communications. As shown in Figure 6, users and applications do not interact directly with transmission services, but rather with a support layer that adapts the information flow to the requirements of the user or application. A half duplex data flow, for example, is appropriate for the interaction of a human user with an application program although transmission services can provide a full duplex data flow. The support layer can provide a consistent user interface even though the distribution of services can vary depending on product configuration. The services can be located in different physical products at different times, but the user should remain unaware of physical network modifications or the redistributing of services to improve total network system performance.

Although the same services may be accessible to different users, the user view of these services can vary significantly depending on user requirements and capability. The structure of SNA products enhances the capability of the network owner to provide an optimum user interface to the services. A simple terminal can be dedicated to a specific application and require minimal training for the operator. The supporting layer shields this class of operator from unnecessary involvement with the network system.

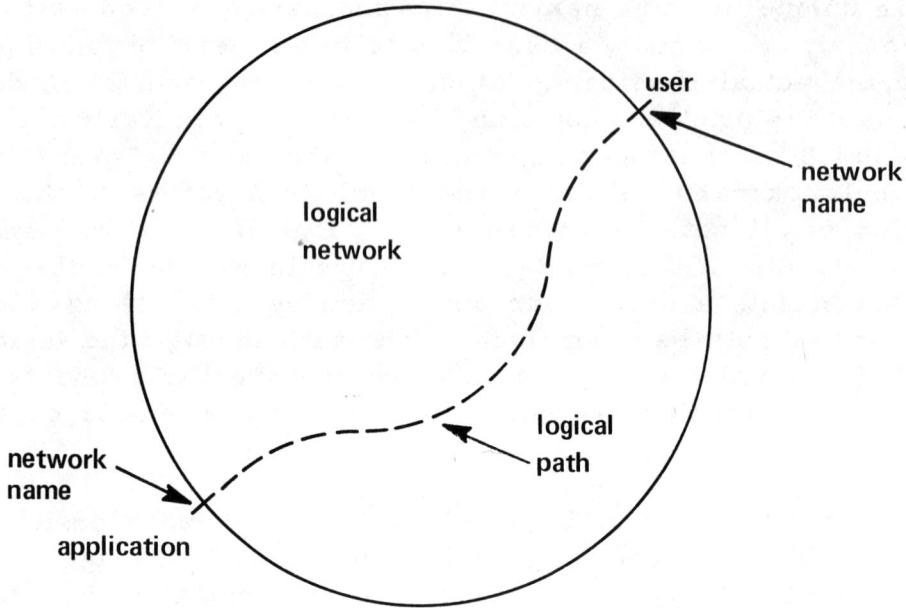

Figure 5. SNA logical network connects a pair of network names

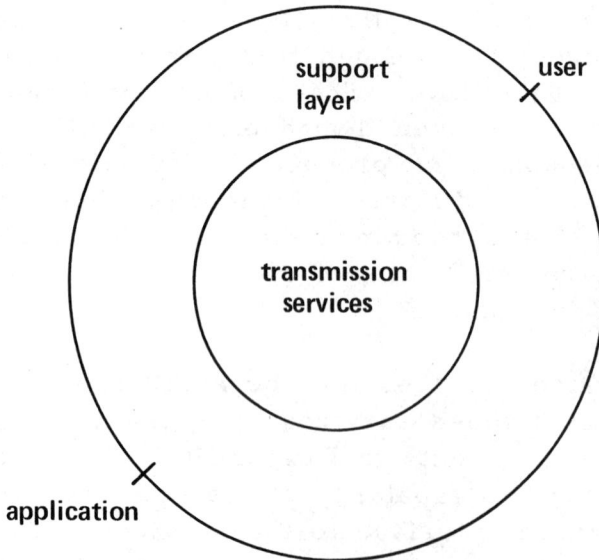

Figure 6. Support layer adapts transmission services to user requirements

At the other extreme the supporting layer can expose a full range of capability to the sophisticated user. This user views the network as a set of services which are immediately available, "Immediate Services," and as a set of services to which he can request connection, "Connected Services."

The user perceives Immediate Services as being supplied immediately by the terminal. These services are defined by SNA; a typical Immediate Service that a user requests is the establishment of a connection to an application. Connected Services, on the other hand, are the information processing services that the user obtains from the network system and are available only after the terminal has established user-to-application communication. These services can be supplied by IBM network products, by the network owner, or by the same or another network system user. The support layer of the terminal ensures that the service request is presented to the network name specified by the user.

The user's input to the network system consists of a request for a particular service and the data associated with that request. The request for Connected Services is sent to the appropriate application which can be located "local" to the user, at some "remote" location, or "distributed" among various programmable products. Data associated with the request can also be local, remote or distributed. The owner of the network may redistribute the services and data, but if the user interface to the terminal remains unchanged, the user continues to view all services as being available directly from his terminal. Since all SNA products have a compatible communication subsystem structure, the network owner has increased flexibility in product selection and configuration.

NETWORKS OF SNA PRODUCTS

In pre-SNA networks, application programs were tailored to support specific teleprocessing products. The terminal user would be limited to communication with only those applications providing specific support for that terminal. In an SNA network the application program supplies only the information processing service requested by the user. The user support layer in the terminal and the counterpart application support layer in the computer adapt the user request to the format for which the application has been designed.   When the user requests a service through a display terminal with minimal information processing capability, the major and complementary portion of the support is located in the computer.   In the simplified SNA network of Figure 7 a 3270 display station can communicate with any application that matches the characteristics of the System/370 support layer.   The 3270 user can access a variety of applications using one terminal with which he is familiar.

As the number of terminals increases, the System/370 computer may lack the processing power to adequately support both the TP network and the locally-attached devices.   Rather than upgrading the computer, the network owner can install a general purpose subsystem like the 3790 Communication System, as shown in Figure 8.   Part of the application programming can be moved to the 3790, easing the processing load on the System/370. The 3790 processes the majority of user requests and passes the remainder to the System/370.   This function redistribution can be accomplished without any alteration in the operating procedure for the 3270 terminal.

The philosophy of function distribution has additional benefits for the network owner.   Function redistribution can lighten TP line traffic, possibly allowing cost reduction through line sharing or the use of lower grade facilities.   TP line failure and computer unavailability have less significant effects on the terminal user since local processing can continue without computer support. Furthermore, local processing may improve system responsiveness to user requests.

The flexibility of an SNA network system is evident in the configuration of Figure 9, which shows a 3270 and a 3790 sharing the same TP line.   The adaptable 3270 SNA terminals can be attached to the computer either through the 3705 Communications Controller or through the 3790 subsystem.   The users of the 3270 terminals supported by the 3790 can be exchanging data with different applications in the System/370.   It appears to the users of all three 3270 display stations that all services are being provided by their individual terminals.

The SNA structure is supported by a diverse set of advanced function hardware and software products possessing several different levels of capability.   Early TP networks were designed

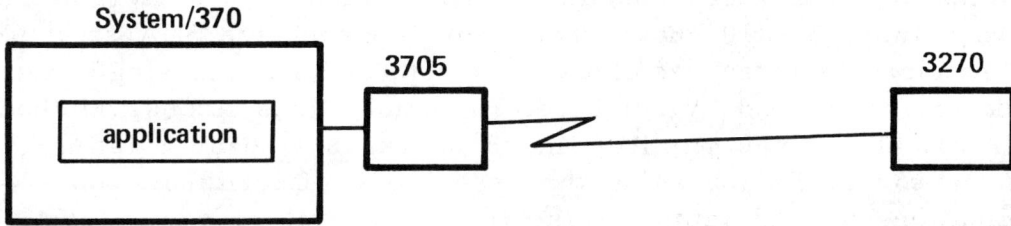

Figure 7. Application programming centralized in computer

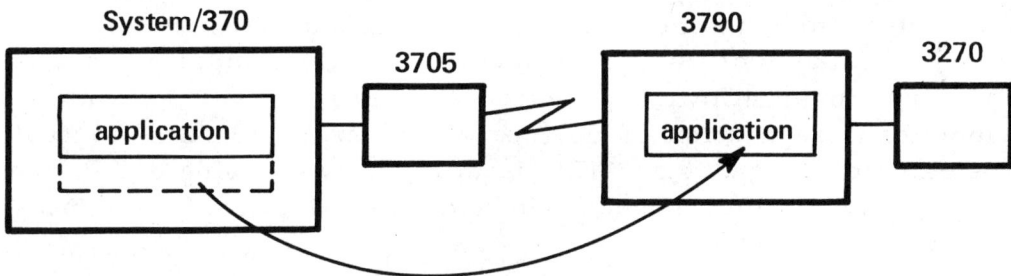

Figure 8. Application programming distributed to 3790

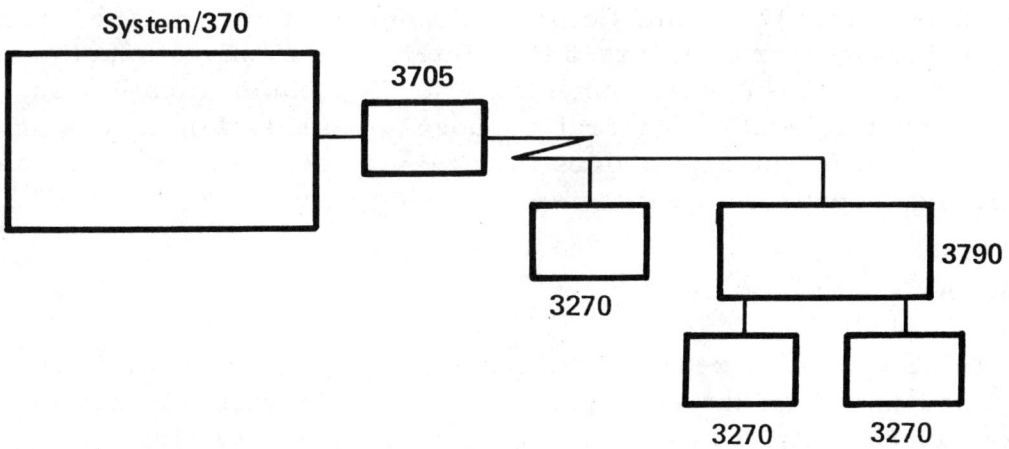

Figure 9. Versatility of SNA products

for a specific application using specialized hardware and software incompatible with other specialized applications. The hypothetical network in Figure 10 shows that the comprehensive SNA structure can satisfy a diverse set of network applications. A single network access method, Virtual Telecommunications Access Method (VTAM), allows new applications to share an already existing SNA network. By managing the association of terminals and applications on a dynamic basis, it also permits a single terminal to access the services provided by multiple applications. VTAM supervises one or more Network Control Programs that control some aspects of physical network operation, reducing the network management load on the computer.

Synchronous Data Link Control (SDLC) is the TP line protocol used to transfer information from one network product to another. Unlike most other protocols, SDLC includes no device control functions, allowing product designers to easily maintain the functional separation of device control from TP line control. The strategic design of an SNA network allows a single TP line to support the various specialized and general purpose products shown in the figure.

In the specialized banking environment, for example, the 3600 Finance System provides an easily-used work station for a teller although this terminal is actually supported by an elaborate teleprocessing system. The 3767 is a general purpose typewriter-like terminal that can provide low cost remote access to information services. For larger volumes of job-oriented information processing, the 3770 Data Communications System combines such I/O devices as card readers and printers to effectively duplicate the local attachment environment. The SNA communication subsystem protocols allow general purpose terminals for accessing a variety of different applications to coexist in the same network as specialized application subsystems.

SUMMARY

The design of recently-announced IBM teleprocessing products was based on the concepts of Systems Network Architecture. Three fundamental concepts are useful for understanding the structure of SNA products and the networks assembled from these products:

Applications:
{
finance
supermarket
retail
etc
}

System/370
Virtual storage
processing unit

Virtual operating system

TP supervisor: Virtual telecommunications
access method

Network control program/virtual system

3704 or 3705
Communications controller

Synchronous data link control

3270 Information display system

3600 Finance system

3650 Retail system

3660 Supermarket system

3767 Communication terminal

3770 Data communication system

3790 Communication system

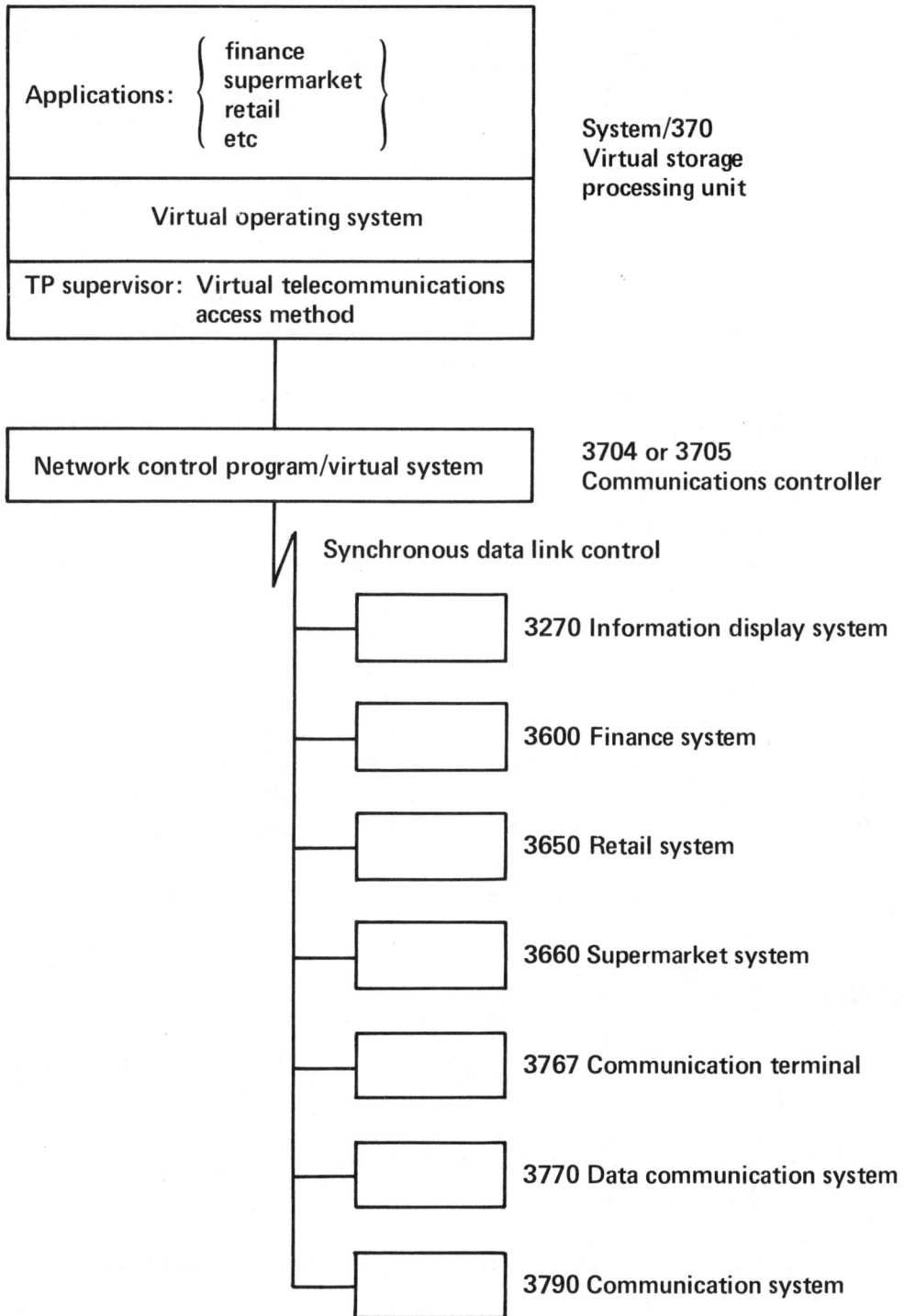

Figure 10. Diverse application support in an SNA network

1.   SNA describes the network functions of each SNA product in terms of a hierarchy of functional layers that perform the communication functions for the network user. Precise definition of the functional responsibility of each product layer permits a variety of products to be integrated into an effective network system.

2.   Each functional layer of an SNA product provides a service to the next higher layer. In particular, the support layer insulates the user from the detailed operation of the network system as it performs communications functions for him. The system user should be concerned only with a specific application and not with the physical configuration and operation of the network. Any service obtained from the network system should appear to be provided directly by the system product with which the user interacts.

3.   For each functional layer of an SNA product there exists a counterpart layer in one or more other products that provides a complementary function. In the user and application layer, the application program provides the information processing services that the user requests. The network owner can assemble a variety of compatible products to meet the requirements of the users of the network system.

The design philosophy of Systems Network Architecture allows contemporary networks to be enhanced and provides a foundation for satisfying the future requirements of network system users.

REFERENCES

Systems Network Architecture: General Information, GA27-3102, IBM Corporation.

Advanced Function for Communication: System Summary, GA27-3099, IBM Corporation.

IBM Synchronous Data Link Control: General Information, GA27-3093, IBM Corporation.

Queueing system with delayed feedback and computer communication networks

by

F.Borgonovo, L.Fratta and F.Maffioli

Istituto di Elettronica and Centro CNR
Telecomunicazioni Spaziali, Politecnico
di Milano, Italy

ABSTRACT

In this paper the analysis of a queueing system with delayed feedback assuming constant service time and synchronous operation is performed via a Markov chain approach. Upper and lower bounds to the time spent in queue are also derived. The motivation of this study has to be found in the necessity to evaluate the influence of the time out on the transit time of packets in a store-and-forward computer communication network.

1. FOREWORD

The main task of a communication network for computers is to transfer data in a preassigned format (packet) among network switching centers (NSC). In order to guarantee a very small error probability ($10^{-6} \div 10^{-9}$) appropriate error control techniques have to be used as for instance error detecting codes. In a store-and-forward network any NSC keeps a copy of the transmitted packets until a positive acknowledgement (ACK) is received from the destination NSC. In such a way it is guaranteed the correctness of the delivered packets and the non-correctly received packets are the only ones undergoing retransmission. The control system of the NSC retransmits a packet if the corresponding ACK has not been received after a preassigned delay r (Time Out). The time out r can be set equal to any value from 0 to ∞ : for both limit values the packet average transit time (i.e. the time a packet spends in the average in the communication network) tends to become very large. In fact, setting r=0, a packet is continously retransmitted until a delivery confirmation i.e. its ACK is received. This will greatly increase the traffic load of the network with a consequent large average transit time. On the contrary for $r \to \infty$ the increase of traffic load is as small as possible, but the average transit time becomes once again too large due to the infinite transit time for the packets which are not correctly received at the first transmission.

The purpose of this paper is to analyse the behaviour of such a system in order to evaluate the average transit time as a function of r. The corresponding queueing model is derived in section 2 and its analysis is attempted in section 3 through a Markov chain approach. Some useful bounds are obtained in section 4 while in section 5 the application to communication networks is discussed.

2. QUEUEING MODEL

The problem stated in the previous section may be modelled by a queueing system with feedback of the kind depicted in fig. 2.1. In this figure, A represents any packet transmitter, i.e. source NSC or User Process connected to the network, and B represents both the communication device and the packet receiver, i.e. the destination NSC or User Process. λ is the average input traffic rate and ρ the average transmitted traffic rate. Any packet joins the queue Q and at its turn it is transmitted by the service S with an average service time s. A copy of the transmitted packet is stored in R for a time r, which is the time out of the system, before being retransmitted by S. Any packet is erased from the transmitter A when its ACK is received. The time at which a packet is erased from A depends on the characteristics of B which are function of the traffic entering B.

Let T_t be the average transit time of a packet, that is the time between its entering A and the delivery to its destination. There are three contributions to T_t: T_q, the average time a packet spends in queue Q, T_ℓ , the average time spent in the service loop (that is in S and R) and T_p, the average propagation time in B, that is the time between the entering of the packet in B and its delivery.

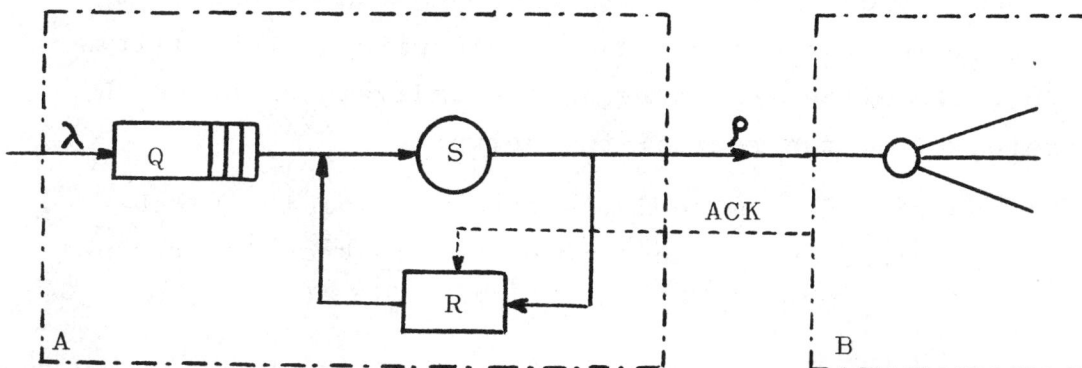

Fig. 2.1

The most relevant parameter of B to be known to study this system is the distribution of the delay in receiving the ACK of any packet.

Finally let us assume that any packet has the same length. This is reasonable since in fragmenting messages into packets the percentage of non complete packets is small with respect to the others [1] . It is then possible to simplify the model letting it be synchronously operating. In this case s is constant and r may be assumed to be an integer multiple of s. As a consequence the effect of the return of an ACK is limited to the erasure of the corresponding packet from R. The problem is then to evaluate T_ℓ and T_q assuming without loss of generality s=1.

3. MARKOV CHAIN APPROACH

When approaching the analysis of the system described in the previous section, the main difficulty is the strong interaction between A and B. In fact the characteristics of B depend on the input traffic and the behaviour of A depends on the distribution of the delay τ in receiving an ACK. In order to be able to carry on the analysis we assume that this interaction may be taken into account simply considering the average input traffic in B, ρ , and the average number of transmissions per packet, n_t, caused by the delay τ . This corresponds to assume that any packet is erased during any cycle with a probability π =1/n_t, and allows to carry on the analysis of system A separately from the rest of the network.

In order to determine π the behaviour of the block B has to be known. In particular we have to know the probability, v, that a packet is not received, the probability u, that an acknowledgement, which has been sent by the receiver, is not received and the distribution function of τ which represents the time between the beginning of the i-th transmission of a packet and the reception of its acknowledgement, conditioned to the fact that it is received.

For what concerns the computation of $\tilde{n}$ the above is enough to describe the behaviour of B provided that different packets travel independently within the communication device as it is reasonable to assume in dealing with large networks. In fig. 3.1 a distribution function $f(\tau)$ is depicted. $T_c = r+1$ represents the cycle time which

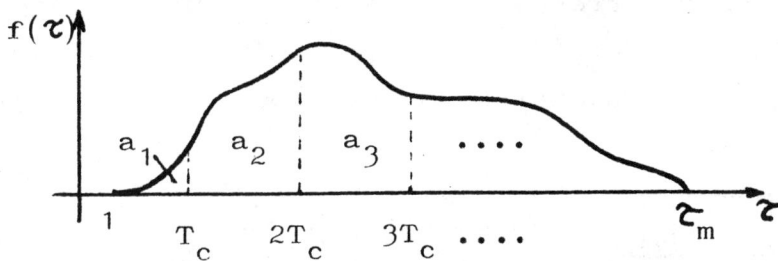

Fig. 3.1

corresponds to the time between the beginnings of two consecutive retransmissions and a_i is the probability that an ACK is received during the i-th cycle time. The probability that the ACK corresponding to the j-th retransmission is correctly received during the (k+j)-th cycle is:

$$b_k = (1-u)(1-v)a_k = (1-u)(1-v) \int_{(k-1)T_c}^{kT_c} f(\tau)d\tau \qquad (3.1$$

and the probability that a packet is erased during the i-th cycle conditioned to the fact that it has not yet been erased is:

$$c_i = 1 - \prod_{j=1}^{i} (1-b_j) \qquad (3.2$$

Furthermore we have that the probability that a packet is erased during the i-th cycle is:

$$d_i = c_i \prod_{j=1}^{i-1} (1-c_j) .$$ (3.3

Finally

$$n_t = \sum_{j=1}^{\infty} j d_j$$ (3.4

To evaluate T_q it is not relevant to know when a packet is erased during the time it is in R. We may then assume that R is nothing but a shift register with r cells and that the packet leaving R either enters the service with probability $\nu = 1 - \tilde{\pi}$, or defitely leaves the system with probability $\tilde{\pi}$. The state of R is therefore defined by the integer m corresponding to the binary configuration of the shift register (fig. 3.2), a 1 in the i-th cell corresponding to a packet being stored there. For example in fig. 3.2, m=39.

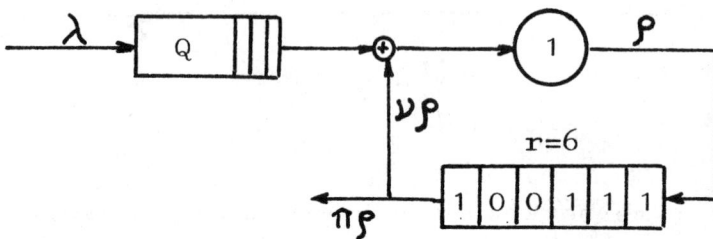

Fig. 3.2

The overall description of the system may be obtained by a bi-dimensional Markov chain. The state of the system is defined by two variables (m,i) where i represents the number of packets both in queue and in service. To find out the steady state probability equations it is useful to group all states in two classes: one contains all states with m=2n even, the other contains all states with m=2n+1 odd. The transition probability graphs for states of the first and second class are reported respectively in fig. 3.3 and 3.4. Note that the general state (2n,i) of the first class can be reached only from states (n,0) and

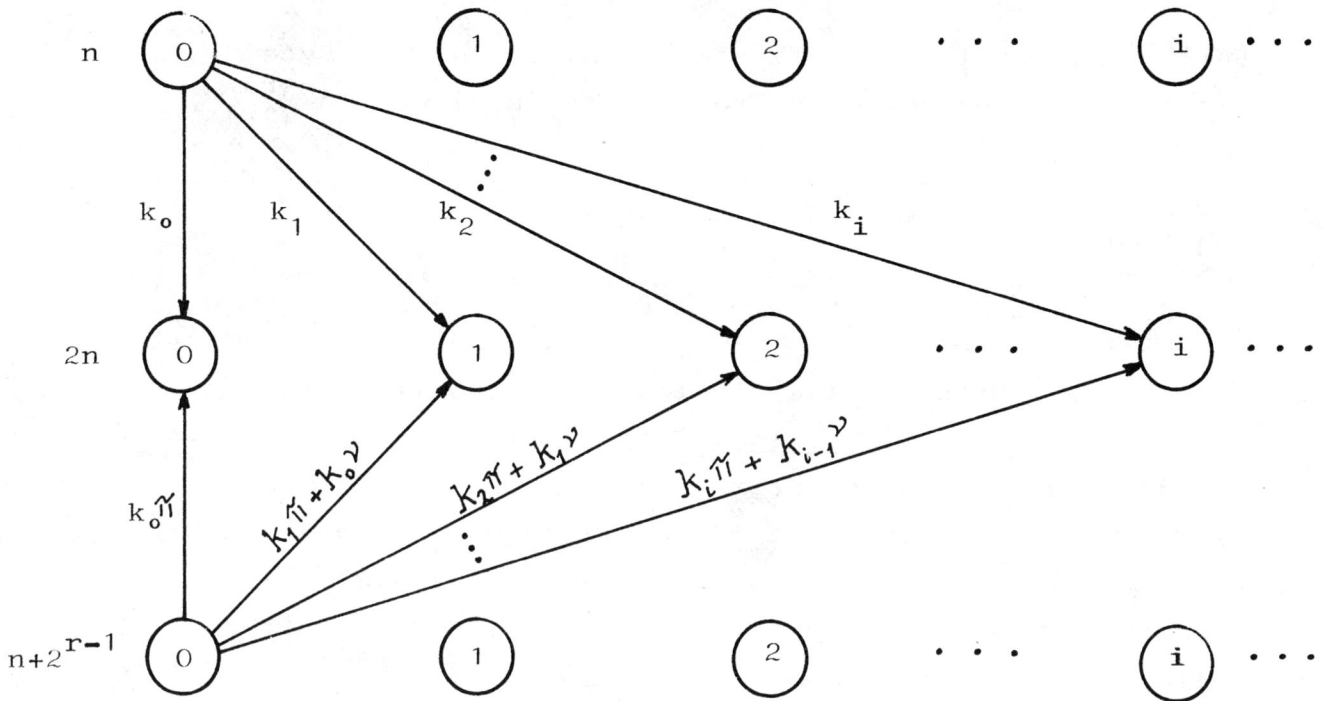

Fig. 3.3

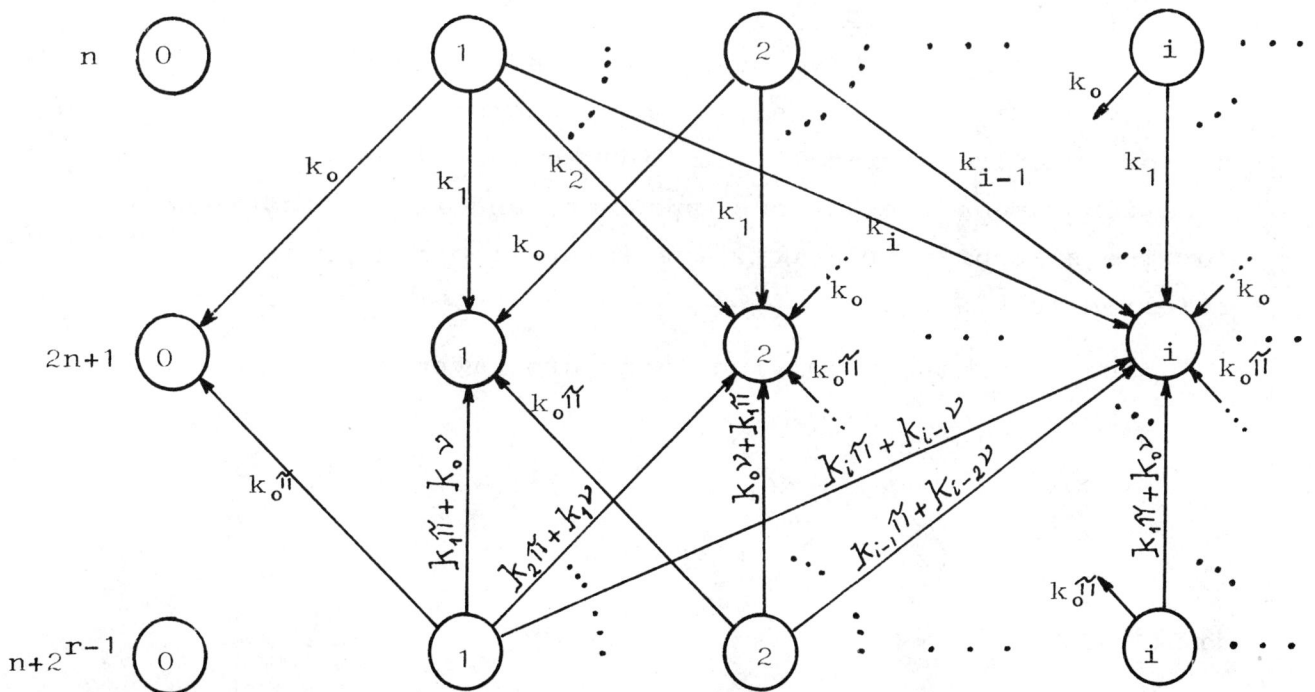

Fig. 3.4

$(n+2^{r-1},0)$ and the general state $(2n+1,i)$ of the second class can be reached only from states (n,j) and $(n+2^{r-1},j)$ for $j \neq 0$. We have therefore:

$$
\begin{cases}
P_{2n,i} = k_i P_{n,o} + (k_i \widetilde{\pi} + k_{i-1} \nu) P_{n+2^{r-1},o} \\
P_{2n+1,i} = \sum_{j=1}^{i+1} k_{i-j+1} (P_{n,j} + \widetilde{\pi} P_{n+2^{r-1},j}) + \nu \sum_{j=1}^{i} k_{i-j} P_{n+2^{r-1},j}
\end{cases} \tag{3.5}
$$

where $P_{m,i}$ represents the stationary probability of being in state (m,i), k_i is the probability of having i independent arrivals during one service time. It can be seen that the first set of equations depends only on the $P_{m,o}$'s, while the second set, except for $n=2^{r-1}-1$, depends recursively upon the $P_{2n,o}$. For $i=0$ we have the following linear system of 2^r equations:

$$
\begin{cases}
P_{2n,o} = f_n(P_{n,o}) & n=0,1,2, \ldots, 2^{r-1}-1 \\
P_{2n+1,o} = g_n(P_{n,o}) & n=0,1,2, \ldots, 2^{r-1}-2 \\
\sum_{j=0}^{2^r-1} P_{j,o} = 1 - \rho
\end{cases} \tag{3.6}
$$

Once the $P_{m,o}$'s have been evaluated through (3.6), (3.5) yield all the $P_{m,i}$'s. The complete solution may be performed only numerically due to the very involved relations among the various unknowns, and is omitted here for the sake of simplicity. The interested reader is referred to [2].

Since the generating functions are given by

$$
Q_m(z) = \sum_{i=0}^{\infty} P_{m,i} z^i
$$

$$
K(z) = \sum_{j=0}^{\infty} k_j z^j
$$

from (3.5) we have

$$\begin{cases} Q_{2n} = K(z) \left[P_{n,o} + P_{n+2^{r-1},o} (\eta + \nu z) \right] & (3.7 \\[2mm] Q_{2n+1} = K(z) \left[Q_n - P_{n,o} + (Q_{n+2^{r-1}} - P_{n+2^{r-1},o}).(\eta + \nu z) \right]/2 \end{cases}$$

The system (3.7) cannot be solved in closed form in general. Therefore, instead of obtaining $Q_m(z)$, we limit ourselves to find $Q_m(1) = L_m$ and $Q_m'(1) = I_m$, i.e. the probabilities that R is in state m and the average number of packets in queue and service, R being in state m. These results may be obtained using the values computed previously for $P_{m,o}$ and solving the corresponding systems obtained from (3.7) by a method similar to that already outlined for (3.5).

The average time spent in queue is obtained by the Little's result as

$$T_q = (I - \rho)/\lambda + 0.5 \qquad (3.8$$

where

$$I = \sum_{m=0}^{2^r-1} I_m$$

is the average number of packets being present in queue and in service, ρ is the average number of packets in sevice and we have to adjoin the constant term 0.5 which represents the average time from the arrival into the system and the first synchronized instant.

4. BOUNDS EVALUATION

From the solution discussed in the previous section it turns out that its computational complexity grows as 2^r. This implies that the exact solution is obtainable in a reasonable amount of time only for relatively small values of r, say up to r=10. An approximate solution is therefore necessary to solve systems with larger values

of r. This is done in the following by deriving upper
and lower bounds to the average number of packets in the
system, I.

The generating function $Q(z) = \sum Q_m(z)$ of the number
of packets in queue and service, i, may be obtained by
adding up separately for all n the equations of (3.7)
leading to

$$\begin{cases} Q_{even}(z) = K(z)\left[P_{e,o} + P_{f,o}(\hat{\eta} + \nu z)\right] \\ Q_{odd}(z) = K(z)\left[Q_e - P_{e,o} + (Q_f - P_{f,o})(\hat{\eta} + \nu z)\right]/z \end{cases} \quad (4.1$$

and

$$Q(z) = Q_{even} + Q_{odd} \quad (4.2$$
$$= K(z)\left\{Q_e + Q_f(\hat{\eta} + \nu z) + (z-1)\left[P_{e,o} + P_{f,o}(\hat{\eta} + \nu z)\right]\right\}/z$$

where $Q_{even}(z)$ is the generating function of $P_{m \text{ even},i}$,
$Q_{odd}(z)$ is the generating function of $P_{m \text{ odd},i}$, Q_e and
Q_f are the generating functions of $P_{m,i}$ when the last
cell of R is respectively empty or full, $P_{e,o}$ and $P_{f,o}$
are the joint probabilities of the last cell being
respectively empty or full and the service being empty.

The upper bound is obtained by solving the system
with r=0. In this case in fact the flow of packets
reentering service is maximally correlated with the flow
of packets leaving service. Such a correlation increases
the average number of packets in queue (see also [3] for
more details). In this case (4.2) becomes

$$Q(z) = K(z)\left\{\left[Q(z) - P_o\right](\hat{\eta} + \nu z) + zP_o\right\} \quad (4.3$$

Solving for $Q(z)$, since $P_o = 1 - \rho$, we have

$$Q(z) = (1 - \rho)K(z)\hat{\eta}(1-z)/\left[K(z)(\hat{\eta} + \nu z) - z\right] \quad (4.4$$

Differentiating (4.4), assuming Poisson input distribution
and setting z=1 gives the required upper bound to I:

$$I^o = \rho + \rho^2(1 + \nu)/2(1 - \rho) . \quad (4.5$$

The corresponding average time spent in queue is from (3.8),

$$T_q^o = \rho(1+\nu)/2(1-\rho)(1-\nu) + 0.5 \qquad (4.6)$$

Converserly a lower bound to I may be obtained assuming that the flow of packets reentering service from R is statistically independent of the state of the queue [3]. This implies that

$$\begin{cases} Q_e(z) = (1-\rho)Q(z) \\ Q_f(z) = \rho Q(z) \end{cases} \qquad (4.7)$$

and

$$\begin{cases} P_{e,o} = (1-\rho)^2 \\ P_{f,o} = \rho(1-\rho) \end{cases} \qquad (4.8)$$

From (4.2) we have therefore

$$Q(z) = (1-\rho)K(z)\frac{(1-z)\left[1-\rho+\rho(\pi \div \nu z)\right]}{K(z)\left[1-\rho+\rho(\pi+\nu z)\right]-z} \qquad (4.9)$$

Assuming Poisson input,

$$I^\ell = Q'(1) = \rho + \rho^2(1-\nu^2)/2(1-\rho) \qquad (4.10)$$

and

$$T_q^\ell = \rho(1+\nu)/2(1-\rho) + 0.5 \qquad (4.11)$$

Note that for $\nu=0$, T_q is independent of r and is given by

$$T_q(\nu=0) = \rho/2(1-\rho) + 0.5 \qquad (4.12)$$

Normalizing (4.6) and (4.11) with respect to (4.12) yields

$$t_q^o = 1 + 2\rho\nu/(1-\nu) \qquad (4.13)$$

and

$$t_q^\ell = 1 + \rho\nu \qquad (4.14)$$

These bounds together with the numerical evaluation of the behaviour of T_q for r=4 are reported in fig.4.1,4.2,4.3 for various values of ρ .

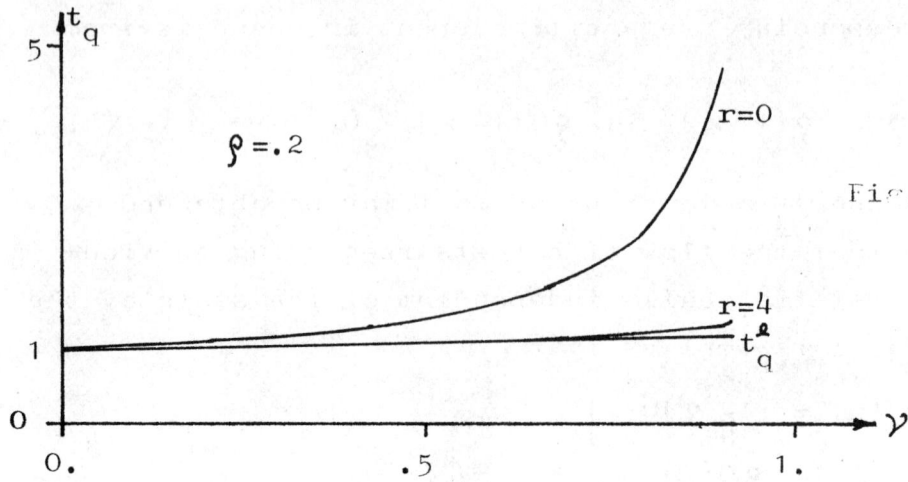

Fig. 4.1

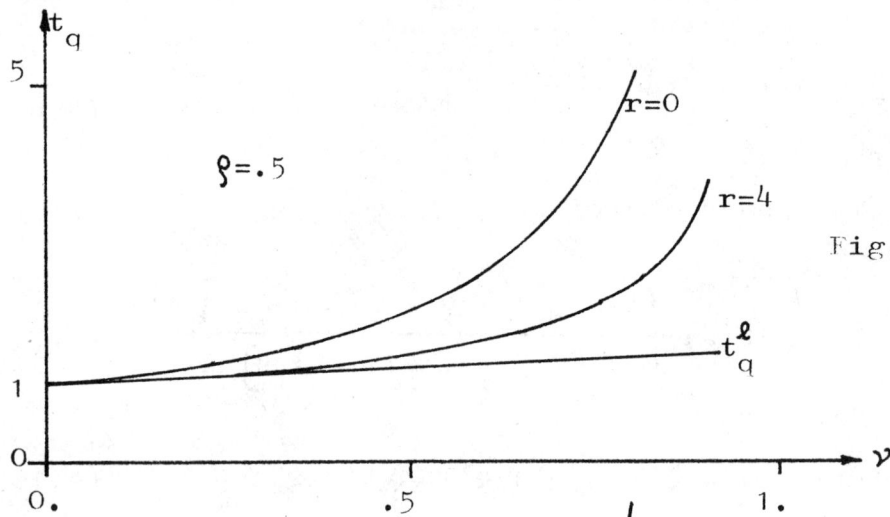

Fig. 4.2

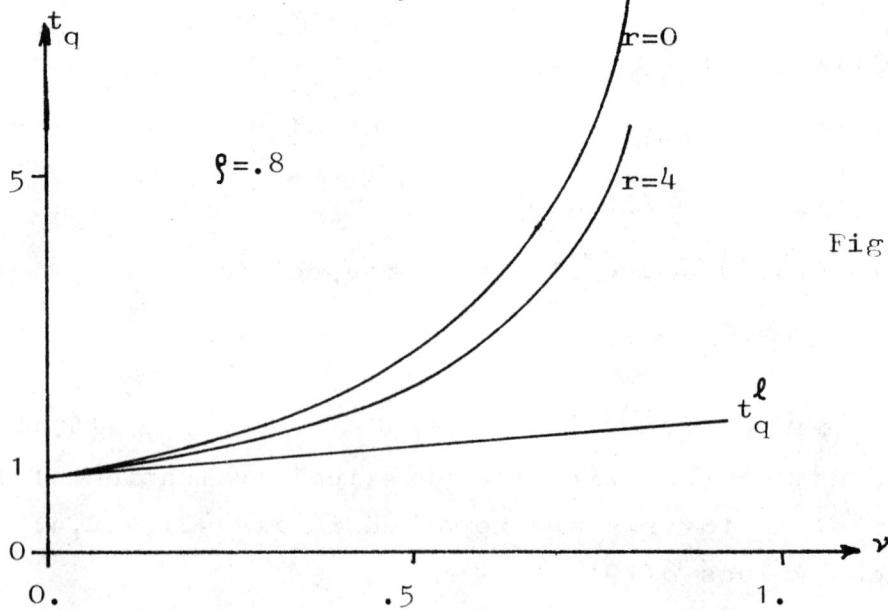

Fig. 4.3

In order to explore more thouroughly the statistical behaviour of Q one can no longer use the Little's result but has to obtain an expression for the Laplace-Stieltjes transform of the distribution function of the waiting time in queue [2].

5. TRANSIT TIME EVALUATION

We are now in position to evaluate the transit time in a store-and-forward communication network as a function of r. This allows to judge of the influence the choice of r has on the overall behaviour of the network.

Once T_q has been evaluated, we still have to obtain an expression for the time between the beginning of the first transmission of a packet and its first correct reception, i.e. $T_\ell + T_p$. Let us recall that the behaviour of B is assumed to be known, so that in particular the propagation time T_p as a function of the input traffic ρ is given. Then we have

$$T_\ell = \sum_{j=0}^{\infty} \left[1 + j(r+1) \right] v^j (1-v)$$

from which

$$T_\ell = (1+rv)/(1-v) \quad . \tag{5.1}$$

From (5.1) we see that T_ℓ increases with r at a rate $v/(1-v)$. On the contrary both T_p and T_q are decreasing functions of r. In fact as r increases the traffic rate ρ entering B becomes smaller since we would have less retransmissions per packet for the same τ. This is even more so since τ cannot increase as ρ becomes smaller. Since the load of the network decreases when r increases, T_p cannot increase with r. From (4.6) and (4.11) we have that T_q is a monotone increasing function of ρ and ν and hence decreases when r increases.

Note however that as soon as r becomes greater than the maximum value τ_m attainable by τ (see fig. 3.1), ϱ reaches its minimum as well as T_p and T_q. Therefore it is not convenient to set r greater than $r_o = \lfloor \tau_m \rfloor$. In practice this will also be the optimum value   of r as long as the contribution of T_ℓ , i.e. $r_o v$, remains negligible.

If this is not the case, the optimum value of r will be smaller than r_o and it may be determined by the procedure sketched in fig. 5.1 and explained in the following. From (3.1), (3.2), (3.3) and (3.4) it is possible to evaluate numerically the behaviour of n_t as a function of ϱ and r, treated as independent variables. Since $\varrho = n_t \lambda$ points A in fig. 5.1 represent the possible working situations for different values of r. This together with the results of section 4, allows to evaluate T_t and hence to find the value of r corresponding to the minimum transit time.

Having assigned the channel capacity i.e. the service time may imply that the system becomes unstable. This may be argued from fig. 5.1 considering that there may be two intersections of the straight line $n_t = \varrho / \lambda$ with any other curve. A more complete design approach would have to consider the channel capacity as a variable: this however is outside the limit of the present work.

ACKNOWLEDGEMENT

It is the authors' pleasure to acknowledge here the friend prof. G. LeMoli for helpful discussions.

REFERENCES

[1] F.Borgonovo, L.Fratta, G.Le Moli & F.Maffioli, "A model
for time out evaluation", European Computer Workshop
Series: Distributed Computer Systems, Darmstadt 1974.

[2] F.Borgonovo, L.Fratta & F.Maffioli, "Synchronously
operating queues with delayed feedback" (in preparation).

[3] F.Borgonovo & L.Fratta, "A model for finite storage
message switching networks", 5th IFIP Conf. on Optimization Techniques, Roma 1973, Lecture Notes in Computer Science 4 – Springer Verlag.

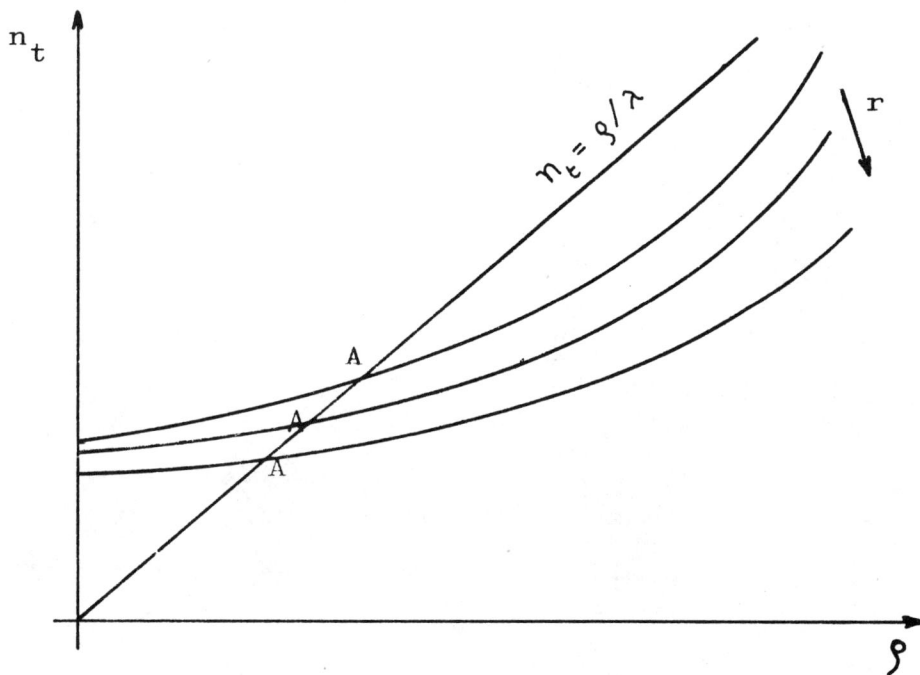

Fig. 5.1

The impact of integrated message processing facilities on administrative procedures and inter-personal interactions

Peter T. Kirstein and Stephen R. Wilbur

Department of Statistics and Computer Science
University College London
UK

ABSTRACT

The paper is concerned with the improvements in personal message services which the use of a computer network can bring. Integration of message composition, distribution, review and filing is not easily possible with existing services provided by the PTTs; the facilities provided on one network (ARPANET) are described. A discussion of the services that could be provided in a commercial message system, the economics of one existing system, and comments on the relation of these activities to the PTT monopolies are also covered.

1. INTRODUCTION

This paper is concerned with communication betweeen people. In particular we are concerned with the impact which computer networks are having on personal communications, on the cost effectiveness of such mechanisation, with the impact these facilities may have on the future development of PTT monopolies, and with the effects PTT regulations may have on the deployment of the facilities.

We discuss message facilities much more powerful than Telex. They include message composition, review, transmission, receiver processing and archiving. Such facilities are now being used on a large scale by many organisations. The bulk of the administrative message traffic, documentation and financial planning of one US Government Agency is now using these facilities; not only does it use them to communicate with its contractors, but most of their proposals, reports and responses come in by the same medium. Where the computer system used for this work is unreliable, the complaints from higher management are immediate and vociferous. One result of the existence of these facilities is a more direct participation of management in the communication; it does not all pass through secretaries. Another is that the secretaries themselves have intimate contact with computer systems. How these facilities will develop, when they are cost effective, and when they use too much managerial time, are not yet quite clear. However, it is clear that the services cannot be ignored since they permit a qualitative change on the whole administrative communication process.

Much of this paper is based on experience with one particular network, the ARPA Network (Ref. 1). This is a network of some fifty nodes, mostly in the US, but also with a node in Norway and the UK. Each node contains a switching computer called a TIP, which may be connected to a service computer (Host), to a number of modem ports, or to both. In general, users dial-in to their nearest TIP or service machine, and from there can make a 'connection' to a remote service machine. From that point on, their use of the service machine is almost identical to the use they would make had they dialled direct. Thus, at first sight, the network appears to be a mechanism for accessing remote machines at local call rates with shared cost of the trunk facilities. Whilst this is a side effect, there are other more pertinent advantages in using a network approach as we shall see later. However, the lack of direct charging for the long distance communication does limit the conclusions which can be drawn from some of the present use made of the ARPA Network.

In providing any new service, one must always attempt to balance both cost and benefits. The services which we are about to describe have been available for several years to users of ARPANET, and are now under serious revision. Because the original user community was mainly computer-oriented university research workers, various cumbersome experimental features are to be found in the services. With the advent of commercial and military international computer networks, the question of what services to provide, or even whether to provide personal communication services at all, has to be looked at closely. Whilst no universal answers are provided in this paper, we hope that many of the examples given will be thought-provoking in both a national and international context.

The PTTs have recently been concerned by the portent of computer networks, especially with respect to their potential in the human communications area. Until comparatively recently there were well defined communication paths, for example, surface mail, telephones and telex. Initially, terminal-computer data transmission posed no real threat, since only one human and one computer system were connected, the object being calculation. Computer networks, however, are considerably different. With users potentially hundreds or thousands of miles distant from the computer system, effective mechanisms have to be provided for the operations staff, applications staff, etc., to instruct the user about the system or to inform him of changes. It is but a short step from this necessity to providing similar services allowing users to communicate among themselves. The question arises at this point, is a computing service being provided, or a message switching service, and how does one define the terms? More fundamentally, do the requirements of these services accord with the 'natural monopolies' which are the basic reasons for the PTTs monopoly charter over message services? If they do, does this monopoly reach to computer-based message services, information retrieval, and all databases? Should the PTTs have this monopoly over all networks, or only those where different organisations inter-communicate? What criteria should be used to differentiate services? Clearly, those based on whether data is processed are becoming increasingly meaningless

We do not presume to try to answer all the philosphical questions here; we merely try to point out the potential of the services from our practical experience, and to give some technical insight. In Sections 2 and 3 the nature of message processing services is considered, with examples from existing services available on ARPANET. In Section 4 we discuss our experience in using the services, and postulate how the elements of a message service should be put together. In Section 5 we discuss the relationship between message services and the PTTs. Our conclusions are presented in Section 6.

2. ASYNCHRONOUS MESSAGE SERVICES

2.1 Introduction

This section is not intended to be an exhaustive catalogue of all message systems on Hosts of ARPANET. It is intended to give an idea of the rudiments which can be provided, and to lead on to some of the desirable features which might be found in a properly integrated message service

There are two forms of communication between people; that which we shall call 'asynchronous', where a sender and recipient deal with the message at different times (a letter is an example of this), and 'synchronous' where both parties are available at the same time and can carry out dialogue (e.g. a telephone call). Most Hosts on ARPANET provide 'asynchronous' facilities, some also provide 'synchronous' facilities. The two forms of communication are not mutually exclusive. In a telephone call it is possible to review a letter which has been received previously; during a synchronous dialogue, it is often expedient to use facilities which have been provided for asynchronous purposes. Examples illustrating this point are given in Section 3. In this Section, we shall review the requirements for, and give practical examples of, asynchronous communications facilities. Those requiring synchronous communication are discussed in Section 3.

2.2 <u>Services Required</u>

Asynchronous facilities are generally provided by mimicking the normal postal system. The sender uses a program to compose his message, which is 'posted' in a file ready for the mail utility program on its next 'collection'. The message is then forwarded via one or more programs to a file of the recipient. He in turn uses another utility program to scan his incoming mailbox, read messages and dispose of them when acted upon.

In general, facilities may be required for the following functions:

    i) Composition and editing of messages,

   ii) Reviewing messages with interested parties before transmission,

  iii) Transmission and routing of messages,

   iv) Archiving of messages,

    v) Status query on the progress of a message, and

   vi) Receiver processing including retrieval.

The current commercial services like Telex usually only deal with transmission and routing of messages. Even here, a number of useful aids like address lists for multi-destination messages are not necessarily easy to include automatically. Many traditional services do have some facilities for archiving, and some ability to query the progress of messages. However, these are still concerned only with backup and recovery in the case where a specific message, identified by some number, has failed to be delivered or is required again. Some facilities for composition and editing have long been provided in time-sharing systems for on-line interactive editing. Until recently, while the facilities required for composition, editing, archival and retrieval were provided in such systems, the implementations have presumed the users to be reasonably conversant with

computer command languages. Tailoring such facilities specifically
for message processing is a recent development; the simplification
of the procedures for naive users, who may have no other contact with
computers, is still in its infancy.

Before we discuss potential services, it is instructive to review some
of the facilities now available over one computer network, ARPANET.

2.3 Rudimentary Message Transmission and Composition

A typical message sending program found on many Hosts on ARPANET is
called SNDMSG, and was developed by Bolt, Beranek and Newman (Ref.2).
It allows messages to be composed, edited, and sent to one or more
users of the Network. The initial system was implemented on a DEC
PDP-10 TENEX system (Ref.3). Because SNDMSG uses the standard File
Transfer Protocol (FTP) designed for bulk data transfer through the Network, messages can be received by most Hosts. Moreover, a Standard
Message Format (SMF Ref. 4) was defined and implemented on many Hosts,
resulting in the implementation of a variety of message reading programs
on different machines.

In its normal form SNDMSG assumes each recipient has a unique account name
on a network Host. However, it is not unusual for several users to share
an account, but wish to separate their 'mail'. Such separation can be
provided by complementary programs to SNDMSG which distinguish recipients
on the basis of, say a line in the message containing the sequence
"Attn: name". SNDMSG is reasonably flexible in the formal list of recipients (account names) for a message. One feature is the ability to
send a given message to each member of a scattered special interest group.
Here a file can be specified as part or all of the addressee list, alle-
viating tedious typing and consequent mistakes. Additionally, it is
possible to give such groups arbitrary names, in which case only the group
name appears in the delivered message, rather than a list of all recipients.

Two other points are worthy of mention. Firstly, SNDMSG requires that all
messages be given a short one line title, which is normally printed by the
mail reading utility as a summary of the message contents. Secondly, while
composing the text of a message it is possible to include the whole of any
other local file, or to enter a text editor to modify such insertions or
correct errors. Simple editing commands permit single characters, words
or linesto be deleted, or allow the current line or the whole text to be
typed out. Alternatively, a much more sophisticated editor can be used.

2.4 Rudimentary Message Reception

A variety of message reading programs exist on most Hosts on ARPANET. This
is partly because the initial programs provided had only a narrow range of
facilities, and partly because extensions to the addressing, classifying and
other facets of a message were deemed necessary by various users. A fairly

typical program called POST, which we developed, is described below (Ref.5).

All incoming mail for a particular account generally is appended to a file with a name such as MESSAGE.TXT in the user's account. For accounts with several users, one wishes to preserve personal mail from accidental deletion by other members in the group, so POST scans through MESSAGE.TXT copying messages to personal files determined by the "Attn:" line mentioned earlier. Any mail not identified by an "Attn:" line is routed to a file called GENERAL.MSG from where it can be manually rerouted if necessary.

Once mail has been 'sorted' a POST user is asked his name, after which a summary of all the messages in his personal file is printed. This summary consists of the message number in the file (for retrieval purposes), the date sent, the sender and the title. Thus the user can read pertinent messages by giving the message number and an appropriate command. Besides commands to print a summary of messages and to type out individual messages, others exist to delete messages once they have been read, to file them elsewhere (e.g. if a reference manual were sent as mail), or to re-route a message to another person using that account.

It is important to note here that we are dealing with a rudimentary system so that the user interface is not ideal, nor are some of the internal mechanisms. For example, messages addressed to several users in the same account (via the "Attn:" line) are in fact copied into each of the recipients' personal files rather than having a single copy of the message with references to that message from each personal file.

2.5 A Structured Message Utility

There is one system on ARPANET which takes a number of different solutions to message processing. This is the NLS system (Ref.6) developed as a sophisticated text and picture processing system. It allows structured text to be composed, edited and displayed on-line using either a printer terminal (TNLS), or a character display, keyset and mouse (DNLS). NLS text is hierarchically structured, so that it is possible to take an overview of a document by looking only at the top 'level' of text. Successive layers give more detail until finally the whole text is viewed. One other important structural feature of NLS allows cross-references to be made within the text to other paragraphs of the file being viewed, or to any other file built by NLS. Whilst the message facilities are set against this structured background, there are other features which are worthy of study. Firstly, messages are dealt with differently depending on their length, or more correctly, how they were submitted to the mailer. For short messages, the whole text is passed to the recipient, whereas only a reference is passed in the case of long messages. Since much traffic in this system is working papers and manuals, this obviously minimises duplicated disk copies of a document. Secondly, all mail sent is

given a unique catalogue number, and a permanent copy of this document is also retained on magnetic tape by the system. This is in
contrast to SNDMSG which leaves the onus on users for ensuring security or longevity of messages.

Since the NLS structured file manipulations are available when reading
messages, such operations as summarising messages become merely requests for output of the top one or two levels of text. Similarly,
finding information within a long message is relatively easy in a
structural environment, but more tedious in the non-structured POST
system.

2.6 Personalised Message Processing

Another message receiving system has been developed at the MIT-Dynamic
Modelling Center (DMC Ref.7). This system includes many of the structured characteristics of NLS, but carries them further. In the POST
system, brief details of new messages are passed to the recipient,
from which messages may be chosen for reading. The DMC system extends
this philosphy considerably. A message is characterised by a number
of fields, some completed by the sender, but some are open to the
recipient to complete. The text of the message is but one of the
sender-filled fields, others include the sender's name, what he considers to be keywords, whether this message is in reply to a previous
message, etc. To these fields, the recipient can add his own fields:
for example, other keywords, whether and when action is required, are
but two possibilities. As of March 1975,the retrieval programs could
then sort by both original and recipient-supplied information. More
complex functions, such as automatic notification of replies, notification of deadlines for actions, etc. have been planned, but not yet
implemented.

2.7 Message Archiving

Most interactive computer systems are chronically short of on-line file
store, but they generally have an archival facility. On ARPANET, there
is at least one resource specifically designed for long term storage of
large masses of structured data. This is the Data Computer (Ref.8)
developed by the Computer Corporation of America. While its present
hardware is on disks, this will soon be supplemented by a 10^{12} bit
direct access store; this is of low cost material (about 10^{-6} cents/bit),
and can hold about 20 million typewritten pages. On an experimental
basis, a connection between SNDMSG, the DMC receiver processing, and
the storage and retrieval services of the Data Computer, has been
implemented.

2.8 <u>The Economics of Message Services</u>

For several reasons it is not possible to go into great detail of the economics of the services mentioned above. Most of the data is not available, little of what exists has been gathered by the authors, and should therefore be published by others; moreover, the data can be interpreted in different ways. As soon as questions of wider utilisation of the message technology were raised, it was realised that it was essential to obtain better information on at least the following factors:

    i) Typical distributions of message size,

    ii) Number of Hosts addressed per message,

  iii) Number of messages addressed to each site,

    iv) Diurnal message traffic variation,

    v) Utilisation of header fields,

    vi) CPU time used in various stages of message processing,

  vii) User interaction time/message, and

 viii) Cost of transmission facilities.

Most of these measurements have not yet been carried out properly (as of 1 May 1975).

For the specific ARPANET environment, speaking from our own experience, the vast majority of messages are shorter than 1000 characters (chars). In early measurements over a limited sample, 55% of the messages were less than 100 chars and 80% less than 200 chars. Some are as long as 10^5 chars. The real message length limit is determined by the transmission time which one is prepared to devote to this purpose. At the present rates (using the 7.2K bps between US and Norway as the bottleneck), a 10^5 char message may take 2 mins to be transmitted.

The message composition phase is clearly dependent on the message length and the amount of editing involved. An early study using one specific implementation and a small sample size, indicates that the CPU use for a PDP-10 in this phase is roughly (5+8 L) secs where L is the message length in thousands of chars. The 'connect' time for the input and composition of a 1000 char message would be about 10 mins. On the same machine, transmission processing takes 1 CPU sec/addressee and 3-10 CPU secs for the message. The rates charged by any computer management for CPU and connect time are partly constrained by financial considerations and partly by which facilities they wish to promote and which they wish to reserve. An example of this can be seen by comparing costs of this message on two similar machines on ARPANET. At BBN CPU time is charged at \$8/CPU/minute and connect time at \$4/hr; at ISI CPU time is charged

at $5/minute peak time and $2.5/minute off peak, while connect time
is free. Thus the 1000 char message would cost $2 in CPU time and
$0.6 in connect time at BBN, whereas it would cost between $1.25 and
$0.63 at ISI.

A different way to reach similar conclusions is the empirical evidence
that a PDP-10 KA TENEX can comfortably support some 30 users involved
only in SNDMSG/POST activities, typically averaging 6 messages/hr each.
The charge made to users working in this way would be about $10/hr each
(based on ISI rates),or about $1.66/message. Thus using the present
TENEX hardware, and the varied charging algorithms, a spread between
$0.63 and $2.6 can be seen for composition and transmission of a
1000 char message.

An indication of the cost of sophisticated facilities is that the NLS
system of Section 2.5 can support only about 10 users simultaneously
on a similar TENEX system. The comparison partly highlights the more
complex tasks done by the typical NLS user, and partly encourages a
realistic value to be put on additional services such as archiving and
structured databases.

The pure data transmission costs are much more difficult to quantify;
for this one needs some information on the tariff and route. Taking as
an extreme case that all message composition is done locally in London,
that the transmission path is London-Washington, that the full cost of
two ARPANET TIPs is dedicated to message processing (one at each end),
that a 9.6K bps line is used at commercial rates, that no other charges
are incurred, and that the line is used on average for 250 days
8 hrs/day at 50% capacity, with a factor of 20% line utilisation (this
low figure is due to the various overheads incurred), the cost of
transmitting messages would be typically $0.50 per message of 1000 chars.
Incidentally, this figure is about one and one-half times that quoted
by Telenet (Ref.9) for transmitting packets through their network,
which is a not unreasonable figure, considering the assumptions made.
On the same basis, a terminal should be costed at about $1.5/hr, assuming
a 300 or 1200 bps terminal is used at 50% capacity on working days. Thus
the different components of the cost of composing and sending a typical
message of 1000 chars are comparable, and reductions in any one are
significant.

3. SYNCHRONOUS COMMUNICATION

Although message transmission and reception as described in Section 2
is fairly efficient, in that it can be easily done by secretarial staff,
there are times when a dialogue is necessary. This Section looks at
the potential of computer networks for various types of dialogue.

3.1 Informal "Chatting"

Many computer systems have a mechanism whereby the troubled user can
send a question to an operator from his terminal, and then wait several
seconds for a reply. A generalised facility of this sort can provide
many services, from advice and collaboration to international tele-
conferencing.

On TENEX machines on ARPANET, a facility known as LINKing exists. By
using a simple command, it is possible to 'link' the output of your
terminal and that of another user on the system. Thus in the linked
state, any output seen on one terminal is also seen on the other terminal
and vice versa. Obviously, if this not organised, chaos results! Linking
has advantages over many similar facilities on other systems for two
reasons. The first is that it is a monitor level command, therefore users
are not limited to plain text communication as a subsystem; LINK is a
system state which is invisible once entered, apart from the obvious
interaction between two users. The second point is that LINK and the
TENEX work on a character by character basis. Therefore, it is possible
for one user to interrupt the other and be noticed immediately. Anyone
who has used a service such as this on a line at a time basis will know
that synchronisation between both parties is difficult, especially if one
is prone to impatience; it is surprising how long it takes for a line
to be typed!

LINK is not limited merely to a dialogue between two people. In fact, up
to four users may participate, but is is then necessary to identify oneself at the start of typed text, since the system does not do this. A
drawback of LINK is that it does not provide a record of the conversation,
other than the console printout. There are ways of getting the system to
provide this, but a number of informal subsystems such as FORUM
(Section 3.3) have been developed.

Since there is a mutual sharing of output from two or more terminals when
they are linked, mechanisms are provided to allow users to prevent linking
when they are producing 'clean' copy on a terminal or working on confident-
ial material.

It is even more difficult to give costs of linking than of the message
service of Section 2. It can be invoked when any other procedure is being
used on TENEX. Thus, for example, all the message composition and retrieval can be carried out with several people viewing all transactions.
The extra overhead due to LINK is small. A typical one hour 'chat', with
no other processing, would occupy perhaps ½ min of CPU time; at BBN
rates the charge per hour would be $8 made up equally of connect and pro-
cessing time, while at ISI the charge would be between $1.25 and $2.50
Here, however, it is essential to factor in also the cost of the time of
the participants, when compared to asynchronous activities.

In typical interactions, using only keyboard originated data, typical data rates are 20-30 words/minute (total) Again, assuming the sort of line loading of Section 2 8, but with only 10% line utilisation instead of 20%, transmission costs come to about $1 30/hr If a considerable amount of computer generated data is passed, this cost could be much higher because of the increased traffic.

3.2 Teleconferencing

It is but a short step from linking and indeed message sending/reading, to thoughts of computer systems which allow specialists who are scattered geographically, to have a conference in the comfort of their own terminal room! A system which goes some way to achieving this is known as FORUM (Ref 10)

FORUM allows both synchronous and asynchronous communication Asynchronous messages are added to a journal file, and when a participant resumes after a break, he is informed of all items which have been appended to this file since he left the conference Its synchronous communication is more organised than that of LINK, in that there is a chairman who rules on the order of speakers and other administrative details It is also possible for participants to have off the record asides, or to butt in to the main discussion at the chairman's discretion Additionally, a good deal of thought has gone into the system to alleviate the frustrations of non-computer specialists

In most respects FORUM is a significant advance in this form of communication; however, it does have its weak points In early versions, there were no keyword search facilities, so that citing previous discussions was difficult without a tedious search Similarly, because of the lack of structure in the journal file, problems of producing abbreviated transactions of a conference were similar in magnitude to a secretary trying to make a precis of a tape recording

FORUM and other similar systems, e g EMISARI (Ref 11) have been used on networks other than ARPANET FORUM, for example, runs on TYMNET; EMISARI, developed by the US Office of Economic Preparedness, runs on a US Government system The authors of these systems cost them as low as $2/user hr

4 THE EFFECTIVENESS AND BENEFITS OF MESSAGE PROCESSING

4 1 General Considerations

From the discussion of Section 2, it is possible to derive some qualitative indications of potential benefits which could be obtained from wider deployment of message processing services It is necessary to discuss the relationship of these services to PTTs' offerings before any real cost advantages can be claimed It is certainly possible, however, to discuss what types of services are required, where they should be located, and how they should be used. Clearly, the optimum choice will depend on the application involved, but some broad principles can be outlined. The figures presented already in Section 2.8 indicate an upper limit to the cost of the services.

We suggest services which should be provided, being in most cases derivatives of those of Section 2. For a large scale commercial service, very considerable changes would certainly be made, but the broad structure should probably be as described below.

4.2 Message Composition

In message composition, several functions are important. Because of the cost and scarcity of computer-trained personnel, it is important to have simple editing facilities available which can be used by secretaries. Systems described above are essentially on-line ones, the cost of connect times (both computer and communication), and the unavoidable complications caused by on-line activity, makes it highly desirable to provide a service which will also read paper or cassette tapes prepared off-line. Such tapes may include such simple editing instructions as delete character, word or line, start new paragraph, etc. An example is the CASSET program of Ref 12. For more complex text manipulation, a sophisticated editor, such as TECO (Ref.13) should be available.

For later review and output processing, messages should include a certain amount of structure. Fields, including the author, title, recipients and keywords must be easily available, whilst text headings and paragraphs should be accessible if desired.

In message composition, there is far less 'economy of scale' than in some other applications. Distributed dedicated editing machines probably make economic sense in the trade-off of communication versus computing costs.

4.3 Document Review

In the case where several authors are collaborating to produce a joint document, there is a clear need to provide facilities for easy transmission of messages. The sort of review facility of FORUM (Section 3.2), where the contributions of each delegate can be seen by a new participant, is useful. A certain amount of synchronous communication is desirable. This is, however, time-consuming and is only of benefit if kept to a minimum.

For some applications it is important to be able to point to parts of the text, and to add one's own observations, without changing the source text. For this, the text structuring of NLS (Section 2.5) and the recipient modified fields of the DMC system (Section 2.6) are very relevant.

The present SNDMSG sends separate copies of a message to each recipient. This is wasteful of transmission bandwidth. At most, one copy should be sent to each recipient site, with that site doing any further distribution. The question of whether to send messages or only citations depends very much on the characteristic message sizes, the average number and distribution of addressees, the capacity of the message processing systems, and the availability of the site holding the reference version of the message.

The questions of authentication of sender and of message privacy are already important, and will be more so in the future. In the review process, the former arises when messages are to be approved for transmission. At the very least the system must append the account name of the sender. This will often not be sufficient, and personal authentication by password may well be required. Added security will sometimes be necessary using message encryption.

4.4 Document Transmission and Retention

This activity is the one best known and understood. SNDMSG gives confirmation if a message is transferred at once, otherwise it keeps trying to deliver it. This is satisfactory, but it is also important that the sender be informed if transmission is impossible. In fact, SNDMSG checks at composition time, on the validity of local recipient names, or on the validity of the remote Host name. If a remote account does not exist the user is informed later. Further facilities for giving the sender information about whether the recipient has read the message can be useful. If a special user process, such as POST, has been run, it is at present not possible to determine whether a specific message has been read, only that the user's message file has been accessed. A simple recipient-operated set of responses, such as 'Message Received', 'I will respond shortly', 'I will respond before ....', would be useful. If the recipient makes the appropriate indication, the response could be returned to the sender, and perhaps to others on the distribution list.

The availability of message service computers, and of the messages themselves will be of great importance. In the case of ARPANET, not all Hosts have had high reliability. Many decisions still have to be made about the level of redundancy which needs to be achieved in the message processors, the degree of backup of messages, and the privacy which must be provided against unauthorised access.

In this context, it is not possible to separate the transmission procedure from file retention or archiving. The really important aspect of this technology is its integrated nature. A key problem will be how to charge for and provide cost-effective services. Different user communities will require different levels of service and privacy   Ideally, their requirements can be reflected realistically in the service provided, and in the relevant tariffs

4.5 Receiver Processing

A key difference between the services described in this paper and Telex is the integrated nature of the sender and receiver processing   Unlike Telex, where a recipient is given his message, here his message is delivered into a special file   Most Hosts then output a short one line message to the addressee when he next accesses the Host to say a message has been received   The recipient can then invoke one of several programs for processing his messages

If the system is used in earnest, either fast display terminals must be used with user files being highly structured with easy search facilities, or a combination of on-line files and hard-copy output will still be necessary   It is our opinion, not shared by some others in the ARPANET community, that it will be a long time before paper can be completely abandoned as an output and archival medium

Like composition, receiver processing is probably done well in a distributed fashion   Assuming a large proportion of the receiver processing requires intensive interactions, one must consider carefully how much of it to centralise   The answer will be entirely dependent on the levels of traffic, the solutions chosen for archival, the geographic characteristics of the message traffic, and the degree of sophistication desired in the message processing   The figures of Section 2.8 indicate that at the present level of technology, computing costs exceed communication costs for this activity in a PDP-10 KA with the files 5000 miles away on ARPANET, but this balance can change very rapidly   There is little doubt that archiving benefits from centralisation, if this allows a cheaper technology to be used, such as 10^{12} bit stores   Care must be taken, however, that in the specific applications, the savings in archival hardware are not more than offset by extra data transmission costs

4.6 Synchronous Communication

So far in this section we have dealt largely with asynchronous transmission of text   Particularly when reviewing documents, synchronous communication can have its advantages   It is our experience that for such coordination there will be at least ten times more asynchronous interactions with individuals than synchronous terminal-oriented ones   This is partly because of the difficulty of synchronising busy peoples' schedules across 5000 miles and up to ten hours of time difference; it is partly because for most purposes synchronous terminal communication takes more of the participant's time for a given information trans-

fer. A typical response for asynchronous use of message services is
1-2 interactions/day. If the subject requires more frequent activity,
synchronous mode is indicated. Even then, it is often best backed up
by previously prepared messages or files.

4.7 Other Communication Media

In some applications, the transmission of line drawing or half-tone
pictures is desirable. If these originate in machine readable form,
there is little problem, except provision of suitable output devices
and an appropriate protocol supported by the Host system. Otherwise,
it is necessary either to use the other excellent asynchronous medium,
the postal system, or to add a facsimile transceiver to the system.
The latter activity is in process at University College London (UCL).
It will lead to the need for at least five times the communication
bandwidth of alphanumeric text per page, but may still be justified in
some applications.

Voice is a very convenient ergonomic medium. For synchronous voice
communication, there is no real substitute for the telephone system,
except perhaps in certain military mobile applications. For asynchronous communication, there is a role for the 'voice-gram' or short prepared
voice message. Even with reasonably efficient coding (as against the
most advanced), twenty seconds of speech contains 200K bits of information (1K=1000), the same as one page of facsimile with reasonable coding,
or five pages of closely written text. The technology of manipulating
voice and facsimile messages has not yet been completely developed.
The disparity of information content between these media and coded text
may mean systems optimised for the latter are not economic or practicable
for the former.

4.8 Ergonomics

Whilst a whole paper could be written on human engineering in this area,
there are two factors which are of overwhelming importance. The first
is that such systems must be acceptable to both secretary and senior
administrator alike. Secondly, the device which most of such users are
familiar with is the keyboard. This is not to say that one should dismiss
other interactive devices completely, but to intermix use of say, a light-
pen and keyboard at an intensive level can only result in annoyance and
confusion to the user.

The difference in ability between a secretary and senior administrator is
probably less than that between a novice and a competent user in the case
of message systems. Where a secretary and administrator probably differ
is in the level of detail they need and their approaches to the information they require. Thus, there is a need for profiles to be built up for
each user of such a system. The profile not only should indicate user

ability in various areas, but also the particular characteristics of
the terminals used, and preferred output formats In other words, the
profiles allow the message system to become (almost) all things to all
men!

Discussion of terminals gives rise to airing of many prejudices, not
only in the form of input, but also output; even the two authors cannot
agree over the use of displays versus printer terminals! Displays have
many advantages, although to make use of random access to characters on
the screen one has to use either cursor buttons or other input devices.

The DNLS system of Section 2.5 uses an integrated display, keyboard,
keyset, and 'mouse'. The mouse can be moved on any flat surface and
causes movement of the cursor, whilst the keyset has five keys which in
conjunction with a shift button on the mouse can give 64 possible characters. Thus an adept user can input characters and point to the screen,
using the mouse in one hand and the keyset in the other This is definitely one form of input which is limited to the well coordinated and dextrous!

Before we leave the subject of human factors, let us return to looking at
synchronous communication. In the absence of facsimile transmission or
voice, communication rates are limited to typing speeds, or at best terminal speeds, if material is recalled from file. Averaged over several
lines, typing rates are of the order of five characters per second, terminal rates are typically between 10 cps to 100 cps, while typical reading
rates are 45 cps. Thus in a synchronous 'chat', there is effectively an
8:1 idle time/useful time ratio for the 'listener'. Moreover, if voice
were used, the information bandwidth would be higher, either allowing
the same information to be passed in less time, or more details to be
sent. All in all, 'linking' is such a time-consuming operation that it
is generally only used where there is urgent need to contact someone or
where other mechanisms (e.g. telephone or messages) are too imprecise.

5. MESSAGE SERVICES AND THE COMMON CARRIERS

In this paper we have sketched some of the ways message services can be
used, and illustrated the development which would make them practicable
We are still left with several very difficult regulatory and political
issues. There is no question but that in most of Europe, the PTTs by law
have a complete monopoly on message traffic They operate the Telex and
telegram systems, and guard jealously against any infringement of their
monopolies The type of services mentioned here, particularly if the
participants are in different organisations, are clear infringements, and
in most countries could clearly only be provided by the PTTs, if they so
insisted. It is not clear to us, however, if the PTTs really want to
provide all these services, or if they would permit others to provide
them if they do not themselves.

The PTTs are already providing message transmission, routing and some archiving. A key property of the message systems outlined in Section 2.4 is their integrated nature. The value contributed by the other functions is considerably greater in some instances than the message transmission itself. Another property of integrated systems is that the whole system must often be tailored to the specific user community. The sheer financial and technical effort of putting in such systems may well strain the limited resources of the PTTs in this area, and may not fit in with their normal operations.

Alternatively, the PTTs could allow private institutions to provide these services under licence. There are already moves in this direction on the data transmission lines themselves, e.g. the recent German tariff structure to charge by volume of traffic.

One problem in charging by volume, in this case, is that for most applications, the services described offer more than Telex; moreover, a tariff structure based on the volume of traffic might distort the technology unnaturally. For example, data transmission can be reduced dramatically by extremely terse commands, highly coded responses and extremely powerful editors, archival and retrieval systems. An arbitrary charge sufficiently heavy to so distort the pattern of usage, would clearly be undesirable. We have not tried to assess what level of charge the PTTs might feel required to impose.

There is another problem; this is not an isolated technology. Many of the subsystems required, already exist on commercial time-sharing systems. If they are not used more widely for message processing services, it is only because the suppliers are careful not to advertise their capabilities; they often neglect to put in tailored packages only because they fear the wrath and retribution of the PTTs. Certainly, it is difficult to distinguish between information retrieval from tailored databases, one person retrieving or modifying another's files, and message processing. Undoubtedly, all these require a considerable amount of computer processing of the information. A tariff structure which would allow one to be economic may kill the other. Alternatively, the regulations may just impose on the user the necessity of tailoring existing systems for the purpose. In this context, the ARPANET experience is interesting: the general purpose TENEX system had ad hoc message services added, users added ad hoc sender and receiver processing modules; later as the services became more heavily used, attempts were made to systemise the service, and it was found that they ran most efficiently on almost dedicated machines. Thus if the regulations encourage or force ad hoc measures, the result will be inefficient use of the communication media, the computers and the time of both implementors and customers.

6. CONCLUSIONS

We have analysed the requirements of interactive message services of a general type, and given examples from ARPANET of different aspects of the services. We have given indications of the costs of the services, though much more needs to be done on the economics, particularly when tempered by reliability, scale, security and concern about simplicity. We have discussed experience of these services in practice, and tried to philosophise about their wider use. Although most of the paper has been concerned with international communications, almost all is directly relevant to national and even local systems, particularly in the area of asynchronous communications. Generally, on a national or local basis, synchronous communication is best carried out using a telephone, except in cases which require accuracy or hard-copy records.

The time is clearly right to introduce such technology, on an experimental basis, to a much wider community. This will probably occur in the US, there the regulatory climate is somewhat different, the distances are larger and the technology better established. We hope methods will be devised to permit attempts to prove the technology in Europe also, since we believe it is potentially very important for both cheaper and better execution of administrative tasks, and may eventually somewhat reduce the requirements for personal travel.

Acknowledgements

The authors wish to acknowledge the following grant awarding bodies, without whose assistance this experience of ARPANET could not have been gained: the US Advanced Research Projects Agency, the Science Research Council, the British Post Office, the Department of Trade and Industry and the British Library.

References

1. Kirstein, P.T., 'UK Experiences with the ARPA Computer Network', in 'Exploitation of Seismographic Networks', ed Beauchamp, K G pub. Noordhoff, pp 55-80, 1974

2. ---- , 'TENEX User's Guide', pp 155-157, BBN, 1973

3. ---- ,'TENEX Executive Language Manual for Users', BBN, 1973

4. Myer, T.H., 'Message Transmission Protocol', BBN, RFC 680, 1975

5. Wilbur, S.R. 'POST - A British Mail System', UCL, Indra Note 330, 1973

6. ---- , 'TNLS Journal System User Guide', SRI, Jul 1973

7. Black, E., 'The DMS Message Composer', MIT Dynamic Modelling Center, 1974

8. ---- , 'Data Computer Version O/11 User Manual', Computer Corporation of America, Datacomputer Project Working Paper No 10, 1974

9. Roberts, L.G., 'Telenet principles and practice', Proceedings of this Conference

10. Lipinski, H.M. and Miller, R.H., 'FORUM: A Computer Assisted Communications Medium', Proc 2nd Int Conf. on Computer Comm, pp 143-147,1974

11. Macon, N. and McKendree J.D., 'EMISARI Revisited: The Resource Interruption Monitoring System',Proc. Int. Conf on Computer Comm, pp 89-92, 1974

12. Wilbur, S.R., 'CASSET - A TENEX Utility Program for the GE Terminet', UCL, Indra Note 356, 1974

13. ---- , 'TENEX TECO - Text Editor and Corrector Manual', BBN, 1973

Document Sources

BBN: Bolt, Beranek and Newman, 50 Moulton Street, Cambridge, Mass. USA.

SRI: Augmentation Research Center, Stanford Research Institute, Menlo Park, California, USA

UCL: Department of Statistics and Computer Science, University College, London, 44 Gordon Square, London, WC1H OPD, England

The state of the art in the evolution of private data communication networks

David W. Mann
Manager, Advanced Systems Group
Logica Limited, UK

Abstract: The paper discusses the current demand for
private computer-based data-communication networks. It
identifies the classes of user requirements that are
currently most difficult to satisfy, and indicates a system
structure appropriate for them. Within this framework the
paper then considers the state of the art in the development
of solutions for specific problem areas.

1.   INTRODUCTION

The term "private network" is conventionally used to describe any system based on communication facilities not
available to the general public. However, in this paper I
am concerned with computer-based data-communication networks, and in particular those that involve private
switching, i.e. the routeing of data over successive telecommunication channels by equipment of the user organi-
sation(s). Moreover I am concerned only with the basic
communications sub-network of such systems, which accepts
data from a source and delivers it to a destination, and not
with the processing of this data at either end. However, I
have included the subjects of computer and terminal interfacing, since these are extremely important in private network development.

The establishment of private networks has been carefully
controlled by the telecommunication authorities because of
its implications for public networks. In general they have
been permitted only within a single organisation, or within
a group of organisations having common interests (e.g.
banks, airlines, or customers of a particular bureau).

Against this background we look first, in Section 2, at the
demand for private networks and the way it is developing.
Then, in Section 3, we identify the kinds of user requirements that it is currently most difficult for a private network to satisfy and indicate the overall structure of a
system generally considered to be most appropriate to meet
such requirements. Within the framework of this overall
design, the state of the art in the development of some
specific aspects of private networks is then considered in
Section 4. Some conclusions are summarised in Section 5.

2.   THE DEMAND FOR PRIVATE NETWORKS

In general an organisation considers the establishment of a
private network with one or both of two objectives in mind:

a)   to see whether it could cater, at an acceptable price,
      for application(s) for which the public switched net-
      works are not adequate, e.g. in terms of privacy,
      transmission rates, error rates, etc., and

b)   to see whether it would be more economical than use of
      the public switched networks.

In either case the private network is likely to be more
attractive if arrangements can conveniently be made for

sharing the leased channels by multiplexing, concentration or switching.

In this section we look briefly at a number of private networks that are in operation or under development to illustrate the kind of applications for which they are currently necessary and/or economical. We also discuss how the demand is likely to develop over the next few years.

2.1   Operational and Planned Systems

Private networks have developed in the two different fields of message switching and on-line data processing, which are gradually merging together.

Message switching systems were originally developed for the transmission of text between paper-tape and teleprinter terminals at slow speeds. The transmission was effected by a store and forward switch to which the terminals were connected in a star network, and from an early stage computers were used to carry out the store and forward operations. (Indeed, this application contributed a great deal to the development of data communications in general.) Clearly private networks in this area have always involved a considerable amount of switching, albeit at low speeds, but there are three trends that are steadily giving rise to even greater demands in this respect.

a)   Message switching systems are now providing facilities for the transmission of data to/from computers, both off-line and on-line. This frequently requires different transmission techniques (involving, e.g. higher speeds, lower error rates, data transparency) and sometimes faster switching.

b)   For reasons of reliability, security, economy or administrative convenience, systems are involving more distributed switching centres with the associated problems of routeing, etc.

c)   Communities of users with similiar activities are finding it convenient and in many cases permissible to share networks, which therefore have to handle larger traffic volumes and provide greater security.

Examples of these trends are to be seen in the SITA network operated for the airlines, the SWIFT network being developed for the banks, and the World-wide Weather Watch network (WWW), which will cater for meteorological messages and data.

In early on-line data processing, many private networks
were set up to overcome the inadequacies and costs of the
data transmission facilities provided on the back of the
public switched telephone networks, and increasingly these
have involved multiplexing and concentration to share
channels. However, in contrast with the field of message
switching, until recently there has been virtually no
requirement for switching per se; a particular terminal has
tended to be used always for communication with the same
remote computer, either for a dedicated application or for
general purpose computing. This position is now changing
as a result of two general trends.

a)   Many organisations are now heavily dependent on the
     proper functioning of their on-line computer centres.
     They therefore wish to ensure that, if a centre fails,
     accidentally or because of sabotage, the terminals
     normally using this centre can readily fall back to
     using another centre. The same facility may be required
     in the event of overload at a particular centre, either
     temporarily or permanently. Private networks are used
     for one or both of these purposes and examples are:
     the Integrated Network System being implemented by
     Barclays Bank in the UK and timesharing networks
     such as Infonet in the US.

b)   Many users require access to special facilities which
     their normal computer is unable to offer, or cannot
     provide economically; for example research workers may
     wish to use special programs, data banks or peripherals
     on computers in other institutions. The other side of
     the coin is that the management of some organisations
     operating several computer centres wishes to have the
     centres specialise in the provision of certain facilities
     rather than be "Jacks of all trades"; for example, they
     may require a centre to focus on the execution of
     scientific programs so that not only the computer runs
     more efficiently, but also the company's expertise on
     the appropriate compilers and packages is concentrated
     at that centre. A number of private networks has been
     set up in the research area with this general objective
     of resource sharing, and the prime example is clearly
     the ARPANET. However, there is increasing adoption of
     the philosophy in the commercial area; for example the
     British Steel Corporation in the UK is implementing
     a major network to link together most of its computers
     and terminals to allow access to specialist services
     and to different kinds of mainframe.

Thus the fields of both message and on-line data processing

are increasingly giving rise to demands for private networks
with significant switching capabilities.

2.2 Scope for Future Development

Trends in the design of both dedicated and general purpose
computer-based data communication systems seem to indicate
quite clearly that any particular computer or terminal is
likely to wish to communicate with more and more other
computers and terminals as time goes by; some of the other
computers and terminals will be within the same organisation,
others in kindred organisations, and others in the world at
large. Moreover, as terminals increasingly acquire storage
and processing capabilities, the kind of communication
facilities they need will become steadily more like those
required for computer-to-computer interaction today. Thus
there will be a need for switched services at higher and
higher speeds.

The data transmission services provided via the telephone
networks are continually being improved, but it is predicted that, even so, they will be unable to cater for a
large section of this demand. There has therefore been
considerable activity throughout the world to provide
radically new public switched data communication facilities.
Such facilities are being introduced not only by the
established common carriers, but also in the US by the
new breed of Value Added Carriers. The plans for some of
the services are being discussed in the next session of the
Conference and the dates for introduction of some of them
are shown in Figure 1 below.

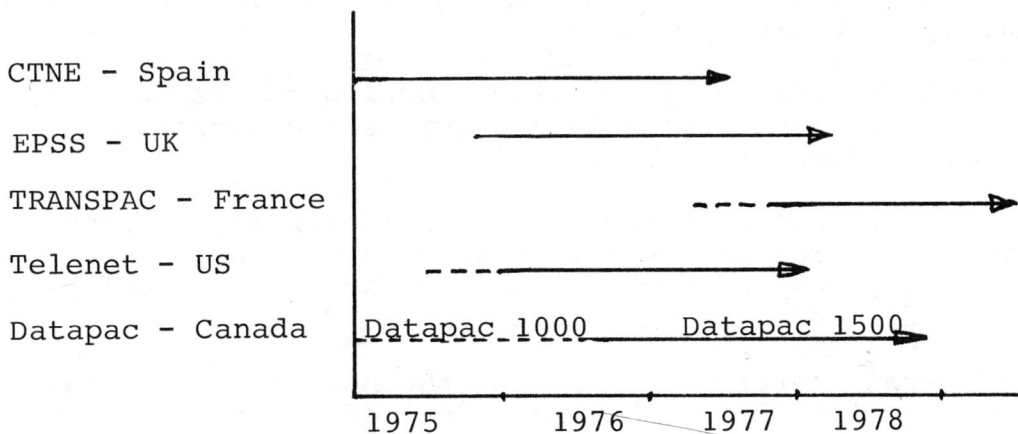

Figure 1: Planned Availability of Some Future Public
           Switched Data Networks

From this it will be seen that, even in countries where
there are firm plans, the networks are unlikely to be
established with extensive coverage until late in this
decade. Moreover, there is considerable lack of standardisation between the different systems (see also Section
4.5). It therefore seems likely that many users will wish
to continue to establish and operate private networks. However, as new public facilities become available, the
position of the telecommunication authorities may be
expected to harden against private networks, especially in
certain countries, and, even where they are permissible,
interworking with the public networks must be anticipated
to be economical or obligatory in an increasing number of
different situations.

3.   TRENDS IN OVERALL DESIGN

From the discussion and examples of Section 2 it is clear
that there are many kinds of private networks, and it is
difficult to discuss problem areas and the solutions available for them without reference to a specific class of network. In this section I therefore first postulate a set
of indicative requirements for a hypothetical network which
would bring together the most demanding aspects of various
existing and planned systems. I then describe an overall
design, which is considered to be most appropriate for such
a network by many workers in the field, including ourselves.
The requirements and overall design are intended primarily
as a background for the discussion of Section 4.

3.1   The Most Demanding Class of Network?

Let us postulate the following indicative requirements for
a hypothetical network.

a)   It must provide for interactive working across the net-
     work, i.e. transmission delays across the network
     should be less than one second.

b)   The network should cater for a considerable switching
     load, i.e. traffic passing through several nodes
     between source and destination and each node catering
     for traffic of several hundred kbit/s.

c)   The overall service provided by the network should have
     a high availability, i.e. in excess of 99%.

d)   The network should provide for transmission within and
     between several different countries.

e)   It must inter-work with other networks, both public and private.

f)   It must provide for communication between a variety of different computers and terminals. In particular it must allow mainframe computers to communicate with terminals that are not supported by the manufacturers' standard software.

g)   It must link computers and terminals that are controlled by a variety of different bodies.

Each of these characteristics is exhibited by one or more of the networks considered in Section 2.

3.2   Overall Design for Such a Network

I think that it is now clear that a private network designed to cater for the requirements listed above should have the structure shown in Figure 2. It is based on four functional modules at the communications level and these have the following characteristics.

a)   The kernel of the network is formed by packet switching node modules which cater for the transmission of data in packets of a standard "network" format. There has been a marked tendency for private networks to use packet switching as their modus operandi and the reasons for this have been discussed extensively in the literature. The standard interface to the remainder of the system facilitates control of the network and simplifies the problem of interworking with other networks (at least at the communications level!)

b)   There is a need for certain protocols (host-host protocols) to be adopted for communication across the network and most of these are implemented in two modules, the HIM and the TIM, which in many ways are logically equivalent. The former interfaces computers to the network and the latter interfaces terminals. The HIMs and TIMs may be regarded as part of an extended communications sub-network which caters for a variety of interfaces appropriate to different computers and terminals.

c)   The fourth module is the NCM, which is used in monitoring and control of the network.

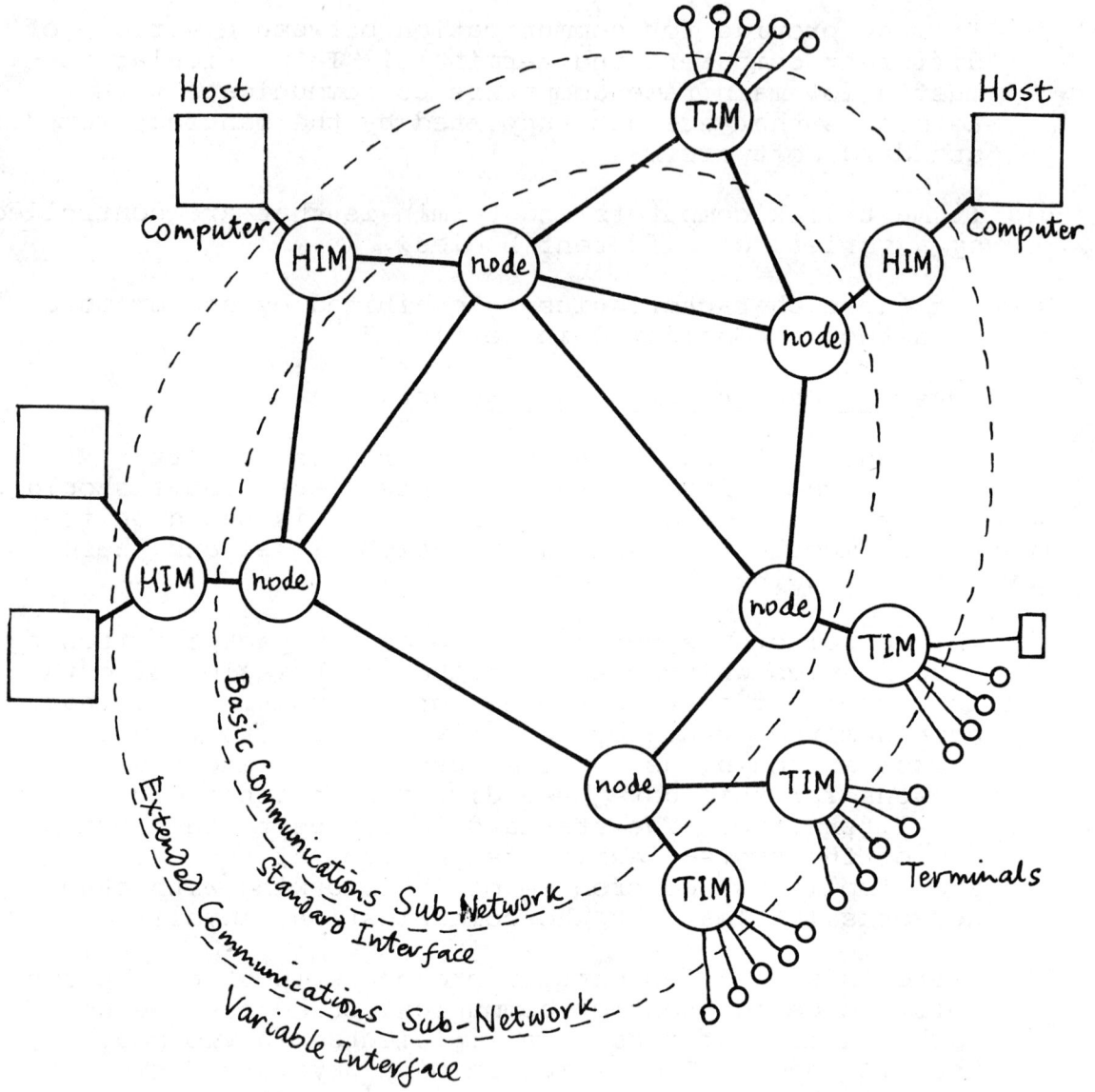

Figure 2:   Overall Design for a Private Network
            to meet the requirements of Section 3.1

The Terminal Interface Module (TIM) may be implemented on
the same computer as the node (cf the UK Post Office
EPSS system or the ARPANET TIP). However, for a number of
reasons we believe it is often sensible to implement these
functions on separate processors. For example, there may
be several different versions of the TIM required and they
may all be changed frequently, whereas the node should be
fairly static; and to interface with other networks the
node and TIM functions will often have to be dealt with
separately.

Similarly the Host Interface Module (HIM) may be implemented on the same computer system as the node or on the
host. We believe the former is frequently undesirable for
reasons similar to those given above. Whether the latter
is sensible is a much more complicated question depending
very much on the nature of the particular host (see Section
4.3).

In each situation, the price for physical separation may be
the duplication of some functions.

4.   SELECTED ASPECTS OF DESIGN AND IMPLEMENTATION

In the previous section, I outlined a philosophy for constructing a particular type of private network to cater for
a demanding class of requirements. What the user ideally
wants, of course, is manufacturers to adopt a common philosophy in this area, together with appropriate standards,
so that he can readily construct networks of components
from different suppliers. However, progress in this
direction is extremely slow and, in view of the significant
marketing implications for manufacturers, it seems very
unlikely that Utopia will ever be reached.

In constructing private networks of the type I have indicated, the user is therefore currently faced with substantial development work. In this section I shall
consider some problem areas of the system and indicate to
what extent solutions exist. I shall only consider the
communications aspects, and in many instances the total
network will involve other problems of much greater extent,
e.g. in the areas of security and back-up for data bases on
the hosts.

4.1   Communication Channels

The procurement of communication channels for an extensive
private network is currently a time-consuming and expensive
activity.

In general only a small proportion of the channels are for
links between nodes or between nodes and HIMs or TIMs (see
Figure 2). However, in order to achieve acceptable
transmission delays across the network, it may well be
necessary to have wideband channels, and on long, perhaps
international, links these are very expensive. Nevertheless, lower cost, high capacity leased circuits based
largly on digital transmission, are being rapidly introduced in North America (MCI, Datran and Bell's Dataphone
Digital Service in the US and TCTS's Dataroute and CNCP's
Infodat in Canada), and there are various plans for the
provision of such facilities in Europe in the near future.
Moreover, it may be possible to share trunk channels with
other forms of communication, e.g. telephony; and satellites may increasingly provide economical channels for use
in a broadcast manner as well as substitutes for other
point-to-point links (References 1 and 2). In general
therefore, it seems likely that, at least in relation to
the remainder of the total system, the cost of the high-
capacity channels will steadily decrease.

On the other hand, it seems that the cost of linking terminals into the network will remain high. Although multiplexing and concentration can be used extensively in these
local networks, there are still many channels that cannot
be shared. Moreover, in some situations it may be necessary
to provide two channels to different TIMs to achieve
adequate availability (see Section 4.4). As in public networks, these local systems can therefore be expected to
require careful planning.

4.2 Packet Switching Nodes

Since the late 1960's the design of packet switching networks has been studied by many different groups, and there
is now extensive literature on the subject, supported by a
reasonable amount of operational experience. From this it
is clear that packet switching is an intricate mechanism
and that the construction of a system based on this
technique requires careful design decisions to be made on
a number of issues, which interact with one another in very
subtle ways. These issues include:

a)   the method of routeing packets through the network,

b)   whether there is to be any limit imposed on the number
     of packets in flight between any particular source/
     destination pair at any one time, and, if so, whether
     these "pipelines" are to be defined for pairs of nodes,
     hosts or processes within hosts,

c)   the method of congestion control,

d)   whether a host is to be permitted to transmit several packets' worth of data into the network in a single message and have this message disassembled into packets by the source node on entry and assembled again by the destination node before delivery,

e)   the method of error detection and correction, and

f)   whether the network is to ensure that packets are delivered to the destination in the correct sequence.

The alternative strategies open to a designer in these and other areas are clearly presented in a recent paper by a number of people at BBN (Reference 3), which also shows the trade-offs that have to be made and the implications for the overall network in transmission delay, throughput, reliability and cost.

The conclusions presented in the BBN paper are not shared by other workers in the field, e.g. on the Cigales Network (Reference 4). The most significant differences of opinion are concerned with what facilities should be provided by the basic communications sub-network of Figure 2 and what should be left to other parts of the total system. This demarcation is clearly vital in the definition of standards for the sub-network. The disagreements are based on strong political as well as technical considerations and are at the root of the slow progress on the production of inter-national standards (see Section 4.5).

In the current climate, the setting of standard interfaces for a private network and the associated decision on demarcation of functions represent the most difficult tasks facing the designer. At best the outcome can be only an uneasy compromise. However, we believe that there are now sufficient guidelines for the remainder of the design and implementation of a packet switching node computer system for this to be a relatively risk free exercise, provided that the developer is content to rely on well-tried tech-niques and does not wish to re-invent the wheel. (The implementation of yet another routeing algorithm can be a temptation that is hard to resist!) The development of the nodal system for the European Informatics Network (EIN) illustrates this point. Its design was based on well-tried techniques and the implementation of the software will be completed about one year from the date of contract with about fourteen man years' effort (of an international team!).

With a packet switching node based on a readily available, modern minicomputer, one can obtain throughputs of the order of several hundred kbit/s and an availability in excess of 99%.   If higher throughputs or availabilities are required, then a multiprocessor configuration is necessary. The straightforward approach to a multi-processor node is duplication with provision for cross-patching lines in the event of a failure (e.g. Telenet). However, the extensive work of BBN on the development of the Pluribus (Reference 5)   shows what can be achieved with full multiprocessing and low-cost hardware. It is in this direction that I believe the future of nodal systems lies, without doubt.

4.3   Host and Terminal Interfacing

Many on-line data processing functions are now carried out by minicomputers and the interfacing of these to a private network is usually straightforward. By contrast, the inter-facing of mainframe computers can present severe problems. A considerable amount of software is supplied by the manu-facturers for use in on-line applications; only a restricted range of terminals (usually the manufacturers' own) is supported by this standard software and they are controlled by a complex mass of telecommunications access software which is fused with the operating system. The modifi-cation of a manufacturer's software to interface to a non-standard network and support non-standard terminals can therefore be very difficult. Moreover, any changes that are made may be incompatible with subsequent releases of the software.

In general there are three different approaches to solving this problem.

a)   The HIM (Figure 2) simulates a terminal normally sup-ported by the host. This has the advantage that no changes are required to the host software. However, it has the disadvantage that not all the mainframe's facilities may be available to the simulated terminal.

b)   The HIM simulates a front-end processor or telecommuni-cations controller supported by the host. This again requires no modification to the host software and will normally provide access to all the host's facilities. One disadvantage is that the interface between the host and its front end may be proprietory and subject to change. It may also be very difficult to ensure that the HIM really does simulate the standard front end or controller in all situations, e.g. on time outs and recovery.

c) The standard software is modified to allow the host to
    handle the network either directly or via a front end.
    With this approach one can bypass irrelevant software,
    but there is the continual problem of maintaining the
    amendments in subsequent releases. This is of great
    concern to a commercial organisation, although often
    not to a research institution, university, etc.

One of these approaches can usually lead to a satisfactory
solution for most mainframe systems. However, in our
experience, the right approach for an IBM S/370 is often
by no means obvious.

The other half of the problem is interfacing terminals to
the network, i.e. the provision of a TIM (Figure 2), and
in general there are two different approaches to this.

a) One can define a Network Standard Terminal (NST) for
    a particular class of terminals and arrange for hosts
    on the network to support the NST. The burden of
    interfacing any particular terminal is then placed
    firmly on the TIM, which must translate to/from the
    codes and procedures of the NST.

b) One can decree that the only terminal in a particular
    class that may be interfaced to the network is a
    specific make and model. All appropriate host software
    is then modified to support this specific terminal.

The ARPANET has paved the way in the definition of a network standard keyboard teleprinter and approach (a) seems
reasonable for this type of device. However, for more
complex terminals, such as VDUs and RBTs, the variation
between products is such that approach (b) may be a more
attractive solution in several situations.

In the whole area of host and terminal interfacing it is
currently difficult to find elegant, general-purpose
solutions: ad hoc solutions are found to specific problems.
However, the emergence of carriers such as Telenet has
added new urgency to this area, since they cannot collect
revenues until the interfaces exist. At the least it can
therefore be expected that considerable effort will be
devoted to the problems and that more ad hoc solutions will
emerge suitable for commercial users.

4.4   Network Performance and Availability

Many networks are designed so that traffic can be diverted
over alternative routes if certain components become
heavily loaded or fail. The performance of the network in
transmitting data between a particular source and destination, and the availability of the service between them,
are critically dependent on the topology of the network
and on the algorithms used for adjusting to loads and
failures. The determination of the optimum design to meet
specific criteria and the investigation of trade-offs
between cost and performance can be complex tasks for a
large network. However, simulation provides an extremely
valuable tool for undertaking these tasks at relatively
low cost.   (References 6 and 7)

One of the major problems in this area is usually the
provision of adequate capacity and fall-back for the links
between hosts/terminals and the nodes of the network. As
indicated in Section 4.1, a single "local tail" can be
expensive. However, if there is only one link to a node and
either this link or the node fails, then the host/terminal
will be isolated from the network. Such failures can
account for most of the unavailability of service across
the network. The availability can then be improved significantly only by increasing the availability of the node
or by arranging for a fall-back link to another node. The
latter arrangement is catered for in some networks, e.g.
EIN and Cigales, and complicates the network algorithms
slightly, e.g. for addressing. It can involve expensive
connections if the next nearest node is a long way away and
the switched network or patching of existing lines will not
serve for fall-back. However, in the short term, it may be
cheaper than duplicating the nodes, although this balance
can be expected to alter in favour of node improvements as
multiprocessor developments progress (Section 4.2).

4.5   Interworking and Standardisation

It has been said earlier that one of the current major
problems of network design is the specification of standards
for the network interfaces. There are two major areas of
concern in this. First, the interface standard should be
chosen so as to minimise the problems of connecting the
hosts and terminals into the network. Second, it should be
chosen to facilitate interworking with other networks.

In the first area the major forces are the computer manufacturers; in the second they are the public carriers.
These forces interact. They also manifest themselves in

two classes of activity.

a) The individual organisations define standards for their
    own services or products, which are thus imposed on
    their customer base. For example, on the computer manu-
    facturer side IBM and DEC have recently produced
    important philosophies and standards, and on the public
    carrier side each of the organisations mentioned in
    Section 2.2 is producing or has produced standards for
    its new network.

b) The organisations participate strongly in committees
    attempting to agree international standards. The most
    important committees in this area at the moment are in
    CCITT (SG VII), ISO (TC97/SC6) and IFIP (WG 6.1).
    Naturally the individual organisations are anxious to
    ensure that the output of these committees conforms
    closely with their parochial standards.

It is to the second class of activity that we look for our
primary guidelines. However, very little progress has so
far been made by the international organisations. It is
therefore necessary for us to look at the standards defined
in the first class of activity and guess how they will be
reflected in the output of the second class.

The standards defined for the European Informatics Network
are presented in another session of this conference
(Reference 8). At the beginning of 1975 it was considered
that these standards represented the best compromise. However, the position is a rapidly changing one.

4.6 Planning and Control

If a private network is to be developed and operated
efficiently, there are many activities that must be coordinated across the network, e.g. releases of new software,
change of addresses, maintenance, installation of new
equipment, etc. There are now good guidelines on the tools
required to monitor and control such activities, e.g. the
Network Control Center of ARPANET. However, I believe that
insufficient attention has so far been given to the kind of
management organisation that is required to develop and
operate a network, and that this accounts for the slow
progress on some projects, particularly those that involve
co-operation between separate parts of the same organisation,
between organisations, or between countries.

Clearly, if a network affects a number of different groups
of people, they should be consulted in its development.

However, it is to be expected that the objectives of the different groups will frequently not coincide and that progress will therefore be extremely slow if all compromises are worked out in committees. For efficiency it is essential that an executive body be appointed with considerable power to make decisions.

Such a body might not meet with much co-operation if it were imposed by senior management, and, in any case, there is no such overlord between different organisations and countries. In general it is therefore necessary for the users of the network to see this requirement, press for the appointment of a strong executive body if need be, and accept loss of some flexibility as a result. The last point is crucial in that in some situations it is not obvious that users have sufficient motivation in forming a shared network to pay the price of lack of flexibility (or the possibility of losing a competitive edge); an interesting discussion of this point in the context of the banks is given in Reference 9. However, some lack of flexibility is inevitable in forming a shared network and unwillingness on the part of a user to delegate responsibility will only delay the inevitable.

In some situations, the establishment of an acceptable executive body might create severe organisational/political problems, e.g. the sharing of a network by different government departments or universities, and in these environments shared networks will be slow to evolve even if they are technically and economically desirable.

5.   CONCLUSIONS

Trends in the design of computer systems are steadily increasing the demand for private networks and in particular, for private switching operations. As new public switched services become available, the position of the telecommunication authorities will undoubtedly harden against private networks, particularly in certain countries, but the common carriers will be unable to cater for the bulk of the demand at least for several years.

The requirements for private networks that are currently most difficult to satisfy include, inter alia, interactive working between a variety of different mainframe computers and terminals. For such a system the overall design now generally considered to be most appropriate is one based on a packet-switched communications sub-network. Extensive research and development in the area of packet switching since the late 1960's has resulted in the production of

good guidelines for the establishment of these networks.
However, significant problems still remain in the setting
of standards for the sub-network, interfacing terminals
and interfacing mainframe computers. Moreover, the
efficient development and operation of a private network
requires a strong management organisation, and in situations
where this is not established, private networks will be
slow to emerge, even if they are technically and economically desirable.

ACKNOWLEDGEMENTS

The opinions presented in this paper have been formed in
numerous discussions with my colleagues at Logica, in
particular Jeremy Tucker, and with our French associates,
SESA. However, they are my own views and are not necessarily
shared by other people in either of these organisations.

REFERENCES

1. L.G. Roberts
    Dynamic allocation of satellite capacity through packet
    reservation
    AFIPS Conference Proceedings, Volume 42, pp 711-716
    (NCC 1973)

2. N. Abramson
    Packet switching with satellites
    AFIPS Conference Proceedings, Volume 42, pp 695-702
    (NCC 1973)

3. W.R. Crowther, F.E. Heart, A.A. McKenzie,
    J.M. McQuillan, D.C. Walden
    Issues in packet switching network design
    AFIPS Conference Proceedings, Volume 44 (NCC 1975)

4. L. Pouzin
    CIGALE, the packet switching machine of the CYCLADES
    computer network
    IFIP Congress, pp 155-159 (Stockholm 1974)

5. S.M. Ornstein, W.B. Barker, R.D. Bressler, W.R. Crowther,
    F.E. Heart, M.F. Kraby, A. Michel, M.J. Thrope
    The BBN multiprocessor
    Proceedings of the Seventh Hawii International
    Conference on System Sciences, Computer Nets Supplement
    (January 1974)

6. H. Frank, R.E. Kahn, L. Kleinrock
    Computer communication network design -
    experience with theory and practice
    AFIPS Conference Proceedings, Volume 40, pp 255-270
    (SJCC 1972)

7. W.L. Price
    Design of data communication networks using simulation
    techniques
    Computer Aided Design, Volume 6, Number 3, pp 171-175
    (July 1975)

8. F. Poncet, J.B. Tucker
    The design of the packet switching network for the EIN
    project
    EUROCOMP 1975

9. C. Read
    Future plans and prospects
    in Money Transmission Today and Tomorrow
    published by The Institute of Bankers

Approaches to controlling personal access to computer terminals

Ira W. Cotton and Paul Meissner

National Bureau of Standards
Institute for Computer Sciences and Technology
USA

Abstract

The advent of time-sharing and computer networking has resulted in a proliferation of computer users, many of whom are located remotely from the computer which serves them. This has been accompanied by increased opportunities for unauthorized users to gain access to computers and has focussed attention on the problem of identifying and authenticating properly authorized users. In the U.S.A., the requirements of the recently enacted Privacy Act of 1974 call for a number of safeguards in the handling of personal information by the Federal agencies, and personal identification is an important aspect of the implementation of this law.

This paper considers the various approaches to personal identification and authentication, on the basis of things known to an individual, things possessed by an individual, and characteristics of an individual, such as appearance, handwriting, voice, fingerprints and hand geometry. A set of evaluation criteria are presented as a guide in selecting personal identification systms for various applications. It is pointed out that currently available systems are vulnerable in varying degrees to erroneous recognition and circumvention; and, therefore, should be incorporated into a hierachical security system which utilizes a variety of safeguards, including auditing features to provide a record of what is accessed, by whom and for what purpose.

There are over two hundred million people in the U.S.
One million of them are directly involved in work relating
to computers, either in computer organizations or in firms
using computers and computer services. Increasing numbers
of these persons are accessing computers via terminals of
one type or another, including programming terminals,
airline reservation terminals, stock broker inquiry
terminals, and supermarket sales terminals.

With so many different people accessing computer systems
in this manner, the problem of validating their rights to
access the various systems is becoming a major concern
[AU74]. Many of these computer systems now store
confidental personal information, which needs to be
protected from alteration by and disclosure to unauthorized
individuals. In the older batch processing days, the
strongest approach was to post a guard at the computer room,
or to otherwise control who could submit jobs to be run.
However, it would be impractical to try to post a human
guard at every remote terminal. Furthermore, human guards
never were particularly effective except for limited
population of users. Thus, we need the technological means
to economically provide the necessary protective features.

There is also a recent legislative mandate for this
need. In the "Privacy Act of 1974" (Public Law 93-579),
Congress has asserted that "the privacy of an individual is
directly affected by the collection, maintenance, use and
dissemination of personal information by Federal agencies."
Congress further recognized the potential of the computer to
intrude upon individual privacy and took steps, through the
Privacy Act, to regulate the handling of personal
information within the Government. Similar measures are
being proposed with regard to the handling of personal
information within the private sector.

The Privacy Act lays down a broad set of requirements
intended to assure adequate safeguarding of personal
information. Included are the following:

  . Control of disclosures;

  . Accounting of disclosures of a non-routine nature;

  . Providing an individual with access to records
    about himself;

  . Inclusion of an individual´s explanation on data in
    dispute;

  . Data should be used only for authorized purposes;
    and should be relevant for those purposes

. Records which are maintained should be accurate and complete;

. Insure integrity, security and confidentiality of records;

. Records should be properly archived and safeguarded when long term storage is required.

Central to the implementation of the safeguards required by the Privacy Act is the ability to establish the identification of individuals: individuals who operate computers, write programs for computers, prepare data, enter queries, receive output, even those who repair computers. Our concern in this paper is with the identification of individuals who access computer systems by terminals, where the terminal is outside of the physical security area of the system being accessed.

By "controlling personal access to computer terminals", we mean both controlling physical access to the terminal as well as controlling access to the computer through the terminal. In the later regard, the environment of a computer network, with terminals remotely connected to computer systems, is inherently different from the batch system environment. First of all there is the additional burden to protect the data while it is in transit, say by encryption. The National Bureau of Standards has just published an encryption algorithm proposed for adoption as a Federal standard which could be used for this purpose [NBS75].

The second problem is the need to perform access validation remotely. This imposes certain constraints on a candidate system, such as size (can it fit on or in a terminal), cost (is it cheap enough for every terminal, or will it be used to control access to clusters), and ease of use (since all operators will need to be able to use the system).

In this paper we will consider a number of approaches to providing protection against unauthorized access based on the personal identification of persons seeking to use a terminal. The intent is to survey in a qualitative way the current state of the art in this technology. The emphasis is on approaches rather than specific devices. We explain how devices can be compared, and introduce a systematic set of criteria that can be used in personal identification system evaluation and/or comparison.

AUTHENTICATION METHODS

In order to use a recognition system for personal
identification, it is generally necessary for the individual
to tell the system who he purports to be. The system then
takes a set of characteristics from a file and compares
these against the same characteristics as derived by the
system from the individual. If these characteristics match
within established limits, the identification is assumed to
be authenticated; if not, the individual is rejected.
Throughout this paper, it is this process of acceptance or
rejection to which the term "personal identification"
refers.

The file characteristics used for the identification
process may reside in a central computer file, or locally
within the recognition station, or they may be obtained from
an artifact supplied to the recognition system by the
individual. As an example of the latter, the individual
might enter a card containing a fingerprint impression into
a reader, and then place the corresponding finger on a
scanning device. The recognition equipment would compare
these two patterns and measure the correlation. If they
matched, he would be accepted; if not, he would be rejected.

If the characteristic data could be readily encoded
digitally, then this data could be transmitted to a central
station, which would be an advantage for performing remote
comparisons. Of course, the encoded data could be read from
an artifact supplied by the individual, rather than reading
an analog pattern from the individual.

The two most well-established systems of personal
identification in use today are: (1) the use of guards,
generally combined with the use of picture passes; and (2)
the use of fingerprints. While fingerprints are well
established as unique personal identification, they are not
generally used for realtime applications because of the
difficulty and time consumed in obtaining good images which
are easy to view and because of the training needed for
making comparisons. Much effort is currently being expended
to overcome these difficulties, and terminal-oriented
recognition systems based on fingerprints may become
widespread in the next few years.

Where the maximum certainty is required regarding users
who are to be allowed access to an information system, it is
necessary to assure that access to the system can only be
achieved from an area which is physically secure, with
access to the area being protected by guards. If the
computer system is accessible via communications facilities
and remote terminals, then the terminals should be in

physically secure areas protected by guards, and the data in transit should be encrypted. Practically, where the constraints such as cost or convenience do not permit full-time guards, automated methods must be implemented.

There are three basic methods by which a person's identity may be established for the purpose of allowing access to an information system:

(1) Something the person KNOWS

(2) Something the person HAS

(3) Something the person IS

The first category includes such things as passwords, the combination to a lock, or a series of facts from one's personal background. The second category includes such things as badges, passes, cards with machine-readable information, and keys to locks. The third category includes physical characteristics, such as a person's appearance, voice, fingerprints and hand geometry.

Something a Person Knows

Something known only to a limited set of persons is among the oldest form of personal validation for strangers (e.g., military passwords). Today, a single password is still the most common access control to timesharing systems. Such systems are easily extended to provide for multiple passwords and catechistic question-answer sequences, perhaps using a random subset of a file of known information (e.g., personal history such as mother's maiden name, high school attended, etc.).

The problem is, of course, that something known by a select few may become known by others. Passwords to timesharing systems are notoriously easy to obtain, and once known, the possessor can penetrate the system. Still, there are design measures that can be taken to improve the security of a password access system.

It is preferable for each user of a system to be assigned his own password rather than using a single password for a set of users. Whenever the system is accessed, it should keep a record of the password used and the nature of the access. This serves as an audit of the activities of various users. In the event that an unauthorized activity should come to light, this audit trail would indicate the password that was involved and would point toward the possible culprit. With individual passwords, a user could not allow his password to be used by

an accomplice without exposing himself to suspicion. Or, if
a password were stolen, the likely source would be evident
and steps could be taken to achieve an increased security
awareness. Individual passwords can be used by the system
in controlling access of users to specific system resources,
including information files and applications.

The generation of passwords ideally should be done under
centralized control [BR73]. The assignment of passwords
should avoid any obvious bases such as the individual's
middle name or initials. In some cases, it might be
desirable to assign them randomly, though in this case, use
of a known pseudorandom algorithm should be avoided.
Passwords should be as long as feasible, consistent with
requirements for memorization and use, thus reducing the
possibility of determining them by trial and error.
Passwords should be changed at intervals and sooner if it is
suspected that they have been compromised.

Systems employing passwords should be designed in such a
way that the passwords can be entered in a concealed manner.
It should not be possible to discover a password simply by
obtaining a scrap printout from the trash. Two main
defenses have typically been employed against this latter
threat: (1) on hardcopy terminals the password may be
obscured by automatically overprinting several times before
the system asks for the password; (2) the password may not
appear at all -- on a softcopy terminal (in full duplex
mode) by not echoing it, and on any type of terminal by
choosing the password from the set of non-printing
characters. A sequence of non-printing characters might,
however, be more difficult to remember than an alphanumeric
sequence.

There is a certain risk of exposure at the time that a
password is actually used. For example, the user might be
observed entering the password, or it might be obtained by
wiretap. Encrypting the data between the terminal and the
computer can protect against the wiretap threat. Another
possibility is to use one-time passwords. The users would
have lists of passwords and would choose the next one in
succession for each use. Alternatively, they could be
supplied with a new one after each use (assuming that a
secure means of delivery could be found).

Something a Person Has

Something possessed by authorized individuals is also an
old and well known method of controlling access. Some
computer terminals have been fitted with physical locks and
keys, but our attention here will focus on cards,
particularly credit-type cards with magnetic stripes. Both

the physical format of the card and the logical format of
the data on the magnetic stripe have been standardized for
particular communities. One example is the American Banking
Association format which provides fields for expiration
date, credit limit, account number and issuer. Current
activity is directed towards building terminals to read
information such as this from credit cards. Simple reading
mechanisms may be built into computer terminals without
great expense.

The problem with this approach is that something a
person has may be stolen or duplicated. For example, credit
card theft is easily accomplished by pickpockets and
burglars, the latter often stealing the cards directly from
the mail.

Theft may even be unnecessary, since credit cards may be
readily duplicated, including the magnetic stripe with its
coded information. A leading college recently held a
student contest ⌄o build duplicators for this stripe. There
were many successful entrants, some with devices using read
and write mechanisms taken from simple home cassette
recorders. An even simpler possibility - and the approach
used by the winning entry - was duplication by heat such as
produced by an iron or a pulse from an electronic flash.
Counterfeiting of fare cards for San Francisco´s BART
railroad system by this method has already been reported
[GI75].

Something a Person Is

Because of the vulnerability. of other methods of
identification to such threats as theft and duplication,
much emphasis is presently being focused on the technology
of personal identification through physiological and
morphological characteristics. Among the characteristics
which are in use or under consideration are appearance,
signature, fingerprints, hand geometry, voice prints, ear
features, dental characteristics, and patterns on the retina
of the eye.

Physical characteristics have long been used as a means
of personal identification; however, they can be quite
ineffective when applied by persons directly -- mistaken
identification is common. An additional problem is that
such characteristics may in some cases be impersonated.
Thus we seek ways of mechanizing the identification process
to make successful impersonation much more difficult. The
four specific examples to be given are general approaches to
identifying individuals. They could be used to control
access to a terminal area, and in certain cases could be
built into terminals themselves.

Hand Geometry

One gross morphological feature suitable for personal
identification is hand geometry. In combination, the
curvature and length of the fingers and translucency
characteristics of the web of the hand between the fingers
may be sufficient to identify individuals. A commercial
hand geometry reader is available which can access
individual stored hand "profiles" and validate real-time
measurements against them. The device costs about $3000 and
is currently in use to control access to food lines in a
university environment, but it has not yet been entrusted
with the protection of more valuable commodities.

Questions as to the suitability of the device for
"sensitive" applications have focused on the speculation
that it could be foiled with an artifact with certain
characteristics of a human hand. The device also seems too
expensive at present to be built into individual terminals,
though it could be used to control access to a terminal
area.

Signatures

A second approach to the automated identification of
individuals is based on the analysis of their signatures.
Signatures are an old and common way of certifying personal
identity, and professional handwriting analysts have been
called on often in the past to appear in court on questions
regarding the legitimacy of particular signatures.

Sophisticated computer systems can perform similar
analyses in real time if programmed with the proper pattern
recognition algorithms. There are two basic types of
automated analysis: static - based on position and direction
changes, and dynamic - based on velocity and acceleration.
Prototype commercial devices exist for online signature
identification, but their validity has not yet been
demonstrated. Industrial research is continuing actively
along this line, particularly based on dynamic analysis.

Speech

The way a person speaks is also a distinguishing
characteristic and may be used for personal identification.
Voice spectrum graphs have been available since the 1930's.
Commonly called "voice prints", these graphs are much more
difficult to compare than fingerprints, and even with an
expert analyst there is some question as to their accuracy.
Their acceptability as evidence in courts of law is

currently the subject of debate [UN72]. Large scale computers may be somewhat more effective than human analysts; prototypes of small devices which can distinguish between limited numbers of individuals have been developed. However, none of these devices has yet been demonstrated really effective for general use.

Fingerprints

The fourth and final personal characteristic to be discussed is fingerprints. While fingerprints are commonly imagined to be a relatively modern scientific form of personal identification, they have actually been known for a long period of time. For example, the ancient Chinese were known to affix fingerprint to deeds and contracts [CU61]. Nevertheless, fingerprints have only been in forensic use for about 100 years.

The well known FBI fingerprint files were initiated in 1924. There are currently about one hundred million living persons (about 50% of the population of the U.S.) with fingerprints stored in these files. The majority of these, interestingly enough, are not criminals, but government employees and resident aliens for whom fingerprinting is a matter of law [WEI74].

Modern fingerprint systems are virtually error-free with good prints, and are the only completely effective personal identification systems at present [EL73]. However, the manual systems which have been in use for years are unwieldy and time-consuming.

Efforts to automate fingerprint identification systems have focused on the use of digital coding techniques and computers. NBS has been one of the leaders in fingerprint technology. NBS has developed coding schemes which permit considerable reduction in the amount of data which ave to be stored for positive computer matching of prints [WEG70, WEG72]. A system which was built based on the work done at NBS is currently being tested by the FBI. This is a rather large computer-
based system (high cost), since it is aimed at automating most of the fingerprint records and file searching at the FBI. Installation of a totally automated system is a very long term project expected to stretch out over many years [BA74].

A similar approach can be built into a terminal system for the identification of a more limited population, say 500 to 1000 individuals. One manufacturer is seeking to introduce such a system commercially [FR74]. Terminals for this system cost about three thousand dollars and the

central station with a minicomputer costs about thirty
thousand dollars.

Combined Technologies

The simpler approachs which have been described are
vulnerable in varying degrees to attempts at penetration.
However, rather than depending on just a single approach,
technologies may be combined for greater assurance.
Considering that there are three basic technological
categories (something known, possessed, or a personal
characteristic), there are three possibilities for pair-wise
combination and one possibility to use all three. In
addition, there is the possibility to use more than one
technique from each category.

As an example, many unattended bank terminals in use
today require both possession of a special card plus
knowledge of a password sequence [WI74]. In this case there
is a problem if the password is stored on the card in
intelligible form, but there are serious proposals to
encrypt the data on such cards.

THREATS

Each of the categories of authentication methods we have
discussed is vulnerable in some degree to circumvention. A
password or the combination to a lock may be learned by
another person. This could happen if a copy were left in
some exposed location, or the user might secretly be
observed while using it. In the case of a remote system, a
password might be obtained via a wiretap. Artifacts, such
as badges, cards and keys, can be stolen and used by an
unauthorized person. If the loss is discovered, it may be
possible to take steps to minimize the potential damage;
however, a clever penetrator might appropriate the artifact
only long enough to carry out a specific action and then
return it without anyone's having been aware of its misuse.
To protect against this threat, an auditing routine should
be incorporated into the system which maintains records as
to what is accessed, under what authentication, and for what
purpose.

Recognition systems based upon physical characteristics
may be susceptible in varying degrees to circumvention. A
voice recognition system depending upon a spoken password
might be spoofed by a recording of the authorized person. A
picture pass might be altered or counterfeited to carry the
picture of a would-be penetrator in place of an authorized
individual. It is possible to mold fingerprint impressions
into thin rubber gloves which might be worn by a would-be

penetrator for the purpose of foiling a fingerprint matching system.

There is also the possibility of an authorized person acting in collusion with an unauthorized person, whereby the authorized person actuates the identification scheme and then passes access to the unauthorized person, or carries out the unauthorized action himself [PA74]. Another possibility is coercion, in which an authorized person is threatened physically or by extortion to actuate the identification scheme. In this latter case, a special provision can be incorporated which allows the user to secretly warn the system than an unauthorized use is being perpetrated. This is known as a hostage alarm.

Even if a recognition system could carry out its function entirely accurately and were immune to deceit, it would still be necessary to assure that it could not be circumvented in some other way. For example, a recognition device might be used in conjunction with a remote terminal, requiring an enabling signal from the device to allow use of the terminal. A would-be penetrator might be able to falsify this signal, thus enabling the terminal without the need for recognition. Another form of circumvention might involve wiretapping, in which the circuit would be switched from the remote terminal to an intruder's terminal after the establishment of recognition and login by a legitimate user. The intruder could send a fictitious message to the legitimate user stating that the computer had gone down in order to avert suspicion. It is thus evident that recognition techniques must be incorporated within complete systems where a hierarchy of provisions are made to assure overall system integrity. This could include the use of encryption for data and control signals.

EVALUATION CRITERIA

There are several factors to be considered in evaluating personal identification systems for a particular application. These include the following:

(1) False Alarm Rate (FAR)

(2) Imposter Pass Rate (IPR)

(3) Resistance to Deceit

(4) Ease of counterfeiting an artifact

(5) Susceptibility to circumvention

(6) Time to achieve recognition

(7) Convenience to user

(8) Cost of recognition device and of its use

(9) Interfacing of device for intended purpose

(10) Time and effort involved in updating (adding and
     deleting users, issuing new passwords, keys,
     changing combinations, etc.)

(11) Processing required in computer system to
     support identification process

(12) Reliability and maintainability

These factors will be discussed briefly in the
paragraphs which follow, the intent being to provide
guidance on collecting and assessing information on specific
personal identification systems. The evaluation of any
given device should center on the experimental or analytic
determination of these parameters. Unfortunately, not all
of these criteria can be expressed on a ratio scale. In some
cases the best than can be accomplished is a rank ordering
of alternatives; occasionally, no quantitative evaluation is
possible.

False Alarm Rate and Imposter Pass Rate

The two parameters which are primarily used to
characterize recognition systems are the imposter pass rate
(IPR) and the false alarm rate (FAR). These are usually
expressed as percentages. The imposter pass rate is
indicative of the degree to which unauthorized individuals
might be accepted by the system. The false alarm rate is
indicative of how often an authorized individual might be
rejected by the system, requiring either that he repeat the
identification process or that he be identified in some
alternative manner. The imposter pass rate is usually of
major concern, since it relates directly to the value of
protection. However, the false alarm rate is also of
concern, since there may be a cost associated with retries
in terms of wasted time and user aggravation.

As a general rule, the operation of automatic
recognition systems involves the setting of a threshold on a
parameter whose value is dependent upon how good a match is
obtained between the characteristics of the individual being
identified and the stored values against which the
comparison is being made. It is generally possible to
improve the imposter pass rate at the expense of the false
alarm rate, and vice versa. In practice, the operating
point generally represents a compromise.

It is possible to use two or more recognition systems in combination, thereby greatly increasing the certainty of recognition. For example, if a system with a 2 percent imposter pass rate were combined with one having a 3 percent imposter pass rate (and the criteria were assumed to be independent), the overall imposter pass rate would be 0.02 X 0.03 = 0.0006, or 0.06%. Of course, there would also be an increase in the false alarm rate with such a dual system.

Resistance to Deceit

The IPR indicates the extent to which a recognition device might allow acceptance of an imposter who was simply purporting to be an authorized individual. It is not intended to reflect cases in which an active effort at deceit is attempted. Such efforts might include attempts to mimic another person's voice, forge a signature, use a hand-shaped template, etc. It should be evident that any recognition device might be vulnerable to deceit by a sufficiently authentic-looking entity embodying a contrived set of input characteristics. Resistance to deceit would depend on the difficulty required to synthesize an entity having the necessary set of characteristics.

Counterfeiting of Artifacts

Recognition techniques which rely on artifacts, such as a key or a plastic card, are vulnerable to being deceived by a counterfeit copy of the artifact. Here, the vulnerability is related to the uniqueness of the artifact.   An artifact requiring very specialized and sophisticated equipment to produce, together with its encoded information, should be correspondingly difficult to counterfeit. It should be noted, however, that it may be possible to copy an artifact much more readily than to reproduce it by the original method. This might apply in the case of recorded codes or holographic images. A further precaution should be noted with regard to ease of alteration. An artifact which might be difficult to produce initially might nevertheless be altered with less difficulty, thereby allowing updating of a discarded or stolen artifact, or allowing an individual with a limited degree of access to masquerade as someone at a higher level.

Susceptibility to Circumvention

Aside from deceiving a recognition device by some artificial means, consideration should be given to the ease with which the device might be circumvented altogether, without the need for deceiving the recognition logic. If the device has an output lead which carries the pass/reject signal, an obvious step would be to tap into this lead and inject a false pass signal. Other more subtle measures might be applied, depending of the manner in which the device operates and the way in which it functions in a system. It is evident that appropriate precautions must be taken to guard against such circumvention.

Time to Achieve Recognition

Different recognition schemes may require differing amounts of time to carry out the recognition process and arrive at a decision. This time is made up of the time required to actuate the device, which may involve keying in some data, such as a combination, password, or personal identifier, the time for biometric sensing to take place, the time to manipulate an artifact, the time for a file retrieval to be carried out, the time for processing to occur, such as a correlation, the time for communications with a central facility, and finally the time to effect the acceptance or rejection. It may be necessary to allow for more than one trial, which further increases the time. In a system utilizing hand-written signatures, about 4 to 5 seconds is required for the signature itself; people are often not aware that ıt takes this long to sign their names. Systems which must be used frequently, or for large volumes of traffic, such as those which admit employees into a work area, may have to work quite rapidly, although this speed requirement may not be compatible with the achievement of a high degree of certainty. User impatience with even moderate inconvenience imposed by security devices is well known, leading to such subterfuges as latches being taped and doors being propped open.

Convenience to User

For a personal identification system to gain acceptance, it must be reasonably convenient to the user; otherwise it will be regarded as an impediment and may even be circumvented by the user as suggested earlier. For example, it should be evident that ∪ system requiring inked fingerprint impressions for each recognition would be objectionable. However, a very satisfactory fingerprint impression for optical scanning can be obtained by placing the finger on the surface of a prism which is designed to achieve total internal reflection.

Related to convenience is the ease of learning to actuate the recognition scheme, including data to be memorized such as passwords and combinations. The possibility for human error must be recognized and

provisions made for starting over and repeating the process.
These provisions should be limited, however, in order to
deny an imposter the opportunity to gain acceptance through
trial and error. Devices which depend on the actuation of
buttons or keys in a coded sequence should be shielded so
that a would-be imposter could not learn the sequence by
observation.

A provision that can be included is a "time penalty," in
which the recognition device is held off for a time interval
after an unsuccessful identification attempt, in order to
impede efforts to gain access by trial and error, especially
by automated means. Also, an alarm indication can be
generated when erroneous identification attempts are made,
in order to call attention to possible intrusion attempts by
an imposter.

Cost of Recognition Device

Some recognition devices are self-contained and can be
used singly, while others require sophisticated support
functions which are best performed centrally and shared
among a number of devices. The support functions might
require a specialized dedicated system, or they might be
programmable on a general-purpose machine, in which case
they could utilize a fraction of the processing capability
of the system for which access protection is being provided.
In any event, there will be a cost for each recognition
device as installed at the points where identification is to
be established, and there may be additional costs for
centralized supporting equipment.

Interfacing of Device for Intended Purpose

The recognition device may be used for controlling
access to an area or it may be used for controlling the use
of equipment such as a terminal or operator's console. The
recognition device must be suitably interfaced for the
intended purpose and this may place certain constraints on
the choice of device. The device should be interfaced in a
manner which meets system requirements and which prevents
the device from being disabled or circumvented. The
installation should be tamper-proof, which involves physical
integrity plus the use of alarm circuits which would be
activated by attempts at circumvention. The device may be
used for enabling local equipment and may also be tied to a
central system which monitors its operation and which may
provide support for the recognition process. The device may
provide only a part of the acceptance process; the user may
also have to employ supplementary procedures, which would
generally be processed by a central system.

Time and Effort Involved in Updating

Good security practices entail periodic reissuing of the variable elements of the system -- passwords, keys, combinations, encoded artifacts, etc. This should be done on a regular basis and should also be done if the system has been or is believed to have been compromised, such as through loss or theft of a key or artifact. Software-implemented provisions, such as passwords (including one-time passwords), may be relatively easy to change and to reissue, as compared to picture badges. Some push-button combination locks are designed to permit new combinations to be entered at will; locks and keys would be more difficult to update.   The choice of an access control scheme would thus be influenced by how often updating would be required and the effort involved in carrying this out.

Processing Required in Computer System

As mentioned earlier, some recognition schemes involve data processing to support the recognition device. This procesing, which could be performed on a general-purpose machine at a central location, may involve such tasks as retrieving profiles of user characteristics, comparing these against values obtained from the individual, coordinating multiple forms of access control, and performing the acceptance or rejection. To carry out these functions requires programs, processing capacity, and storage in the central facility. These requirements could be significant where an attribute is represented by several hundred sampled values and a correlation must be performed between the file set and the "live" set. Routines for supporting the recognition devices would generally work in conjunction with other security programs in the central facility, such as those which established access rights of users and device identity and which perform various monitoring functions.

Reliability and Maintainability

The reliability of the personal identification system will have an important influence on system security. The personal identification equipment should be designed so that it is fail-safe, in that it should deny access if a failure occurs or if the power is cut off. It should be provided with indicators for displaying its status, and should have test circuits for monitoring its performance. It should be provided with detectors to warn against tampering. For maintenance purposes, there must be a method for disabling these protective circuits, but this method itself must be secure enough to prevent its being used in attempts at

cirrcumvention. The need for allowing multiple
identification attempts was stated earlier; however, the
number of retries should be limited to thwart an imposter
who might try to gain access by trial and error.

CONCLUSIONS

In closing, we would like to point out that ,here is no
single scheme best ,uited to all applications. At least
three primary tradeoffs must be considered. First of all,
it is necessary to trade off the cost of protection against
the value of the information being protected. Secondly, the
probability of accepting imposters (the primary threat) must
be traded off against the costs (in inconvenience or in
time) of false alarms. Finally, required physical and
temporal characteristics (e.g., terminal system, rapid
search), should be considered.

Reviewing the different approaches available for
personal identification systems, it can be seen that there
is a spectrum of obtainable security levels. Table 1 [EL73]
illustrates the relative completely effective of some of the
technological alternatives in this spectrum. The key
tradeoff here is the difficulty of penetration. We would
have to say that at the present time, positive personal
identification does not yet appear to be economically and
technically feasible for the majority of computer users.

The NBS effort in personal identification is part of a
broader computer security program. The work on controlling
access to computers via terminals is directed at identifying
and evaluating different approaches, including experimenting
with different devices, but not including product testing.
NBS is preparing to issue guidelines for Federal agencies to
assist them to make effective use of the available
technologies and to help them match particular technologies
to their requirements.

REFERENCES

AU74   Autrey, Vaughn M.   "Will the real terminal user
please stand up." <Telecommunications>, May 1974, pp.
23-26.

BA74   Banner, Conrad S. and Robert M. Stock.   "Finder
-- the FBI's approach to automatic fingerprint
identification."   Presented at a Conference on The
Science of Fingerprints at the Home Office, London,
England, September 24-25, 1974.

BR73   Branstad, D. K.   "Security aspects of computer
networks."   AIAA Computer Network Systems Conference,
Huntsville, Alabama, April 16-18, 1973.

CU61   Cummings, Harold and Charles Midlow.   <Finger
Prints, Palms and Soles: An Introduction to
Dermatoglyphics>.   New York: Dover Publications, 1961.

EL73   Eleccion, Marce.   "Automatic fingerprint
identification."   <IEEE Spectrum>, September 1973, pp.
36-45.

FR74   French, Nancy.   "Identification system utilizes
digitized fingerprint images."   <Computerworld>,
September 11, 1974.

GI75   Gilder, Jules H.   "The insecure computer
problem: Ways sought to foil unlawful entry."
<Electronic Design>, March 1, 1975, pp. 26-32.

NBS75   National Bureau of Standards.   "Encryption
algorithm for computer data protection: request for
comments."   <Federal Register>, 40:52 (March 17, 1975),
pp. 12134-12140.

PA74   Parker, Donn B.   "Computer security: some easy
things to do."   <Computer Decisions>, January 1974, pp.
17-18.

UN72   "Voice identification based on spectrographic
analysis."   <University of Baltimore Law Review>, Vol. 2,
No. 1, Winter 1972, pp. 114-124.

WEG70   Wegstein, Joseph H.   "Automated fingerprint
identification."   National Bureau of Standards Tech Note
538, August 1970.

WEG72   Wegstein, Joseph H.   "Manual and automated
fingerprint registration."   National Bureau of Standards
Tech Note 730, June 1972.

WEI74   Weisinger, Mort.   "Your fingerprints on file
-- good or bad?"   <Parade Magazine>, September 8, 1974,
pp. 12-14.

WI74   Wiseman, Toni.   "Grand central commuters catch
cash on way to the train."   <Computerworld>, September
11, 1974.

                    Additional Reading

    American Federation of Information Processing
Societies.   <AFIPS System Review Manual on Security>.
Montvale, New Jersey: AFIPS Press, 1974.

    IBM Corporation.   <The considerations of physical
security in a computer environment>.   Manual G520-2700.
White Plains, New York: IBM Corp., 1972.

    U. S. Department of Commerce.   <Guidelines for
automatic data processing physical security and risk
management>.   Federal Information Processing Standards
Publication 31.   Washington, D.C.: National Bureau of
Standards, 1974.

    U. S. Department of Commerce.   <Controlled
Accessibility Bibliography>.   NBS Technical Note No. 780.
Washington, D. C.: National Bureau of Standards, 1973.

    U. S. Department of Commerce.   <Controlled
Accessibility Workshop Report>.   NBS Technical Note No.
827.   Washington, D. C.: National Bureau of Standards,
1974.

_____

Note: This paper was also presented at "Computer Networks --
      Trends and Applications", a symposium held at the
      National Bureau of Standards on June 18, 1975.

Table 1. Technological Alternatives for Personal Identification

Security Level	Requirement for Security Breach	Example Basis for Identification
Minimum	No forgery needed	Code-only system Household quality key system
	Straightforward amount of forgery	Card system Sophisticated key system Card-code system
	Readily duplicatable personal attributes	Personal appearance system Hand geometry system
	Difficult-to-duplicate personal attributes	Voice print system Fingerprint system
Maximum	Presently non-duplicatable personal attributes	Genetic code system

The problems of linking several networks with a gateway computer

Peter L. Higginson and Andrew J. Hinchley

Department of Statistics and Computer Science
University College London
UK

ABSTRACT

The paper outlines the practical network gateway environment at University College London. The use of an internal connection protocol is discussed, together with the operating system environment for the gateway. The use of the gateway function and associated problems are then evaluated.

1. INTRODUCTION

At University College London (UCL) a number of bilateral connections have been made on a DEC PDP-9 between the US ARPA computer network and UK star networks. These connections allow either the Rutherford Laboratory (RL) IBM 360/195 or the University of London Computer Centre (ULCC) CDC 6000/7000 complex to communicate with ARPANET (Ref.1). The PDP-9 acts as a gateway between the networks by a fairly complete mapping of protocols (including higher level protocols), of one network onto the other.

To combine these systems and to allow for current developments, which include the addition of the Cambridge Computer Aided Design Centre (CADC), a UKAEA CULHAM system, and the British Post Office Experimental Packet Switched Service (EPSS), requires both some formalisation of the switching function to connect a single user on any one of the six systems mentioned above, to any other, and also refinement of the operating system to cope with the demand for large amounts of·software to operate as reliably as possible.

This paper discusses the solutions found for these problems, the resulting benefits for future network connection and measurement, and the remaining problems to be investigated. Our approach has been to devise an internal set of protocols for initiating connections, and by suitable software development, concentrate the handling of this protocol into one software segment, which can then act as a key data area for subsequent normal or abnormal behaviour of any network connected via this segment (hereafter called SWITCH).

2. INTERNAL PROTOCOLS FOR SETTING UP DATA CONNECTIONS

As can be seen from the diagram (Fig.1), the gateway machine appears as a Host computer or satellite to each network, so that connections to the PDP-9 are made in the appropriate protocols for that network. To set up network-network contact within the system requires a common protocol for all connections; furthermore the gateway must receive enough information at this interface to suitably allocate system resources, and to allow for recovery procedures to be succesful in the event of a break in contact.

To establish a connection, send and receive data paths must be set up, and some form of internal buffering is of course desirable, to smooth the net-net data flow. On the PDP-9, we are using a drum/disc queueing facility, whereby a large number of FIFO queues can be allocated with a common process to swop buffers between core and backing store, and allocate additional free space as queues lengthen.

The protocols (described fully in Appendix I) can be divided into a user and server set.

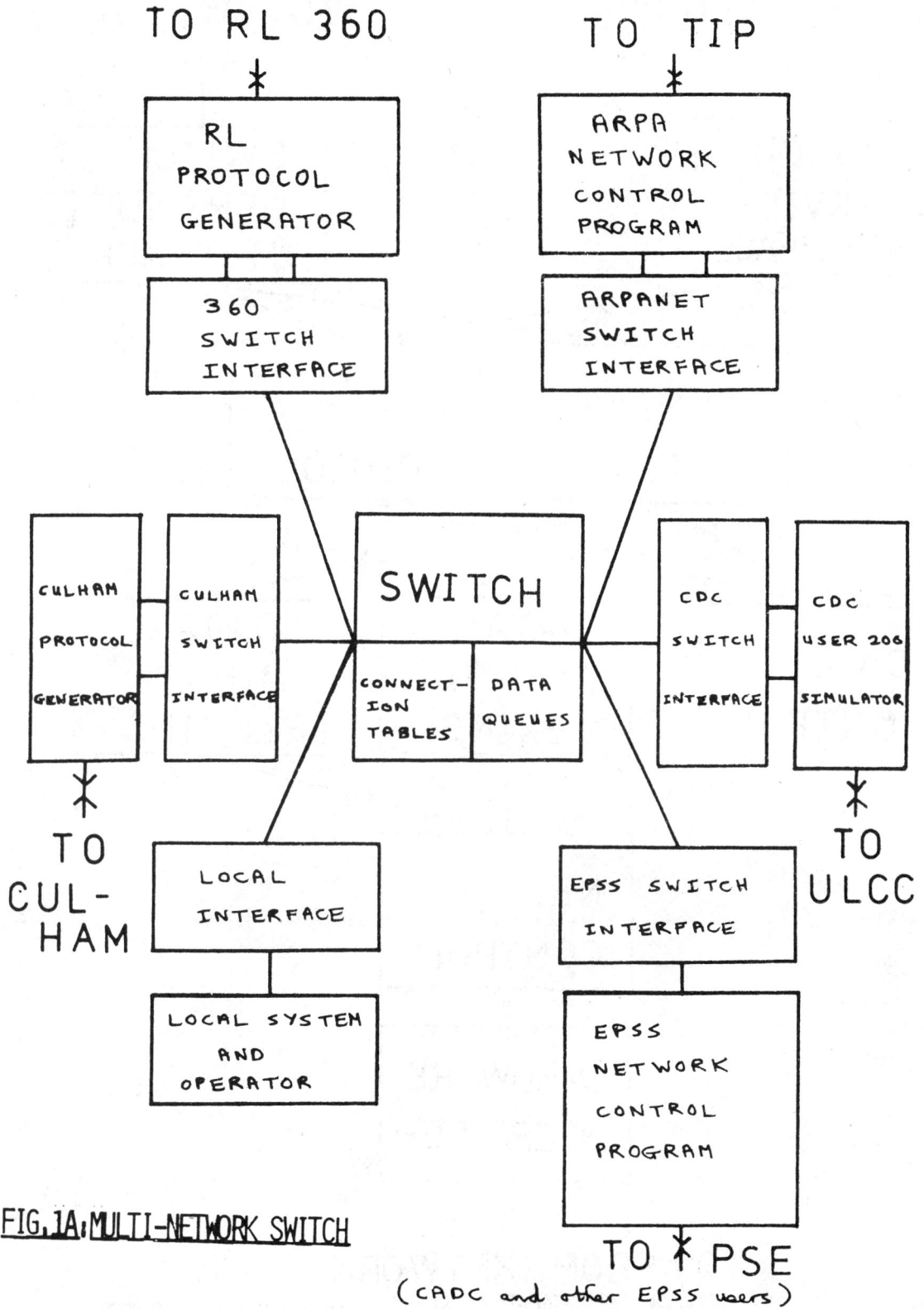

FIG. 1A: MULTI-NETWORK SWITCH

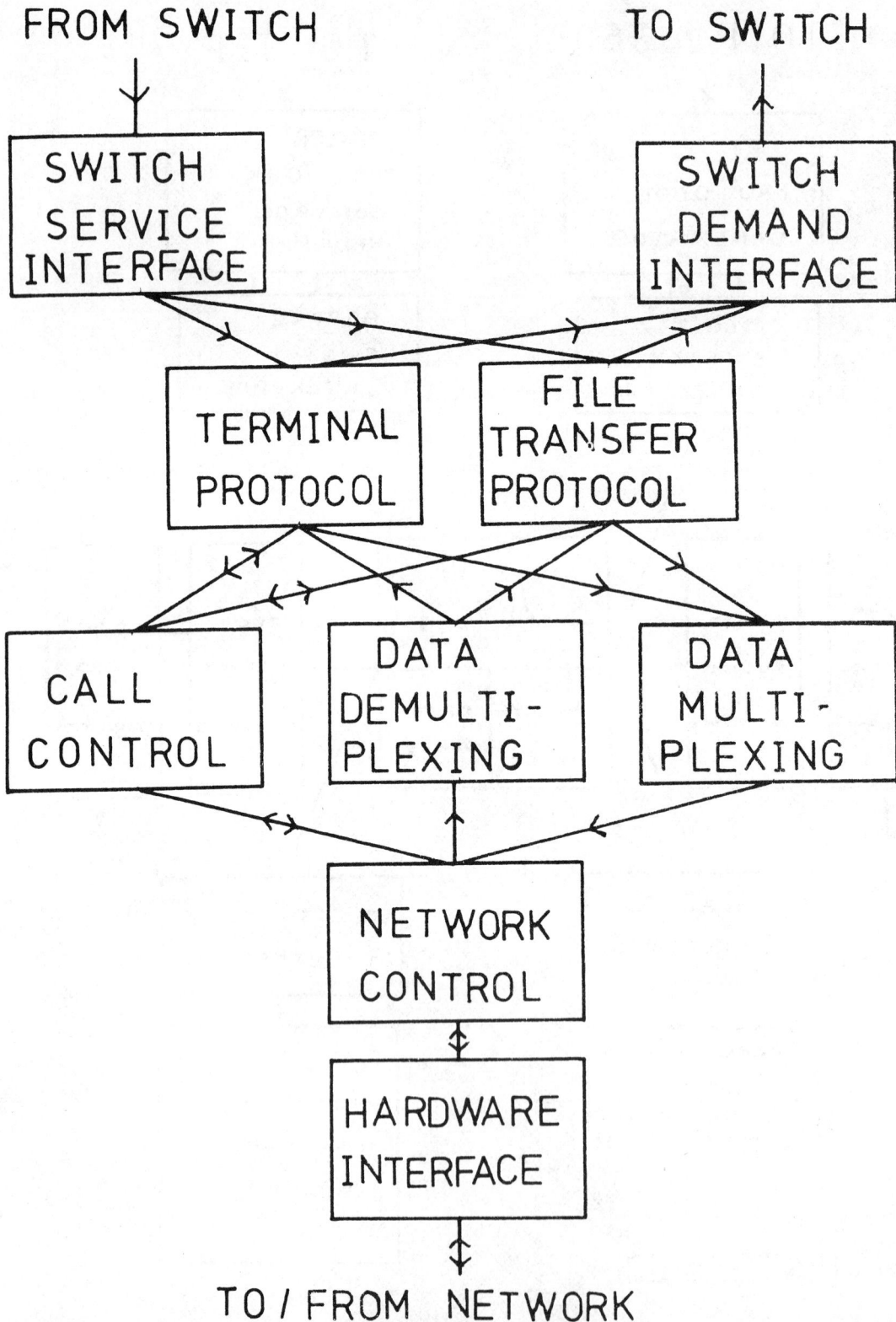

FIG.1B:A TYPICAL NETWORK INTERFACED TO SWITCH (EXPANSION OF A NETWORK CONTROL PROGRAM OF FIG.1A)

2.1   Demand Interface

The demand interface is a set of calls on the SWITCH segment to initiate
and send/receive data on the connection. SWITCH will allocate the queueing resources indicated above, and by means of the <u>server</u> protocol set,
attempt to open the connection. Once opened, traffic can continue without further demands on the switching function, until either end has requested the connection to be closed.

2.2   Service Interface

The service interface is a set of procedures which can be called by SWITCH to
progress a connection in response to <u>user</u> demands.

It is now clear that for each network, this basic protocol set will establish
connection in a very practical fashion, allowing the possibility of built-in
recovery, buffering, and monitoring facilities. The problems of higher-level
protocols and net-net addressing are discussed elsewhere in this paper.

3.   NECESSARY OPERATING SYSTEM FACILITIES

The operating system we had developed for our PDP-9 already had dynamic
program segment loading and some multi-programming facilities (Ref.2). Our
early work in the ARPA to RL network interface had resulted in the operating
system being made more rugged without changing its basic concepts.

The problem of a many-network interface simultaneously running in a small
machine, can be likened to selecting at random, n programs from a larger
population m. Because of the randomness, an overlay system is not good
enough; a paging system would have solved the problems, but we do not have
any paging hardware, or even any program relocation possibilities. In the
two network case, m was 31, of which about 5 were resident in core, and the
rest demand loaded; n averaged about 8 when the system was lightly loaded.
In the six network case, m will rise about 90 without a comparable rise in
either n or the amount of core available.

To cope with this unforeseen rise, the segment linkage system had to be re-
designed so as to minimise the amount of resident information for segments
which were part of a system, but not currently in core. While this was being
done, the speed of program loading was improved, and the size of run files
was reduced; since it was obvious that these could also become important
factors with a larger number of program segments.

We are currently investigating whether it is possible to make some of the
more important programs re-entrant, so as to improve multi-programming, or
whether it is better to keep more data in core (or predict which data will
be needed), so as to reduce the amount of time the system spends waiting for
data that is stored on the drum. The second option is more complex, since

it means that less space is available for segments to be in core, but
of greater benefit, and its trade-offs have yet to be assessed. We expect to report some results of these investigations at the conference.

4. OVERALL SYSTEM BEHAVIOUR

It is almost impossible to remove all bugs in real-time software above
a certain complexity. We do not have the manpower available to take our
software beyond a certain (fairly good) level of reliability, and in
addition, we have a mixture of applications: some experimental and some
of a service nature. Considerable effort has therefore gone into making
the underlying system inherently robust so that the effects of sub-system
failure can be mitigated. Each Host or network sub-system has been totally separated, and the sub-systems communicate via SWITCH. We realise that,
in a larger machine, this would be normal practice; however, in our case,
we neither have hardware which could separately protect each sub-system,
nor do we have sufficient core to be able to dedicate an area to each sub-
system.

Failure or lock-up of a sub-system is detected by a high-level watchdog
timer which first dumps the current status, the global area and the program
segment status of the sub-system, and then proceeds to clear out the core
areas occupied by that sub-system, and to reinitialise it. Meanwhile, the
switching system notifies all other sub-systems that had had calls with the
failed sub-system. All queues to the failed sub-system are cleared.

The system as a whole is protected by a low-level watchdog in the operating
system, which initiates a total restart (from backing store), if it detects
that the high-level watchdog is not functioning. A hardware addition under
construction will restart the machine unless it is polled frequently by the
low-level software watchdog. This addition will detect some of the remaining failures: those due to power failure, CPU failure, and gross software
failure.

The implications of one sub-system shutting down are obviously less grave
than the implications of total restart. Our procedure allows for a greater
error rate in more experimental or newer sub-systems, without degrading the
service ones. Fortunately, the simple protection system we have, does allow
us to protect the operating system, and tends to trap bugs before they cause
damage to other programs. Terminal users see a short interruption of service,
and can be told what is happening. When the sub-system is available again,
they can reconnect and continue. A possible later improvement might be to
save enough connection status information so that users of Hosts could be
connected automatically to the port they were previously using; for networks
they could only be reconnected to the Host they were using, and would have
to find and reconnect to their job themselves.

5. APPLICATION OF SWITCH TO KNOWN NET-NET CONNECTION PROBLEMS

The implications for internetworking of the work described so far in this paper, can now be discussed. Our direct mapping of the protocols of each network onto the SWITCH protocol implies that two machines on different networks may communicate using the protocol applicable to their local network. Note that we have not tackled the general problem of network-network addressing; thus EPSS users must address our gateway as an EPSS Host, and supply an agreed ad hoc address for a machine in the destination network. This arrangement is obviously unsatisfactory beyond the two network case.

In the longterm, either all networks must use substantially the same network protocol (tending to one global network), or a gateway of considerable complexity is required. This subject is dealt with in a UCL paper at this conference (Ref. 3).

In our practical situation, every Host and network has a different protocol, and our objective is to link these Hosts and networks. Just as anyone on EPSS will gain by not having to implement special protocols to access (for example) the ARPA Network, so the method we have chosen restricts the inter-network access to a fairly high level. This means that there is only inter-network access above the virtual call level; the lowest level that will be provided will be a mapping of the Network Virtual Terminals of the constituent networks. For example, the TELNET protocol of ARPANET (Ref. 4) will be mapped onto the Interactive Terminal Protocol (ITP) of EPSS (Ref. 5).

To provide what is essentially a datagram service connection appears to be more simple, but would require us to define our own protocols for 'datagram over ARPANET' and 'datagram over EPSS', for example. These protocols would not be compatible with any in current use, and hence would require both ends to write new protocols. We shall not be implementing a connection of this type, except for the (Cerf-Kahn) INWG protocol (Ref. 6), which takes into account and allows for the gateway function. We can, if necessary, implement a VIRTUAL CALL level connection between networks. In this type of connection the call control and flow control are done by the gateway separately for each network, but the data is passed through unchanged. For example, this would allow Hosts on EPSS access to ARPANET high-level protocols and vice-versa.

It is, in fact, impractical to map the existing ARPA and EPSS protocols below the virtual call level, since in the ARPA case, the call control messages all arrive on the same sub-channel, and one needs to have the status of all calls in progress to be able to interpret them. In EPSS a virtual call is all that is provided.

6. A MULTI-PROCESSOR ENVIRONMENT

Before going on to look at other areas of interest, it is worth examining one other system problem, which is of interest to us from the research
point of view, but would be mandatory for commercial reliability of an internet switching environment. We are currently planning to run our two PDP-9
machines as a dual-processor system by use of a common communication channel
with joint access to a 45M byte disc. The complex has been designed with the
ability to add additional processors at a later stage.

The switching program will be modified to extend its capability from just
within one machine to be able to connect to any Host or network, through either
local machine. We tend to use one machine as the 'service' machine, and keep
the other for experimental purposes. Until now we have taken advantage of
the fact that both machines are Hosts on ARPANET, and tested new software in
conjunction with the ARPA software only. In cases where this has not been
possible we have had to take the service machine out in order to do testing.

The advantages of SWITCH are threefold: firstly, we can add a new Host to
the existing set easily, and run it in an environment (the other machine)
where it cannot interfere with the existing service functions. This will
allow us to test a new Host interface under operational conditions, without
as previously happened, degrading the operational service; secondly, we get
some re-routing capabilities; both machines can be connected to any of the
lines to other networks, and in some cases, alternative paths are available
to the same destination. This will be important in the initial use of EPSS,
since connections will be able to be selected either through EPSS at certain
times of the day, or via the alternative leased lines when EPSS is not
available. The third advantage of SWITCH is that it can provide an interprogram interface where new protocols are being developed within a network or
Host front-end software. A new protocol generally has a clear interface with
the existing protocol programs. The amount of testing required for a new
protocol should not be under-estimated: what works with one other network
Host may not work with another, and to 'prove' a protocol requires that it
be tested with a large cross-section of other Hosts on the network.

7. HIGHER-LEVEL PROTOCOLS

We have shown that SWITCH is a useful tool for basic connection protocol mapping of one network to another. When we apply the same philosophy to higher-
level protocols, we run into compatibility problems more severe than those
already existing between different Hosts in the same network. An obvious example is file transfer on ARPANET, an interactive service using several
simultaneous connections between file origin, file destination, and file transfer request site. EPSS will probably use a batch type of bulk transfer, and
a network-network file transfer must inevitably bring a number of problems
The practical role of the gateway machine must depend on the available resources.

At UCL, as in any gateway situation, we have no wish to commit ourselves
to buffering complete file transfers because of the large amount of storage
this would take. In our current system when the user requests a transfer,
both end machines must be available, and the data transferred directly
end to end.

We provide a few kilobytes of buffer to smooth out the data flow, but are
limited to the lower of the two mean file transfer rates The time to transfer a file would not matter if it were not for the fact that user interfaces
to file transfer programs on ARPANET demand that the user is present during
the file transfer. The best solution to this may be for the gateway to provide a file transfer queueing system so that transfer requests may be queued
and carried out when possible. This allows the gateway to attemtpt to set-
up both sides of the connection and not start moving the data unless both
are available

The problem of protocol incompatibility becomes severe with protocols more
complex than file transfer. The ARPA RJE protocol, for example, is based on
their FTP, and exchanges file names for RJE control, and then ships files
using the FTP. This is unlikely to map easily onto the EPSS model of a mainframe talking to an intelligent workstation. We have not so far implemented
the ARPA RJE protocol, nor have many other organisations, because little use
of it is made on ARPANET. We can route files to the 360 job-well, but the
user must organise his own output routing.

8. GATEWAY HOST FUNCTIONS AND MEASUREMENT

Implementation of a central switching system has allowed us to standardise
our user interface and centralise the code for dealing with it. This was not
the prime aim of SWITCH, but it was an obvious sequel to centralisation of
the switching control, to provide as far as reasonable, one user interface
rather than one for each network.

Previously, each front-end system had its own set of commands and facilities
arranged in a rather ad hoc manner. Thus the operator was able to monitor
use by ARPANET of the 360, and talk or broadcast messages to the people on
ARPANET, but had none of these facilties with regard to use by the 360 of
ARPANET We could have implemented a set of operator control facilities in
each interface, but this would have lead to more complexity and near duplication of code than was necessary. This would have been difficult to implement
without a standard interface between the various network front-ends

We have two purposes in monitoring what users are doing; one is short-term
'live' observation of users in order to provide assistance, and the other is
long-term measurement of types and periods of usage, message lengths, etc
The first is obtained by copying both sides of one conversation to the operator s
console, and can be set up by the operator The second is effected by storing
messages complete with identification, of which channel they were passing along,
and reconstructing conversations by post-processing the stored data To date

this has only been done experimentally, and the raw output has been used for debugging and evaluating system performance only.

Until now we have regarded it as sufficient that users have an account on the Host they wished to access. However, we are considering implementing an accounting function within the gateway-Host, so that we may more accurately identify individual users and groups of users, and hence improve the usability of our measurement data, and be in a position to control access of users from one network to another.

APPENDIX I:

SWITCH PROTOCOLS

1 The set of procedure calls to establish a connection through SWITCH

   i) Allocate ⟨network⟩ ⟨socket⟩

      An initial communication channel is required prior to any further
      action. The gateway machine (in our implementation) is not com-
      pletely transparent, and has a number of functions, some of them
      outlined below, allowing preliminary contact for the user

  ii) Command ⟨network⟩ ⟨socket⟩ ⟨buffer⟩

      The command set are identified from the actual data buffer, and are
      the same for all Host/networks initiating connections:

          STATUS

          HELP

          OPERATOR

There are local PDP-9 functions allowing respectively status information,
help files on system usage, and operator communication. These all use the
data path set up by an initial allocate.

          LOGIN ⟨destination network identifier⟩

LOGIN will attempt to set up a connection to the required network, by calling
the login process for that network on the PDP-9   This in turn will attempt
to make connection with the remote site   A set of fail codes will be returned if unsuccessful, otherwise the connection can now be successfully
mapped across SWITCH, and retained until further notice.

          CLOSE

CLOSE connection will place the connection in a closing status at the SWITCH
level, and will initiate closing procedures which will vary from net to net.
Only when both ends of the connection have acknowledged the request for closing
the connection, will it be broken.

          INTERRUPT

An interrupt condition will be conveyed across the connection, the result
will be system-dependent, but SWITCH will flush existing data queues.

          DISCONNECT

This is an abnormal interruption of service, or alternatively a response to a
previous CLOSE   Actual breaking of the connection can now take place

iii) <u>Data forward</u> ⟨network⟩ ⟨socket⟩ ⟨buffer⟩

   <u>Data pick-up</u> network   ⟨socket⟩ ⟨buffer space⟩

Having set up a connection. we are now able to use the data paths mapped by SWITCH by a <u>data forward</u> or <u>data pick-up</u> command Socket identification is now sufficient for connection to be identified from resident connection tables, and the relevant data queue accessed to obtain or send the next message buffer

  iv) <u>Status</u> ⟨network ⟩ ⟨socket⟩

This allows full connection information to be returned to a calling process, and can be used either for flow control or for the kind of measurement information indicated later in this paper

2 <u>The set of procedures to allow SWITCH to establish a connection to a network</u>

This procedure set allows SWITCH to convey the   connection requests (made in the form of the preceding section) to the required destination network   This is essentially the server side of the connection

   i) <u>Login</u> ⟨ buffer ⟩

   The buffer will contain a login message suitable for the remote Host on the destination network   A login procedure will be initiated, and if successful, a socket number will be returned which will serve as identification for this connection at the interface

   ii) <u>Interrupt</u> ⟨socket⟩

   The interrupt condition will be conveyed in the appropriate defined form for the Host/network

  iii) <u>Close</u> ⟨socket⟩

   The connection has been put in closing status, and this information is to be conveyed to the Host/network No further data exchanges will now be expected

   iv) <u>Disconnect</u> ⟨socket⟩

   An exchange of <u>close</u> protocols has taken place, or service has been broken abnormally The connection can now be broken, and all participating processes (source, destination, SWITCH) can reallocate the resources used for the connection

Acknowledgements

We acknowledge gratefully the support of the British Post Office the Department of Industry, the Ministry of Defence, the Science Research Council, and the US Advanced Projects Agency which has made this research possible

References

1 Stokes, A V and Higginson, P L , The Problems of Connecting Hosts into ARPANET', Proceedings of this Conference

2 Gould, I H and Higginson, P L , 'A Multiprogramming Operating System for the PDP-9', Proc DECUS 7th European Seminar, pp 31-36, 1971

3 Lloyd, D and Kirstein, P T , 'Alternative approaches to the interconnection of computer networks', Proceedings of this Conference

4 ---, 'TELNET Protocol Specification', ARPA Network Current Network Protocols NIC 7104

5 Adams, C J et al, 'An interactive Terminal Protocol' EPSS Liaison Group, Study Group 2, HLP/CP (74) 12, Issue 2, March 1975

6 Cerf, V and Kahn, R , 'A Protocol for Packet Network Intercommunication' IEEE Transactions on Communication, Vol C-20, No 5, p 637, 1974

Security and design considerations in a
distributed criminal justice computer network:
the State of Missouri's approach

Sarwar A. Kashmeri
Director, Planning and Control
Regional Justice Information System (REJIS)
U.S.A.

This paper, the first to be presented on the criminal
justice information system in the state of Missouri,
describes the state's network in terms of its hardware,
connections and files. It then describes the security
features that have been built into the network from a
software and site point of view. It describes the policy considerations that control this network and attempts
to show the effectiveness that has been achieved with
this distributed (3 computers) system. The state of
Missouri is characterized by two large metropolitan areas
on either side (Kansas City and St. Louis) and a more
rural area in between. The network that has evolved
reflects this and is a leading example of a statewide
system tuned, at the same time, to service the specialized metropolitan needs.

I. INTRODUCTION

In 1965 the Metropolitan St. Louis Police Department became the first police department in the world to use the
computer for providing on-line information to the policeman on the street. This historic event in the law enforcement field was to have an effect on every major criminal justice information system that has since been developed. It preceded the FBI's NCIC system, and the latter
drew on the expertise of the St. Louis Police Department
for its design.

In July 1968 the Kansas City Police Department implemented
the ALERT (Automated Law Enforcement Response Team) system.
This system, which addressed itself to the operational
information that must be available to each police officer
in the field on a "right now" basis soon became internationally known as the most progressive one anywhere.

These two metropolitan systems of Missouri were soon to be
joined by a computer at the Missouri State Highway Patrol
(MSHP) at the state capitol in Jefferson City. In a logical evolution, the three machines were interconnected in
1973 and a statewide system was created. The system,
while providing statewide information, is highly tuned to
the local environments which contain the computers. This
is its strength and originality. MULES (Missouri Uniform
Law Enforcement System) as this network is called, now
serves every component of the criminal justice system in
the state: police, courts, corrections, prosecutors, probation and parole.

This paper, the first presented on this system, will provide a comprehensive overview. It will concentrate on the
applications that are operational now.

Before getting into the subject matter of the paper, I
would like to give you an idea of the state of Missouri
and then acquaint you with some of the acronyms now preva-
lent in the criminal justice information system field in
America today.

Description of Missouri

Missouri is a predominantly rural state located within
fifty miles of the population center of the United States,
in the area known as the "Middle West." It is approximately 1,000 miles west of New York City and is flanked on
the east by Illinois and on the west by Kansas. The
Mississippi River forms its eastern boundary; the Great
Plains lie to the west. There are about 4,750,000 people
living in approximately 69,700 square miles. There are

two metropolitan areas, Kansas City and St. Louis on either end of the state, which between them account for 58% of the population and 71.4% of serious reported crime.

Missouri is the 19th largest state in the union. It became a possession of the United States in 1803 (when the Louisiana Territory was purchased from France), and a state in 1821.

Commercially, it is noted for its automobile assembly centers, aerospace industries (McDonnell-Douglas), beer producing (Busch Breweries), livestock slaughtering, meat packing and flour milling. Its most important crop is corn. It is also a great livestock market and a center for hog raising and cattle feeding. It is noted for its fine saddle horses and ranks high in mule population. During World War I it furnished most of the mules used in the European theatre of operations.

Sir Winston Churchill visited Missouri in 1946 and delivered his famous "Iron Curtain" speech at Westminster College in the sleepy little town of Fulton. Twenty years later, the bombed-out remains of the historic church of St. Mary Aldermanbury were shipped from London to Fulton to be reassembled, and they now contain the Winston Churchill library and museum. Missouri was the birthplace of Harry Truman, president of the United States during the closing years of World War II, who gave the order to drop the first atomic bomb. It is also the birthplace of the ice cream cone (1904) and "The St. Louis Blues," which brings us back to the problem of criminal justice.

Acronyms

I would like to describe briefly some of the acronyms used in this paper. The National Crime Information Center (NCIC) is a division of the Federal Bureau of Investigation (FBI). Their computer acts as a national index and provides information on stolen property, wanted persons, etc. Every state in the U.S.A. is tied to it. The NCIC also compiles statistics on crime throughout the country and issues monthly uniform crime reports.

NLETS (National Law Enforcement Teletype System) is a telecommunications network for exchange of administrative messages between all the states, with the exception of Hawaii.

ALECS (Automated Law Enforcement Telecommunications System) is a special network of 8 states in the midwest for the exchange of administrative messages and drivers' license, vehicle registration and license plate information.

II. SYSTEM DESIGN CONSIDERATIONS

To place the network in Missouri in proper perspective, it
should be remembered that the criminal justice system itself in the country exists at three broad levels: local,
state and national. For this reason, the information systems that have been created tend to reflect this hierarchy. At each of these levels, data files are maintained
from which records are selectively passed on to the next
higher level information system. These files, because of
the interconnections between the system, can be checked by
terminals throughout the country. This, in effect, is the
criminal justice information system that serves the United
States.

For a most enlightened description of this see Chapter 3,
Jurisdictional Responsibility, in Volume I of Reference 1.

The three computers and the interconnections that form the
criminal justice computer network in the state of Missouri
are shown in Figure 1. The system is called MULES for
Missouri Uniform Law Enforcement System. The name is an
anachronism, as every agency in the criminal justice area
uses the network now. A fourth computer, which will eventually be part of the MULES network, has recently been
purchased by the state's Supreme Court. It will be used
to support a statewide Judicial Information System, using
the communication facilities already in place. Interestingly enough it is a Burroughs computer; the three other
machines are all IBMs.

The Department of Revenue (DOR) computer which supplies
motor vehicle and drivers' license information to the network is not classified as a criminal justice computer.
This is a reflection of the fact that the DOR is not a
criminal justice agency.

The Kansas City and Jefferson City computers are run by
the Kansas City Police Department (KCPD) and the Missouri
State Highway Patrol (MSHP) respectively. This is the traditional manner in which such systems are administered,
i.e. by a functional criminal justice agency. In the
St. Louis area, the local governments have chosen a unique
approach to the administration of criminal justice systems.
They have set up a separate agency (called REJIS) to perform this function. REJIS, the first such independent
agency in the nation, is described in somewhat more detail
in the section titled Policy Considerations. For a full
description, see Reference 5.

The two metropolitan systems support the local areas,

FIGURE 1

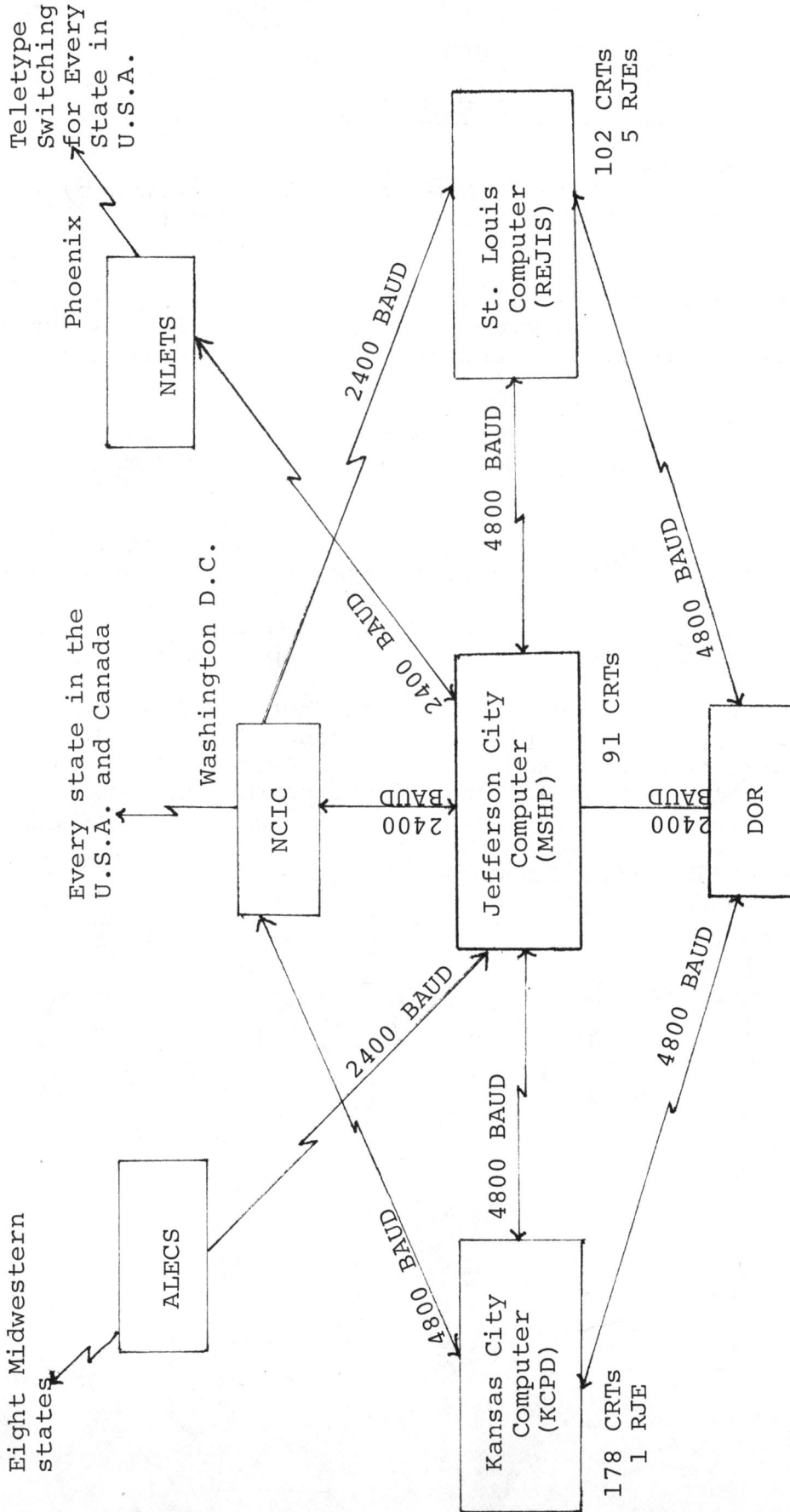

STATE AND NATIONAL NETWORK DIAGRAM. FOR HARDWARE DETAILS
SEE FIGURE 2 NEXT PAGE

FIGURE 2

HARDWARE SPECIFICATIONS

Kansas City: One 370/158, 1M memory, VS1; operated by the
Kansas City Police Dept. Serves Kansas City metropolitan
area.

Jefferson City: One 370/155, ½M memory, DOS. Operated
by the Missouri State Highway Patrol (MSHP). Serves rural
areas between Kansas City and St. Louis metropolitan
regions.

St. Louis: One 370/155 - II, 1M memory, DOS (VS1 in
November). Operated by REJIS. Serves St. Louis metropolitan area.

DOR: Department of Revenue (State of Missouri) computer.
UNIVAC Series 70 (SPECTRA 70). Located in Jefferson City.

NCIC: Operated by the FBI from Washington D.C.   IBM
360/65, 2M memory. Complete dual back-up system.

NLETS: Operated by NLETS, Inc. from Phoenix, Arizona.
Dual processor configuration. 64K each. Action tele-
controllers. Modification of the Data General Nova 840
Series. Utilizes AT&T end to end for communication
facilities.

ALECS: One 370/155, 1M memory.

where the heaviest workload exists. They also forward information to the MSHP computer which thereby maintains a statewide data base.

There are two statewide files[1] maintained at the MSHP presently. They are:

a) Wanted Persons File; this contains descriptive name information and an associated list of charges. As of April 1975 this file contained 36,772 records, contributed by the St. Louis and Kansas City areas.

b) Wanted Vehicle File; this contains a description of the vehicle and why it is wanted. As of April 1975 there were 43,392 records in this file, contributed by the St. Louis and Kansas City areas.

These two files then, are available to each one of the 371 terminals on the network. In addition to these files, the three computers allow messages to be switched between any of the terminals. Consequently a rapid statewide communications network is realized.

Some idea of the large scope of local processing can be obtained by a brief narrative of the activity on the St. Louis network. Again, the statistics refer to the month of April 1975. The description is in terms of files.

1) Arrest File - This file contains information on arrests made over the past eight years. Each logical record in the file defines one arrest incident. (291,740 logical records)

2) Business File - Records are maintained on business firms in the St. Louis area so police agencies can quickly determine information, such as who should be contacted in case of emergency, by checking the file by either address or business name. (14,865 logical records)

3) Criminal History File - This is an historical file containing name-related information concerning criminals. The data is saved for purposes of identification and information. (88,219 logical records)

4) FIR File - The mnemonics FIR refer to the field interview reports which are recorded in this file. Information from interviews conducted by police officers is recorded

---

[1]The word file in this paper means on-line file.

on this file for six months. It is used to determine information about possible suspects in criminal cases. (21,440 logical records)

5) Known Persons of Interest File - This file is maintained by the St. Louis City Police Department for informational purposes and contains identification information. (278 logical records)

6) Personnel File - The St. Louis City Police Department maintains a roster of its employees in this file along with pertinent information about them. (3,640 logical records)

7) Wanted Persons File - This file contains persons wanted on local charges. The more serious charges, which qualify for entry into the statewide files, are also passed on to the MULES system. (33,324 logical records)

8) Vehicle File - In addition to duplicating the St. Louis portion of the statewide file, information on towed vehicles is maintained. (30,716 logical records)

9) Juvenile Court File - The use of this file is restricted to the Juvenile Courts of the area. It serves the administrative, judicial and correctional needs of these courts. (67,212 logical records)

REJIS statistics show that 95% of the inquiries against the local data base are handled within 15 seconds; 90% within 10 seconds. A total of 691,627 transactions were handled by the REJIS computer in April. The corresponding Kansas City figures would be about 15% greater and the MSHP figures about 15% lower.

With this overview of the network and files the question of security can now be addressed.

III. SYSTEM SECURITY CONSIDERATIONS

Security of the data and the equipment is of prime concern in the criminal justice environment. Since the information kept is related to people, a tremendous responsibility to safeguard it rests upon the designers and operators of the system.

I am going to divide the subject into two categories: Software Security and Site Protection.

Software Security

Every terminal on the MULES network is connected by means
of leased (dedicated) lines. Thus the need to pass
through switchboards is totally eliminated. Three levels
of security protect access to the data base.

LEVEL #1: Each terminal identifies itself to the software
by means of a unique code which is hardware-generated.
The software then makes use of this code to positively
identify the terminal that is making this particular on-
line transaction.

LEVEL #2: After the terminal has been identified, a second level of security is involved which insures that the
requested access program for this particular transaction
can be made available to the terminal that is making the
transaction. If the program is not authorized for use by
the terminal, a message is returned to the terminal in-
forming it of the same.

LEVEL #3: The third level of security is maintained within the access program itself. Because many agencies can
have legitimate access to the same program and have their
records stored on the same file, the ultimate integrity
and security of the file is maintained at the access program level. Every police agency has a unique nine character code ("authority code") assigned by the FBI which is
known to all criminal justice agencies throughout the
country. Before a record is entered into our files, the
agency is required to enter this nine character code, and
the software verifies that the "authority code" being used
by the terminal is indeed valid for use by that terminal.
(More than one code can be validated for use by terminals
authorized to enter records for agencies that do not yet
have their own terminal.) Once a record has been successfully entered, its data integrity is maintained by the
on-line programs that have capabilities of modifying records.

Before any modification is allowed, these programs cross
check the authority code of the record against the pre-
verified code submitted by the terminal. Thus only the
agency creating a record can modify it. Further, selective entry and display by agency is made possible.

It is interesting to note that with so much file security
dependent upon the access program, control over these programs can itself guarantee a high level of security. For
instance, in our case, the fact that REJIS programmers
have no knowledge whatsoever about access programs belong-
ing to the St. Louis area courts makes the court data

highly secure.

The remote job entry (RJE) terminals on the network have their security handled on an individual basis. Since the RJE's belong to agencies that have created records and therefore have legitimate need for them, access to on-line records for report generation and statistical purposes is provided for. Our procedures for doing this require an operator at REJIS to dump records that belong to the agency on tape which can then be processed by the RJE's. In this way we further restrict access to on-line records.

A continuous log tape is produced on a dedicated tape drive. This log tape contains a copy of every transaction (both inquiry and response) that was made against any of the on-line files. In case of disaster, the log tape can be used to restore the on-line files from the last check-point. Since the log tape contains the inquiry, the response and other pertinent information about the transaction including terminal identification, kind of transaction, time it occurred, operator I.D. (person using the terminal), the tape also becomes an invaluable audit tool. Using it, we can answer questions like: Were any checks made against name XYZ on the 25th of July between 3 and 7 P.M.? This audit function, we feel, has tremendous potential for preventing misuse of terminals and the resulting compromise of our data and file security.

The log tape can be used in case a disastrous situation would cause a current on-line file to be destroyed. All on-line data files are checkpointed at least weekly onto both a backup disk pack and tape. Because of the rotation schedule established, three backup copies to the on-line file always exist. If the current disk file should be destroyed, these backup files can be used to re-create a past version of the file on disk. A special program can then be run, using the log tapes, to update the past version of the file.

Presently, the log tapes and the backup copies are stored on site, in fireproof safes. Off-site storage and the logistics to make this practical are being investigated.

Site Protection

The Kansas City Police Department and Missouri State Highway Patrol computers are located in these agencies' buildings. Consequently they are as well protected as any other sensitive material at any police site.

REJIS on the other hand operates from a commercial office building in downtown St. Louis. We have had to provide our own security arrangements. These will now be described. (For a more complete description see Reference 6)

REJIS occupies two floors, the 3rd and 4th, in an office building. The computer and telecommunications equipment, together with the entire Operations Division, occupy the 4th floor. The rest of the agency is located on the 3rd floor of the building.

Because it has the hardware, the 4th floor is the most secure part of the facility. It is also the hub of REJIS's security operations. Upon getting off the elevator on the 4th floor, one finds a two-door "mantrap" type of entrance. There is no other way to get into the 4th floor. The first door to the mantrap is controlled by an electric strike which can only be released from the computer operator's console. One identifies oneself via an intercom system to have the first door opened, then walks into the "mantrap" in front of a television camera which is monitored from the operator's console. One then confronts a second door, with a combination lock, which opens into the 4th floor. All windows and doors on the 4th floor are electronically treated against forced entry. The same applies to the freight elevator access area on the 4th floor and the fire exit. There is a central operations console from which the entire security system on both floors can be monitored and controlled. There are silent alarms on the 4th floor that can be triggered in case of emergency, which are connected directly to the Dispatch Room of the St. Louis Police Department, only a quarter of a mile away.

The 3rd floor, which also serves as the main entrance and reception area for the company, is protected by a normal locking door. The 3rd floor work area is protected by an ultrasonic alarm system after hours. Again, all windows and doors are electronically treated against forced entry.

We require that an identification badge be prominently displayed by anyone within the REJIS facility. REJIS employees have an identification badge with their picture on it and their signature on the reverse side. We made a list of all the people who need access to REJIS and who are considered essential for our operations (e.g. customer engineers, programmers from user agencies, etc.) and have issued them badges that clearly indicate who they are and the name of their agency. All visitors are required to log in and out at the entrance to the facility.

The identification badges themselves are in 2 colors: red and blue, which indicate the level of security classification granted to the wearer. Not everyone is allowed into the area containing the computer equipment, the telecommunications equipment, the tape library and the two control

terminals. In addition we require pre-employment checks
of all employees by the St. Louis Police Department.

All hard copy information that has criminal justice information on it is shredded. The same is done with computer
printouts containing code of any kind that could be used
to violate software security.

We are already analyzing the physical security arrangements to see whether they will meet our long-term needs.
In particular, card-controlled access and a method of restricting passage through the mantrap to one person at a
time are some of the items under investigation. An automatic Halon gas fire extinguishing system is under consideration. For the time being, Halon hand-operated exting-
uishers have been installed.

The enforcement of all security procedures has been entrusted to one person: the Administrator of Control and
Security. He was also instrumental in devising all our
physical security systems and procedures. We see security
as a line responsibility, with the Administrator playing
an audit and control function.

All of the terminal operators are now being certified.
And security is an essential part of both the basic and
advanced courses. The basic course itself is of one
week's duration.

The REJIS staff is (as this paper was written) conducting
a security audit of every terminal on the REJIS network.
This will result in a security profile on each site which
will be updated annually.

Our commitment to security and the protection of individual rights is total. And we are constantly educating ourselves, our users and policy makers on issues that affect
these areas.

IV.   SYSTEM POLICY CONSIDERATIONS

It is appropriate at this time to look at the administrative mechanisms that run the three MULES computer centers,
and how this policy making is coordinated.

The Kansas City computer is run by the Computer Systems
Division of the Kansas City Police Department. This is a
line function of that police department and, as such, is
budgeted for as a line item in the department's budget.
The police department in Kansas City is run by a board of
police commissioners through a police chief. The budget
for the department comes from local taxes in the Kansas

City metropolitan area, but the Board of Police Commissioners is appointed by the governor of the state.

The computer in Jefferson City is managed by the Information Systems Division of the Missouri State Highway Patrol. The MSHP is an agency of the Missouri State Department of Public Safety. Its budget, therefore, derives from state allocations which are made by the state legislature every year.

In the St. Louis area a completely different structure exists. The computer is managed by an independent agency that has been set up by the local governments. This agency, called REJIS, is a not-for-profit corporation, incorporated under the laws of the state of Missouri. It is managed by a board of directors that is appointed by the local governments and whose members are representatives of the criminal justice system in the area. The concept of this agency is new, and REJIS is the first one in the United States.

This concept reflects a growing awareness of a twin-pronged problem that has plagued criminal justice planners for many years:

a) Most criminal justice information systems begin in the largest police department in the area. This department continues to develop the now regional system until it becomes obvious that the surrounding smaller departments are using a significant portion of the computer's capabilities and are paying very little if anything at all to support the operations. At the same time, other components of the criminal justice system, i.e. the courts, the corrections and probation and parole agencies, start requiring computerized services, and must get these from this particular police department, or buy computers of their own. These two facets can stifle growth and/or contribute to a proliferation of computers.

b) The problem becomes particularly acute in the case of the courts. Under the American Constitution, the Executive and Judicial branches of government are equal and independent of each other. State constitutions reflect this independence. For a court, therefore, to rely on a police department (part of the Executive branch) to provide computer services which in course of time become critical to the court's operations, and the curtailing of which could curtail the court's independence, is viewed increasingly as repugnant by the courts around the country and in Missouri in particular.

Exactly these circumstances, in the St. Louis metropolitan area, led to the creation of REJIS. The St. Louis Police

Department, which had pioneered the use of the computer
and was paying for its ongoing operation, supported the
numerous municipal police departments. They were, by the
early 70's, using over a quarter of the computer's total
workload. In addition, the courts and corrections agencies
were looking for computer services as their operations
reached critical levels.

MCCJ-Region 5[1], from whom money was being requested for
these computers, funded a study to find a more cost-
effective solution. This study and the resulting negotia-
tions between area government leaders led to the creation
of REJIS.

REJIS, as an independent agency[2], arrives at a budget
every year for its operations and allocates this to all
the agencies that use its services: police, courts, prosecutors, corrections, probation and parole. No one agency,
therefore, is faced with the burden of picking up most of
the cost.

What we have then in Missouri is a network of three computer systems, each run by separate and independent agencies which are connected and must follow certain basic
policies.

An informal committee of representatives from the St. Louis
Kansas City and Jefferson City areas, people from different parts of the criminal justice system, have been meeting
since the inception of the MULES network to coordinate policy and progress. There is no one supreme authority which
directs them to do this. Local jurisdictional entities are
too many and too diverse to permit such an authority within
the state. It is a common need that drives them towards
this common endeavor, and history has shown that they have
been successful to date.

Recently, especially at the national level, there has been
increasing awareness of the need for legislation, vis-a-vis
criminal justice information systems. Two bills are pend-
ing before the U.S. Congress on this subject. The Depart-

---

[1]The Missouri Council on Criminal Justice (MCCJ) distributes federal (LEAA) funds in the state of Missouri; its
branch, Region-5, allocates this money in the St. Louis
area.

[2]By independent is meant not located in, or controlled by
the police, prosecutors, courts or corrections agencies.

ment of Justice has issued a set of regulations which will
affect criminal justice information systems in the future.
All of these laws will, in course of time, have a profound
impact on criminal justice information systems in the
United States. I would be surprised, were I to speak to
you again in a few months, if I could not tell you of a
more formal organization that we have had to set up in the
state because of these necessities. But as of now it is
this cooperative spirit at the policy-making level, and a
reflection of it at the technical level, which has held
this state of the art system together. And who can
quarrel with demonstrated success!

V. CONCLUSION

In conclusion, the criminal justice agencies of the state
of Missouri are served by a distributed computer system
which has now been operational for some three years. It
incorporates the oldest and most innovative criminal justice information systems in the world, namely those of
St. Louis and Kansas City. It provides round the clock
service to its users. It aids the policeman, prosecutor,
judge and corrections official in their respective work.
And in so doing, it serves the citizens of Missouri by reducing crime, saving lives and providing them services of
the highest quality that the state of the art, tempered by
economics, will allow.

The only available literature in the United States on
criminal justice systems standards are the six volumes
specified in Reference 1. These publications of the
National Advisory Commission on Criminal Justice Standards
and Goals provide criminal justice planners with a wealth
of excellent reference material.

For example, standard 7.8 in Volume I specifies that, based
on a 24 hour/day, 7 day/week operation, a criminal justice
information system must be operational at least 90% of the
time. Again standard 4.4 in the same volume specifies a
maximum of 10 seconds response time in a critical activity.
An example of this is a vehicle stop where a police officer's life is in potential danger.

The four hundred criminal justice agencies in Missouri are
being provided computerized information service that meets
or exceeds these national standards.

VI.   REFERENCES

The following are either referenced in the text or were
relied on for information contained in this paper.

1.   Report of the National Advisory Commission on
     Criminal Justice Standards and Goals, 6 Vols.,
     (Manager, Public Documents and Distribution Center,
     5801 Tabor Ave., Philadelphia, Pa. 19120) 1973

          I.   Criminal Justice System
         II.   Corrections
        III.   Courts
         IV.   Police
          V.   Community Crime Prevention
         VI.   A National Strategy to Reduce Crime

2.   Hindelang, M. J.; Dunn, C. S.; Sutton, P.; Aumick, A.L.
     Sourcebook of Criminal Justice Statistics,
     (Washington, D. C.: National Criminal Justice Reference
     Service, Law Enforcement Assistance Administration)
     1973

3.   Records, Computers and The Rights of Citizens: Report
     of the Secretary's Advisory Committee on Automated
     Personal Data Systems (Washington, D.C.: U.S. Dept. of
     Health, Education and Welfare) 1973

4.   ALERT (Automated Law Enforcement Response Team) Kansas
     City Missouri Police Department: An IBM Application
     Brief, (White Plains, N. Y.: IBM) 1972

5.   Kashmeri, Sarwar A., REJIS: A New Concept for Regional
     Criminal Justice Agencies, Project SEARCH: Second
     International Symposium on Criminal Justice Informa-
     tion and Statistics Systems (Sacramento, Calif.:SEARCH
     Group Incorporated, 1620 35th Ave., 95823; also
     available from the author) 1974

6.   Kashmeri, Sarwar A., Security Considerations in an
     Independently Operated Criminal Justice Information
     System, IBM Data Security Forum, Denver, Colorado
     (White Plains, N. Y.: IBM Corp., Data Processing Div.,
     Dept. 62Y, 1133 Westchester Ave., 10604; also availa-
     ble from the author) 1974

(The author can be contacted at REJIS, 1017 Olive St.,
 Saint Louis, Missouri, 63101, U.S.A., Tel. 314 421-1956)

A minicomputer network to enhance computer security

DR. JAMES A. PAINTER
TECHNICAL DIRECTOR
JOINT TECHNICAL SUPPORT ACTIVITY
DEFENSE COMMUNICATIONS AGENCY
DEPARTMENT OF DEFENSE
USA

This paper addresses the problem of unauthorized
changes in hardware and software in a hypothosized computer network system which has implemented an acceptable
degree of computer security. Computer security consists of
hardware and software used to provide controlled sharing
and isolation in a resource-sharing multi-user environment.
A system of minicomputers, called "minimonitors," is
described which can provide the function of detecting
deliberate or unintentional modifications. The minimonitors
can also provide a security surveillance capability. An
additional unit, called an "analyzer," is also described
which does the network control and analysis for the minimonitor network. A development program is described which
can lead to such a network of minimonitors and analyzer.

I. Introduction.

Computer security is only one component of the total effort required to prevent (1) unauthorized receipt of data ("theft"), (2) unauthorized manipulation of data ("spoofing") and (3) unauthorized denial of data processing services ("interference"). The total security effort is normally divided into six components; administrative or procedural security, physical security, personnel security, communication security, emanation security, and computer security.[1] Computer security consists of the hardware and software used to provide controlled sharing and isolation in a resource-sharing multi-user environment. Controlled sharing and controllable isolation are the technical attributes required of a computer system's hardware and software in order to provide protection against theft, spoofing, and interference.

Security is a total problem, and computer security is only one facet of it. It should be noted that the components of security are complementary in the sense that a weakness in one component can usually be alleviated by additional strength in another. For example, assume a computer strongly radiates intelligible signals, i.e., it has a weakness in emanation security. The system can still be made secure by increasing the amount of physical and administrative security applied, e.g., by controlling access to a larger volume of space surrounding the computer or by utilizing a shielded enclosure. Likewise, a computer which does not adequately implement controlled sharing and isolation, i.e., has weak computer security, may require that personnel security be increased to ensure that all users are allowed to access and modify all data in the system. In one sense, there need be no computer security problem since by utilizing sufficiently rigorous controls via the other security components, the system can be secured at an acceptable level of risk. However, the controls may be too onerous, and a higher capability for computer security may be required in order to obtain acceptable levels of the other controls.

One of the major problems in computer science at the present time is the development and certification of a computer system which implements controlled sharing and isolation.[1,2,3,4,5,6,7] When such hardware and software are available, the computer security component should be strong enough to permit realistic and useful trade-offs in the other security components. The basic plan for developing and certifying a system consists of (1) producing a model of a secure system, (2) verifying that the model agrees with intuitive concepts of security (including formal and informal policy and procedures), (3) producing an implementation of the model, and (4) verifying that the implementation agrees with the model. Different researchers put different degrees of importance upon these four steps, but this appears to be the uniformly agreed upon plan. It should be noted that certification is the final goal of this plan (and of most current research).

Computer networks, especially those using a common-user communications facility, compound the security problems. [8,9,10] As noted above, much current research is aimed at providing computer security at a single site or node of a network. At least three intuitive arguments can be given that indicate that as computer networks proliferate the computer security problem will get worse, no matter what rate of success attends present efforts to secure a node. First, a network "obviously" contains more items of value, hence is a more tempting object of deliberate penetration attempts. The ratio of reward to penetration effort seems better. An analogy would be the fact that a home safe is built very weakly compared to a bank vault because the vault normally contains and protects more valuable contents.

A second argument is the observation that penetration and subversion of a single node of a network permits utilization of a more or less powerful computer to aid in the attack on the rest of the network. Even if the remaining computer nodes can resist penetration, it is still probable that the communication facility can be overloaded, thus denying service to all users of the communication facility. It is also probable that network terminals, i.e., those not protected by a secure host, can be subverted.

The third argument is the observation that a computer network involves at least two technologies (ADP and communications) and usually many administrative units. It has long been recognized that security is a problem in system integration ("A chain is only as strong as its weakest link.") A computer network, both technologically and administratively, is rife with opportunities for overlooking details and misplacing confidences, hence failing security.

II. The Problem.

This paper is an attempt to address one aspect of the computer security problem in a computer network. For expository reasons, the problem and a solution will be described first in terms of a single node on a computer network. However economies of scale obtained by a network are required to make the solution feasible except possibly in cases of very high threat or risk. Following the usage of the

ARPANET, the term "host" will be used interchangeably with "node of a computer network" or simply "node."

Several assumptions are made in the following discussion. The first is that the environment is post-certification. That is, at each node in a computer network there is in operation a combination of hardware and software which has been certified as providing computer security. This assumption implies that the technology is such that a rigorous mathematical proof of the correctness of the system is not available, but, in common with the other security components, a probabilistic approach has been used. A second allied assumption is that the security implementation involves both hardware and software. That is, a failure in either hardware or software might cause a computer security failure. No assumption is made regarding the homogeneity of the nodes in the network. For the economies of scale mentioned above to obtain, the network cannot be completely heterogeneous; but the utility of such a network is not too evident. The main reasons for the existence of a computer network mitigate against a completely heterogeneous network.

A further assumption is that the maintenance support for hardware and software or both required by the site has not changed from current commercial practices. That is, all of the group of hardware/software fabricators or installers or both are not under the administrative control, i.e., complete security system, of the site. This seems to be a reasonable assumption. There is an industry-wide trend away from hardware and software produced and maintained by an individual user or even collection of users. It must be conceded that there is room for doubt about the validity of this assumption. The obvious security risks must be weighed against the economic realities. This assumption is based upon the observation that very few people construct their own safes in modern society. To summarize, the assumptions are that the world is about as it is at present, except that initial computer security involving hardware and software has been achieved.

The first aspect of the problem to be considered is that of unauthorized modifications to the hardware. Note that the only modifications being discussed are those which modify the hardware operation. "Bugs" or passive surveillance devices are not included. Protection against such devices is traditionally supplied by other security components, e.g., emanation or physical security. In the sense that they do not interfere with controlled sharing and controlled isolation, they are not a proper problem for computer security. There are two obvious ways by which the modifications can be introduced. First, site maintenance personnel can deliberately make unauthorized modifications. This is clearly a failure of personnel security. Second, modified hardware can be introduced into the supply system serving the installation. This effort could be made either on a circuit module/logic board basis or on a major component/subassembly basis. The first would presumably be a statistical attack while the second would probably be specifically targeted. The site maintenance personnel would be unaware they were introducing modifications, and the normal techniques of site personnel security would be circumvented.

The second aspect to be considered is that of surveillance of the computer system and its users for security purposes. Here the intent is to ensure that (1) the system is not penetrated and (2) the software is not modified (presumably to enable a latter penetration). As with the first problem, the system could be modified intentionally by the site maintenance personnel or unwittingly by them using modified software introduced into the software distribution system.

This method of dividing the problem into a hardware and software aspect is based upon historical and technological grounds. As will be described shortly, there are two independent technologies which can be used to attack these two separate aspects. The problem then can be addressed by borrowing from existing knowledge. There is one other obvious partitioning of the problem. This is to view one part of the problem as being that of guaranteeing that no unauthorized changes are made in either the hardware or software. The argument can be made that if the system were originally certified, and if all authorized changes were recertified, then the only problem is the detection of unauthorized changes. Typically, personnel and administrative security measures are used to address this view of the security problem. The other part of the problem is essentially surveillance to detect successful and unsuccessful penetration attempts. The question might arise that if the system were certified, is not surveillance just a case of "security for security's sake"? The answer is "No," since failure in other security components, e.g., intruders, disgruntled employees, etc., can cause unanticipated stress upon computer security. Surveillance is intended as a mechanism to alert the security system that a failure has occurred and that corrective action is required. This view of the problem, however, while interesting, seems sterile at present. There is no parent body of technology to draw upon.

III. Local Solution.

The problem can be attacked by a combination of two

existing technologies. The first aspect of detecting modifications in specified hardware is routinely solved today
by computer manufacturers during testing after manufacture
and also during maintenance. The intention is to detect
errors introduced by faulty components or workmanship in
either manufacturing or installation. This is not viewed
as a security problem, but as just the real world observation that components and humans occasionally fail.

This aspect of computers has a long and distinguished
history.[11,12,13,14] However, as the population of computers has grown over the past years, the testing procedures have changed. Just as it is no longer possible to
require programmers to be graduate scientists, it is no
longer possible to require test personnel to be graduate
engineers. One of the first steps taken was the introduction of Automatic Test Equipment (ATE). This is equipment
which would (1) establish a known state (environment), (2)
initiate a known input, and (3) verify that the output is
as expected. The next step was the incorporation of a
relatively sophisticated control device, e.g., a minicomputer, to control the ATE. Such a system is the present
state-of-the-art. This then is the solution to the first
problem, a minicomputer which can establish a known state,
initiate inputs, and determine outputs. It obviously must
also be able to validate the outputs and take appropriate
actions. As is usually the case, this description over-
simplifies reality. Such a system is usually called an
Automatic Test System (ATS).[15] One of the conceptually
simple, but practically difficult, problems associated with
an ATS is that caused by a large number of different types
of circuits or components. This diversity naturally introduces a data base of tests representing different tests for
different components and faults. The typical engineering on
a large number of components guarantees that there is a
significant amount of change introduced into the data base.
It also guarantees that the changes continue over time. All
of a sudden, the ATS has a data base maintenance problem.
Cheap large volume data storage devices are an aid to this
problem.[16]

The second problem of providing system surveillance
and detecting software modifications has exactly the same
solution. Here the source technology is that of the hardware monitors used for Performance Evaluation Monitoring
(PEM).[17,18,19] A hardware monitor system consists of a
set of "probe points," i.e., data collection points, data
collection recording devices, e.g., counters, and data
analyses capabilities. PEM hardware monitors have become
more sophisticated and now usually include a control mechanism, e.g., a minicomputer, to control the data collection

and analysis. This PEM system thus consists of a minicomputer which accepts inputs from its host and takes appropriate actions.

Two types of data are required for the solution of the surveillance problem. First, a rough "statistical" set of measurements is needed which can be compared against "normal" operation. The basic intent is to grossly monitor normal operations and detect aberrations statistically. This is similar to the "management" type reports which PEM normally reports on a recurring basis. The second type of data is detailed examination of registers, memory, etc. The intent is to detect specific violations, intentional or not. For example, this capability can verify that the software has not been modified by examining memory directly. This is the analog of the "tuning" or "sizing" reports which PEM produces as a response to a specific request and which usually involves detecting specific events or classes of events.

It is obvious that a minicomputer cannot perform all of those functions required by ATS and PEM simultaneously due to a lack of computing power and memory size. In addition, a typical minicomputer cannot control all of the data collection points which would be required to perform the functions. One solution would be to use several minicomputers dedicated individually to ATS and PEM functions or a rather large conventional system. However, this turns out not to be necessary. The hardware testing function need not be performed continuously. It takes a relatively long time to modify the hardware, and the testing cycle time can use this fact. Likewise, the "statistical" monitoring by nature is spread over a relatively long time. The detailed monitoring is the only function which appears to require a very short cycle. This is more apparent than real, however. A suspect user program can be placed into a dormant status ("sleep" or "roll out"), permitting a more leisurely examination. A suspect operating system program can cause a reinitialization of the program from a "secure" read-only copy. Thus there is the obvious solution, to utilize the single minicomputer on a time-sharing basis among these functions.

The time-shared minicomputer ("minimonitor" is the term used hereafter) is thus a technically feasible solution to both halves of this security problem. The fact that it is physically isolated and distinct from the host enhances its security, since no attack on the host (other than physical seizure) would also attack the minimonitor. It should be noted that the minimonitor is not the same concept as that of encapsulation.[20] Encapsulation addresses the problem of automating the concept of "period processing" and thus reducing the overhead associated with this technique for computer security.

It must be remarked that neither of the two parent technologies are directly applicable without modification. Also there are two trends apparent today which may make the problem more difficult, analogous to the worsening trend introduced by networks into the present problem of computer security. The first trend is that toward diversified computer architectures.[21] The architecture of the node influences the solution in two ways. First, although Automatic Test Systems are in widespread use, the diagnosis and testing of digital circuits and systems is still an open field of study. Furthermore, an ATS normally executes its tests on a system which is not operating, and often not operational. The ATS establishes its known environment without consideration of the anticipated usage of the equipment or the operational impact of the test. This raises problems of interference by the ATS with an operational system. There is an alternate strategy which is normally used for fault detection in situations when continuous operation is required. This is the technique of majority-voting systems. This technique provides a diagnostic ability under all operational conditions. However, such a system is designed to permit continuous operation, not to detect faults per se.

Conceptually there is a solution to the problem of fault detection in an operational system. It is to establish a mechanism whereby the minimonitor can isolate, or at least stabilize, a subsystem or component from the control of the node. It can then establish its desired environment, test, and verify outputs. Then the minimonitor can release the component, isolate another component, and continue testing. This scheme is practical, but requires a degree of component duplication and external control which is not provided in normal computers of today. Thus there is the practical problem that the solution may require modification of some present computers if they are to be nodes in a network.

There is a very similar problem in adapting hardware monitoring technology. There must be a capability to probe any register or storage location, as well as control circuits. It is clearly impractical to instrument every storage location in primary and secondary storage. The obvious answer is to permit the monitor to force the host hardware to provide the requested data. This implies the monitor can initiate data fetches from both primary and secondary storage, and furthermore that the resultant fetches do not cause catastrophic results to the host. A system architecture where any user on a memory bus can initiate a memory fetch by providing an address and a fetch command and where the results of such a fetch are placed on a bus for any user's utilization would be transparent to such a probe system. A system where the memory and the arithmetic/control unit are intricately interwined would not be satisfactory. Again, the solution proposed may not apply to all present computers, but there are systems extant which are so designed as to be acceptable. Thus computer architecture changes may make this solution very difficult or impossible.

The other trend is the advent of Large Scale Integrated (LSI) which may cause further problems. First, it may be possible for manufacturing personnel to hide "Trojan Horse" penetrations in a very complicated circuit. LSI is characterized by a very large number of internal circuits and relatively a very few inputs and outputs. This makes testing (even for manufacturers) very difficult since the component has a very large number of states, and there is no convenient means to subdivide the testing problem. When a "computer-on-a-chip" stage is reached, testing such a system utilizing a very few input-output probe points is equivalent to diagnosing a computer using the operator's console. LSI also raises problems for the surveillance aspect. Probes can only be inserted at the input and output points. There is no way to attach a probe to the inside of a chip, hence the number of places which are even accessible to the surveillance program is drastically reduced.

In summary, the local problem can be attacked by utilizing a minimonitor as a mechanism to detect hardware/ software modifications and to provide a surveillance of programs in execution. Technologies are presently in hand which implement these two mechanisms. The integration of the two technologies is the major problem, although there are visible trends which may imply future problems.

IV.   Network Solution.

There are still two problems evident. The programs are very large for a minicomputer to store, and the analysis processing is very demanding. Both of these problems are solved by using a conventional system as program storage and (time-shared) processing capability for the set of mini- monitors which are attached to the host. This concept of a network of minimonitors monitoring a conventional computer network appears to be an attractive means of enhancing com- puter security in a network. (See Figure 1.) Thus the eco- nomies of scale available to a network provide an opportunity to utilize present technologies and provides a ground for further work. The term "analyzer" will be used to denote

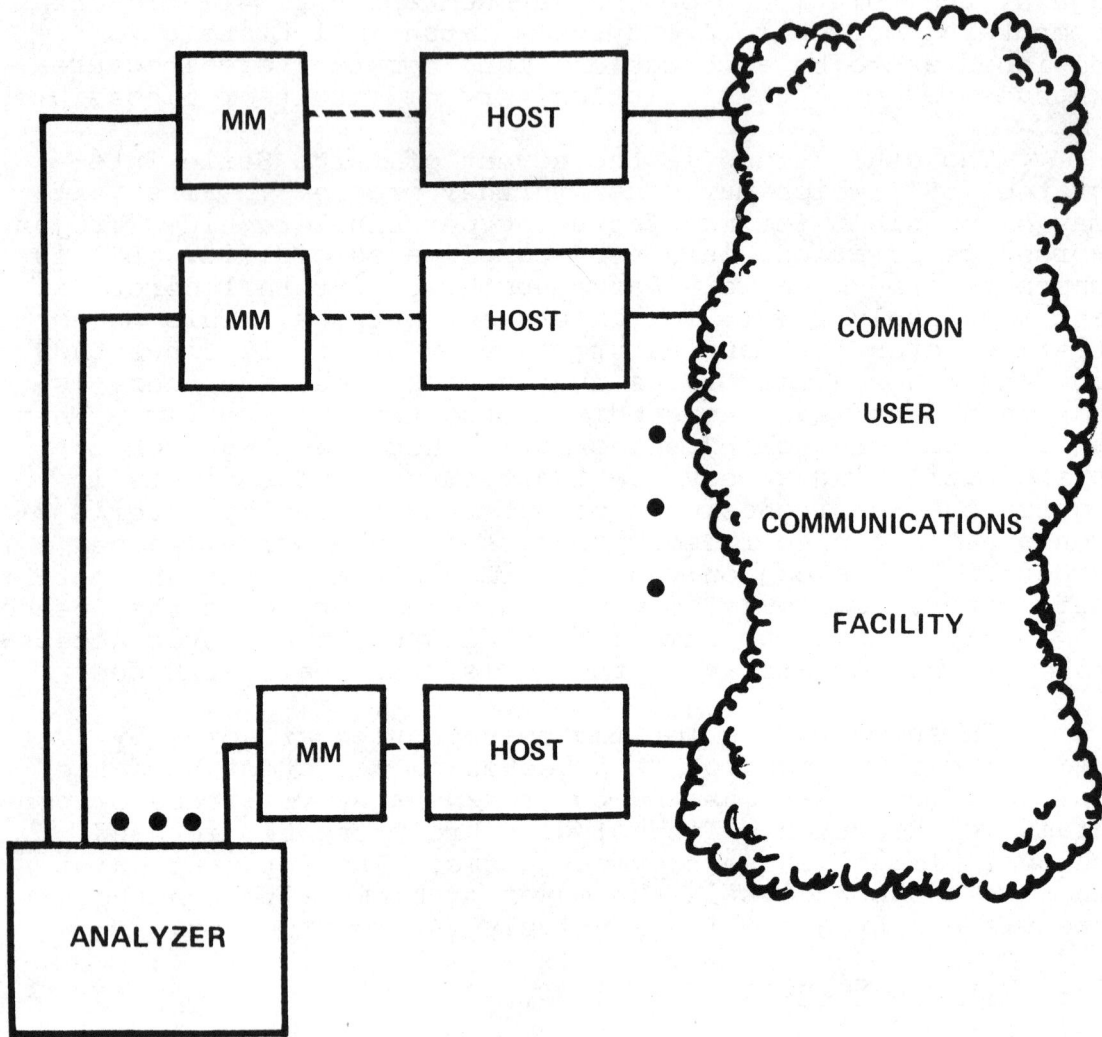

ANALYZER/MINIMONITOR NETWORK
USING HIGH SECURITY
DEDICATED COMMUNICATIONS

MM   MINIMONITOR

━━━━   DEDICATED COMMUNICATIONS

━ ━ ━   PROBE/CONTROL CONNECTIONS

FIGURE 1

the system which services the minimonitors. The name is
chosen to denote the fact that the appropriate analysis is
its major task. This idea of an analyzer and a collection
of minimonitors is superficially similar to that of a security controller and a collection of intelligent crypto-
graphic devices.[22] However, the objectives (surveillance
and end-to-end encryption) are distinct, and the system/
communication organizations are different.

One aspect of a network of minimonitors which needs
discussion is the question of the communication facility to
be used. The assumption has been made that the computer
network utilizes a common-user communication facility.
Thus evidently with appropriate interfaces, the minimonitors
could use the same communication facilities. The other
choices would be to utilize another communication facility,
either dedicated (this is the choice shown in Figure 1) or
shared with another set of users. The cost and security
would be lowest if both the minimonitors and the host computers utilize the same communications. The cost and security would be highest if the minimonitors utilized a dedicated communication facility. The use of another common
user facility would probably be intermediate in cost and
security, but not necessarily. The solution selected in
each case will have to be the subject of a trade-off analysis in terms of acceptable risk and cost. The analysis will
also have to consider the problem introduced by changes in
the nodes' workload. Clearly as the workload increases, the
monitoring load will tend to increase (particularly if the
analyzer is used as a work leveler for the minimonitors).
Thus the communications load (minimonitors plus hosts) will
tend to increase faster than the computational load (hosts).
Unfortunately, the choice of a communication facility can
only be made once, and will have to be feasible over all
threats, costs, and workloads for a given network. Note that
a related problem is the relationship of the hosts and the
analyzer, e.g., the analyzer may be a host. These variations
are obvious and are not diagrammed except for the choices
made in Figure 1.

V. Minimonitor/Analyzer Development.

A little consideration of the previous arguments shows
that the development of the proposed system can be made by
traveling an alternative route. The use of an ATS is well
established, but the use of the host system to run its own
diagnostic routines is even more time honored. Likewise
hardware monitors are an important tool in performance evaluation, but software monitors are the other tools normally
used. This raises the obvious alternative of using host
software to perform both the hardware diagnostic and the
software surveillance functions.

The following development program is feasible:

1.   Develop, as part of the basic operating system, an executive system to perform diagnostic functions.

2.   Utilize the same system to perform surveillance functions. A software monitoring system would presumably be incorporated into the diagnostic executive developed above.

3.   Develop the analysis routines required to do the statistical monitoring and to choose the explicit monitoring requirements. It must be recognized that functionally the above development program is identical with the proposed security enhancements. It must also be recognized that such a development does not provide the security that is inherent in the general system of independent minimonitors. On the other hand, there are quite a few unresolved questions in the transfer of the present technologies to this function. This methodology can be used to develop the required functions and to provide a basis for programming the attached minimonitors and the analyzer. Obviously a fourth step involves developing the software techniques on a suitable minimonitor and analyzer. This proposal has the advantage that the functionality can be developed independently of the hardware and programming costs.

VI.   Summary.

The problem of ensuring the integrity of a secure computer system and of providing a surveillance capability in a computer network can be addressed by providing a minimonitor at each host and an analyzer to control them. The minimonitor would be physically connected directly to the host at appropriate points, e.g., memory bus, data registers, control elements, etc., and would have at least the following capabilities:

1.   Establish a known environment. This may include the abilities to isolate a component, ensure quietude, and initialize the state of components.

2.   Initiate input data. This may include the ability to initiate control sequences, as well as data sequences. It might also include modification of control elements, e.g., microcode programs.

3.   Accept output data from the probes in the host.

4. Perform rudimentary analysis of the output data including comparing it against expected values.

5. Initiate appropriate alarm actions.

6. Interchange data and programs with the analyzer. Data flow, e.g., test cases and results, would be bidirectional, while program flow would be from analyzer to minimonitor.

7. Accept control commands from the analyzer, e.g., to change test programs, to initiate more intensive monitoring of a suspicious activity, initiate alarm actions locally, etc.

The analyzer would be the chief control component of this security system. Although it has been described as a single component, reliability and physical security considerations argue for some degree of replication. These techniques are well understood however, and need not be discussed further here. Whatever sets of equipment are used to achieve it, the analyzer needs at least the following capabilities which were not mentioned above:

1. Schedule minimonitors for routine and priority activities.

2. Maintain the data base of minimonitor programs and data.

3. Initiate netwide alarms.

4. Maintain profiles of "normal" activities to be matched against statistical monitoring data.

5. Perform necessary analysis.

Such a minimonitor network would be a positive enhancement to computer security in a network environment.

VII. <u>References</u>.

1. Data Security and Data Processing, Vol 5, Study Results: TRW Systems, Inc. (G320-1375)

2. J.P. Anderson, "Information Security in a Multi-User Computer Environment," <u>Advances in Computers</u>, Vol 12, Morris Robinoff (ed.), Academic Press 1972, pp 1-35

3. R.S. Fabry, "Dynamic Verification of Operating System Decisions," Communications of the ACM, Vol 16, Nov 1973, pp 659-668

4. R.R. Schell, P.J. Downey, and G.J. Popek, "Preliminary Notes on the Design of Secure Military Computer Systems," Tech. Rpt. MC1-73-1, ESD/AFSC, L.G. Hanscom Field, Bedford, MA, Jan 1973

5. W.L. Schiller, "Design of a Security Kernel for the PDP-11/45," Tech. Rpt. 2709, MITRE Corp, Bedford, MA, Jun 1973

6. M.J. Spier, "A Model Implementation for Protective Domains," International Journal of Computer and Information Sciences, Vol 2, 1973, pp 1-23

7. M.J. Spier, T.N. Hasings, and D.N. Cutler, "An Experimental Implementation of the Kernal/Domain Architecture," ACM/SIGOPS Fourth Symposium on Operating System Principles, Yorktown Heights, NY, Oct 1973, pp 8-21

8. W. Wuff, E. Cohen, W. Corbvin, A. Jones, R. Levin, C. Pierson, and F. Pollack, "HYDRA: The Kernal of a Multiprocessor Operating System," Communications of the ACM, Vol 17, No. 6, Jun 1974, pp 337-345

9. T.N. Pyke, Jr. and R.P. Blanc, "Computer Networking Technology - A State of the Art Review," Computer, Vol 6, No. 8, Aug 1973, pp 13-19

10. S. Winker and L. Danner, "Data Security in the Computer Communication Environment," Computer, Vol 7, No. 2, Feb 1974, pp 23-31

11. J. vonNeumann, "The General and Logical Theory of Automata" in Collected Works, Vol 5, A.H. Taub, ed., New York, Macmillan, 1963

12. C.V. Ramamoorthy, ed., "Special Issue on Fault-Tolerant Computing," IEEE Transactions on Computers, Vol C-20, Nov 1971

13. W.C. Carter, ed., "Special Issue on Fault-Tolerant Computing," IEEE Transactions on Computers, Vol C-22, Mar 1973

14. D.R. Schertz, ed., "Special Issue on Fault-Tolerant Computing," <u>IEEE Transactions on Computers</u>, Vol C-23, Jul 1974

15. K. To and R.E. Tulloss, "Automatic Test Systems," <u>IEEE Spectrum</u>, Vol 11, No. 9, Sep 1974, pp 44-52

16. A. Toth and C. Holt, "Automated Data Base - Driven Digital Testing," <u>Computer</u>, Vol 7, No. 1, Jan 1974, pp 13-19

17. "Update on Hardware Monitoring," <u>EDP Performance Revue</u>, Vol 2, No. 11, Oct 1974

18. J. Morris, "Hardware Monitors, Past, Present and Future," Selected Papers of SHARE Computer Measurement and Evaluation (CPE) Project, Vol 2, pp 308-332, 1974

19. J.A. Scull, ed., "Performance and Evaluation Bibliography," <u>Performance Evaluation Review</u>, Vol 2, No. 2, Jun 1973, pp 37-49

20. R.L. Bisbey and G.J. Popek, "Encapsulation: An Approach to Operating System Security," Information Sciences Institute, RR-73-17, Oct 1973

21. M.D. Schroeder and J. Saltzer, "A Hardware Architecture for Implementing Protection Rings," <u>Communications of the ACM</u>, Vol 15, Mar 1972, <u>pp 157-170</u>

22. D.K. Branstad, "Security Aspects of Computer Networks," Paper 73-427, <u>AIAA Computer Network Systems Conference</u>, Apr 1973

Alternative approaches to the interconnection of computer networks

David Lloyd and Peter T.Kirstein

Department of Statistics and Computer Science
University College London
UK

ABSTRACT

There is growing interest in the interlinking of computer networks to allow their users to intercommunicate or to share each others resources. The alternative methods of achieving this have to be evaluated against a background of political, technical and economic factors. This paper outlines the main alternative approaches to interconnection, and the factors which will determine their relative importance in practice.

1.   INTRODUCTION

Several research groups are actively engaged in experiments on Inter-
networking- the interlinking of individual networks so as to permit
users of one network to communicate with, or share the resources of,
those of another. Several alternative approaches are being explored.
The physical entity placed between two or more networks for the purpose of interconnection has become known as a Gateway, but the range
of functions it must perform varies from one approach to another. The
level at which interconnection should be made, the services to be provided to Internet users, and the centralisation or dispersion of the
functions to implement them, all have to be decided against a background of political, technical and economic factors.

One approach envisages that all host computers wishing to engage in
internetworking would implement a common host-host protocol, which
would become an international standard. This would be in addition to
their own local network protocols. The facilities to be provided in
this internet protocol are still under discussion, but they concern
primarily the interconnection of hosts, and any user facilities such
as virtual calls are provided at host level. Another approach, fa-
voured by the PTTs, considers that virtual calls are most significant
at the communications sub-net level. They usually prefer to ignore
any host-level protocols as being of convern only to the users (or
customers). A third approach advocates that all network interconnections should be made at the communications sub-net level.

We take an intermediate position. International standardisation is a
desirable goal, and could lead to a very simple gateway between networks. However, we cannot afford to wait until international standards
have been agreed, and until all networks have been converted to be compatible. From past history, that is unlikely to happen in any medium
term. Moreover, for many practical users the majority of the traffic
will be confined to a single network, with only a small proportion
needing to cross network boundaries. For these applications, a more
sophisticated gateway, mapping the protocols of one network onto those
of another, seems an optimum solution. The different approaches will
be compared in our paper, but we shall concentrate on our preferred
solution.

We shall discuss the facilities that we believe should be provided
at such a gateway. It should appear like a host to both networks, and
will probably interconnect on a virtual circuit basis. It will make
full use of the local routing, flow control and error control facilities
in each network. The gateway will be more complex in order to offer
these facilities, but this will be offset by a reduction and simplification of the extra software required for internetworking in every
other host.

We shall present practical examples of our ideas, and we shall describe some comparative experiments which are now being prepared.

2. THE DEVELOPMENT OF COMPUTER NETWORKS

In this section we first discuss the considerations which led to the development of centralised computer networks, and how those considerations affected the technology used. We then outline the development of distributed networks, and the particular technical decisions which govern their implementation. Finally, we discuss the new issues which arise when different computer networks are connected together.

Centralised Computer Networks

Early on-line computer systems began life as batch-processing systems with communications added almost as an afterthought by the mainframe manufacturer, but eventually users came to appreciate that their new communications-based computer systems were an entirely new tool. This lesson was learned at the expense of some very costly failures. Attention was then concentrated on careful total system design to realise the full potential of the new systems. Communications received special attention, because their effectiveness was a major factor in overall system performance. Moreover, communications links had proliferated, but the cost of communications had increased and, although the computer was still the major cost item, it was increasingly attractive to be able to make moderate savings on communications at the expense of relatively little design effort, and to provide better facilities than those offered by the mainframe manufacturer. The advent of cheaper mini-computers provided the communications designer with a new tool, and a whole new range of options for producing more cost-effective total networks. The portion of the system dealing with data communications was becoming an entity in its own right - the Data Communications Subnetwork. In this paper we shall refer to it as the Subnet. Many different topologies and modes of operation were studied. Algorithms were devised for comparing star, multidrop and ring networks, and much research effort went into extending the potential of circuit and message switching operation.

There was a general trend in the use of on-line systems towards centralisation. Small machines have always had some spare capacity to allow for future contingencies, but in dedicated applications this could not be exploited by the general user. On the other hand, if several small machines were replaced by one large installation, the resulting total of spare capacity would be significant. The general picture was of a collection of functionally separate on-line systems, which had made use of the available technology to pool the common parts of their operation, and so to reduce costs. Many systems in this category are in operation today, and some of them have been very successful indeed.

Distributed Computer Networks

Further developments in technology have created new design options, and changed the relative importance of those we already had. Also, new approaches to data base technology have the potential to provide higher management with immediate overall data on the running of their organisation which, if it was available at all from previous fragmented filing systems, could be extracted only at the cost of much time and effort.

The present state of the technology is summarised as follows:

- the cost of processing power has decreased dramatically.

- the relative cost of communications is therefore becoming much more significant

- very large resources can be built which were not previously available (eg 10^{12} bit stores).

- processing power can be cheaply decentralised in the network and allows the potential of packet switching subnets to be exploited.

- higher management will require immediate access to the main data base as an aid to overall policy decisions. This is the "high risk" area in the organisations's operation, and there is a powerful incentive to meet the need to the full.

- data bases can be decentralised at reasonably low cost, or their capability extended on a centralised basis using the new resources.

- specialist sections of organisations can operate autonomously using their own sub-set of the corporation's data base, updated as often as the application demands. The updating, and even partial processing, may require information exchange between autonomous subsets of an organisation or even between different organisations.

Against this background, there is now a strong incentive, in many organisations, to set up distributed computer networks. These consist of different computer systems, and even computer centres, linked by an almost autonomous data communications Subnet. To allow the different computer systems, hereafter called Hosts, to be connected into a single Computer Network, rigid criteria must be defined for the hardware and software interfaces between the Hosts and the Subnet; these interfaces are called Protocols. To allow a process in one host to communicate with a process in another host, a further level of protocols must be defined, and similarly terminal protocols are necessary to allow terminal users connected directly to the subnet to communicate with hosts in a uniform way. Brief descriptions of these protocols for one network, the ARPA computer network, are given in Refs (1,2).

In dedicated computer networks there is often a predominance of one type of traffic. It might be the transfer of large files for RJE operation, or the exchange of many short messages over a period of time where interactive terminals are used, or simply a set of short, discrete, control or status messages. These types of traffic present conflicting requirements when one tries to optimize the design of a system that has to cater for them all.

The practice has been to optimize for the predominant traffic type, and to accept a lower grade of service for the minority traffic types.

The development of larger, general purpose networks, in which there will necessarily be a more even distribution of traffic types, means that we must seek ways of designing and operating the networks so that any type of user will have a high probability of obtaining the grade of service that he needs at a given moment. A very large network should be able to take full advantage of any economy of scale· part of this economy comes from the ability to bulk-buy the network elements at discount prices, but the greatest saving comes from the sheer size of the user population and the resultant smoothing of the instantaneous demand on any one type of resource.

The user who gains access to the large network should thus be able to make use of the processing power or other resource that he needs at a cheaper rate than if he had bought the same resource for his dedicated use. On the other hand he will expect the network resources to be so managed as to guarantee him a high grade of service and a very high availability. This means that the network must cater for all traffic types and modes of operation, and that it must be able to adapt to changes in the traffic mix which will occur with time. Users may come and go, but the large network is a general purpose utility which, once established, will have to provide the desired service for a very long time.

Interconnected Computer Networks

Internetworking is a natural extension of the process which led to the setting-up of individual large computer networks. It poses the same design problems as any single network, plus a whole range of additional problems. The study of internetworking began with various research organisations, but its aim is to satisfy the desire or need of real-world users – government, military, commerce – to intercommunicate or to share each other's resources.

In some cases it will be acceptable for all the relevant Host systems to agree together to use a single subnet; in this case a single Computer Network would be formed, according to our terminology. In other cases this solution will be impractical. The separate organisations may have such an investment in their existing or proposed Computer Networks, that a fresh start will be out of the question. It is in this case that interconnecting different Computer Networks, or Internetworking, becomes a firm requirement.

Individual networks always have a central authority responsible for their design and operation. There is thus the opportunity of conceiving the network as a total system. In some cases hardware and software may be compatible throughout a network. In others, or where a new user wishes to be attached, there is the option of buying compatible equipment, or developing other arrangements to match the existing equipment to the official network standard. The ARPA Computer Network (Ref.3) is an example of a very large network in which there is commonality of hardware and software within the communications subnet. On the other hand the attached Host computers represent a very wide range of machines which differ greatly in the manner of their parochial operation, but which communicate readily with one another through a common set of network protocols. Each host, on joining the network, had to agree to implement a standard interface, which included the Network Control Program (NCP).

When we attempt to extend this principle to internetworking, the problems are much harder to solve. Here there is no central authority responsible for the overall design, and indeed it is not always possible to define what we mean by the 'overall system' in this case. The individual networks may exist already, which in future will have to be interconnected. The networks have developed already along individual lines to suit their own needs, and represent a wide variation of size, purpose, hardware, software, topology, and method of operation. An obvious approach would be to devise and seek agreement for a set of international standard protocols which all networks would have to implement. This may be a worthy long-term aim, but it is hardly a realistic approach to the immediate problems of internetworking because:

- International agreement is always a protracted process, and success is by no means certain.

- Many existing networks, and those which are under development, have their own service requirements and protocols, and a considerable political and financial interest in preserving them.

- Some very large users, notably the PTTs, are proceeding independently with their own experimental systems, and in some cases have already announced their eventual commercial systems (Ref.4.5)

The PTTs' concern, so far, is only with the subnet. No body yet exists which has any real power or charter to bring any standardisation to the high level protocols. Around specific subnets like ARPANET, CIGALE (Ref.6), the European Informatics Network (EIN) (Ref.7), or EPSS (Ref.8), the Host operators are determining the high level protocols. The only body so charged is the Internetwork Working Group (INWG) of the International Federation for Information Processing (IFIP), but this is not a standardising body, nor representative of all interested parties.

A more realistic goal is to develop a set of protocols for Internet use which can be superimposed on those of individual networks without detriment to normal operation of any local Network. This goal has been approached in several ways:

- All hosts that wish to take part in internetworking could be asked to implement a standard host-host protocol for internet use, in addition to their local Network protocols. The Transmission Control Program (TCP) (Ref.9), and two protocols (Ref.10,11), have been produced to meet this requirement.

- Networks could be left to operate in their normal fashion, but there could be agreement on a standard user service - a type of interchange that could be presented as an entity at the gateway to a neighbouring network and be passed on correctly without either network needing to become involved in the detailed working of the other. In cyclades (Ref.12) this basic service is the "datagram", while the BPO EPSS (Ref.8) and the French PTT RCP and Transpac systems (Ref.13,4) have selected the "virtual call" as their basic services.

- Networks could be invited to provide a more comprehensive range of basic services, using local network procedures and controls. A much simpler internet Transmission Control Facility module would then be added to each host and gateway to provide necessary controls at internet level, or to add any common facility that might be unavailable in a specific intermediate network.

Each of these approaches is associated with a specific gateway concept. and we shall discuss each of them in turn, as well as the set of basic internet services that we propose. There is however one major constraint that may affect any or all of these approaches, and that is the presently unknown policy of the PTTs towards internetworking. The policy may well differ according to whether the networks are private, public or both, and whether they cross international boundaries when connected. The PTTs have a necessary and legitimate interest in accounting for all public or international traffic, but the way in which they choose to gather their accounting information or to exercise their controls will have a profound effect on the design of any facilities for internetworking. For example, tarriffs might be based on any combination of traffic volume, traffic type, connection time, circuit length, time of day or use of network facilities. Accounting data would constitute a massive overhead both for the PTT and the user who exercised his right to check the accuracy of his charges. In the case of internetworking there would be the even more difficult question of charge sharing, and the status of transit networks. These are all very complex issues, but their resolution is long overdue if meaningful designs for internetworking are to proceed.

3. USER SERVICES IN INTERCONNECTED NETWORKS

Many users have developed their own highly sophisticated interprocess communication for specialised purposes. It would be impossible to cater for them all at internet level. However, it should be possible to provide a basic service for the general user. and to do it in such a way that more complex exchanges can be readily synthesised by suitable combination of tne basic service 'building blocks'. This approach has the advantages that even the simplest networks could engage in internetworking, while networks which already use more sophisticated techniques could continue to do so for intra-net purposes.

We consider that a user could build up whatever kind of communication he might require, given this set of three basic facilities:

- A simple, single message, with comprehensive control header, which can be delivered reliably without further action or intervention by the user. (Datagram).

- An ordered sequence of messages in each direction which, thanks to an end-to-end set-up procedure, requires fewer control fields per packet. (Virtual Circuit).

- A longer sequence of messages in one direction, which has a minimal overhead of control information per packet, This requires a special end-to-end set-up scheme. (Bulk Data Transfer).

We assume that this is the total internetworking requirement, and that the source, destination, and any intermediate local networks, have the flow, error, and sequencing controls as well as the routing ability to give all three services. It does not concern us that certain of these functions may be performed at Host level in some networks and at Subnet level in others. The fact that they are defined and standardised would allow them to be offered as Subnet services in certain types of system; they would however be available as services from all systems.
We shall now discuss the attributes of these three services.

The Datagram Service

The Datagram is one of the services being considered by CCITT, and the one which has received the widest acceptance (Ref.14). The user will deliver to the network a message up to 255 bytes in length, together with control information in a standard format. The network will then deliver the message to the addressee (or gateway in the case of internet messages), guaranteeing a high probability that the message will be delivered success-fully and undamaged, and inform the user of success or failure to deliver.

An essential feature of the datagram is that it is treated as a unique message, No attempt is made to preserve the order of a set of datagrams exchanged between a pair of users, no resources need be reserved for a datagram in transit, and indeed intermediate nodes can forget the existence of an individual datagram once they have received an acknowledge-ment that their neighbour has received it. It follows that the datagram has to take with it all the control data needed to ensure successful delivery. Where the user's datagram is genuinely a single message, this necessary overhead may amount to 10 or 12 bytes. The datagram in this form may well satisfy the needs of many users.

More usually, however, the datagram will not by itself be able to meet the user's needs because the order of transmission and reception has to be preserved. If the network cannot do this, then the user must do it for himself by adding sequencing information, and so reducing the space left for data in his 255 byte field. If the user needs a virtual circuit, or special facilities for file transfer, then if the network does not provide them he must take up even more of the data field to carry the extra control information needed. This adds to the communication overhead, which is already larger than it need be because each packet in a multi-packet message has to carry all its own control data, including addresses. In the case of internet messages, extended addressing is needed in any event, and the space left for the user's message is further reduced. One proposal for an internet protocol (Ref 10) that would permit each packet to carry control data for flow and error control as well as sequencing and duplicate detection information, requires a total of 32 bytes of the user's data field to be surrendered.

Virtual Circuit Service

A Virtual Circuit service was also outline in Ref.14 but there is as yet little agreement on the details that such a service ought to provide. In principle the service is designed to help users who wish to exchange ordered sequences of messages between the same locations. Individual messages may be either single or multi-packet, but they will be logically linked to other messages. The most obvious case of this is an interactive terminal dialogue, where the individual messages are separated by the system's response time, or the thinking time of the operator. This type of traffic is growing faster than any other, and it is particularly important to be able to handle it in an efficient manner. The user may well want to specify facilities and controls in addition to those provided by the basic datagram service, and there is no reason why he should have to specify these, or the source and destination addresses, more than once.

In operation, a virtual circuit may be requested by a form of control datagram which give the source and destination addresses, and the other parameters of the virtual circuit. The network allocates a "connection number" and as the datagram finds its way through the network in the usual way each node and gateway takes note of the parameters. In this way a route is established which subsequent packets must follow, but because of the advance warning given, such packets can carry a much reduced header with the address fields, for example, replaced by the connection number.

Bulk Data Transfer

At present the subnets do not normally make provision for bulk data transfer. It has been considered essentially a Host function, so that bodies, like CCITT, who are considering subnet facilities, have ignored it. The need has been recognised both by ARPANET and by the EPSS User community, but in neither case is the protocol part of the subnet; we believe that such a standard is necessary for internetwork use. Nowadays most on-linetransaction processing tends to use short messages to interrogate or to update some central file system, but RJE operations already need bulk data transfer facilities. There is, moreover, a trend towards the creation

of very large Data Bases to meet the total information needs of large
organisations. With the relative costs now in favour of remote processing
rather than simply remote communication, it will become more and more
attractive for individual sections to run an appropriate sub-set of the
organisation's data base on a local mini-computer, and to update it by
bulk data transfer as often as the particular application demands. There
will thus be a general requirement for a bulk data transfer service.

With bulk data we are very interested in reducing the communications
overhead per packet still further. Ideally the user might wish to send
one comprehensive header, and then inject the whole file without further
packet headers. This, however, would be unmanageable from the error control
point of view, and retransmissions when errors did occur would offset any
advantage so gained. Moreover, a really large block of data passed in this
way would monopolise network channels at the expense of other users for
an unacceptable time.

Both of these problems may be alleviated by dividing the bulk data into
"records" for transmission. The optimum record size could be determined
by prior agreement, in the simplest case, or dynamically if a particular
network used a suitable flow-control algorithm. In either case, the
principle would be that a comprehensive header would precede each record,
containing sufficient data to ensure correct sequence of the record and
provide data integrity within it. The record header would identify the
record as a serially numbered part of a particular bulk data transfer,
while each packet within the record would need only a count to show its
sequence within the record.

4.   THE REQUIREMENTS FOR CONNECTION OF TWO OR MORE NETWORKS

We have sketched in $2 how user demands are forcing the implementation
of systems allowing users in one computer network to access services
in another. In $3 we have outlined the basic user services which should
be provided to such users in general. To achieve connection requires a
Gateway between the networks. The term "Gateway" arouses extreme concern
in the minds of representatives of the PTTs, because of the specific
connatations a Gateway has in the international telephone network. By
our use of the term "Gateway", we mean the entity which is placed between two or more networks to allow them to communicate with each other.
In reality a Gateway may be sited physically in the premises of the
operators of one of the subnets, it may be an extension of one of the
Switches of one Subnet, it may be distributed over several networks, it
may be in a special site, or even at a user's premises.

Here we discuss first the basic requirements for connecting networks
and hence the facilities required in a network. Next we consider where
Gateways might be connected to the subnets of the separate Networks.
Finally we contrast the advantages of the different forms of connection.

Basic Facilities

We shall now consider the basic common facilities that must be provided
in any viable concatenation of networks: Instructions for use of processes, Addressing schemes, Handling of Internet Packets, Routing between gateways, flow and error controls, and access control and accounting.

- Instructions for Use of Processes. In order for two processes to
  communicate usefully, each will need to know what facilities are
  available at the other, and the detailed procedures for using them.
  The provision and updating of appropriate user directories will be
  a major problem in internetworking.

- Addressing. For internetworking, host and process names within
  one network may follow any convenient local scheme; it is the total
  address that must be unique. Agreement is therefore needed on the
  designation of networks, and the format of address fields to be
  used in an internet header.

- Formation of Internet Packets. Any source process must supply to its
  local host the data to be transmitted, and control data including
  the total destination address. This will be used by the Internet
  Transmission Control Facilities (TCF) within the host, which will
  generate an Internet Packet (IP) of agreed format. The Internet TCF
  passes IPs to and from the local subnet by the appropriate host-
  subnet protocol.

- Delivery of IPs through local networks. An IP in transit through the
  subnet will be indistinguishable from local intra-net traffic; it
  will simply be delivered to the gateway address using the measures
  adopted by that network to ensure reliable delivery. Any extra controls added at internet level must not interfere with these local
  controls.

- Routing Between Gateways. Whatever the method of interconnection,
  the gateway will need to scan the internet header of the IP. In
  general, the gateway will look like a host to both networks. Routing may be done by static routing tables, in the simplest case, with
  specified alternate paths. Dynamic routing would be possible in those
  systems which could accept the higher control overhead.

- Flow and Error Control Functions. In any method of connection, some
  measure of control will be needed at internet level. Implementations
  which by-pass the local network controls will have to do everything
  at internet level. Those which make full use of the facilities
  provided by local networks to ensure reliable delivery between gateways will have a simpler task. In either case the cost-effectiveness
  of the simplest scheme should be carefully considered against the
  higher performance, but greater overhead and complexity, of the more
  elegant schemes.

- Access Control and Accounting. There must be accounting for the
  traffic between networks. There will be cross-billing in most
  cases, and the gateways are the natural point for collecting the
  accounting data. A related function is user identification, which
  is needed for correct submission of bills and also for regulatory
  purposes by the network operators.

Possible Gateway Configurations

We have defined the "Gateway" as the physical entity placed between
computer networks for the purpose of interconnection, and have set
out the basic features which must be present in any interconnection
scheme. We shall now consider the possible gateway configurations, and
comment briefly on the advantages and disadvantages of each. It is
convenient to classify a gateway according to the level at which an
attached network will see it. Thus, a gateway connected directly to
a communication sub-net will have to look like a local sub-net
switching node, while a gateway connected to a switching node
will have to look like a local host (or other device which can
locally be connected to the node).

Gateways at Switching Node Level. A gateway at switching node level
is shown in Figure 1.

  - This is the most complex method to implement; it involves simu-
    lating in the gateway a local subnet switching node for each
    attached network. The gateway is complicated because it has to
    map the entire node-node protocols of one subnet into those of
    the next. These may not both be packet switched. If the two net-
    works are very different in operation, mapping could be very diffi-
    cult indeed.

  - A major disadvantage is the lack of flexibility that this scheme
    affords. Several PTTs, for example, have implemented systems
    which at subnet level use an interim technology or operating
    technique. They plan on updating them later, but there is a
    fundamental requirement that they shall be able to do so without
    changing the user's view of a system. This is not difficult if the
    gateway is at host level, but if the gateway is at lower than
    host level, then changes to either attached subnet will require
    the gateway to be modified, with consequent interruption in
    service.

  - This method also requires a universal addressing scheme for hosts,
    which can be used by the sub-net. Otherwise the IP would have to
    be extracted and scanned, and the gateway would no longer be
    at switching node level. This would impose an extra burden on the
    sub-net protocols, either by addition of fields in some header for-
    mat, or by the need for extra control information to accompany the
    message or packet.

Parellel Connection at Host Level. A host-level gateway, connected
to each network in parallel to local hosts, is shown in Figure 2.

- This has been the most popular approach until now, although there
  is considerable variation between tne ways in which various groups
  have invisaged its practical implementation. The gateway contains
  a complete Internet Host for each attached network (this does not
  exclude the possibility that common functions may be shared between
  the various parts of the gateway). Connection to each network is
  made direct to a local switching node, and all local net host-host
  facilities and controls are by-passed.

- The need to provide all facilities at Internet level means that
  there will be duplication wherever a given facility is also provided by a local sub-net. This will not affect the Internet traffic,
  but may be considered as an unnecessary and therefore unwelcome
  imposition on the local network. This method is however perfectly
  viable, and in principle could be made as comprehensive or as basic
  as the situation demands. The scheme is conceptually simple, but the
  implementations proposed for it have become very complicated, for
  reasons that will be discussed later.

Series Connection at Host Level. A rather special case of a host-level
gateway is where the connection is made in series with a local host.
This is shown in Figure 3.

- In this case connection to each network is made within a local
  host, by the addition of an extra TCF element for internetworking.
  This element is added in series with the local host, and the local
  network therefore sees the gateway as a local host which has been
  given additional responsibility. The gateway common routing and
  formatting functions comprise a special kind of process shared by
  the two halves of the gateway.

- This approach takes full advantage of whatever facilities may be
  already present between hosts in an individual network (sequencing,
  error and flow control, etc.). There is no loss of flexibility by
  this arrangement; on the contrary, where some facility is missing,
  there is the option of adding it between pairs of gateways, where
  the facility is lacking from individual networks only, or of adding
  it to every internet TCF where a new end-to-end facility is required.
  End-to-end controls would be added only to the degree required
  (either generally, or by specific users).

Comparison of Alternative Methods of Connection

The idea of gateways at switching node level is attractive where adjacent
networks have communications sub-nets of identical or very similar characteristics. This does not however apply generally, because not all networks
are packet switched, and those that are do not share a common type or make
of switching node. This method of connection would generally be very difficult to implement, and the detailed implementation would be different for
every gateway. This method is also very inflexible to change.

Either method of connection at host level is viable, but each has its advantages and disadvantages. The method of parallel connection (Figure 2)
appears most attractive to the system designer because he has complete freedom to create whatever internet protocols he may wish, without taking too
much account of what is provided in individual networks. The protocols
required are necessarily comprehensive, and the resulting TCF that has to
be implemented at every internet host and at the gateways is not a small
package. We therefore have to consider, whatever the technical advantages,
whether it will be politically or economically acceptable to individual
networks to implement an internet TCF of this type. After all, the internet
traffic in any one network is likely to be a small proportion of that network's total traffic. The network users may therefore be unwilling to allocate disproportionate resources for internetwork facilities, especially if
it offers to internet traffic a better grade of service than that available
to local traffic.

The protocols of Refs.10,11 are both designed to support the parallel type
of connection. In principle either type, if reduced to its most basic
features, could also be used with the series connection. In practice, this
has not been attempted because each protocol has become associated with one
particular implementation. This is perhaps because there are so few workers
in this field, and because they have to pursue parallel interests which
sometimes conflict. For example, the Transmission Control Program (Ref.9),
proposed as an implementation of the protocol of Ref.10, has become very complicated indeed over the past few months, as a result of efforts to make
it compatible with these requirements:

- Internetwork experiments between Stanford University and UCL (the
  first between workers in the UK and US).

- The search for a replacement host-host protocol for Arpanet.

- The special demands of packet radio work (Ref.15).

- Other internetwork experiments internal to the US.

It is because of our doubts over the willingness of real-world users to
accept complex schemes for internetworking that we at UCL have put forward
the idea of the series connection at host level (Figure 3). We feel that it
has promise as a practical method of internetworking, and that it should be
investigated to the same degree as the parallel connection method.

The advantage of this scheme appears to be its simplicity, and the ease with which it could be incorporated in even the smallest host of gateway machine. What happens to a particular message as it makes its way through individual networks may appear rather complicated, but that need not concern us. The series connection is at a slightly higher level than the parallel connection, and as such is independent not only of the local subnet protocols, but of the local host-subnet protocols as well. The TCF construction is completely modular in terms of extra facilities that can be added at internet level, and we believe that it is an ideal vehicle for evaluating the most important tradeoff in internetworking: the penalty in practical terms of accepting a performance less the ideal, versus the cost and complexity of the extra control mechanisms needed to approach ideal performance.

We think it important to try and evaluate the relative performance of the series and parallel methods of connection. This will have to be done with the protocols stripped to their bare essentials, and repeated as each basic function is added or augmented. We believe, though only experiment will tell, that in those networks which implement the virtual circuit (such as EPSS and RCP), and for a given level of complexity in the internet software, the series method will prove the more cost-effective solution.

5.   CONCLUSION

Our conclusions are few and simple:

- There will be an increasing demand to provide interconnection facilities between existing and planned computer and data networks.

- There will be a requirement for three basic services to users: datagram, virtual circuit, and bulk data transfer. Not all of these will necessarily exist at subnet level.

- Facilities which must be provided to allow concatenation of networks include: Instructions on how to access foreign processes; an agreed addressing scheme; an agreed internet header, which must be part of the data to be passed between networks; at least one gateway common to the two networks; routing between gateways; control functions at internet level; access control and accounting.

- It is application dependent whether to have the gateway connected to the networks at subnet level, or as special gateway Hosts with special internet protocols, or as normal Hosts with slightly increased functions. Particularly for connecting existing networks, or where there are serious incompatibilities, we believe the third method to be a simple and practical solution.

- The optimisation of network design depends greatly on the constraints imposed by PTT tarriff structures and regulatory policy. It is vital that the PTTs should consider and announce as soon as possible their intentions towards internetworking.

ACKNOWLEDGEMENTS

This work was carried out under a Defence Fellowship awarded by the
Ministry of Defence. The authors wish also to acknowledge the fruitful
exchange of ideas they have enjoyed with workers at ARPA, Stanford
University, the National Physical Laboratory and the BPO, and the facilities of ARPANET which made possible much of the discussion.

REFERENCES

1.   "Current Network Protocols", ARPA Network Information Center,
     NIC 7104, 1973.

2.   S.D.Crocker et al, "Function Oriented Protocols for the ARPA Computer
     Network", SJCC 40, p 271, 1972.

3.   ..G.Roberts and B.D.Wessler, "The ARPA Network", Computer Communication
     Networks, Prentice Hall, 1973, p 485.

4.   ---, "Protocols Standards d'access au Reseau Transpac", Centre Commune
     d'Etude de Television et Telecommunications, TCF/R/DT/6/75.

5.   "DATAPAC" preliminary specification, Trans Canada Telephone System
     (Computer Comms Group) November 1974.

6.   L.Pouzin, "CIGALE, The Packet Switching Machine of the CYCLADES Computer
     Network", Proc IFIP 74 Congress, Stockholm p 155.

7.   D.L.Barber, "Progress with the European Information Network", ICCC,
     proc 2nd Int Conf on Computer Comm, 1974, p 215.

8.   D.Pearson and D.Wilkin, "Some Design Aspects of a Public Packet Switched
     Network", ICCC, proc 2nd Int Conf on Computer Comm, p199.

9.   V.Cerf et al, "Specification of Internet Transmission Control Program",
     INWG 72, December 1974.

10. V.Cerf and R.Kahn, "A Protocol for Packet Network Intercommunication",
     IEEE Trans, vol C-20, No 5, p 637, May 1974.

11. H.Zimmermann and M.Elie, "Transport Protocol. Standard Host-Host Proto-
     col for Heterogenous Computer Networks", INWG 61, April 1974.

12. L.Pouzin, "Presentation and Major Design Aspects of the CYCLADES Com-
     puter Network", IEEE Proc 3rd Data Comms Symp, 1973, p 80.

13. R.Despres, "RCP,the experimental packet switched data transmission ser-
     vice of the French PTT", ICCC Proc 2nd Int Conf on Computer Comm,
     1974, p 171.

14. "Proposal for some basic elements of Public Packet Switched Services", CCITT Study Group VII, Question 1/VII point C, April 1974.

15. R. Kahn, "The organisation of computer resources into a packet radio network", Proc NCC 1975, p

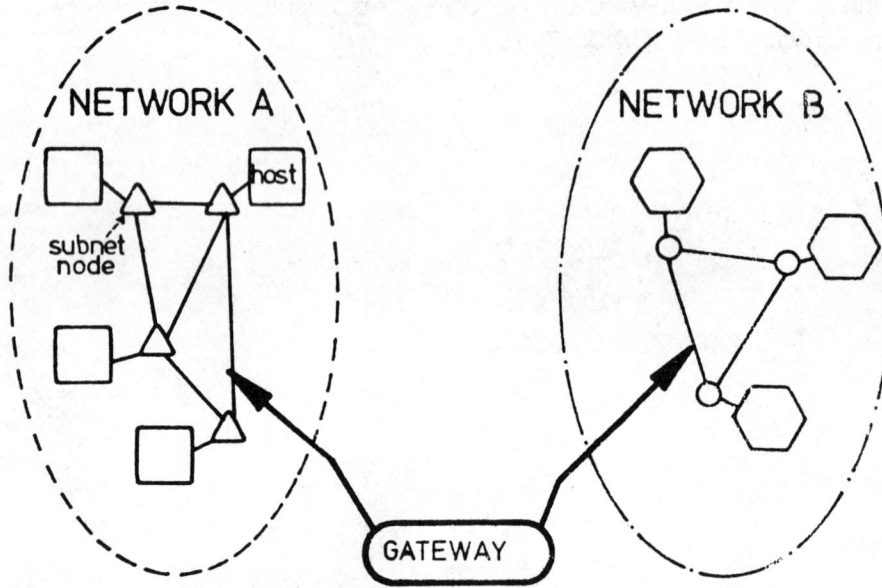

Fig.1a. Gateway at Switching Node Level.

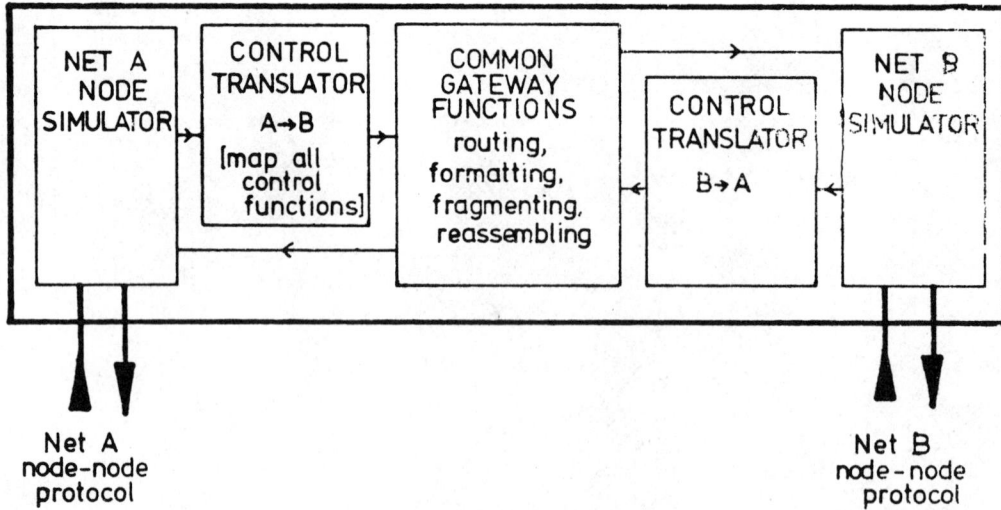

Fig.1 b. Schematic of Gateway.

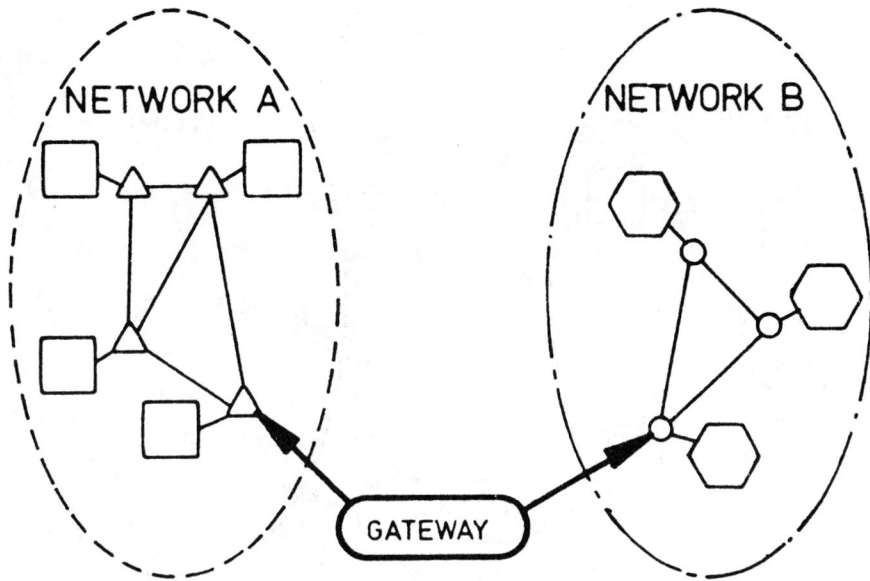

Fig.2a. Parallel Connection at Host Level.

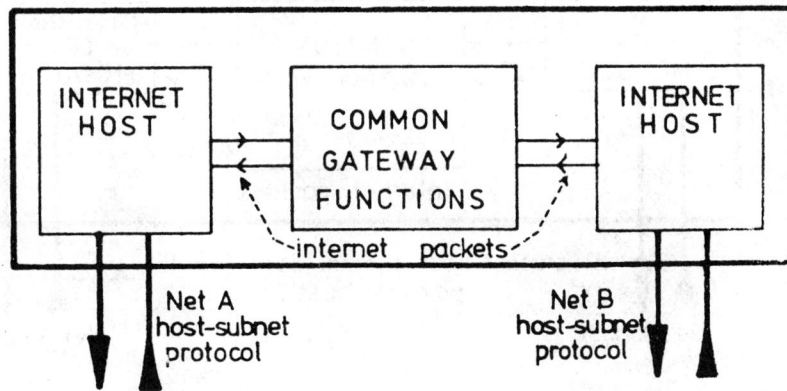

Fig.2b. Schematic of Gateway.

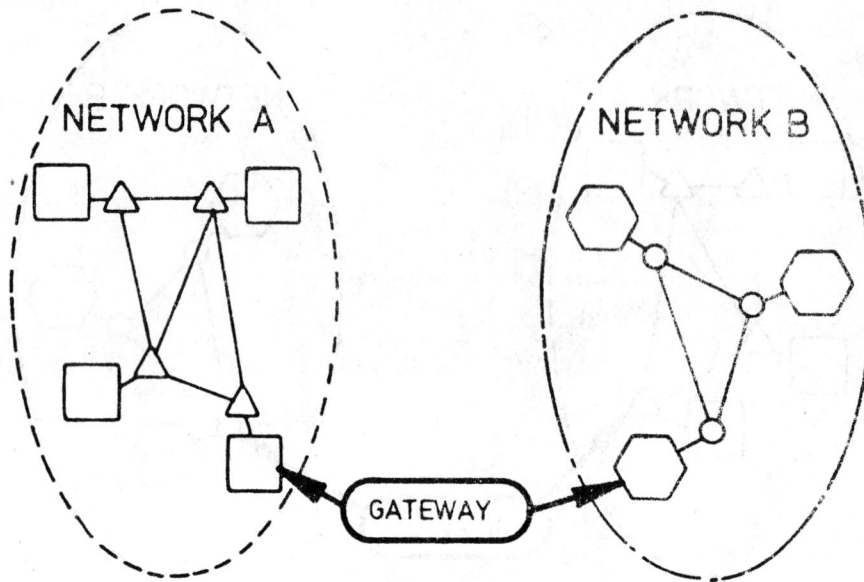

Fig.3a.Series Connection at Host Level.

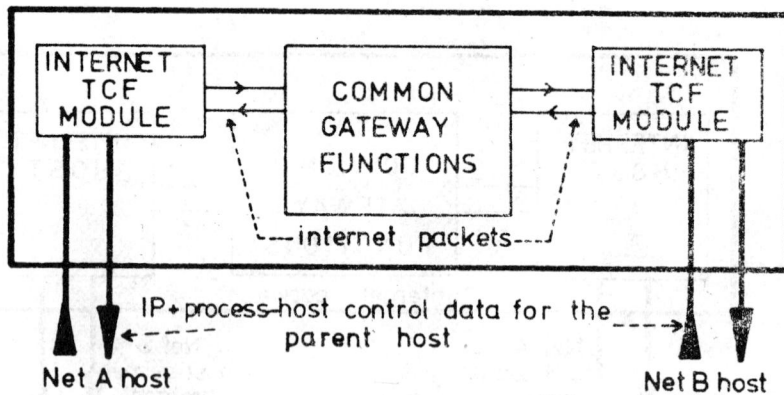

Fig.3b. Schematic of Gateway.

Command language design for networks of processors

Dr. I.A. Newman, Senior Lecturer,
Mr. N.S. Fitzhugh, *
Computer Studies Department,
Loughborough University of Technology
UK

ABSTRACT

This paper is concerned with the problems of designing a unified command language for use on a network of dissimilar processors. The requirements of the user are studied to produce a conceptual structure of a command language. From this basis and a consideration of the ways in which a network can be used, a sub-model suitable for the specification of network commands is developed. Finally, examples of typical network commands are given illustrating how the ideas proposed would appear to the user.

*This author wishes to acknowledge the support of the S.R.C.

1. INTRODUCTION

The design of a suitable command language for a network of dissimilar processors is self-evidently closely related to the search for a universal job control language which has been engaging the efforts of a large number of research workers over the last few years.

The work on the subject has been impelled by the realisation that converting job control, when machines were changed, was becoming an order of magnitude more time consuming than converting the programs which actually do the work [1]. Three main types of approach to the problem are evident, 'the pure research', 'the general solution to a particular problem', and 'the pragmatic compromise'. The first two are the province of the individual or of a small group at one site while the last is the 'committee' solution.

Committees to study possible common command languages have been set up by:- CODASYL, who, at the moment, are attempting to find a common functional subset of existing control languages; BCS, who have defined various types of computer use and are attempting to define the require- ments of users who use the computer in each of these ways; Dutch Group, who defined job control in terms of data flow and are attempting to formulate a language in these terms.

IFIP Technical Committee 2 is also concerned with this problem, sponsoring a conference in the summer of 1974 to provide an international exchange of information [2] and deliberating the formation of a co- ordinating group.

The individual efforts to solve specific problems with reasonable generality have both been in this country. The General Command Languages (GCL) was produced at the U.K. Atomic Energy Laboratories at Culham to provide a suitable language for translation on a satelite machine for transmission of jobs to remote hosts using the standard remote job entry interface to the mainframe [3].

The UNIQUE command language was designed at Nottingham University to interface users painlessly with the George 3 system on an ICL 1906A and to give them access to other machines through remote job entry links[4,5].

The research efforts have been more numerous but it is worth noting in particular the ABLE language produced at Bristol University which provides a general purpose high level language incorporating job control[6].

Three other high level, but machine dependent, starting points are worth mentioning in the context of a search for a suitable job control language:- The Job Organisation Language (JOL) designed for IMB 360/370 machines, which translates to O.S. and is probably the only marketed job control language; the Burroughs Workflow Language (WFL); and the ICL new range job control language. All three, although designed for a particular machine, are of a high enough level to be a possible starting point for a machine independent command language.

The developments and discussions described above are all concerned with providing batch processing facilities, the BCS group, the UNIQUE command language and the ICL SJCL are also concerned with providing facilities for users of interactive terminals.

None of the groups or individuals mentioned above have been explicitly concerned with the problems of job control for a network. Two existing networks, the ARPA network and the French network, have 'solved' the problem by providing a network command language which has to be used in addition to (or on top of) the host JCL at the target site. This has not proved very satisfactory and ARPA users are studying the problem of providing a general interface language. The one approach which appears to be ruled out on the evidence of a study in Germany [2] is the translation of existing job control languages into one another; the result, even for simple jobs, is too voluminous.

The remainder of this paper will follow the user oriented approach to command language design. The basic tenets of the approach and the model of a computer system on which it is predicated are both explained for a single computer. It is then demonstrated that the same framework can be applied to the general problem of a network of (basically self-sufficient) machines. The advantages of the method in terms of simplicity, self-consistency, and coherent security of information are stressed. One possible form of the network command language interface is introduced in the final section.

2.   USER ORIENTED COMMAND LANGUAGE DESIGN

The most promising approach to the design of a command language which would work on a network consisting of a variety of dissimilar machines appears to be to start from the user requirements and to map these on to the computers.

Most users are aware only of the externals of any operating system. A new approach to operating system design seems likely to emerge incorporating this fact [7]. Currently, however, it seems that the user is offered JCL facilities which fit the existing operating system. It would seem to be a sound notion to design the operating system upon the basis of an abstract Command Language. In this way the user-machine interface provides the model for the operating system actions, (i.e. the semantics of the operations carried out by job control commands are determined by considering the user expectations of the commands rather than deciding what the code does and then specifying the job control language).

This paper outlines the requirements of a command language as related to the uses to which it will be put and develops a command language model which it is argued would satisfy these requirements. The technique of studying the use of the system is applied to provide a model of a network. The command language requirements for the network are then expanded in terms of the preceeding models. It is demonstrated that structures developed in the model should be applicable to any real system.

2.1 Requirements of a Command Language

The command language is essentially an interface between the user
and the computer operating system with communication in both directions.
Once it is accepted that this is the raison d' etre for a command
language then it follows that it must be designed to satisfy user needs.
The user is not, of course, the only determinant of the requirements for
a command language, since the needs of the system manager have to be
considered, but the user is certainly the prime consideration, (if there
were no users then there would be no system and therefore no system to
manage!)

Thus the manner in which the user population use the computer
systems will be taken as a starting point for determining the requirements.

2.2 Use of Computer System by its Users

It can reasonably be assumed that everyone who uses the computer
has a problem to solve, be they DP men, engineers, or computer scientists.
It follows that they are generally interested in the solution and not, in
the first instance, in the internal processes which are employed by the
system to achieve that solution.

If a computer system is to be used as a tool in aiding problem
solution, the problem itself must first be expressed in a form such that
an algorithmic solution is possible. This has then to be coded into a
form acceptable to the computer. Having done that, the user must supply
this coded form to the system and wait for results. The initial problem
he wanted to solve has now been replaced by three (often equally
different) problems:-

a) The 'language' to code the algorithm in

b) The mechanics of accessing the computer

c) The instructions to the computer system which enable his
     coded solution to be executed.

The instructions to the computer on how to carry out the task in
hand are the last but often the most difficult part of the problem solving
process. As far as the user is concerned there is no obvious need for any
such "rubbish" as it does not really relate to either his problem or to
him.

For many users the problem of job control is worse when they do not
have a program they have written themselves, merely the specification of
a package, the names of some files, and some data. They have to bind
these components together with job control commands to produce a
meaningful result in a finite time.

Thus no matter what the user background, academic, industry, or
commerce he invariably begins his computing career with what can be
termed - Simple Jobs. These consist of card deck (or paper tape),

program (or package call), with appropriate data. The job is input,
(compiled) and run, with line printer output. He becomes more aware of
the facilities he can use through observing what the computer does to
his Simple Job, conversing with other users, through formal courses, and
by the demands of his work. He may require additional facilities to
help him solve his problem, in which case he is motivated (or forced) to
discover how to use them himself. As a consequence the user may develop
his expertise from the Simple Job through definite phases to become a
proficient user. However, not all users by any means attain this pinnacle.
In fact a large number never progress past the Simple Job stage, and
those that do, still frequently use Simple Jobs.

The user population profile can be built upon this basic premise.
Thus as the facilities become more complex and esoteric fewer people try
to make use of them. In fact, it is possible to place the facilities in
a loose order having the property of natural extensions - the deeper you
go the fewer people there are. This model can never be complete due to
the continuing developments, but it can reflect the current state of the
abstract ideal.

It is this model that forms the basis for developing the primitive
notions of command language in the following section of this paper.

Having studied the uses of the system it is possible to summarise
the user requirements as:-

1. Simplicity - Most users are running 'simple' jobs most of the
    time. Simplicity implies ease of use, understanding and
    readibility. All too often in the past languages have been
    bedeviled by special control symbols such as brackets, commas,
    asterisks, slashes and ampersands. These symbols have no
    counter part in the natural languages and only serve to confuse
    the user. Sensible and well defined responses from the system
    are also essential if a simple user interface is to be
    maintained. Nothing is more dismaying than an incomprehensible
    message in reply to an apparently correct (from the book)
    request. Responses should clearly be related to the commands
    used to avoid this situation.

2. Extendability - If the straightforward job should be simple to
    do, it also follows that a slightly more complex job should not
    be a lot more difficult. Current job control languages cope
    with the simple job by introducing macros, or catalogue
    procedures, (this provides the simple user-machine interface
    although it does not usually solve the machine-user message
    problem) however the slightly more difficult task still requires
    much more work. Extensibility should in the ultimate allow the
    full facilities of the system or any subset of them to be
    available to the user by building on his previous knowledge.
    He should not be required to discard what he has already done
    just because he wishes to access a new facility.

3. Machine Independence - It is self-evident that the user does not care, nor does he wish to be aware of the actual machine that is solving his problem, thus the current necessity for him to learn a different interface language (and to learn to interpret different system messages) for each new system he comes in contact with seems highly undesirable.

2.3 Use Of The System by the System Manager

The system manager (and his team) may, and usually is, a user(s) like any other user with the same requirements. In addition however he has the task of sharing the available resources between the 'proper' users and of maximising the useful work done by the system as a whole.

The existance of the system manager, or rather the fact that computing resources are limited, and a system manager is needed adds two more requirements to the list:-

4. Efficiency - Time spent carrying out job control commands is time wasted.

5. "Schedulability" - The language must permit (even require) the user to state his computer resource requirements with the understanding that the original criteria of simplicity and machine independence are not violated.

3. HIERARCHICAL MODEL OF A COMMAND LANGUAGE SYSTEM

The previous section introduced the requirement for a simple extendible command language. It was suggested that a hierarchical structure would be the most effective way of satisfying the criteria specified.

The conventional command language is shown in Fig.1. This commences with the system facilities, then at the sole other level, the user commands are added.

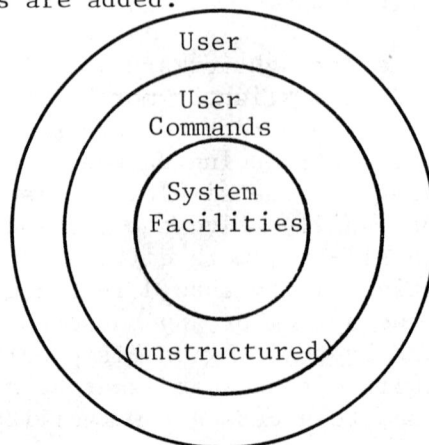

FIG 1 : CONVENTIONAL SYSTEM

A hierarchical model for a command language system has been devised at Loughborough in order to examine the feasibility of the 'top down' approach for providing a command language interface to existing computer systems. The approach commences with a small subset of commands at an inner-most (least complex use) level (Fig.2).

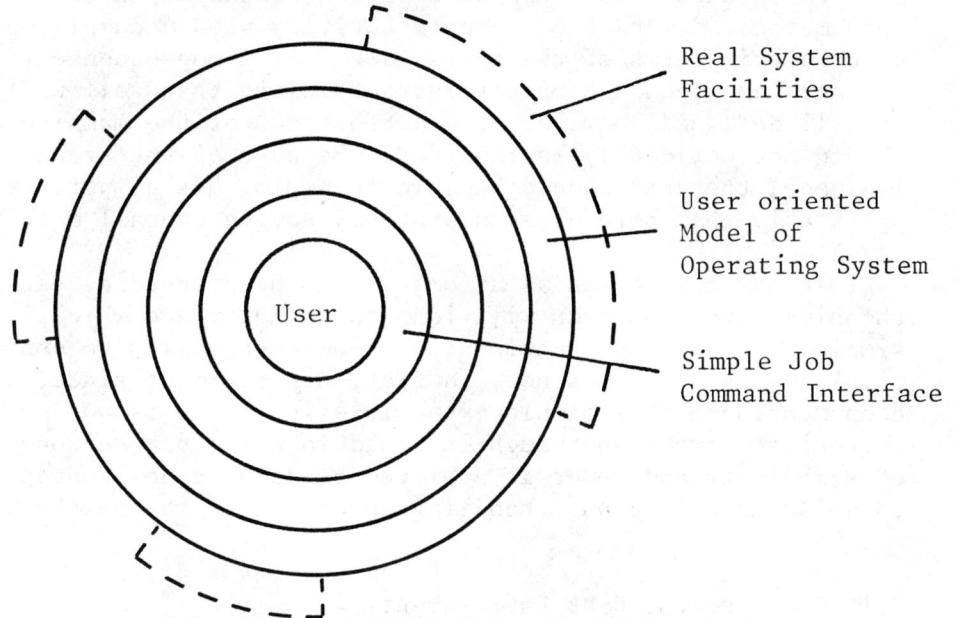

FIG.2 : HIERARCHICAL COMMAND LANGUAGE MODEL

The subset is then continuously and coherently extended to encompass more complex facilities. Each level in the model encompasses all inner levels (i.e. is a superset of inner levels), conversely each inner level is a true subset of the preceeding level. The outer-most level of the model is thus the complete representation of a user oriented operating system. This must in turn be interfaced to real systems which is indicated in Fig.2 by an extra broken ring (broken since any real system may have some restrictions in terms of the facilities which can be implemented).

This method satisfactorily solves the problem that no language can ever be designed to encompass all possible uses now and in the future, however it is the outer-most (most rarely programmed) facilities which normally need to be added to the model, while the subset presented at the inner-most level changes very rarely. Thus it is our contention that a user of a single computer can receive all the benefits of the connection of his computer to a network without needing to make any changes and without being explicitly aware of the enhancement. This is justified in the following section.

The model implies a high level user oriented command language approach such that a user with a simple job only requires to know a very small subset of the possible commands (and command uses). Both the number of commands and the scope of a given command can be extended as the usage requirements become more complicated.

Communications Networks

This paper does not make proposals about implementation in the theoretical design, (the step from the model to the real system in Fig.2) but the practicalities have not been ignored. As computing stands at present it is necessary for the Command Language to be mapped on to existing JCLs. This is not the most convenient method as the commands have to be either interpreted or else translated into the target JCL. Both methods demand the converse activity when decompiling system messages which are in terms of the target JCL. As a consequence the High Level Command Language is probably less efficient than well written host JCL. If well designed, however, the performance of the machine and users should not noticeably be impaired. Because of the transparency of the language, the user should be able to employ his computer time more profitably than before, even probably saving overall machine time.

It has been taken as axiomatic in the preceeding paragraph that the high level approach will lead to an interface which is minimal for simple tasks but is capable of piecewise expansion to cope with more complex jobs. This is not, in fact, self-evident since, as has already been mentioned, the simple extensible interface is not provided by current systems even though it could in principle be done. The combination of simplicity and power is achieved by using a new conceptual approach to defaults and default handling described in the next section.

3.1 Creating the User Environment

In conventional systems the user environment is produced from the defaults, and the associated parameter values, specified in the job control file. If a facility is required the user has the option of using the default values provided by the system or he may overwrite some or all, with his own values. The macro and catalogued proceedure systems are unstructured so both the simple and the complex jobs use the same procedures. Thus the simple-minded user needs to be aware of the default values that exist for the general and more complex cases. Thus the user environment is a hotch-potch of macros or catalogue procedures calls with some, or all, of the default parameter values replaced by user specified values.

The hierarchical user orientated model shown in Fig.2 can be employed to create the user environment by mapping it onto a tree structure as shown in Fig.3. As the user moves up the structure more system variables which can be manipulated are apparently exposed to him.

He need not be aware of the variables unless the facilities used demand knowledge of this level of the user model. If he employs a facility at level n say, then he "sees" only a box at this level. Levels n+1 etc. will have the variables pre-set according to the current system default values and these will be masked from the user. Should he wish to modify a default value at level n+1 then he, figuratively, is now allowed to look inside the box at level n and thus is made aware of the parameters representing the facility at level n+1.

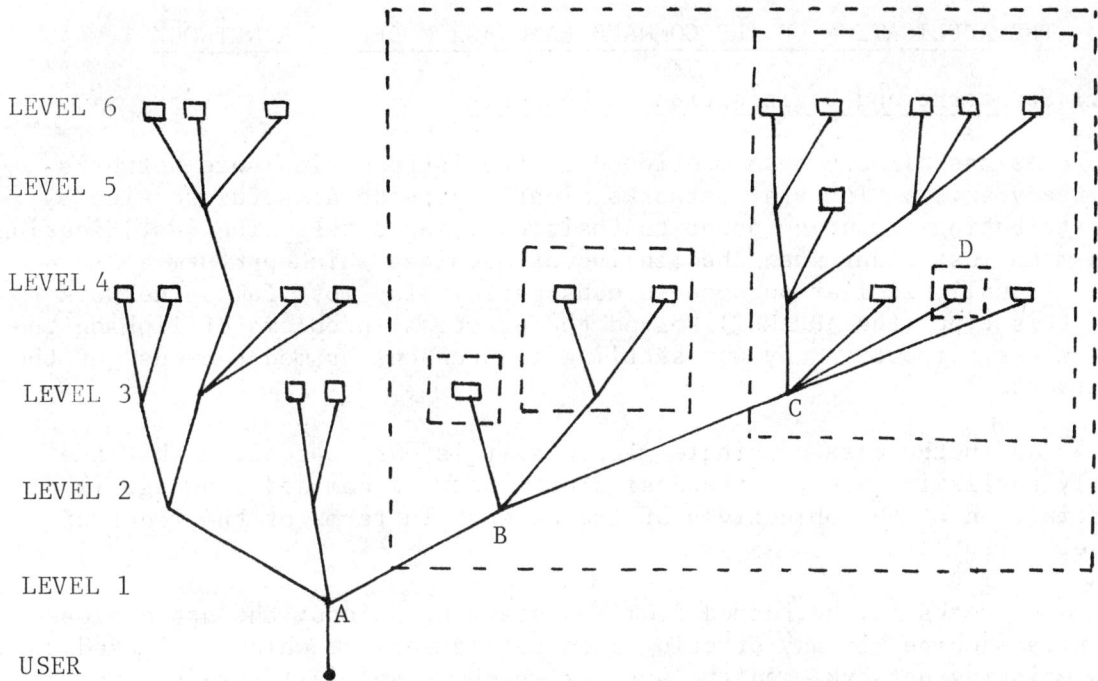

FIG 3 : THE USER ENVIRONMENT

The small square boxes represent the terminal leaves of the structure.
These can be thought of as being the default values provided by the
system. The user at LEVEL 1 (the node A) is aware of three facilities
one of which is indicated by the large dotted rectangle. If he uses
the facility at B then he sees the next level which again consists of
three facilities each of which possess default values. At point C
he sees three further default values, and so on.

The establishment of a user environment which can vary with the
user and his different uses is the fundamental prerequisite of an
'intelligent' user oriented command language. Ideally the system
could keep a history of the interaction of each user and anticipate
his likely needs, more pragmatically a number of likely scenarios
can be established, either by the system or by the user, and the user
can choose one of these at the start of an interaction. The defaults,
so established, must be modified in the light of the actual commands
issued by the user to supplement and replace the default stream.

4. THE APPLICATION OF THE COMMAND LANGUAGE MODEL TO A NETWORK

4.1 Structure and Organisation in Networks

As has already been mentioned in the introduction some networks already exist. The star networks clearly provide a useful service by distributing computing power to their outlying sites. The justification is much less clear when the linking of machines which perform a functionally similar purpose is considered. The most famous network of this type (the ARPANET) solved the practical problems of linking the machines without in any way settling the reasons or modes of use of the network.

As in the case of single machines it is our contention that the only realistic base for the design of a network command language is a definition of the objectives of the network in terms of the modes of use.

Networks may be formed from two starting points: the stand-alone single machine already offering a computing service which is linked to an existing network; and the network which is specially created to serve some existing need. In the first case the user of the existing machine sees an increase in the facilities offered to him, he can do all that he could before with something else in addition; either he can now do some jobs that he could not do before or he can now be more certain that his results will arrive when he wants them. In the second case the network may have been chosen as a solution to the problem for many reasons. The most likely ones are that the multimachine configuration offers more flexibility, greater reliability and more facilities cheaper than a single machine. In either case the user does not really envisage a whole network; at the worst he is forced to see interfaces to a few different machines; at best, and certainly conceptually, he sees a more powerful (computer) system.

4.2 The Network Model

In order to formulate the user-network interface, it is first necessary to define a model of a network in which the interface could be implemented.

The model chosen for this paper is the loosely coupled network [8] which assumes that the network is formed from a collection of machines, all of which can operate independently if the network is severed. Each machine provides a standard set of basic services for its local user population and each machine also offers one or more special functions as its contribution to the functioning of the total network. The advantage of this type of network is that the flow of jobs between machines is minimised and the amount of computer resources wasted in operating system and network control overheads is also reduced. This type of network has an extra advantage in the case where the network consists of a number of widely dispersed sites. The user at a particular site will probably have had his work processed at that site,

if any problems arise the computer staff will be in a much better
position to advise and help him than if his work were being processed
at a site miles away over which they had no control.

The network model is particularly suited to the case where a
single machine is linked to a network but is also applicable where a
new network is created with the goals of minimum software development
and maximum flexibility.

In order to achieve these goals for both types of network it is
necessary to ensure that the work involved in transmitting information
is minimised.

4.3 The User Interface

The loosely coupled network should look to each user as if it is
a single system, being indistinguishable from a self-consistant extension
of facilities on each of the stand alone computers which it links. The
user may require facilities which are only available at a particular site
(other than his own) but the information about the site would normally be
deduced by the system from a study of the facilities he requests rather
than by requiring him to specify the machine explicitly. The knowledge
of the existence of separate machines is equivalent to the detailed
knowledge of the hardware involved in a card reader, say, when all one
wants to do is read an existing pack of data cards.

The consequences of the network and user models described above are
most apparent in the consideration of the storage of information on a
machine and in the handling of the transfer of information (data, jobs,
and messages) between machines. The basic unit of storage and for
transfer is the (text) file and it is the contention of this paper that
this is the principal object manipulated by any command language. The
ramifications of this contention are explored in the following sections.

4.4 Files and the Filestore in a Network

Before this topic is discussed it is necessary to state what is
meant by the term, "filestore". A general definition is required to
deal with all situations.

The concept of a logical file space is adopted in this paper. The
filestore is then analogous to a collection of mathematical sets, where
each set corresponds to a file. Thus a file can be defined as a
collection of objects having at least one common property. In this
definition "object" refers to the composition of the file. For instance,
the "object" in a text file would be the individual words. The
properties range from the trivial case, where the single property is
that the file is composed of the components of that file, to more
complex relations. Thus a file may be a collection of files, or a
component of one file may appear in several other files, or a file may
impose a mapping on another file. In this way the logical file space
encompasses many possible structures from the simple sequential files

to the data base. The filestore is conceptually merely a collection of
sets. Using this as a basis many problems normally associated with
filestores and data bases and tackled as special cases are logically
integrated and a single conceptual solution sufficies for them all.

The logical file concept is not self sufficient. Files to be
useful, must be accessible to the users, and they must be stored on
real, rather than logical devices.

The association between the logical file system and the hardware
is accomplished by a mapping function(s). The choice of mapping
function, and all the other properties of the file, which enables the
user to access the information (or not to if the system security does
not permit it) are conceptually contained in the file directory space.

The combined structure allows for all the normal file handling
requirements including multiple copies, aliases for the same file, plus
various integrity and security classifications for the files.

A conceptual approach incorporating the offline and on-line files
is adopted in this paper. All files are assumed to exist in virtual
store with a mapping function which projects each file onto one or more
physical storage media (e.g. card decks, tapes etc.) When the separate
machines are interconnected, the conventional view allows only online
files to be accessible to each user. Each file that is required, but
not available in the filestore associated with the users local machine,
has to be explicitly fetched. This creates problems of renaming to meet
the uniqueness criteria, ensuring the security of duplicate copies, and
the integrity of the files when updated. This is because the files are
explicitly manipulated across system boundaries.

If the boundaries are removed then the conceptual problems of the
user largely disappear, and the task of the system implementor is
greatly reduced.

The logical filestore approach permits the user to see the
concatenation of the individual filestores with no explicit boundaries
The user accesses the file he requires 'directly' (the implementor
provides different mapping functions to connect the user request to
the physical instance of the file requires). For the simple minded
user he will only "see" the filestore of the machine which he uses.

The files are accessed through a directory which provides the unique
filename composed of machine identifier, user identifier and user
filename. This points to a conceptual file. This in turn, through
the mapping function, provides the physical location, or locations,
of the file. It is seen that the filename provides the link between the
directory and the logical file space. For each directory entry there
is one, and only one entry in the logical file space.   The mapping
function links the filename to the physical devices.   There may be

none, one, or several entries in the physical file space depending on the file being a name only, a single copy, or many copies (for security or because it is being used on several machines).

4.5 System Control

The jobs in the network would normally be performed by the machine connected to the physical device where the job entered. If this machine could not perform the job, probably because of scheduling or hardware requirements, the network would be interrogated to determine if any other machine would accept the job. If the job is accepted by the network, the JCL file is transmitted to the accepting machine. However, if no machine can take the job, the user is informed that this situation has arisen, either immediately, or after an interval of time in which the job has been constantly refused by the network. A mechanism to ensure that no job remains in the queues indefinitely is necessary. This may be the simple time limit, or a more complex algorithm.

Scheduling and accounting are more fully discussed in a companion paper [9].

4.6 Messages and Job Control

If the major item transferred between machines is the file, then it is necessary to explain how the concept could be implemented in terms of the processing of jobs submitted by a user.

The job control supplied by the user would be semi-compiled by the machine at the location where the job had been entered. The semi-compiled form is necessary as the job scheduling requirements must be determined before the job can be performed and it would not be sensible or reasonable to demand that the scheduling requirements be supplied in machine terms in the high level language written by the user. The job control could not however be fully compiled into a machine dependent code as the machine on which the job will run is not determined at this stage.

The scheduling requirements are extracted from the problem oriented commands specified by the user for the job step(s), within the job. The job is then either, queued in this machine, or presented as a whole, or as job steps, to the other machines in the network with a request for assistance. The presentation of the job would be as a file consisting of the scheduling requirements only. If 'agreement' is reached for another machine to accept the job, then the job itself would be transferred as a file to that machine, which then treats it as one of its own jobs.

Messages generated by the job would be stored as a job 'log' file. At the end of the job these messages must be anticompiled to an intermediate form related to the semicompiled command language originally transmitted. This new file is then transmitted to the

originating machine which would generate suitable user orientated
messages. The semicompiled form for the job control and messages has
the same advantage as the single internal code for storing text
information in a filestore and as the single transmission code for
the network linkage. Each machine has only to provide one routine
which will convert to the semicompiled form and one which can convert
from the semicompiled form and <u>not</u> 100 routines for each machine on the
network.

5. COMMAND LANGUAGE FOR THE NETWORK

It is possible to design a command language model for the network
applications. The model must reflect all the points made earlier in
this paper. In particular, the model must demonstrate the principle
of extendibility in relation to the network usage. The other design
objectives proposed in the introduction can only be dealt with in the
implementation of the model as a command language.

The structure is shown below. As the user progresses down the
levels the facilities become increasingly detailed. Of the four levels
shown below the top-most level (1) does not involve the user in any
knowledge of the network at all and corresponds to the inner-most
ring(s) of Fig.2. (By hypothesis this satisfies most of the user-uses
of the system). Although the user does not know about the network this
does <u>not</u> imply that he will not be using it. If a user request a run
of a particular package, and it is not available on the machine at
which his job was input, then the job will be transmitted to a machine
which does run the package and the results will be returned to him
later. The network may also help him if the machine he is connected
to is overloaded and cannot handle his job within the timescale he
specified, provided he gets his output back in time it is immaterial
to him which machine processed his job.

The three levels of network usage can be thought of as:-
working progressively down; the user exercising a choice between
facilities, user knowledge of the existence of subsystems, and user
knowledge of the detailed structure of the network.

Hence the model is as shown.

LEVEL 1   Single machine with potential knowledge of processor, files
          and their dispositions and peripheral devices

LEVEL 2   Resources at   Definable Processor
          many sites   Characteristics

LEVEL 3   Files linked to   Resources at
          particular machines   particular machines

LEVEL 4   Network topology   Physical details of
                                                processor and devices

The parallel structure at the levels indicates components to be
independent yet requiring approximately the same degree of expertise
The serial structure, on the other hand, implies that knowledge of
any level is more complex than preceeding levels, although knowledge
of the upper levels is not always a necessary condition for use of a
lower level.

The commands required to use the network facilities are partly
extensions of existing commands and partly new commands that apply
to the network environment alone. Some examples of the commands
follow. The examples would normally appear in a command language
file but for the sake of simplicity the examples are taken out of
their usual context.

For the purpose of illustration the commands are expressed in
a metalanguage. It is not intended that this should be implemented.

5.1 Processor Characteristics (Level 2)

The processor characteristics form part of the scheduling
requirements of the job or job-step. Thus any combination of the
following commands could be employed and appear as the first set of
commands in the appropriate job step.

        STACK PROCESS
        REAL ARITHMETIC
        PRECISION INTEGER <number>
        PRECISION REAL <number>

5.2 Resources at Different Sites (Level 2)

The resource commands at level 2 form additions to existing
commands. Thus if on a single machine

        PRINT <filename>

prints the named file on the line printer then

        PRINT <filename> AT <location>

will print the file on the line printer at the specified machine
site. Similarly

        PUNCH <filename> becomes
        PUNCH <filename> AT <location>

If

        PUNCH <filename> ON <punch device specification>

where the punch device is a standard punch device, punches on the
appropriate local device then

534 Communications Networks

    PUNCH <filename> ON <punch device specification> AT <location>

will punch out the file at the specified remote site.

    Other similar commands are available for other devices. The
terms INPUT and OUTPUT have been avoided because they are rather
nebulous, PRINT, PUNCH, etc. have been preferred. This does not mean
that these terms may not be used however, for instance if a file is
to be stored on a magnetic tape

    OUTPUT <filename> ON <magnetic tape description> AT <location>

5.3   Resources on a Particular Machine

    For use of particular resources, such as a 96 character line
printer, or special character set devices the same form of command
may be employed as for level 2 resources (the magnetic tape description
could be expanded for example). The device specification in this case
demands a non-standard resource. It is the users responsibility to
ensure that a suitable device exists at the given location, if he
'specifies' both together - clearly if it does not then an error must
be reported.

5.4   File Manipulation on Specific Machines (Level 3)

    The type of commands required for file manipulation on the
network are extensions of the single machine commands. Typically

    CREATE <filename> AT <location>
    DELETE <filename> AT <location>
    STORE <filename> AT <location>
    APPEND <filename$_1$> AT <location$_1$> ONTO <filename$_2$> AT <location$_2$>
    COPY <filename$_1$> AT <location$_1$> FROM/INTO <filename$_2$> AT <location$_2$>

The metasymbol <location> has a range of possible meanings. It
could apply to a geographical site within the network. At the other
extreme it may specify the physical device or devices, and position,
or positions, on that device, or devices. Again, this implies
extendibility of the metasymbol in addition to the language.

    At level 4 the user is so involved with the physical attributes
of the system that he must manipulate the components at a low level.
Consequently it does not appear sensible to attempt to specify the
commands for this level. The language would merely provide a framework
through which access to this level could be obtained.

6. CONCLUSIONS

The paper has proposed a hierarchical command language structure oriented to the requirements of the user. It has been shown that such a structure is well suited to the needs of users of a network, since most users can gain most of the facilities of the network without needing to be aware of its structure. It has also been shown that the same conceptual approach greatly simplifies the problems of filestore access and file integrity in the network and reduces the problems of file security to the same level of difficulty as on a single machine. Finally it is demonstrated that the system is flexible enough to offer different levels of complexity to different users and ultimately to allow users to access any network facility explicitly should they require to do so.

7. REFERENCES

1. Steel, in "Command Languages" ed. C. Unger, North Holland 1975.

2. Krayl, Unger, Weller "On the portability of JCL programs" in "Command Languages" 1975.

3. Dakin, "A General Control Interface for Sattelite Systems" in "Command Languages" 1975.

4. Newman, "The UNIQUE command language"- Portable Job Control" Proceedings DATAFAIR 1973.

5. Newman, McConachie, "A Guide to the UNIQUE command language", University of Nottingham 1974.

6. Parsons, "A High Level Job Control Language" Software - Practice and Experience, Vol.1 March 1975.

7. Morris, "Job Control on the Atlas and MU5" in "Job Control Languages" ed. D. Simpson, NCC 1974.

8. Evans, Newman, "Usage Considerations in Multiple Processor Systems" Proceedings Software 74.

9. Newman, Taylor, "Maximising System Performance by Optimising Scheduling and Accounting Algorithms" (To be published in the Proceedings of Eurocomp 75).

Job control in a heterogenous computer network

P Schicker
W Baechi
A Duenki

Cost 11 (EIN) Project
ETH Computer Centre
Switzerland

ABSTRACT

A distributed stack machine is built on a structure of network services. The machine allows the user to execute a distributed job and solves synchronization problems of concurrent operation. The job control, written in a uniform high level job control language, allows the user to reference virtual devices anywhere in the network. A bulk transfer service extends the I/O systems and enables access to these virtual devices.

Using a Pascal-like notation, an example of a network control job is the vehicle for illustrating language needs at the user level, for suggesting an environment in which the job should run, and for demonstrating problems such as file transfer, error-handling, process creation, parameter passing.

KEYWORDS: job control language, heterogenous computer network, remote file access, file transfer, distributed network application
CR-CATEGORIES: 3.50 4.22 4.32

INTRODUCTION

Resource sharing in a computer network depends on distributed services. We call a service distributed if it is implemented in local stations which communicate with each other according to a fixed protocol. The basic service of the network is the communication facility (in the European Informatics Network this service is implemented in a packet-switching sub-network). Other services make use of this basic one, thus becoming themselves distributed services.

The human user, through a batch or interactive job, wants to access resources. To do this he is aided by services which the operating system provides and which he directs with his job control tool. If he uses distributed services then he has access to remote resources, thus becoming a network user. If he wishes to execute part of his job on a different host computer then his job control must be distributed.

At the same time the user should be to a large extent unaware that he is using a network; and his tool, the job control language, should not be too complicated.

Therefore, we want to give the user a uniform job control language which is supported by each operating system and which makes use of the underlying distributed services.

GENERAL CONCEPT

The basic concept for the control language is its interpretation by a stack machine. This is essentially an arbitrary decision which at the moment seems adequate. A job executing on a single (local) system is directed by an interpreter (interpreting job control statements) which in turn interfaces to the operating system and uses a stack handling mechanism. With the aid of a special protocol the interpreter can request the creation of a subsidiary job somewhere in the network. The subsidiary job, on its turn, has the same structure as the primary job, i.e. executed by an interpreter with interfaces to the operating system and uses a stack handler. To facilitate communication between the primary and subsidiary job we allow the subsidiary job access to the stack variables of the primary job; in other words, the subsidiary job is treated like an inner block, and the standard interpretation of scope of variables is maintained. We have therefore two stack handlers , each handling a different portion of the stack. We want to give these two handlers the possibility to communicate. Hence, we introduce a simple stack handler protocol. If the subsidiary job performs an operation on a variable in the remote portion of the stack then it is only necessary to address the remote stack handler, sending the primitive operation descriptor, the variable reference and a value. Because of the distributed stack handling mechanism, it is advantageous to include a compilation phase. This, e.g. eliminates the need to carry along a symbol table. In turn, the compilation phase invites the possibility of using a high level language.

SYNCHRONIZATION

Variables of type semaphore are defined in the language and the two possible operations, P and V, on these objects are primitives executed, like fetch and store, by that stack handler where the respective portion of the stack resides. Operations on this variable are, therefore, localized (manipulated by a single stack handler) while requests for such operations can originate from any portion of the job which has access to such a variable.

For the high level control language we anticipate constructs which will allow the compiler to assume the burden of synchronizing operations on shared variables and calls on shared procedures. That is, the compiler could introduce a variable of type semaphore and insert the necessary primitives.

DEVICE REFERENCES

Most control jobs will also need to coordinate access to objects which we cannot put on the stack. A file is such an object; the only thing we can put on the stack is a reference which is related to the file. But this is easy to do: In a local environment the user normally supplies sufficient information to identify a file and asks the operating system to create a path to the file and to supply a reference to the start of the path. Typically, the system has a list where it maintains an entry for the file with indications for the device on which it resides, the position, the status, etc. With the addition of a subscriber identification this same reference value would describe a path first to a specific subscriber, where operations on the file can be coordinated, and then within the subscriber to the file. The local I/O system must address the proper remote service, and supply the reference value. Since the transfer may be long and physical data representations may differ between the two subscribers, we introduce a bulk transfer service which offers the local I/O system a (driver-like) interface to the remote service and which also maintains and monitors control and data paths, assists in recoveries, and which places the access control in the hands of the referenced subscriber's bulk transfer service.

Since remote job entry/retrieval, file-to-file transfers, device-to-device transfers, and processes mimicking files all require the same services, we generalize the concept and define a class of objects, virtual devices, which are referenced from the control job by variables of type deviceref. These virtual devices are manipulated by the local operating systems and supported by the bulk transfer service.

Because the bulk transfer service must also support the file-to-file transfers without the assistance of a controlling process, it is desirable to make the data conversion function in, or available to, the bulk transfer service. For simply structured files, e.g. file of integer, the 'data description' can be readily supplied at this level, with, for example, the reference value (this will be our initial approach).

LANGUAGE

If a compilation phase is anyway needed, then a high level language (in the ALGOL class of languages) would be preferable. Basic features would include data types and declarations, structured variables, structured statements (case, while, if, for) which provide good flow control, a sophisticated procedure facility, and a syntax suitable for easy extension. A well designed language and a clever compiler contribute to both simplicity and reliability by

     a)   making unnecessary the manipulation or knowledge of low-level features

b) facilitating   hierarchical   ordering   of
    concurrent processes and data structures
c) analyzing syntactically operations on well
    defined data types and
d) adding   for   syntactically   recognizable
    constructs declarations   and operations which
    implement often used logical concepts.

Since many language constructs will reflect overall
design considerations we will not offer a language
definition now but instead provide an example of a
typical control job and then use this job to demonstrate
some problems such as file transfer, error handling,
process creation, and parameter passing. To do this, we
will use a PASCAL-like notation.

```
    job                                               (1.0)
        var f:deviceref,                              (1.1)
            subB:subscriber ;                         (1.2)
        ..........
        at subB do                                    (1.3)
            f := retrieve ( ...fileX... ) ;           (1.4)
        at find(PASCAL) do begin                      (1.5)
            var lgo: deviceref ;                       (1.6)
            PASCAL ( input=f,object=lgo ) ;           (1.7)
            execute ( object=lgo ) ;                  (1.8)
        end ;                                         (1.9)
    end                                               (1.10)
```

The intention is to submit at any subscriber A a job
which wishes to compile and execute a PASCAL program at
any subscriber C in the network where a PASCAL compiler
exists. The source statements to this PASCAL program
exist on a file at a particular subscriber B. We can now
examine these statements in detail.

TYPES OF VARIABLES   (1.1)(1.2)

A type deviceref allows us to reference remote and local
files, and a type subscriber allows us to designate a
specific subscriber of the network.

REMOTE SUBSIDIARY PROCESSES   (1.3)

The general form of the at statement is

$$\underline{\text{at}} \ \langle\text{subscriber}\rangle \ \underline{\text{do}} \ \langle\text{statement}\rangle \qquad (2.0)$$

It means that the statement is executed at the subscriber specified. There are three actions involved:

a) Transfer of the internal language representation of the ⟨statement⟩ to the indicated subscriber.

b) Creation of a subsidiary job at the subscriber.

c) Execution.

OPERATING SYSTEM VARIABLES

If we allow statements of the job to execute on more than one subscriber then problems arise concerning operating system variables, where we define such a variable to be a means of referencing values supplied and maintained by the operating systems. These variables, which are implicitly declared, would include:

a) global variables such as device references indicating global default files. Such variables are in the primary stack and are accessible by all portions of the job.

b) allowances, such as normally issued for time, cost, resources. These variables are qualified by the primary or subsidiary job, and reside in the local portion of each job's stack. Only local access to these variables is necessary, but the initialization, which is really resource allocation, is a function of either the compiler (static) or of that job which creates the subsidiary (dynamic).

c) Current state variables such as current time consumed, cost incurred, resources owned.

d) ON conditions, error flags.

These last two (c and d) contain information of interest to the preceding or relatively primary jobs. However, the normal scope of variables dictates that these variables are not accessible to the primary job. But job monitoring would need some means of assessing the current running state and accounting needs the sum of the completed states. And the user himself may wish to monitor subsidiary jobs. Therefore, these variables should be qualified by a job reference variable declared in the primary job.

Definition of the operating system variables is essentially a specification of the initialization, monitoring, and completion handling of a distributed job.

ACCESS MECHANISM FOR FILES   (1.4)

The parameters to the function ´retrieve´ identify a file which is known to subscriber B. The reference value returned by retrieve serves as a mechanism for access to the file. Assignment to the variable ´f´ makes this access mechanism available via the distributed stack handler service to subscriber A as f is declared in a block which is executed at subscriber A.

The <statement> part of the at statement terminates, the subsidiary job (at subscriber B) ceases to exist, and the primary job resumes. It is important to note that the value assigned to ´f´ continues to have meaning. Because ´f´ is declared in an outer block the assignment must ensure that the association between the reference value and the file itself exists beyond the life of the subsidiary job which establishes the reference.

It is sufficient within the language only to identify our file; thus files themselves are not objects of the language. The subscriber on which a job statement executes is responsible for the actual data access. The extended input/output system uses the device reference value to address that port of the remote bulk transfer service corresponding to file access and to supply sufficient information to allow the remote input/output facility to find the file. The logical connection is established between the job requesting access to the file and the file itself. With the help of the bulk transfer service the process may now manipulate this file, e.g., read or write it partially or entirely, perform elementary positioning operations, etc.

FAILURES

Suppose now that at subscriber B the file does not exist and therefore the ´retrieve´ is unsuccessful. This is an error and, in our example, it causes termination of the job at B, and then of the job at A. The termination state of the subsidiary job, contained in its operating system variables, is returned to A as part of the normal job completion. There the state of the job at A is adjusted to reflect this additional information.

The language should allow the user to inhibit such terminations and to continue executing at some outer statement. The control job then assumes responsiblity for inspecting and testing the appropriate operating system variables.

If, instead, the job at B is executing and a network bisection occurs which cuts communication between subscibers A and B, then the job at B cannot access the stack variables at A; it can neither continue nor properly terminate. The network should intervene and notify the job at A - essentially simulating an abnormal termination of the subsidiary job. At B the situation is somewhat different. Normally the job should terminate because execution is hampered and no results can be returned to the primary job. However, if the job at B (or some portion thereof) executes some task which should not be interupted, e.g a data base update, and the task is a closed procedure (one which needs no non-local variables) then the user should be able to declare such a state, and the compiler should be able to validate the locality of the procedure.

PROCEDURE CALLS

´lgo´ is of type deviceref, but here the declaration is in an inner block. ´PASCAL´ and ´execute´ both call procedures - procedures which are not compiled with the control job but rather exist as local facilities on one or more subscribers. Since such external procedures have no access to the stack of the job control, they have no access to execution variables except through passed or default parameters. The calling sequence for such procedures should have the same format as for library procedures or any internal procedure. But we need also to standardize parameter conventions, at least for well known facilities. Without this, the user is subjected to the anomalies of the various local implementations of, for example, Pascal. Such a statement as 1.5 cannot exist; the user must tailor his PASCAL call to that Pascal which he actually will use.

PARAMETERS

Parameter conformance has two aspects: one must recognize the significance of each parameter passed and one must consider default parameters. The first problem is easily resolved if one adopts a keyword only convention and require that the local implementation be clever enough to ignore superfluous or meaningless keys.

For parameters that are defined in the procedure but not supplied with the procedure call we would allow two kinds of defaults: values (expressions), and variables. For example, the Pascal compiler which we call in statement 1.7 could generate output onto a file which is, by default, referenced through an operating system variable (e.g., Sysout, Output). On the other hand, if the output file reference is by default the value nil then no output would be generated. It is also conceivable that Pascal establishes for its output a new file which later on could be made accessible by `retrieve`. If not, then this file cannot be referenced by the control job.

OBSOLETE INFORMATION

Let us introduce the following statement into our original job control program:

$$f := lgo ; \qquad (1.8A)$$

Through this statement we encounter problems of cleanup and obsolete information. The variable `f` had contained a reference to a file, namely, to the source file of the Pascal program. Upon assignment of `lgo` to `f` we lose any reference to the original source file and implicitly cancel the access mechanism created by the retrieve function in (1.4). But does the ability at subscriber B to associate between the original reference value (which we no longer have) and the actual file still exist? We would like, at least, to destroy this association upon completion of the job, but having lost our reference value, i.e. our access mechanism, we can no longer do this. Therefore, we might allow reassignment to `f` to also destroy the association; i.e. implicit in reassignment is connection to subscriber B and request to erase this link. But then, we could not swap two variables of type deviceref as example:

```
a := f ;                                          (4.0)
f := g ;                                          (4.1)
g := a ;                                          (4.2)
```

Although the reference values would remain, the meaning
would not. A better solution is needed.

One might also remark that statement (1.8A) causes the
device reference in ´lgo´ to become known in the outer
block, i.e. at subscriber A.

SUMMARY

Resource sharing is achieved in the most complete sense
by providing a facility for executing a job in a
distributed way.   The job is written in a uniform high
level language and is compiled and executed on a
distributed stack machine. We accomplish this by making
the interpreter of the job control language distributed.
This means that job creation and stack handling are
distributed   services.   The   user   identifies virtual
devices (files and devices – local and remote) to be
used in the high level language by means of variables of
type <u>deviceref</u>. These virtual devices are accessed
through the local I/O system which is extended by a bulk
transfer service to a network wide I/O system.

BIBLIOGRAPHY

[1]

Gram,C. and Hertweck,F.,
Command Languages: Design Consideratinns and Basic
Concepts,
Proceedings of the IFIB Congress 1974,
North Holland Publishing Company, Amsterdam,
Netherlands

[2]

Hansen, P. B.
Concurrent Pascal,
Report from California Institute of Technology,
April, 1974

[3]

Raymond, J. and du Masle, J.,
NJCL, A Network Job Control Language,
Proceedings of the IFIP Congress 1974,
North Holland Publishing Company, Amsterdam,
Netherlands

[4]

Sergeant, G. and Farza, M. N.,
IGOR, Machine Interprétative pour la Mise en OEuvre
d´un
Language de Commande pour le Réseau Cyclades,
Thèse,
Université Paul-Sabatier de Toulouse, France

[5]

Wirth, N.,
The Programming Language PASCAL (Revised report),
Berichte der Fachgruppe fuer
Computerwissenschaften,
Swiss Fedreal Institute of Technology Zuerich,
Switzerland.
july, 1973

[6]

Zimmerman, H. and Elie, M.,
Transport Protocol. Standard Host-Host Protocol for
Heterogeneous Computer Networks
Reseau Cyclade, Sch 519.1
Iria, Rocquencourt

Maximizing system performance by optimizing scheduling and accounting algorithms

Dr. I.A. Newman, Senior Lecturer,
Mr. D.W. Taylor, Computer Officer,
Computer Studies Department,
Loughborough University of Technology
UK

Abstract

This paper commences with an examination of the difficulties of defining system performance in a service environment. Several approaches to the task are studied and a case argued for the use of an accounting and scheduling system linked to an overall resource allocation policy. A model of such a system is presented and practical examples are given to show its effectiveness in satisfying users and increasing the utilisation of machine resources in both batch processing and interactive environments. The application of such a system to networks is discussed and it is suggested that an equally successful result should be obtained.

1.   Introduction

The subject of increasing the utilisation of a particular piece of
equipment will come under discussion whenever the annual capital cost
(either in discounted cash flow terms, or as a lease or hire charge)
and   the annual running costs of the equipment, become a noticeable
fraction of the annual budget. The size of the annual budget
administered is usually a function of the seniority of the management
concerned. The more costly the equipment the higher the level of
involvement in terms of seniority and therefore also in terms of the
number of people concerned.

Some equipment, such as buildings, is costly but the use is well
defined and acceptable and this is not subject to major improvements.
The use of such equipment is 'kept under review' but does not merit
much management attention. Most other individual pieces of equipment
are kept below the 'attention threshold' by their relatively low cost
unless and until they cause problems and thus intrude on the
consciousness of the higher management echelons.

Unfortunately for computer services staff both the 'cost' and the
'problems' tend to bring the computer to the notice of everyone. The
position is made even more difficult because there are no well defined
and acceptable modes of use for computers. Since there is no saleable
end product (excluding computer bureaux) of computing, the measurement
of the benefits must, ultimately, be in the hands of the users rather
than being evaluated by the computer services staff or by empirical
measurements of performance.

The foregoing description should help to explain why computer
services managers have had to adopt a 'two way' stance: on the one
hand they must please the users, no easy task when users normally only
comment on the service when it is bad; on the other hand they must
describe the performance of the system in a quantifiable manner for
the benefit of their superiors. The only way out has been to do their
best to provide a good service using skill, judgement (and guess work) and
to demonstrate the success of their effort by providing pages of
figures describing the use of the machine (which is relatively easy to
measure). The question which this approach raises of the relationship
between the use of the computer and the usefulness of the computer
system is examined in section 2 of this paper.

Turning back to the aspect of pleasing the users, section 3
examines the problems of controlling the use of the computer system
to stop one group of users consuming resources to the detriment of the
rest (if one cannot please them at least one can minimize the displeasure),
and section 4 discusses the task of meeting user requested priorities
within the constraints of the limited actual resources. Both sections
note the difficult role which must then be fulfilled by management;
trying to administer resource control or attempting to decide the
relative merits of several users demanding ultimately high priority runs.

The common factor, behind the management decisions which are required in both cases, is the problem of resource allocation to the users. In a conventional (non-computing) environment this is normally handled by policy decisions regarding the disposition of finances for future periods. The same method can be used in a computer system if the cost of all resources is expressed in a single unit. The distribution of the units describing the computing power available should then be the only explicit management operation required, since the computer system itself can be trusted to administer the routine accounting and scheduling operations. Furthermore, now that the relative priorities allowed to the users are a direct function of the availability of resources, the scheduling strategy can be directed towards the optimisation of the workflow in the machine.

A suitable model which can be used to describe the action of a complete resource allocation, scheduling and accounting system is presented in section 5 and the usefulness of practical examples of such systems are studied.

The final section demonstrates that the model of user and computer system described is equally applicable to a network and thus that the user – resource allocation aspect of the problem is still adequately covered by the preceeding discussions. The problems of the practical implementation of integrated accounting and scheduling schemes on a loosely coupled network are studied and it is demonstrated that there should be no significant difficulties in achieving high resource utilisations in such networks.

2.   The Definition and Measurement of Performance

A number of techniques have been proposed that attempt to measure the performance of an existing computer system or to estimate the expected performance of a proposed system. They are nearly all more or less elaborate variations on a single theme: the measurement of the level of activity of one or more components of the system.

Early examples of this technique were based on the idea that a simple measure of C.P.U. activity was a sufficient indicator of system performance. This was manifested in 'wait-light watching' and simple hardware or software monitors that reported the percentage of C.P.U. utilisation. Prior to the mid 60's this was a reasonable technique, but, with the advent of more sophisticated operating systems, measurement of object program C.P.U. utilisation was taken as more meaningful. Indeed a statement such as 'the operating system uses 40% of available mill time' is still taken as a valid description of the performance of a complete computing system.

It is easy to see that, in the days when the price of the C.P.U. dominated the cost of a system, the attraction of such a single,

simple measure was overwhelming. However, as software became more
sophisticated and as the functions of the C.P.U. were usurped by other
sub-systems (notably channels), this measure was no longer independent
of the performance of the other components of the system. A multitude
of measures are now taken: core utilisation, channel loading, seek time
statistics on random access devices, etc. The importance of the
software sub-system has not been overlooked, and many performance
measures are available: supervisor transient routine usage, compiler
object code performance, etc.

The volume of possible statistics is enormous, but as more figures
are presented it becomes more and more difficult to estimate the
performance of the total system. The real value of system instrumentation
lies not with quantifying 'total system performance', but 'sub-system
performance'. In this area it is extremely valuable, especially for
uncovering design errors in both the hardware and software.

There is a need for a simple yardstick of total system performance.
The ideal measure would be some expression of the effective user
throughput of the system, because then the amount of useful work done
is being measured instead of simply the amount of work done. User
throughput, however, is a rather vague, unquantifiable term and is thus
impossible to measure directly. It is an expression not just of machine
specific items like processor power but of items such as the ease of
access to the system or the quality of documentation supplied to the
user. The relative importance of such factors can only be assessed by
the individual user, and in many cases it is purely a subjective
assessment.

Actual user utilisation is already measured to some extent by most
operating systems as part of an accounting package. These figures,
interpreted in relation to requirements specified by the users and
management of the system, provide a reasonably accurate estimate of
effective user throughput and can, therefore, be used as the basis for
the measurement of performance. One problem is that utilisation
statistics do not differentiate between work that is directly useful
and work that is indirectly useful to the user and 'work' that he did
by mistake. Many activities such as compiling or data vetting are not
useful work in themselves (except, perhaps, in a training situation),
but are merely part of the overhead imposed by the system in getting
some useful work done. Although such facilities are not currently
available, it would be extremely useful if separate statistics were
maintained for directly useful and indirectly useful work. The directly
useful work statistics then provide the basis for the performance
estimate and the indirectly useful work statistics would provide a
mechanism for monitoring the results of changes that were made in order
to reduce the amount of indirect work performed, e.g. better documentation
or a more humane job control language. Studies at Nottingham University [1]
have shown that, as far as the system is concerned, the proportion of
directly useful to indirectly useful work is fairly constant except when

explicit attempts are made to change the amount of indirect work performed.

For most systems, the performance measure will be derived from the total utilisation statistics and will therefore include these extraneous components. This is not entirely satisfactory, but any measure of performance that attempts to include an estimate of the effectiveness of the system for each user is bound to be imprecise because of the subjective nature of 'effectiveness'. It should be pointed out that the set of measures produced by an accounting system are not the same as the set produced by a system instrumentation package because the accounting statistics are taken on a per user job basis instead of being an absolute measure of activity over a period of time. In both cases one has a multitude of figures describing the performance of the system, however, in the case of the utilisation statistics the concept of useful work makes it possible to perform a meaningful reduction to a single performance value.

The reduction is achieved by taking the weighted sum of the individual resource utilisations for all users in some fixed period of time. Whilst this may seem to be crude, it should be remembered that we are not expecting a very precise measure because of the nature of what we are measuring. The values given to the weights are, of course, vitally important; incorrect weights can give a totally inaccurate picture. On the other hand the weights only have to be correct within the degree of accuracy expected of the final sum. Weighting the components enables management to express the relative priorities of different resources.

The measure of performance, P, is then,

$$P = \sum_{i=1}^{n} U_i W_i \; ,$$

where n is the number of resources, U_i is the level of utilisation of resource i and W_i is the weight attaching to resource i.

The level of utilisation, U_i, of resource i is determined by,

$$U_i = \frac{\sum_{j=1}^{m} q_{ij} v_{ij}}{E_i}$$

where

m   is the number of utilisations of the resource i.

q_{ij} is the quantity of resource i consumed at the utilisation j. This value is as produced by a standard accounting package.

v_{ij} is the 'value' to the user of using q_{ij} of resource i at the jth

utilisation. The evaluation of 'value' is, for the moment, left
undefined. Mechanisms whereby a user attaches a value to a
resource request are discussed in a later section. It is this
value that enables some regard to be given to the more subjective
aspects of performance. For an example a high value can be
applied to figures for turnaround time if the actual time was less
than or equal to that requested by the user. On the other hand,
if the actual turnaround was considerably longer than that
requested, then a small (or even negative) value can be applied,
thus reflecting the loss in user throughput in the final
performance value P. It is very difficult to incorporate this
sort of item into a purely technical model of performance.

E_i is the expected utilisation of resource i. $\sum_j q_{ij} v_{ij}$ is simply

the sum of the actual quantities of resource i utilised, weighted
by the value at each utilisation. E_i is the expected value of

this sum if resource i is neither under nor over-utilised. The
value of E_i may be assessed subjectively, or possibly,

stochastically. It is unreasonable to assume that any equipment
should operate at 100% of its technical capacity. Indeed the
expected utilisation of some equipment would be quite low otherwise
under or over-utilisation might occur in the rest of the system.
In addition, due regard to the quality of service given to users
dictates that a certain degree of under-utilisation is required,
see Sizer [2].

The A_i then, are dimensionless quantities whose values will
normally be < 1.

A further restriction in the weights, $\sum_{i=1}^{n} W_i = 1$, ensures that
P $\leqslant$ 1, unless some over-utilisation occurs.

The value of the weights, W_i, have still to be determined. These
depend on how P is to be used. If P is used to assess the ongoing
performance of an existing system then the W_i may be set to express the
relative importance of one resource to another. It is still highly
subjective, but at least the measurer has quantified his feelings about
what are the important components of his system. The quantification
can then be discussed and a case for the selected weightings argued.

An alternative use of P is to help decide the most effective
enhancement to a configuration for a given budget. In this case the
weights relate directly to the real cost of resources. It is only
necessary to calculate P for those resources that are under consideration
for enhancement. The various alternative enhancements each give rise to
a different set of weights, the set that maximises P might be assumed to
be the most cost-effective enhancement in terms of the given utilisation
levels. If the enhancement is fairly simple then the history of

utilisation levels can be used in obtaining a value for P. If the enhancement is such that a drastic change in the mode of user is expected (e.g. converting from batch to timesharing) then this method is of little value. Large changes in user characteristics are not determinable by any form of measurement of existing characteristics.

Management still, however, need to know the effect of a change before it is made in order to judge the likely effects of the change, but to do this a feedback loop is required that allows users to demonstrate their likely behaviour in the event of each change before that change is made. The subject of user characteristics and feedback are discussed in a subsequent section.

3. Accounting -the control of usage

As has been suggested in the introduction users do not want to be controlled at all, ideally they would like to have freedom to use as many computing resources as they require, but in practice this conflicts with the requirements of other users. Management thus has a duty to 'control' one user in the interests of the others.

Most modern operating systems contain an accounting package of some sort to provide management with statistics on computer usage. These statistics are used by commercial computer bureaux to invoice their customers for resources used, and by other installations (either in-house commercial or educational) as a means of policing the use of computer resources. For the commercial bureau the economics of the market place determines the allocation of resources, whereas other installations must rely on a management judgement. It is with such judgements that we are concerned in this section.

The simplest, and most common, method of using accounting statistics to control resource utilisation is for the computer manager to review the statistics, looking for unusually high, or low, levels of utilisation. The judgement of what is unusual is often completely undefined. When such a level has been found then the problem situation has to be resolved by negotiation, persuasion or threat. The major difficulty with this system is that it relies completely on the manager. Unless he is extremely astute and knows his users well, he is unlikely to detect shifts in user behaviour until they become glaringly obvious. At this stage it is probably too late to persuade the user (department) to change his (its) ways. He will have become too heavily committed to his accustomed way of doing things.

The solution to this is to pre-allocate resources to users or groups of users. This is often done by setting maximum levels of use for each resource. When a user transgresses one of these thresholds, a report is produced for management action. A problem with this approach is that the mechanics of setting the allocation levels are technically detailed and error-prone, especially when a large body of

dissimilar users are involved. In a computer service situation the
allocation of resources amongst competing users is a policy decision
that should be made by an overall management committee and not by the
computer centre management. However, this is extremely difficult for
a committee to do when the units to be allocated are of a technical
nature. Ideally this committee should be able to say that department X
will have 1/3 of the resources, department Y will have 1/2 of the
resources available, etc.. Another problem is that this method of
allocation imposes a very inflexible regime on the user in that it
assumes that the type and level of his resource requirements do not
vary between allocations (quarterly, or even annual, committee
meetings?). This is not normally the case in practice, so that the
operation of this type of scheme usually results in either frustrated
users, or gross over-allocations being made to avoid potential trouble,
or continuous jiggling of the allocations (by computer management) in
an attempt to adapt to changing usage patterns.

Accounting reports, per se, can thus be seen to be inadequate as
a method of control without detailed intervention by the systems
manager. This sort of management effort is tolerable for a small,
closed, community but clearly unrealistic if a user population in the
hundreds were to be considered.

4. Scheduling

The role of the scheduler is of great importance in any
discussion on performance and resource allocation. It is the scheduler
that actually implements policies on these two issues. In terms of the
broad definitions of performance and resource allocation that have been
adopted in this paper, the type of scheduler that is involved is the
'high-level' scheduler. There will, of course, exist some machine-
dependent low-level scheduler that attempts to keep the system running
at a maximum (technical) efficiency; avoiding contention for common
resources, allocating core space and mill time, and other short timescale activities. The high-level scheduler on the other hand selects
a set of jobs for the low-level scheduler to run, working on a longer
timescale to implement strategic decisions.

Until recently scheduling of this type has been a largely manual
task. The crudest technique is to service work on a first in first
out basis. This method is not without merit; it is simple and it makes
demand self-regulating in that while a program is in the queue, it is
out of the hands of the programmer and he can, therefore, generate no
more input for that job. The resource allocation policy generated by
this scheduler is a simple reflection of user demand, however the most
demanding user is not necessarily the most effective or the most
deserving.

Another simple scheduling system is to always select the shortest
job first. This is justified on the grounds that user satisfaction (and

hence performance in the broad sense discussed above) is proportional
to 'turnaround time', so giving a good turnaround to as many users as
possible will maximise performance. Resources are allocated to users
in proportion to the frequency of job submission and the inverse of the
shortness of his jobs. The man with long jobs suffers very badly under
this system.

The most common scheduling scheme consists of some combination of
the two schemes already outlined. These schedulers are usually operated
manually, so there is always the possibility for some form of ad-hoc
implementation of a management policy about the importance of various
classes of work. This is often manifested in giving priority to those
users who can convince the management (or operations staff) of their
claim to a larger share of the available resources.

Schedulers can be automated if there is a suitable job control
language to describe a job's resource requirements and if the system
maintains an input well large enough to hold all jobs awaiting
processing. Early automatic schedulers consisted of a first-come-first-
served queue together with a priority system to overide this ordering
for urgent jobs. Elaborations of this type of scheduler consisted of
several queues, one for each type of work; short, small jobs, cpu-
bound jobs, jobs requiring magnetic tapes, etc. The scheduler then
tries to keep all of the queues moving forward. The problem now is to
ensure that the use of priority codes is not abused, although such
schedulers are automatic, a degree of manual intervention is required
to ensure that users do not completely defeat the intentions of
management by manipulating the priorities to gain extra resources.

These manual and semi-automatic schedulers are usually quite
satisfactory where the user population is small, and when they are
prepared to co-operate with each other. When large, open groups of
users are involved, it becomes increasingly difficult to maintain a
consistent scheduling strategy without a much greater degree of
automation. In order to gain this greater degree of automation the
scheduler needs more information than is supplied to the schemes
already described. It needs to know what resources have been allocated
to each user, and how much of these resources he has already consumed.
The scheduler can then select jobs for execution based on the criteria
that users shall not exceed their allocation.

The George III standard high-level scheduler is an example of
such a scheme. There is a set of 26 priority levels (A-Z) or 'urgencies',
and each user is allocated an amount of processor time at each level.
When he submits a job he specifies its urgency, and if he has not already
consumed his allocation at that level then the job is given that urgency.
If he has used the allocation at the requested urgency then the job is
given the highest urgency, below that requested, for which he does have
some allocation remaining. The scheduler then selects jobs for running
based on their urgency and the length of time that they have been
waiting. When the job is complete the processor time allocated to the

urgency at which the job was run is reduced by the actual processor time used.

Another example of an automatic scheduler is the one implemented at Cambridge University for their 370/165, Larmouth [3] . Each user, or project group, is allocated a 'share' of the machine and the scheduler attempts to give him this proportion of the machine's resources averaged over some suitable period. In order to achieve this, the scheduler controls the rate of working of each project by varying the turnaround given to jobs run on that project. Work is defined as STORE times COMPUTATION TIME. Users can give individual jobs a high priority in order to get a good turnaround, but this priority is relative to other jobs on the same project, not an absolute priority, so users cannot claim more than their allotted share by consistently requesting high priority. There are other facilities built in to ensure that users cannot cheat the system, e.g. there is no advantage to be gained by splitting a large job into several smaller jobs (c.f. scheduler where smallest jobs are run first).

Both these schedulers are of the type necessary to control a large computer service, but they both have some shortcomings. The George III scheduler only uses processing time requirements to determine if a job is given the urgency requested by the user. The allocation of this resource to the various urgency levels is then crucially important in determining the level of service that each user receives. There seems to be no obvious way of making this allocation that will reflect a consistent resource allocation policy. Facilities are provided for individual George III sites to write their own high-level schedulers, so potentially the scheduling requirements of individual sites, and the shortcomings of the supplied system can, in principle, be partially overcome, although it has not been managed in practice. The Cambridge system works on the assumption that the rate of working as expressed in terms of turnaround time and job size (mill time and store occupancy) is an accurate indicator of the rate of overall resource consumption. This is not usually the case. The system as it stands favours those jobs that are I/O bound over those jobs that are processor bound (as does the George III scheduler), this could be rectified by including I/O transfers in the definition of work. However this still does not account for those resources that are not directly associated with the execution of a program, e.g. filestore occupancy and terminal connect time. Presumably these may be allocated by fixed allotments, although the inherent (user) inflexibility and implementation difficulties attendant on this means of resource allocation have already been discussed.

The next section discusses a linked scheduling and accounting system that overcomes this problem by controlling the overall rate of resource consumption instead of the rate of working. It is further suggested that the total system approach is simpler to implement and is more meaningful to the user.

5.   Linked Accounting and Scheduling

The preceeding two sections have demonstrated that neither
accounting nor scheduling on their own can be used to please the user
(by controlling individuals or by meeting user stated priorities) or
to maximise system performance. Both require extensive management
effort in an attempt to ensure that the work done reflects the
organisational strategies. The only system where this management
effort is not required is the Cambridge University scheduler which,
despite its drawbacks, operates with a minimum of human intervention.
This observation leads to the realisation that the scheduler is not
simply a scheduler it is in fact a total resource allocation, scheduling
and accounting system. The scheduler has available information about
the share of the machine owned by the user and also about the computing
resources consumed by the user. The former comes from a (manual)
resource allocation procedure, the latter is feedback from an accounting
system.

The total system approach can be formalized and extended to
include all the resources consumed by users. The amount of each resource
available over a control period is estimated, an effective 'price' for the
resource fixed in terms of computing units (funny money) and a total value
for the system is calculated by summation (exactly analogous to the
calculation of the use of the system in section 2). Users are then
allocated an income of computing units and are charged for resource
consumption according to the prices set for the resources used. The
unit of allocation is simple enough for all major allocations to reflect
the management committee policy on the relative importance of different
work. Effectively each user or group of users is given a fraction of the
total system. The scheme is very flexible in that users may work in any
way they choose as long as they remain within their overall budget. If
it suits them, at one stage of a project, to use a large amount of
processor time and very little mass-storage then this is a trade-off
that they are free to make. The day to day levels and type of resource
consumption are controlled entirely by the user, only he knows the true
urgency of a particular job and consequently how much of <u>his</u> resources
he is prepared to commit to it. It is this aspect of resource allocation
that enables the user values, v_{ij}, specified in section 2, to be
determined.

Several systems of this kind have been implemented in recent years.
In 1970 Nielson [4] published a paper outlining the principles of
resource allocation by pricing and more recently Lehman [5] expanded on
this subject. These and other implementations differ greatly from each
other in many respects (see examples in section 5), although the basic
principle, of allocating to each user a fraction of the <u>total</u> resources
available, remains the same. One of the advantages of this technique
is that it is robust enough to accommodate wide variations in allocation
philosophies and yet still be successful. Pricing policy, for example,
has been the subject of some discussion. Users require a reasonably

stable price structure in order to make long-term plans, but, on the other hand, the varying of price levels is the mechanism used by computer centre management to influence the use of the machine to optimise performance, consequently the price-levels are subject to change. Shaftel and Zmud [6] have recently proposed that prices should be reviewed periodically, but that during that period they should be completely fixed. Under these constraints Shaftel and Zmud have developed an analytic method of determining the most resource-effective set of prices for a control period based on the history of usage over preceeding control periods. This method is satisfactory for an installation where there are no substantial variations in demand over shorter intervals than the control period, which implicitly includes the (unrealistic) constraint of 'no breakdowns'. Lehman [7] has applied the technique of allocation and accounting to a system where uniformity is not apparent. In order to try to smooth demand over the day, he uses a technique in which prices are varied according to the machine load.

The concentration on pricing policy ignores the important rôle of the scheduler in satisfying the user requirements and in maximising the effectiveness of the computer system. The difficulty arises because the two requirements appear to be in conflict since the optimisation of the use of the computer requires, in terms of a batch system, a large pool of jobs from which a suitable job mix can always be maintained, while the satisfaction of the users means meeting user stated priorities.

There has, however, been a considerable amount of work done at Nottingham and Loughborough Universities which demonstrates that the two constraints on scheduling can be separated. The approach is based on charging policy which reflects both the resources used by the user and the inconvenience caused to other users (and to the system). Since the amount of resources available to each user is fixed by management decision at the beginning of the control period he can get more computing power (more C.P.U., transfers, disc space) by choosing to use the system 'politely';(by giving a lower priority or a later deadline time, by logging in when there are few other people around, or by moving files from disc to tape when they are not required), than he will by making urgent demands (immediate return of information, large disc based files).

This approach encourages the individual user (or user group) to evaluate the real requirements of this job relative to his other work and to assign it a priority accordingly. The effect is to 'spread the load' allowing a steady pool of available jobs to be maintained without many 'critical deadline' jobs restricting the scheduling choices.

The model which is presented to the user is a simple one reflecting his view of the computing system as a black book which in some way does his work for him. The work is presented at an entrance and collected at an exit. The two controls which the user may want to exercise on his job, while it is in the box, are the length of time it remains in the box and the maximum resources it can consume. The job is then charged for on exit related to the actual resources consumed and the inconvenience caused to other users in meeting the requested turnaround-time. Thus each user has the responsibility for 'spending' his resource allocation in the most effective way for him. One may choose to use it all on one big high priority job run at a peak period (maximun inconvenience) while another may use fewer resources running three or four similar jobs but allowing them to remain in the system longer or choosing to enter them at off peak periods (minimum inconvenience).

The distributed value of the computer system is calculated using an average inconvenience factor. It is therefore anticipated that the statistical result of this user freedom will be that the system can maintain a pool of jobs from which to choose for scheduling (system optimisation) purposes.

The other requirement for effective use of machine resources, is that the resources that the job is likely to use are known to the scheduler before it presents the job for execution. These are usually related to the maximum resources as specified by the user but it would be advantageous if they could be known explicitly, for example by the system keeping records of resource utilisations for common types of work.

The effectiveness of the system depends on the common-sense of the users, but this is encouraged first by the control on input (if all resources are spent then no more input can be accepted for the control period), second by the feedback to the resource allocation system (if a user manages to spend all his resources on high priority work perhaps he does not deserve such a high allocation).

Despite the difficulty of proving theoretically that the system will both achieve user satisfaction and increase the throughput, it has been operated successfully in practice. Two such systems are described below, the first (Nottingham University Computer Centre) a primarily batch system, the second (Loughborough University Computer Studies Department) an interactive system.

5.1 Nottingham University

The background to this system has been described previously [8]. The basic objective was to share the available resources (which were insufficient to meet demand) fairly amongst the users without restricting all jobs to an unacceptable delay. The system is basically geared to batch working although interactive file handling (file input, listing, editing and deletions are allowed). Users specify a return time for batch jobs and this return time is used as a measure of inconvenience for the purpose of charging. Total resources available are calculated from a consideration of expected (desired) utilisation of each resource, which is converted to a 'money' value by defining a price per unit used, and these resources are distributed on the basis of resources used during the previous control period, which is done automatically, and a special allocation, by request to a university management committee.

The system gives a response of between 25 minutes and 45 minutes for jobs requested in one hour even during peak periods and yet maintains between two and twelve hours of work waiting to be processed. System utilisation, in terms of mill time spent performing work submitted by the user, is normally between 70% and 80% over a four week period running 24 hours a day 5 days per week. Since a similar loading occurs on disc channels it can reasonably be inferred that the system is being used quite effectively with little waste.

Several extra points about the Nottingham system are relevant. First that it has been found to be necessary to maintain a very low priority and consequently charge (possibly 0) category of job in order to ensure that the system will never idle, because all users have exhausted their resources. Second that the compilable job control, which is another facet of the total user system allows the resources required by the job to be assessed before the job is scheduled for execution (this in turn enables 'awkward' jobs to be referred to the operator for manual scheduling). Thirdly, the arrangement of distributing available resources, which allows for variations in planned service time in different control periods, has also been adapted to cope with unplanned system breakdown by forcing a percentage reduction in each user budget to compensate for the 'lost' resources.

Finally, when offered, an increased number of runs on the limited facility student service which was not within the normal accounting and scheduling system, the committee of users refused on the grounds that this was to the detriment of paying customers. (The student service is, now, also charged for in the normal way).

5.2   Loughborough University

The accounting and control system implemented at Loughborough University is for a mini-computer (PDP 11/40) system. The service provided is wholly interactive and there are no operators or supervisory staff in attendance. The manufacturer supplied operating system includes a reasonable set of accounting routines for reporting usage and, in addition, it is possible to set a maximum limit to the amount of disk space that an individual user can retain when he logs out. It is not possible to set limits on the utilisation of other resources. These controls proved to be of only marginal assistance in managing the system and as it was heavily over-loaded almost from the day of installation, it was decided to implement an accounting and control system based on the principles described above.

With an interactive system users are free to change their use of the machine from second to second once they are connected to the system. The user control aspect of scheduling is thus much more intangible in a interactive environment than in a batch environment. The pool of user jobs is replaced by a pool of users waiting to use a terminal, The scheduler cannot directly control the pool as it can under a batch system, but it can detect its existence (by examining the system load level) and it can take action to coerce the pool of available users into an order that enables the system to perform well, i.e. to keep the load to a level which can be handled efficiently. The mechanism for doing this is embodied in the pricing policy described below. If this is effective then it should rarely be necessary to take more drastic measures to control workflow (forcible logging out of users, degraded modes of service).

It was intended to change as little of the manufacturer's software as possible, consequently the choice of resources to be priced was dictated by what statistics were already kept by the operating system (disk space, connect time, cpu time, number of log-ins and line-printer paper used). Although these were sufficient, at least two additional measures would have been useful: number of disk transfers and the number of terminal lines output during an interactive session. The first because the main bottleneck in the system is the queue for disk accesses, and the second because paper costs real money.

Besides the equitable allocation of resources the objective of the pricing policy used at Loughborough is to encourage short terminal sessions and to persuade users to avoid the system when it is heavily loaded. This is effected by making the charge for terminal connect time increase dramatically for long continuous sessions, and by varying the charge for connect time and C.P.U. time according to the load (determined by the number of active jobs) on the system. In an extreme case it would be possible for a user to be charged 100x as much for a 2 hour session at peak loading as it would for a $\frac{1}{2}$ hour dession during a slack period.

In practice the system has performed extremely well, the queues for terminals have almost completely vanished and many users have acknowledged that they are now getting a more effective service from the machine.

The use of the system is spread over a longer time period and less machine and human effort is spent in controlling usage at peak periods. Thus it can be concluded that the system is being utilised more effectively. The only remaining problem is to find an effective method of ensuring that the system does not idle when there are users (albeit overdrawn) who could use it. This is more a theoretical than a practical point since users normally learn not to exhaust their resources and simple remedies, such as permitting overdrawn users on to a few terminals if no-one else is using the machine, have proved to be quite adequate in practice.

The fact that the major problem now is how to handle under-load conditions, rather than coping with over-load or increasing efficiency serves to underline how powerful the overall technique is in controlling usage and improving the system performance.

6.   Application to a Network

The linked resource allocation scheduling and accounting system described in the previous section is very suitable for application to a network of computers. The concept of the computer system as a black box into which users submit work and from which they collect output is unchanged whether the box contains one machine, several machines or an army of clerks with calculators. The methods of scheduling jobs once they are submitted and of calculating a total value of resources available for use, are also straightforward if the whole network (collection of machines) is under the control of a single management structure which sets objectives and can thus decide relative priorities between users and prices for resources. However a problem could occur in the case of the loosely coupled network where each machine (or at least each sub-network) is capable of free standing operation and is controlled by an independent management committee. In this case common pricing and allocation strategies are unlikely to be achieved and thus scheduling for the network appears untenable.

These apparent difficulties can be resolved if the assumption made in the companion paper [9] is adopted, viz. that each sub-network will itself handle the bulk of work being submitted to it. The necessary requirement is then that each management will operate resource allocation, pricing, accounting system internally for their own users on their own system. An agreement must then be reached about the conversion between the unit of resource adopted by each establishment and the network 'computer' unit. Since by definition only the users of a given system will have resources on that system (even if this is managed by system effected transfers invisibly to the user), the normal resource allocation and accounting methods can be adopted for each system. Furthermore, if the network connection is treated like any other input source, the flow of jobs from the network can be controlled and scheduled in exactly the same way as the flow of jobs from a card reader. Each system can therefore optimise its own performance in accord with the aims of its management with the additional benefit that the method of interconnection described does not generate much unwanted network traffic thus keeping system overheads, for organising the network, to a minimum.

7.   References

1.   Ratcliffe, Levers, "Variations in usage patterns", Internal Report, Cripps Computing Centre, Nottingham University, 1973.

2.   Sizer, "Computers as a Resource to be Allocated by a Money Budget", Computer Weekly, No.429, January 23rd, 1975.

3.   Larmouth, "Scheduling for a Share of the Machine", Internal Report, Computer Laboratory, Cambridge University, 1973.

4. Nielson, "The Allocation of Computer Resources - Is Pricing
        the Answer?", CACM, Vol.13, No.8, August, 1970.

5. Lehman, "Principles of Computer Usage and Control",
        Online, 1973.

6. Shaftel, Zmud, "Allocation of Computer Resources through
        Flexible Pricing", Computer Journal, Vol.17, No.4, Nov. 1974.

7. Lehman, "Computer Usage Control", Computer Journal, Vol.16,
        No.2, May, 1973.

8. Newman, McConachie, "Improving the Performance of an ICL 1906A
        Computer Under the George 3 Operating System", Datafair, 1973.

9. Newman, Fitzhugh, "Command Language Design for Networks of
        Processors", Eurocomp 75.

UK Post Office DDS Proposals: user and DP industry implications

R D Bright
Head of Market Development: Digital Services
Post Office
UK

D L Hebditch
Director
Pliener Associates Ltd.
UK

Abstract:

This paper describes the background to the objectives,
the methodology and some preliminary results of work
being carried out by the UK Post Office, into the
likely demand for its proposed range of Digital Data
Services.

INTRODUCTION

Following the 1970 decision to begin detailed technical investigation and to lay plans for developing a range of Digital Based Functional Data Communication Services, the UK Post Office put in hand arrangements for establishing a close liaison with its customers and the general dp industry in order to obtain reactions to these important and far ranging proposals.

In more recent times these comprehensive proposals constituting the "Digital Data Services" (DDS) have been separately identified as consisting of the following key elements:-

    i   Enhance and augment the Datel Service Range.

    ii   Open an Experimental Packet Switched Service (EPSS).

    iii Develop a leased Digital Data Service (PCDDS).

    iv   Develop a Pilot Circuit Switched Digital Data Service (PSDDS).

    v   In the larger term develop and integrate these and other forms of communication services.

Figure 1 summarises the main features and facilities of the three main services under study, ie:-

    Private Circuit DDS   (PCDDS)
    Public (Circuit) Switched DDS (PSDDS)
    Packet Switched DDS   (PkSDDS)

EARLY STAGES OF MARKET INVESTIGATION

By the end of 1971 the shape and form of the proposed Digital Data Services was emerging and their inherent features were defined sufficiently to permit the following major parameters to be assumed:-

    . Synchronous Transmission.
    . Full Duplex Working.
    . Byte Timing (from the network).
    . Interworking with Foreign Public Data Networks.

This latter feature reflected the growing momentum of international studies notably at CCITT, where already the synchronous User Classes of service were being stated as:-

    600   bit/s
    2400 bit/s
    9600 bit/s
    48000 bit/s

However the position on the asynchronous User Classes of service (also to be covered by Recommendation X1) was less clear.

In pursuance of its declared intentions to seek user views on the nature of the facilities to be offered by the proposed services, the UK Post Office initiated a series of "Consumer Research Panels" composed of well-informed individuals drawn from a cross-section of interests, ranging from dp managers

```
┌──────────────────────────────────────────────────────────────────────────────┐
│ POST OFFICE TELECOMMUNICATIONS: PROPOSED DIGITAL DATA SERVICES                  │
│ A summary of possible facilities.                                              │
├──────────────────────────────────────────────────────────────────────────────┤
│ User Classes                          Features:                                │
│                                                                                │
│         )   110 bit/s)                Three services as shown overleaf         │
│ 1 and 2 )   200 bit/s) Asynchronous   *Digital Technology                      │
│         )   300 bit/s)                *Target error rates of less than 2.6 bit/s in 10⁷ │
│                                       *Timing provided by the network (ie bit and byte timing) │
│     3       600 bit/s)                *Eight bit ch with bit-sequence independence for data │
│     4      2400 bit/s)                *International Alphabet No. 5 used for control purposes │
│     5      9600 bit/s) Synchronous    *Network Terminating Units (NTUs) supplied as part of │
│     6       48K bit/s)                     the circuit - modems not required   │
│                                       *Interworking with Foreign Data Networks │
│                                                                                │
└──────────────────────────────────────────────────────────────────────────────┘
```

Figure 1

Post Office Telecommunications: Proposed Digital Data Services

PRIVATE LEASED CIRCUITS	CIRCUIT SWITCHED SERVICE	PACKET SWITCHED SERVICE
INHERENT FEATURES	**INHERENT FEATURES**	**INHERENT FEATURES**
*Point-to-point private leased circuits User Classes 3, 4, 5 and 6.	*Circuit switching User Classes 3, 4, 5 and 6 *Fast connect times (1 second)	*Packet mode operation User Classes 3, 4, 5 and 6 *Error control *Data signalling rate conversion *Simultaneous bothway packet operation *Variable length packets
FACILITIES	**FACILITIES**	**FACILITIES**
*Multipoint circuits *High-speed multiplexing *Half-duplex operation	*Packet assembly *Closed User Groups (with or without outgoing access) *Incoming calls barred *Remote line identification *Autocalling and autoanswer *Multiple lines at the same address *Call transfer *Call redirection *Changed address interception *Network supplied status information *Interface for User Class 1 *Half-duplex operation *Direct calling *Abbreviated address calling *Mnemonic calling *High speed multiplexing (9.6K and 48K links) *Polling *Multiple address calls	*Packet disassembly *Closed user groups (with or without outgoing access) *Incoming calls barred *Autocalling and autoanswer *Multiple lines at the same address *Changed address interception *Network supplied status information *Multibuffer packet operation *Delivery confirmation

Figure 1 (contd)   POST OFFICE TELECOMMUNICATIONS: PROPOSED DIGITAL DATA SERVICES

(NB It should be noted that not all the facilities described in this section would be available at the opening of a service)

and planners to computer scientists. Each panel was separately constructed and
the views expressed were not disclosed to subsequent panels, but all were
presented with an identical list of possible facilities, complete with definitions
and descriptive material some time prior to the day of discussion, in order to
allow time for consultation with colleagues.

Of the fifteen or so facilities researched in this way approximately 75% resulted
in a consensus - many being a unanimous verdict. For example, it was recommended
not to provide network "gateways" between the proposed circuit switched DDS and
the Public Switched Telephone Network on the grounds of cost, conceding that
some users would have to rent access lines to both networks.

The results of these discussions were of vital interest to the UK Post Office in
steering the direction of its on-going technical and cost studies and considerable
effort was subsequently devoted to testing these initial conclusions on a wider
audience of users. In parallel with these National Market Investigations, the
views of other common carriers were canvassed and this culminated in the UK
Post Office submission to CCITT Study Group VII - Customer Services and Facilities
Working Party - in January 1974. This document has since served as a model for
all contributions relevant to CCITT Recommendation X2.

DDS USER COST BENEFIT PROJECT

From the earliest days of its market investigations into the user reactions to
DDS it has been apparent that, for a variety of reasons, conventional market
research would not be adequate in fully assessing likely reactions to the DDS
should it be implemented. These factors included:-

   i   The complexity of the "product" being investigated was too great to
   expect the majority of customers to devote sufficient time to considering
   and evaluating its potential.

   ii   The cost benefits of the new facilities could impact central site
   design to an extent which would make straightforward tariff comparisons
   of limited value. The real need would be to evaluate communications costs
   in the context of changing total systems costs.

   iii   The implications of item (ii) would be heavily dependent upon the dp
   industry's attitude and willingness to expoit the potential benefits in
   designing future products. Would new terminals for example, support the
   PCDDS onto calling forcility?

To overcome these problems the only course open to the UK Post Office was to
mount an extensive User Cost Benefit Studies in which it would reflect all
these factors, including those relevant to dp activities involved in data
communications. The objective of the study was stated as:-

   "To identify, assess and report on the potential User Cost Benefit
   implications of the proposed Digital Data Services".

Implicit also was the need to compare and contrast these proposed services
not only with each other, but also the constantly developing range of
Datel Services.

To ensure that up-to-date commercial dp/data communication trends were fully
reflected and to inject an experienced 'user' viewpoint at all stages, it was

further decided to engage the full time services of a consultant well versed
in these aspects. After a series of discussions the services of
Mr David Hebditch (a Director of Pliener Associates Ltd a firm specialising in
the design and implementation of teleprocessing systems) were obtained for an
initial period of twelve months. A key condition of the contract was his full
time commitment involving secondment to work as a member of the UK Post Office
marketing team, engaged on the several facets of this task.

PLAN OF ACTION

After some initial deliberations the broad outline of the various stages
involved in the study were identified. An important basis for the futuristic
work was to formally structure the present data communications environment which
meant a co-ordinated study of the technical and system relationships existing
each side of the traditional modem interface. Once this was properly formalised,
the study could progress into the likely future pattern based not only on new
data communication services, but also emergent dp industry ranges of front-
ending devices and terminals. A later phase would inject this accumulated
knowledge into some form of system cost model which would need to be specially
developed for the purpose.

Meanwhile, a separate comprehensive survey of users' future plans was
commissioned to provide information on the state of the data communications
market, likely to emerge by about 1980. But this would need to be measured in
terms of 'teleprocessing systems' as much as the conventional terminal 'yardstick'
and yet still be able to provide information on traffic flows, regional
distribution, industry sectors and applications.

The final stage would be to combine all this information into a final report
which should attempt to provide the UK Post Office with a comprehensive overview of the potential market shares expected for each of the services, including
the existing and planned Datel Facilities in the period ending 1983.

We would like to take this opportunity to thank all those representatives of
users, dp industry, research groups and central government who gave unstintingly
of their time throughout the various phases of the study.

THE TELEPROCESSING USER SURVEY

As mentioned above, an exhaustive survey of users and dp industry achievement
and trends was undertaken in parallel with the staged programme described above.
This was conducted by the UK Post Office Data Communications Market Research
Group and elicited an 80% response rate from nearly one thousand UK data
establishments equipped with or capable of supporting data communications.

As many of the findings were published during 1974 under the heading of the
'Teleprocessing User Survey' there is little point in elaborating on the
results in this paper suffice to say that equipped with this information, it
is possible to take the specific findings of the cost models used in the
Cost/Benefit Study and to scale these up to represent national patterns and
allocate market shares.

METHODOLOGY FOR THE COST BENEFIT STUDY

At the end of 1973, the Data Communications Division of Post Office Marketing Department, set up a Project Team to study the User Cost/Benefit aspects of the Digital Data Services being formulated at that time.

The project comprised three major phases (as shown in Figure 2):-

      Phase 1: Study of Existing Systems.
      Phase 2: Scenario Study on Future Systems.
      Phase 3: Cost/Benefit Modelling.

The output from each of these became the input to the final report. The output from Phases 1 and 2 were also input to Phase 3.

PHASE 1: V SERIES STUDY (Figure 3)

Phase 1 included a detailed investigation of how Data Terminal Equipment (DTE) manufacturers implemented their hardware interfaces to the existing telephone-based facilities, as well as a study of technology forecasts and an assessment of how such techological trends will influence data communications hardware, software and the architecture of networks. This phase was essential in order to isolate the benefits of 'inevitable' techological developments from those which might be brought about by the introduction of Digital Data Services. In summary, Phase 1 was a look at the present 'state of the art' and how that state might change if we continue to use the telephony network for data transmission. Appendix 1 summarises some of the main features of the techology forecasts. Figures 6 and 7 itemise the more important trends identified.

PHASE 2: X SERIES STUDY (Figure 4)

Phase 2 presented particular problems. Whereas existing systems could be documented by complementing our own experience with reading manuals, visiting suppliers and so on, such techniques are obviously impossible when one is trying to determine the nature of future systems. How, for example, does one design a commercial system using a packet switched network? How do we know that such commercial systems will choose packet-switching in preference to, say, fast circuit switching? We decided the best approach currently available was to use a variation of the Delphi technique. Instead of asking participants to time-scale developments, we would fix the time on 1985 and ask them to agree the state of the techology. To establish a starting point for the formalised discussion, project team wrote Scenarios describing on-line systems in five major existing and potential application areas:-

      1   Commercial order-entry.
      2   Time-sharing service.
      3   Large-scale bank network.
      4   Environmental monitoring system.
      5   Credit Card readers.

A group of 35 informed individuals within the DP profession were then asked to read the scenarios and to respond to questionnaires which would enable them to express their agreement/disagreement with the propositions made. In addition to the questionnaire on each scenario, there was a general set of questions on the DDS proposals as a whole. In total, there were over 50 primary questions with 'sub-questions' accounting for about 100 additional answers. Additional

DDS COST/BENEFIT STUDY: STRUCTURE OF PROJECT

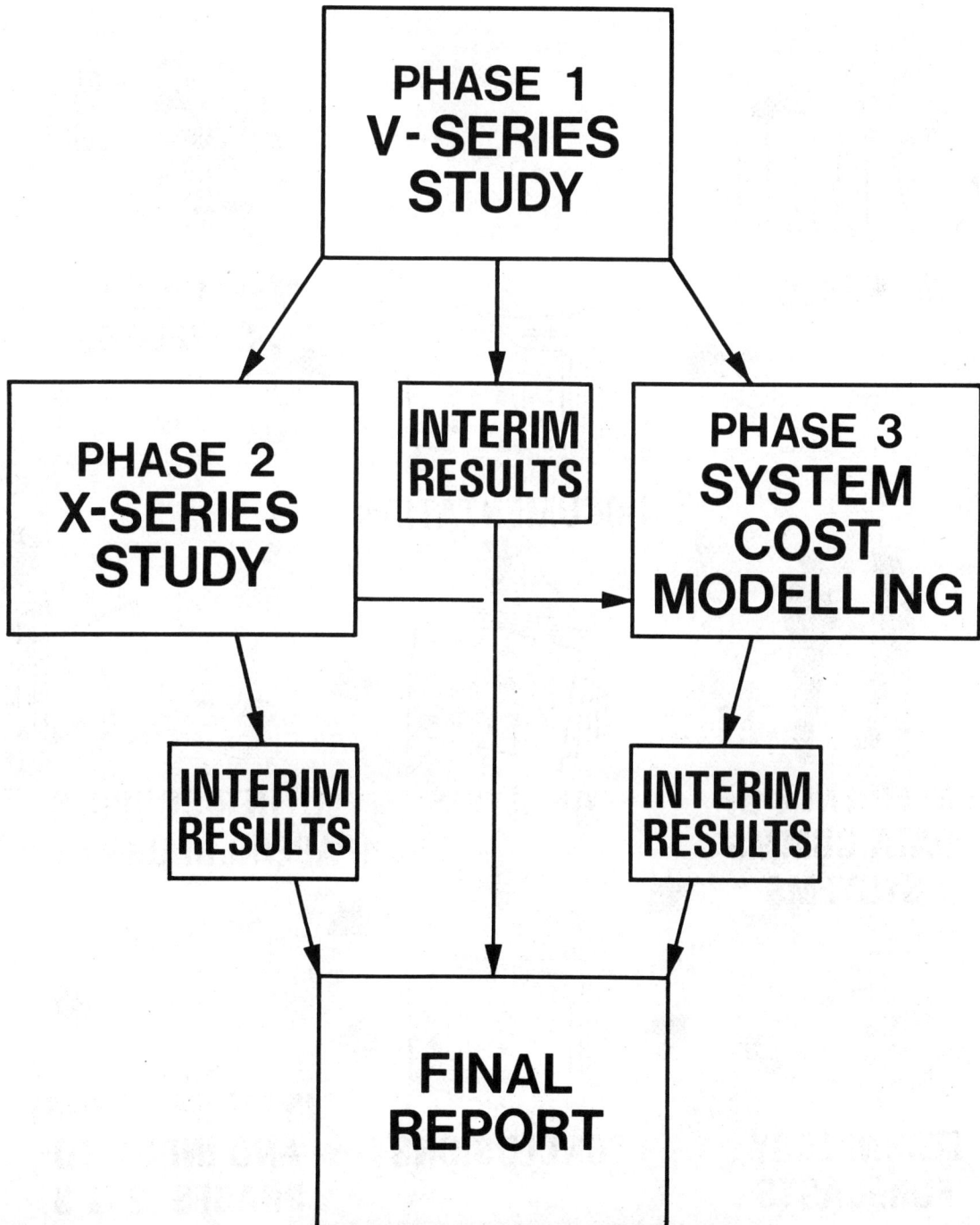

DDS COST/BENEFIT STUDY:
PHASE 1 STRUCTURE

V-SERIES STUDY

MANUALS

MEETINGS WITH SUPPLIERS

DOCUMENTATION

EXPERIENCE OF DATA COMMS SYSTEMS

ANALYSIS

OTHER SOURCES (PAPERS, BOOKS ETC)

TECHNOLOGY FORECASTS

CONCLUSIONS

INTERIM REPORT AND INPUT TO PHASES 2 & 3

DDS COST/BENEFIT STUDY:
PHASE 2 STRUCTURE

X-SERIES STUDY

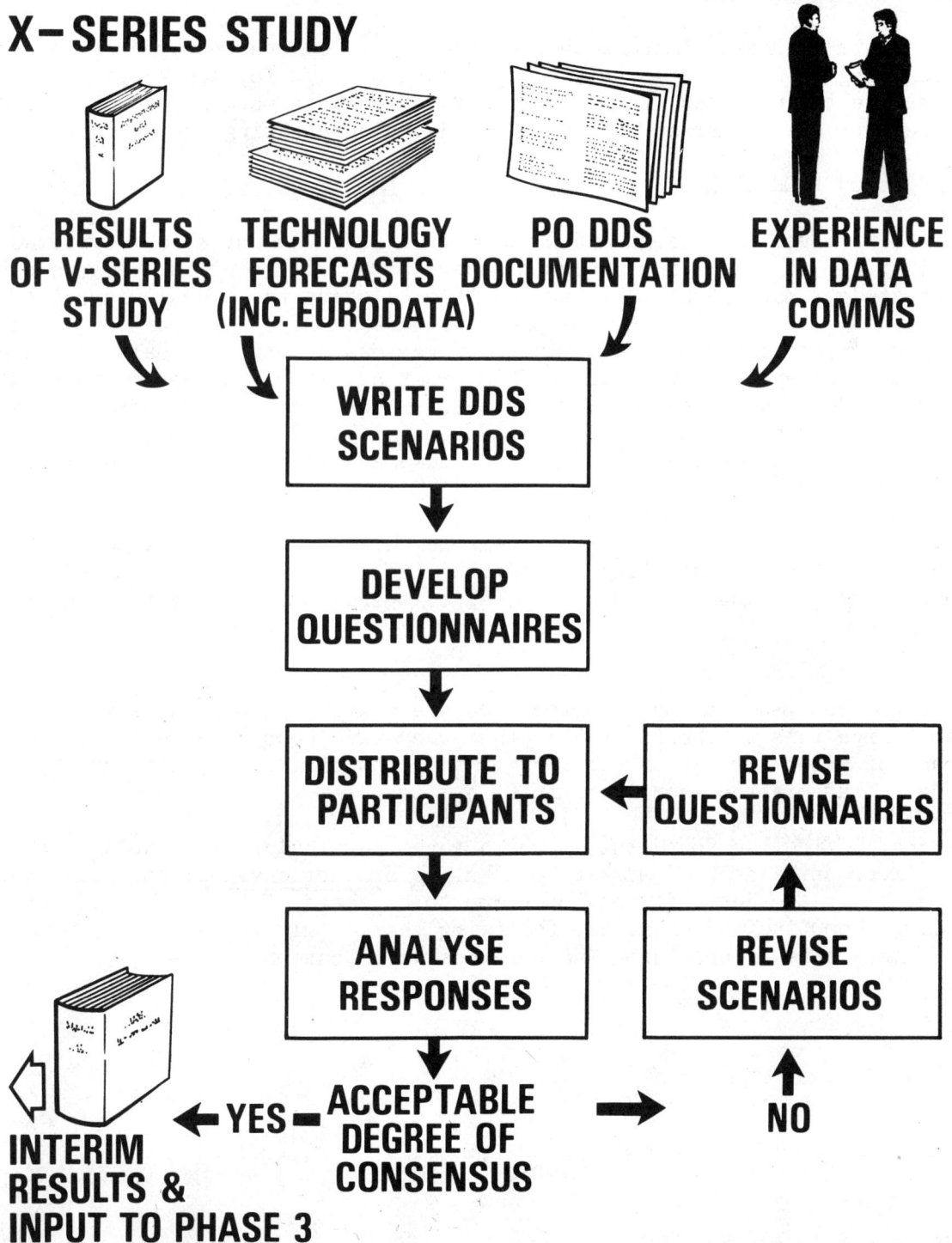

RESULTS OF V-SERIES STUDY | TECHNOLOGY FORECASTS (INC. EURODATA) | PO DDS DOCUMENTATION | EXPERIENCE IN DATA COMMS

WRITE DDS SCENARIOS

DEVELOP QUESTIONNAIRES

DISTRIBUTE TO PARTICIPANTS ← REVISE QUESTIONNAIRES

ANALYSE RESPONSES | REVISE SCENARIOS

← YES — ACCEPTABLE DEGREE OF CONSENSUS → NO

INTERIM RESULTS & INPUT TO PHASE 3

comments volunteered by participants totalled nearly 20,000 words. After the responses were consolidated, the results were cycled back and the respondents asked to review their initial answers in the light of the total response. This enabled the project team to achieve a higher degree of consensus than might otherwise be the case. (Incidentally, the identity of each respondent was not discolsed to the others.)

The results of Phases 1 and 2 thus enabled us to be reasonably confident about redesigning existing networks (and designing systems for new application areas) to utilise the proposed Digital Data Services. This work was supplemented by the results of the Market Research Group's Teleprocessing User Survey.

PHASE 3 COST MODELLING (Figure 5)

Phase 3 involved the design and writing of a Data Communications System Cost Model. This is a tool for assessing the cost structure of the various systems under study. For example, it was possible to study the overall impact of substituting DDS tariffs for telephone network tariffs in a particular network. Also, we investigated the sensitivity of various sub-system costs to the charge of certain independent variables. (In practice, it was necessary to input over 40 independent variables for each system.) Such modelling techniques enabled the team to identify the likely user financial benefits of such facilities as packet or byte interleaving. Figure 8 shows a small section of the model output for a test run.

Inevitably this 'left over' those items which were difficult if not impossible to cost, eg fast connect time and remote line identification. These factors reduced to a "How much are you prepared to spend for ...?" type of question.

SUMMARY

Although Cost Benefit Analysis techniques are well established within the UK Post Office this is the first time that they have been used to assess the impact of a total range of services on the financial feasibility of the use of data transmission techniques in DP systems.

The Post Office has found the approach to be particularly valuable in the most important aspect of marketing, that is product development. In other words, it is the Post Offices intention to be ahead of trends (if not actually leading them) instead of merely following them. Only in that way can we be absolutely sure of providing the services which customers need.

DDS COST/BENEFIT STUDY:
PHASE 3 STRUCTURE

COST MODELLING

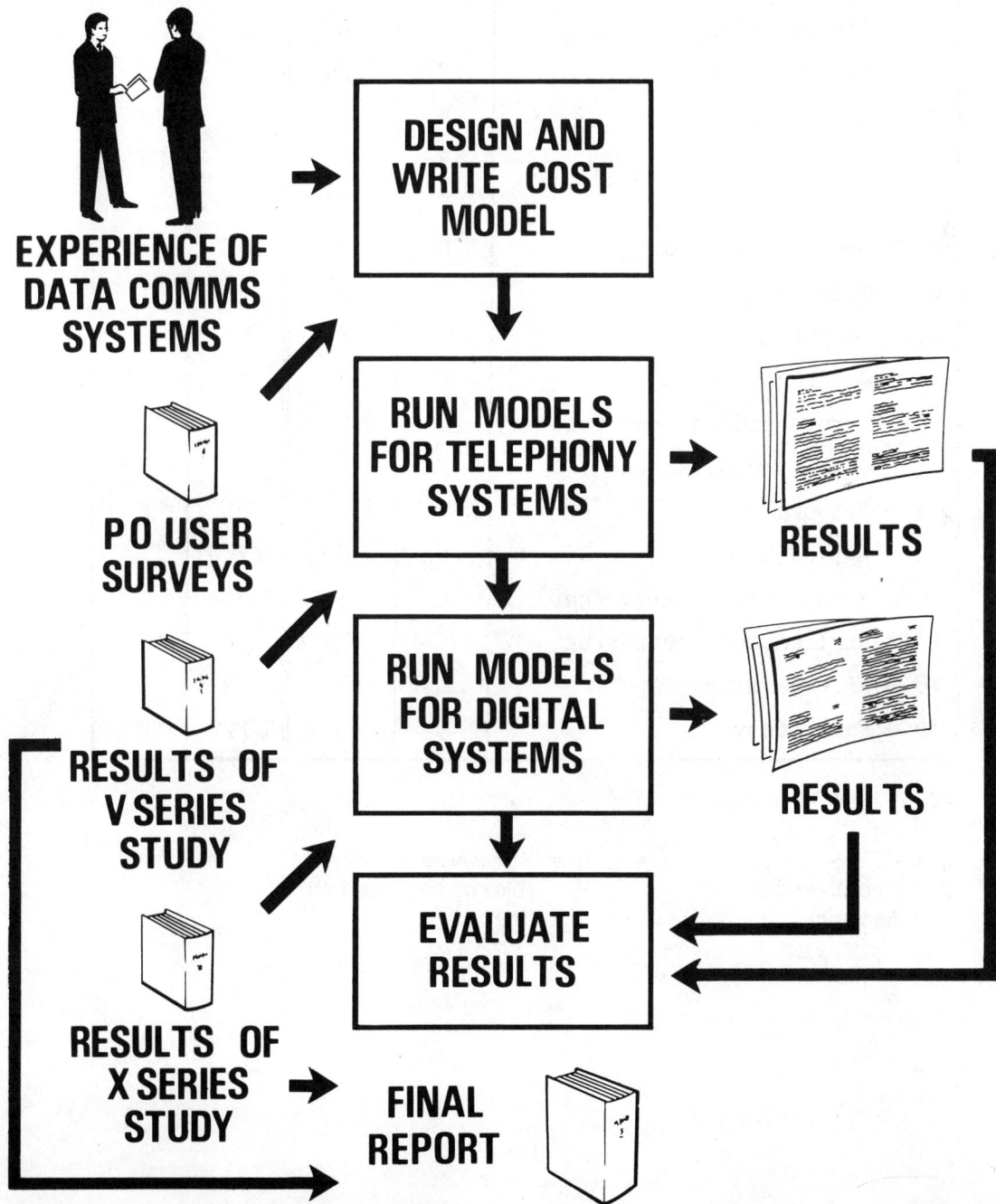

EXPERIENCE OF
DATA COMMS
SYSTEMS

DESIGN AND
WRITE COST
MODEL

PO USER
SURVEYS

RUN MODELS
FOR TELEPHONY
SYSTEMS

RESULTS

RESULTS OF
V SERIES
STUDY

RUN MODELS
FOR DIGITAL
SYSTEMS

RESULTS

RESULTS OF
X SERIES
STUDY

EVALUATE
RESULTS

FINAL
REPORT

FIGURE 6: LIKELY TRENDS IN DATA COMMUNICATIONS TECHNOLOGY

	FUNCTION	PRESENT		TREND	
		UNIT	TECH	UNIT	TECH
1	P-S S-P Conversion	F	H	F	H/M
2	Framing with SS bits	F	H	F	H/M
3	Ins/Del of syn chars	F	H	F	M/H
4	ID of control chars	F	S/M	F	M
5	Error detection	F	H/S	F	M/H
6	Auto-dialling	F	H+S	F	H+S
7	Auto-connect	F	H+S	F	H+S
8	Protocol control	C	S	F/N	S+M
9	Code conversion	C	S	F	S
10	Buffering	C	S	F	S
11	Queuing	C	S	F	S
12	Error handling and recovery	C	S	F	S
13	Collation of stats	C	S	F	S
14	Network mod	C	S	F/N	S
15	Msg editing (in)	C	S	C/F/N	S
16	Formatting of msgs (out)	C	S	C/F/N	S
17	Application processing	C	S	C/N	S
18	File handling	C	S	C/N	S
19	Failsafety	C	S	C/F/N	S

KEY:

C = CPU   H = Hardware
F = Front-end   M = Microprogramming
N = Network   S = Software

FIGURE 7: LIKELY TRENDS IN TERMINAL TECHNOLOGY

	PRESENT	FUTURE
INTERFACE HANDLING	H ———————⟶	H
CONTROL (COMMS)	H ———————⟶	M
CONTROL (PERIPHERALS)	H ———————⟶	M
PROCESSING	S ———————⟶ (and increasing)	S/M
TIMING	ASYNCH ———————⟶	SYNCH
SPEEDS	INCREASING ———⟶	
BUFFERING	INCREASING ———⟶	
INTEGRAL MODEMS	INCREASING ———⟶	

KEY:

H = Hardware

M = Microprogrammed

S = Software

FIGURE 8: SECTION OF A SPECIMEN DDS COST MODEL OUTPUT

COST MODEL SUMMARY	£	PERCENTAGE OF TOTAL
TOTAL CAPITAL COST	2,012,423	42.26
TOTAL CONTINUING COST	2,576,600	54.11
TOTAL ONE-TIME COST	173,100	3.63
TOTAL PROJECT COST	4,762,123	

ANALYSIS

TERMINAL SUB-SYSTEM	665,828	13.98
CPU SUB-SYSTEM	3,820,523	80.23
COMMUNICATIONS SUB-SYSTEM	275,772	5.79

TRAFFIC COSTS

	COMMS SUB-SYSTEM	TOTAL SYSTEM
COST PER KILOBIT	0.00268	4.62791E-2
COST PER MESSAGE	0.00938	0.161977

END OF MODEL RUN

UK POST OFFICE COST BENEFIT STUDY

SOME FEATURES OF THE TECHNOLOGY FORECASTS

Some of the major items of the Post Office (TMk4.4.2) and Eurodata technology
forecasts are summarised below, together with the teams comments upon them.
All prices are quoted in 1973 £s.

*MOS and Core Storage will decrease in cost from 0.3-0.5 per bit to 0.5-0.1
per bit in 1980. This will significantly influence the feasibility of
incorporating buffers in all terminals.

*The cost of mini and micro-processors will decrease by a factor of five
between 1973 and 1980. The implication of this is that 'processors on a chip'
could be readily available for much less than £200 thereby facilitating the
incorporation of programmability in even low-cost terminals.

*The increasing use of mini and special purpose processors will yield cost
reductions of 50% or above for CCUs of equivalent line capacity. This will
not necessarily change the way in which systems are configured but, obviously,
will reduce costs, and should make many more systems feasible.

*Selling price of general purpose intelligent terminals will decrease by over
50% between 1973 and 1980. This is much more substantial than the decrease
anticipated for hardwired devices (c 25%) and should cause increased popularity
for programmable terminals.

*Although the cost of software development is identified as being a major
obstacle to the increased use of 'soft' components, much work is now taking
place to reduce the problem (eg through the use of high-level real-time
compilers such as CORAL and RTL/2). Once development costs can be controlled,
software has the advantage that production (or 'reproduction') costs are very
low compared with hardware.

*As the cost of hardware components decreases, the network costs will inevitably
assume greater importance. This is particularly so as line rentals are
continuing costs which are susceptible to inflation, government revenue policies
and so on.

Network independent high level protocols

A.S. Chandler, Section Head, Network Technology,
Computer Aided Design Centre,   UK

To make effective use of any communication sub-system, there has
to exist a high level of protocol with which the user can
communicate. In established methods of communication - for example
an RJE terminal working over a leased line into a mainframe - the
high level protocol is well integrated into the operating system.
A similar situation applies to terminal access to the mainframe.
Since this level of protocol is a part of the operating system
it follows that there is a major problem when one attempts to
link to mainframes of different manufacturers.

The EPSS protocols laid down by the British Post Office cover the
interface to the network, but do not define any further how the
system should be used. Bearing in mind that EPSS is experimental,
and that the form of a permanent public network in the U.K. will
almost certainly differ from the present proposals in some degree,
it is sensible to design links to the network to be as insulated
from the mechanics of the network as is reasonably possible.

This paper describes the hierarchical structure of a set of
protocols proposed to implement a basic file transfer protocol on
EPSS. A brief description of the operational characteristics of
the file transfer protocol is given, and its interface with the
lower levels of protocol.

OVERVIEW

Traditionally the user has communicated with his mainframe via a
terminal or an RJE station using a direct connection, a leased
line or a dial-up link through the public switched telephone
network (PSTN). Alternatively, he might use either a satellite
or a work station. In the context of this paper a satellite
computer is regarded as a machine dependent upon its host
processor whilst a work station is a stand-alone machine with its
own operating system and high level language compiler. The work
station is able to be free-standing for the interactive part of
the work, but can be linked to a mainframe to do the remainder of
the computing and to access data banks and specialised software;
typically this would apply to a graphics application.

The main concern of the end user is to be free to use the same
terminals in the same way whether by direct connection or via a
switched network of datel or data type. He does not want to be
bothered by the interfacing or communication problem so long as
he can get his work done as cheaply and efficiently as possible
and, equally importantly, has some flexibility to start small and
grow as his needs expand, from terminal to work station, without
incurring expensive software overheads or radically changing his
mode of work.

A network is regarded as the means of "joining together" mainframes,
satellites, work stations, intelligent terminals, etc., to give the
user access to distributed computer power in as simple and flexible
way as possible.

The User Interface

Ideally the user wants the same interface to be usable at the
highest possible level. All that is required is a simple interface
which is capable of presenting data in a form acceptable to existing
operating systems. User requirements fall into a number of distinct
categories, each having radically different functional requirements:

1. interactive terminal traffic.

2. file transfer. Broadly speaking, data is transferred
   between user processes in different machines. In this
   context the user process might be an input or output
   peripheral, a file system or a user program. A further
   possibility would be to use the file transfer facilities
   to submit a job to the job stream of a remote host,

,without incurring the overhead of the more complex relationship that exists between an RJE station and its remote host.

3.   Job transfer. This would include "log-on" protocols for RJE stations, facilities for submitting jobs to the remote host, facilities for making enquiries to the remote host and inputting job control information.

Other areas have been identified, such as graphics protocols, data-base access, and no doubt more will emerge in the future. However the above are of immediate interest, in that they can be directly related to facilities provided by existing operating systems. There are a number of clearly identifiable components in a multi-discipline network, which reflect the overall structure of the network:

I   Communication sub-system:

This is communication at the lowest level and provides a "vehicle" for data transfer. It covers the line protocol and defines the procedure for transferring data between machines connected to the network. Further, as in the case of EPSS, it might define virtual calls, and mechanisms for the detection of and recovery from error situations. It might be regarded as the firmware of the network.

II   Bridging Interface:

Defines the interface between the vehicle and the higher levels of protocol and provides a layer of insulation between the vehicle and the high level protocol. The bridge should provide a number of primitives to high level protocols, and it is these which provide a network-independent interface for the high level protocol, and hide the particular method of operation of the network firmware.

III High level protocol:

Defines a series of functionally oriented high level communication protocols between sites on the network. The existence of level II allows this component to be totally independent from the vehicle to be used for data transfer. Without this independence the functions of computer communication and data transfer mechanism will inevitably merge. The ability to extend the system to offer new functions becomes difficult and

leads to a more complex software interface. More
important, the possibility of working with different
organisations connected to the sub-network is
correspondingly diminished, and the ability to work
with organisations using a different (but interconnected) network becomes impossible, for all
practical purposes.

IV   Gateway:

This is the interface between two or more networks.
The gateway would probably take the form of a host
computer connected to each network, and dedicated to
the task of operating as a gateway. A less practical
approach might be to perform this gateway function in
a host which is offering the normal range of user
facilities in parallel.

Its function would be to map between the protocols of
one network and the protocols of the other. The
complexity involved at this level depends on the degree
of compatibility between the two networks. If the
components at level III are identical then mappings
at levels I and II only will be involved. Conceptually
this sits above level III and, as it is not the subject
of this paper, will not be further discussed.

Thus, for a host connecting to a network, there have been identified
three discrete levels of protocol. They may be summarised by the
following figure 1.

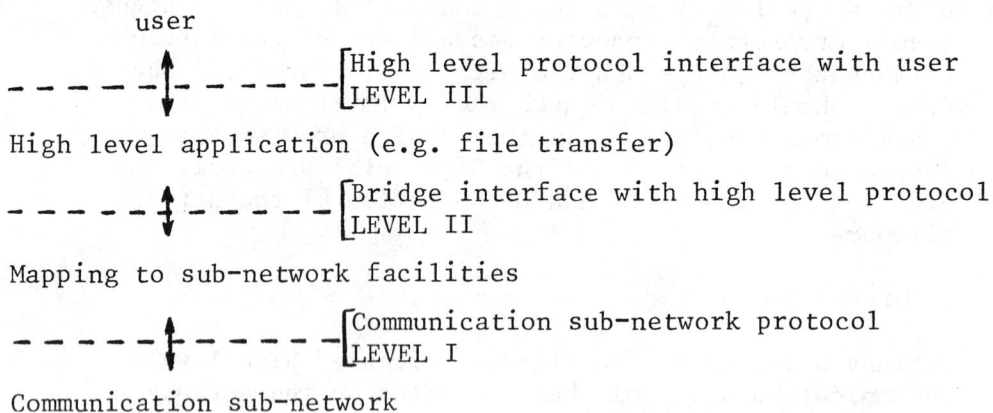

```
            user
                ↑
 — — — — — ─┼─ — — — — ─┌High level protocol interface with user
                ↓        └LEVEL III

High level application (e.g. file transfer)

                ↑
 — — — — — ┼ — — — — ─┌Bridge interface with high level protocol
                ↓        └LEVEL II

Mapping to sub-network facilities

                ↑
 — — — — — ┼ — — — — ─┌Communication sub-network protocol
                ↓        └LEVEL I

Communication sub-network
```

FIG. 1   Hierarchical structure of levels of protocol

The Experimental Packet Switched System (ref. 1) proposed by the British Post Office defines the facilities of a communication sub-system. This includes the hardware interface to the network, the packet structure and the concept of a virtual call. The system does not, however, consider the manner in which a real user might communicate a request for a transfer, perform that transfer and terminate in a satisfactory fashion on completion. Study Group 2 of the EPSS Liaison group was established to consider the problems, and recommend a solution. For a variety of reasons it was obvious that any high level protocol proposed by this group should ideally be independent of the communication sub-system (in this case, EPSS). The overriding consideration was the experimental nature of the system, coupled with the possibility of modifications to the characteristics of the network in any permanent service that might be offered.

The Study Group identified the functional requirements of a number of high level protocols, in particular interactive terminal access, remote job entry and file transfer. In the initial implementations of EPSS it is clear from discussion with other users, and within the group, that these will be the three areas of immediate interest. Without doubt, protocols to satisfy requirements in other areas will be developed as more experience and confidence is gained in EPSS.

Another group (Study Group 3) was charged with the task of defining the bridge between the network independent high level protocols, and the EPSS network. In practice this entailed a joint activity between the two groups to define the bridge functions as required by the high level protocol, and subsequently for Study Group 3 to define a way of implementing these functions on the EPSS network.

BASIC FILE TRANSFER PROTOCOL

This description of a basic file transfer protocol proposed for use on EPSS is not intended to be complete, and is fully defined elsewhere (ref. 2). The intention is to illustrate the basic concepts in order to place in context the functions required at the bridge. The first proposal made to the Study Group was based on the protocols used on the Computer Aided Design Centre's star network (ref. 3), a network of distributed computer systems which has been operating in a commercial environment since mid-1974. The functional characteristics of that system were subsequently modified to produce the present protocols.

The file transfer protocol provides an infrastructure to enable one process to transfer a data stream to another process. This data stream might contain directives to enable the receiving process to

interpret correctly the information received. Prior to sending the
data stream, a transfer request would have been sent from the
initiating process, which starts the interchange, to the initiated
process, giving details of the proposed transfer. In the network
the two processes would be implemented in two host computers
connected to the network. The actual form of a process within a
host is not discussed here. The process might be considered always
to be present, but dormant until a transfer request is received from
a higher level, or from the network. Alternatively the process might
be initiated on receipt of the transfer request. For the purpose of
this paper, this is unimportant, and is regarded as a local
implementation problem. Similarly the interface between the
operating system of the host computer and the file transfer process
resident in it is not defined here, and again this is a local
problem. However, guidelines to the solution of both problems will
be provided by the operating system.

FTP control path and parameter transfer

While this file transfer protocol is not presented using a theoretical
formalism, an important concept of the protocol is the "thread of
control". Throughout this paper the process initiating the file
transfer is referred to as process P. Process Q is the initiated
process. At the start of the interaction, process P sends a command
specifying the direction of the data transfer. Two such commands
are available in the FTP proposed for EPSS – GIVE (data Q→P) and
TAKE (data P→Q). The command is followed by a series of keyword
parameters with qualifying values giving attributes of the file to be
transferred. Some of these keywords can quote alternative values
which may subsequently be reduced by process Q. For simplicity
only one (TAKE) will be described in this paper, in order to
establish the concept. However, it should be borne in mind that
although the directives exchanged are essentially the same, the
thread of control is necessarily different. It is important to
appreciate that at the end of the transfer, control is always
returned to the initiating process P, whether or not the transfer
was successful. Also, during the actual transfer of data, that
the thread of control remains at the process which is actually
sending the data.

Process P will always send an END to indicate the end of the
transaction, whether or not it has been successful. This is not a
transfer of control but is used to complete the procedure, and
to provide a means of indicating that a new command can be issued
to start another file transfer, or that the link between process
P and process Q may be closed.

In the diagrams used to illustrate the following paragraphs the
keywords used have been chosen for their descriptive qualities,
and are not the keywords used in the protocol. Arrows crossing
boundary between P and Q are used to indicate the direction of
the transfer of control, when it occurs. Shorter arrows are used
to indicate when a single directive or keyword is transmitted,
but is not associated with a transfer of control.

1. Process P sends the command with the associated keyword
   parameters, and this list is terminated with a request
   for a REPLY. This action will pass control over to
   process Q. At this point process Q might choose to
   reject the proposed file transfer, in which case a
   REPLY will be returned, quoting a reason for the failure.
   Control has thus been returned to process P. Process
   P sends an END finally terminating the transfer. Figure
   2 illustrates this situation.

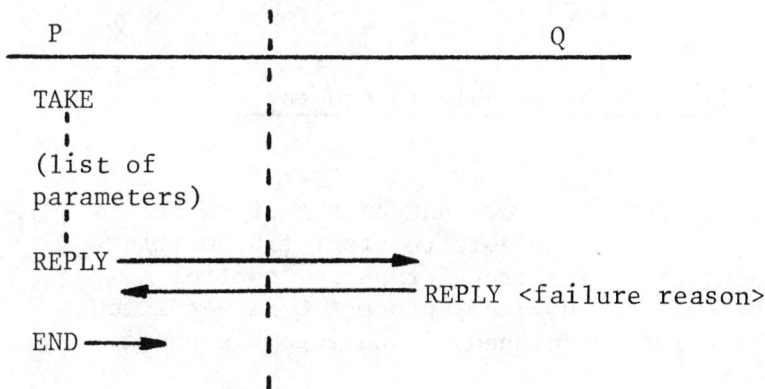

FIG.2   File transfer rejected by process Q

2. Having received the transfer command with its associated
   keyword parameters, process Q is now at liberty to reduce
   some or all of the quoted values. A list of keyword
   parameters with the reduced set of values is returned
   to process P, again terminated with REPLY. Control is
   back in process P, which may be content to accept the
   reduced values (see 3. below) or may find them
   inadequate. If this is the case, process P sends a
   REPLY to process Q giving a failure reason. Process Q
   is expected to return a dummy REPLY to pass control back
   to process P, and again the interaction is completed
   by an END. Figure 3 summarises this interchange.

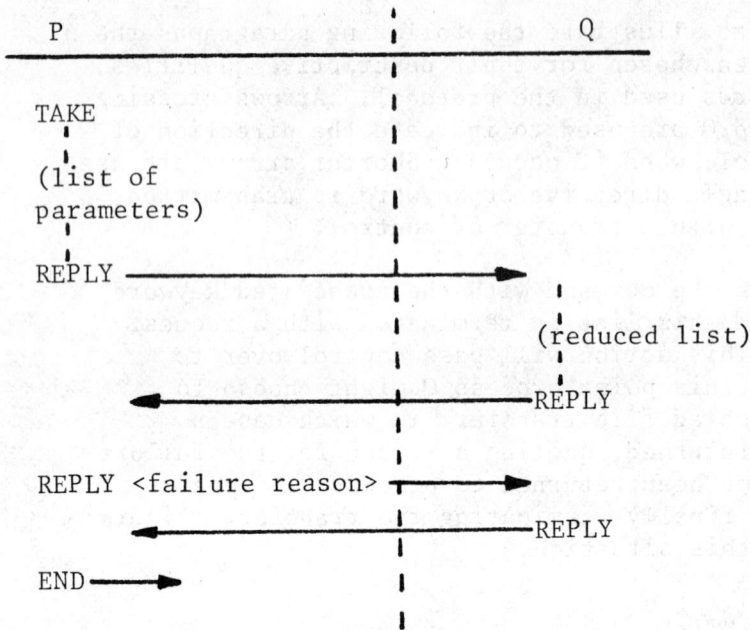

FIG.3   Reduced values unacceptable to process P

3. If the originally quoted set or reduced set of values is
    acceptable, process P is now able to start transmitting
    data.   Throughout this data transfer phase, control
    remains with process P.   However, process Q is permitted
    to transmit directives spontaneously during this phase:

    (i)   A restart request to process P, to back up to
           an earlier restart marker.

    (ii)   A directive to acknowledge the acceptance of data,
           up to the restart point whose number is quoted.

    (iii) A request to process P to skip forward to the restart
           point whose number is given.   This mechanism is used
           should process Q wish to abort the file transfer.
           Process Q issues a request to skip to the end of
           file, and will ignore all incoming data, until the
           appropriate restart marker and end of data directive
           is received.   Then process Q confirms end of data,
           giving a failure code, indicating the reason for
           the abort.

Process P will send an END to complete the interaction.
Figure 4 shows this interchange.

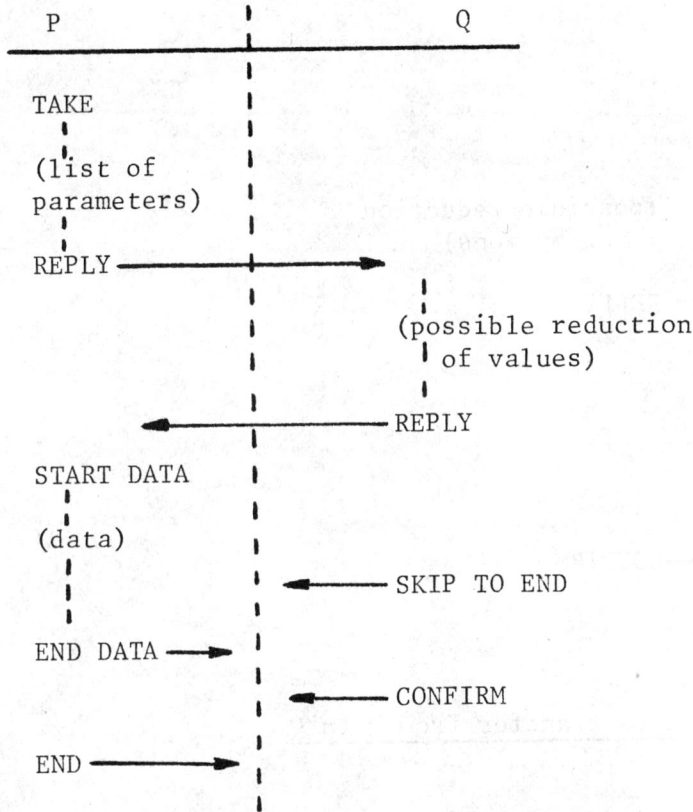

```
        P                    │              Q
                             │
   ─────────────────────────┼────────────────────────
                             │
   TAKE                      │
    ▌                        │
   (list of                  │
   parameters)               │
    ▌                        │
   REPLY ────────────────────┼──────────────▶
                             │
                             │
                             │      (possible reduction
                             │        of values)
                             │
         ◀────────────────────────────── REPLY
                             │
   START DATA                │
    ▌                        │
   (data)                    │
    ▌             ◀───────── SKIP TO END
    ▌                        │
   END DATA ────▶            │
                  ◀───────── CONFIRM
                             │
   END ─────────▶            │
                             │
```

FIG.4   <u>File transfer aborted by Process Q</u>

At the end of the data transfer an end of data marker
is transmitted to process Q. Process Q confirms end
of data to process P. This last interaction is
necessary to ensure that data has been received
satisfactorily and to check that no restart requests
are in transmission. Naturally no restart requests
should be sent after end of data has been confirmed
by process Q. Process P finally terminates the
interaction with an END, as before. Figure 5
illustrates this interchange.

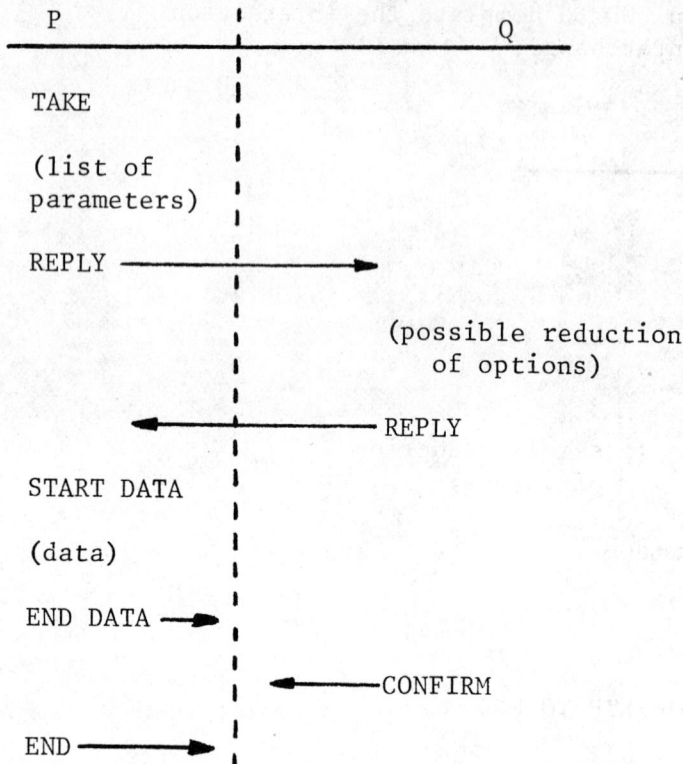

FIG.5   Complete data transfer from P to Q

FTP Data transfer

The policy adopted for the data transfer phase has been that it is
desirable to mix directives for the high level protocol (e.g. restart
points, code changes, etc.) with the actual data being transferred,
in order to synchronise the two. Accordingly, there has to exist a
mechanism to differentiate between control directives and data.
This could be done by introducing each directive with a special
character (or sequence of bits) but this leads to a number of
problems, notably:

1.   The entire data stream has to be scanned for this character
     when received.

2.   Occurrences of this character within the users data stream
     will have to be "escaped out" in some way, possibly by
     repeating the character. The obvious implication therefore
     is that the entire stream has to be checked before trans-
     mission.

The mechanism eventually recommended by the Study Group uses a record structure, of the form:

        <zero separator><directive><argument><terminator>
  or   <record separator><data>

The record separator is a single byte, six bits of which are used to specify the length of the record in 8 bit bytes. In order that records of length >63 bytes may be transmitted, a sub-record facility exists. Thus, each record or sub-record is preceded by a single byte, six bits being used to give the length of the record or sub-record, and a single bit is used to indicate that the last byte of the following sequence of bytes is the last of the current record. (The remaining bit is used to indicate a compressed sequence of data.) Provided then, that the protocol does not allow sub-records of zero length to be transmitted, there is no possibility for confusing directives and data, and the distinction is achieved with a relatively small overhead.

BRIDGE INTERFACE

Closer consideration of the file transfer protocol reveals a number of characteristics of the interface:

1. A logical link has to be made between the local and the remote high level processes.

2. This link is used to establish contact in the first instance by passing the transfer command, and subsequently to pass the parameters of the transfer.

3. A response is received from the remote high level process, either rejecting the proposed transfer, or accepting it with a possible reduction in the parameter values.

4. A flow of actual data occurs, possibly with directives injected into the data stream.

The bridging protocol has to provide facilities to allow the high level process to establish, use and relinquish logical links. The logical link provides a full duplex data transmission capability between the two processes. The interface to the process is referred to as a port. A port is a local entity and may be assigned in a number of ways:

1. by the high level process when communicating to the bridge.

2. by the bridge, as a result of an action by the high
    level process.

3. in a simple system, ports may be preassigned.

Communications from the high level process to the bridge can be
expressed in the form of a procedure call, with data, to which
the bridge is expected to return a result. Some calls will
expect no results, but they will still require a signal from the
bridge to indicate acceptance. Some will have results returned
immediately, while others will be suspended, awaiting a response
from the remote system. A high level procedure call is expressed:

> operation (data); →result

Communication from the bridge to the high level process can be
regarded in the form of an interrupt, which will produce no direct
result. However, it may subsequently lead to a procedure call
from the high level. Bridge initiated communication is expressed:

> *operation (data);

Link creation

The following sequence is used to establish a logical link:

> open(calling address, called address); →port or refusal error

This informs the bridge of the requirement to establish a new logical
link. As previously mentioned the port may be allocated by the
bridge as shown in this call, or by the high level process, in which
case it would be passed in the argument, rather than being returned
as a response.

This procedure call will cause the bridge to pass a message through
the sub-network to the bridge at the specified address. This will
signal the remote high level process with:

> *create(calling address, called address, port);

The call will be rejected with:

> close(port, errorcode); →null

or accepted with:

> accept (port); →null

This information will be transmitted over the sub-network to the bridge which started the interchange, and subsequently the high level process will receive its results.

In addition, the logical link may be rejected at any level (e.g. at the local bridge if the sub-network is not available) and a suitable response will be returned to the high level process.

Figure 6 summarises a successful interchange.

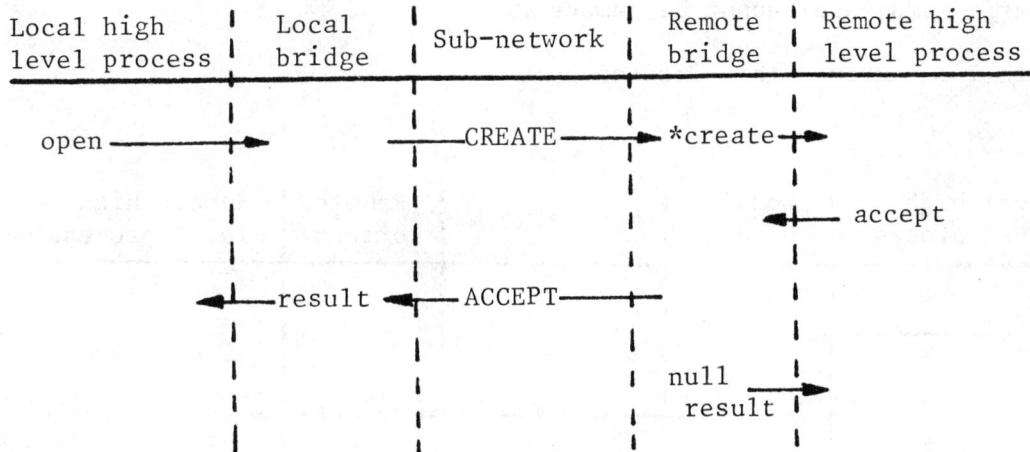

```
Local high    | Local    |              | Remote  | Remote high
level process | bridge   | Sub-network  | bridge  | level process
──────────────┼──────────┼──────────────┼─────────┼──────────────
              |          |              |         |
  open ───────────▶      |──CREATE──────▶ *create─▶
              |          |              |         |
              |          |              |         | ◀─── accept
              |          |              |         |
         ◀────┼──result ◀┼──ACCEPT──────┤         |
              |          |              |         |
              |          |              |  null   |───────▶
              |          |              |  result |
              |          |              |         |
```

FIG.6   Successful link establishment

Link termination

The following sequence is used to relinquish an existing link. It is assumed that in normal circumstances the two high level processes have already completed their interactions, and that any data remaining in the sub-network may be discarded. The high level process terminates the link with:

     close (port, errorcode); →null

Either high level process can terminate the logical link, and the problem of both processes closing at the same time can be circumvented by suitable implementation at the bridge level. In the file transfer example previously described, it would be appropriate for the initiated process to close the call on receiving the final END.

This procedure call will cause the bridge to pass a message
through the sub-network to the remote bridge. The remote
bridge will signal its high level process with:

        *close (port, errorcode);

Any subsequent attempt by the high level process to use that
port will be rejected by the bridge.

This last signal can also be generated by the bridge if the
sub-network fails or has indicated that this logical path no
longer exists, and cannot be remade.

Figure 7 summarises this interchange.

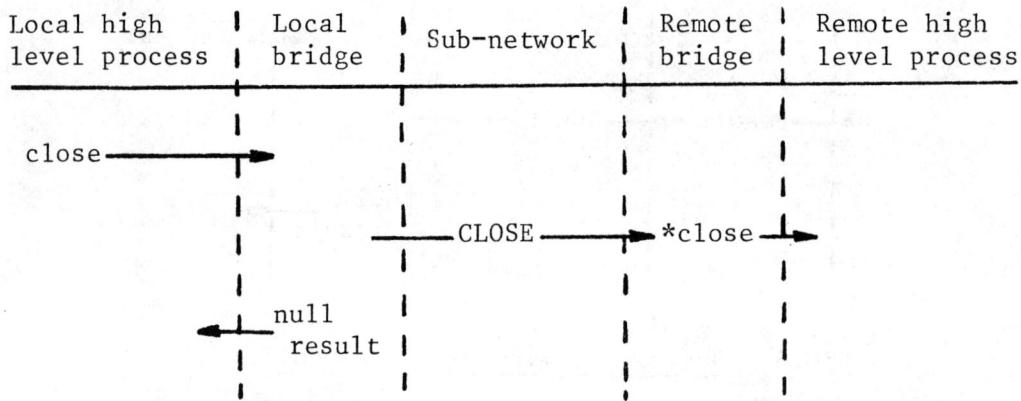

```
Local high      | Local  |              | Remote | Remote high
level process   | bridge | Sub-network  | bridge | level process
────────────────┼────────┼──────────────┼────────┼──────────────
                |        |              |        |
    close───────────►    |              |        |
                |        |              |        |
                |        ───── CLOSE ──────► *close──►
                |        |              |        |
             ◄──│ null   |              |        |
                │ result |              |        |
                |        |              |        |
```

FIG.7   Link termination

Data transfer

The protocol for data transfer to and from the bridge has proved
a difficult issue to resolve, and there are several schools of
thought. Also some details are implementation-dependent and
the particular solution adopted can, to a large extent, be

governed by the characteristics of the operating system. The
two major areas are:

1. When receiving data, should the high level process
   issue a "read" procedure call, and receive the data
   as the results, or should the bridge inform the high
   level protocol that data has arrived? Each method
   has points in its favour. If the high level process
   issues reads, then it would do so at the rate at
   which it could dispose of the information, and
   therefore the bridge would use this to control the
   rate of incoming data. If the bridge informs the
   high level process that data has arrived, then this
   would remove the onus of having to make speculative
   reads from the high level process. In fact, a
   hybrid approach is quite workable. If the high
   level process is expecting data (e.g. receiving a
   file) then it would issue a read of the form:

   read (port, volume of data); →data OR error code

   This assumes that responsibility for resource
   allocation rests with the bridge. If the buffers
   are to be allocated by the high level process,
   then the procedure call would have to quote a
   buffer address, in addition to the other parameters.
   (Again this is a local problem.)

   If data arrives unexpectedly, for example a restart
   request in the reverse direction to the main data
   flow, then the bridge might spontaneously pass
   the data to the high level process with:

   *read (port, buffer address);

   The same arguments can be applied to writes from a
   high level process. However, for simple implementation,
   it is only necessary to issue reads and writes from the
   high level process, and it is this mechanism which is
   described.

2. Should the interface between the high level process
   and the bridge be a byte stream, or should a record
   structure be used? A record structure has an apparent
   advantage in that error recovery is made more simple,
   and that the bridge is dealing in positive units of
   information. However a record structure confirs
   advantages when implemented at the higher level, and
   would have to be duplicated at the bridge interface.

Within EPSS, a substantial error recovery mechanism
exists at the sub-network level, and more meaningful
error recovery facilities will have to be designed
within the high level process, making use of restart
points injected into the data for this purpose.

A byte interface is necessarily more simple, and
can be provided as a sub-set of a record interface.
In an experimental system, this in itself has a
number of advantages in that it provides a formal
interface for testing a variety of record interfaces.

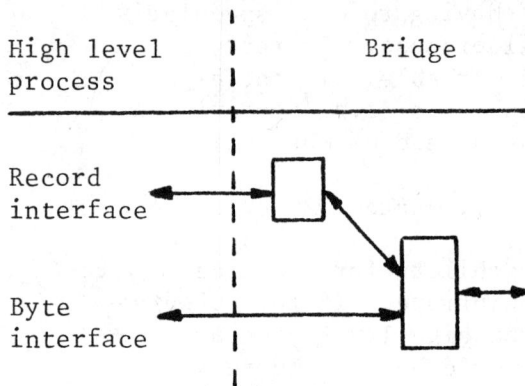

High level   Bridge
process

Record
interface

Byte
interface

FIG.8   Byte and record interface between bridge and
         high level process

To send data to the remote high level process, the local process
makes a procedure call to its local bridge:

        write (port, data, end of sequence); →null OR error code

will immediately accept the data (or will reject it with an error),
and will assume responsibility for ensuring that the data is
correctly transmitted over the sub-network. The bridge will also
be responsible for making the most efficient use of the sub-network.
For example it might withhold transmission of a small amount of
data until it has a complete packet to send. However, if the end
of sequence flag is set, then the bridge must transmit all the
data that it is holding for that port, and further, that flag
must be propagated through the network. Its primary use by the
high level process is to indicate that it has reached the end
of a sequence (for example the end of the parameters of a file
transfer request) and that some action is required by the remote
high level process.

Received data will be held by the bridge, until the high level
process issues a read. If a maximum volume of data has been
accumulated, the bridge will prevent further transmission by use
of its own flow control facilities. The read issued by the high
level process is of the form:

    read (port, volume of data); →data OR error code

The procedure call will be completed by the bridge when sufficient
data has arrived to fulfil the read or when data arrives which is
flagged as the end of sequence.

Figure 9 summarises this situation.

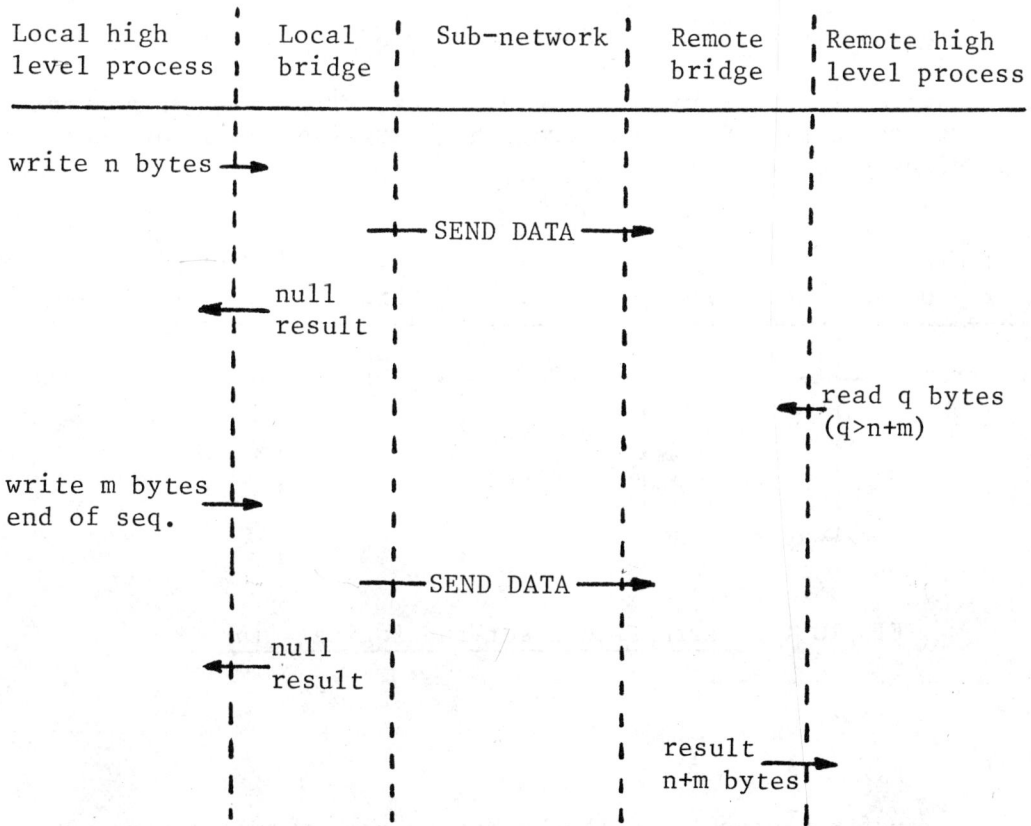

FIG. 9   Data transfer

Error Control

A number of situations can arise in which errors will be detected
by the bridge, resulting in loss of data or a failure of the
logical link. These will be returned to the high level protocol
with an interrupt-like function:

        *error (port, error code);

There is also a requirement for the high level process to be able
to request that the bridge performs a 'reset' on this logical
link, to clear any data in either direction, and to re-synchronise
with the remote bridge and high level process. This is of the
form:

        interrupt (port, error code); →acknowledge   OR error

and in addition to resetting the logical link, will cause an appropriate error to be passed to the remote high level process (of the
form previously described).

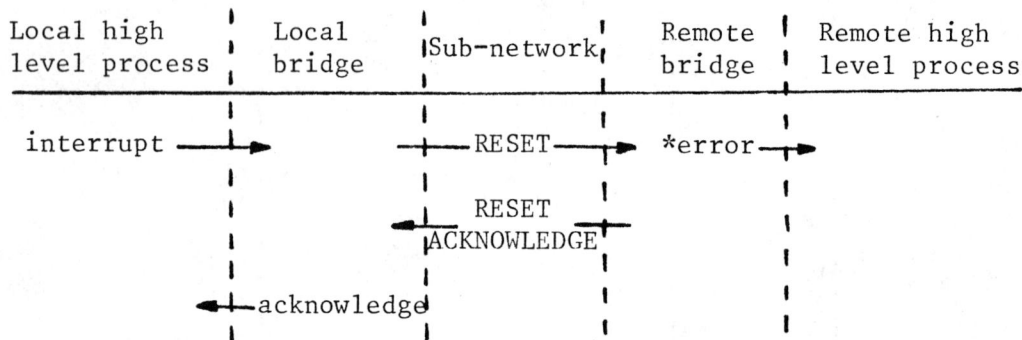

Local high level process	Local bridge	Sub-network	Remote bridge	Remote high level process
interrupt ⎯⎯→		⎯⎯RESET⎯⎯→	*error ⎯→	
		RESET ACKNOWLEDGE		
←⎯acknowledge				

FIG.10   Interrupt to reset the logical link

SUMMARY

The file transfer protocol and the bridge to the communications sub-
system, as proposed for initial use on EPSS, are extremely simple
in both function and operation. A number of more complex facilities
could be provided at both levels, and indeed functions such as
recall, and a record interface to the bridge have been discussed
at length. However, a simple approach in the first instance will
give implementors the opportunity to gain confidence in EPSS and
to accrue more experience in networking problems. In the long term
this will lead to the design of facilities to solve the actual
problems encountered when using a network.

ACKNOWLEDGEMENTS

The author wishes to acknowledge the considerable time and effort of the members of the working groups of Study Groups 2 and 3, all of whom have made significant contributions to the discussions and subsequent design of the protocols recommended for use on the EPSS network.

Acknowledgement is also due to the Director of the Computer Aided Design Centre, for permission to publish this paper.

REFERENCES

1. EPSS Customer Document (Issue 4) - British Post Office

2. A Basic File Transfer Protocol. EPSS Liaison Group Study Group 2
       HLP/CP(75)3

3. CAD Centre's Star Computer Network - CADC R/255/74.

Virtual call issues in network architectures

Louis POUZIN

Director of the CYCLADES Network

Institut de Recherche d'Informatique et d'Automatique

France

ABSTRACT

The concept of virtual circuit is mainly used to designate a set of end-to-end control mechanisms in packet switching networks. Similar mechanisms called liaisons may be found at higher levels in a computer network. Their properties are reviewed, specifically with regard to port access, error and flow control.

Various forms of virtual circuits are included in existing or planned packet networks. But some networks have none. Since end-to-end control mechanisms always exist at higher levels, it is not clear that virtual circuits in packet networks are worth their cost.

Interfacing computer systems with virtual circuits raises a number of problems specifically in splicing with liaisons at a higher level. Another approach is a gateway mimicking terminals. Finally, the least interfering approach is to consider virtual circuits as a substitute to real ones.

DEFINITIONS

Terms such as virtual call, virtual circuit, logical link, logical
path, are used synonymously in the computer communication literature.
What is actually meant is the existence of an association between two
entities, (often referenced as <u>ports</u>) along with a set of rules for
transferring information from one entity to the other in an orderly
and reliable manner.

By definition, a virtual call (VC) has only two ends. Therefore barring
abnormal behaviour, all information sent from one end over a VC is
delivered only to the other end. In some sense, a VC behaves like a
pipe, (fig. 1).

Port A   Port B

O━━━━━━━━━━━━━━━━━━━━━━━━━━━━━━━━━━━━━━━O

Fig. 1 - Virtual call

SOME CONFUSING ASPECTS

In the area of packet switching networks (PSN), there seems to be a
fairly good understanding of the datagram (DG) service. On the other
hand the concept of VC raises a great deal of confusion, as many people
mean different things, while arguing with evident conviction.

E.g. for the French P & T, a VC is a set of resources allocated throughout a PSN, allowing the transfer of indefinite streams of characters
on a fixed route. It is actually a FIFO queue.

For the UK Post Office, a VC is a protocol between a pair of PSN end-
nodes allowing the delivery of sequenced packets, which are transferred
on possibly different routes.

For Bell Canada, a VC is an end-to-end (E-E) protocol implemented within
subscriber computers, allowing the transfer of sequenced messages in
fragments not necessarily delivered in sequence.

For some computer manufacturers, a VC is the closest substitute to a
physical point to point circuit, which allows to maintain their existing
hardware and software, without changing their network structure.

For users, VC's are just a dragging tug-of-war between some sects in
Packetistan.

In this paper we shall attempt to review various aspects of the VC concept, and to place it in a proper perspective within a network structure. Indeed, most of the controversy about VC's stems from the way they are inserted at a particular functional level, not just the way they are designed or implemented.

THE NEED FOR LIAISONS

Since the terms virtual call, or circuit, have been mostly associated historically with PSN's designed by some PTT's, it seems appropriate to introduce a more general term, which can apply to other forms of VC implementation as well.

We shall term liaison a temporary or permanent association between two ports, for the purpose of transferring information according to the rules of an E-E protocol.

The concept of liaison results from several requirements :

. segregate information received according to its source.

. set up error and flow control schemes end-to-end.

. handle independently the traffic between any pair of ports.

These requirements stem for the modern approach of structured design, which aims at decoupling the various logical layers of a system. The liaison protocol should not interfere with lower level communication mechanisms, and should provide a basic layer upon which higher level protocols can be built.

The concern for security introduces the need for well defined areas of responsibility in traffic control. E.g. PTT's cannot rely entirely on subscribers to protect public PSN's from tampering or congestion. Similarly, subscribers cannot rely entirely on PTT's to ensure the correctness or the balance of traffic between their correspondents. In other words, areas of responsibility must be reflected in system boundaries, and self-reliant mechanisms.

As can be verified easily, in existing systems any automated information transfer relies on some form of E-E protocol between distant entities.

When traveling from one port to the other, the information transferred may be constrained to pass through lower level protocols controlling the traffic between intermediate ports. This may or may not bring some advantages. But, to keep with sound design principles, these lower level mechanisms should be invisible at the E-E level.

LIAISON PROPERTIES

In the following we shall examine typical technical properties attached to liaison mechanisms, regardless of the level of system at
which they are located.

1 - Transit delay

When using real or physical circuits for data transmission over a
telephone line, there is always some delay between sending and receiving a particular bit. This is usually small enough (a few μs to a few
ms) to be neglected as compared to the time it takes to transmit a
whole message of a few hundred bits on a regular telephone line. In
this case the data link is not referred to as a liaison or VC.

Store and forward communication systems require an E-E delay longer
than the transmission time of a message by the sender. This is due
to intermediate queueing and transmission delays. This environment
is typically the one in which liaisons are considered to control
information transfer.

Since delays are substantial several messages may be simultaneously [1]
in transit on a liaison. Consequently half-duplex control procedures
 commonly used over physical circuits (alternating message sending
and acknowledgement) become inefficient, as they waste a significant
ratio of the potential throughput. More effective procedures such
as HDLC[2] are required to make use of the available rate.

2 - Uni- or bidirectional

Some implementations offer only unidirectional liaisons, such as
socket to socket connections in Arpanet [3]. Others include bidirectional liaisons, such as Cyclades [4]. Practically there are very few
applications where unidirectional liaisons would be sufficient.
Most of the time some feedback is required. Thus, bidirectional
liaisons are more convenient and take less overhead.

3 - Permanent or transient

In order to exist a liaison requires an association between two
existing entities. When entities are permanent, it can be considered
that there exists a permanent association between any pair. This is
the case in Cyclades. Another approach is to open and close an
association on a dynamic basis, as in Arpanet. Maintaining an active
liaison requires more information than when it does not exist, due
to the state variables representing the instantaneous traffic activity. Consequently, it saves on overhead to open/close liaisons just
for the time they are sufficiently active. E.g. in Cyclades, liaisons
are permanent, but without status information, for basic message
transfer only. Additional properties requiring state variables may
be activated, but they are bracketed with open/close states.

4 - Sharable or busy ports

If no more than a single liaison can be anchored on a single port, the latter is put in a busy state, like a phone set engaged in a conversation. E.g. in Arpanet, a socket allocated to a connection is unavailable for establishing other connections. But one may allow any number of liaisons to be anchored onto the same port, as in Cyclades (fig. 2).

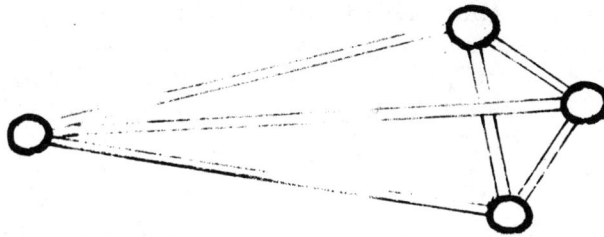

Fig. 2 - Multi-connected ports

The first approach is satisfactory when entities linked through a liaison are non-sharable resources, such as a card reader or a simple terminal. But if the entity is sharable, e.g. a transaction system, a data base manager, a remote job entry service, a multi-device terminal, the second approach is more efficient, as it does not require additional machinery to allow several liaisons to be attached to a single port.

Accessing a sharable resource with single liaison ports requires one of the following schemes :

a) Each potential caller is allocated a unique port (or set of ports). Thus the number of ports may grow unmanageable, and it is not convenient to call the same entity by different names.

b) Callers access dedicated ports, which switch quickly liaisons over to free ports. The total number of ports need only be set for the maximum number of simultaneous callers. But there is an additional machinery and set of conventions. In Arpanet this is the Initial Connection Protocol (ICP)[5].

c) Other schemes might be imagined : random calls, queueing and call back. But they are even more involved.

None of the previous schemes is completely satisfactory, due to increased overhead and devious error conditions resulting from the caller unpredictable behaviour, during the port selection process.

On the other hand making a multi-liaison port restricted to a single liaison is trivial. Therefore multi-liaison ports are more suitable in all circumstances.

5 - Call collision

When two ports attempt to establish a liaison with one another, the logic may be such that both fail, like in the telephone system. This is undesirable, as it induces delays and overhead traffic in multiple attempts. Schemes exist that avoid call collisions through a symmetrical handling of requests and responses (Arpanet, Cyclades). Other variants are based on port priority. But they introduce additional parameters and complexity with no obvious advantage.

6 - Sequencing

Most usually liaisons are implemented in such a way that information is delivered to the receiver end in the same sequence as it has been sent. This property may result from the characteristics of the transmission medium (e.g. a telephone line). But if the transmission sequence is not guaranteed by the medium (e.g. a PSN), a specific mechanism often called reassembly is in charge of piecing together fragments of received information so as to deliver the whole traffic stream in sequence.

7 - Error control

Since no transmission medium is actually error-free, some mechanisms are customarily introduced to detect errors and perform recovery. Typically these mechanisms fall in two categories :

a) Stepwise control implemented along the path taken by the information carried over a liaison (Fig. 3). This is a useful but not sufficient technique. Indeed, detecting and correcting errors locally

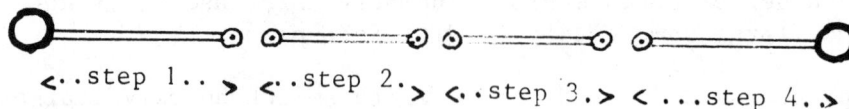

<..step 1.. > <..step 2.> <..step 3.> < ...step 4.>

Fig. 3 - Step-wise control

improves E-E reliability and reduces the loss of throughput. As a by-product it is also an effective tool to monitor the behaviour of physical components of the transmission medium. But there are uncontrolled gaps between the sections under control. Thus the reliability of the whole liaison is not any better than that of these weaker links. If in addition the transmission medium is under various responsibilities, no one is clearly in charge of the global reliability.

b) <u>End-to-end control</u>. A single mechanism extends its domain over the whole liaison, thus making it as reliable as this mechanism allows (fig. 4). The major advantage is to define more clearly areas of responsibility for insuring reliability. As long as mechanisms located at

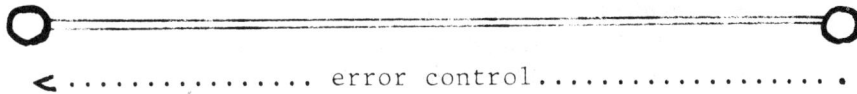

Fig. 4 - End to end control

both ends can be held safe, then the reliability of the whole liaison is independent of the transmission medium. However, error detection and recovery may be affected by transit delays, if they rely upon an acknowledgement scheme. Some throughput degradation occurs whenever an error must be corrected by retransmission. Thus it is all the more desirable to have a low error rate in the transmission medium that transit delays are longer.

Practically the most satisfactory scheme is a superposition of both techniques. Low error rates are brought about by step-wise control, while high reliability is enforced through E-E control.

Typically error control relies upon two basic mechanisms[6] : - checksumming fragments of information, - a naming and acknowledgement scheme for fragments. Incidentally, this requires a well defined relationship between fragments sent and received. Otherwise there is no content independent way to make sure that all fragments are received correctly.

8 - Flow control

This term is confusedly taken to mean two different things. One is the set of rules whereby a sender at one end of a liaison is restricted from flooding the receiver end beyond its capacity of accepting traffic. The other is the set of rules whereby a transmission medium prevents itself from being overloaded with incoming traffic. In order to prevent confusion we shall refer to the latter as <u>congestion control</u>.

Although both problems may present some intuitive similarities, there is no evidence that they are strongly inter-dependent. Thus only E-E flow control will be considered for the moment.

As opposed to error control, whose well defined objective is to
catch all errors of a certain type, there is no such clear cut
objective for flow control. Indeed, curbing, sender output so that
in no circumstances there occurs information loss is technically
simple to implement, but can be disastrous in terms of throughput
and delay. Idle state or rejected traffic have the same effect in
reducing throughput. Therefore the objectives of a good flow control
scheme may be diversified, e.g. :

  - minimize response time in conversational traffic
  - maximize useful throughput
  - minimize transmission cost
  - keep the receiver busy at all times
  - minimize sender overhead
  - etc.

A conclusion is that there can be no single good flow control scheme.
Depending on the environment some objectives will be considered
essential, while others will be immaterial, or just secondary. But
it would be unpractical for users and manufacturers to support a
multitude of application tailored implementations. Therefore a
practical objective is to devise parameterizable schemes lending
themselves to particular tunings and strategies.

Similarly to error control, flow control schemes may be step-wise or
end-to-end.

a) In a step-wise implementation information to be delivered is
stored in intermediate queues cascading into one another along the
transmission medium (Fig. 5). The longer the queues, the longer
the delay and the more asynchronous are sender and receiver. As long
as the storage capacity of the transmission medium is large enough
to maintain non-empty queues, the advantage of this scheme is to
decouple sender and receiver traffic rates, at least over a certain
period of time. Each one can work at its own pace without being
constrained by continuous interactions. But this is true only to the
extent that the transmission medium has a large enough buffering
effect so that it does not interfere continuously with the sender
or the receiver. The ideal case is when the transmission medium can
be considered as an infinite sink, e.g. a conventional message
switching system.

Fig. 5 - Step-wise flow control

The other side of the coin is increased transit delay and overhead
in the transmission medium, due to storage, control procedures, and
individual liaison management. Therefore step-wise flow control is
not particularly suitable for inter-active traffic, nor for handling
large amounts of liaisons.

b) <u>End-to-end flow</u> control mechanisms are part of the set of rules governing traffic exchange between sender and receiver over a liaison. They are located at both ends and interact directly with one another.

As for error control their logical working is independent from the transmission medium, but not their efficiency. Since flow control schemes are only good as long as they are efficient, there is actually much dependency between flow control tuning and transmission medium characteristics such as : error rate, transit delay, storage capacity. It is fair to say that a lot more experimentation, simulation and research are necessary to have a more scientific understanding of the relations between sender/receiver traffic and transmission medium characteristics. This effort is under way.

Nevertheless, E-E mechanisms are fairly predictable in simple cases, which account for most typical applications.

- Conversational traffic requires a strong coupling between sender and receiver, since their input and output rates may be highly different, and one may want to use flow control mechanisms to direct precisely the alternation of the conversation. This can be obtained by interacting at the message or fragment of message level, assuming that the transit delay is small as compared to the sender/ receiver response time. There is no problem if transit delays do not exceed 500 ms.

- Steady traffic such as in the case of remote batch terminals requires intermediate buffering to damp out the effects of bursty computer systems. If we assume an irregular transit delay, this is another reason for intermediate buffering. On the data center end there is normally no problem in having enough capacity to keep up with the terminal traffic. But the transmission medium can introduce an uncertain delay which might degrade the performance of an out-putting device, such as a line printer. Simple analysis shows that buffering at the terminal end is necessary to compensate for variations in sending rates and transit delays, unless the latter are insignificant.

E-E flow control can be regarded as isomorphic of error control in terms of resource management[6]. Both are no more than producer-consumer schemes in the message name space. As a result they may be implemented economically with the same mechanisms, and are often associated in communications protocols.

In conclusion, flow control is still an area where improvement is definitely needed. No scheme can be guaranteed as always effective, but E-E schemes are more economical in implementation and overhead. They can also be built independently from transmission media, and this adds one level of flexibility.

An approach, which does not seem to have received much attention so far, is to draw upon strong analogies between information transfer and distribution of perishable goods, to be consumed fresh. Principles of industrial dynamics[7] would seem to apply well to the subject.

9 - Priority channel

Due to the pipe-line effect of a liaison, it is often necessary to send signalling information to be processed as soon as possible, ahead of the normal information in transit. This is the closest equivalent to an interrupt in conventional systems. Furthermore, a relation must be established between signalling information and the normal flow, in order to mark the point where some action is to be resumed.

10 - Purging

For various reasons, such as error recovery, it is necessary to be able to wipe out all information in transit, without closing a liaison. However, if several independant traffics are multiplexed over the same liaison, this may be handled more conveniently in a higher level protocol.

NETWORK STRUCTURES

Some networks have placed the liaison machinery at the boundaries of their own responsibility. In other words, every organization, or project management, is keen on offering a supposedly error-free and efficient E-E transport service to the outside world. E.g :

- Arpanet and Cyclades host-host protocols
- Bolt, Beranek and Newman's PSN (Arpa subnet)
- EPSS (UK Post Office).

Other networks exhibit a different approach :

- Cigale[8] and the EIN PSN's offer a DG service, without liaisons. But it might be argued that they are just sub-systems of computer networks under a single project management.

- Datapac (Bell Canada) is a simple DG PSN. Liaisons are supposed to be implemented within the subscriber equipment.

- Tymnet and Transpac (French P & T), offer   step-wise controlled liaisons on fixed routing, which seems to be most appropriate for handling character terminals. In this environment E-E control relies primarily on human users. There is also a DG service in Transpac which will likely be similar to Datapac.

There have been no conclusive facts in support of a particular network structure. The network technology is still at an age of high diversity. Presumably Darwinism will gradually eliminate the less adaptive dinosaurs.

Technical arguments, without figures, may be advanced as follows :

- a PSN is only a sub-system of computing services.

- computing services require control mechanisms that are independent from transmission media.

- since E-E protocols at subscriber level insure reliable information transfer, there is no need to introduce duplicate mechanisms at PSN level.

However, PSN's might be used for other purposes than subsystems, (which ones ?), and liaison mechanisms may be essential to insure proper operation, (or are they ?).

At this point, we have to wait for feedback from experience in order to compare objectively the cost-effectiveness of the various networks mentionned above.

While liaisons are an intrisic part of network computing service responsibility, it is not yet clear that liaisons at PSN level (or VC's) play an essential role in the total network structure.

INTERFACING WITH VC'S

It might be argued that even if VC's are not essential, they don't hurt either. Thus it is worth investigating how typical computer systems may interface with a VC service in a PSN.

Presently no commercial computer software is designed for general purpose heterogeneous computer networks. Typical architectures are star, or tree, networks of terminals with centralized control. Nevertheless, remote concentrators, or satellites, or intelligent terminals, have already brought the need for a software structure that decouples applications,transmission and terminals. Application programs deal with abstract entities such as ports. All the tasks of information transfer and terminal handling is taken care of by manufacturer standard software.

It is quite predictable that application programs must not be modified so that they work indistinctly with local or distant terminals, through switched or leased lines, or a PSN.

The only acceptable ways to interface with a PSN will likely be :

- adaptation of the host computer software by the manufacturer.
- gateway interposed between PSN and subscriber computer (Fig. 6), without changes to the computer software.
- substitution of physical circuits with PSN services.

1 - Adaptation of the host software

Since manufacturers must deliver software adaptable to a variety of network topologies, they cannot afford to bias the whole of their network software in view of a particular PSN. The largest possible part of the software must be independent from the transmission medium. Thus, interfacing with a PSN will tend to be located within modules at a lower level, between line handlers and message transport.

Traffic at this level is a multiplexing of various independent data streams between ports and terminals and/or concentrators. PSN services offer typically two choices, VC's or DG's.

Using PSN services requires in any case the formatting of packets according to PSN conventions. If only the DG service is used, it may be required to fragment and reassemble blocks exceeding the PSN packet size. In addition, sequencing is to be performed on the receiver end. Error and flow control are already part of higher level protocols and need not be duplicated. If a standard line procedure is offered by the PSN, e.g. HDLC, it will probably be available from the manufacturer. Altogether, the cost of interfacing with the DG service is quite limited.

Using VC's requires to embed the PSN E-E protocol within the host E-E protocol. Practically, this means that every property of a host liaison has to be matched by some equivalent mechanism of the VC service. Here follows a series of problems that are to be solved.

a) Mapping liaisons onto VC's will generally require a multiplexing of liaisons over VC's, and a dynamic allocation of VC's in relation to traffic activity. Indeed, it is predictable that idle VC's will not be free.Queueing for VC's may also occur when the host subscription is exhausted.

b) Opening/closing VC's requires a specific protocol to be called on demand. In some PSN's this scheme is rather involved, and may result in call collisions.

c) So far VC ports in PSN's are not sharable. When host ports can establish several liaisons, they have to be allocated separate VC's. Then, there is the problem mentionned earlier of finding out a free VC to reach a sharable port.

d) While PSN's perform detection, and possibly correction, of transmission errors over VC's, none of them takes care of VC loss. Thus, recovery procedures must be implemented at host level. In existing PSN designs, there seems to be no provision for finding out VC status from a host.

e) Flow control protocols do not match perfectly, as they usually

deal with different entities : characters, buffers, packets, etc.
Some extra buffering is needed to take care of allocation mismatches.

f) Purging a liaison takes additional steps to clean up extra buffering, and may be cumbersome when several liaisons are mapped onto a VC.

g) It appears that no PSN offers priority channels over VC's, except
the Arpa subnet. Thus, priority messages must be extracted from
liaison traffic and routed onto separate VC's, or sent as DG's.

In summary, adapting the host software to VC's requires a specific
VC management, as VC's are non trivial resources. Furthermore, mapping
liaison properties onto VC's is not trivial. Except for the simple
VC's of the Arpa subnet, there has not been to our knowledge any
report about interfacing a host software with VC's. This is all the
more disturbing that some public PSN's appear to be strongly biased
to VC's.

2 - <u>Gateway between host and PSN</u> (fig. 6)

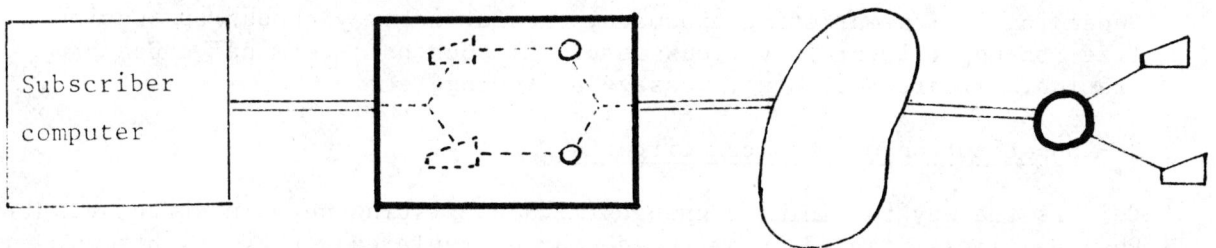

Fig. 6 - Gateway

The basic objective is to avoid any modification to the host software.
Since the only devices that can communicate with the host are usually
friendly terminals, or concentrators, the adaptation is engineered so
that all traffic mimics data streams exchanged with remote devices.

Mimicking device traffic requires a precise understanding of the protocols used by the host software. This may or may not be easy, depending on the relationship between the computer manufacturer and the
implementer of the gateway. Even if this information is readily available, protocols may be dependent on system parameters that may change
with software releases, or system generations.

In order to decouple as far as possible the gateway implementation
and the host software, one may choose to mimic physical non intelligent
terminals, because they are likely quite stable.

As seen from the host, the gateway is a cluster of terminals. The other
part of the gateway maps the terminal data streams onto PSN services.

If there exist terminal concentrators which do not belong to the PSN organization, they may communicate with the gateway via any E-E protocol handling liaisons, using e.g. DG's across the PSN.

In another case, gateway and terminal concentrators belong to the PSN organization, e.g. a common carrier. E-E protocols between concentrators and gateway appear to the host as a VC service, even though the PSN may use DG's to carry out data transmission.

In a third case, the gateway belongs to the host and concentrators belong to the PSN. In other words, the carrier provides one end of the E-E protocol, and requires that the customer implement the other end. Again, this appears to the host as a VC service, regardless of the transmission technique used.

It is worth noting that interfacing a PSN through a gateway is actually an additional layer of system structure, which turns the PSN into a subnet. Services offered are no longer PSN services; they are E-E services built on top of a PSN.

Depending on its marketing approach, the carrier may choose to specialize its upper layer in various services, such as : terminal concentration, circuit switching, message switching, etc.

3 - Substitution of physical circuits

This is the way to minimize changes within existing network structures. Physical links, leased or switched, may be replaced with VC's, permanent or transient.The only changes required are a substitution of line procedures used to control data links with the PSN protocol for VC's. This protocol may even be embedded in a line procedure such as HDLC, in which case the adaptation might be implemented in the I-O hardware, or in black boxes replacing conventional modems.

A COMPARISON OF INTERFACE POLICIES

If the objective is always to minimize the PSN impact on existing network structures, it is quite predictable that the third approach will be preferred by users. However there are other aspects which are to be taken into account. This can be summarized as follows :

Substitution of physical circuits
  . minimum changes
  . better transmission quality
  . reduced transmission costs (?)
  . same constraints as existing networks

Gateway
  . no change to the host software
  . possibility of using terminals not directly compatible with the host

- possibility of accessing several hosts from the same terminal
- restrictions due to the characteristics of the simulated terminals, conversion overhead, and VC services available from the carrier.

Adaptation of the host software

- computer-to-computer communications
- more efficient adaptation
- possibility of standards for host access·
- software supported by manufacturer
- some manufacturers may be reluctant

The three approaches have their own merits, and may even be combined consecutively or simultaneously.

However there is one area in which the only constructive approach is to adapt the host software, viz. standardization. As long as hosts handle communications in a specific way, there are limited chances of getting beyond the concept of network of equipment. The future of such networks is obviously handicapped by the difficulty for users to learn many systems.

Standard host access would open the way to networks of services, in which hardware and software makes would become invisible from the end user. This may be unrealistic as long as competition is based on gadgetry rather than cost-effectiveness. But it is even less likely to happen if adaptations to PSN's are costly, inefficient, and non standard. This is why VC's are a matter for concern, as they can be a good deterrent from host access standards;

SYSTEM ARCHITECTURE

In summary, VC's may be looked at from different viewpoints, and it is likely that their use may turn advantageous or troublesome depending on their proper placement in a total system architecture.

- Substitute to real circuit

  They appear as physical transmission devices at the lowest levels of a system

- Interface with simple remote terminals

  They act as device handlers providing for a simple and limited set of control functions. This is only suitable for conversational non intelligent terminals, simple single-stream I-0 devices.

Communication tool between system components
_____

The responsibility for insuring meaningful communications
belongs to the end correspondents, which are the only ones in
a position to know their traffic and error control requirements.
Therefore, E-E control mechanisms in VC's are not useful, as they
are at a different level. In addition, the VC interface is not as
simple and convenient as it would be desirable. Practically, it is
tempting to mask it out with an additional layer of logic, in
order to turn it into a simple message transfer service.

REFERENCES
_____

1 - IBM Systems reference library. General information - Binary
    synchronous communications. GA 27 - 3004-2 (oct. 1970) 40 p.

2 - ISO/TC97/SC6 - High level data link control procedure.
    Doc 1005 (oct. 1974) 54 p.

3 - CROCKER SA, McKENZIE A, POSTEL J - Host-host protocol for the
    Arpa network, NIC 8246 (Jan 1972) 37 p.

4 - ZIMMERMANN H, ELIE M - Transport protocol : Standard host-host
    protocol for heterogeneous computer networks, IFIP WG 6.1, doc
    61 (apr. 1974) 31 p.

5 - POSTEL J - Official initial connection protocol. NIC 7101
    (jun. 1971) 5 p.

6 - POUZIN L - Network protocols. NATO International advanced study
    institute on computer communication networks. Univ. of Sussex,
    Brighton (sep. 1973), 231 - 255.

7 - FORRESTER J W - Industrial dynamics. IT press (1961) 464 p.

8 - POUZIN L - CIGALE, the packet switching machine of the CYCLADES
    computer network, IFIP congress, Stockholm (Aug. 1974) 155 - 159.